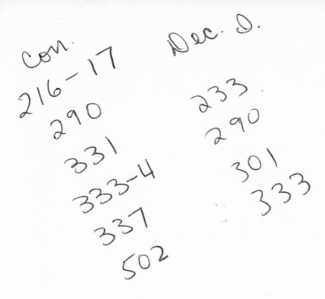

Con.
216-17
290
331
333-4
337
502

Dec. D.
233
290
301
333

A HISTORY
OF PHILOSOPHY
IN AMERICA

A HISTORY
OF PHILOSOPHY
IN AMERICA

Volume I

Elizabeth Flower
and Murray G. Murphey

Capricorn Books, New York
G. P. Putnam's Sons, New York

Vol. I SBN: 399-11650-8
Vol. II SBN: 399-11743-1

Library of Congress Cataloging in Publication Data

Flower, Elizabeth.
    A history of philosophy in America.

    Bibliography.
    Includes indices.
    1. Philosophy, American—History. I. Murphey,
Murray G., joint author. II. Title.
B851.F56   1976   191   75-40254

Acknowledgments

We are grateful for permission to quote from the following:

The Manuscript Journals of Amos Bronson Alcott, by permission of The Houghton Library, Harvard University.

"The Technometry of William Ames," by Lee W. Gibbs, unpublished dissertation, Harvard University, 1967, by permission of the author.

Freedom of the Will, by Jonathan Edwards, edited by Paul Ramsay, by permission of Yale University Press.

Images and Shadows of Divine Things, by Jonathan Edwards, edited by Perry Miller, by permission of Yale University Press.

The Philosophy of Jonathan Edwards, edited by Harvey Townsend, University of Oregon Monographs, 1955, by permission of University of Oregon Books.

"The Mind" of Jonathan Edwards, by Leon Howard, copyright © 1963 by The Regents of the University of California, by permission of University of California Press.

The Papers of Benjamin Franklin, edited by L. Labaree, by permission of Yale University Press.

The Thought and Character of William James, by Ralph Barton Perry, by permission of Alexander R. James.

Samuel Johnson, President of King's College, His Career and Writings, edited by Herbert and Carol Schneider, volumes I, II, and III, Columbia University Press, 1929, by permission of Columbia University Press.

The Manuscripts of Charles Sanders Peirce, by permission of the Department of Philosophy, Harvard University.

The Collected Papers of Charles Sanders Peirce, volumes 1-6, edited by Charles Hartshorne and Paul Weiss, The Belknap Press of Harvard University Press, 1931-1935; volumes 7-8, edited by Arthur Burks, The Belknap Press of Harvard University Press, 1958, by permission of Harvard University Press.

Royce's Logical Essays, by Josiah Royce, edited by Daniel Robinson, by permission of The Christopher Publishing House.

Fugitive Essays, by Josiah Royce, Introduction by J. Loewenberg, 1920, by permission of Harvard University Press.

The World and the Individual, Second Series, by Josiah Royce, by permission of Dover Publications, Inc.

For both inspiration and the forging of the tools with which the writers have worked there is a preeminent obligation on the part of both of us to Herbert Schneider and Perry Miller.

Contents

Volume I

Volume II

Preface

This book began, more than a dozen years ago, as a joint venture into the understanding of the course of philosophic thought in America. In 1963 we published a brief preliminary volume for the Union Panamericana entitled *Principales Tendencias de la Filosofia Norteamericana*. Since that bantling appeared, our enterprise has progressed through an unbelievably perilous and circuitous route to its present form, helped on at critical junctures by the kindness of a variety of samaritans. Although we have both contributed to every chapter, each author bears a primary responsibility for some chapters. Elizabeth Flower bears primary responsibility for chapters 4, 5, 6, 8, 11, 14, and 15; Murray Murphey is chiefly responsible for chapters 1, 2, 3, 7, 9, 10, and 12. Chapter 13 was a joint product.

It is a pleasant duty to thank publicly those who have given so freely of their help. Herbert Schneider has given us the benefit of his unparalled knowledge of the history of American philosophy, and has saved us from many mistakes. Francis Clarke spent many hours with us poring over Latin texts. Max Fisch's invaluable suggestions brought us many leagues closer to our objective. Bruce Kuklick, Finbarr O'Connor, and Phillip Mullin made a number of important criticisms. To Abraham Edel we owe not only much substantive aid, but also innumerable subtle touches which only his wit and grace could have provided. Those who have studied with Perry Miller will have no difficulty in detecting echoes of his reverberating voice in these pages. Ann Goolsby and Mrs. Forest Smith typed and edited early drafts of this work. Shirley Ann Eriksson and Harry Jackendorf contributed their special skills toward improving the readability of many parts. Finally, we would like to thank Richard Balkin, who has played the part of midwife to this book and materially eased the pangs of labor.

Introduction

In a book as long as this one, there is considerable danger that one may become lost among the trees and never find the forest. It may therefore be helpful to the reader to have a preliminary indication of some of our major findings. Surveying the career of philosophy in America, perhaps the most striking characteristic of this history is the complexity and intimacy of the relationships among science, religion, and philosophy. So complex and so intimate have been these ties that it is often unclear what if any distinction can be made among them. If the impetus for change has more often come from the sciences, particularly in such cases as the Newtonian and Darwinian revolutions, still religious movements such as the Great Awakening have also had important philosophic consequences, and philosophy has often served as a mediator or synthesizer of the two. But there are also cases—e.g., Locke—in which it is impossible to say whether one is dealing with philosophy or science, and cases—e.g., Emerson—in which it is impossible to say whether one is dealing with philosophy or religion; here the very distinctions seem of dubious value.

Philosophy in America really begins with the Puritans of old and New England. Surely it is clear that Puritan society was thoroughly wedded to a religious world view, and that the Puritan life was lived in intimate relation to what we would call supernatural entities. Yet the Puritans were also committed to science, and saw no basic conflict between the scientific study of God's works and any other mode of approach to the Lord. Their science of course was Aristotelian, modified by the influence of Ramus, to whom so much of their specific world view was due. And Ramus in their eyes was an educational reformer and methodologist whose work had improved and clarified scholastic thought by making it more empirical, more practical, more precise, and more easily learned. In this sense, Ramus was perceived by the Puritans as a pioneer in what we would call scientific method, and therefore as a comrade in arms of men like Bacon and Descartes. The ease with which the Puritans accepted the scientific revolution, their admiration for Bacon and hospitality to Descartes and Cartesian logic must be seen in this light. For them, the scientific revolution was a step forward in the continuing search for an understanding of God's works.

These same factors account for the ease with which Puritans accepted the work of Newton, Boyle, and Locke. Newton's physics and Boyle's chemistry were eagerly embraced because they were advances in knowledge—all knowledge, whether of God or nature or man. Even men of such radically different stamps as Cotton Mather and Jonathan Edwards were equally enchanted by Newton. Much the same is true of their view of Locke, for Locke was perceived by the Puritans as a psychologist—the most thorough and precise scientist of the human mind—not as a "philosopher" in our sense of arguing a speculative position. Americans by and large read *Essay Concerning Human Understanding* as a scientific account of how, not as a justification of what, we know. And accordingly men as disparate as Edwards and Franklin were equally able to follow Locke just as they followed Newton, and to build interpretations upon the one as they did upon the other.

The Puritans have usually been presented in the history of the American mind as though their world view served as the paradigm for all subsequent American thought. One of the things we have found is that this is not so, or at least not wholly so. The introduction of Scottish philosophy marks a watershed—a paradigm shift, if you like—of major importance. The Scottish philosophers and their American followers have not won high praise from American historians, but this we believe was largely owing to the fact that their work has been misconstrued. Scottish writers have been reviled because of what their critics have seen as the weakness of their realism. For the Scots, the external world was guaranteed by the testimony of consciousness that we do in perception know real qualities of real things, and when a warrant for that testimony has been demanded, the Scots have appeared to retreat to the pious hope that our creator would not deceive us. But this view fails to do justice to the Scots because it demands of them answers to questions which were not theirs, and ignores the questions they did ask. The Scots took Locke as a psychologist and a realist who was seeking to answer the question, how, if the world really is as Newton, Boyle, and the new sciences say it is, do we come to have the knowledge of it that we do? This inquiry was both epistemological and psychological. It was not concerned with proving the validity of knowledge; it assumed the validity of knowledge, and asked rather how such valid knowledge was possible. Hence the great concern of Scottish writers with perception, and particularly with its physiological aspects; hence also their great admiration for Berkeley, not because they were idealists, which they were not, but because Berkeley's new theory of vision was such an acute psychological study of the process of perception. To the Scots, epistemology was the empirical study of how we know, not the attempt to prove by some metaphysical demonstration that what we think we know is really so. Scottish writers envisioned no more conclusive proof of the truth of our theories than that which science provides; they were not speculative metaphysicians but empiricists who sought a science of knowledge just as they sought a science of mechanics or a science of electricity.

The influence of this Scottish orientation has been pervasive. When C. S. Peirce wrote the famous series of papers in the *Popular Science Monthly* from which eventually pragmatism was extracted, he followed very much the Scottish model. Responding to the new evolutionary theories and attempting to develop a theory of cognition congruent with them, Peirce did not there attempt to demonstrate the validity of knowledge but to show how an organism situated in an environment goes about the process of learning what it must learn to survive. Functional patterns of thought and action which have become habitual for the organism Peirce called beliefs; these patterns relate action to need satisfaction with enough reliability to form a basis for conduct. Disruption of belief, because it threatens survival, forces the organism to seek new beliefs, and that process of search is defined to be inquiry. The problem then is to find the method of search which is most successful, and that method Peirce argues is the scientific method. Hence knowledge arises as an evolutionary necessity for organisms underendowed with instinct, and the question is to determine which method of inquiry is in fact the most successful in producing adaptive knowledge. Here again epistemology is conceived as an empirical study of knowing, taken as a type of adaptive behavior; the reality of the environment and the organism are assumed rather than argued, and the theory is properly seen as a branch of psychology.

That James's psychology and his philosophy are hardly distinct will be clear from the analysis presented in chapter 11. Indeed pragmatism in its Jamesean form, radical empiricism, and pluralism are direct consequences of the doctrines which James laid out in the *Principles of Psychology*. But what needs to be stressed is that in so developing his philosophy James was following a tradition which goes back at least to Reid and Locke. James was of course much more concerned with the warrant of knowledge than the Scottish writers had been—he was a child of Kant as well as Reid—and he found that warrant in the successful functioning of knowledge, following the lines marked out by Peirce. Yet it is clear that for James epistemology was very much an empirical discipline built upon the psychology of perception rather than a prior or antecedent philosophy.

This tradition reaches its culmination in Dewey. When Peirce criticized Dewey's logic for being a "natural history of thought," he failed to see that it was exactly this emphasis which Dewey had taken from his own *Popular Science Monthly* papers. For Dewey the distinction between epistemology and psychology simply did not exist; the problem was to determine how the mind knows, and to use that knowledge to correct and refine the knowing process. Dewey assumed the biological model developed by Peirce and the Jamesean psychology as a basis for developing this "natural history of thought" and elaborated his own theory of inquiry as a refinement of them. Dewey's "naturalism" lay in just this refusal to permit philosophical problems of knowledge to be separated from the empirical question of how the mind does in fact work.

The cordiality with which Americans of every stamp welcomed science and the intimacy of the relation between their science and their philosophy should not be permitted to hide the fact that innovations in science raised serious religious difficulties. At the center of these difficulties were three fundamental questions: what is God's relation to the world, what proof have we of the existence of the soul, and what knowledge have we of the soul? The first was raised by the success of science in predicting natural phenomena without reference to God, for it was unclear how events which could be predicted and explained in purely natural terms could be interpreted as having a religious meaning. The second was raised by the Darwinian revolution, for the demonstration of evolutionary continuity between man and animal called in question the traditional claim that man differed absolutely from the animals by the possession of an immortal soul. The third was raised by the new psychology of Locke and his successors, for in this psychology not only was it difficult to identify unambiguously the action of the immortal soul but the concept of ideas of reflection raised serious question of our ability to know such a spiritual principle. It is these problems which have provided the drive behind the idealistic tradition in America. There were of course idealistic elements in Puritanism, including the implicit Platonism of the theory of archetypal ideas and the theory of conscience, but these elements were integrated into a predominantly realistic position drawn from Aristotle and Ramus. But after the new scientific works became known here, full-fledged idealism appears almost simultaneously in Johnson and Edwards. That Johnson drew his doctrine from Berkeley shows that these problems were not unique to America, and also indicates another reason for Berkeley's historical importance. Edwards and Berkeley and Johnson all found in idealism a solution to the problem of God's relation to nature; by making the world ideal and God its cause, the immanence of God in nature could be maintained maugre Newton, and His total governance of the world upheld. All three struggled with the problem of ideas of reflection, but they reached different solutions, Berkeley and Johnson reverted to a quasi-Platonism while Edwards developed a view of such ideas as repetitions of the original acts. Both theories, however, have the function of guaranteeing genuine knowledge of a spiritual principle.

The triumph of Scottish realism arrested the development of idealism for some time, but in the 1830s it erupted again in the Transcendentalist movement. Although the absolute idealism of the Transcendentalists was an indigenous development, it was powerfully stimulated by British romanticism, which in turn drew heavily upon German idealism, and the influence of the Germans rapidly increased thereafter. This is obviously true of the Hegelian movements in the Midwest, but such men as Peirce and Royce were also deeply indebted to the Germans. For Peirce and the rest of the pragmatists the direct influence of Kant was paramount, but all of the idealists were also influenced by writers such as Schelling, and of course by Hegel. This type of American idealism reached its finest formulation in Royce, although it had many other adherents. And certainly it served to provide a philosophic position for these men which would permit them to accommodate the discoveries of science within an overall metaphysic which guaranteed their religious commitments.

In the period since Royce, idealism has continued to play this role in America. Royce's own synthesis, while it had enormous influence over men such as Lewis, has not become the paradigm for contemporary idealism; that role has been played by the work of A. N. Whitehead, whose arrival at Harvard in the 1920s was an event of major importance in the recent history of American philosophy. An accomplished mathematician and a great logician, Whitehead combined a mastery of science and the formal disciplines with a strongly idealistic philosophic outlook which made him a formidable champion of the idealist cause. His following remains strong today, though few of his progeny have exhibited the command of logic, mathematics, and science for which he has been so justly acclaimed.

As this account suggests, the central role of philosophy in American thought has been that of a mediator between or synthesizer of science and religion. This was obviously true of the Puritan technologia. It is equally obvious with respect to Scottish realism, which provided the second dominant paradigm in the history of philosophy in America. Convinced that conflict between true science and true theology was impossible, the Scots were at once fearlessly empirical and naively sure that the results of such empiricism would always turn out to support Protestant theology. Idealism, too, despite its special sympathy for religion, always sought to do full justice to science. But this synthetic role becomes particularly evident in the Darwinian revolution. No scientific theory in our history has so thoroughly overturned established doctrines as Darwin's. In the wake of the *Origin of Species*, there is an explosion of intellectual energies in philosophy as men sought desperately to repair the shattered world view. Spencerian materialism, Hegelianism, positivism, romantic idealism, refurbished realism, and pragmatism all sought with varying success to find some solution to the problems posed by evolution. Of these, pragmatism emerged as the most successful. Of the genesis of this remarkable movement much has been written, and its ancestry is indicative of its central concern. Partly inspired by Berkeley, but also by the English empiricist Alexander Bain, more deeply indebted to Kant, but no less so to the Scottish realists, pragmatism was a movement which sought to create an empiricism rigorous enough to qualify as a philosophy of science but broad enough to embrace ethics and aesthetics, and even metaphysics and religion as well. It was and has remained a synthetic philosophy designed to stop the war between science and religion and restore a unified world view.

In the modern world, pragmatism is viewed as a variant of empiricism, and even as a hardheaded empiricism; its connections with religion are forgotten. But it needs to be stressed how important these connections were historically, and how much modern pragmatism is indebted to the religious concerns of men like Peirce and James. Both of these men were fundamentally religious, and Peirce was an idealist; both vigorously rejected any form of reductionist empiricism and laid great stress on the freedom and spontaneity of the mind. Both abhorred materialism—then so popular as an alleged implication of science—and fought to maintain a view of man as a creature of values and interests, of imagination and insight far transcending anything possible in the crude mechanistic psychology of Spencer and his followers. Most important, both men saw science as a tool by which the mind creates order and beauty out of the chaos of experience. The validity of that view is of course independent of the specific motives which led its founders to its formulation, but from the historical point of view the role of those religious motives in the development of pragmatism should not be forgotten.

One of the most interesting areas of interaction among scientific, religious, and philosophic ideas has been ethics. Puritanism viewed ethics as applied theology and vigorously denied the legitimacy of any form of secular ethics. This tradition, of which Ramus was the founder, is still strong in Edwards, who criticized Hutcheson, with whom in other respects he has much in common, for failing to base his ethics upon the love of God. But this Ramist tradition was overturned by the Scottish philosophy, and in this respect the influence of the Scots has been absolutely decisive. The Scottish position made ethics an empirical discipline to be approached, like any other empirical subject, through the scientific method. Although the perception of moral attributes was assigned to a distinctive moral sense, this sixth sense was not a transcendental intuition but was conceived in analogy to the five exterior senses as an organ of perception. The result was an ethical position which denied any distinction in kind between ethics and other forms of empirical knowledge—a view which they also extended to aesthetics. "Moral science" as they often called this field of inquiry thus became an early form of social science—empirical, comparative, and independent of theology and revelation. Although the Scots said, and believed, that the results of this secular moral inquiry would necessarily be congruent with the findings of theology and Biblical exegesis, they insisted upon the propriety of keeping the two fields distinct.

In their revolt against the Scottish philosophy, idealists sought to tie ethics more closely to theology, but the empiricists who succeeded the Scots in America retained their emphasis upon ethics and aesthetics as empirical disciplines. The pragmatists to a man accepted this view, Peirce no less than James, but it was particularly Dewey and Lewis who elaborated it into full-scale theories of valuation. And while a major concern of these writers has been with ethics, they have treated aesthetics in a parallel fashion, as an empirical discipline to be pursued by essentially scientific methods.

Two further features of our findings require particular note. First, throughout the period of our study Americans have constantly assumed that philosophy had a practical role in shaping not only the personal structure of the spirit but the character of human institutions. There are no stout defenders of the purity of philosophy, its neutrality, its studied irrelevance to practice. On the contrary, all schools—idealism as well as materialism and pragmatism, religious as well as inclining to the secular—regard it as furnishing the principles for the guidance of life and social institutions. In the eighteenth-century revolutionary period, in the St. Louis Hegelians of the Civil War period and its aftermath, and again in Deweyan instrumentalism of the first half of the twentieth century, the aspect of institutional reconstruction becomes almost of the essence. Not till the mid-twentieth century—beyond our period—does philosophy in America toy with ideals of purity and impracticability.

Second, the history of philosophy has often been written as though it consisted of isolated giants who, as it were, shouted to each other across the centuries. Any history which emphasizes the importance of individual thinkers, as ours also does, is to some degree liable to this interpretation, but we have tried to supplement these studies of the major figures by detailed attention to the institutional contexts in which at least some of them worked—contexts composed not only of the institutional setting itself, but also of institutional philosophic traditions which provide much of the continuity between one thinker and another. Thus our extended study of Princeton, our treatment of logic at Harvard, and our emphasis upon the problems of church polity at least serve to suggest the importance of this dimension of the history of philosophy. Limitations of space have prevented us from carrying this theme further, but it is surely one which must figure prominently in any subsequent treatment of this subject.

It is well to state at the outset the limits of our study. American thought is of course richer all along than we have been able to present it, in even the confines of these two volumes. We should be content if this serves as a starting point for the immense and very rewarding recanvass of our philosophic tradition. At almost every point there were ideas, works, and figures—large as well as small—that we had to pass by. We made our selection in several ways: by significant movements, by dominating figures, by academic institutions. Our aim was rather to do a thick study of a more restricted domain than a thinner study of a more extensive domain. What is more, some sacrifice of American materials had to be made to provide space for tracing the continuities with the European philosophic traditions, a relationship central to a genuine understanding of our philosophical tradition itself. We hope that the method of analysis employed in dealing with individuals and movements will be found worthwhile in the avenues of research that we see as opening up in the current growth of interest in American philosophy. We welcome the contemporary efforts to provide definitive editions of our significant philosophers and the increasing studies of individuals in their fuller context. Meanwhile, in our work, individuals will have to stand for broader movements, and movements for the fuller range of their participants. Thus James has to stand for many dimensions of philosophical psychology: for Mark Baldwin, among others, whose enormous influence Piaget acknowledges; as well as for G. Stanley Hall whose contributions were clearly larger than the vituperation of Scottish realism we cite; and, with some stretching, for the New Realists who tried to carry through his neutral monism to get rid of dualism in epistemology. (The Critical Realists, who in reaction reinstated a paler form of dualism in a new garb, should have to stand on their own.) Royce has to stand for a multitude of philosophical idealists as diverse as Palmer and Hocking at Harvard and Urban and Sheldon at

Yale, Cunningham and Bowne at Cornell, and Brightman at Boston University. And Dewey holds proxies not only for the varieties of naturalistic moral philosophers such as Ralph Barton Perry and Stephen Pepper, but also for the ever-enlarging work in social philosophy. But even Dewey's mantle is not ample enough to include the variety of strong and interesting naturalisms of the first half of the twentieth century in America—from Woodbridge's Aristotelian naturalism at Columbia to Singer's naturalization of Kant at Pennsylvania. (We do include Santayana's fusion of Plato and materialism at Harvard.) In the wider reaches of naturalism as a distinctive American movement—quite different from the biologistic naturalisms that stemmed from Spencer in the Old World—one would include Morris Raphael Cohen at New York's City College, and Roy Wood Sellars at Michigan (who matured a critical type of emergent materialism). There is no one to stand for Whitehead's organic idealism—it would be stretching Royce too much to throw this burden on him! We regret particularly Whitehead's absence from our volumes, but as we suggest in the epilogue, his influence in American thought has had its greater growth in the period beyond our scope.

It speaks for the vitality of American philosophy in this century that even in relation to its first half we cannot here begin to exhaust the list of its contributors.

Chapter One

Early American Philosophy: The Puritans

Chapter One

Early American Philosophy: The Puritans

1. Introduction

The men who settled America were not philosophers. Some were soldiers, some were philanthropists, and some were religious zealots, but most were plain Englishmen seeking to better their economic situation. Although religious motives were often mixed with economic ones, colonization was by and large a commercial undertaking, and it was expected to justify itself in terms of the laws of trade. Accordingly, those who came as settlers were chiefly practical men who lacked the inclination, even if they had had the time, to indulge in more intellectual pursuits. It is not surprising, therefore, that little philosophy was done on these shores before the eighteenth century was well under way.

There is, however, one colony which forms a clear exception to this rule—Massachusetts. The men who founded the Massachusetts Bay Colony in 1630, and subsequently the Connecticut colony as well, were not primarily interested in commerce, and their colony was unlike any other, either in conception or in execution. No other colony was so well organized or so well led; no other brought over so many people in so short a time; no other was so successful in establishing in the wilderness the kind of society its planners desired; and in no other colony was so much importance attached to intellectual pursuits. It is therefore with the Puritans of Massachusetts that the story of philosophy in America begins.

3

The settlement of the Massachusetts Bay Colony was a by-product of the Puritan struggle to reform the Church of England. When Henry VIII broke with Rome, he thereby made the Church of England a Protestant church, but since he was more interested in politics than in theology, he made little change in the church's doctrines and ritual. The church therefore remained very similar to the Roman Church. Protestant churches of the Lutheran and Calvinist persuasions, on the other hand, adopted far more sweeping reforms of both theology and ritual, and to these radicals the conservative Church of England seemed scarcely Protestant at all. Accordingly, the radicals demanded that the English Church be "purified" of its Catholic elements—hence the name "Puritan" which was given to the English Calvinists. After Henry's death, Edward VI was more sympathetic to Puritan plans, but Edward's brief reign was followed by that of Queen Mary who was determined to return England to the Catholic Church. Under Mary, the more extreme Protestants faced severe persecution, and many of them found it expedient to flee to Europe, particularly to Geneva, where they found Calvinism in firm control. But Mary's reign also was brief, and Elizabeth had no intention of surrendering the independence of the English Church which her father had established. From the return of the Marian exiles in 1558 on, the number of Calvinists in England grew rapidly, and, as their power increased, so did their demands. Throughout the late sixteenth and early seventeenth centuries, the religious controversy grew in intensity, and although the fortunes of the Puritans varied, they continued to believe that their cause might prevail by peaceful means. But when Charles I succeeded to the throne in 1625, the Puritans found themselves confronting the most hostile monarch since Queen Mary. Charles appointed the Puritans' archenemy, William Laud, as Archbishop of Canterbury, and supported Laud's vigorous persecution of the dissenters. By 1629, when Charles dismissed Parliament and declared his intention to rule alone, the Puritan prospects looked black indeed. It was then that a group of Puritan leaders resolved to found a colony in New England as a refuge for their faithful, where their cause might be preserved and protected against the return of better days in England. The New England undertaking was therefore conceived from the beginning as the planting of a large religious community in the New World, and it was planned accordingly. From the founding in 1630 until the revolution ended the persecution of the Puritans in England, a steady stream of immigrants flowed across the sea, so that by 1640 Massachusetts had a population of twenty thousand and was the largest colony in America.[1]

All Puritans were Calvinists, but within the Calvinist camp there were divisions over questions of both theology and polity. The New England settlement was the work of men who held distinctive views on both these matters: in theology they were Federalists; in polity they were nonseparating Congregationalists. As Federalists they believed in a peculiar contractual theology, the nature of which will be discussed below. As Congregationalists they believed that every church

should be an independent and autonomous body of believers subject to no ec-
clesiastical authority beyond itself, and they therefore objected to the hierarchical
structure of the Church of England. Separating Congregationalists (such as the
Pilgrims of Plymouth) simply withdrew from the Church of England and formed
their own churches; nonseparating Congregationalists (such as the Puritans of
Massachusetts Bay) stayed within the English Church and sought to remake it on
Congregational lines. Hence the churches of Massachusetts were thoroughly
Congregational, although technically within the Church of England.[2]

New England's leaders were an unusually well-educated and articulate group of
men who were proponents of an elaborate and comprehensive system of belief[3]—a
system which attempted to supply a unified, coherent view of the universe.
Although this system was theologically oriented, it also dealt with related scientific and philosophic questions, so that like scholasticism it is a combination of
science, philosophy, and theology all in one. This system was taught to the people
of Massachusetts and Connecticut by every means available to the leadership. It
was taught in the schools and colleges, in the sermons, attendance upon which was
required of all, in books and pamphlets, and even in the home and shop. Dissent
from the official creed was rigorously suppressed, and obedience to its mandates
was enforced through a strict system of surveillance.[4] We do not know, of course,
how effective the leaders were in their program of indoctrination, but there is good
reason to believe that on the whole they were successful.[5] The New England
Puritans are therefore a rare phenomenon in American history—an entire society
formally committed to a specific body of thought. Accordingly, one can speak of
"the" Puritan doctrine—meaning, of course, the position advanced by the
leaders—with reasonable assurance that one is discussing a system of belief which
was accepted by the society as a whole. And since this Puritan system forms the
intellectual background for virtually all early American philosophy, it requires
discussion in some detail.

2. Physics and Theology

The Puritan system was formulated before the Puritans came to America, and its
sources are therefore to be sought in Europe. There are, in fact, three major sources
from which the Puritans drew their peculiar views—medieval scholasticism;
Protestantism, particularly Calvinism; and the Renaissance humanism of the
Ramists.[6] Although the final doctrine is a unique Puritan achievement, it is
probably most easily approached through its sources.

The Puritans owed most of their science to scholasticism. At least until the latter
part of the seventeenth century, Aristotelian physics and Ptolemaic astronomy
were the accepted doctrines in New England, and not until the arrival of Charles
Morton in 1686 did the new science seriously challenge the old.[7] Puritan theology

was thus integrated into a view of the physical universe based on Aristotle, and this fact helps to explain certain important aspects of Puritan thought.

Scholasticism conceived of physics as the study of changeable being.[8] Following Aristotle, change was conceived in terms of three principles: substance, form, and privation. Thus, when an unmusical man becomes musical, a substance (man) which lacks a form (musicality) acquires it.[9] The problem then is to state the necessary and sufficient conditions for the occurrence of such changes. Aristotle's answer to this problem is the doctrine of the four causes. In every change, he holds, there is matter undergoing change (material cause), a form which the matter acquires in the change (formal cause), an agent who produces the change (efficient cause), and an end sought in the change (final cause). So in the building of a house, the building material is the material cause, the form of the completed house is the formal cause, the builder is the efficient cause, and the creation of a habitable dwelling is the final cause.[10] All change is therefore teleological, since every complete causal explanation requires the stipulation of the final cause.

The doctrine of the four causes provided the paradigm of scientific explanation for scholasticism. But when this paradigm was applied to nature in an effort to give order and predictability to our phenomenal experience, the results were not wholly satisfactory. This is perhaps most easily illustrated in the case of motion. A causal explanation of motion on Aristotle's grounds must specify the material cause which is the thing moved, the formal cause which is the place to which it is moved,[11] the efficient cause which is the mover or force impressed, and the final cause which is the objective sought and so is here identical with the formal cause or place to which it is moved.[12] When this paradigm is applied to the observed motions of the classical four elements—fire, air, water, and earth—it yields an apparently adequate and simple explanation. In terrestrial experience we find that earth sinks through water, and water through air; we also find, if we trust naive observation, that fire rises through air. Accordingly, Aristotle gave to each element a place to which it moves by virtue of its nature: earth is placed at the center of the universe, water above earth, air above water, and fire in one of the heavens. For the elements, then, we have the rule that each body has a natural motion to its natural place, and when in that place remains there at rest unless displaced by a force. The natural motions of compound bodies are then easily seen to be the resultants of the natural motions of their elementary constituents.[13]

This theory accounts neatly for an immense range of observed data. But it involves fundamental problems. First, it divided space into absolute places having intrinsically different properties, so that the homogeneity of space is destroyed. Second, it distinguished two different kinds of motion—natural and unnatural—which obey quite different laws. Natural motions are always vertical with respect to the earth's surface, and a body in natural motion accelerates uniformly as it moves toward its natural place. Unnatural motions, which include some vertical motions (e.g., upward motion of a stone) and all horizontal motions, are interpreted as due to the action of a mover, and continue only so long as the mover acts. Hence to produce uniform motion horizontal to the earth's surface, there must be a constant force acting continuously. Third, a causal explanation of an unnatural motion requires identification of the efficient cause or mover. Where there is a visible mover no problem arises, but where no visible mover is in evidence an invisible mover must be postulated, and the class of invisible movers most readily available to the scholastics—and to the Puritans—was spirits. The spirit may be considered as located in the moving object, as is the case with the "motive soul" of animate things, or as external to the object but acting upon it, but in either case it is the spirit which supplies the missing efficient cause required to explain the motion. Thus the scholastics explained the motions of heavenly bodies as due to "intelligences" operating upon inanimate objects, the Puritans as due to a motive soul in the star ("A star is animated by a single soul, *viz*., the motive."[14]), but both had to invoke a spiritual efficient cause.[15]

In our day, we conceive the world in "naturalistic" terms. To give order and predictability to our experience, we use theories which postulate the existence of subatomic entities connected to each other and to observables by relations capable of precise, impersonal, and objective statement. We believe in the existence of these entities because the theory which postulates them gives stability and coherence to our sense experience, and since we believe in them, we interpret our sense experiences as signs or indications of the action of these entities. In a similar fashion, the physical theory held by the Puritans required the postulation of spiritual entities to explain certain phenomena, and since this theory was supported by a vast amount of empirical data and was far superior to any alternative then available to them, they accepted its consequences. That such entities were invisible was no more an objection in Puritan eyes than the invisibility of subatomic particles is in ours, and the fact that explanations involving spirits had to be couched in terms of purpose seemed logical enough to men who believed that all explanation required final causes. So for the Puritan sensible change was produced by, and was a sign or indication of, spiritual agents. For him, the spiritual world lay always just behind the phenomenal veil. What held his world together and gave regularity and predictability to it was not the intricate interplay of particles but the mighty hand of God.

Since control of the world rested finally in the hands of God, it was essential for the Puritans to know all that they could about Him, and the general outline of this knowledge was provided by Calvinist theology. For a Calvinist, God is above all the locus of power. It is God Almighty, creator, lord, and master of the universe, who is depicted in Puritan sermons. His sovereignty is unconditional, His power is infinite, and His will, arbitrary and unconstrained. It is God who completely determines all events, so that ultimate causality resides in God alone. He is omniscient, with absolute foreknowledge, and is transcendent, so that human knowledge can never adequately depict Him. The Puritan God is therefore always mysterious and inscrutable: His ways are past our finding out; His wisdom is hidden; His will is to us inexplicable.[16]

But however much the Puritan stressed God's transcendence and mysteriousness, he never doubted that some knowledge of Him was possible. The Lord has revealed Himself to man both in the creation itself and in the Bible, and from the study of these some knowledge of God can be attained. So from contemplating the extent of the creation we can learn something concerning the power of God, and similarly for the other attributes. Of course these attributes as we conceive them do not describe adequately the true character of the deity: to conceive accurately the power, or justice, or mercy, or other attributes of God is beyond human power. Yet we can reason about these attributes analogically. We can know, for example, that God must possess an attribute which is to Him as power is to an earthly king, although the actual power of God must be as much beyond that of a king as God is beyond mortal rulers. By such analogical devices we can describe and reason about the Lord, although it must never be forgotten that we see through the glass but darkly.[17]

Why should God have chosen to hide Himself so completely from human eyes? The answer is that He did not, or at least He did not do so originally. When God created Adam in His own image, He endowed him with intellectual powers far beyond those of men today. Adam could not, of course, know God directly, but he possessed an immediate intuitive understanding of nature (illustrated by his naming of the animals) and of the law.[18] But the fall so corrupted Adam's nature, including his mind, that this great intellectual power was destroyed both in him and in his progeny, and while this degradation affects all the capacities of the mind, it is particularly severe with respect to man's ability to perceive the law and moral distinctions. Sinful men no longer have the capacity to attain knowledge either of nature or of the law in the way Adam did.[19] Therefore God has mercifully granted to them a second source of knowledge, the Bible, in which He dictated to scribes such portions of His wisdom as it was necessary for men to know. Accordingly, the Puritans regarded the Bible not only as true, but as written by God. It did not surprise them, therefore, that there were problems in interpreting this revelation, for our minds are but ruins and the Scripture is God's own wisdom. For the Puritan, what the Bible asserts is fact, just as what his senses tell him is fact. The sun's standing still was no more puzzling to him than its brilliance or heat, but he did not deny that the sun was bright because he could not explain the source of its brilliance, and he did not deny that it stopped for Joshua because he could not explain just how the trick was done. Many facts were inexplicable in his world, and the Bible had no monopoly on mysteries.[20]

Puritanism interpreted Adam's sin in the traditional Protestant manner as the sin of pride: instead of seeking to please God, Adam sought to gratify himself, and so to usurp God's place. The consequences of this sin were catastrophic. Adam's nature was so transformed that thereafter he became inherently sinful, seeking for and delighting in evil. The fall involved a loss of intellectual acuity, but it is not due to ignorance or stupidity that the fallen sin. Rather, the Puritans conceived the effect of the fall as a complete corruption or depravity of human nature such that the fallen delight in evil and lust after sinful pleasures even when they fully recognize what they are doing and strive to do otherwise. Moreover, the corruption which afflicted Adam is transmitted to all his progeny without mitigation. All men are therefore born innately depraved, predisposed to sin by their corrupt nature and unable to resist its lure by any effort of their own. "In Adam's fall," says *The New-England Primer*, "We sinned all."[21]

If all men commit sins, then they must pay the penalty for those sins. God's justice demands that sinful men be damned, but His mercy demands that some be saved. Most will be damned; a few—a "saving remnant," as the Puritans called them—will be saved. In traditional Christian fashion, the Puritans explained this redemption of the chosen through the atonement, whereby Christ satisfied the demands of God's justice. But with respect to who shall be saved, they are unflinchingly Calvinists. Since God is all powerful, and determines all that is to be, He also decrees, or predestines, who is saved and who is damned. This decree is eternal and irrevocable: no act of the individual can affect it in the slightest. For all eternity God has immutably decreed each man's fate and most men's damnation. Of this stark doctrine, even Calvin remarked, "It is an awful decree, I confess."[22]

The doctrine of predestination means that some men go to heaven and others go to hell, come what may. Since those chosen for sainthood are children of Adam, they are born depraved like everyone else, but before they are fit for heaven their depravity must be removed. Complete sanctification of the elect is only achieved after death, but the process begins in this life with the experience of conversion. According to Puritan doctrine, man cannot alter his own nature: what can alter it is the grace of God. When grace is given to a man, the object of his affections is changed from himself to God, so that thereafter he loves the Lord above himself and seeks to obey God's will. Grace is therefore the love of God, and its reception is often spoken of as falling in love with God. Moreover, grace is irresistible: God redeems whom He chooses, and the chosen are passive recipients of grace. Grace is not earned; it is given, and once given it is given forevermore. The Lord chooses His own, and the Lord is faithful to His chosen. One can neither bargain nor argue with the Lord.[23]

The paradigm case of conversion for the Puritans was of course the conversion of Paul on the road to Damascus. Here grace came in a blinding flash, as a devastating spiritual rape. But the New England Puritans did not regard all conversions as sudden or violent. There is within Puritanism a variety of views on this point, but the prevailing view in New England allowed for a temporally extended process of conversion as well as for the blinding flash. Hence enormous labor and erudition were expended in trying to define the "stages" of conversion, beginning with the first conviction of sin, progressing through despair and humiliation to the final conversion when faith is truly achieved. At exactly what point in this process grace is present, and just what is due to man in his natural state and what to the action of the Holy Spirit are points upon which Puritan divines never achieved perfect accord. Yet by the mid-seventeenth century the New England leaders admitted both the cataclysmic conversions exemplified by Paul and the more extended step-by-step conversions which they found so frequently among the members of their congregations.[24]

Conversion is followed by sanctification—i.e., by the life of the converted being made holy. For since the elect love God and strive to do His will, they will lead more holy lives than sinners. But sanctification remains imperfect in this life: while they are still in this world the saints still sin and still fall short of perfect obedience. Grace does not therefore restore the elect to Adam's high estate, but it makes them holier than sinners, it gives them an ability to strive for holiness which sinners have not, and it restores in some measure that superior power of discernment which Adam had before the fall.[25]

The Puritan theory of grace leads to the conclusion that the lives of saints will differ in certain identifiable ways from those of sinners. Saints will experience conversion and they will undergo a partial sanctification. Are these signs sufficient to enable men to know while yet in this life who is saved and who is damned? The traditional view is that they are not—that only God can know the state of a man's soul. The New Englanders did not quite reject this traditional view, for they admitted that only God can know with certainty who is elect, but they held that from these visible signs men can know with high probability who is elect. By careful questioning and examination, by requiring a detailed account of the conversion experience, and by observing the degree to which in fact a man did live a sanctified life, one could judge with reasonable accuracy whether or not he had grace. This doctrine permitted the New Englanders to redefine the basis of church membership. The Congregational Church was a church of believers: in New England it became a church of visible saints—of men who were judged to have received grace. Everyone who wished to join the church was examined by the members and had to satisfy them that he, too, had been genuinely converted. Of course the Puritans admitted that some men might be accepted who were not saints, and that some might be rejected who were, but they were confident that such errors were rare. Thus the visible church in New England was for them a realization of the invisible church of true saints.[26]

Upon the visibility of the distinction between saint and sinner the culture of New England was based. Puritan New England is often called a theocracy. In a strict sense it was not—the ministers never held political office and church and state were clearly distinct. Yet it was certainly a state ruled by saints, for membership in the church was a condition for voting and holding office. The reasons for this restriction of power to the elect are obvious from the theology. In Eden the only social institution was the family—no state was necessary. But after the fall, government was instituted as a means of restraining the rapaciousness of sinful men. Clearly the control of the government ought not to be given to the wicked, since that would defeat its purpose. Power should be in the hands of those who are least likely to abuse it, and these are obviously the saints, for although the saints are not yet sinless, they are at least partly sanctified. There is in Puritan thought no doctrine of natural rights: the Puritans called their legal code the *Laws and Liberties*.[27] A natural right is a claim based upon the inherent nature of the individual; a liberty is something granted by a supreme power. In Puritan eyes the inherent nature of man was evil: to speak of rights in such a context was not only absurd, it was presumptuous. What freedoms men had they enjoyed as liberties granted by God, and granted (as one grants liberties to a child) according to the recipients' ability to exercise the liberty without abusing it. It was, therefore, only common sense in the Puritan view that saints should enjoy more liberty than sinners.[28]

The Puritan doctrines of predestination and irresistible grace add up to a stark assertion of complete determinism. Not only physical nature but also human thought and action are absolutely determined by divine decree. One might therefore expect that such doctrines would be enervating. Indeed, such a doctrine may appear at first to provide an excuse for sin, for surely if a man is by his nature determined to be evil, he can well claim that his sins are not his fault since he had no choice. Yet the Puritan doctrine was not enervating; in fact, it had a remarkable energizing effect upon its adherents, for it was precisely the state of the will that was the crucial sign of grace. The sinner not only does sinful acts, his sin is a willful sin, for however he may protest, the sinner loves his evil ways and *will* not leave them. The sinner is a willful sinner; like the neurotic who so loves his neurosis that he cannot bear to give it up, the unregenerate man cleaves to evil as the light and love of his life.[29] To be regenerate—to have grace—is therefore to have a regenerate will, to be able to strive for the good and turn away from sin. It is not that by striving one acquires grace—rather the fact that one can strive to do good is a sign that grace has been given. Yet since sanctification is never complete in this life, since even the saints still sin, even the regenerate will is not wholly freed from the fatal attraction of evil, and every such failure, every such breach of the law, may also be a sign that grace was never given at all. It is not that grace is revocable, for it is not—once grace is given, it is given forever—it is rather that you can never be wholly certain that you do have grace. The state of the soul must therefore be inferred from signs, and in even the purest saint the signs of grace are still mixed with those of sin. It is true indeed that God has decreed each man's damnation or salvation from all eternity, but for the individual, the question is, which? The doctrine of visibility means that there are signs by which a man can attain some assurance—though never complete certainty—regarding his state. Accordingly, the Puritan had to scrutinize his life and behavior, watching for the crucial signs, and among these the most critical is the ability to strive to live a sanctified life, perfect in every respect. And since no mere man can do this continuously, there is always cause for doubt, and so a necessity to prove and reprove oneself every day. And if a man should ever attain complete certitude, so that at last he feels absolutely certain of salvation, in that moment he has most horribly sinned, for he has presumed to know what only God can know. Thus, far from being an enervating doctrine, Puritanism drove its adherents to a ceaseless struggle to attain an unattainable goal, and made every failure to reach the goal a fresh motive for renewed effort.[30]

Except for the doctrine of visibility, the theology thus far described is fairly orthodox Calvinism. But the New Englanders belonged to a particular group of Puritans who subscribed to a peculiar theory of the covenant which has little warrant in Calvin, and which sets them apart from most other Calvinists. The term "covenant" occurs repeatedly in the English Bible in passages which spell out the terms which God has set for his people. Thus one of the most critical Puritan texts is Genesis 17:2-14, King James Bible:

> And I will make my covenant between me and thee, and will multiply thee exceedingly. And Abram fell on his face: and God talked with him, saying: As for me, behold, my covenant is with thee, and thou shalt be a father of many nations. Neither shall thy name any more be called Abram, but thy name shall be Abraham; for a father of many nations have I made thee. And I will make thee exceedingly fruitful and I will make nations of thee, and kings shall come out of thee. And I will establish my covenant between me and thee and thy seed after thee in their generations for an everlasting covenant, to be a God unto thee, and to thy seed after thee.

The Puritans utilized the concept of a covenant relationship to describe God's behavior to men. So it was held that the original agreement between God and Adam was a covenant—the Covenant of Works, which Adam broke by eating the apple. In this covenant, so the Puritans believed, Adam acted not as an individual but rather as the "Federal" representative of all mankind, and so when he fell his sin was justly imputed to his constituents. Thus the covenant doctrine serves to explain, or at least define, the mystery of original sin and its imputation. Similarly, redemption is formulated in terms of a covenant. The covenant with Abraham described in Genesis 17 is the Covenant of Grace in which God promises salvation to Abraham and his seed upon the condition that they believe. Once the covenant concept was thus enshrined in the theology, the Puritans extended it to all manner of other relationships. The formation of the church was conceived in terms of a church covenant made between the members and God in which the members pledged to worship God according to His ordinances and God in turn received them as His people; similarly, the foundation of the state was conceived to lie in a covenant between the citizens and God—this was the meaning of the famous

Mayflower Compact. Even the agreement between God and Christ, which is the basis of the atonement, was conceived as a covenant—the Covenant of Redemption. In fact, the use of the covenant concept as a way of conceiving the relation of God and man became so characteristic of the New England Puritans that their theology has become known as the "Federal" theology.[31]

The use of the concept of the covenant to describe the relation between God and man does not alter the fundamental doctrines of Calvinism—rather it serves to explicate certain problems of the theology. The covenant as the Puritans conceived it in no sense diminishes the absolute sovereignty of God. When God offers the covenant to man, He does so freely in an act of mercy. God is not constrained to make this offer, and man, having sinned, has no right or claim upon God. It is solely because God has arbitrarily chosen to manifest His mercy in this fashion that the covenant exists. The New England Puritans also believed that the offer of the covenant must be willingly accepted by man, for there can be no contract among parties unless both agree to its terms. But the emphasis upon willing acceptance does not necessarily contradict either God's sovereignty or the doctrine of predestination, for a man who will accept the covenant is, by the Puritan theory of grace, a man in whom grace is already working. Not only the offer but the acceptance are then from God. Puritan theologians did not fully agree on the question of the degree to which unregenerate men could prepare themselves for the acceptance of the covenant, but they did agree that the willing acceptance which sealed the covenant was the work of the spirit.[32]

The use of the concept of the covenant does not impugn the sovereignty of God, but it does serve to give a stability to the world which Puritans greatly needed. What God has promised in the covenant He will perform—that was the pledge upon which New Englanders built their lives and their society. Not because He owes man anything, nor because man can claim anything from Him, but simply because being God He will do what He has pledged, the covenant promises were taken as a secure basis for predicting both the course of individual life and the course of history. In a world which often seemed to have gone mad, the covenant helped to guarantee order and stability.[33]

Calvinist theology and scholastic physics defined for the Puritans the broad outlines of the world within which they lived. It was a world completely dominated by the overpowering presence of a deity upon whose will every event depended, and it was therefore essential to know as exactly as possible the nature and the desires of this monstrous God. For the Puritan, the acquisition of knowledge was a duty from which no man who dreamed of salvation could shrink. Few societies have revered learning more or sought it more diligently than the New Englanders. Of course the knowledge they sought was theological, but since to them all nature and history were works of God, there was no field of study which did not reveal something of the Lord's ways, and the Puritan savant therefore took all the world for his subject. Accordingly, questions of philosophy, science, and the liberal arts received detailed treatment in Puritan writings, and the Puritan views on these matters are drawn not only from scholasticism but also—and in some areas, chiefly—from the writings of Peter Ramus.

3. Ramus

Pierre de la Ramée, whose Latinized name was Peter Ramus, was born in 1515 in northern France and died in 1572, a victim of the St. Bartholomew's Day massacre. He attended the University of Paris, and remained there for most of his life as a teacher and writer. Repelled by what he considered the uselessness and aridity of scholasticism, Ramus set himself to reform the traditional arts curriculum. In 1543 he published the first of many editions of his *Dialecticae*,[34] in which he undertook to reform the art of logic. In subsequent writings he extended his crusade to grammar, mathematics—particularly geometry—physics, and theology, while his friend and co-worker Omer Talon undertook the reconstruction of rhetoric, but logic remained the heart of the doctrine, for it was from logic that Ramus derived the principles upon which he refashioned the other arts. The writings of Ramus and Talon were immensely influential throughout Europe in the century following 1543, and a vast controversial literature developed around them. Modern scholarship has only recently rediscovered the Ramist movement and begun to assess its significance, but it is already clear that Ramism was one of the important intellectual movements of the Renaissance. New England's debt to Ramus was second only to its debt to Calvin.[35]

Ramist logic was not what we would call logic today. It is a method of argumentation designed for use in disputation, and its purpose is persuasion rather than demonstration.[36] It therefore differs fundamentally from true deductive logic, but it is nevertheless the outgrowth of a long tradition in medieval logic which has its origins in Aristotle's *Topics* and the Platonic dialogues. It will be recalled that Aristotle distinguished sharply between demonstrative reasoning, which aims at proof and is the logic of science, and dialectical reasoning, which aims at persuasion and is the logic of opinion and debate.[37] His major concern in the *Organon* is with demonstration, but in the *Topics* he gives an extensive treatment of dialectic. Since the purpose of dialectic is to dispute problems or theses, a method which will serve this purpose must rest upon some characterization of the nature of a problem. In Book I of the *Topics*, Aristotle uses the predicables and the categories to define the subjects about which dispute is possible and then in the next six books enumerates a series of "topics" or "commonplaces"[38] which can be used in formulating or analyzing a disputation. These topics might best be described as rules of thumb for debating—e.g., "Another commonplace is to make definitions both of the accident and of that to which it belongs, either of both separately or one of them, and then see if anything untrue has been assumed as true in the definitions.''[39] The last book considers the practice of dialectical reasoning, strategy in dispute, methods of presentation, and similar considerations. The *Topics* therefore is not so much a logic as a debating manual, and although it is concerned with valid reasoning, what genuine logic it contains is subordinated to the goal of persuasion.

Medieval logic was thoroughly Aristotelian, and while the great scholastic logicians like Jean Buridan were extending and developing Aristotle's deductive logic,[40] dialectic also received considerable attention. The importance of disputation in the curriculum of the medieval university ensured attention to works on rhetoric and debating,[41] and dialectic in the form given it by Aristotle was a combination of the two. Since both dialectic and logic deal with modes of reasoning, the line between the two was not always clear, and, as Ong has pointed out, it is badly blurred in such highly influential works as the *Summulae Logicales* of Peter of Spain.[42] This confusion of logic proper and dialectic became more marked in the late scholastic and early Renaissance periods, and is particularly marked in the work of Rodolphus Agricola—in many ways the direct precursor of Ramus.[43]

In the writings of Rodolphus Agricola, the term "dialectic" is extended to include all logic, so that Aristotle's distinction between logic and dialectic is abandoned.[44] Agricola divides dialectic into two parts, invention and judgment.[45] The objective of dialectic is the formation or analysis of convincing disputations, and the two-part division reflects this concern. Invention is concerned with "thinking out the middle term or argument"[46] by which a conclusion may be drawn, while judgment is the process of combining the terms to form propositions and discourses.[47] So to prove that "All men have lusts," one uses a syllogism to derive the assertion from two premises, and to formulate these two premises one requires a middle term so related to "men" that if this middle term holds of all men then they must have lusts. One might therefore argue, "All men are animals," "All animals have lusts"; hence "All men have lusts."[48] The middle term here is referred to as an "argument" on the ground that it enables one to "argue" a conclusion concerning man, and the problem of invention is to find such middle terms. Now, obviously, given any term A, any other term B is a possible argument with respect to A if it is related to A in a "significant" way. So in the broadest sense, the problem of invention is the problem of discovering all the terms "significantly" related to a given term, while the problem of judgment is that of combining these terms into true propositions, syllogisms, and discourses.

How then can such arguments be found? The answer is given by the doctrine of the *loci* or places, which is drawn ultimately from Aristotle's *Topics*. As Agricola conceives the places, they are a classification of all the possible ways in which one term could be an argument with respect to another, i.e., of all the relations which can obtain between two terms which are significant for the purpose of argument. The specific list he gives contains twenty-four places: definition, genus, species, property, whole, parts, conjugates, adjacents, act, subjects, efficient agent, end, consequences, intended effects, place, time, connections, contingents, name, pronunciation, compared things, like things, opposites, differences.[49] The list is conceived as exhaustive; thus, whatever is an argument to a given term must be its genus, or its species, or its property, or a whole of which it is a part, etc. Agricola calls the places ''seats'' of the arguments, and he describes their nature and use as follows:

> . . . greatly gifted men have cut out from this profuse variety of things these common headings *(capita)*, such as substance, cause, result, and others which we shall treat of, so that when we set ourselves to thinking about some certain thing, following these headings, we may go immediately through the whole nature and parts of the thing in question, through all the things which agree with it and which disagree with it, and draw out from these headings the arguments adapted to the matters proposed. These things, common in that since they contain within themselves whatever can be said on any matter, they thus contain all arguments, were called by these men places *(loci)*, because all the instruments for establishing conviction are located within them as in a receptable or a treasure chest. A place *(locus)* is nothing other than a certain common distinctive note of a thing, by the help of which it is possible to discover what can be proven (or what is probable) with regard to any particular thing. Let that be our definition of a place *(locus)*.[50]

Invention, therefore, may be reduced to a methodical examination of the places, with the certainty that whatever arguments there may be can be so discovered.

The problem of invention bears an obvious relation to the problem of induction —both are concerned with the formation of true statements. But in Agricola and Ramus the differences are more significant than the similarities. The objective of dialectic for them was the formation and analysis of discourse, not the pursuit of science, and while these are not exclusive goals they are not identical either. Invention was a tool for analysis as well as a means of discovery—essentially, the places were a scheme of categories for the content analysis of other discourses— but in practice it was both simultaneously, since it was in other discourses that they looked for knowledge. Indeed, as Howell has pointed out, it was in the traditional wisdom that these men sought for knowledge, not in nature, and invention was for them a means of culling the content of that wisdom so that it could be applied to current problems.[51] Nevertheless, as we shall see below, the analogy between invention and induction was not lost, and it later had important consequences.

Ramus was the intellectual heir of Agricola, and his logic falls squarely within the topical tradition.[52] Like Agricola, he regards logic as identical with dialectic, and so as a part of the theory of discourse. Dialectic, he asserts, is ''the ability to discourse''[53] and is a natural capacity of all men. Hence, even the unlettered possess a natural dialectic which is sufficient for ordinary tasks. By reflecting upon this natural dialectic, we can discover the rules of reasoning, and when these rules have been systematized into the art of dialectic, we can employ them to cultivate and refine our natural powers.[54] Thus the art of dialectic is not something given a priori, but something learned from observation and experience. Ramus reproduces the division of dialectic into invention and judgment,[55] and his concept of these processes is very nearly identical with Agricola's. Ramus does differ from Agricola in his specific list of places, and he varied his list in different editions of the *Dialecticae*. He also differs in calling the places themselves "arguments" instead of "seats" of arguments, and then deriving the specific arguments as species of the more general places.[56] But his concept of what a place is and how it functions is identical with Agricola's, and so his theory of invention differs in no important respect from that described above.

Agricola devoted little space to judgment; Ramus dealt much more fully with this division of logic. He divides judgment into two parts—axiomatics, which deals with the combination of terms to form true propositions, and deduction, which deals with the combination of propositions. Deduction in turn is divided into two parts—syllogistic, dealing with logical deduction in a strict sense, and method, which deals with the ordering of propositions to form a discourse.[57] This scheme of divisions itself tells much about Ramist logic. Invention gives us the terms out of which propositions are made: axiomatics combines these terms into axioms, or true propositions. That this can usually be done without appeal to either deduction or induction means that Ramus regards these axioms as self-evident. We simply perceive by the power of our natural reason that certain combinations of terms are true. Syllogistic reasoning, therefore, is necessary only with respect to doubtful propositions, and its function is to clear those propositions of doubt by deriving them from self-evident axioms.[58]

The objective of dialectic is discourse, and the task of combining propositions into a discourse is assigned to method.[59] It is not assigned to syllogistic, for Ramus does not conceive of discourse as a series of syllogisms but as a series of axioms. The proper method of discourse, which is for him synonymous with the method of teaching,[60] is described as follows:

> The method of teaching, therefore, is the arrangement of various things brought down from universal and general principles to the underlying singular parts, by which arrangement the whole matter can be more easily taught and apprehended. In such method, this alone has to be prescribed: that in teaching the general and universal explanations precede, such as the definition and a kind of general summary; after which follows the special explanation by distribution of the parts; last of all comes the definition of the singular parts and clarification by means of suitable examples.[61]

There appear to be four major characteristics which define a Ramist discourse. First, it should contain only statements which are true, universal, necessary, and affirmative.[62] Statements true only at certain times or at certain places are to be excluded. Second, these statements should be homogeneous—i.e., they should all deal with the same subject matter. Third, the statements should be ordered in terms of universality, beginning with the most general and proceeding to particular cases.[63] Fourth, these statements are very often either definitions or partitions of the subject, and in the latter case the partition is usually a dichotomy.[64] Thus a Ramist discourse typically begins with a definition of its general subject, e.g., "Grammar is the art of speaking well and of writing well."[65] Then the subject is divided into its constituent "parts," e.g., "The parts of grammar are four: orthography, etymology, syntax, and prosody."[66] Each "part" is then defined and further divided, and so on until the "ultimate parts" are reached and defined, at which point the presentation of the art is complete. Accordingly, a Ramist discourse can be laid out in tabular form as a continuously branching tree, and such presentations were extremely common.[67]

Ramist dialectic was designed both as a means of analyzing discourses and as a means of formulating them. Ramus conceived the process whereby a discourse is produced (genesis) as simply the converse of the process whereby it is analyzed (analysis). Thus in genesis, one begins by inventing terms, then combines these into axioms, and then methodically arranges the axioms into a discourse. To analyze this discourse, one simply reverses the procedure, picking the discourse apart into its constituent propositions, and resolving these into their component terms. A single system of dialectic therefore suffices for both purposes.[68]

Ramus applied his method to the reform of the traditional arts curriculum. In theory, this curriculum consisted of the trivium—grammar, rhetoric, and logic— and the quadrivium—arithmetic, geometry, physics, and music—but in fact music had been virtually dropped, and other "arts" such as medicine, law, and theology added.[69] The Ramist reform of the arts involved a new concept of the origin and function of the disciplines.

> Dès le commencement Ramus a posé ce principe fondamental qu'il y a trois formes successives de toute science: la nature, l'art et l'exercice. En dialectique, la nature c'est la raison ou la faculté naturelle de raissoner; l'art se compose alors des préceptes pour bien user de cette faculté, et l'exercice consiste à mettre en pratique les préceptes de l'art, afin de les convertir en habitudes.[70]

Similarly, in the other arts the rules of art are first discovered by the analysis of concrete examples and are then codified to serve as directives for the improvement of practice. Thus the student must first learn the arts from the analysis of particular cases. He must then use the arts so acquired to generate (by genesis) new works of his own. As one might expect from a Renaissance humanist, the concrete examples which Ramus used to establish the rules of the arts were drawn chiefly from the classical authors, but with respect to such arts as physics and astronomy he also emphasized the importance of direct observation of nature. Thus Ramist doctrine involves an empirical approach both to classical literature and to nature, and emphasizes the practical utility of the arts.[71]

It follows from the Ramist doctrine of method that each art must be homogeneous, in the sense that all its statements must deal with a single subject or its parts. But Ramus also held that the same subject matter should not appear in two different arts.[72] This does not mean that the arts are not related, for, after all, logic furnishes the ordering principles for all the others, but it does mean that redundancy should be avoided. And since Ramus's logic is a method of persuasion, it is not surprising that he found considerable overlap between his logic and traditional rhetoric. Following Cicero, the scholastics divided rhetoric into five parts—invention, arrangement, style, memory, and delivery.[73] That processes of invention and arrangement (or judgment) also occurred in logic presented no problem for them, for they thought of logic and rhetoric as producing discourses of different kinds: the former a learned disputation, the latter a popular oration. There was, therefore, a parallelism between logic and rhetoric, but no redundancy.[74] But Ramus recognized only one basic form of discourse, although it might be varied superficially to fit the audience. To Ramus, dialectic was the theory of rational discourse, while rhetoric was the theory of communicating the results of such discourse to others.[75] Hence Ramus put invention and arrangement into dialectic, and restricted rhetoric to style and delivery only.[76] Accordingly, rhetoric is conceived of by the Ramists as the embellishing or ornamentation of a discourse, the content and structure of which are provided by dialectic.[77] Ramus himself loved eloquence and so did not draw out the implications of this peculiarly nonorganic theory of style, but his Puritan followers did. If the purpose of discourse is didactic, as both Ramus and the Puritans believed, then the important thing is to communicate the content of the discourse. Ornamentation, except as illustration or example, must be avoided lest it distract attention from the message itself. Thus the famous "plain style" is one of the many debts the Puritans owe to Ramus.[78]

Ramus was both a philosopher and an educational reformer. As a philosopher, he drew from both the Platonic and Aristotelian traditions, and although he referred to himself as a Platonist,[79] his position seems to have been a moderate realism. But it was the desire to reform education rather than traditional philosophic problems which inspired Ramus's work. Ramus worked and thought within the context of the medieval university. It was his revulsion from scholastic pedagogy which led him to devote his life to the attempt to refashion the arts curriculum into a form which would be simple, clear, and easy to learn and remember. Thus the characteristics of a Ramist discourse were largely determined by this concept of teaching: the movement from general to particular was designed to illustrate abstract truths by concrete cases, and the emphasis on plain style and orderly arrangement were intended to make the instruction as swift, easy, and natural as possible. Moreover, the emphasis on utility and empiricism in Ramist doctrine marked a sharp break with the metaphysical debates of the schoolmen. Ramus was not a scientist in the modern sense, and in his own writings he drew his examples from classical literature rather than from nature, but his reforms of method and teaching did help to prepare the way for Bacon, Descartes, and the scientific revolution.[80]

4. Technologia

Ramist doctrine reached England about 1550[81] and spread rapidly thereafter. By the 1570s it already had proponents at the University of St. Andrews in Scotland and at Cambridge,[82] and was known at Oxford.[83] Cambridge became a center of Ramism in England, as it was of Puritanism, and of mathematics, and subsequently of physics and Platonism. William Perkins, Alexander Richardson, and William Ames, all of whom were leaders in the development of the Federal school of Puritan theology, were also Cambridge Ramists.[84] Their relation to New England is quaintly but accurately put in Samuel Johnson's synoptic view of the intellectual history of medieval Europe, written just after his graduation from Yale in 1714:

> From Greece philosophy was introduced into Italy and thence into Germany, Holland, Spain, France, and England. In these countries not a few of the greatest men were found; for their doctrine was Christian. Among these innumerable men the principal sects were Platonists, Peripatetics, and Eclectics. The leader of the eclectic sect was that great man, Ramus, at whose feet, as it were, there followed Richardson and then Ames, the greatest of them, followed him and we follow Ames.[85]

The system which Richardson and Ames developed was called "technologia," "technometrica," or "encyclopedia," and it was the official philosophy of the New England Puritans. It was taught to generations of students at Harvard and Yale, and formed the intellectual core of Puritan writing and preaching until the eighteenth century was well under way.[86] In this system are brought together all the strands discussed above—the heritage of scholastic arts and sciences, the theology of Calvin, and the doctrines of Ramus—and the synthesis so created forms the background against which the development of eighteenth- and even nineteenth-century American philosophy must be seen.

"Technologia," or "technology," means literally knowledge of the arts; "encyclopedia" means the circle of the arts. But what the Puritans meant by "art" requires some explanation. Aristotle regarded science and art as distinct, the former being concerned with demonstration, the latter with making things. "All art is concerned with coming into being, i.e., with contriving and considering how something may come into being which is capable of either being or not being, and whose origin is in the maker and not in the thing made . . ."[87] It is true that Aristotle's careful distinction was not always preserved during the Middle Ages: Peter of Spain used the terms art and science interchangeably, and so did many of his successors, Ramus included.[88] Nevertheless, the distinction was still clear in the curriculum at Cambridge in the early seventeenth century, where a "science" meant a body of abstract knowledge and an "art" meant a discipline involving action.[89] Yet in technologia the term "art" is extended to include science, so that all knowledge is referred to as art.[90] The Puritan meaning of Art is therefore equivocal: it can mean abstract knowledge, or it can mean a set of practical rules for making something. The emphasis in the formal definitions is on the latter aspect—thus, Richardson writes, "Art is the rule of the making and governing of things to their end"[91]—yet the Puritans also intended the former. What harmonizes these two meanings for them is the belief that what is science to us must be art to God, since our science can be at most a description of God's mode of acting in creating and governing the universe. But if art is synonymous with knowledge, our approach to God must be through the creation (including the Bible). *Ens primum*—i.e., God as He is—is unknowable—an assertion which reiterates the Augustinian notion that the essence of God transcends human knowledge. But *ens a primo*—God manifest in the creation—can be known.[92] So Richardson remarks, "The proper subject of Art is *Ens a primo* . . ."[93] Thus technologia as the theory of art is in some ways the Puritan equivalent of metaphysics, and it occupies the place of metaphysics in the Puritan curriculum.[94]

"Every art and every inquiry . . . is thought to aim at some good . . ."[95] wrote Aristotle, and the Puritans fully concurred. The good aimed at they called "*eupraxia*," which means well-doing or good conduct.[96] As Ames put it, "Art is the idea of ε$\grave{υ}$πραξία, eupraxia or good action, methodically delineated by universal rules."[97] So Richardson argues ". . . there is no Art but is an eternal rule in the Idea of God, as a precept of that thing whereof it is an Art, to guide it to its *Eupraxie*";[98] and Johnson asserts, "Art is the idea representing and directing *eupraxia*."[99] Moreover, every art aims at the production of some artifact. This artifact is called the euprattomenon or good work; as Ames put it, "since something made by motion (or some *thing* (*res*), as the logicians say, made by motion) necessarily and immediately follows every motion, the thing or ε$\grave{υ}$πραττόμϵνο$ν$, euprattomenon or good work, made by the motion of art or any kind of eupraxia must follow."[100] In the case of the mechanic arts, this artifact will clearly be tangible, but in the case of the liberal arts it may not be discernible by sense—i.e., one may by dialectic create a discourse which is never spoken or written but exists only in the mind. Nevertheless, Ames and Richardson insist that the euprattomenon is the invariable result of the practice of art, and their insistence underlies their denial of the distinction between theoretical and practical arts. For the Puritans, all arts are practical; all involve practice (praxis), albeit good practice (eupraxia), and all produce an artifact—something made by art. The intensely practical thrust of these Puritan Ramists—their insistence that ideas must issue in action and their antipathy to contemplation and speculation—is evident in their basic definition of art as the idea of eupraxia.[101]

God is the supreme artificer, whose euprattomenon is the creation. The nature of this artistry is described by Ames:

> In every artist, or anyone who expresses himself after taking counsel, there exists beforehand an idea which he keeps in mind as he is about to work so that he may fit his work to it. So also in God, since he does not work naturally nor rashly nor by constraint, but with highest perfection of reason, such an idea is to be understood as preexisting, as the exemplary cause of all things to be done. Heb. 11:3. *Those things we see were made of things that do not appear.*[102]

Accordingly, the entire scheme of creation must preexist in the divine mind as an archetypal pattern—in their terms, an "exemplary cause"—from which existing things were copied. These archetypal ideas are eternal and immutable, so that they are essentially Platonic Ideas,[103] although they do not exist except in the mind of God. And since all things are made according to this platform, the divine ideas themselves are both archetypal science and archetypal art: "in regard to the truth of particular things it [the divine idea] is called *scientia*, knowledge, which in extent is omniscience; . . . in actual practice it is called *ars*, art, whereby he (God) knows how to accomplish all things most skillfully."[104] Hence God is truly Art, and the creation a work of art of which God's ideas are both the "platforme" and the governing rules.

> Now if *Ens primum* be the cause of *entia a primo*, then he hath the Idea of them in him: for he made them by counsel, and not by necessity; for then he should have needed them, and they have a parelion of that wisdom that is in his Idea. Again, it must needs be that this wisdom is his, because he governs them by the rules of Art, for so every rule of Art is a Statute-law of God, by which he made the things, and whereby he governs the things, whose Art it is. Now seeing it is so, therefore this Law hath God for the Author, and look what Idea was in the making of the thing, the same Idea is in the governing of it: for if the Lord should make it by one rule, and govern it by another, it would not serve the turn to guide the thing to the *eupraxie*, whereunto it was made. So that hence it follows, that every rule of Art is eternal . . . So that if *ens a primo* be divided into parts, this wisdom also will be divided into parts: and as in a Looking-glass that is broken, look how many pieces it is broken into, so many images shall you see: So for the Arts, look into how many parts the thing is divided, into so many parts will the Arts be distributed.[105]

Archetypal art is one, but as the creation in which that art is embodied is various so it appears fragmented to us into the diverse arts. Only in the circle of all the arts do we have a true representation of the divine art. Hence encyclopedia or technologia portrayed the arts as a circle with God at the center.[106]

The creation itself—*entia a primo*—is a copy of the divine archetype, and so makes manifest or embodies the divine art. This holds of course not only for physical nature, but also for the course of history as well. As embodied in created objects or events, art is called entypal, and the thing or event is called the entype.[107] It follows at once that all nature and all history symbolize the divine wisdom, so that, as Johnson put it, "Things are God's words in print."[108]

It is precisely here that the significance of Ramus for the Puritans becomes evident. Technologia holds in effect that the creation is God's discourse which we must try to interpret, and Ramist dialectic and rhetoric are designed for the analysis of discourse. All that need be done is to apply Ramist technique to the interpretation of nature, history, and the Bible, and we should be able to read out the Lord's meaning. The immense appeal that Ramus had for the Puritans was due to the fact that his peculiar dialectical logic so exactly met this need for a method of interpreting the creation. Thus a system of analysis designed to function on human discourses is applied to nature, and what had been a means of culling the received wisdom of the past becomes a tool for the study of nature.[109]

> And this teacheth man thus much, that he is to seek out, and find this wisdom of God in the world, and not to be idle; for the world, and the creatures therein are like a book wherein God's wisdom is written, and there must we seek it out.[110]

In Puritan hands, the dual empiricism of Ramus—the empirical study of literature and of nature—becomes effectively one, for nature itself is God's discourse and science is the study of God's art. And by thus focusing attention on the interpretation of natural phenomena, the Puritans opened a path for the new science. Detailed empirical observation of nature now became a duty; new discoveries were sought and prized as revelations of the divine wisdom. For the Puritans, science and religion were one: the early scientists of New England were chiefly ministers.[111]

Art in the mind of God is archetypal; when embodied in the creation it is entypal; and when it is in our minds it is said to be ectypal.[112] The ectype is thus our copy of the archetype, obtained by a correct reading of the entype. Since God is a Ramist too, the discourse of the creation is constructed according to the rules of art by genesis—i.e., having "invented" the arguments He chose to embody, God has joined these arguments in nature, as we would in propositions, to spell out His message. So as we find the arguments in nature, they are "in disposition"—in combinations—and we must resolve these by analysis.

So that for Arithmetick, Geometry and nature, man was to learn them by the creatures, as he was also to learn the knowledge of Logick, Grammar, Rhetorick and Divinity. The reason is this, the *Genesis* of every thing is Gods, and man must see the rules of Art, therefore man must see them from singulars, by *analysis*: now then if man must learn these, and know them by his senses observation, induction and experience, then he must seek, and find out these, for they are not written in him: again, whereas every thing is in disposition, it is requisite that man find them out, and see them severally, therefore in this respect is this Art of reason called Invention, namely as he is sent by God to find out these things in his creatures; now if man must find them out with this act of his eye of reason, then it is fitly called invention.[113]

The divine plan is to be discovered by the analysis of particular objects and events. So invention here becomes the problem of discovering the significant properties and relations of real things, and the places of Ramist logic serve to direct the search. The problem of induction was not a problem for Puritans precisely because this system not only furnished them with a set of well-entrenched predicates, but also guaranteed them that all the relevant concepts were to be found in this set.

When invention has gathered in the terms, judgment combines them into "axioms." Richardson spells out the significance of this word:

The word in his proper signification is, worthiness, or dignity, and by a metonomie of the adjunct for the subject, it signifies such a truth as is worthy the receiving, or believing: now *axioma dubium* is not worthy this worthy name *Axioma*, because it is not *per se manifestum*, but we are fain to demur upon it, so that some axioms are not so plain as others: others also there are which are so plain, as he that cannot see them, or doubteth of them, deserveth the whip. Now because this first part of disposition is of a clear truth, *ergo*, he [Ramus] calls it *axioma*, as if he should say an honorable truth: putting us in mind thereby, that though this name be common to all axioms, yet it is principally to them which are *per se manifesta*. . . .[114]

Axioms are, or should be, self-evident. If they are not self-evident, we must prove them syllogistically, for ". . . syllogisms serve but for the clearing of the truth of axioms,"[115] but for the most part the truth of the axioms is *per se manifesta*. That this should be possible was no more surprising to the Puritans than that in reading a man should correctly understand the meaning of a sentence, for truth with respect to nature means simply understanding the meaning of things.

Now man not being able to take this wisdom from God, which is most simple, therefore it hath pleased the Lord to place it in the things, and as flowers do send out a scent, or odor that doth affect our sense of smelling, so every precept of Art doth *spirare* a sweet science to our glass of Understanding, which is indeed that irradiation, which we heard of in Divinity in the Creation of things . . .[116]

God creates the discourse which is nature by genesis; we derive our ectypal knowledge from singulars by analysis. Unlike God, who has no need of analysis, we must start from the particulars of sense and derive our knowledge from them.[117] Ramus and his followers were empiricists who subscribed to a moderate realism; universals never exist in nature except embodied in particulars, and we must learn them by induction and abstraction from these particular things.[118] But Ramus also held that universals are clearer to reason than singulars. Hence when we come to systematize our knowledge for purposes of teaching, we must order it from universal to particular, following the rules of method Ramus laid out in the *Dialecticae*. The order of teaching is thus the opposite of the order of discovery—a dictum which emphasizes how much Ramist dialectic was oriented to classroom instruction rather than to actual discovery. Indeed, this contrast is particularly striking in Ames, who, in describing the process of analysis by which we acquire our knowledge from individual things, cites Bacon's discussions of method in the *Novum Organum*[119] as exemplifying the Ramist method of analysis. It is therefore important to distinguish the Ramist method of analysis, by which we learn the arts from the entypes in nature, from the Ramist doctrine of method dealt with under judgment in dialectic which defines how the completed art is to be taught to students.

When we have formed the axioms which constitute ectypal art and cast them into series according to the doctrine of method, we then have an "encyclopedia" or circle of the arts which the Puritans believed to contain the whole of the liberal arts.[120] In this "circle" there are six arts which stand in a fixed order. Since the object and end of art is eupraxia, the distinct arts are given by the species of eupraxia, which are discoursing well, speaking well, communicating well, measuring and numbering well, doing the work of nature well, and living well. The corresponding arts are dialectic, grammar, rhetoric, mathematics, physics, and theology.[121] One is at once struck by the omissions; the trivium is present, but the quadrivium has been markedly altered, and such arts as law and medicine, metaphysics and ethics—subjects which bulked large in the university curriculum —do not appear at all. Clearly, the Puritan theory of the arts differs in some rather striking ways from the traditional one.

Let us look first at the order which the Puritan Ramists specified among the arts. Following Ramus, Ames divides the six arts into four groups: most general art, which is dialectic; less general arts, which are grammar and rhetoric; less special art, which is mathematics; and more special arts which are physics and theology. The basis of this ordering is described by Ames in terms of "becoming concrete"—e.g., "general eupraxia becomes concrete in use in all other eupraxiae and in itself, and this from absolute necessity so that the remaining eupraxiae cannot be known, or exist, or be exercised without it."[122] When Ames says that a given art "becomes concrete" in another, what he means is that the former is presupposed or utilized by the latter. Thus dialectic is presupposed by all the other arts, but mathematics, although presupposed by physics, is not presupposed by dialectic, grammar, or rhetoric. Thus Ames's classification of the arts is a classification based on presupposition.

Dialectic is the art of discoursing well. Since for Ramus, dialectic and logic are all one, dialectic may also be thought of as the art of reasoning well,[123] and it is perhaps most appropriately conceived as the art of rational discourse. The resulting discourse, however, need not be spoken discourse; when a man thinks to himself, he invents arguments, formulates axioms, and arranges his thoughts in a coherent fashion, but he need never put his thoughts into speech or communicate them to others. Dialectic is therefore prior to both grammar and rhetoric as well as to the special arts. The divisions of dialectic—invention, judgment, etc.—have been described above in some detail, but it should be noted that dialectic also includes what might best be called the theory of real definition. Mere nominal definition, which concerns merely conventional relations among words, belongs to grammar, but real definition, which "is the means by which is explained what a thing really is"[124] belongs to dialectic. Similarly, real definition must be distinguished from etymology, which is again a grammatical category, even though the examples of real definition given by Ames and Johnson involve reference to Greek and Latin roots. The important point for dialectic is that names of the thing in question may furnish arguments by which some conclusion can be argued about that thing, and this will be the case if the definiens consists of words (in whatever language) which explicate the semantic content of the name. Thus "*cadaver* is so called because of *caro* (flesh) *dato* (given) *vermibus* (to worms)."[125] "Name" is in fact a place (locus) because arguments can be found there, at least in the case of some types of definition.[126]

Grammar and rhetoric are less general than dialectic. The eupraxia of grammar is speaking well, while that of rhetoric is communicating well. Both therefore depend upon dialectic to provide the content which is to be spoken or communicated, and rhetoric clearly presupposes grammar since only what has been formulated in speech can be communicated. The generality of these arts is described by Ames as hypothetical; they are presupposed by the special arts on the hypothesis that the content of these arts is to be spoken or communicated, but since in theory at least one could pursue logic without either formulating one's work in speech or communicating it to others, the presupposition is hypothetical only. Grammar is divided into etymology and syntax, and is concerned with relations among words; rhetoric is divided into elocution and pronunciation and is concerned with the "embellishment" of discourse to make it more elegant and more persuasive.[127]

Mathematics is divided by Ramus into two branches, arithmetic and geometry, which have respectively the eupraxiae of numbering well and measuring well. The

Ramists gave much more attention to geometry than to arithmetic. Ames omits arithmetic altogether and identifies mathematics with geometry,[128] but this course was certainly extreme—neither Ramus nor Ames's New England followers went so far. Nevertheless, as Johnson's encyclopedia shows, geometry was certainly the more important branch. In that work, arithmetic is covered in two pages: it deals only with the positive integers and fractions, subtraction is restricted so as not to yield negative integers, and real numbers are undreamed of. The treatment of geometry, on the other hand, is far more extensive, and includes incommensurable lengths, but it is chiefly concerned with naming and classifying plane and solid figures, finding areas and volumes, and similar elementary problems.[129] While the disparity between the treatment of arithmetic and that of geometry is great, this fact must be viewed in the context of the sixteenth- and early seventeenth-century mathematics. Despite the work of men such as Vieta, geometry was at this point by far the best developed field of mathematics, and the Ramist emphasis upon it was an accurate reflection of the state of the art.[130]

Mathematics is described by Ames as the less special of the special arts, meaning that it is presupposed by the more special ones—notably by physics. As will become clear below, neither Ramus nor his followers conceived of mathematics as a purely formal system in the modern sense; they saw mathematics, as every art, as something to be learned from the empirical investigation of the entypes. But the Ramists did clearly draw a distinction between "pure" mathematics as an art to be studied in its own right, and the applications of mathematics which are involved in the study of physics. Thus the use of mathematics to solve problems concerning the locomotion of a material body was for them a problem of physics in which certain theorems of mathematics were applied, whereas the study of the relations among the angles of an abstract triangle was a purely mathematical question. So while the Ramist distinction between mathematics as a less special art and physics as a more special art presupposing mathematics is not precisely the modern distinction between pure and applied mathematics, it nevertheless involved a very important clarification of the relation between mathematics itself and its applications and one which certainly had very important implications for future developments.[131]

The eupraxia of physics is doing the work of nature well.[132] The meaning of this statement is not obvious, and to clarify it two important points must be grasped. First, as we saw above, the Ramists distinguished sharply between *ens primum*—God as first being—and *ens a primo*—created being or the creation. The "nature" with which physics deals is created being only, but it deals with the whole of created being. Thus physics for Ramus includes much more than inorganic nature—it includes all that is except God, and so embraces all animate things but God as well as all inanimate things. Indeed, as Ames is at pains to point out, physics includes even the study of the angels.[133] Hence Johnson distinguishes nature into perishable and eternal, the latter including even the highest heaven, and

further distinguishes the perishable into the animate and the inanimate.[134] Thus
Ramist physics is a combination not only of Aristotle's physics and astronomy,
with a considerable dash of alchemy, but also of Aristotle's biology, including the
whole of the *De Anima*. To some of the specifics of these doctrines we will return
below—what must be stressed here is that, in the Ramist catalog of the arts,
physics accounts for the whole of created being, and so—by the rule that no two
arts should deal with the same subject matter—excludes any other art from this
domain. Second, when the art of physics has been learned by analysis, man
thereby acquires not only understanding, but also the capacity to act according to
the precepts of the art, and so to produce a euprattomenon. In this action, the
Ramists conceive of man as imitating the work of nature, for as natural things are
the euprattomenon of God's artistry, and our art is an ectypal copy of God's
archetypal art, so we in acting under the rules of art are in fact imitating, however
feebly, the actual artistry of God. Hence the eupraxia of physics is to do the work
of nature well—i.e., to imitate successfully the divine art. It is particularly
noteworthy here, though it is also true elsewhere, how completely the Puritan
Ramists thought of ectypal art as copying what is "really out there" in the entypes
of nature. This imitative view goes far beyond the obvious platitude that tech-
nological processes must be in accordance with the laws of nature; instead of the
manipulative orientation which characterizes modern technology, the Ramists
thought of art as imitating nature and of the product of human art as an "entype"
too, albeit one inferior to God's.

Nevertheless, it is important to keep in mind the fact that Ramus and his
followers such as Ames were the heralds of a new age. The Renaissance, after all,
involved not only the recovery of classical learning, which, bursting upon Europe
after so long a period of relative "darkness," filled men with an often too great
awe for the monumental achievements of antiquity, but also a rejection of that very
classical learning in favor of new ideas and new formulations, particularly in the
sciences. Both of these processes proceeded simultaneously; the year 1543, in
which one of the most important translations of Archimedes' work was published,
is also the year in which Copernicus' *De Revolutionibus* was published—and the
year in which the first edition of Ramus's *Dialecticae* appeared. This mixture of
reverence and rejection is clear in Ramus and even clearer in Ames. Ames was a
humanist and a "literary empiricist" who derived his knowledge of physics from
reading rather than from experiment.[135] Nevertheless, he was intensely interested
in physics, and he praised Bacon's efforts to reform scientific method even as he
sought to assimilate these efforts to the Ramist techniques of analysis. Moreover,
in what Lee Gibbs has pointed out as one of the most remarkable passages in the
Technometry, Ames wrote:

From these things it becomes clear, secondly, although respect and honor are
owed to the ancients' writings of this kind [physics], how much respect and

honor are owed. Other things being equal, the writing of more recent men should certainly be placed before, not after, the writings of the ancients. For several eyes may see better than one; day may teach day; and second thoughts may be better than first thoughts.[136]

In that statement there rings the authentic voice of the scientific revolution, not from Bacon or Descartes, but from the master theologian of the Puritan Ramists.

The eupraxia of theology is living well or living to God. It is not, as one might have expected, the understanding of God, for although theology deals with God, God as He is is transcendent and no accurate knowledge of Him is possible for mere humans. Hence theology, like all other arts, must be derived from God's works, and in this case from Scripture. Even though, as we shall see, something of God can be learned from nature, Ames is insistent that the theological knowledge acquirable from nature is trivial in comparison with that available from Scripture, so that Scripture must be the true basis of theology.[137] There is therefore for Ames no justification for Christians to develop a "natural theology" or a theology drawn from the study of nature rather than Scripture. But in theology as in all the arts, the aim and object are eupraxia or action well done, not contemplation or mere speculation. What theology teaches, therefore, is how to live well or live to the glory of God. It should be stressed that this view of theology as living to God does not exclude the search for happiness as a proper human goal, but rather defines it as a goal subordinate to the chief end of man which is the glory of God. Since God made all things and made them for His own glory, it is obvious that in one sense the whole creation necessarily serves that purpose. But the Ramists distinguish between the behavior of nonrational things, which serve God's glory by virtue of their nature, and rational creatures, whose conduct is by council and for whom God has through revelation provided a set of rules to walk by. Ames spells out the function of theology in two theses.

111. Theology alone homogeneously transmits (1) the universal teaching about God, not as he is in himself (for he is not known in this manner by anyone except himself) but as he has revealed himself to us more clearly in the book of Scripture and more obscurely in the book of nature so that we might live well. . . .[138] 113. Theology alone homogeneously transmits (2) the universal teaching of virtues (i.e. of honesty, law, and equity). Theology alone homogeneously delivers the whole revealed will of God for directing our morals, will, and life. This whole revealed will of God alone is that right reason—if absolute rectitude be looked toward, as it must be looked toward here—in which alone, by the consensus of all who are of sound mind, the norm or rule of honesty, law and equity (and therefore of virtues) is constituted.[139]

The omitted thesis—112—qualifies the last sentence of thesis 111 by insisting that "anything of truth and certainty which is known about God by natural light has likewise been divinely revealed . . .'' and therefore reliance upon the book of nature is unnecessary and redundant for those to whom Scripture is available.[140] Thus Ames holds that Scripture contains all that can be known of God and His will, and that Scripture is sufficient to provide us with all the rules and precepts necessary for living to the glory of God. All virtues, all laws, positive and negative, all instruction necessary to mortal man for the guidance of his life are to be found in Scripture.

The Ramist encyclopedia was intended to provide a complete circuit of knowledge. It begins with dialectic or the art of rational thought, then proceeds through the arts of speech and communication to mathematics. Then follows physics, dealing with all created being, and theology, dealing with uncreated being, at least so far as uncreated being is knowable by men. Specifically excluded from this circle of the arts are metaphysics, natural theology, and ethics, and this exclusion is deliberate and supported by a carefully drawn argument. The Ramists are particularly virulent in their attack on metaphysics; both Ramus and Ames wrote tracts against metaphysics, and no opportunity is lost to assail this ''pretended'' art. The enemy here is Aristotle, of course, but the attack is broader than that, for what the Ramists seek to show is not that Aristotle's metaphysics is wrong, but that there is no such legitimate subject. ''There is a science which investigates being as being and the attributes which belong to this in virtue of its own nature''[141] wrote Aristotle. The Ramist reply is that there is no such science, but that what is called metaphysics is an illicit congeries of concerns pilfered from other arts. Insofar as metaphysics is concerned with the determination of the terms which can be applied to being, it is involved merely in the construction of a lexicon, which is properly the task of grammar, so that for metaphysics to claim such a function is to fall upon Charybdis. ''But if metaphysics should contend that these or other similar appellations are owed to itself not as appellations but with respect to their reasons, it surely falls upon Scylla. For then logic, from which alone the reasons of these or any other general appellations of being are taken, will justly bring action against it.''[142] For since as we have seen real definition belongs to logic, metaphysics is again an interloper. Thus so far as metaphysics deals with terms or definitions, the Ramists hold it redundant. Insofar as it deals with created being, it obviously overlaps physics and is again redundant. But the real animus of the Ramists against metaphysics arises from their belief that it overlaps theology. This fact is made very clear by Ramus himself.

The God of Aristotle has not created the world and providence does not govern all the greatest and least parts of the world; rather, God moves an eternal world as a magnet moves iron. The God of Aristotle is neither the best nor the greatest . . . because God may think nothing about the genus of men, nor may he deliberate upon human things with any charity, beneficence, or piety; because he lacks all power, he can undertake or do nothing new.

Therefore, how does such wretchedly atheistic theology appear other than as a gigantic struggle against God? . . . Therefore, theologians, drive away such a pest from the realms of the Christian religion; set forth for the Christian youth the holy gospel of Christ; define the light apart from this darkness; seek piety apart from this impiety. . . .[143]

What really outraged the Ramists was the fact that metaphysics appeared to them to be a form of pagan theology which purported to deal with God and divine things without benefit of Christian theology. Metaphysics was not only redundant—it was wrong and worse yet it was blasphemous. This theme is picked up by Ames in a particularly interesting passage in the *Marrow*. In speaking of faith and observance, Ames writes

Out of the remnants of these two parts have sprouted among certain philosophers two new theologies—Metaphysics and Ethics. Metaphysics, in fact, is the faith of the Peripatetics, and ethics is their observance.[144]

As this passage makes clear, the Ramists' attack on metaphysics is closely related to their attack on ethics. For the Ramists, ethics is a part of theology, for as we saw above it is theology alone which lays down the rules of right living. A naturalistic ethics or any ethics derived from non-Scriptural sources is therefore either redundant (if it agrees with theology) or heretical if it does not. Of course the enemy here is again Aristotle, but it is also the whole canon of classical pagan writers. Writing as a Renaissance humanist, Ramus was heir to that adulation of the classics the recovery of which had provided so vital an impetus to the rebirth of learning. But Ramus was also a Christian intent upon the defense of Christian doctrine against the paganism of the classical writers. Whatever his debts to classical learning— and they were immense—he had therefore to insist that Scripture alone provided the road to knowledge of God and to living the good life, and to banish metaphysics and naturalistic ethics from the circle of the arts. The importance of this view, boldly asserted by Ramus and strongly reiterated by Ames, upon subsequent Puritan thought needs to be particularly stressed, for no follower of Ramus or Ames could write a metaphysics, a natural theology, or a naturalistic ethics.[145]

The Ramist encyclopedia also excluded law and medicine, not to mention a host of "practical" arts such as carpentry, stonecutting, farming, etc. But the exclusion of these "arts" from the encyclopedia rests on quite different grounds than the exclusion of metaphysics, natural theology, and ethics. In the medieval and Renaissance university, the liberal arts formed the heart of the curriculum which a student pursued to acquire the master of arts degree. Beyond that lay doctoral degrees in medicine, law, theology, and philosophy. These advanced studies Ames regarded as improperly called "arts," or rather as so called only by a metonymy of the effect for the cause. Thus medicine does not add new principles, but rather shows further applications of physics (in the very broad sense defined above) to the treatment of the ill. Similarly, jurisprudence, however it may emphasize the study of the *Corpus Juris* and other writings upon civil law, borrows all its fundamental principles from theology, in which alone the rules of right conduct are to be found. Human codes of law, classical or other, must on this view be seen as applications of precepts drawn from theology to particular situations—a thesis which goes a long way to explain the character of the legal codes of New England. Thus for Ames the higher "faculties" of law, medicine, theology, and philosophy are extensions and applications of the six basic arts rather than new arts to be included in the circle.[146] Very much the same view applies to the manual arts such as carpentry or shipbuilding, which again are "arts" only by the metonymy of the effect for the cause. Most of these represent applications of physics, often combined with mathematics, although some, like printing or calligraphy, represent applications of grammar or rhetoric too. So the mechanic "arts," like the advanced studies, rest upon a foundation provided by the core curriculum of the liberal arts. Thus one sees again how fundamentally the whole Ramist movement was oriented to particular problems of curriculum reform in the Renaissance university.[147]

According to the Ramist view, the ectypal arts are learned from singulars by analysis. That means that the arts must be empirically discoverable from the study of the entypes. That this should be so is not surprising, for God created the entypes by genesis and so by analysis we should be able to discover the art. But how is it that we actually derive the specific arts from the entypes? Ames remarks:

This [en]type, which we have said is things themselves or being itself, is concrete from all the arts' principles, which not only appear and shine forth around the [en]type but also in it.[148]

By a locution which seems at first peculiar, Ames says that the "principles" of the general arts shine forth "around" the entype while those of the special arts shine forth "in" the entype. By "principles" here Ames means "arguments," for genesis proceeds from invention of arguments to their disposition and analysis from disposition to invention, so that what must be found is not only the specific arguments but, if logic itself is to be learned from the entypes, the very places themselves. In the *Dialecticae*, Ramus specifies two types of arguments— artificial and inartificial. Artificial arguments are those which are the results of artifice and embrace "all that can be constructed by system and by our own efforts."[149] Inartificial arguments are "all those which have not been furnished by ourselves but were already in existence, such as witnesses, tortures, contracts, and the like. . . ."[150] This distinction, which Ramus credits to Aristotle,[151] is reflected in the list of places Ramus gives: the first six—causes, effects, subjects, adjuncts, opposites, and comparatives—are defined as primary artificial arguments; the next three—reasoning from names, reasoning from distribution, and reasoning from definition—are classed as derivative primary artificial arguments, and the last—witness or testimony—is inartificial. As Howell has pointed out:

> The ten basic entities in Ramus' theory of logical invention are in reality the ten basic relations between predicate and subject in the logical proposition, or the ten basic relations among the objects of knowledge in the human environment.[152]

When therefore Ames says that the arguments "shine forth around" the entype rather than "in" the entype, the distinction he is making is between relations in which the object stands to other things and components constitutive of the object itself. The distinction is indeed forced, and the forcing is most obvious with respect to the category of cause, as we shall see below, yet this appears to be his meaning. When by analysis we search the entype to learn from it the art of logic, what we must be concerned with are those characteristics of the object by which we can prove something, and proof being always in propositions we must search for those categories which must be true of objects if they are to be known in propositions. This is no Kantian deduction; the characteristics are really there in the entype where God put them, and we learn them by systematic observation, induction, and experience. Similarly, since grammar and rhetoric are concerned with what can be propositionally formulated about objects, the "principles" of these arts are also said to "shine forth around" the object rather than "in" it.[153]

When we come to the special arts, however, Ames says that the "principles" shine "in" the object. Thus he writes:

> First, quantity is seen in the (en)type. For all things are primarily made from matter (so that they thus immediately differ at the first from God) and are therefore quantities. Hence the principles of measuring.[154]

Ames is here following Ramus in holding that in the order of generation efficient and material causes precede formal and final. The efficient cause, being a relation between the object and some other thing, belongs to logic, but the material cause, being constitutive of the object, is "in" the thing. Accordingly, the object has quantity, and the Ramists quite clearly view mathematics as the art of measuring quantity, whether discrete and so subject to arithmetic, or continuous and so subject to geometry. Thus despite the Ramists' remarkably clear-cut distinction between mathematics per se and its applications in physics, they thought of mathematics as learned by observation and induction from the quantitative characteristics of empirical objects.[155]

Physics is marked off from mathematics by the addition of form.

Secondly, natures are seen in the (en)type. For things are secondarily distinct from each other especially through form, which is the particular nature of things. Hence the principles of doing the work of nature.[156]

It is the addition of form to matter which constitutes the nature of the thing. Ames spells out the role of form as follows:

Form has three functions: (a) to establish a thing determinately (and hence it is called form); (b) to distinguish a thing essentially (and hence it is called difference); and (c) to effect the operations and actions of which it is the principle (and hence is called act).[157]

Physics then is the art which deals with the whole nature of things, and since form, like matter, is constitutive of the thing, the principles of physics are also said to "shine in" the entype. It is therefore from observation and induction that we learn the art of physics. And yet one cannot help remarking the peculiar limitations of the physics so described. A Ramist physics is basically a taxonomy in which various classes of objects—e.g., minerals, plants, etc.—are described by their matter and form. Only where the form is the principle of action of the thing (as, e.g., with animate things) is dynamics treated, for the Ramist classification of the arts does not treat efficient causes as part of physics. The eupraxia of physics— doing the work of nature well—certainly involves the notion of efficient cause, but in the sense of the agency of the artist, not of invariable antecedents, and since in Puritan eyes the efficient cause of the natural entype is God, it is to theology that we must look for such causes.

Thirdly, (wrote Ames) the end is seen in the (en)type. The end is that universal goodness (namely, the glory of God) which is seen in all things and toward which all things look like some arrow shot in a straight line.[158]

Ames elaborates this position as follows:

The end rises up from the union of matter and form: it is that goodness or perfection of a thing by means of which it is fitted for operation and use. This goodness in the intention of the efficient is a helping cause; the use toward which it tends is the effect; the thing or person it serves in use is the object.[159]

Thus both the efficient cause, which is God, including God's intention in the making of things, and the final cause, which is primarily the glory of God and secondarily our own blessedness, enter into the entype. And since the entype is made for this end and governed by God to that effect, these characteristics of the entype are "in" it and discernible by analysis.

There is however a fundamental difference between our ability to learn theology from the entype and our ability to learn the other arts. As we have seen, the fall had catastrophic consequences for the whole of human nature, including our purely intellectual faculties; what was intuitively obvious to Adam must now be laboriously searched out by analysis. But nowhere was the effect of the fall as destructive as upon our ability to perceive goodness in created things. "But after man has fallen, the goodness not only of the remaining creatures (which have been subjected to a curse and vanity because of man), but also of man himself (in whose conscience it had especially shone), has been so obscured and darkened that its principles remain to be comprehended there by us only as very few and indeed very corrupted."[160] This is the fundamental reason why neither a natural theology nor a natural ethics is possible: the corruption introduced by the fall has so diminished man's powers of discovering goodness and his duty from the entypes that not even by analysis can we learn to live to the glory of God. Unlike the other arts, therefore, theology is not learned from singulars by analysis—it is learned from Scripture, for God, having taken pity upon our miserable state, has given to us an explicit revelation of what we must know to live well. Alone of the arts, theology rests upon the inartificial argument of testimony, although, since the testimony is divine, it is also certain. For this reason, Ames demurs at calling theology an "art" and prefers to call it a "teaching" or "doctrine,"[161] although he and his followers felt no hesitation in including it in the circle of the arts.

Finally, there remains the status of the technometry itself. Both Miller and Gibbs have commented that technometry or technologia fulfills the role of metaphysics in Puritan thought. As Miller has commented, "In place of metaphysics there was now technologia, which was not another art but a preface or prologue to the arts, one of the 'praecognita.' "[162] Ames thought of technologia as a theory of the arts which was itself abstracted from the particular arts and so is equally empirical in origin. It is thus more than an introduction to the arts; it is a meta-discipline concerned to order and systematize the arts rather than an art itself.

From the modern standpoint, there is another omission from the circle of the arts which is perhaps even more remarkable because it is not even remarked—viz., neither Ames nor his followers refer to an art of history. This does not mean of course that these men were ahistorical in their thinking; rather it means that they did not conceive of history as we do. In fact, it seems clear that Ames regarded history as subsumed under theology. There are several reasons for this conclusion. First, as God made all things by art, according to the archetypal plan in his mind, so events, like objects, must be entypes embodying the divine plan. Indeed, the doctrine of predestination and the Puritan emphasis upon the providence of God guarantee that whatever has been, is, or will be is what God determined. Yet the entypal status of events alone does not differentiate history from the other arts, for physics too deals with entypes, and so this fact does not serve to explain why, unlike physics, history should be included under theology. The heart of the matter lies rather in a second factor—the peculiarly historical character of Puritan theology. When one turns to a work such as Ames's *Marrow*—certainly the most important single work of Puritan theology for the understanding of early seventeenth-century New England—one finds a book divided, in true Ramist fashion, into two parts dealing respectively with faith and observance. But the content of the first section, on faith, is heavily historical, and depends completely upon the presumed historicity of a series of concrete events which may be categorized as the creation, as detailed in the Mosaic account, the fall of man, "the Administration of the Covenant of Grace before the Coming of Christ," the person, life, death, and exaltation of Christ, "the Administration of the Covenant from the Coming of Christ to the End of the World," and "the End of the World."[163] These events are the bedrock of the Puritan faith: the doctrines of Christianity derive their authority from the historical fact of their utterance by Jesus Christ, or their communication by God to specific individuals at specific times and places, not from any a priori certainty or their "agreeableness" to reason. Indeed, Puritan Christianity is a doctrine built upon a specific historical framework. Although God himself is eternal and immutable, the terrestrial creation is in fact a stage created for the express purpose of allowing the enactment of the drama of salvation. The duration of this drama, at least of the terrestrial acts, is extremely short, beginning about six thousand years ago and ending at a point in time which, although as yet unknown to man, was expected to come "soon" and might well be imminent. Thus for the Puritan time was not an undifferentiated continuum; it possessed a specific structure determined by its contents. Puritan "history" was therefore not concerned, as ours is, solely with the past, but with the entire temporal drama, for the future on their view is just as fixed and certain as the past. The "historical" certainty of the second coming was no less than the historical certainty of the first, although we cannot now measure our distance from the former as we can from the latter. Puritan history was thus theological because Puritan theology was so overwhelmingly historical. And it is this temporal framework with its certainties and expectations which gave meaning to Puritan life, both public and private. For the Puritan, the crucial historical questions were not "what has happened?" or even "what will happen?", for both of these questions are already answered, but "where are we now in relation to the unfolding drama?" If the Puritans studied the past, and the present, as indeed they did, it was above all because they wanted to know the hour of Christ's return.[164] Finally, there is another factor which binds theology and history together—viz., their mutual reliance on Scripture. Almost all of the crucial events of the Puritan time frame rested solely upon the warrant of Scripture. This is obviously true of the creation and the fall, and of the administration of the covenant before Christ; it was, and is, very nearly true of the person, life, death, and exaltation of Christ, for the amount of non-Scriptural but nonapocryphal material concerning Jesus is very slight; it was largely true of the history of the early church, and it was certainly true of all the Puritans knew about what was to come. Thus history like theology rests upon the inartificial arguments furnished by testimony. In the case of secular history, these testimonies are of course fallible, but the overall historical framework of Puritan thought rested upon Scriptural testimony and therefore had the certainty of divine sanction. History cannot therefore be an art in the strict sense since it does not rest on artificial arguments; like theology, it must be a teaching.

Yet to work even the details of Scriptural history into the Christian time frame proved to be no simple task. Viewed from the Puritan perspective, the coming of Jesus was the culminating fact of Scriptural history and the climax to which the whole of the Old Testament built. Fortunately for the Puritans, this was also the perspective of the early church and particularly of those who wrote the New Testament, so that the later writers were able to build upon a foundation laid by the apostles themselves. Christianity, after all, began as a movement within Judaism, and the problem confronting the early church was to ensure the acceptance of Jesus as the Messiah of the Jews. Given the character of the Messianic tradition within Judaism, and particularly the prophecies respecting the Messiah contained in some of the prophetic books, the method of doing this was fairly clear—viz., to prove that Jesus had fulfilled these prophecies. We know that Jesus Himself, and Paul after him, used this technique,[165] and of course when addressing a Jewish audience for whom the authority of the Old Testament was already established beyond question, the logic of this approach was clear. But logical or not the approach failed, and in due course the church under the leadership of Paul turned its primary efforts to the Gentiles. Here of course the situation was virtually reversed; instead of relying upon the established authority of the Old Testament, the Christians had to justify its acceptance as authentic Scripture in addition to the then current accounts of the life and actions of Jesus—whatever these accounts may have been. Hence it became increasingly necessary to tie the Old Testament to the career of Jesus. The Messianic prophecies provided the basis for doing this, but they were hardly enough to justify the acceptance of the whole of the Old Testament as an indispensable prologue to the advent of Jesus. There therefore emerged very rapidly a set of methods of interpreting Old Testament figures and events as symbolic prophecies foreshadowing the coming of Jesus. Such methods are evident in the writings of Paul and the other New Testament authors, particularly Matthew, but it was Paul who first referred to the Old Testament event which prefigures the later one as a "type." Thus in Romans 5:14 Paul says, "Nevertheless, death reigned from Adam to Moses . . . who is the figure [typos] of him that was to come." Such "typological" readings, as they came to be called, opened a way for integrating Old and New Testament history. As Thomas Davis has remarked:

Although the references to typology in the Gospels and Epistles indicate that the terminology for describing the typical event has not been completely established, the basic concepts of typology are clearly illustrated. Writing before there is any New Testament canon, the authors view the Old Testament in the light of divine history. The Hebrew Scriptures, they believe, are not simply the sacred books of the Jewish people, and, as such, to be read in reference to that faith alone; they are the records of God's dealings with his people, and in these relationships, the advent of his divine son is foreshadowed. To the New Testament authors, typological exegesis is a method of reading history; it is centrally rooted in history itself.[166]

The development of typology was soon followed by a much more elaborate set of exegetical methods. Building upon the allegorical tradition of Old Testament exegesis which already existed among Jewish scholars, and which reached its most influential formulation with Philo of Alexandria, Origen developed a threefold method of Scriptural interpretation, involving first a literal level, then a moral level, in which the literal facts are read allegorically, and finally a spiritual or mystical level, open only to those especially enlightened by grace. Origen's work in turn led to the famous fourfold method, developed by St. Jerome and St. Augustine and given its classic formulation by Cassian, which distinguishes the literal level, the tropological (moral) level, the allegorical level, and the anagogical level. Blessed with this exegetical apparatus, the church throughout the Middle Ages had little difficulty in demonstrating intimate relations between the Old and New Testaments or in developing suitable interpretations for Scriptural passages which seemed crude or obscure. Indeed, the exegetical methods allowed so free a play of ingenuity that many came to regard them with suspicion.

The Reformation brought a renewed emphasis upon the Scripture as the basis of faith and a demand for the cleansing of the church of all the "corruptions" which human ingenuity had imposed upon the primitive order. This demand for purification affected exegesis as it affected everything else, and made Protestants hostile to the allegorical methods of the scholastics. But the Protestants still faced the interpretative problems which had given rise to such methods, and as they returned with new vigor to the study of Scriptural texts, they found there warrants for typological readings which they did not see for allegorical or anagogical ones. Calvin made extensive use of such typological readings, and so did his followers, including Ames.

Typology, as these men conceived it, is not an allegorical method, and does not depend upon human fancy. It is rather a method of relating one or more earlier historical events or things to a later one. The earlier events or things are said to be "types" of the later one; the later event is said to be the "antitype." Both type and antitype are real historical events; Moses could not be a type of Christ if he had not been a real historical figure. Moreover, the relation between type and antitype is a real similarity between the two events or things. But of course the similarities which relate a type and an antitype are not just chance resemblances; the types are created by God for the explicit purpose of indicating the antitype, and as only God creates and determines events of history, so in reading the types we are again explicating the discourse of God. Because Protestants believed that Scripture was the Word of God, that there was but one meaning to Scriptural passages, and that that meaning could be correctly explicated by gracious men through study and counsel, they believed that it was also possible to distinguish clearly what was and what was not a type-antitype relation.[167]

Compared to some Puritan writers, Ames is quite moderate in his use of typology. Yet he takes typological exegesis for granted, and uses it freely in developing his historical account of the covenant. By Ames's time of course the authority of the Old Testament was hardly an issue, but the problem of harmonizing the two Testaments remained, and so did the problem of accounting for the fact that Jews before Jesus had been saved. Samuel Mather put this issue succinctly in a later work:

> Either the Gospel was preached unto them of old, or else it will follow, that they were all *damned*, or else that they were saved *without Christ*; which to imagine were infinitely derogatory and dishonorable to the Lord Jesus Christ. The Fathers before the coming of Christ were saved and went to Heaven. But without Christ there is no salvation . . . Therefore if the Old Testament Saints were *saved*, it was by *Christ*, and if by Christ, they had the *Gospel* preached to them as well as we.[168]

Ames's answer of course is that the Covenant of Grace is revealed in the Old Testament (after all, Genesis 17 was the text usually cited by Puritans as the foundation of the covenant) but that it was revealed through types and figures. But as Ames develops this view, the covenant is unfolded progressively in time, the types becoming clearer and clearer in the course of the Old Testament history until the appearance of Christ Himself. Thus Ames writes:

> 1. Although the free, saving covenant of God has been one and the same from the beginning, the manner of the application of Christ or the administration of the new covenant has not always been so. It has varied according to the times during which the church has been in process of being gathered.
> 2. In this variety there has always been a progression from the imperfect to the more perfect.[169]

Ames distinguishes a series of stages in the administration of the covenant, the first extending from Adam to Abraham, the second from Abraham to Moses, the third from Moses to Christ, the fourth from Christ to the end of the world, and the last at the end of the world. In each succeeding stage the covenant is revealed more clearly, and in those preceding the advent of Christ the revelation is by prophecy, types, and signs. Thus for those whose minds the spirit illuminated, the new covenant was available, even though it was expressed "in types and shadows."[170]

Amesian typology was conservative; he viewed the Old Testament types as representing New Testament antitypes only, so that typology figures only in the analysis of Scriptural history. But it is not difficult to see that a much broader use of typology was possible. The Bible, and particularly the Book of Revelation, contains predictions about the future and the end of the world which Ames accepted without question. Why should not the Scripture contain types of things and events after the first coming of Jesus—indeed, why should it not contain types of all significant historical events? Ames did not extend the doctrine in this way, but a number of New Englanders did, including such highly influential leaders of the first generation as John Cotton and Richard Mather. By the use of typology, these men were able to read recent history, including their flight from England, as antitypes to such Old Testament events as the calling of the Israelites out of Babel, and so to tie secular and sacred history together in a way which allowed them to see their own role in the drama of salvation. The New Englanders were by no means the only ones to make such extensions of typology, and many New Englanders, such as Roger Williams, violently disagreed with such a use of typology. Nevertheless, such typological readings are to be found in virtually all the early New England histories, including Bradford's and Cotton Mather's. Thus when in the eighteenth century Jonathan Edwards undertook a yet more daring extension of typology, he built upon a foundation already securely laid.[171]

5. Epistemology and Psychology

If the circle of the arts is the sum of ectypal knowledge, how adequate is that knowledge? Is the ectype an accurate copy of the archetype, and if not, how serious are the discrepancies? In seeking to answer these questions, the Puritans found themselves on the horns of a dilemma. There are, on the one hand, good reasons in Puritan theory to believe that the ectype is not a particularly accurate copy of the archetype. First, Puritan theology laid great emphasis upon the transcendence and inscrutability of God. The distinction between *Ens primum* and *ens a primo* was of course designed to protect God's transcendence while still making a portion of the divine wisdom available to men, but even with respect to the archetypal "platforme," no Puritan would assert that human ideas could exactly replicate the Platonic forms in the divine mind. The most that they could ever claim for the ectype, therefore, was that it was an imperfect copy of the archetype, and this imperfection applied even to the ectypal knowledge possessed by Adam. Second, the Puritans held that as a result of the fall the power of the mind had been sadly reduced. So if even Adam's ectypes were imperfect, those of sinful men must be much more so. Third, in point of fact, Puritan knowledge of nature was exceedingly imperfect and gave them very little predictability or control. If, as their theory asserted, all creation was intelligible and revealed one plan, then it was painfully clear that they understood very little of that revelation. Puritan beliefs in the inscrutability of God and the ruin of the mind rest not only on theological doctrines but also on their patent inability to predict or control experience. For all of these reasons, therefore, the Puritans were disposed to stress the inadequacy of their ectypal knowledge. But on the other hand, there were equally strong reasons to stress the adequacy of the ectype. First, Ramist theory gave extraordinary powers to the mind. Not only does Ramist logic stress the natural dialectical ability of man, but it also endows him with a remarkable ability to perceive truth immediately. In fact, the whole Ramist doctrine of judgment adds up to the assertion that proof by reasoning is less important than proof by immediate, direct perception. We know that axioms are true because they are self-evident, and persuasiveness in discourse does not result from rigorous proof but from the orderly exhibition of self-evident truths. The appeal throughout is to an intuitive apprehension of truth, which is very like that intuitive insight which Adam manifested in the naming of the animals.[172] Second, in the theory of the covenant and in the Puritan receptiveness to science, there is clearly evident a felt need for a more stable and intelligible world. If, as technologia pledged, the creation was a work of art and so manifested a stable and intelligible plan, the Puritans wanted desperately to know what that plan was, and the more faith they could put in ectypal knowledge the more hope they could have of achieving that goal. The Puritan dilemma, therefore, was a real one, and it centered upon the problem of how the mind knows.

Puritan views of the nature of the mind and the knowing process were drawn from both Platonic-Augustinian and Aristotelian-scholastic sources. Following these traditional views, the Puritans held that all life depends upon the existence of a soul, and as living things form a scale running from mere vegetative life up to rational creatures, so the corresponding souls must form a series ordered with respect to increasing powers.[173] The vegetative soul accounts for nutriment and reproduction—the basic faculties of plants. The motive soul accounts for locomotion; it may be combined with the vegetative soul, as in moving plants, or it may exist alone, as in the stars. All animals possess both vegetative and motive souls, but they also possess a sensitive soul which gives them the power of sensation and the faculties of common sense, imagination, and sensitive memory.[174] These faculties provide the basis for the process of knowing in animals, which may be described as follows. External objects produce images, or phantasms, of themselves in the five exterior senses—sight, hearing, taste, touch, and smell. These phantasms are then carried by the animal spirits to the common sense, located in the center of the brain.[175] The common sense apprehends the phantasms, and contrasts, compares, and distinguishes them, "whereby the *Sensitive Creature* as it were, doth conclude *Sensibly*; and accordingly either embraceth, or avoids the Object."[176] Phantasms then pass to the fancy or imagination, which is located in the forebrain. The fancy has several functions: it is "to preserve them [the phantasms] in the absence of their objects,"[177] and to vivify them; but it can also synthesize new phantasms from the old.[178] Moreover, the devil can insert phantasms directly into the fancy without the mediation of the senses, so that fancy is the Achilles heel of the mind.[179] The fancy and common sense then sway the sensitive appetite (i.e., the sensual passions and affections) located in the heart, and these in turn activate the muscles to produce action.[180] Finally, from the fancy phantasms pass to the sensitive memory, located in the rear of the brain, where they are stored until needed.[181]

Man is an animal, so he possesses the vegetative, motive, and sensitive souls. But he is a rational animal, and so he also possesses a rational soul. The rational soul adds to the sensitive faculties two new ones—reason and will. Phantasms are transmitted from the fancy to the reason, which is located in the upper portion of the brain.[182] The reason or intellect is both active and passive. As active or agent intellect it abstracts from the phantasms the intelligible species, which is then received in the passive intellect in the act of knowing.[183] Rational knowledge is therefore knowledge of intelligibles, not of mere sense. In distinction from the Thomists, the Puritans hold that pure intelligibles may be completely abstracted from sensible phantasms, so that no phantasms remain associated with the pure concept. God, angels, the soul itself, and all spiritual things are known as such pure intelligible objects wholly free of sense imagery. We do indeed obtain these conceptions by abstraction from phantasms, but not until we wholly free the intelligible from the sensible have we reached a true concept of a spirit.[184] This point is important for two reasons. First, it was one of the chief grounds on which the Puritans distinguished true religion from superstition.

> And hence the Grossness of popery, and all sorts of Idolatry appears in that the Objects of their devotion must be Gross materiall, and Sensible, and the Acts of it consist much in bodily Exercise and outward rites, meanwhile the Spiritual worship which God requires is accounted too fine for them because they will not truble themselves in any abstracting Labour. And this Shews the true reason why Corruption inclines them naturally to Superstition, and Idolatry. Which Else would appear too Gross, fulsom, and absurd for any reasonable Creature.[185]

A man who cannot conceive an angel without a phantasm of a winged creature has in Puritan eyes no concept of an angel at all. Second, the rational soul is the immortal soul, and it is therefore essential that its operations should not be necessarily dependent upon sensation. In this life, reason operates on sensible phantasms, but these serve only to convey the intelligible species to the reason— they do not qualify the knowledge of intelligible species itself. "The *Act of understanding* is immediately from the soule, without any least concurrences of the body thereunto, although the things whereon that Act is fixed and conversant, require, in this estate, bodily organs to represent them unto the soule . . .''[186] Similarly, there are in effect two memories—the sensible memory, which is a faculty of the sensible soul and cannot survive death, and the intellectual memory, which is a faculty of the rational soul and is independent of phantasms.

The rational soul is self-conscious, and is not only aware of its own acts in sensation, which are known by the common sense,[187] but also knows both its own intellectual acts and itself as acting in those acts. The soul can reflect upon itself and its own nature, for since it is itself a spiritual or intelligible being, it is a proper object to itself; but whether this self-knowledge comes by direct intuition, or by inference from its awareness of its own acts about other objects, is not made clear.[188]

The second faculty of the rational soul is the will, which is located in the heart. It is the function of the will to choose good or evil, and this choice should be based upon the information furnished and the decisions made by the reason. But the choice of the will is not a mechanical effect of the decision of the reason. Ideally, reason and will concur, but the concurrence is by counsel and not necessity, and disagreement is possible. Having chosen, however, the will then commands the passions and affections and so carries its decision into action.[189]

This description of the process connecting stimulus and response is a description of how the mind should function—of what would be the case if the mind functioned as it was intended to function. But since the fall, the mind has not functioned perfectly, and the Puritans had therefore to describe psychologically what sin did to the mind. What was destroyed in the fall was not, they held, any of the faculties themselves, but rather the due order and subordination among them. The imagination now misleads reason, either by synthesizing false images or by relaying to it images directly inserted by the devil.[190] Reason, therefore, becomes confused and fails to judge rightly of the matters brought before it. Moreover, the will, which ought to be completely ruled by reason, is now in rebellion, and not only does it sometimes refuse to do reason's bidding, but it also initiates sinful actions and carries reason in its wake.[191] Thus the consequence of sin is essentially a derangement of the psychological mechanism which produces false judgments and irrational actions. Conversely, what grace restores is, from the psychological point of view, the due order among the faculties, and, particularly, reason's control over the will. Since regeneration is imperfect in this world, this restoration is never perfect and the rebellious will is never wholly subdued, but in the saints the rule of reason is more perfect than in ordinary men.[192]

These Puritan doctrines lead to certain peculiar consequences. As Miller has shown, the psychological description of the results of the fall does not accord well with the theological description. Theologically considered, depravity is a corruption of the whole nature of man—a corruption resulting from man's exaltation of himself as the supreme value, so that in every act he seeks self-gratification. Such a concept is not translatable into the crude doctrine of the faculties, and the attempt to so translate it leads to a substitution of irrationality for evil. Grace, theologically speaking, is a sense of the glory of God and an adoration of Him so complete that the demands of the self *can* be subordinated at least in part to service to the Lord. But grace, psychologically speaking, becomes rational control of impulse. Thus Puritan thought involved from the very beginning conflicts between moralism and piety—between a concept of virtue as repression and control of emotion, and a concept of virtue as passionate devotion to the ideal.[193]

If the psychological effect of sin is the derangement of the faculties, what are the epistemological consequences of this fact? The Puritans thought of this derangement as affecting not the accuracy of sense impressions but the adequacy of the knowledge derived from them.[194] If imagination is lawless and reason confused, it obviously cannot be claimed that the ectypal knowledge derived from sensory sources is an accurate copy of the archetype. This inadequacy affects all knowledge, but it particularly affects our knowledge of good and evil, for as we have already seen, it was particularly our ability to learn the moral law from the entypes which was impaired by the fall. For Christians, this special deficiency is made up by God's gift of Scripture. But for the heathen who lacks Scripture, it would seem to follow that no knowledge of the law is possible. How then can the heathen be justly damned?

The official Puritan epistemology is Aristotelian: all knowledge comes through the senses and there are no innate ideas.[195] But the official doctrine is repeatedly compromised, as it is in the following passages from Ames:

21. In this beginning of spiritual death, God imparts a certain moderation, which is either internal or external.
22. Internally this takes the shape of vestiges of God's image, Jas. 3:9. These vestiges appear both in the understanding and in the will.
23. In the understanding, there remain the principles of truth which direct both the theoretical and the practical judgment.
24. The theoretical principles deal with the true and the false, of which all men who have any use of reason have some knowledge, Rom. 1:20; Ps. 19:2, 3.
25. Practical principles distinguish between honest and dishonest, just and unjust—that God is to be worshipped, or that something is not to be done to another which one would not have done to oneself.
26. This is the law written in the hearts of all men. Rom. 2:15, *They show the mark of the law written in their hearts . . .*
28. In the will, the vestiges appear in a certain inclination to dimly known good. Although vanishing and dead, the inclination is found in all people in some degree; for this reason it can be said that at least the shadows of virtue are approved and cultivated by all. 2 Tim. 3:5, *Having a show of godliness.*[196]

God created Adam in His own image, and this image included, so the Puritans believed, an innate knowledge of God's law. The fall indeed desolated man, but it did not wholly destroy the image of God.[197] There remain even in fallen men some vestiges of that original image, and these vestiges constitute an innate knowledge of both truth and right. Thus reason is more than just a capacity for dialectic—it is also a source of truth which is tapped through the Ramist doctrine of axioms. And the conscience now becomes not just a capacity to judge respecting right and wrong, but also a source of moral principles. "This is the law written in the hearts of all men," and since it is written there all men must know it. The heathen is justly damned because he, too, has the law written in his heart, and his failure to obey it is therefore willful and not a product of ignorance. Thus the fact that Peripatetic epistemology could not guarantee the truth and universality of the moral and religious doctrines to which the Puritans were committed forced them to seek assurance in other quarters, and, like Augustine, they found it in Platonic innatism. The reason itself is thus an internal source of ideas. The Puritans limited this source severely, and hedged it about with the cumbrous psychology of the faculties, but they could not do without it.[198]

Notes — Chapter One

¹The background of the settlement is described in Perry Miller, *Orthodoxy in Massachusetts, 1630-1650* (Cambridge, Mass.: Harvard University Press, 1933); Edmund Morgan, *Visible Saints: The History of a Puritan Idea* (New York: New York University Press, 1963); Charles M. Andrews, *The Colonial Period of American History* (New Haven, Conn.: Yale University Press, 1960), Vol. I, chaps. 17-18; Edmund Morgan, *The Puritan Dilemma: The Story of John Winthrop* (Boston: Little, Brown and Co., 1958); Everett H. Emerson, *English Puritanism from John Hooper to John Milton* (Durham, N.C.: Duke University Press, 1968).

²Miller, *Orthodoxy*, esp. chaps. 3-4.

³In the last decade, questions have been raised concerning the amount of agreement which actually prevailed among the New England Puritans, even at the level of the leadership (Michael McGiffert, "American Puritan Studies in the 1960's," *William and Mary Quarterly*, ser. 3, 27:36-67 [1970]). Some of these disagreements among the leaders have long been known, but have recently received increasing emphasis—e.g., the Antinomian controversy (David Hall, *The Antinomian Controversy* 1636-1638 [Middletown, Conn.: Wesleyan University Press, 1968]); the Cotton-Williams controversy (Sacvan Bercovitch, "Typology in Puritan New England: The Williams-Cotton Controversy Reassessed," *American Quarterly* 19:166-91 [1967]); the arguments surrounding the Half-Way Covenant (Robert G. Pope, *The Half-Way Covenant: Church Membership in Puritan New England* [Princeton, N.J.: Princeton University Press, 1969]), etc. Others are somewhat less familiar, or involve reinterpretations of the issues involved in the better-known controversies (Norman S. Fiering, "Will and Intellect in the New England Mind," *William and Mary Quarterly*, ser. 3, 29:515-58 [1972]; Norman Pettit, *The Heart Prepared: Grace and Conversion in Puritan Spiritual Life* [New Haven, Conn.: Yale University Press, 1966]; Paul Lucas, "An Appeal to the Learned: The Mind of Solomon Stoddard," *William and Mary*

Quarterly, ser. 3, 30:257-92 [1973]). There is no question that such disagreements did exist, but one cannot avoid the suspicion that the emphasis they are now receiving has more to do with the efforts of a new generation of scholars to assert its independence of the ghost of Perry Miller than with the magnitude of the disagreements themselves. The disagreements are important; but many were solved: Hutchinson was banished, Cotton did compromise, Williams did leave Massachusetts, etc. Moreover, they are all arguments within the limits of a single world view; e.g., Cotton and Williams certainly disagreed about certain issues of typological interpretation, but both thoroughly accepted typological exegesis as a method of Biblical and historical analysis. In asserting therefore that the Puritan leadership held a single belief system or world view, we do not of course claim that absolute agreement prevailed on every detail, but that a broad consensus existed on fundamental points and that arguments were conducted within the limits of that consensus. To overwork once more Thomas Kuhn's much overworked notion of paradigm (Thomas Kuhn, *The Structure of Scientific Revolutions* [Chicago: University of Chicago Press, 1962]), the leadership agreed upon a single paradigm, and the problems upon which debate was focused were of the sort which arise in normal research.

[4]Miller, *Orthodoxy*, chap. 7; Edmund Morgan, *The Puritan Family* (Boston: Boston Public Library, 1956), chap. 5.

[5]The evidence is both positive and negative. On the positive side, we have clear evidence of widespread acceptance in the diaries and letters which have survived. On the negative side, studies of deviance in New England show no widespread opposition to the regime. Violations of the Puritan code of course occurred, but neither in number nor in kind do they indicate serious alienation from the Puritan system (Emil Oberholzer, *Delinquent Saints* [New York: Columbia University Press, 1956]). The same conclusion appears justified by the Court records.

[6]Perry Miller, *The New England Mind: The Seventeenth Century* (New York: Macmillan Co., 1939), p. 92. This work is hereafter cited as *New England Mind I*.

[7]Samuel Eliot Morison, *Harvard College in the Seventeenth Century* (Cambridge, Mass.: Harvard University Press, 1936), pt. I, p. 236.

[8]William Thomas Costello, "The Scholastic Curriculum at Early Seventeenth Century Cambridge" (Ph.D. diss., Harvard University, 1952), p. 145.

[9]Aristotle, "Physics," I.6.189b34ff, in *The Basic Works of Aristotle*, ed. McKeon (New York: Random House, 1941), p. 230.

[10]*Ibid.*, II.3.194b16-195a27.

[11]W. D. Ross, *Aristotle* (New York: Meridian Press, 1963), p. 99.

[12]*Ibid.*, p. 77.

[13]Herbert Butterfield, *The Origins of Modern Science, 1300-1800* (New York: Macmillan Co., 1956), p. 14.

[14]Samuel Johnson, "An Encyclopedia of Philosophy," in *Samuel Johnson, President of King's College, His Career and Writings*, ed. Herbert and Carol Schneider (New York: Columbia University Press, 1929), II:149.

[15]Butterfield, *Origins*, pp. 2-18.

[16]Miller, *New England Mind I*, pp. 10-21.

[17]*Ibid.*, p. 12ff.

[18]*Ibid.*, pp. 111, 133, 182ff.

[19]Samuel Willard, *A Compleat Body of Divinity in Two Hundred and Fifty Expository Lectures on the Assembly's Shorter Catechism* (Boston: B. Green and S. Kneeland for B. Eliot and D. Henchman, 1726), pp. 15, 211; Miller, *New England Mind I*, pp. 30-32, 111. Cf. also John Calvin, *Institutes of the Christian Religion*, trans. Allen (Philadelphia: Presbyterian Board of Education, n.d.), I:282-308; Jaroslav Pelikan, "Cosmos and Creation: Science and Theology in Reformation Thought," *Proceedings of the American Philosophical Society* 105:464-69 (1961); Lee Wayland Gibbs, "The Technometry of William Ames" (Ph.D. diss., Harvard University, 1967), pp. 340ff.

[20]Miller, *New England Mind I*, pp. 19-21.

[21]*The New-England Primer*, ed. Ford (New York: Teachers College, Columbia University, 1962), unpaginated; Miller, *New England Mind I*, pp. 21ff. William Ames, *The Marrow of Theology*, trans. Eusden (Boston: Pilgrim Press, 1968), pp. 116ff.

[22]Calvin, *Institutes*, II:207.

[23]Ames, *Marrow*, pp. 149-60; Miller, *New England Mind I*, pp. 25ff.

[24]Pettit, *Heart Prepared*.

[25]Ames, *Marrow*, pp. 167-71; Miller, *New England Mind I*, pp. 49ff.

[26]Miller, *New England Mind I*, pp. 49f, 435ff; Morgan, *Visible Saints*, chap. 3.

27 *The Book of the General Laws and Liberties Concerning the Inhabitants of Massachusetts* (Cambridge: Printed according to order of the General Court, 1648).

28Morgan, *Puritan Family*, p. 78; Miller, *New England Mind I*, chap. 14; Perry Miller and Thomas Johnson, *The Puritans* (New York: American Book Co., 1938), pp. 180-94. As time went on the franchise was broadened. See Richard C. Simmons, "Freemanship in Early Massachusetts: Some Suggestions and a Case Study," *William and Mary Quarterly*, ser. 3, 19:422-28 (1962).

29Robert Middlekauff, *The Mathers* (New York: Oxford University Press, 1971), pp. 4-5.

30Miller, *New England Mind I*, pp. 387f.

31Cf. Perry Miller, "The Marrow of Puritan Divinity," in *Errand into the Wilderness* (Cambridge, Mass.: Harvard University Press, 1956), pp. 48-98 and Miller, *New England Mind I*, chaps. 13-15, for a detailed exposition of the Federal theology and its social ramifications. The Federal theology was not confined to New England, nor did it originate there. See Miller, *New England Mind I*, app. B.

32Pettit, *Heart Prepared*; Gerald Goodman, "The Myth of 'Arminian Calvinism,' in Eighteenth Century New England," *New England Quarterly* 41:213-37 (1968).

33Miller, *New England Mind I*, pp. 379ff; Miller, *Errand*, pp. 71ff.

34Petri Rami Veromandui, *Dialecticae partitiones, ad celeberrimam et illustrissimam Lutetiae Parisiorum Academiam* (Parisiis: Iacobus Bogardus, 1543).

35Miller, *New England Mind I*, chap. 5; Frank Pierrepont Graves, *Peter Ramus and the Educational Reformation of the Sixteenth Century* (New York: Macmillan Co., 1912), chaps. 1-4; Walter J. Ong, S. J., *Ramus, Method, and the Decay of Dialogue* (Cambridge, Mass.: Harvard University Press, 1958), chap. 2. On the Ramist literature, see Miller, *New England Mind I*, app. A, and Walter J. Ong, S.J., *Ramus and Talon Inventory* (Cambridge, Mass.: Harvard University Press, 1958). On the Ramist movement in England, see Wilbur Samuel Howell, *Logic and Rhetoric in England, 1500-1700* (Princeton, N. J.: Princeton University Press, 1956).

36Howell, *Logic and Rhetoric*, pp. 9-11; Ong, *Ramus Method*, pp. 92ff, 100-102, 154ff; Norman E. Nelson, *Peter Ramus and the Confusion of Logic, Rhetoric, and Poetry*, University of Michigan Contributions in Modern Philology, no. 2 (Ann Arbor, April 1947).

[37]Aristotle, *Topica*, I.1.100a18-100b23; Ong, *Ramus Method*, pp. 60-62, 101; Howell, *Logic and Rhetoric*, pp. 154ff.

[38]"The subject of the Topics are [*sic*] essentially the so-called *loci* . . . Aristotle never defined them, and so far no-one has succeeded in saying briefly and clearly what they are. In any case it is a matter of certain very general prescriptions for shaping arguments." I. M. Bocheński, *A History of Formal Logic*, trans. Ivo Thomas (Notre Dame: University of Notre Dame Press, 1961), p. 51.

[39]Aristotle, *Topica*, II.2.109b30-33.

[40]Ong, *Ramus Method*, pp. 53-54, 62; Ernest Moody, *Truth and Consequence in Mediaeval Logic* (Amsterdam: North-Holland Press, 1953); Philotheus Boehner, *Medieval Logic* (Chicago: University of Chicago Press, 1952).

[41]Ong, *Ramus Method*, pp. 60, 154ff; Costello, "Scholastic Curriculum," pp. 9, 15ff.

[42]Ong, *Ramus Method*, pp. 55f.

[43]*Ibid.*, pp. 94ff.

[44]*Ibid.*, p. 101.

[45]*Ibid.*, p. 112; Howell, *Logic and Rhetoric*, pp. 15-16.

[46]Agricola, quoted in Ong, *Ramus Method*, p. 112.

[47]Howell, *Logic and Rhetoric*, p. 15.

[48]Ong, *Ramus Method*, pp. 112ff.

[49]*Ibid.*, p. 122.

[50]Agricola, quoted in *ibid.*, pp. 117-18.

[51]Howell, *Logic and Rhetoric*, pp. 23-24.

[52]Ong, *Ramus Method*, pp. 115, 123-30, 182ff.

[53]*Ibid.*, p. 176.

[54]*Ibid.*, pp. 177f; R. Hooykaas, *Humanisme, Science et Réforme: Pierre de la Ramée (1515-1572)* (Leyde: E. J. Brill, 1958), p. 22; Peter Ramus, "The Meaning of Dialectics," in Dagobert Runes, ed., *Classics in Logic* (New York: Philosophical Library, 1962), pp. 641-42.

[55]Ramus, "Dialectics," pp. 642-43, 649.

[56]Ong, *Ramus Method*, p. 183; Ramus, "Dialectics," pp. 649-50.

[57]Graves, *Ramus*, p. 155.

[58]Miller, *New England Mind I*, pp. 133-36.

[59]*Ibid.*, pp. 139ff; Ong, *Ramus Method*, pp. 245ff.

[60]Ong, *Ramus Method*, pp. 245ff. The method of prudence is given only minor importance.

[61]*Ibid.*, p. 245.

[62]Howell, *Logic and Rhetoric*, pp. 151f.

[63]*Ibid.*, pp. 151-53.

[64]Ong, *Ramus Method*, pp. 260f; Miller, *New England Mind I*, pp. 127ff.

[65]Ramus, quoted in Ong, *Ramus Method*, p. 246.

[66]*Ibid.*

[67]Cf. the diagrams in the beginning of Ames's *Marrow*.

[68]Ong, *Ramus Method*, pp. 263f.

[69]*Ibid.*, pp. 136-39; Costello, "Scholastic Curriculum," chap. 2.

[70]Hooykaas, *Humanisme*, p. 22.

[71]*Ibid.*, pp. 20-50.

[72]Ong, *Ramus Method*, pp. 262, 270; Howell, *Logic and Rhetoric*, pp. 151-52.

[73]Howell, *Logic and Rhetoric*, pp. 6-7, 66ff.

[74]*Ibid.*, p. 165.

[75]*Ibid.*

[76]*Ibid.*; Ramus, "Dialectics," pp. 647-48.

[77]Howell, *Logic and Rhetoric*, pp. 165ff; Ong, *Ramus Method*, pp. 277ff; Ramus, "Dialectics," p. 648.

[78]Ong, *Ramus Method*, pp. 283-84; Miller, *New England Mind I*, chap. 12.

[79]Graves, *Ramus*, pp. 24-25; Ong, *Ramus Method*, pp. 42-44; Hooykaas, *Humanisme*, p. 23.

[80]Hooykaas, *Humanisme*, pp. 20-32; Neal W. Gilbert, *Renaissance Concepts of Method* (New York: Columbia University Press, 1960), pp. 129-44; Graves, *Ramus*, pp. 160-72.

[81]Howell, *Logic and Rhetoric*, pp. 173f.

[82]*Ibid.*, pp. 178ff.

[83]*Ibid.*, pp. 189f.

[84]*Ibid.*, pp. 206-17; Miller, *New England Mind I*, pp. 502-5; Miller, *Errand*, pp. 57-60.

[85]Johnson, *Writings*, II:61.

[86]Morison, *Harvard College*, I:161-64; Miller, *New England Mind I*, p. 161.

[87]Aristotle, *Nicomachean Ethics*, VI.4.1140a11-13.

[88]Ong, *Ramus Method*, pp. 156, 160ff; Ramus, "Dialectics," p. 646.

[89]Costello, "Scholastic Curriculum," p. 59.

[90]See Johnson's "Encyclopedia" where physics, mathematics, and theology, which were classed as sciences at Cambridge (Costello, "Scholastic Curriculum," pp. 59-62) are treated as arts. Johnson, *Writings*, II:115 (axiom 532), 137 (axiom 777).

[91]Richardson, quoted in Miller, *New England Mind I*, p. 164.

[92]Miller, *New England Mind I*, p. 163.

[93]Alexander Richardson, *The Logician's School-Master: or, A Comment upon Ramus Logick* (London: Gartrude Dawson, 1657), p. 14.

[94]Miller, *New England Mind I*, p. 161.

[95]Aristotle, *Nicomachean Ethics*, I.1.1094a1-2.

96Miller, *New England Mind I*, p. 164.

97Gibbs, "Technometry," p. 157.

98Richardson, *Logician's School-Master*, p. 5.

99Johnson, *Writings*, II:63.

100Gibbs, "Technometry," p. 165.

101*Ibid.*, pp. 271-73.

102Ames, *Marrow*, p. 95; partially quoted in Miller, *New England Mind I*, p. 167.

103Miller, *New England Mind I*, p. 177; Johnson, *Writings*, II:65ff.

104Ames, *Marrow*, p. 97.

105Richardson, *Logician's School-Master*, pp. 15-16.

106Miller, *New England Mind I*, pp. 160-61; Gibbs, "Technometry," pp. 192, 538f.; Johnson, *Writings*, II:65.

107Miller, *New England Mind I*, p. 165; Johnson, *Writings*, II:67.

108Johnson, *Writings*, II:67.

109Miller, *New England Mind I*, pp. 165-66.

110Richardson, quoted in Miller, *ibid.*, p. 162.

111Samuel Eliot Morison, *The Intellectual Life of Colonial New England* (New York: New York University Press, 1956), chap. 10; Miller, *New England Mind I*, p. 217ff.

112Miller, *New England Mind I*, p. 165; Johnson, *Writings*, II:69.

113Richardson, quoted in Miller, *New England Mind I*, p. 162.

114Richardson, *Logician's School-Master*, p. 253. Note the ambiguous use of "axiom" to refer to true propositions and to propositions in general.

115*Ibid.*, p. 335.

116*Ibid.*, p. 22; Miller, *New England Mind I*, pp. 168-69.

[117]Gibbs, "Technometry," p. 300.

[118]*Ibid.*, pp. 213-14.

[119]*Ibid.*, pp. 376ff.

[120]The best example of such an encyclopedia which is easily available in English is Samuel Johnson's, cited in n. 14 above. Johnson's work includes a brief technologia as an introduction. The most extensive and instructive statement of the technologia doctrine however is in William Ames's technometry, which has been translated by Lee Gibbs in pp. 157-208 of the work cited in n. 19 above, and to which Gibbs has added a splendid and invaluable thesis-by-thesis commentary which ought to be better known.

[121]Gibbs, "Technometry," pp. 245ff.

[122]*Ibid.*, pp. 252ff.

[123]Johnson, *Writings*, II:69.

[124]*Ibid.*, p. 83.

[125]*Ibid.*, p. 79.

[126]Gibbs, "Technometry," pp. 318ff.

[127]*Ibid.*, pp. 255ff.

[128]*Ibid.*, p. 186.

[129]Johnson, *Writings*, II:115-37.

[130]Eric T. Bell, *The Development of Mathematics* (New York: McGraw-Hill Co., 1945) chap. 6.

[131]Gibbs, "Technometry," pp. 260ff.

[132]*Ibid.*

[133]*Ibid.*, pp. 476ff.

[134]Johnson, *Writings*, II:141, 145.

[135]Gibbs, "Technometry," p. 387.

[136]*Ibid.*, pp. 387f.

137*Ibid.*, p. 494.

138*Ibid.*, p. 187.

139*Ibid.*, p. 188.

140*Ibid.*

141Aristotle, *Metaphysics*, IV.1.1003.21-22.

142Gibbs, "Technometry," p. 318.

143*Ibid.*, p. 313.

144*Ibid.*, pp. 316, 184n.

145*Ibid.*, p. 312. This does not mean however that such subjects were never studied in New England or at Harvard. The technologia of Richardson and Ames was the dominant intellectual system of New England, but other systems were also studied. Both metaphysics and ethics were certainly studied at Harvard fairly early in the seventeenth century, as S. E. Morison has shown (Morison, *Harvard College*, I:252, 260f). Nevertheless, it is also true that no American Puritan wrote either a metaphysics or a naturalistic ethics during that century.

146Gibbs, "Technometry," pp. 547-62.

147*Ibid.*, pp. 562-95.

148*Ibid.*, p. 172.

149*Ibid.*, p. 449.

150*Ibid.*

151Howell, *Logic and Rhetoric*, p. 115.

152*Ibid.*, p. 156.

153Gibbs, "Technometry," pp. 328-32.

154*Ibid.*, pp. 172-73.

155*Ibid.*, pp. 332-34.

156*Ibid.*, p. 173.

157*Ibid.*, p. 335.

158*Ibid.*, p. 173.

159*Ibid.*, p. 336.

160*Ibid.*, p. 173.

161*Ibid.*, p. 267.

162Miller, *New England Mind I*, p. 175.

163Cf. contents of Ames, *Marrow*.

164Miller, *New England Mind I*, chap. 16; Miller and Johnson, *Puritans*, pp. 81-90.

165Luke 24:27; Acts 17:2-4.

166Thomas Davis, "The Traditions of Puritan Typology," in *Typology and Early American Literature*, ed. Bercovitch (Amherst: University of Massachusetts Press, 1972), p. 17.

167Perry Miller, Introduction to Jonathan Edwards, *Images and Shadows of Divine Things*, ed. Miller (New Haven, Conn.: Yale University Press, 1948); Bercovitch, "Typology in Puritan New England"; Davis, "Traditions of Puritan Typology."

168Samuel Mather, *The Figures or Types of the Old Testament* (New York: Johnson Reprint Corp., 1969), p. 7.

169Ames, *Marrow*, p. 202.

170*Ibid.*, p. 206.

171Bercovitch, "Typology in Puritan New England."

172Miller, *New England Mind I*, p. 133.

173Johnson, *Writings*, II:147ff.

174Miller, *New England Mind I*, p. 240.

175*Ibid.* There is disagreement respecting both the location of the faculties in the brain, and the order in which phantasms reach them. Morton places the imagination in the center of the brain and the common sense in the forebrain (Charles

Morton, *Compendium Physicae* [Boston: Publications of the Colonial Society of Massachusetts, 1940], vol. 33, pp. 180ff). Willard has the phantasms go first to the imagination and only then to the "cogitation" or common sense (Willard, *Compleat Body*, p. 120).

176Willard, *Compleat Body*, p. 120. On the common sense, see Miller, *New England Mind I*, pp. 240-41; Morton, *Compendium*, pp. 180-81.

177Miller, *New England Mind I*, p. 241.

178*Ibid.*, pp. 246f; Morton, *Compendium*, pp. 181-82. Willard gives this function to the common sense (*Compleat Body*, p. 120).

179Miller, *New England Mind I*, p. 257.

180*Ibid.*, pp. 241f.

181*Ibid.*, pp. 240-41; Morton, *Compendium*, pp. 182-84; Willard, *Compleat Body*, pp. 120f.

182Miller, *New England Mind I*, p. 241.

183Edward Reynolds, *A Treatise of the Passions and Faculties of the Soul of Man* (London: for Robert Bostock, 1640), p. 403. See Miller, *New England Mind I*, p. 515.

184Reynolds, *Soul*, pp. 403-8; Morton, *Compendium*, pp. 200ff.

185Morton, *Compendium*, p. 203.

186Reynolds, *Soul*, p. 403.

187Morton, *Compendium*, pp. 180ff.

188Reynolds, *Soul*, p. 404. Aristotle's position on this point is far from clear. Cf. Ross, *Aristotle*, pp. 178ff; Aristotle, *Metaphysics*, XII. 9.

189Miller, *New England Mind I*, pp. 247ff; Morton, *Compendium*, pp. 203-4.

190Miller, *New England Mind I*, p. 257.

191*Ibid.*, pp. 250, 260.

192*Ibid.*, pp. 260ff.

193*Ibid.*, pp. 256f, 260ff.

[194]*Ibid.*, pp. 268-69.

[195]*Ibid.*, p. 269; Richardson, quoted in *ibid.*, 162.

[196]Ames, *Marrow*, pp. 123-24.

[197]Johnson, *Writings*, II:59.

[198]Miller, *New England Mind I*, pp. 269ff; Willard, *Compleat Body*, pp. 40, 573-74.

Chapter Two

The Impact of Science

Chapter Two

The Impact of Science

1. Newton and Locke

In 1543—the year that Ramus published the *Dialecticae*—a posthumous work of an obscure Polish priest named Nicholas Copernicus was published. This work, *De Revolutionibus Orbium*, is justly celebrated in the history of science as the first modern assertion of the heliocentric theory in astronomy. Nevertheless, the book was not widely celebrated in its own day, for the heliocentric theory as Copernicus conceived it was highly unsatisfactory. Copernicus still believed in circular orbits, and to fit heliocentric circular orbits to the six known planets on the basis of the astronomical data then available required a total of thirty-four cycles, including epicycles. To be sure, Copernicus's theory was simpler than Ptolemy's—Ptolemy had needed a total of eighty cycles—but simplicity was not the deciding factor. The major objection to the Copernican system was the fact that it flatly contradicted the physics of Aristotle, for there was no way within Aristotle's theory to explain either the motion of the earth, or why if the earth were moving the objects on its surface did not fly off. The Copernican theory might be a simple and elegant calculating device, but as a true account of celestial phenomena it was impossible—so long as Aristotle's physics ruled.[1]

This situation was modified somewhat by Kepler's work. On the basis of astronomical observations, Kepler finally succeeded in discovering the true nature of the planetary orbits and so replaced the thirty-four cycles of Copernicus with six simple ellipses. Kepler's laws constitute one of the greatest triumphs of descriptive astronomy: they yield a correct description of the shape of the planetary orbits and of the variation in a planet's velocity as it moves along its path. Yet despite the great simplicity of Kepler's description, the fundamental objection remained: what Kepler described was impossible in terms of Aristotelian physics.[2]

But even as Kepler worked, Galileo was laying the basis for the new physics. We have seen above that in Aristotelian physics uniform motion horizontal to the earth's surface requires a constant force acting continuously, so that where no visible mover is in evidence a spiritual efficient cause had to be postulated. The inadequacy of this account was clearly evident in the case of projectiles: they continue to move after contact with the mover ceases, yet it can hardly be held that they are moved by spirits. Galileo undertook the investigation of this anomaly, and so was led to his researches on the law of falling bodies and ultimately to the formulation of the first law of motion. This law, as Butterfield has pointed out, "is the great factor which in the seventeenth century helped to drive the spirits out of the world and opened the way to a universe that ran like a piece of clockwork,"[3] for it made unnecessary the spiritual causes which the older physics could not do without.

Important advances were also being made in mathematics, chemistry, and theories respecting the structure of matter. Descartes's discovery of analytic geometry made it possible to put equations to the orbits, and so laid the basis for an adequate mathematical attack on physical problems. And other mathematicians— Pascal, Fermat, Wallis, Barrow, and many more—were slowly groping their way toward the calculus.[4] Meanwhile, the classical theories of the atomic structure of matter were experiencing a revival of interest. Bacon called attention to them in his *Thoughts on the Nature of Things*, and Gassendi and other European writers elaborated theories of matter which were atomic and mechanical. But the most persuasive champion of the "corpuscular" theory in England was Robert Boyle, whose brilliant attack on the Aristotelian theory of the four elements and the alchemical theory of the three principles revolutionized chemistry and redirected chemical research toward the analysis of compounds and the discovery of their elementary components. Boyle's formulation of the corpuscular theory greatly influenced both Newton and Locke, and it was from Boyle that Locke derived the theory of primary and secondary qualities.[5]

Thus when Newton appeared, many elements of his theory were already in existence. But these elements remained separate until he put them together, and it was not until then that his contemporaries grasped the significance of these elements. The Copernican theory was known in New England in the mid-seventeenth century, as was Kepler's work, but Aristotle's physics continued to be the accepted doctrine.[6] In hindsight, we can see that the situation was being prepared for Newton from 1543 on, but to his contemporaries his work came as a magnificent surprise.

Newtonian mechanics was the first great scientific synthesis achieved by man. Newton brought the physics begun by Galileo to full development. He clarified the basic notions of time, space, and mass, and formulated the three fundamental laws of motion and the law of universal gravitation. He then proved that if the sun and planets obeyed these laws, the orbits described by the planets would have precisely the characteristics described by Kepler's laws, and he succeeded in showing that the orbits calculated by his theory did in fact fit the known empirical data. Moreover, in order to give an exact mathematical formulation of his system, Newton invented the calculus, and stated the laws of motion in the form of total differential equations—a feat which Einstein called ''perhaps the greatest advance in thought that a single individual was ever privileged to make.''[7] Newton thus created a mathematical physics capable of explaining not only terrestrial phenomena like the flight of projectiles but the flight of the planets as well.[8]

Without attempting here a review of the *Principia* or of its influence, there are certain features of Newton's work which must be noted. First, Newton's theory proved to be amazingly accurate. For over two hundred years it continued to furnish remarkably adequate explanations of mechanical phenomena and to lead to new and important discoveries. Not until the twentieth century was any significant revision of it attempted. Second, Newton's theory was extremely powerful and dealt with fundamental aspects of nature. The problem of the motion of material bodies had always been the most prominent problem of physics, and in giving a solution of it which extended to such striking and impressive elements of our experience as the motions of the planets and of the moon, the behavior of falling bodies, and of the tides, Newton seemed to have probed to the very heart of nature. Moreover, his theory was so seemingly complete, and permitted such absolute predictability that he seemed to have solved these problems once and for all.

Third, Newton's work brought about an expansion of the intellectual horizons of his age greater even than that produced by the discovery of the New World. In solving the riddle of the skies, he pushed the frontiers of human knowledge out into the heavens themselves, and gave his contemporaries the first convincing demonstration of what science—and the mind of man—could achieve. When Roger Cotes wrote the preface to the second edition of the *Principia*, he concluded his argument in favor of experimental science with the following words:

> Fair and equal judges will therefore give sentence in favor of this most excellent method of philosophy, which is founded on experiments and observations. And it can hardly be said or imagined, what light, what splendor, hath accrued to that method from this admirable work of our illustrious author, whose happy and sublime genius, resolving the most difficult problems, and reaching to discoveries of which the mind of man was thought incapable before, is deservedly admired by all those who are somewhat more than superficially versed in these matters.[9]

No one had doubted that there was a plan to creation or that it could be known in part by man, but no one had ever thought that man could actually grasp the

fundamental laws of the universe—until Newton published. Pope's famous line—
"God said 'Let Newton be,' and all was light"—accurately mirrors not only the
awe which his achievement inspired, but also the sense of enlightenment which it
brought. The blank wall of unintelligibility which nature had always shown to man
was suddenly gone, and a new world lay open to investigation.

Fourth, and perhaps most important of all, Newton provided his age with a
model of nature which was to prove the most fruitful model ever devised.

> According to Newton's system, physical reality is characterized by the
> concepts of time, space, material point, and force (reciprocal action of
> material points). Physical events, in Newton's view, are to be regarded as the
> motions, governed by fixed laws, of material points in space. The material
> point is our only mode of representing reality when dealing with changes
> taking place in it, the solitary representative of the real, in so far as the real is
> capable of change. Perceptible bodies are obviously responsible for the
> concept of material point; people conceived it as an analogue of mobile
> bodies, stripping these of the characteristics of extension, form, orientation in
> space, and all "inward" qualities, leaving only inertia and translation and
> adding the concept of force. The material bodies, which had led psychologi-
> cally to our formulation of the concept of the "material point," had now
> themselves to be regarded as systems of material points. It should be noted
> that this theoretical scheme is in essence an atomistic and mechanistic one.
> All happenings were to be interpreted purely mechanically—that is to say,
> simply as motions of material points according to Newton's law of motion.[10]

In the Newtonian view, nature consists of time, space, material points, and forces
acting among them. These forces act always between pairs of points, in the
direction of a right line connecting the two points, and vary inversely with the
square of the distance. The forces between points are wholly determined by
intrinsic characteristics of the points (mass) and by the distance between them.
Moreover, given any isolated system of material points, if the position, velocity,
direction, and mass of the points are known at any one time, the entire future, and
past, behavior of the system is absolutely determined and can in principle be
calculated—i.e., the system is absolutely deterministic.[11] Strictly speaking what
Newton had shown was only that this model could account for the motion of
material bodies, but neither Newton nor his age conceived the model so narrowly:
"up to the end of the nineteenth century it formed the program of every worker in
the field of theoretical physics."[12] Newton's work convinced his contemporaries
that nature possessed the simple intelligible structure represented by this model, so
that all physical phenomena were regarded as explicable in these terms. The one
and two fluid theories of electricity and magnetism and the caloric theory of heat,
the corpuscular theory of light, and even the wave theory of light were based on
Newton's laws; similarly, the kinetic theory of heat, the kinetic theory of gas, and

even the revolutionary developments in electricity, magnetism, and optics due to Faraday, Boltzman, and Maxwell were conceived and governed by the Newtonian model.[13] How completely this model governed men's minds may be indicated by the fact that even in the late nineteenth century reputable scientists could assert that what can never be explained by Newton's laws is incapable of scientific explanation.[14] Certainly no other single achievement in the history of science has proven so remarkably successful and fruitful for so long a time.

But despite the scientific success of the Newtonian model, the philosophic problems which it raised were appalling. In Aristotle's substance-and-attribute model of nature, there is no reason to question the accuracy of sense impressions, for everything in the model assures us that we do know what we seem to know—that the world really consists of substantial things which we know by their attributes. But in the Newtonian model we are presented with a description of nature which does not correspond to our sense experience. What Whitehead has called the bifurcation of nature emerges full blown with the Newtonian model.[15] For the material objects of experience must now be interpreted as systems of material points—yet we do not perceive the points while we do perceive continuous colored surfaces. As Whitehead has observed, "It seems an extremely unfortunate arrangement that we should perceive a lot of things that are not there";[16] and it is still more unfortunate that we should not perceive things that are there— nevertheless, on the Newtonian model this is the case. The question therefore becomes critical—how is what we perceive related to reality as defined by the model? And how is knowledge possible?

It was the great virtue of John Locke's *Essay Concerning the Human Understanding*[17] that it provided a seemingly clear and adequate answer to these questions. Locke begins his *Essay* with an analysis of the nature and source of our ideas. By an "idea" Locke means that which is the object of thought—"that which his mind is applied about whilst thinking."[18] These ideas come to us from two sources—sensation and reflection. By "ideas of sensation" Locke means ideas of qualities perceived through the five external senses, such as red or yellow;[19] by "ideas of reflection" he means ideas of the operations of our own minds, such as thinking or believing.[20] These two sources, Locke holds, account for all our ideas—there are no other organs of perception and no innate ideas.[21] But in denying innate ideas, Locke meant that no man is born with ideas already consciously before the mind: he did not deny that men are born with the capacity to form certain ideas upon the presentation of particular stimuli in experience, for he saw no difference between this assertion and the assertion that all knowledge originated in experience.[22] All our knowledge, therefore, is knowledge of ideas derived from sensation or reflection. But how accurate is that knowledge?

Locke fully accepted the Newtonian model, including its implicit atomism, as defining the nature of physical reality, and like Boyle, Newton, and others, he assumed that the mass-points must be material particles. Accordingly, Locke asked himself what qualities we must assume these particles to have if they are to behave as the model requires. Following Boyle,[23] Locke asserted that the particles must possess "solidity, extension, figure, motion or rest, and number," and these qualities, since they qualify the ultimate particles themselves, he calls "primary qualities,"[24] or sometimes "mathematical qualities." So far as the model is concerned, these qualities suffice, and there is no need to postulate any further qualities.

It is clear that we do not directly perceive the ultimate particles themselves, for they are too small to be detected by our senses. Yet we do perceive aggregates of such particles, which we call bodies, and these bodies produce effects in us, called sensations. As these sensations are produced in us by bodies even at some distance from us, "it is evident some singly imperceptible bodies must come from them to the eyes, and thereby convey to the brain some motion; which produces these ideas which we have of them in us."[25] The action of the particles upon us thus produces the sensations which are the source of our ideas of the primary qualities in the object, and "the ideas of primary qualities of bodies are resemblances of them, and their patterns do really exist in the bodies themselves . . ."[26]—that is, our ideas of these primary qualities are accurate replicas of the primary qualities themselves. But we have ideas of other sensible qualities besides these, such as color, scent, heat, etc.—what is the origin and status of these ideas? Locke's answer is that these other sensible qualities are not replicas of anything in the external objects themselves, but are effects produced in us by the action of the particles upon our senses, and depend upon the particular motion, size, number, and figure of the particles.[27] Our ideas of colors, therefore, are not copies of any quality in the object, but they do correspond to the object as effects to causes; hence the object may be said to possess "secondary qualities" which may be defined as powers of the object to produce certain sensible effects in us, where by "powers" what is meant is that the particular particles which come from the object affect our senses in a certain manner. Thus all our sensible ideas do correspond to reality, as described by the Newtonian model, but only our ideas of primary qualities are truly descriptive of that reality—our other sensible ideas result from the secondary qualities of objects, and correspond to those objects as effects to causes.

Locke's assertion that our ideas of the primary qualities "resemble" the primary qualities in the objects was an extremely unfortunate way of stating his case, for it is obvious that Locke could not prove that this resemblance obtained. Later critics—notably, Berkeley, Edwards, and Hume—had no difficulty in showing that the ideas themselves can give no warrant for this assertion, and were so able to reduce all qualities to secondary ones. Yet this criticism, while true, still misses the point, for what really differentiated primary and secondary qualities for Locke was not any inherent difference in the ideas per se, but their relation to the Newtonian model. The bifurcation of nature arises from the assertion that nature is atomic whereas our perceptions are not of atoms but of qualitative continua.

Locke's intent was to eliminate the bifurcation by showing that if we postulate primary qualities as true of the atoms, we may then explain our sensory experience as due to the action of systems of such atoms upon our senses. Our ideas of primary qualities are true of the atoms because we so postulate the atoms to be—not because the ideas carry some inherent warrant. In this sense, Locke was really a physiological psychologist of considerable sophistication, and the acclaim which he received as the greatest psychologist of his age was not misapplied.

Our ideas of sensible qualities such as red or cold or hard, Locke holds to be unanalyzable, and he therefore calls them "simple ideas."[28] Similarly, we have ideas of reflection, such as thinking or willing, which appear to be incapable of analysis, and these Locke terms "simple ideas of reflection."[29] A "simple idea," therefore, is one which cannot be analyzed into component ideas, and in the perception of which the mind is entirely passive—the mind cannot refuse to perceive bodies which affect the senses nor can it fail to perceive its own operations.[30] Simple ideas thus refer to two very different types of objects—sensible qualities and mental operations, and this diversity of extension was to become a serious problem for Locke's followers.

Out of our simple ideas the mind generates complex ideas. Locke distinguishes three basic types of complex ideas—ideas of modes, relations, and substances. Ideas of modes are complex ideas, such as "beauty" or "theft," which are combinations of simple ideas but which are themselves qualitative descriptions of objects.[31] Ideas of relation involve the "comparison" of other ideas and so involve more elementary ideas.[32] Ideas of substances are the ideas of those things which have the qualitative characteristics described by simple ideas or ideas of modes—it is the idea of a subject of inhesion taken apart from the inhering qualities. Locke makes it very clear that the idea of substance has no other content than this, viz.:

> So that if any one will examine himself concerning his notion of pure substance in general, he will find he has no other idea of it at all, but only a supposition of he knows not what *support* of such qualities which are capable of producing simple ideas in us; which qualities are commonly called accidents. If any one should be asked, what is the subject wherein colour or weight inheres, he would have nothing to say, but the solid extended parts; and if he were demanded, what is it that solidity and extension adhere in, he would not be in a much better case than the Indian before mentioned who, saying that the world was supported by a great elephant, was asked what the elephant rested on; to which his answer was—a great tortoise: but being again pressed to know what gave support to the broadbacked tortoise, replied— *something, he knew not what.*[33]

Substance is thus for Locke a construct postulated to explain the coexistence and covariation of ideas: "*because we cannot conceive how they should subsist alone, nor one in another*, we suppose them existing in and supported by some common subject; which support we denote by the name substance, though it be certain we have no clear or distinct idea of that thing we suppose a support."[34] Since what Locke means by a "clear or distinct idea" is an idea resolvable into simple ideas, and since simple ideas are either of qualities or operations, it follows that we can have no simple ideas of that which has the qualities or does the operations—in this sense Locke describes the idea of substance as "confused" or "obscure."[35] It thus was easy for later critics to argue that Locke's concept of substance was a gratuitous metaphysical postulate, since it added nothing perceptible to the co-varying simple ideas, and so to rob Locke's world of material particles of its substantiality.

From particular complex ideas we obtain general or abstract ideas by a process which Locke describes as follows: "Words become general by being made the signs of general ideas: and ideas become general, by separating from them the circumstances of time and place, and any other ideas that may determine them to this or that particular existence."[36] Lockean abstraction is thus a process which proceeds by the elimination of particularizing determinations: the general or abstract idea is the idea of what is common to the members of a class. Abstract ideas in this sense are fundamentally distinct from the intelligible species of Puritan theory, whether the abstraction extends to spiritual or sensible objects. For Locke, all ideas, abstract or other, are reducible to combinations of simple ideas: hence the abstract idea of table involves simple ideas of sensation, and the abstract idea of spirit involves simple ideas of reflection. In Puritan theory, on the other hand, abstraction is the process whereby the intelligible species is gleaned from the phantasms of the entypes we experience.[37] Abstract ideas, therefore, are never sensible nor are they class concepts only—"the abstract is the form of the concrete, as justice is of the just, i.e., that because of which the just is just."[38] This concept of the intelligible species as the standard or archetype is totally lost in Locke, nor does there exist any concept of an intelligible entity in the Puritan sense. For Locke, a spirit is a something which thinks and wills—not a purely intelligible being. Locke's theory is thus fundamentally incompatible with the Platonic doctrines of the American Puritans, although this incompatibility was not at first understood.

As Locke and Newton conceived of the world, the bodies we experience are systems of particles. If we could know the precise configuration and characteristics of these particles which constitute the object, we would be able to predict all its behavior perfectly, including its effects upon us. Hence, as Locke argues, the atomic structure of the body is its real essence.[39] But that real essence is unknown to us—we must deal with the objects of experience by "nominal essences" or abstract ideas defining classes to which the objects belong.[40] We deal with the objects, therefore, through groupings which we impose upon them and which are arbitrary in the sense that although they rest on experienced similarities among objects, those similarities may be accidental or insignificant. Yet since Locke defines knowledge as the perception of the agreement or repugnancy of ideas with each other,[41] we may obtain knowledge of bodies by determining the relations among their nominal essences. This knowledge can be at best only probable, for the relations must be found in experience rather than derived from our knowledge of the nature of the object as would be the case if we knew the real essences— nevertheless, the knowledge so obtained is a sufficient basis for dealing with the world.

With respect to mathematics and morality, and God, however, Locke held that demonstrative certainty was possible. For Locke holds that mathematical and moral ideas are "not intended to be copies of anything, nor referred to the existence of anything, as to their originals . . .":[42] they have, therefore, no referent to which they can be false. But "certainty being but the perception of the agreement or disagreement of our ideas, and demonstration nothing but the perception of such agreement, by the intervention of other ideas or mediums . . . ,"[43] we can have certain and demonstrable knowledge in mathematics and morality, for we can know the agreement or disagreement of our own ideas, and as these ideas refer to nothing beyond themselves, certainty respecting our ideas is in this case complete certainty. Yet our ideas are not simply subjective, for they are applicable to whatever real things there may be which conform to the definitions of the moral or mathematical entities. So Locke holds that if there is a real triangle, its angles must total 180 degrees, and "if it be true in speculation, i.e. in idea, that murder deserves death, it will also be true in reality of any action that exists comformable to that idea of murder."[44] Thus, for Locke, the nature of right and wrong, like mathematical theorems, is known by reason—a fact which shows a certain lingering rationalism which his empiricism had not extinguished.

Locke also holds that we can have certain knowledge of God, although such knowledge is of quite a different sort than our knowledge of morality or mathematics. For as God is a real substance, our ideas of God must conform to that external reality and so must rest, not on relations among our ideas simply, but upon truths regarding substances of which we are intuitively certain. Thus from the intuitive truths that the self exists and that nothing cannot produce something, Locke infers the existence of an eternal being.[45] Again, since we are intuitively certain that we perceive and know,[46] Locke infers that "there has been also *a knowing being from eternity*,"[47] since only a knowing being could create a knowing being. Hence he argues "from the consideration of ourselves, and what we infallibly find in our own constitutions, our reason leads us to the knowledge of this certain and evident truth,—*That there is an eternal, most powerfull and most knowing Being*."[48] That this argument assumes the absolute certainty of the causal principle, which elsewhere Locke regards as an empirical generalization from observation,[49] shows again a certain lingering Rationalism.

Locke was known as the greatest psychologist of his age, yet from the modern point of view, it is clear that his psychology was highly intellectualized. Locke is concerned primarily with how the mind knows, and he gave scant attention to the emotions. Indeed, aside from his very brief comments in the chapter on pain and pleasure,[50] his only treatment of a psychological process which is not entirely intellectual is his discussion of the will. Locke holds that the will is determined by *"the uneasiness of desire*, fixed on some absent good"[51]—nevertheless, he holds that men are free because they can suspend that determination temporarily for further consideration.[52] Thus Locke is still technically a believer in free will, although the range of freedom is narrowly circumscribed and desire does determine the will whenever it is determined.

For most men of his time, Locke's theory appeared to resolve the outstanding problems of the Newtonian model. The theories of substance and primary qualities enabled Locke to describe physical reality in a manner consistent with that model, while the theory of secondary qualities enabled him to explain the relation of our sense experience to the real world in a way which appeared to be consistent with both physics and physiology. And the theory of real and nominal essences and of knowledge enabled him to assert both that probable knowledge of the world is possible, even though we cannot perceive the essential atomic structure as it really is, and that we have demonstrable knowledge of God, morality, and mathematics. Moreover, by introducing a separate category of spiritual substances and by specifying a separate but equal category of ideas—those of reflection—by which we perceive the action of our own spirit, Locke seemed to show that our spiritual knowledge is both empirical, i.e., based on observation, and secure. Thus it is not surprising that so many men regarded Locke "on the mind" as the definitive treatment of knowledge. Yet the immense influence which Locke had upon European and American thought was not due simply to his success in providing answers to these questions: it was due equally to the ambiguity of his answers and to the further problems which they involved. There are not many philosophers of whom it can be said that their ideas led at once to materialism, realism, and subjective idealism: nevertheless, this can be said of Locke, for he was certainly an important source for the materialism of the eighteenth-century French philosophers and of Jefferson; he was the major source for the idealism of Berkeley, Edwards, and Hume; and the Scottish realists to a man thought of themselves as following in Locke's steps. Such diversity of interpretation indicates that on many points Locke was something less than clear, and those who happily accepted his theories soon found themselves entangled in a series of problems which neither they nor Locke had foreseen. Because these problems were to occupy the philosophers we shall deal with for the next two hundred years, it will be well to mention some of the major ones here.

First, as Berkeley and Hume showed, Locke's theory of primary and secondary qualities was not sufficient to establish realism. Those realists who came after Locke had, therefore, to revise his doctrine, and the theory of representative ideas upon which it rested, so as to reestablish the existence of an external world.

Second, Locke's argument for the freedom of the will was hardly one to inspire confidence in the advocates of human liberty. The freedom Locke gave to men was far too narrow to satisfy the Arminians, while it was far too broad for the necessitarians. Third, Locke's concept of experience was so narrowly intellectual that most of man's emotional life was ignored. It became, therefore, an interesting question for those who came after him what happened to his doctrines when the concept of experience was broadened to give due weight to the affections, passions, and sentiments. Fourth, Locke considered himself an empiricist, and was so considered by his contemporaries. Yet his empiricism was not as thoroughgoing as at first appeared. Locke did indeed claim that all knowledge came from experience, yet he could not supply an experiential warrant for the distinction between primary and secondary qualities or for his theory of substance, and these failings left him open to the attacks of Berkeley, Hume, and the commonsense realists. Moreover, the concept of experience itself was far from clear. If sensation and reflection are both experienced, does it follow that what is known by reflection is observed in the same sense that what is known by sensation is observed? If so, does it then follow that spiritual and moral properties are observable and describable in natural terms? Locke is certainly not clear on this issue, and his obscurity left the choice to those who followed him. Thus were moral properties to be taken as observable, we would have a naturalistic ethics of the sort developed by Hutcheson, and if spiritual properties are similarly given naturalistic treatment, we have a materialism of the sort developed by Condillac. Indeed, for all his vaunted empiricism, Locke did not even close the door securely against innate ideas, for nothing in his argument excludes the existence of innate dispositions to the evocation of a given idea upon the presentation of a certain stimulus. Fifth, in Puritan psychology, certain faculties, e.g., reason, will, and conscience, are specific to the immortal soul, while others, e.g., common sense, imagination, and memory, are faculties of the sensitive soul and so are common to man and beast. It is, therefore, perfectly clear in Puritan thought which psychological phenomena represent the action of the immortal soul and which do not. But Locke's rejection of the faculty psychology has the consequence that the human understanding becomes a unitary agent: hence, the dual nature of man is not clearly reflected in the operations of his mind. Locke asserted that thinking is the action of a spiritual agent, yet since it is only the power of framing abstract ideas which "puts a perfect distinction betwixt man and brutes,"[53] the result is that the categorical division between spiritual and animal functions of the mind, upon which the Puritans insisted, becomes much less clear in Lockean psychology. Indeed, by treating the mind as a unit, Locke virtually demands that it be all spiritual or all animal: thus one line of development leads from Locke to a purely mechanistic conception of man, while another leads to pure idealism. Finally, as Locke declares himself to be an empiricist, he is committed to the claim that our knowledge of spiritual beings can be derived from observation. Our ideas of such beings are for Locke not the pure intelligible species of Puritan and scholastic theory but complex ideas of substances which are constructed from simple ideas of reflection. But Locke's claim that simple ideas of reflection are empirical observations in the same sense in which simple ideas of sense perception are empirical observations was to prove a mare's nest for those who came after him—particularly to those who conceived of simple ideas as involving images of some sort. Thus not only did Locke confuse the question of just which mental functions are spiritual in character, but he also left it quite unclear just what sort of ideas we have of these operations. Accordingly, the adequacy of Lockean epistemology as a support for a supernatural religion was open to serious doubt. Thus, Locke's bequest to his philosophic posterity was not only a brilliant and original analysis of the mind and knowledge, but also a sheaf of problems which were to occupy British and American thinkers for two hundred years.

Contemporary with Locke's work, and in part influenced by him, came a series of developments in ethics which had great importance for all thinkers in Europe and America. In part these developments were simply extensions of the general secularization which had grown continuously since the Renaissance. Calvinism itself marked a change of emphasis from the virtues of resignation, acquiescence, love, and charity, to initiative, sobriety, thrift, and worldly success as a mark (though never a cause) of salvation. But during the Enlightenment there is evident a shift in emphasis away from the spiritual state of the individual toward a concern with a broader concept of universal benevolence. In contrast to the Puritan view that the good works of sinners are doubly damned, Cumberland argued in *De Legibus Naturae*[54] in 1672 that the benevolence of each toward all was the supreme principle of morality. Cumberland gave this principle a religious base, for he interpreted benevolence as a commandment of God, but the common good is nevertheless asserted unambiguously to be the supreme law of morality. Moreover, Cumberland's benevolence, although it remains tied to older concepts of virtue, is also very largely a concept of happiness to be found in this world. Nor was Cumberland alone in turning to a more secular view. Even his fellow Platonist, Henry More, who conceived moral principles as eternal truths known by pure reason, still included among these principles the maxim that "if it be good that one man should be supplied with the means of living well and happily, it is mathematically certain that it is doubly good that two should be so supplied, and so on"[55]—a rule which clearly points along the way toward utilitarianism.

Locke's contributions to ethics were less through his own ethical doctrines, which, as we have seen, contain elements of rationalism, than through his redirection of speculative activity along psychological lines. Writing in 1711, Shaftesbury turned to psychology to find answers to moral problems and particularly to Hobbes's assertion that man is purely egoistic. Shaftesbury stressed the importance of the social affections, which he held to be as natural to man as the self-regarding, and held that both types of affections are equally necessary to human happiness. Thus disinterested benevolence is for Shaftesbury as much a source of happiness for the doer as any egoistic impulse, and mere self-regard must be controlled and balanced by benevolence if the maximum of happiness is to be attained. The ultimate motive for moral behavior remains the happiness of the individual, but this motive is fulfilled in part by disinterested benevolence. Shaftesbury also introduced the concept of the moral sense by which the moral properties of acts are perceived, thereby according to moral properties the same natural status that colors and tactile qualities possess, and laying the basis for a purely naturalistic treatment of ethics.[56] Shaftesbury's work was further developed by Hutcheson, to whose achievements we will turn below.[57] It was Hutcheson whose sophisticated formulation of the moral sense theory and the psychological approach to ethics became the basis for the work of the Scottish school of realists. But Hutcheson also carried the development of ethics a step closer to utilitarianism by distinguishing between formal goodness, meaning the goodness of the motive producing an act, and material goodness, referring to the goodness of the objective consequences of the act. With respect to the latter, Hutcheson is explicitly utilitarian, holding that "that action is best which procures the greatest happiness for the greatest numbers."[58] By the second half of the eighteenth century, David Hume and Adam Smith were advancing social utility as the law underlying even the spontaneous private appraisal of a virtuous character.[59] Virtues thus became characteristics valued as instruments to the attainment of happiness, with the primary emphasis upon the objective social consequences of acts. Such a concept of benevolence implies a corresponding broadening of the moralist's task to include political economy, the theory of institutions, and the study of the state, for social organization may now be planned and assessed in terms of the happiness achieved. Thus when Jefferson replaced Locke's natural right to property by the pursuit of happiness, he was summarizing a course of development of central importance in the eighteenth century. In contrast to Smith and Hume, Jefferson still regarded the pursuit of happiness as a natural right and perforce unobservable, but happiness was fast becoming the measure of social utility and of moral worth itself.[60]

2. The Christian Philosopher

Although reports of the new scientific developments in Europe began to reach New England soon after 1650, Harvard remained wedded to the older theories until 1686.[61] But in that year—the year before the *Principia* was published—Charles Morton arrived from England. Morton had been master of the dissenters' academy at Newington Green and was thoroughly conversant with the latest scientific developments in England and Europe. In the course of his teaching he had prepared a text on natural philosophy called the *Compendium Physicae*, and this book became the standard text at Harvard. The *Compendium Physicae* was pre-Newtonian, and still contained Aristotelian views, but it also contained expositions of the newer theories of physics, astronomy, chemistry, anatomy, and physiology. Morton favored the views of Copernicus and Kepler, described the work of Galileo and Descartes, and was greatly influenced by Boyle who more than anyone else was his master. Thus although the *Compendium Physicae* was at best a transition work and represents an unstable synthesis of old and new theories, it nevertheless brought to New England reasonably accurate and detailed accounts of the new developments in Europe and so helped to emancipate the Puritans from the chains of scholasticism.[62]

The *Compendium Physicae* remained the text in natural philosophy at Harvard until 1728, and not until the 1750s was technically adequate instruction in Newtonian mechanics introduced; nevertheless, popularized versions of the Newtonian theory were circulating long before that time, and scientific interest and activity increased rapidly after Morton's advent. Of course in scientific attainment the colonists lagged far behind Europeans: American scientists were observers and collectors rather than theoreticians. But in astronomy and natural history observations and collections made in the New World were of particular significance in Europe, and colonial amateurs soon learned to exploit the opportunities geography gave them.[63]

The impact of the new science upon the Puritans must be viewed in the context of other changes which were transforming New England society. In 1684—two years before Morton arrived—the Massachusetts charter was annulled by the English government, thus forever ending the absolute control of the colony's social and intellectual affairs which the Puritans had so long enjoyed. It required all the ingenuity of Increase Mather, the colony's leading minister and diplomat extraordinary, to obtain the new charter of 1692, but, with a royal governor and a pledge to abide by the Toleration Act of 1689 granting liberty to all religious factions, the old power was gone forever. Thereafter, the Calvinist orthodoxy could not enforce consensus, with the result that voices of dissent were soon raised, and if unity remained it was more formal than real. The Puritan ministry thus lost the basis of much of its power, and had to rely upon persuasion where once coercion sufficed. With its ultimate means of social control gone, with factions proliferating at home, and with the influx of new scientific, philosophic, and religious ideas from abroad, the Puritan ministry faced its greatest challenge.[64]

Of the ministers who met this challenge, the greatest was Cotton Mather. This remarkable man was the grandson of John Cotton and of Richard Mather—two of the ministerial leaders of the Puritan settlement in New England. His father, Increase Mather, was the greatest Puritan minister and leader of the second generation.[65] Cotton Mather was born in 1662 and, of course, was educated at Harvard. He wished to become a minister but he was so afflicted with stammering that for some time he contemplated a medical career, but the impediment was finally overcome and he became a minister at the Second Church of Boston. Despite an active career as a churchman, Mather wrote more than four hundred and fifty books and was the foremost intellectual leader of New England in his day. To describe Mather's response to the new situation of New England would be to write a biography of Cotton Mather, for his whole life was devoted to the task of refashioning the New England way to make it serviceable in the eighteenth century. But two aspects of his response particularly concern us—his intellectual response to the new science and philosophy, and his response to the problem of factions and social control. As to the first, the answer is clear: Mather embraced the new science and became one of its leading champions in New England. He was chiefly responsible for the introduction of smallpox inoculation in America during the Boston epidemic of 1721, and he was an eloquent advocate of the new theories. But Mather was more than this—he was a scientist of singular ability. His writings on natural history and medicine are extraordinarily perceptive and amply justified his election to the Royal Society. He was the first person in America, and one of the first in the world, to espouse the theory that bacteria were a cause of disease, and his attempt to explain the success of inoculation in terms of this germ theory was remarkable, even though the explanation itself was erroneous.[66] Mather was a thorough student of the scientific literature of his day, and wrote copiously on scientific subjects, but his most extended treatment of physical science is to be found in a work published in 1721 entitled *The Christian Philosopher*.[67]

It may strike the modern reader as odd that Puritan ministers such as Mather should have so readily accepted the new science. Nevertheless, such was in general the case, and there are at least four reasons for it. First, even though political leadership had left the clergy with the loss of the old charter, the ministers were the undisputed intellectual leaders of New England. Believing as they did that knowledge formed a consistent and unified whole represented by the circle of the arts, Puritans looked to the ministers for leadership in all areas of knowledge. For the ministers to have permitted the rise of a separate intellectual elite in the sciences that could challenge their own leadership was unthinkable. Mather's scientific work, his anxiety to become a member of the Royal Society, and his role in the smallpox controversy, where he championed inoculation in the face of the leaders of the Boston medical profession, must be seen in this light. Second, there is within the Puritan tradition an injunction to the scientific study of nature which had the authority of Ramus and Ames. Third, the new science was extremely useful to the ministers. Technologia pledged that nature is a revelation of the divine plan—that behind the seeming chaos of experience there lies a coherent intellectual order. As the intellectual leader of his people, it was the task of the Puritan minister to explain the meaning of events and their relation to this divine plan. From the minister's point of view, therefore, the primary problem was to demonstrate that there was a rational explanation to the phenomena of experience, and with the tools furnished to him by Aristotle and Ramus this was by no means an easy task. Indeed, the ministers were often hard pressed to find any intelligible order at all in the seemingly random workings of nature. What a blessing, then, was Isaac Newton! Here was a proof of order and plan in nature beyond anything the ministers had dreamed of. For the Puritan ministers such as Mather, Newtonian science was a splendid confirmation of their doctrine and a marvelously useful tool. And fourth, very quickly after the publication of the *Principia*, there emerged in England a group of religious interpreters of Newtonian physics. This group, led by Richard Bentley and by such men as William Derham, produced a natural theology in which Newtonian science was used to support a set of theological propositions about the attributes and actions of God. Such religious uses of the new science could not be ignored by the Puritan clergy, and it fell to Cotton Mather to take the lead in meeting them.

The Christian Philosopher is a work in the natural theology genre. As such, it marks a sharp break in the Amesian tradition which had dominated New England thought up to that time. But the situation Mather faced in the early 1700s was very different from the situation William Ames had faced a century earlier. The rise of the new science, and especially Newton's magnificent work, achieved without recourse to hypotheses about divine purposes or plans, now presented the danger that mere human reason might find the creation understandable apart from its creator. Ames had denigrated natural theology because he believed the study of nature could tell us nothing of God or the law which was not better known from Scripture; Mather had to embrace natural theology lest it should turn out that the study of nature told us nothing at all about God. Hence Cotton Mather's natural theology was by no means an uncritical celebration of the glories of human reason and science; quite the contrary, it was an attempt to harness the new science to the service of the Puritan God.

Newton, like Laplace, had no need of the hypothesis of God in the *Principia*, and his system, at least as published, is notably lacking in teleological explanations. To make the Newtonian system yield support for religion, Mather had to make certain additions to it, and what he added were four axioms in terms of which the new science was to be interpreted. These were (1) that order implies an intelligent orderer, (2) that order is always a means to an end, (3) that the effect resembles the cause, and (4) that the laws of nature describe God's mode of action with respect to material things.[68] These assumptions were adopted as self-evident in part because they seemed to be supported by enormously convincing arguments from analogy. The order which Newton's laws defined upon a system of material points is extremely simple, and the motions of the points are capable of being represented by simple mechanical devices such as an orrery or a watch. In fact, the analogy between the solar system and a watch became one of the clichés of the eighteenth century and is repeated *ad nauseam* in every work on natural theology. From this analogy it seemed to follow, at least to the expositors of the natural theology, that the solar system like the watch must have been produced by an intelligent craftsman whose ingenuity, skill, etc., were evident from the study of the contrivance itself. Hence the laws of physics could be integrated with the propositions of theology by regarding them as descriptions of the mode of divine action or of the behavior of devices made by God. The laws of motion so became laws of God by which He governed the creation[69] and directed it toward the ends ordained by His decree. Thus Mather can refer to a "*Twofold Book* of GOD; the Book of Creatures, and the Book of the Scriptures,"[70] and summon his readers to the task of eliciting the Lord's intentions from the study of nature.

But the fourth assumption in particular has a deeper meaning which Mather makes quite explicit. Newton let the laws of motion and the law of gravity stand as axioms, and treated notions such as mass and gravity as primitive. But Mather insists that these primitives and axioms be carried back to God. How are we to account for the laws of motion if not by the hypothesis of God?[71] And what explanation is to be given for the existence of gravity?

> 'Tis enough to me what that incomparable Mathematician, Dr. *Halley*, has declar'd upon it: That, after all, *Gravity* is an Effect insolvable by any *philosophical Hypothesis*; it must be religiously resolv'd into the *immediate Will* of our most wise Creator. . . .[72]

What is called gravity is therefore the will of God in action, and the law of gravity is simply a description of how God chooses to act. Similarly, Mather asks, if we assume, as the Newtonian model requires, that nature is atomic, who formed and shaped the atoms?[73] The order of nature is not self-subsistent; it is nothing but the arbitrary decree of God that swings the planets in their orbits, nothing but His mere pleasure that holds us from plunging into the sun. No knowledge of nature can be complete which does not lead us back to its mysterious and awful cause.[74]

Once it is clear what the laws of nature are—viz., God's decrees—it is also clear that they are contingent rather than necessary, and so that they can be abrogated by God in certain cases, i.e., in miracles. That the sun really stopped for Joshua, Mather has no doubt; "The same *Infinite Power* that gave the *Motion*, gave the *Check*."[75] Similarly, "The *Strength* for which a *Samson* has been so fameous, was indeed owing to a Possession and Assistance of a *Spirit* entering into him from above."[76] The order of nature, being God's pleasure, is not inviolable, however rarely God is pleased to violate it.

Mather's use of nature for religious purposes takes two quite different forms. The first may be called the spiritualizing of nature. Thus after describing some natural fact, as, e.g., the motions of the planets, Mather reflects upon the cause of these motions and so is led to reflections upon God.[77] Or in discussing some natural fact, as, e.g., the child's love of fruit, Mather interprets it as symbolizing some spiritual truth—e.g., the innate depravity of the child.[78] In these cases, nature illustrates or points to a spiritual truth, but the natural fact or event is not a punishment or reward for specific human behavior. But there is a second use which Mather makes of nature which involves what the Puritans called "special providences." A special providence is a natural event which serves as a judgment upon human conduct. The special providence is not a miracle, because it is the result of secondary causes and so lies within the ordinary framework of nature, but God has so ordered the secondary causes that this event will follow upon a particular human act and serve as a divine judgment upon it.[79] Now since the Puritans believed in absolute predestination, there is no reason why God might not have so ordered the world that certain natural events (as, e.g., eclipses) should always follow hard upon certain human transgressions and Mather does suggest just this view when he comments that comets may be "Ministers of Divine Justice, sending baneful Steams, from their long Trains, upon the *Planets* they come nigh."[80] Yet almost all of the events which Mather interprets as special providences have this in common—that the science of that day could neither predict their occurrence nor control them nor fully explain them. Thus droughts,[81] lightning bolts,[82] earthquakes,[83] volcanic erruptions,[84] and vermin,[85] are regarded as judgments on men, and although all are interpreted as natural events accomplished through secondary causes, no adequate explanation of them existed at that time. The reasons which guided Mather's choice of special providences are fairly obvious. If an event can be predicted twenty years ahead without reference to human behavior, it is difficult to regard that event as occasioned by a particular human act, even though in an abstract sense the coincidence of the two events may be perfectly determinate. There is, therefore, an intrinsic difficulty in the Puritan theory of the relation between natural and social phenomena which is thrown into bold relief by Newtonian science. Puritans, of course, believed in absolute determinism, but they believed that natural phenomena and human phenomena were so bound in a single scheme of causation that natural events may serve as judgments upon human events. But if the course of nature is predictable without reference to human affairs, then this doctrine breaks down. And since the Puritan's sense of the immediate presence of God rested in no small part upon the belief that many natural events were God's judgments upon him, the collapse of this belief has serious consequences for Puritan piety. In Mather's day the issue was not critical, because the range of phenomena which could actually be predicted by Newtonian science was relatively narrow. Mather could abandon eclipses as special providences because he had so many other events to call upon that the loss was trivial. But in terms of the wider implications of the new science—of the possibility that all physical phenomena would be rendered predictable—the issue was very critical indeed. In fact, it seems clear that Mather was able to embrace the new science so readily just because its explanatory power was so great in some areas and so very limited in others.

This same ambivalence appears in Mather's comments on human reason. On the one hand, he lauds Newton and his achievement, urges the rational study of natural phenomena, and emphasizes the power of reason.[86] Yet on the other hand Mather stresses the incomprehensibility of God and the weakness of human reason:

> Gentlemen Philosophers, the Magnet has quite puzzled you. It shall then be no indecent Anticipation of what should have been observed at the Conclusion of this Collection, here to demand it of you, that you glorify the infinite Creator of this, and of all things, as incomprehensible. You must acknowledge that Human Reason is too feeble, too narrow a thing to comprehend the infinite God.[87]

Not content with this, Mather tries to prove how feeble reason is by citing a series of conundrums (the problems of infinite divisibility, continuity, and the Zeno paradoxes) which he asserts are too deep for the human mind.[88] These considerations lead him to the conclusion:

> But then to the natural Imbecility of Reason, and the moral Depravations of it, by our Fall from God, and the ascendant which a corrupt and vicious Will has obtain'd over it, how much ought this Consideration to warn us against the Conduct of an unhumbled Understanding in things relating to the Kingdom of God?[89]

Here again Mather is seeking a middle way. Even Newton is a child of Adam, and however much Mather might praise the triumph of reason in science, he had also to insist upon its weakness and imbecility. It is not an accident that these reflections on the weakness of the mind follow a discussion of the magnet rather than a discussion of the planetary orbits. If Newtonian science is the product of fallen reason, then the fall might not seem so serious after all, and so Mather must find fresh proof of human imbecility.

In his response to the philosophical implications of Newtonian science, Mather shows the same ambivalent pattern of acceptance combined with continued adherence to the older doctrines. Thus he adopts the Newtonian model of nature, including the atomic structure of matter,[90] with no apparent reservation. Moreover, he cites Newton's work on light and color, and comments:

> It is not Bodies that are coloured, but the Light that falls upon them; and their Colours arise from the Aptitude in them, to reflect Rays of one Colour, and to transmit all those of another. 'Tis now decided, No Colour in the dark![91]

Yet there is not the slightest evidence that Mather recognized the epistemological problems raised by the subjectivity of color. He evidently held without question to the Aristotelian epistemology and psychology he had learned in college; the accuracy of the sense images is simply never questioned.[92]

Mather accepted the new science and sought to incorporate it into his own theologically oriented world view. He did so because his own world view sanctioned science and assured him of its consistency with theology, and because the new science was so obviously useful to him. But he also accepted it because by doing so he was able to vindicate the claim of the clergy to intellectual leadership in the colony. The sciences represented a new learning, and in a society where learning was revered, he who commanded the new learning would lead (as Benjamin Franklin was to prove). Mather was determined that the ministry should retain its position of leadership, even if it meant ramming smallpox inoculation down the throat of a reluctant medical profession. Thus Mather's ready embrace of the new sciences was part of his overall effort to maintain clerical leadership of the society and to move New England into the eighteenth century without compromising the fundamentals of either doctrine or social order.

In 1710—eleven years before *The Christian Philosopher* appeared—Mather published a slim book entitled *Bonifacius. An Essay upon the Good, that is to be Devised and Designed, by those who desire to Answer the Great End of Life, and to Do Good while they Live*,[93] but which soon became known as *Essays to Do Good*. At first glance, the book appears to involve little that is new. That it is the duty of Christians to do good in the world was hardly an original observation on Mather's part and certainly not one likely to be contested. Mather is strictly orthodox in his assertion that the "*first-born* of all *devices* to *do good*, is in being *born again*."[94] Without conversion, whatever works a man may do will be "*dead works*,"[95] for "no *good works* can be done by any man until he be *justified*."[96] Mather is at particular pains to emphasize that good works cannot justify any man,[97] but are rather the mark or sign that the man is saved.

> A *justifying faith* is a *jewel*, which may be *counterfeited*. But now the *marks* of a *faith*, which is no counterfeit, are to be found in the *good works* where unto a servant of God is inclined and assisted by his *faith*.[98]

Hence good works should not only follow upon faith, but they also are one sure sign of election. But Mather does not rest the whole incentive to doing good upon this theological basis—he also argues that good should be done for the joy of doing it. Thus he describes doing good as an "incomparable pleasure,"[99] a "ravishing satisfaction,"[100] and remarks:

> Yea, the *pleasure* in doing of *good offices*, 'tis inexpressible; 'tis unparalleled; 'tis *angelical*; more to be envied than any *sensual pleasure*; a most *refined* one. Pleasure was long since defined, *the result of some excellent action*. 'Tis a sort of *holy Epicurism*.[101]

Mather's benevolence is thoroughly imbedded in a religious framework, but his appeal is nevertheless to the emotional satisfactions of benevolent action—to the doer's happiness as the immediate reward of doing good. This Epicurism may be holy but it is also a long step toward the morality of benevolence of the eighteenth century.

Having grounded his enterprise in orthodox doctrine, Mather turns to the business of doing good. "Our *opportunities to do good* are our TALENTS,"[102] and we should reflect upon our abilities to see what particular good we may do. Every man has duties to himself, to his family, to his kin, and to his neighbors, Mather asserts, and ought to apply himself to doing good in these relations. Moreover, particular groups of men have special opportunities to do good because of the positions they occupy. Ministers, magistrates, schoolmasters, doctors, officers, lawyers, and rich men each receive a detailed analysis of how and where they may do good. But Mather's most arresting suggestion is that "reforming societies" be organized by good men which will undertake not only to watch over their own members but to oversee the society as a whole and attempt to suppress disorder and immorality. Mather proposed that at each meeting of these societies a series of ten "points of consideration"[103] be recited and discussed, each point being directed to some activity to do good which the society ought to undertake— e.g., "Is there any sort of Officers among us, to such a degree unmindful of their duty, that we may do well to mind them of it?" or "Is there any *special service* to the interest of religion, which we may conveniently desire our Ministers, to take notice of?"[104] The suggestion that such societies be organized was not original with Mather; similar proposals had been made in England, and such societies had been organized there with some success, as Mather points out.[105] But in Mather's hands the reforming societies represent an attempt to organize voluntary associations which could supply the social sanctions necessary to fill the vacuum left by the removal of the government of the old charter. Indeed, the whole book is an attempt to mobilize what resources the Toleration Act and the new charter had left for the purpose of maintaining Christian discipline in the Puritan society. And in seeking to rally the troops Mather adroitly played down the ever-proliferating doctrinal dissent within the society by turning to a social gospel based on practical piety, active good works, and the morality of benevolence—points on which all pious men could unite. Thus *Essays to do Good*, like *The Christian Philosopher*, was an attempt to forge a Christian community under the leadership of an enlightened ministry—an attempt which used in a bold and creative way the new materials which the Enlightenment brought to Mather's hand. Newtonian science, the morality of benevolence, and voluntary societies were the weapons with which Mather hoped to defend Puritan doctrine and the Bible Commonwealth.[106]

3. *Samuel Johnson*

The Enlightenment did not reach all parts of America at the same time. Even when the names of Newton and Locke were well known in Boston and Philadelphia, they were still unheard of in the wilds of darkest Connecticut. There Yale College had been founded to serve as a stronghold of Calvinist orthodoxy,[107] and how well the new institution succeeded in this endeavor is shown by the fact that as late as 1714 its students were still learning technologia in exactly the same form in which it had been taught at Harvard prior to Morton's advent.[108] But in that year Jeremiah Dummer, the colony's agent in England, sent the college a gift of books, including works by Newton, Boyle, Locke, Tillotson, Barrow, Whitby, and many more, which for the first time made modern English thought available to Yale scholars.[109] The books fell upon fertile soil, for among the young men at Yale in the years between 1714 and 1720 were Samuel Johnson and Jonathan Edwards.

Samuel Johnson was born on October 14, 1696, in Guilford, Connecticut. He belonged to the fourth generation of his family in America, his great-grandfather having been one of the original settlers of New Haven, and the family was both substantial and respected. The Johnsons were fully of the Congregational way; both his father and grandfather had been deacons of the church, and Samuel was given a thoroughly orthodox upbringing. He early showed a delight in reading Scripture, and an unusual interest in scholarly subjects—notably the Hebrew language—which signs prevailed upon his family to send him to Yale in 1710.[110] There he received a pure Congregational education. In the year he graduated—1714—Johnson drew up what he called an "Encyclopedia of Philosophy," a compendium of all knowledge as it was then understood at Yale. The 1271 theses of this Ramist document simply recapitulate the seventeenth-century Puritan doctrines of technologia, Ptolemaic astronomy and all. Such was Johnson's preparation for the role of an intellectual leader in New England.[111]

In 1715 Johnson became a tutor at Yale—a position he kept until 1720—and was thus able to continue his own studies.[112] In 1714 he somehow acquired a copy of Bacon's *Advancement of Learning*; it was this book which brought home to him for the first time the appalling inadequacy of the system in which he had been trained, "so that he found himself like one at once emerging out of the glimmer of twilight into the full sunshine of open day."[113] Stimulated by Bacon, he began an intensive study of the Dummer collection. Some of the books, such as Newton's, were beyond him, and although by hard work he mastered enough mathematics so that he could make out the general doctrine, it seems clear that he never attained full mastery.[114] But others, such as Locke and many of the Anglican writers, he devoured whole, and so found opening before him a new intellectual world of whose existence he had hitherto been wholly ignorant.[115]

The effect of this intellectual revolution upon Johnson is complex. On the simplest level, it forced a drastic intellectual housecleaning, in which his out-moded scientific and philosophic beliefs were scrapped and the more modern ones of Newton, Boyle, and Locke substituted for them. But clearly more was involved here than the substitution of Copernicus for Ptolemy. The discovery that New England was one hundred and fifty years behind the times in science could not fail to raise questions about the adequacy of its beliefs in other areas. By 1722 Johnson had not only become a Newtonian, he had become a rationalist and an Anglican as well.[116]

The external facts of Johnson's conversion to the Church of England are clear enough. Johnson claimed that the study of the sources convinced him that the Episcopal mode of organization was the one originally obtaining in the primitive church, and therefore the only correct one.[117] By 1719 he put this conclusion on paper in a memorandum to himself,[118] and this conviction was evidently shared and expressed with several friends who subsequently converted to the Church of England with him. In 1720, for reasons not wholly clear, Johnson left Yale to become Congregational minister at West Haven, but he did not at this time feel called upon to break openly with the Congregational Church despite his Anglican sentiments. For the next two years Johnson preached at West Haven. Then in 1722, as the result of a too obvious friendship between Johnson and his fellow apostates and an Anglican clergyman named George Pigot at Stratford, an inquiry was held and Johnson and his friends were forced to declare themselves. To appreciate the difficulty of this position, one must remember that an Anglican in Connecticut was as welcome as a Communist in the American Legion. But Johnson and his friends held to their convictions and declared for the Church of England, to the scandal of the colony. With the break now finally made, Johnson and two others sailed for England to take orders in the Anglican Church.[119]

These are the recorded facts, but there is more to it than this. Although the issue was joined on the question of church polity, it is clear that there were theological differences involved as well.[120] The first of Johnson's sermons which we have, dated 1715, shows Johnson to be an orthodox albeit moderate Calvinist subscribing to the usual doctrines of original sin, irresistible grace, etc.[121] But the sermons of 1716-18 show a marked change. Doctrines such as irresistible grace disappear: instead one finds an overwhelming emphasis upon reason and rationality. At least by 1720 Johnson had abandoned predestination and was clearly in the Arminian camp.[122] The antiquity of bishops, therefore, was not all that was involved: Johnson was questioning not only the legitimacy of Congregational ordination, but also the rationality of Calvinist theology.

Johnson's account of his trip to England reads like the record of a triumphal procession. The knowledge of the crisis in Connecticut had reached England before him, and he was greeted with particular delight by the Anglican clergy. The kindness shown to the young man by the leading English clerics, not to mention the master's degrees given him by Oxford and Cambridge, quite overwhelmed him, and he returned to America to assume his duties as minister at Stratford more than ever confirmed in the Anglican persuasion.[123]

Having discovered the Enlightenment so late and so suddenly, it is not surprising that Johnson bought it wholesale. Dazzled by the staggering achievements of Bacon, Newton, Boyle, and Locke, he too quickly depreciated the value of his

own seemingly obsolete heritage, and so was easily led down that road toward
rational theology that English divines had been traveling since the Restoration.[124]
But after his return to America in 1723, with crisis past and his course settled,
Johnson had time for reflection and for a nearer view of the consequences of the
rationalist doctrines. No sooner was he back than Governor Burnet called his
attention to the controversy over the nature of the Trinity raging in English
theology.[125] Hard upon this appeared Anthony Collins's famous *Discourse of the
Grounds and Reasons of the Christian Religion*,[126] which greatly disturbed
Johnson and set him upon the intensive study of the evidences of Christianity. The
result of these controversies was to shake Johnson's faith in reason and so-called
rational theology, and to lead him to the conviction that the text of Scripture,
elucidated by scholarly historical and philological inquiry, is the court of appeal to
which reason itself must bow. Thus in 1727, Johnson asserted that ''after all the
light of nature will be found extremely insufficient to instruct us in the knowledge
of God and the right method of worshipping and serving Him, and what course we
must take to please Him and gain his acceptance,''[127] and stressed the superiority
of revelation over reason as a source of religious knowledge.[128]

This was Johnson's frame of mind when in February 1729 Bishop Berkeley
arrived in America. Johnson had read the *Principles* in 1728,[129] so that Berkeley's
doctrines were not entirely unfamiliar, but it was not until he met Berkeley that he
became converted to his philosophy. As one of the few Anglican clergymen in
New England, it was natural that Johnson should pay his respects to the bishop.
Berkeley received him very kindly, presented him with copies of his works, and
engaged in philosophic discussions with him which made Johnson his disciple.[130]
The reasons which led Johnson to adopt the Berkeleyan philosophy are stated in an
extremely interesting passage in Johnson's *Autobiography*:

> His [Berkeley's] denying matter at first seemed shocking, but it was only for
> want of giving a thorough attention to his meaning. It was only the unintelli-
> gible scholastic notion of matter he disputed, and not anything either sen-
> sible, imaginable or intelligible; and it was attended with this vast advantage,
> that it not only gave new incontestable proofs of a deity, but moreover the
> most striking apprehensions of his constant presence with us and inspection
> over us, and of our entire dependence on him and infinite obligations to his
> most wise and almighty benevolence.[131]

Johnson was not a great thinker either in theology or in philosophy, but he had seen
the central problem with complete clarity. Like the deists, Johnson could go into
raptures contemplating the great order and beauty of the Newtonian universe, the
wondrous machinery of the heavens, and the matchless design of nature. Johnson
too could wield the argument from design to make science support theology.[132]
But what Johnson had learned from the Deist debate in England was that rational
proof was not enough. The heart of Puritan piety was the constant sense of the

immediate presence of God. It was just because the Puritan saw the hand of God so clearly evident in nature that he felt this presence ever with him. But while the new science had presented a description of nature which confirmed its character as God's artistry, it was an artistry curiously detached from man. That God had indeed created the point-masses and ordained the laws of mechanics was true, but the operation of the system was predictable without any reference to human affairs. Because the Newtonian model was limited in scope and could not explain lightning and plague, war and drought, men like Mather could persuade themselves that the direct superintendence of the world by God and man's complete dependence upon His will were still proven by special providences.[133] But Johnson had read the deists and had learned that other doctrines could be drawn from the new science—doctrines which in his view exalted human powers at the expense of the divine. Berkeley's philosophy, by dissolving the world machine into immaterial ideas, offered Johnson just the means he needed to restore that immediate presence and dependence.[134]

After Berkeley returned to England, Johnson exchanged several letters with him which give us considerable insight into Johnson's response to idealism.[135] From these letters, it is quite clear that Johnson interpreted Berkeley in terms of the Ramist Platonism in which he had been reared. Thus Johnson regards the ideas in the divine mind as archetypes (in the Ramist sense) to which our ideas conform,[136] and so has no difficulty in interpreting Berkeley's statement that nature is a universal language in terms of the Ramist doctrine that "Things are God's words in print."[137] In his replies to Johnson, Berkeley graciously but firmly refused to be drawn into Platonism.[138] Yet in the years following 1730, Berkeley moved slowly toward Johnson's position. Berkeley's early writings are a clear-cut attack on extreme rationalism and deism and are highly empirical and antimetaphysical in tone. But as Berkeley became older he became more and more conservative, until in *Siris* he adopted a view which goes a long way toward Platonism.[139] Johnson read *Siris* twice,[140] and although he was not converted to tar water, he found its doctrines thoroughly congenial.[141]

Johnson's career after 1729 was a notable one. From his pulpit in Stratford, he fought to extend the prestige and power of the church, and he was often involved in religious controversies, particularly during the Great Awakening. Johnson was a bitter enemy of Whitefield, Edwards, and the other revivalists and wrote effectively against them—a particularly important service since many of the people who were revolted by the revivals turned to the Anglican Church as a haven. For his writings and leadership in this cause, Johnson was awarded a doctorate from Oxford in 1743.[142]

Johnson's retreat from reason to Scriptural history and philology became more pronounced as he grew older and finally led him to embrace the system of John Hutchinson, sometime steward of the Duke of Somerset.[143] In 1724 Hutchinson had published a slender volume called *Moses's Principia* in which he tried to show, by highly dubious interpretations of the Hebrew text, that the Book of Genesis contains the fundamental principles of science. The work is an open attack on the Newtonian system, in which Hutchinson holds, "Gravity had got the better of Revelation,"[144] and seeks to substitute for it an interpretation based on the direct action of God. Johnson became acquainted with Hutchinson's work in 1744 or 1745 when he read Lord President Forbes's "Letter to a Bishop"—a work which is devoted to the description of Hutchinson's system.[145] In 1750 or 1751 he read the entire twelve volumes of Hutchinson's works,[146] and was won over to the system. Hutchinson's assertion that Scripture was superior to science as a source of knowledge and his antirationalist views made his work all too appealing to Johnson, and despite the warnings from his friends that Hutchinson was a humbug, Johnson remained captivated to the end of his life.[147]

In 1754 King's College was established in New York City, with the provision that its president was to be an Anglican clergyman. To this position, Johnson was elected in 1754—a singular honor which signalized his position as the leading Anglican scholar in America. He continued in the post for a decade during which time he succeeded in putting the college on its feet. In 1764 he retired again to Stratford where he continued as pastor until his death in 1772.[148]

Johnson's reputation as a philosopher rests chiefly upon his correspondence with Berkeley in 1729 and 1730[149] and upon his *Elementa Philosophica* which was published in 1752.[150] This correspondence is chiefly of interest for its indications of Johnson's interpretation of Berkeley's views and for Berkeley's answers:[151] for the statement of Johnson's own position it is to the *Elementa Philosophica* that one must look. This book consists of two parts: the *Noetica* which contains Johnson's theory of knowledge, and the *Ethica* which contains his theory of morality. The *Ethica* was first published separately in 1746 under the title *Ethices Elementa*.[152] It was then republished with slight revisions in 1752 as the second part of the *Elementa Philosophica*.

The *Elementa Philosophica* is dedicated to Berkeley,[153] and the influence of Berkeley's ideas is evident throughout. Accepting from Locke and Berkeley the definition of an idea as that which is before the mind,[154] Johnson follows Berkeley in dividing the world into two classes of "things"—ideas, which are the things perceived; and spirits, which are the things which perceive. The *esse* of ideas is *percipi*; the *esse* of spirits is *percipere*. Ideas, we are told, are passive and inert; spirits are active.[155]

In his treatment of ideas, Johnson follows Berkeley very closely. All ideas are sensible, and all that we immediately know by the senses is ideas. Simple ideas are such things as colors, shapes, sounds, smells, etc.—in other words, they are unanalyzable phenomenal qualities given directly in experience.[156] When these simple ideas are combined, they form complex ideas, as, e.g., the idea of the sun is composed of the simple ideas round, bright, hot, etc. Like Berkeley, Johnson rejects the Lockean theory of abstraction: an abstract idea of a triangle cannot be obtained by simply successively deleting particularizing determinations. On the other hand, Johnson no more than Berkeley is rejecting universality: both understand universality to be a relation whereby a given concrete idea may stand for all of a class.[157]

Johnson further accepts Berkeley's doctrine of the dual nature of causality. Ordinarily what we mean by causality in science is an invariable association among observed phenomena—the fire that I see is the cause of the heat that I feel, because whenever the fire occurs I have the experience of heat. But on the Berkeleyan analysis, the perceived fire and the felt heat are merely two ideas—two passive inert images—which happen to be invariably conjoined. The relation among them is, therefore, like that between a word and its object: they occur together, and either may stand for the other. So causality in the sense of invariable association Berkeley and Johnson regard as a noncausal, semiotic relation among ideas. On the other hand, true efficient causality, Berkeley and Johnson hold, is to be assigned only to spirits. Only spirits are active; only spirits are self-moving voluntary agents capable of initiating action; hence "only intelligent active beings or spirits, can be truly efficient causes, which alone are properly called causes . . ."[158] The existence of such causes is known to us from our own experience of ourselves, and is projected thence to all like spirits.

From this position it is a short step to Berkeley's new theory of vision. What we perceive in nature is clusters of sensible ideas, some visual, some tactile, some derived through other senses. These clusters are relatively stable: the ideas which compose them are either invariably associated or alter only under given conditions. Accordingly, these ideas may be regarded as signs of each other, so that upon the perception of some we may infer the presence of the rest. But never do we perceive any material substratum supporting these ideas, and, since the *esse* of ideas is *percipi*, what is never perceived is not. Matter and substance may, therefore, be dispensed with. The objects of nature thus become simply groups of ideas which happen in fact to occur together, and so the substantiality of common sense is dissolved into an arbitrary juxtaposition of immaterial ideas.[159]

But these ideas which we perceive must have a cause. For in the perception of sensible ideas we find that our minds are passive and that the ideas are imposed regardless of our will. They are, therefore, not caused by us, and since Berkeley and Johnson both affirm that whatever is either is or has a cause, and since ideas themselves are inert, we must look for a cause in the realm of spirits.[160] Some few of the ideas of nature might owe their existence to subordinate spirits like ourselves, but certainly not all of them can be so caused and it is therefore necessary to suppose that they are produced in us by the direct agency of God. Accordingly, in all our perceptions we do feel the direct action of a God who stands just behind the phenomenal curtain and whose hand every moment governs our experience.[161]

If ideas are defined as sensory images, it is obvious that we can have no ideas of our own minds or their operations. For spirits are both immaterial and inherently active, while ideas are static and passive, and no idea can adequately represent a spirit. To explain how we can know ourselves, Berkeley was forced to admit a new vehicle of knowledge which he called a "notion": we have no ideas of spirits or their acts but we do have notions of such things.[162] The admission of notions marks a transition in Berkeley's thinking toward the more Platonic views which characterize *Siris*, and these views find full expression in Johnson. At the very beginning of the *Elementa Philosophica*, Johnson restricts "ideas" to sensible effects and introduces "notions" to signify the objects of consciousness and pure intellect.[163] This concept is further defined as follows:

> But besides these powers of sense and imagination, we are conscious of what is called the pure intellect, or the power of conceiving of abstracted or spiritual objects, and the relations between our several ideas and conceptions, and the various dispositions, exertions and actions of our minds, and the complex notions resulting from all these; of all which we cannot be properly said to have ideas, they being entirely of a different kind from the objects of sense and imagination, on which account I would rather call them notions or conceptions.[164]

This statement might suggest that notions are to be regarded as simple class concepts, but this is not what Johnson intends. A notion for him is any nonsensible object of the mind. Thus the concepts of numbers, spirits, consciousness, and the good are all notions in Johnson's usage.[165] A notion is known not by sense but by reason. It may be an abstraction from something but it need not be: the concepts of consciousness and affection are notions,[166] but they are not class concepts nor are they abstracted from sensible objects: rather they are what Locke mistakenly called the "simple ideas" of reflection. When Johnson speaks of notions such as the concept of the soul as "abstracted,"[167] what he means is that the soul is considered without reference to its usual sensible concomitants, e.g., the body— not that the concept of the soul is some sort of class concept. The soul is conceived as a thing devoid of or taken apart from any sensible manifestations.

The structure of the realm of notions parallels that of the realm of ideas. Just as there are simple ideas such as red, cold, or hard, so there are simple notions such as perception, consciousness, volition, affection, and action. And just as simple ideas are compounded to form complex ideas, so are simple notions compounded to form complex ones such as spirit, soul, God, cause, and justice.[168] Similarly, abstraction can be applied to either realm. For the operation of abstraction, as defined by Berkeley and Johnson, consists in assigning a name which stands ambiguously for all individuals of a particular sort.[169] So we can abstract as well from sets of notional things as from sets of sensible things. Thus Johnson's philosophy contains two primary sorts of objects—sensible and notional—and neither is reducible to the other.

But if notional and sensible things are neither reducible to the other, they are nevertheless so related that inferences can be made from one realm to the other. For in the first place, all causes are spirits, and therefore notional things. So from the existence of ideas, or their existence in a particular manner, we can infer notional causes.[170] But beyond this, notional and sensible things have a specific and peculiar relation in that God has conjoined to each spirit a cluster of sensible ideas called the body, the behavior of which is causally related to the various states and acts of the soul. Thus although the connection of soul and body is purely arbitrary and depends only upon divine decree, the relation is stable and regular, and the sensible behavior of the body becomes a sign of the state or intent of the soul. We first learn to interpret this sign from our experience of ourselves and our own bodies, and we then interpret the behavior of comparable bodies on the assumption that they are governed by spirits analogous to ourselves. It is by this means that we come to know of and understand other spirits. And we come to know God in the same way. We first form our notions of Him by idealizing those attributes which we find in ourselves, and we then interpret the behavior of sensible nature as if it were related to Him as the body is to us.[171]

> I say, we both see and feel his universal presence; for it is manifest, that He may as truly be said to be an object of sense as any human person; for, what do I see when I behold a king: not the spirit or soul, which is properly the person, and which, in the nature of it, cannot be an object of sense; I see only the shape and color of a man, clothed with gorgeous robes. In like manner, I cannot see God, as He is a spirit, and, as such, is invisible; but I as truly see Him, as I see a man like myself; nay, indeed, more manifestly than I can behold any mortal man; for I see Him in every visible shape and form in all nature; I behold Him in all the infinitely various modifications of light and colors throughout the whole creation; in all which, He is every where present, being, as it were, clothed with light, as with a garment; . . . In the same manner, I may truly say, I feel Him in the heat and wind, and in every tangible figure and motion, etc., I hear Him in every sound, and taste Him in every morsel, etc. In a word, I must again say, it is He who is All in All.[172]

In this sense, it may be affirmed, as both Berkeley and Johnson do, that sensible nature is a language through which God communicates with us.[173]

In defining the character of sensible ideas, Berkeley asserted that the *esse* of ideas is *percipi*. But this assertion leads to a problem: if ideas exist only when perceived, then they cannot exist when not perceived; accordingly, the sensible world must cease to exist when no one is looking at it and must be re-created *de novo* when next perceived. To avoid this consequence, Berkeley introduced his doctrine of archetypes. If nature is to have continuous existence it must be continuously perceived and such perpetual vigilance is possible only for God. So Berkeley held that the sensible world exists in archetypal form as ideas in the mind of God.[174]

The doctrine of archetypes is one of the most obscure and ill-developed parts of Berkeley's philosophy, and it involves a host of difficulties which Berkeley did little to solve. If the archetype guarantees the existence of the idea when it is not perceived by created spirits, how is the archetype related to the idea when it is perceived by a created spirit? Is my idea identical with the divine archetype during the time I perceive it? If so, does it not then follow that God, too, has sensible ideas? And if not, how can I know that my idea is true? Indeed, if God's ideas are not sensible, how can there be any similarity between my idea and His? Yet again, even if truth exists, is it the same for different spirits, and if not, how can it be said that different spirits know the same world? All these difficulties and more, Berkeley bequeathed to his adoring New England disciple.

Having been raised a Ramist, Johnson was thoroughly familiar with the Platonic theory of archetypes, so it is not surprising that he gave the doctrine of *Siris* a strongly Platonic interpretation. In so doing, he drew heavily on the writings of Cudworth, Norris, Malebranche, and Fénelon, where he found formulations of the Platonic theory which were particularly useful.[175] Thus Johnson defines truth as follows:

> God's infinite intellect, comprehending all that is, is the original standard. He himself is said to be infinite truth, or the truth itself, as being infinitely intelligible and perfectly known to his own infinite intellect, and conformable to it in all that he is and does; and all things that exist, are what they are originally in his eternal archetypal idea, or as they are known to him, whether they be things necessary or contingent. And the truth of things created consists in their conformity to their archetype, as they actually exist in nature and fact, partaking of so much truth and reality as the great Author of them thought fit to assign them. That is, what is called, metaphysical truth . . . And now, this existence of things as they really are, whether in the eternal mind, if they are things necessary, or in the nature and fact, if they are things contingent, must be the standard to our minds, and our knowledge or judgment of them is then truth, when we conceive and affirm of them as being what they really are. This is called logical or mental truth.[176]

The archetypes for which Johnson here contends are clearly Platonic ideas in the mind of God. Such Platonic ideas are notions: they are intellectual objects known by reason, not by sense. Like the Cambridge Platonists, Johnson conceives these ideas not as creations of God, but as identical with the divine essence, so that God Himself is the true archetype of the world, and so the "truth itself."[177] The ideas are related to the created world, both notional and sensible, in that they are the standards of which created things are imitations. The archetypes are therefore more than mere class concepts: they are also ideals. The archetypal horse, indeed, defines the class of horses, in the same sense that the original Mona Lisa defines the class of copies of itself; but it is also the ideal standard according to which the particular horse is judged, just as a given reproduction of the Mona Lisa is judged by its similarity to the original. So "truth" for created things (metaphysical truth) lies in the accuracy with which they copy their archetypes—a "true" horse is one which closely imitates the ideal horse. Correspondingly, the truth of our knowledge (mental truth) must lie in its accurately imitating its archetype, whatever that may be.

And it is just here that difficulties arise. Clearly, there must be archetypes of simple ideas—otherwise, something would exist without God's knowing of it. But since all archetypes are notional, the archetypes of sensible qualities must be notional: God's idea of pain cannot be a feeling of pain.[178] But in what way can a purely sensible quality be like a purely nonsensible notion? This is a question to which neither Berkeley nor Johnson ever gave an answer, yet it is obviously a critical one for their philosophy. Indeed, it is so critical that the fact it is unanswered must mean that Johnson regarded the answer as obvious. And such appears to be the case. Johnson repeatedly emphasized that in the perception of both simple ideas and simple notions the mind is entirely passive.[179] These ideas and notions are, therefore, caused by some agent other than the soul, and this must be God. The truth of simple ideas and notions is, therefore, not a question for Johnson: however they are related to their archetypes they are given by God and so must be adequate for God's purposes and ours. Thus Johnson remarks of simple ideas:

> . . . in him they must exist, as in original intellect; in us, only by way of sense and imagination; and in him, as originals; in us, only as faint copies; such as he thinks fit to communicate to us, according to such laws and limitations as he hath established, and such as are sufficient to all the purposes relating to our well-being, in which only we are concerned.[180]

For these simple elements of knowledge, whether sensible or notional, we have God's warrant and no further question need be asked.

But if the mind is passive in all perception, both of sensation and reflection, wherein is it active? Johnson spells out his position as follows:

> Our minds may be said to be created mere *tabulae rasae*; *i.e.*, they have no notices of any objects of any kind properly created in them, or concreated with them: yet I apprehend, that in all the notices they have of any kind of objects, they have an immediate dependence upon the Deity, as really as they depend upon Him for their existence; *i.e.* they are no more authors to themselves of the objects of their perceptions, or the light by which they perceive them, than of the power of perceiving itself; but that they perceive them by a perpetual intercourse with that great Parent Mind, to whose incessant agency they are entirely passive, both in all the perceptions of sense, and in all that intellectual light by which they perceive the objects of the pure intellect. Notwithstanding which, it is plain from experience, that in

consequence of these perceptions they are entirely at liberty to act, or not to act, and all their actions flow from a principle of self-exertion.[181]

It is clear from this passage that God causes all our simple ideas and notions, and that in those perceptions the mind is wholly passive. But the mind is active in consequence of those perceptions. And among these activities of the "pure intellect"[182] are all acts of comparison and abstraction, judging, willing, affecting, ordering, and reasoning.[183] The mind therefore is passive in the reception of the elementary constituents out of which knowledge is constructed, but in the synthesis of these elements into the propositions which form our knowledge it is active.

A proposition, according to Johnson, expresses the judgment of the mind that the attribute named by the predicate is true of the things denoted by the subject. If the judgment is correct, the proposition is true; if not, not.[184] Some propositions, Johnson holds, are known to be true by intuition: they are self-evident and cannot be doubted.[185] To establish propositions which are not self-evident we must resort to demonstration. But Johnson regards demonstration as reducible to self-evidence, since he thinks all demonstrations consist of a series of self-evident steps. Thus we can prove $A = C$ if we know by intuition that $A = B$ and $B = C$ (and that equality is transitive!). Hence, "the certainty of demonstration is always ultimately resolved into the certainty of intuition."[186]

But how do I come to have this intuition which permits me to know what is true? Johnson appears to recognize two sources of this intuition. With respect to propositions about sensation he agrees with Locke that we have an innate power to make intuitive judgments.[187] So he would regard the truth of the proposition "white is not black" as intuitively certain. But with respect to concepts and notions, Johnson appeals to what he calls the "intellectual light":

. . . no sooner does any object strike the senses, or is received in our imagination, or apprehended by our understanding, but we are immediately conscious of a kind of intellectual light within us . . . whereby we not only know that we perceive the object, but directly apply ourselves to the consideration of it, both in itself, its properties and powers, and as it stands related to all other things. And we find that as we are enabled by this intellectual light to perceive these objects and their various relations, in like manner as by sensible light we are enabled to perceive the objects of sense and their various situations; so our minds are as passive to this intellectual light, as they are to sensible light, and can no more withstand the evidence of it, than they can withstand the evidence of sense. Thus I am under the same necessity to assent to this, that I am or have a being, and that I perceive and freely exert myself, as I am of assenting to this, that I see colors or hear sounds. I am as perfectly sure that $2 + 2 = 4$, or that the whole is equal to all its parts, as that I feel heat or cold, or that I see the sun when I look full on it in the meridian in a clear day; *i.e.* I am intuitively certain of both. This intellectual light I conceive of as it were a medium of knowledge, as sensible light is of sight: in both there is the power of perceiving, and the object perceived; and this is the medium by which I am enabled to know it. And this light is one, and common to all intelligent beings, and enlighteneth alike every man that cometh into the world, a Chinese or Japanese, as well as an European or American, and an angel as well as a man: by which they all at once see the same thing to be true or right in all places at the same time, and alike invariably in all times, past, present, and to come.[188]

This light, Johnson holds, is derived "from the universal presence and action of the Deity, or a perpetual communication with the great father of lights."[189]

Therefore, tho' I cannot explain the manner how I am impressed with it (as neither can I that of sense) I do humbly conceive that God does as truly and immediately enlighten my mind internally to know these intellectual objects, as he does by the light of the sun (his sensible representative) enable me to perceive sensible objects.[190]

It is obvious that what Johnson is describing here is a variant of the Augustinian theory of illumination. Like all idealists, Augustine was faced with the dual problem of explaining how judgments can be true, and how different men can have the same truth. As a neo-Platonist, he held that the Platonic archetypes are the ideas in the divine mind, and that these serve as the standard of truth. But Augustine rejected Plato's doctrine that the soul knows the divine ideas by recalling what it had seen in a preexistent state. And he also rejected the view that the ideas are somehow innate in the soul, like seeds awaiting the proper occasion to grow.[191] Rather, we discover the ideas because God continues to teach the soul and it is by illumination that the teaching is done. Augustine thinks of the mind as discovering truth by an act comparable to that by which the eye sees an object. Just as the object must be made visible by the light of the sun, so the truth must be made intelligible by the "light" given by God.[192] This illumination is confined to intelligible objects: it does not deal with sensible objects; for any man can discover by reflection alone that $2 + 2 = 4$, whereas only a man who has seen a table knows that it has a flat top. By illumination then, we can acquire knowledge of such rational objects as numbers or the good, but not of tables or chairs.[193] But what we actually know by the illumination is only the truth of certain judgments, not the content of ideas.[194] Thus we know that the proposition "charity is good" is true. We do not know by illumination what goodness is, but by reflecting upon our true judgments as to what is good we can discover the idea of goodness which served as the standard for those judgments. This does not mean, however, that we know goodness by abstraction from the things which we judge good, since the idea of goodness had to be virtually present as a standard in order that they could be judged good to begin with. The idea, therefore, comes from within and is the basis of our knowledge of truth, but what we know directly by illumination is only that certain judgments are true.[195] And what is true of ethical judgments Augustine holds to be true for all universal or necessary judgments respecting intelligibles. The truth of such judgments rests upon their correspondence to the divine archetypes, and that they so correspond we can know only by illumination.[196]

Illumination takes place due to the direct action of God upon the soul. But this does not mean that the human mind is simply a mode of the divine mind. God is the "inner master"[197] who teaches, not the student who learns. The divine light accounts for the fact that we have true judgments, but it is the human reason which judges and which, by reflecting upon the judgments which it makes, discovers the rules of its operation.[198] The Augustinian theory does not compromise either the independence or the freedom of man.

There is no evidence that Johnson was well acquainted with Augustine's works,[199] but he had access to this theory from a variety of other sources. It can be found in the writings of Cudworth and particularly of Norris, sometimes called the English Augustine,[200] and in the French writers Malebranche and Fénelon, all of whom Johnson cites as sources.[201] But the theory is particularly prominent in Fénelon's work, and it was evidently Fénelon who was the chief source of the passage quoted above.[202]

But knowing the source from which Johnson derived the theory does not tell us what he meant by it, and the latter is no easy task. For what is it that the intellectual light enables us to perceive? Is it the truth of judgments, or the objects of the intellect? Johnson actually says both: sometimes he says we know intellectual objects by the light, and sometimes only truths.[203] This ambiguity apparently arises from the fact that he uses the concept of the intellectual light in two senses, one broad and one narrow. In the broad sense, Johnson evidently means by the light simply consciousness or awareness. Thus although consciousness is not itself an act, it is a condition of virtually all operations of thought, and so Johnson can hold that the light is given and that we are passive with respect to it, yet active in consequence of it. And in this sense it is clear that the light enables us to perceive not only truth but all "objects of the pure intellect"[204] as well.

In the narrow sense, however, Johnson uses the light in a more Augustinian sense to mean that by which we know the truth of certain propositions concerning morality, aesthetics, and other notional subjects. Among these Johnson lists all propositions of mathematics, all propositions concerning the contents and operations of our own minds, all analytic propositions (including evidently those involving sensible ideas as well as notions), and a variety of statements which can only be classed as synthetic a priori statements, such as the proposition that whatever is either is or has a cause.[205] One may infer, therefore, that Johnson uses illumination as Augustine did to account for the truth of those statements which can be known to be true without recourse to empirical evidence. But even here

Johnson's use of the light is ambiguous. In giving intuitive certainty to proposi-tions respecting the operations of our own minds, he is appealing to an intuition respecting simple notions which exactly corresponds to our intuition respecting simple ideas. I know that I am conscious just as I know that I see black, and the appeal in both cases is to an immediate awareness, not to an archetypal standard. On the other hand, judgments of morality and aesthetics do involve reference to such a standard and are impossible without it. Thus, e.g., when I am presented with certain combinations of ideas, I discern at once that they are beautiful. If I analyze this judgment, I discover that the beauty consists in the proportion and harmony among these ideas, and by idealization of this proportion and harmony I can approach the concept of true archetypal beauty as it exists in God.[206] But clearly the standard of true beauty had to be virtually present in the original judgment or I would not have considered these ideas beautiful in the first place. In this usage, therefore, Johnson is employing the concept of the light in a correct Augustinian sense.

Johnson's use of the intellectual light is designed to solve two problems. The first arises from the division between ideas and notions. Locke admitted simple ideas from both sensation and reflection and posited intuitive certainty respecting both. When Berkeley denied that there were simple ideas of reflection and insisted that we have instead something called "notions," he left unsettled the problem of truth respecting these notions. To solve this problem, Johnson generalized the notion of the intellectual light to include immediate consciousness or awareness and attributed to it the function of Locke's immediate intuition respecting simple ideas of reflection. But, secondly, Johnson has to deal with problems of truth which cannot be solved by immediate perception but which involve reference to the divine archetypes. Here Augustinian illumination in the strict sense comes into play and affords a basis for judgments of morality, aesthetics, mathematics, and similar a priori truths.[207]

The propositions of which we are certain consist of those which are warranted by intuition of some sort and of those demonstrable from such self-evident truths. Yet in defining mental truth, Johnson says, "this existence of things as they really are, whether in the eternal mind, if they are things necessary, or in the nature and fact, if they are things contingent, must be the standard of our minds. . . ."[208] Now to exist in nature and fact means for Johnson to exist in idea. So what is being asserted here is that the truth of propositions respecting contingent things, i.e., of empirical propositions, consists in their agreement with sensible experience. But for the truth of such propositions we have no intuitive warrant. Empirical state-ments, excepting judgments of sensation, are not certain; at best they are merely highly probable. So the empirical sciences, though they may presuppose necessary truths, as, e.g., the axiom of causality, afford only probable knowledge.[209]

Part two of the *Elementa Philosophica* sets forth Johnson's position in ethics. First published independently in 1746, this was the first treatise on ethics published by an American, and the very fact of its publication shows the extent of Johnson's break with the Amesian traditions in which he had been reared.[210] Yet Johnson's *Ethica* is no rationalist tract; just as his epistemological position in the *Elementa Philosophica* represents a retreat from his early rationalism, so his ethical position represents a retreat from the mild deism of Wollaston. Johnson read Wollaston's *Religion of Nature Delineated* in 1726 or 1727,[211] and the influence of Wollaston's ideas is clear and obvious in the *Ethica*.[212] Johnson cites Wollaston as a source several times in his text,[213] he included a final prayer modeled on Wollaston's,[214] and he adopted some of Wollaston's doctrines for his own. Thus like Wollaston he regards our own happiness not only as the end sought in action but as that end which God intends us to seek,[215] and he borrows from Wollaston the principle that "our good and happiness in the whole, does necessarily coincide with, and even result from, the truth and nature of things, or things, affections and actions, considered as being what they really are."[216] Johnson even follows Wollaston so far as to identify ethics with the "religion of nature,"[217] but his interpretation of the term "religion of nature" is in marked contrast to Wollaston's. Wollaston regarded natural religion as that part of religion which is discoverable from nature by reason without recourse to revelation. Johnson defines the term rather differently.

> What is here attempted, is a short system of ethics and morals . . . which have, of late, been called The Religion of Nature; by which I would not be understood to mean a system of truths and duties which mere natural reason would ever, of itself, have discovered, in the present condition of mankind, without the assistance of revelation or instruction; for it is but a very little of God and religion, or of truth and duty, that man, in his present state, utterly uninstructed, is able to discover by his mere natural powers . . . What I would therefore be understood to mean by Ethics, or the Religion of Nature, is, that system of truths and duties, which, tho' they are not obvious to our weak reason, without revelation and instruction, yet when discovered, whether by the one or the other, do evidently appear, upon the consideration, to be founded in the first principles of reason and nature; in the nature of God and man, and the various relations that subsist between them; and from thence to be capable even of strict demonstration.[218]

The primary and fundamental source of such revelation is the Bible, for the prophets play a role in the moral realm not unlike that of Newton or Archimedes in the scientific realm—they are the discoverers of the great moral truths.[219] Johnson is thus distinguishing between the ability to discover true propositions of ethics and the ability to demonstrate such propositions once they are discovered. The latter ability is allowed to human reason,[220] but not the former which requires supernatural aid. This distinction is made even in the *Ethices Elementa* which Johnson published in 1746, but it is drawn much more sharply in the *Elementa Philosophi-*

ca in 1752 after he had become a follower of Hutchinson. Thus in the later work he added to the advertisement defining the scope of the religion of nature the statement that "as our reason in these things, is, at best, but very dark and weak, it is of the greatest importance to us, that we diligently study the holy oracles. . . ."[221] Johnson's position then is quite distinct from Wollaston's, for the scope of reason, and so of rational ethics, is limited to the demonstration of principles already discovered by supernatural assistance. Reason is thus distinctly subordinate to revelation, and no conflict of reason and revelation is possible so long as reason is limited to its appropriate realm.

Ethics is the science of the good, but what is meant by the goodness of something?

> . . . its truth consisteth in its conformity to its plan or archetype, which is its standard; and its goodness is its fitness to answer its end. And as the plan is formed with a view at the end to be answered, they are in effect only the same thing under diverse considerations; and a thing is true, considered as intelligible, and good as eligible.[222]

Johnson's assertion that the "good must therefore consist in freely choosing and acting conformable to the truth and nature of things"[223] is verbally similar to Wollaston's doctrine but it is also thoroughly Ramist, for as this passage makes clear, it involves the assertion that the archetype is the idea of God which serves as a rule of art to direct things to their appointed ends. As the mind of God is the standard of all things, so He alone is perfect good, and created things have goodness only as they conform to Him—i.e., fulfill the ends for which He has designed them.[224] So to determine in what the good of man consists, one must determine the end for which man was created.

Johnson bases his argument concerning man's true end upon the principle that God cannot act in any manner which contradicts the divine attributes. Now among these attributes of God is complete self-sufficiency: God is perfect and contains within Himself everything which He desires. Therefore, Johnson argues, the end of man cannot be God's happiness, for that would violate God's self-sufficiency and make the creator dependent upon the creature.[225] Yet Scripture tells us that God made all things for His own glory.[226] Accordingly, if we are to avoid contradiction, we must "conceive it to be the Glory of God to communicate His perfections in various degrees . . . and to display His goodness to His creatures. . . ."[227] That is, we must regard it as God's aim in the creation to display and exercise His attributes. Now as respects the spiritual creation, it is obviously the moral attributes that will be displayed, and these include the benevolence, goodness, kindness, etc., of God. And the display of these attributes will consist in making the creature happy. Hence, it must be the happiness of man which is the chief end for which God made him.[228]

If man's happiness is his true end, in what does that happiness consist? Most assuredly, Johnson held, we were not intended for food, drink, and sex only.[229] It was one of the features of the Berkeleyan system which recommended it most strongly to Johnson that the relation between our spiritual and material selves there appears as purely arbitrary and temporary. For on the ideal hypothesis the material body through which all sensible knowledge is derived is merely a cluster of sensible ideas associated with the spirit. The very arbitrary nature of this association was for Johnson one of the strongest proofs of immortality, and all the higher powers, being spiritual, must clearly survive the loss of the body which occurs at death.[230] Sensible pleasures must therefore end, but the "noble powers of reason, reflection, self-exertion and self-determination"[231] survive, and it must be through these powers that our eternal happiness is to be found. Not creature comfort then, but spiritual and intellectual joys are the true ends of man.

Since eternal bliss will consist in perception of and conformity to God, it is clear that the creature's happiness depends upon his acquiring both the knowledge and the disposition of the will required for such obedience. It is not surprising, therefore, that Johnson thinks of our experience as an extended course of instruction whereby God teaches us the lessons necessary for eternal happiness. Thus the primary function of the sensible world is to exemplify the spiritual.[232] Similarly, God has so ordered the world that in the usual course of events sin leads to misery and virtue to happiness, and from this fact we can learn some of the elements of morality.[233] But the world is, Johnson admitted, a hard school, for the vicious often prosper and the good often suffer. The reward is not here but hereafter, and likely children need correction too. It is, therefore, not possible to learn by earthly experience alone all that is needed of the law, for our education continues after death, and earthly experience is too brief and incomplete a segment of the training process. Reason and experience can aid, but revelation is indispensable.[234]

It is the educational character of life which gives Johnson his explanation of sin. God could have made us so perfect that a transgression of the law would have been impossible, but we should then have been mere automata. Instead of that, God has made us moral agents capable of freely choosing whether or not to obey. Without the possibility of disobedience there could be no freedom, so that sin is in fact a necessary consequence of the freedom of the will. But since the whole course of our experience conspires to lead us toward virtue, and since we are always free to choose the good if we so wish, Johnson believed that the road to salvation lay ever open to all men.[235]

Viewed in the context of the Enlightenment, the intellectual career of Samuel Johnson tells a great deal about eighteenth-century New England. Born and bred a Puritan, thoroughly indoctrinated with technologia, Johnson found his intellectual world shattered by the new learning which the Dummer collection brought to Yale. Johnson's response to this situation was a radical break with his past and a wholesale adoption of Newtonian science, Lockean psychology, and rational religion. But Johnson soon saw that his Enlightenment threatened not only tech-nologia but the piety in defense of which Richardson and Ames had created their system. Appalled by deism, Johnson began to realize that unbridled reason might endanger Christianity itself, and strove to find a secure intellectual basis on which to rest his faith. In turning to idealism, Johnson chose a path which many after him were also to choose—most notably, and with far greater originality, Edwards and Emerson. Through idealism Johnson was able to find an epistemology permitting both natural and spiritual knowledge, and through illumination theory to base his ultimate convictions upon divine teaching. He was thus able to confine the morality of benevolence within the domain of Scripturally sanctioned action, and with Hutchinson's help, to subdue reason to revelation. Johnson's philosophy was thus a remarkable synthesis of new ideas and traditional doctrines, forged to meet the emotional needs of a man to whom life without immediate intercourse with God was unthinkable. That need was the ultimate legacy of Puritanism.

4. Benjamin Franklin

Benjamin Franklin was born in Boston in 1706. His father was a candlemaker, a professing member of the Old South Church, and an orthodox and devout Puri-tan.[236] Franklin was given a thorough Puritan upbringing, and his precocity and early love of reading led his father to hope that the boy might become a minister. But lack of money made it impossible for the elder Franklin to give his son the necessary formal education, and so young Benjamin was apprenticed instead. After trying several trades without success, he was finally apprenticed to his brother James, who had returned from England to set up as a printer in Boston in 1717.[237] James Franklin was, if not a free thinker, at least a man who had adopted the standards of contemporary English journalism as his own, and who aspired to give Boston the benefits of the newer styles. In 1721 he brought out the first issue of a newspaper entitled *The New-England Courant* in which he tried to imitate such English models as the *Spectator*. The paper's attempts at satire and wit and its irreverent treatment of the local scene made certain a conflict with the ruling powers of the city, but Franklin also chose the anti-inoculation course during the smallpox epidemic of 1721, and so made himself particularly obnoxious to the Mather group.[238] In this environment, Benjamin found himself with access to a much different sort of reading than the works on polemic divinity which stocked his father's meager library, and during his teens he read widely in the literature of the Enlightenment—particularly Locke, Shaftesbury, Collins, and above all the *Spectator* on which he strove to model his own style.[239] These works, together with the attitudes of his brother's faction toward the Puritan leadership, under-mined Franklin's faith in the Puritan creed and he soon became a deist.[240] As James Franklin's relations with the authorities deteriorated, Benjamin became actively involved in the controversy. He wrote a series of letters under the name of Silence Dogood which he slipped under the office door and which so pleased James Franklin and his friends that they were published, no one suspecting that they were the work of a sixteen-year-old boy.[241] The letters are Franklin's first significant writing, and they were a calculated attack on Cotton Mather. Franklin had read *Essays to do Good* thoroughly, and the choice of the pseudonym Silence Dogood was a skillful thrust at the loquacious author of the *Essays*. Some of the letters, notably the fourth, which is a vicious attack on Harvard, were leveled against the sacred cows of orthodoxy, and the character of Mrs. Dogood is the personification of the sort of busybody to which Dogoodism at its worst could lead. From these letters it is clear that by 1722 Franklin was thoroughly alienated from the ruling order of Boston and New England, and as James Franklin became increasingly embroiled in difficulties with the authorities, it became increasingly clear to Benjamin that the path of wisdom was to leave town. Accordingly, in 1723, Benjamin Franklin, age seventeen, set off for Philadelphia to seek his destiny.[242]

In 1724, Franklin went to London, and while working there as a printer happened to assist in printing Wollaston's *Religion of Nature*.[243] Franklin disliked the work, and wrote a brief reply to it entitled *A Dissertation on Liberty and Necessity, Pleasure and Pain*,[244] which he published in 1725 when he was nineteen years old. The *Dissertation* was his first philosophic work, and therefore deserves detailed discussion.

The *Dissertation* is divided into two parts, the first dealing with liberty and necessity, the latter with pain and pleasure. In the first part, Franklin takes the necessitarian position. If it is true, he argues, that there is a creator of the universe called God who is all-wise, all-good, and all-powerful, then whatever happens must be by His will and therefore must be good. This is obviously the case for events which God directly decrees, but it is also so, Franklin argues, for events which God only permits.

> If God permits an Action to be done, it is because he wants either *Power* or *Inclination* to hinder it; in saying he wants *Power*, we deny Him to be *almighty*; and if we say He wants *Inclination* or *Will*, it must be, either because He is not Good, or the Action is not *evil*, (for all Evil is contrary to the Essence of *infinite Goodness*).[245]

This thesis Franklin applies not only to ordinary events in nature, but also to human acts as well: these too must be according to God's will. Therefore, "if the Creature is thus limited in his Actions, being able to do only such Things as God would have him to do, and not being able to refuse doing what God would have done; then he can have no such Thing as Liberty, Free-Will or Power to do or refrain an Action."[246] What Franklin calls "liberty" here is the self-determination of the will: he admits that we can do as we will, but he does not regard that ability as constituting liberty.[247] Moreover, Franklin asserts that "if there is no such thing as Free-Will in Creatures, there can be neither Merit nor Demerit in Creatures,"[248] and so claims that God must esteem all Creatures equally, there being no difference in merit among them. Thus for Franklin, the fact that the will is determined destroys responsibility, for the creature cannot be praised or blamed for doing that which it has no choice but to do.

In the second part of the *Dissertation*, Franklin deals with pain and pleasure. The capacity to experience pain, he argues, is what distinguishes the quick from the dead: it is the defining characteristic of living things. Moreover, Franklin holds that pain is the sole cause of desire: every desire is a wish to escape from some pain, and its intensity is proportional to the amount of the pain. And since voluntary action is action directed to the satisfaction of desire, Franklin concludes that pain is the sole cause of voluntary action: without pain "all the Animal Creation would immediately stand stock still, exactly in the posture they were in the Moment Uneasiness departed; not a Limb, not a Finger would henceforth move; we should all be reduc'd to the Condition of Statues, dull and unactive."[249] Franklin next defines pleasure as the satisfaction of desire: thus "it follows that *Pleasure* is wholly caus'd by *Pain*, and by no other Thing at all."[250] He then gives his argument a unique twist. Every desire is fulfilled, he claims, for every pain does end, if only at death. Therefore, the amount of pleasure a man experiences always equals the amount of pain he endures, so that with respect to the net balance, all men are equal. One man may have more pleasures in life than another, but he must also have more pain; conversely, one man's pains may exceed another's, but so then do his pleasures. Thus God deals equally with all men, for all accounts are evened at death.[251]

The argument that the net balance of pain and pleasure is zero is directed squarely against Wollaston's argument for immortality. Wollaston held that since the amount of pain endured in this life exceeds the amount of pleasure, there must be an afterlife in which the balance is made up, or else God would not be benevolent.[252] As Franklin remarked wryly, the equality of pain and pleasure means "that there is not, on that Account, any Occasion for a future Adjustment."[253] But Franklin is not content to leave the matter there: he also attacks the argument that the immortality of the soul is proven by its immateriality. For even if the soul is immaterial, still it can think of nothing but ideas, and these ideas, Franklin asserts, are received by the senses and imprinted on the brain. Destruction of the brain also destroys its ideas, as is proven by cases of brain damage, so that at death all ideas must be destroyed, and hence all memory, too. So even if the soul does continue to exist after death, it cannot think, since it has no ideas, and its existence must be perpetual unconsciousness. Such a state may indeed be immortality, but it is hardly the sort of Elysium Wollaston had in mind.[254]

Franklin's *Dissertation* marks a drastic break with his Puritan past. His denial of immortality and of merit and demerit in men of course implies a wholesale rejection of Christianity. The discussion of the soul's action in thinking is drawn chiefly from Locke, and shows his complete acceptance of the Lockean theory of ideas—a theory from which, so far as we know, he never deviated. But the notion of ideas physically imprinted on the brain is crudely mechanistic. So, too, is the treatment of pain and pleasure, and the whole approach to organic beings ("Thus is the Mechine set on work; this is life."[255]). His necessitarianism is not derived from Calvinism, but stems from an attempt to explain all action by the laws of mechanics, thus incorporating the moral order in the natural order under a single deterministic scheme.[256] The *Dissertation*, therefore, represents an extreme form of mechanistic deism in which the only function left to God is that of creating the machine; once that is done, history unwinds like clockwork. For a sometime candidate for the Puritan ministry, Franklin had come a long way.

Franklin returned to Philadelphia in 1726.[257] During the next two years, while occupied in establishing himself in business, he was also occupied with the religious and ethical questions treated in the *Dissertation*. In November of 1728 he drew up the following statement of his religious convictions.

I BELIEVE there is one Supreme most perfect Being, Author and Father of the Gods themselves.

For I believe that Man is not the most perfect Being but One, rather that as there are many Degrees of Beings his Inferiors, so there are many Degrees of Beings superior to him.

Also, when I stretch my Imagination thro' and beyond our System of Planets, beyond the visible fix'd Stars themselves, into that Space that is every Way infinite, and conceive it fill'd with Suns like ours, each with a Chorus of Worlds for ever moving round him, then this little Ball on which we move, seems, even in my narrow Imagination, to be almost Nothing, and my self less than nothing, and of no sort of Consequence.

When I think thus, I imagine it great Vanity in me to suppose, that the *Supremely Perfect*, does in the least regard such an inconsiderable Nothing as Man. More especially, since it is impossible for me to have any positive clear Idea of that which is infinite and incomprehensible, I cannot conceive otherwise, than that He, *the Infinite Father*, expects or requires no worship or Praise from us, but that he is even INFINITELY ABOVE IT.

But since there is in all Men something like a natural Principle which enclines them to DEVOTION or the Worship of some unseen Power;

And since Men are endued with Reason superior to all other Animals that we are in our World acquainted with;

Therefore I think it seems required of me, and my Duty, as a Man, to pay Divine Regard to SOMETHING.

I CONCEIVE then, that the INFINITE has created many Beings or Gods, vastly superior to Man, who can better conceive his Perfections than we, and return him a more rational and glorious Praise. As among Men, the Praise of the Ignorant or of Children, is not regarded by the ingenious Painter or

Architect, who is rather honour'd and pleas'd with the Approbation of Wise men and Artists.

It may be that these created Gods, are immortal, or it may be that after many Ages, they are changed, and Others supply their Places.

Howbeit, I conceive that each of these is exceedingly wise, and good, and very powerful; and that Each has made for himself, one glorious Sun, attended with a beautiful and admirable System of Planets.

It is that particular wise and good God, who is the Author and Owner of our System, that I propose for the Object of my Praise and Adoration.

For I conceive that he has in himself some of those Passions he has planted in us, and that, since he has given us Reason whereby we are capable of observing his Wisdom in the Creation, he is not above caring for us, being pleas'd with our Praise, and offended when we slight Him, or neglect his Glory.

I conceive for many Reasons that he is a *good Being*, and as I should be happy to have so wise, good and powerful a Being my Friend, let me consider in what Manner I shall make myself most acceptable to him.

Next to the Praise due, to his Wisdom, I believe he is pleased and delights in the Happiness of those he has created; and since without Virtue Man can have no Happiness in this World, I firmly believe he delights to see me Virtuous, because he is pleas'd when he sees me Happy.

And since he has created many Things which seem purely design'd for the Delight of Man, I believe he is not offended when he sees his Children solace themselves in any manner of pleasant Exercise and Innocent Delights, and I think no Pleasure innocent that is to Man hurtful.

I *love* him therefore for his Goodness and I *adore* him for his Wisdom.

Let me then not fail to praise my God continually, for it is his Due, and it is all I can return for his many Favours and great Goodness to me; and let me resolve to be virtuous, that I may be happy, that I may please Him, who is delighted to see me happy. Amen.[258]

This document reveals an interesting development since the *Dissertation*. The root idea is of course the classical theory of the Great Chain of Being—that the whole creation forms a scale ordered in terms of perfection and extending from God down to the lowest inanimate objects. According to this theory, God created creatures exemplifying every possible degree of perfection, so that the scale is complete and continuous, and the creation is fixed and unchanging—there are no evolutionary implications to the Chain of Being. Traditionally, man is the halfway point in the scale, above the beasts but below the angels. What Franklin has added to this is the elevation of some angels to the status of subordinate Gods—a modification which was certainly religious heterodoxy—and the suggestion that the lesser Gods may share the passions of men. The suggestion that each subordinate God creates and rules a solar system may not be original with Franklin. There is in the first place the medieval theory which assigned the planets and stars to the care of particular groups of angels, so that some traditional warrants exist for such a theory.[259] And in the second place, there is a fair chance that Franklin got this idea from Newton. As Parton has noted,[260] in March of 1725, while Franklin was still in London, Newton is reported to have remarked in conversation that he thought the revolutions of the heavenly bodies might be superintended by various beings superior to us, under appointment by God. Parton suggests that Franklin knew of this conversation from Dr. Pemberton, and that it was the source for his excursion into polytheism. Although Parton's theory is conjectural only, it is an appealing one, for in view of Franklin's mechanistic deism, as evidenced in the *Dissertation*, he would probably have been greatly impressed by anything Newton said about religion, and this would help to explain why he adopted so unlikely a view. Whether Newton is in fact the source or not, it is clear that by 1728 Franklin had developed the idea of the Chain of Being in such a way as to yield a polytheistic account.[261] What is of particular interest here is that by doing so, Franklin managed both to preserve the remote spectatorial God of the *Dissertation* and to add a God more closely interested in human affairs, and capable of responding to human praise or neglect. Franklin does not explicitly impute direct providential intervention in human affairs even to the inferior God, although the description of that being certainly implies such a possibility. But Franklin does very clearly break with the major theses of the *Dissertation*. In resolving to be virtuous, Franklin in effect denies the total determinism which would make such a resolution meaningless; in asserting virtue to be a real and effective property, he reverses the view on virtue and vice which he had taken in the *Dissertation*; and in claiming that virtuous men lead happy lives he implicitly rejects the theory of pain and pleasure which he had previously espoused. The 1728 statement therefore shows that Franklin was in retreat from the mechanistic deism of the *Dissertation* and was groping for a new and more satisfying formulation of his religious ideas.

By the end of the next four years, Franklin had achieved such a reformulation, and had rejected both the views of the *Dissertation* and the polytheism of his 1728 statement.[262] In the *Autobiography*, he says that the arguments of the *Dissertation*

> perverted some others, particularly Collins and Ralph: but each of them having afterwards wrong'd me greatly without the least Compunction and recollecting Keith's Conduct towards me, (who was another Freethinker) and my own towards Vernon and Miss Read which at Times gave me great Trouble, I began to suspect that this Doctrine tho' it might be true, was not very useful. My London Pamphlet . . . appear'd now not so cleaver a Performance as I once thought it; and I doubted whether some Error had not insinuated itself unperceiv'd into my Argument, so as to infect all that follow'd, as is common in metaphysical Reasonings.[263]

This is a curious and interesting passage, which recalls Samuel Johnson's second thoughts about the value of rationalist principles.[264] Franklin was not the last American to discover that whether virtue and vice are "empty distinctions" or not, social intercourse is impossible without them. But Franklin did not leave the matter here: if his doctrine was not useful, he did not really think it true, and he reexamined his position. As he wrote to Vaughan in 1779,

> In 1730, I wrote a piece on the other side of the question, which began with laying for its foundation this fact: "That almost all men in all ages and countries, have at times made use of prayer." Thence I reasoned, that if all things are ordained, prayer must among the rest be ordained. But as prayer can produce no change in things that are ordained, praying must then be useless and an absurdity. God would therefore not ordain praying if everything else was ordained. But praying exists, therefore all things are not ordained, etc. This pamphlet was never printed, and the manuscript has been long lost. The great uncertainty I found in metaphysical reasonings disgusted me, and I quitted that kind of reading and study for others more satisfactory.[265]

Franklin was wrong: the paper was written in 1732 and read before the Junto, and it has survived. It is entitled "On the Providence of God in the Government of the World,"[266] and is a direct answer to the *Dissertation*. Franklin begins with the same premises he used in the *Dissertation*: the existence of a God who created the world, and his possession of the attributes of perfect power, goodness, and wisdom.[267] He then asserts that one of four situations must obtain: either (1) God has completely determined everything, or (2) God has determined nothing, or (3) God had determined some things and left other things undetermined, or (4) some things are determined and some are not but God sometimes "interferes by his particular Providence and sets aside the Effects which would otherwise have been produced by any of the Above Causes."[268] Now, says Franklin, which alternative will you choose? If you choose the first, then it follows that God has ordained "some things contrary to the very Notion of a wise and good Being,"[269] for he must have ordained the evils in the world, "and, which is still more highly absurd that he has decreed the greatest Part of Mankind, shall in all Ages, put up their earnest Prayers to him both in private and publickly in great Assemblies, when all the while he had so determin'd their Fate that he could not possibly grant them any Benefits on that Account, nor could such Prayers be any way available. Why then should he ordain them to make such Prayers?"[270] The first alternative, therefore, leads to the conclusion that God has ordained evil, which contradicts His goodness, and that He has ordained useless prayers, which denies the economy of nature and so contradicts His wisdom. But if you choose the second alternative, that all is governed by chance, then God must care nothing for the creatures He has made and must be indifferent toward the sorrows of the virtuous and the triumph of vice. "How is it possible to believe a wise and an infinitely Good Being can be delighted in this Circumstance; and be utterly unconcern'd what becomes of the Beings and Things he has created?"[271] Nor is the third alternative any better, for it still makes God become wholly inactive once the creation is complete. But this, Franklin says, is absurd: why should a being with the power and knowledge to act, and the goodness to act rightly, sit idle?[272] Such a position is "an Absurdity, which . . . cannot be swallowed without doing the greatest Violence to common Reason. . . ."[273]

We are left, then, with the last alternative. This hypothesis requires both a particular providence and free agency in men—both of which Franklin had previously denied. In the *Dissertation*, Franklin denied free will on the grounds that if God is all powerful then nothing can occur which is contrary to His will, and therefore men can do only what God wills. But Franklin now replies, why cannot God will that men should have freedom of choice? Since God is, Himself, free, and all-powerful, He can certainly make men free agents if He chooses, and if He does so then there is no contradiction between man's freedom and God's power. Nor does the doctrine of a particular providence contradict God's attributes.

> If God does not sometimes interfere by his Providence tis either because he cannot, or because he will not; which of these Positions will you chuse? There is a righteous Nation grievously oppress'd by a cruel Tyrant, they earnestly intreat God to deliver them; If you say he cannot, you deny his infinite Power, which [you] at first acknowledg'd; if you say he will not, you must directly deny his infinite Goodness.[274]

But once the existence of a particular providence is granted, "I conclude, that believing a Providence we have the Foundation of all true Religion,"[275] for we should love, fear, and obey God, "and pray to him for his Favour and Protection; and this Religion will be a Powerful Regulator of our Actions, give us Peace and Tranquility within our own Minds, and render us Benevolent, Useful, and Beneficial to others."[276]

This short paper is a complete repudiation of the *Dissertation*. Whereas in the *Dissertation* Franklin took the ground that God is the standard of goodness, so that whatever God wills is good, in the Junto paper he assumes a standard of goodness independent of God by which God's actions are judged. Thus it is now an argument against determinism that if everything is decreed then God has decreed evil, whereas in the *Dissertation* it is an argument against the existence of evil that God has decreed all things. This standard of goodness is clearly benevolence— i.e., the promotion of the happiness of others—but no justification of the standard is presented. Franklin uses the argument from design to show that God is benevolent—an argument which implicitly rejects the whole treatment of pain and pleasure in the *Dissertation*—but the assertion that benevolence is good stands as an unsupported premise. Moreover, by asserting free agency and a particular providence together, Franklin is able to give men liberty without compromising God's power or control over the creation. In so doing he adopts a position which is exactly that of Wollaston, against whom the *Dissertation* was directed.[277] Thus by 1732 Franklin had abandoned his early and extreme deism, and moved to a much more conservative position. For Franklin had recognized the basic issue involved in the relation between Newtonian science and traditional Christianity. The Newtonian model could admit God only as a creator: once the work of creation was done, every further event in the system was wholly determined by natural laws. But as Franklin saw clearly, a God who has no influence on human affairs is a God to whom humans need pay no heed. A sense of the presence of God and of man's dependence upon Him can only be maintained if God must be taken into account in man's plans. Franklin made this view very clear in a letter which he wrote to "Mr. J. H.," who had asked him to read and evaluate his deist tract. Franklin remarked:

> I have read your Manuscript with some Attention. By the Arguments it contains against the Doctrine of a particular Providence, tho' you allow a general Providence, you strike at the Foundation of all Religion: For without the Belief of a Providence that takes Cognizance of, guards and guides and may favour particular Persons, there is no Motive to Worship a Deity, to fear its Displeasure, or to pray for its Protection.[278]

Moreover, Franklin argues, without belief in a providential religion the chief spur to morality is lost. "If Men are so wicked as we now see them *with Religion* what would they be if *without it*?"[279] You, yourself, he told this unknown author, probably acquired your habits of virtue from your religious training, and, "among us, it is not necessary, as among the Hottentots that a Youth to be receiv'd into the Company of Men, should prove his Manhood by beating his Mother."[280] The sharpness of Franklin's reaction to this tract—he advised the author to burn it[281]—shows the strength of his own commitment to this doctrine of providence. Like Cotton Mather,[282] Franklin insisted upon the necessity of special providences and recognized that without them religion could not endure. But unlike Mather, Franklin did not seek those providences in acts of nature. He seems to have accepted fully the fact that the physical universe is ruled by invariable natural laws, and his own work on electricity, particularly the invention of the lightning rod, had the effect of removing one of nature's most startling phenomena from the class of providential events.[283] Special interventions of God were to be sought only in human affairs, but there, Franklin believed, they must and do occur.

It seems clear then that after his return from England, Franklin, like Samuel Johnson, had serious second thoughts about the more extreme versions of deism. But Franklin's reaction was much less extreme than Johnson's. In 1731 Franklin drew up a brief statement of his religious creed:

> That there is one God Father of the Universe.
> That he [is] infinitely good, Powerful and wise.

That he is omnipresent.

That he ought to be worshipped, by Adoration Prayer and Thanksgiving both in publick and private.

That he loves such of his Creatures as love and do good to others: and will reward them either in this World or hereafter.

That Men's Minds do not die with their Bodies, but are made more happy or miserable after this Life according to their Actions.

That Virtuous Men ought to league together to strengthen the Interest of Virtue, in the World: and so strengthen themselves in Virtue.

That Knowledge and Learning is to be cultivated, and Ignorance dissipated.

That none but the Virtuous are wise.

That Man's Perfection is in Virtue.[284]

He continued to hold this creed until his death.[285] It marks a complete rejection of the polytheism of his 1728 statement, and an explicit acceptance of the doctrine of immortality, of postmortem reward or punishment for actions performed in life, and of a particular providence—doctrines which had been denied in the *Dissertation*. But the complete absence of any mention of Jesus shows that Franklin had not returned to conventional Christianity. He never accepted the divinity of Jesus, although he did regard him as the greatest moral teacher who ever lived,[286] so that Franklin can at most be regarded as some form of Unitarian and more likely as a conservative deist.

Nevertheless, during the 1730s Franklin returned to the Presbyterian Church. It seems clear that what attracted Franklin to the church was not its doctrine but the preaching of Reverend Samuel Hemphill, who had arrived in Philadelphia from Ireland in September of 1733 and whose views were far more liberal than those of the orthodox Presbyterians. Indeed, so liberal were Hemphill's views that he was tried for heresy by the orthodox in 1735 and permanently suspended from his duties. Franklin took an active part in the controversy, publishing a series of papers in Hemphill's defense which reveal a good deal about Franklin's own position.[287] He attacked the orthodox viciously, comparing their actions to the Spanish Inquisition, lashing their intolerance and use of what he called lies and deceit in the proceedings against Hemphill. Franklin openly rejected the doctrines of original sin and sudden irresistible conversion, and denied the authority of the church to impose any articles of belief or test of orthodoxy. Every man, Franklin argued, must have complete liberty of judgment in questions of religion and should be free to say what he believes. Moreover, Franklin baldly asserts that it is by good works that a man is saved, and that faith is only one means to lead men to the practice of doing good: "Morality or Virtue is the End, Faith only a Means to obtain that End: And if the End be obtained, it is no matter by what Means."[288] Hence Franklin argues heathens who are virtuous may be saved by their good works even without

faith, and faith alone without works is of no value, for even the devils believe![289]
Clearly, Franklin was no Presbyterian.

The Hemphill affair ended Franklin's relations with the Presbyterians, but not
his attendance upon public worship. Thereafter he often attended Anglican services and urged his family to do so as well. There is no evidence that Franklin ever
accepted Anglican theology, and his subsequent support for David Williams's
deist liturgy[290] indicates that he would have preferred a form of public worship less
committed to Christian doctrines. But it is an indication of the conservatism of
Franklin's deism that he preferred attendance upon Anglican services to no
attendance at all. After all, in his view it mattered relatively little what faith one
held as long as it was conducive to virtue, and Anglican doctrines could lead to
moral behavior as well as any other.[291]

For Franklin, it was virtue rather than faith which led to salvation. But what is
virtue? In a paper which he wrote in 1735, Franklin gives an explicit statement of
his views respecting the aims of human action. No knowledge is wisdom, he
asserts, "but the Knowledge of our *true Interest*; that is, of what is best to be done
in all the Circumstances of Humane Life, in order to arrive at our main End in
View, *Happiness*."[292] And not only do we seek happiness, but God intends that
we should seek it.

> I believe he [God] is pleased and delights in the Happiness of those he has
> created; and since without Virtue Man can have no Happiness in this World, I
> firmly believe he delights to see me Virtuous, because he is pleas'd when he
> sees me Happy . . . Let me then not fail to praise my God continually, for it
> is his Due, and it is all I can return for his many Favours and great Goodness to
> me; and let me resolve to be virtuous, that I may be happy, that I may please
> Him, who is delighted to see me happy.[293]

It is thus our duty to promote the happiness of God's creatures, including ourselves. There is no opposition for Franklin between benevolence to others and
seeking happiness for oneself: both are parts of the same broad injunction to
maximize the happiness of all God's creatures.

The next problem is to define the nature of happiness. Franklin spelled this out
in 1732:

> Quest(ion). Wherein consists the Happiness of a rational Creature?
> Ans. In having a Sound Mind and a healthy Body, a Sufficiency of the
> Necessaries and Conveniences of Life, together with the Favour of God, and
> the Love of Mankind.
> Qu. What do you mean by a sound Mind?
> A. A Faculty of reasoning justly and truly in searching after [and] discover-
> ing such Truths as relate to my Happiness. Which Faculty is the Gift of God,

capable of being improv'd by Experience and Instruction, into Wisdom . . .

Q. What do you mean by the Necessaries of Life?

A. Having wholesome Food and Drink wherewith to satisfie Hunger and Thirst, Cloathing and a Place of Habitation fit to secure against the inclemencies of the Weather.[294]

The root meaning of happiness involved in this passage is the satisfaction of natural wants, and the other components cited all involve reference to that. Thus "a Sound Mind" means the ability to discover "such Truths as relate to my Happiness," which happiness cannot, therefore, consist in the first instance in possession of a sound mind, although, happiness being otherwise defined, the possession of a means to that end may well be a secondary source of happiness. Similarly, the favor of God is to be attained by promoting the happiness of His creatures, which happiness, to avoid circularity, must be first definable independently of the favor of God, although that favor may be a secondary source of happiness of more ultimate consequence than the primary one. Since the same remarks apply to the love of mankind, it is finally to health and the satisfaction of natural wants that we are brought.[295] The satisfaction of these needs (health included) is thus the primary source of happiness: benevolence consists in helping others to attain their satisfactions, thus winning the love of men and the favor of God, which favor, as the doctrine of particular providence suggests, is likely to find expression in augmented need satisfactions. Knowledge is wisdom only if it is useful for the satisfaction of needs: hence in all his schemes for the promotion and diffusion of knowledge, Franklin emphasized "useful knowledge."[296] But Franklin did not interpret utility narrowly: the emphasis on practical application is aimed at metaphysics, not theoretical science. It is true that he was not satisfied with his work in electricity until he could produce useful applications,[297] but it is also true that when he began his research no useful application was known or in prospect. Franklin was the best theoretical scientist in America before Willard Gibbs, and if he valued science chiefly for its practical results, so, after all, did Newton.[298]

In his creed, Franklin asserted that "none but the Virtuous are wise."[299] In view of his statements above concerning wisdom and his assertion that "without Virtue Man can have no Happiness in this World,"[300] it is clear that he regarded virtue as an indispensable means to happiness. Franklin therefore set himself "the bold and arduous Project of arriving at moral Perfection. . . . As I knew, or thought I knew, what was right and wrong, I did not see why I might not *always* do the one and avoid the other."[301] But he quickly found that "mere speculative Conviction" that one should be virtuous was not enough to guarantee virtuous behavior. To attain "uniform Rectitude of Conduct"[302] he therefore formulated the method which he called the "art of virtue." Franklin's discussion of the "art of virtue" in the *Autobiography* is too famous to require more than a brief summary here.[303] He selected thirteen virtues which he wished to acquire: viz., temperance, silence, order, resolution, frugality, industry, sincerity, justice, moderation, cleanliness, tranquillity, chastity, and humility. He then drew up a score card on which he could record day by day every failure to act in accordance with these virtues. He devoted a week to each virtue in turn, repeating the whole process after thirteen weeks, and although he did not acquire perfection, he did manage "to acquire the *habitude* of all of these virtues."

The "art of virtue" is a fascinating document for a number of reasons. In the first place, it perfectly illustrates Franklin's view that speculative thought which has no practical application has no value. Metaphysical dogmas which do not yield empirical consequences, religious faith which does not issue in good works, and ethical convictions which do not affect conduct he considered worthless.[304] It is not enough, Franklin asserts, to know what virtue and vice are; one must know "also *how* to resist the Temptation to those Vices, and embrace Virtue with a hearty and steady Affection"[305] and that is what the "art of virtue" teaches.

Secondly, the doctrine of the "art of virtue" is a curious combination of Arminianism and behaviorism. The induction of virtuous behavior in a person is for Franklin simply a question of creating the necessary habits of conduct, and he approaches this task in terms of what amounts to a reinforcement theory of learning. But the training is self-imposed and self-directed throughout, and represents the triumph of free will over all other determinants of behavior. Not grace but conditioning, not divine decree but method is the secret of virtue. Thirdly, as Schneider has pointed out,[306] the virtues specified in the "art of virtue" are purely instrumental: they are means by which happiness can be achieved, and this is all that they are supposed to be. But they are means to the happiness of the performer only: philanthropic virtues such as charity, mercy, kindness, and benevolence are conspicuously lacking from the list. Indeed, the "art of virtue" completely ignores the question of the happiness of others, despite the fact that the promotion of the happiness of others is an essential part of Franklin's creed. Accordingly, it is clear that the "art of virtue" is not a complete statement of Franklin's moral position.

In his creed, Franklin proposed the formation of a league of virtuous men—what he later called the United Party for Virtue.[307] The basic reason for the formation of such a party Franklin described in a paper of 1731:

> That few in Public Affairs act from a meer View of the Good of their Country, whatever they may pretend; and tho' their Actings bring real Good to their Country, yet Men primarily consider'd that their own and their Country's Interest was united, and did not act from a Principle of Benevolence.[308]

The United Party, therefore, was to further the practices of disinterested benevolence in public affairs. In his *Autobiography* Franklin described how he had planned to form the party. He wanted each member to agree to a religious creed essentially identical with that described above, and to train himself in the thirteen virtues according to the method of the "art of virtue."[309] That is, he regarded a training in virtues which are means to satisfying one's self-interest as a fit preparation for the practice of disinterested benevolence.

The crux of the problem here is the relation between self-interest and the interests of others. Franklin regarded true self-interest as including both provision for oneself and benevolence to others, for both are components of happiness. But which component has priority? Franklin's statements and his conduct both attest that he thought a man's first duty was to provide adequately for the satisfaction of his own needs. This is why the members of the United Party were first to learn the "art of virtue." Franklin did not believe that all who practiced these virtues would become rich, but he did believe that they would become "free"—free of debt and able to provide for their own needs.[310] And this degree of financial independence Franklin regarded as a necessary condition for disinterested benevolence. Like practically all men of his time, Franklin believed in the moral value of property. A man without property, who has no security respecting the necessities of life, was not in Franklin's eyes a free man. Thus to be "free" for him meant to be free from imperious domination by one's own wants, and free from dependence on others for their satisfaction. A hungry man cannot be disinterested; a debtor cannot preserve an independent judgment; "it is hard for an empty Sack to stand upright."[311] Only the man who has achieved this degree of independence is free to act "from a Principle of Benevolence."[312]

Such a position gives a peculiar emphasis to the concept of benevolence. If every man ought to provide for himself, charitable and philanthropic activities which encourage dependence in the recipient are not benevolent. Franklin did support ordinary charities, but this was not his preferred form of doing good. What was most conducive to the happiness of others was that they should learn to provide for themselves, and it was once again through the "art of virtue" that Franklin hoped to teach them how to do so. Thus although the "art of virtue" does not teach benevolence, the teaching of the "art of virtue" was a benevolent act, and Franklin preached that doctrine in his papers and almanacs, and in his *Autobiography*.[313] The same approach to benevolence is evident in many of Franklin's schemes for the promotion of the public interest. Franklin was a brilliant organizer, and much of his public benevolence took the form of organizing voluntary associations to achieve some beneficial end. But it is usually the case that these associations are made up of those whose own interests benefit from the association's activities, so that the function of the association is to enable each member to provide better for himself rather than to confer gratuitous benefits on all.[314] Once more, benevolence consists in showing people *how* to achieve happiness.

In the light of today's cynicism, it is difficult to accept the fact that Franklin's morality was not hypocritical. We are still too close to an era of moralistic apologetics for economic ruthlessness to see the difference between Franklin and Horatio Alger. But the difference is there, and our difficulties in seeing it reflect the fact that we no longer believe the premises upon which Franklin's theory rested. Franklin's ethical and social philosophy is based upon the assumption that a harmony of individual interests is possible in which all men can achieve happiness, and what guarantees for him the possibility of such a harmony is the divinely appointed economy of the world. It is not correct to say that Franklin secularized the Protestant ethic, because Franklin's ethic is not secular: it rests upon the belief that God has so ordered the world that every man's natural wants can be satisfied, that each man can do this largely for himself, and that virtuous conduct is the most efficient way to do it. God is benevolent, and having made man to seek happiness, He has also provided the means by which that search can be successful. The moral order is not the same as the deterministic natural order—the mistake of the *Dissertation* was to think it was—but it is no less perfect. Virtue does bring happiness and vice, misery—both here and hereafter. For Franklin, true self-interest is never inconsistent with benevolence, because every man can attain an adequate standard of living without hindering anyone else from doing the same, and beyond that point he has more to gain from benevolence than from selfishness.[315]

The intellectual careers of Cotton Mather, Samuel Johnson, and Benjamin Franklin were certainly disparate, yet all three were born and bred orthodox Puritans and all three were forced to modify their ancestral creed by the impact of Newtonian science, Lockean psychology, and the morality of benevolence developed by Cumberland, Shaftesbury, and Hutcheson. As a theological leader of New England, Mather had to deal with the challenge the new science presented to the established doctrine. Instead of attacking science, Mather had the wisdom to embrace it, and rapidly made himself as able a scientist as could then be found in America. From that position, he was able to utilize the natural theology as a means of showing that science supported Puritan religious beliefs, and his *Christian Philosopher* was the first such work written in America. At the same time, Mather found himself faced with proliferating doctrinal divisions within New England, and bereft of the Old Charter's stern means of achieving uniformity. Again Mather showed his metal, not by digging in his heels, but by trying to use the existing resources and the new morality creatively to achieve a program on which all factions could unite. That this program took the form of moral reform—of doing good—rather than of enforcing belief was an indication of how astutely Mather had calculated the drift of the times. But Mather's complex defense of Puritan doctrines was not entirely successful, and when Samuel Johnson encountered the new learning in science and rational divinity, his response was to reject Puritanism entirely and to embrace Anglicanism and rational religion. But Johnson soon found that once reason was made supreme more than Puritanism was in danger, and so turned to idealism on the one hand and Hutchinsonian Scripturalism on the other to find a secure defense for Christian doctrine. Yet like Mather, Johnson saw in good works and morality a basis for a wider agreement than could be obtained on doctrinal issues. Johnson was the first American to publish a work on ethics and to emphasize its central place in the curriculum. For Johnson, ethics remained closely tied to revelation, but the break with the Amesian tradition was clear; moral truths might be discovered in Scripture, but they were capable of demonstration by reason. Franklin's response to the new learning was in certain respects similar to Johnson's. Having rejected Puritanism, and become an enemy of Mather's, he turned first to extreme deism, but he too soon saw the dangers of this position and retreated to a much milder form of deism, emphasizing particular providences and good works. It is a peculiar fact that in this course of development Franklin was probably guided to some degree by Mather. Despite his early attacks on Mather in the Dogood letters, Franklin later wrote to Mather's son Samuel:

> When I was a boy, I met with a book, entitled "Essays to do Good", which I think was written by your father. It had been so little regarded by its former possessor, that several leaves of it were torn out; but the remainder gave me such a turn of thinking, as to have an influence on my conduct through life; for I have always set a greater value on the character of a doer of good, than any other kind of reputation; and if I have been, as you seem to think, a useful citizen, the public owes the advantage of it to that book.[316]

This letter has been interpreted as thinly veiled sarcasm,[317] yet it is not unlikely that it is true. Certainly Franklin took Mather's proposals respecting voluntary reforming societies very much to heart, and the use of voluntary associations to accomplish good works became the hallmark of Franklin's social activity. Moreover, the "standing queries" for the Junto were based upon Mather's "points of consideration" for those societies, and the plan for the United Party for Virtue probably has the same source. But more important is the fact that Franklin adopted and carried out the strategy Mather had begun of devising a program of moral reform upon which men of differing beliefs could unite. Mather would have been aghast at the degree to which Franklin secularized this program, but the underlying point was the same—in a society of multiple religious groups having irreconcilable doctrinal differences, agreement was possible only upon moral principles and concrete reforms. If piety became moralism, it was because the pious could agree on nothing else but morals. The problem then was to find the system of morals which could command universal assent.

But the road we have traced in this chapter was not the only possible road. There was another way, although it was a more difficult way. If new science and old doctrines did not perfectly blend, there remained the possibility of reconstructing the old doctrines upon the foundation of the new science—of devising a new Puritan theology based not on Calvin and Aristotle and Ramus but on Calvin and Newton and Locke. To do that would clearly require a man of remarkable gifts—a man such as Jonathan Edwards.

Notes — Chapter Two

[1]Butterfield, *Origins*, chap. 2; Thomas S. Kuhn, *The Copernican Revolution* (New York: Random House, 1959), chap. 6; J. L. E. Dreyer, *A History of Astronomy from Thales to Kepler* (New York: Dover Press, 1953), chap. 13; A. Wolf, *A History of Science, Technology, and Philosophy in the Sixteenth and Seventeenth Centuries* (London: George Allen and Unwin, 1950), chap. 2.

[2]Butterfield, *Origins*, pp. 42-52; Dreyer, *History of Astronomy*, chap. 15; Wolf, *Sixteenth and Seventeenth Centuries*, chap. 6.

[3]Butterfield, *Origins*, p. 7. On Galileo, see Butterfield, *Origins*, chaps. 1, 4; Wolf, *Sixteenth and Seventeenth Centuries*, chap. 3; Sir Willaim Dampier, *A History of Science* (New York: Macmillan Co., 1949), pp. 128ff.

[4]Carl Boyer, *The Concepts of the Calculus* (New York: Hafner Co., 1949), chap. 4; Wolf, *Sixteenth and Seventeenth Centuries*, chap. 9; Bell, *Development of Mathematics*, chap. 7.

[5]Butterfield, *Origins*, pp. 91-105; Louis Trenchard More, *The Life and Works of the Honourable Robert Boyle* (London: Oxford University Press, 1944), pp. 234ff, 254, 285ff.

[6]Morison, *Harvard College*, I:223-34; Theodore Hornberger, *Scientific Thought in the American Colleges, 1638-1800* (Austin: University of Texas Press, 1945), pp. 38ff; John J. McCarthy, "Physics in American Colleges before 1750," *The American Physics Teacher* 7:100-104 (1939).

[7]Albert Einstein, *Essays in Science* (New York: Philosophical Library, n.d.), p. 42.

[8]Dampier, *History of Science*, chap. 4; Wolf, *Sixteenth and Seventeenth Centuries*, chap. 7; Bell, *Development of Mathematics*, pp. 145ff.

[9]Roger Cotes, Preface in Sir Isaac Newton, *Mathematical Principles of Natural Philosophy*, ed. Cajori (Berkeley: University of California Press, 1947), p. xxxii.

[10]Einstein, *Essays*, pp. 41-42.

[11]John T. Merz, *A History of European Thought in the Nineteenth Century* (London: William Blackwood, and Sons, 1923), vol. I, chap. 4.

[12]Einstein, *Essays*, p. 32.

[13]A. Wolf, *A History of Science, Technology, and Philosophy in the Eighteenth Century* (London: George Allen and Unwin, 1952), chaps. 7-10; Merz, *History*, vol. I, chap. 4; Einstein, *Essays*, p. 33.

[14]Emil Du Bois-Reymond, "The Limits of Our Knowledge of Nature," *Popular Science Monthly* 5:17-32 (1874).

[15]Alfred North Whitehead, *The Concept of Nature* (Cambridge: University Press, 1920), chap. 2.

[16]*Ibid.*, p.27.

[17]John Locke, *An Essay Concerning Human Understanding*, ed. Frazer (Oxford: Clarendon Press, 1894).

[18]*Ibid.*, I:121.

[19]*Ibid.*, I:122-23.

[20]*Ibid.*, I:123.

[21]*Ibid.*, I:bk. I.

[22]*Ibid.*, I:19-20.

[23]More, *Boyle*, pp. 263-64.

[24]Locke, *Essay*, I:170.

[25]*Ibid.*, I:172.

[26]*Ibid.*, I:173.

[27]*Ibid.*, I:178-79.

[28]*Ibid.*, I:145ff.

[29]*Ibid.*, I:159ff.

[30]*Ibid.*, I:142.

[31]*Ibid.*, I:215-16.

[32]*Ibid.*, I:216-17.

[33]*Ibid.*, I:391-92.

[34]*Ibid.*, I:395.

[35]*Ibid.*, I:392.

[36]*Ibid.*, II:16-17.

[37]Johnson, *Writings*, II:67.

[38]*Ibid.*, II:79.

[39]Locke, *Essay*, II:26ff.

[40]*Ibid.*

[41]*Ibid.*, II:167ff.

[42]*Ibid.*, II:230.

[43]*Ibid.*, II:232.

[44]*Ibid.*, II:233-34.

[45]*Ibid.*, II:307-8.

[46]*Ibid.*, II:308.

[47]*Ibid.*, II:309.

[48]*Ibid.*

[49]*Ibid.*, I:433ff.

[50] *Ibid.*, I:302-7.

[51] *Ibid.*, I:334.

[52] *Ibid.*, I:348-49.

[53] *Ibid.*, I:208.

[54] Richard Cumberland, *De Legibus Naturae* (London: Flesher, 1672).

[55] Henry Sidgwick, *Outlines of the History of Ethics* (London: Macmillan, 1954), p. 172.

[56] Anthony, Earl of Shaftesbury, *Characteristics of Men, Manners, Opinions, Times*, vol. II, *An Inquiry Concerning Virtue, or Merit* (London, 1711).

[57] See pp. 224-26.

[58] Sidgwick, *Outlines*, p. 203.

[59] *Ibid.*, pp. 207-18.

[60] For an excellent analysis of the development of moral philosophy throughout this period, see Norman S. Fiering, "Moral Philosophy in America, 1650 to 1750, and its British Context." Unpublished Ph.D. dissertation, Columbia University, 1969.

[61] Morison, *Harvard College*, I: 214ff.

[62] Morton, *Compendium*; see the biographical sketch of Morton prefaced to this volume. Cf. Morison, *Harvard College*, I:236-49.

[63] Morison, *Harvard College*, vol. I, chaps. 10-11; Perry Miller, *The New England Mind: From Colony to Province* (Cambridge, Mass.: Harvard University Press, 1953), chap. 26 (this work is hereafter cited as *New England Mind II*); Frederick Brasch, *The Newtonian Epoch in the American Colonies, 1680-1783* (Worcester: American Antiquarian Society, 1940); Frederick Kilgour, "The Rise of Scientific Activity in Colonial New England," *Yale Journal of Biology and Medicine* 22:123-38 (1949); Frederick Kilgour, "Thomas Robie (1689-1729), Colonial Scientist and Physician," *Isis* 30:473-90 (1939); McCarthy, "Physics in American Colleges"; Lao Simons, "The Adoption of the Method of Fluxions in American Schools," *Scripta Mathematica* 4:207-19 (1936); I. B. Cohen, "The Beginnings of Chemical Instruction in America—a Brief Account of the Teaching of Chemistry at Harvard prior to 1800," *Chymia* 3:17-44 (1950); Brooke Hindle, *The Pursuit of Science in Revolutionary America, 1735-1789* (Chapel Hill: University of North Carolina Press, 1956).

[64]Miller, *New England Mind II*, esp. chap. 11.

[65]Kenneth B. Murdock, *Increase Mather: the Foremost American Puritan* (Cambridge, Mass.: Harvard University Press, 1926).

[66]Otho Beall and Richard Shryock, *Cotton Mather, First Significant Figure in American Medicine* (Baltimore: Johns Hopkins, 1954), esp. pp. 113ff, 176ff.

[67]Cotton Mather, *The Christian Philosopher: A Collection of the Best Discoveries in Nature, with Religious Improvements* (London: printed for Eman. Matthews, 1721); Kenneth B. Murdock, "Cotton Mather," in *Dictionary of American Biography*, ed. Malone (New York: Charles Scribner's Sons, 1946) vol. XI, pp. 386-389. Beall and Shryock, *Cotton Mather*, pp. 87-92, 96-122, 176-186. See also Theodore Hornberger, "The Date, the Source, and the Significance of Cotton Mather's interest in Science," *American Literature* 6:413-20 (1935); Miller, *New England Mind II*, chap. 26; George H. Daniels, *Science in American Society: A Social History* (New York: Knopf, 1971), pp. 77-83.

[68]These assumptions are exemplified in such works as William Derham, *Astro-Theology: or a Demonstration of the Being and Attributes of God, From a Survey of the Heavens* (London: W. Innys, 1715); William Paley, *Natural Theology*, in *The Works of William Paley, D.D.* (London: Henry Fisher, Son, and P. Jackson, 1828), vol. II.

[69]Mather, *Christian Philosopher*, p. 9.

[70]*Ibid.*, p. 8.

[71]*Ibid.*, pp. 8-9.

[72]*Ibid.*, p. 82.

[73]*Ibid.*, p. 96.

[74]Middlekauff, *Mathers*, pp. 285ff.

[75]Mather, *Christian Philosopher*, p. 76.

[76]*Ibid.*, p. 279.

[77]*Ibid.*, p. 34.

[78]*Ibid.*, p. 141.

[79]Miller, *New England Mind I*, pp. 228ff.

[80]Mather, *Christian Philosopher*, p. 45.

[81]*Ibid.*, p. 53.

[82]*Ibid.*, p. 63.

[83]*Ibid.*, pp. 101ff.

[84]*Ibid.*, pp. 100-101.

[85]*Ibid.*, p. 162.

[86]*Ibid.*, pp. 5-6, 56, 283.

[87]*Ibid.*, p. 111.

[88]*Ibid.*, pp. 112ff.

[89]*Ibid.*, p. 114.

[90]*Ibid.*, pp. 10, 88ff.

[91]*Ibid.*, p. 11.

[92]*Ibid.*, p. 291.

[93]Cotton Mather, *Bonifacius. An Essay upon the Good, that is to be Devised and Designed, by those who Desire to Answer the Great End of Life, and to Do Good while they Live* (Boston: Printed by B. Green for Samuel Gerrish, 1710).

[94]*Ibid.*, p. 22.

[95]*Ibid.*, p. 27.

[96]*Ibid.*

[97]*Ibid.*, pp. 27-28.

[98]*Ibid.*, p. 29.

[99]*Ibid.*, p. 59.

[100]*Ibid.*, p. 152.

[101]*Ibid.*, pp. 150-51.

[102]*Ibid.*, p. 31.

[103]*Ibid.*, pp. 135-36.

[104]*Ibid.*, p. 136.

[105]*Ibid.*, p. 132.

[106]Miller, *New England Mind II*, pp. 395-416; Middlekauff, *Mathers*, chap. 12.

[107]Miller, *New England Mind II*, p. 246.

[108]Johnson, *Writings*, II:23-186.

[109]*Ibid.*, I:7.

[110]*Ibid.*, I:3-6; Joseph Ellis, *The New England Mind in Transition: Samuel Johnson of Connecticut, 1696-1772* (New Haven, Conn.: Yale University Press, 1973), pp. 1-16.

[111]Johnson, *Writings*, II:55-186; Ellis, *Johnson*, 16-33.

[112]Johnson, *Writings*, I:7ff.

[113]*Ibid.*, I:7.

[114]*Ibid.*, I:9; See *ibid.*, II:289, where Johnson discusses his mastery of the calculus.

[115]*Ibid.*, I:7; E. Edwards Beardsley, *Life and Correspondence of Samuel Johnson, D.D.* (Boston: Houghton Mifflin and Co., 1887), pp. 13f.

[116]See Johnson, *Writings*, I:6, for Johnson's discussion of his disillusion with the New England way. For a discussion of Johnson's revision of his system, see Theodore Hornberger, "Samuel Johnson of Yale and King's College: a Note on the Relation of Science and Religion in Provincial America," *New England Quarterly* VIII:378-97 (1935). See also Beardsley, *Johnson*, pp. 12-23; Ellis, *Johnson*, chap. 3.

[117]Johnson, *Writings*, I:13.

[118]*Ibid.*, III:3-8.

[119]*Ibid.*, I:11-16; Miller, *New England Mind II*, 471; Beardsley, *Johnson*, 12-23; Perry Miller, *Jonathan Edwards* (New York: Meridian, 1959), pp. 5-6; Franklin Dexter, *Documentary History of Yale University* (New Haven, Conn.: Yale University Press, 1916), pp. 226-30; Ellis, *Johnson*, chap. 4.

[120]Johnson, *Writings*, I:11.

121 *Ibid.*, III:293-312; Ellis, *Johnson*, pp. 56-61.

122Johnson, *Writings*, III:315-57, esp. 317, 321, 324, 331-33.

123 *Ibid.*, I:16-19; Beardsley, *Johnson*, pp. 23-54; Ellis, *Johnson*, pp. 82-88.

124G. R. Cragg, *From Puritanism to the Age of Reason* (Cambridge: Cambridge University Press, 1950).

125Johnson, *Writings*, I:20-23.

126Anthony Collins, *A Discourse of the Grounds and Reasons of the Christian Religion* (London, 1724).

127Johnson, *Writings*, III:372.

128 *Ibid.*, III:372ff.

129 *Ibid.*, I:507.

130 *Ibid.*, I:24-26.

131 *Ibid.*, I:25.

132 *Ibid.*, II:457.

133See p. 78.

134Hornberger, "Johnson," pp. 387-90; Paul Anderson and Max Fisch, *Philosophy in America* (New York: D. Appleton-Century Co., 1939), pp. 51-53.

135Johnson, *Writings*, II:261-84.

136 *Ibid.*, II:264ff.

137 *Ibid.*, II:67.

138 *Ibid.*, II:282. See Herbert Schneider, *A History of American Philosophy*, 2d ed. (New York: Columbia University Press, 1963), pp. 21f.

139G. Dawes Hicks, *Berkeley* (London: Ernest Benn Ltd., 1932), pp. 205-29; John Wild, *George Berkeley: A Study of His Life and Philosophy* (Cambridge, Mass.: Harvard University Press, 1936), pp. 399-479.

140Johnson, *Writings*, I:521, 524.

141Berkeley devoted the first part of *Siris* to an exposition of the medicinal virtues of tar water. See *The Works of George Berkeley, D.D.*, ed. Fraser (Oxford: Clarendon Press, 1871), II:358-508.

142Johnson, *Writings*, I:27-30; Beardsley, *Johnson*, chap. 5; Ellis, *Johnson*, pp. 117-19.

143Johnson, *Writings*, I:30-31; *The Dictionary of National Biography* (London: Oxford University Press, 1917), X:342.

144John Hutchinson, *Moses's Principia of the Invisible Parts of Matter: of Motion: of Visible Forms: and of their Dissolution and Reformation* (London: J. Betterhan, 1724), p. 74. On Hutchinson, see Leslie Stephen, *History of English Thought in the Eighteenth Century* (London: Smith, Elder and Co., 1876), I:389f.

145Duncan Forbes, "Letter to a Bishop, concerning Some Important Discoveries in Philosophy and Theology," in *The Works of the Right Honourable Duncan Forbes, late Lord President of the Court of Sessions in Scotland* (London: J. Morton, 1810), pp. 281-348.

146Johnson, *Writings*, I:523.

147Anderson and Fisch, *Philosophy*, pp. 53-54; Beardsley, *Johnson*, pp. 127-28; Hornberger, "Johnson," p. 394; Ellis, *Johnson*, pp. 228ff.

148Johnson, *Writings*, I:32-42; Beardsley, *Johnson*, chaps. 8-12.

149Reprinted in Johnson, *Writings*, II:261-84.

150Reprinted *ibid.*, II:357-518; Ellis, *Johnson*, chap. 8.

151Wild, *Berkeley*, pp. 311-19.

152*Ethices Elementa, or the First Principles of Moral Philosophy. And Especially That Part of it which is called Ethics. In a Chain of Necessary Consequences from certain Facts* (Boston: Rogers and Fowle, 1746). Johnson published it under the pseudonym "Aristocles."

153Johnson, *Writings*, II:359.

154*Ibid.*, II:373; R. F. Alfred Hoernlé, *Idealism as a Philosophical Doctrine* (London: Hodder and Stoughton, n.d.), pp. 33f, 63f.

155Johnson, *Writings*, II:372-76, 382; Hicks, *Berkeley*, p. 77.

156Johnson, *Writings*, II:373-76.

157*Ibid.*, II:400-401; Hicks, *Berkeley*, pp. 88-96.

158Johnson, *Writings*, II:385.

[159]*Ibid.*, II:376, 423; George Berkeley, "An Essay Towards a New Theory of Vision," in *The Works of George Berkeley Bishop of Cloyne*, ed. Luce and Jessop (London: Thomas Nelson and Sons, 1948), I:141-239.

[160]Johnson, *Writings*, II:384-86; Hicks, *Berkeley*, pp. 129-30.

[161]Johnson, *Writings*, II:374-75.

[162]Hicks, *Berkeley*, pp. 145-46, 161f.

[163]Johnson, *Writings*, II:373-74.

[164]*Ibid.*, II:378.

[165]*Ibid.*, II:378, 380.

[166]*Ibid.*, II:378.

[167]*Ibid.*, II:402.

[168]*Ibid.*, II:378.

[169]*Ibid.*, II:400-401.

[170]*Ibid.*, II:385.

[171]*Ibid.*, II:373, 402-4, 424-25, 432.

[172]*Ibid.*, II:466-67.

[173]*Ibid.*, II:466; Berkeley, "New Theory of Vision," p. 231.

[174]Hicks, *Berkeley*, pp. 130-57, 207-8ff.

[175]Ralph Cudworth (1617-1688) and John Norris (1657-1711) were members of the group of philosophers at Cambridge University who were called the Cambridge Platonists (cf. John Muirhead, *The Platonic Tradition in Anglo-Saxon Philosophy* [London: George Allen and Unwin, 1931], chaps. I-V). Nicolas de Malebranche (1638-1715) was a French metaphysician whose philosophy involved controversial use of the Augustinian theory of illumination (see below). François de Salignac de La Fénelon (1651-1715) was Archbishop of Cambray.

[176]Johnson, *Writings*, II:406-7.

[177]Muirhead, *Platonic Tradition*, pp. 83ff. Johnson's view is explicitly based on Norris's (Johnson, *Writings*, II:377n). Norris held that the divine Ideas are

identical with the divine essence. But since the divine essence is simple, there cannot be a plurality of Ideas, so the Ideas must be seen as diverse aspects of one undifferentiated entity. We have then the classic problem of how to derive the many from the one, and Norris solves it by regarding the many as different degrees of the one. As God is all being, so each creature is a partial being or contains a certain degree of being. All creatures therefore form a scale ordered with respect to degree of being and the Idea of any creature is simply the Idea of the degree of being which that creature has, or rather, is (John Norris, *An Essay Towards the Theory of the Ideal or Intelligible World* [London: Printed for Edmund Parker, 1722], I:247ff.).

[178]Johnson, *Writings*, II:377; Norris, *Ideal World*, II:496-502.

[179]Johnson, *Writings*, II:374-75.

[180]*Ibid.*, II:377.

[181]*Ibid.*, II:374.

[182]*Ibid.*, II:381.

[183]*Ibid.*, II:381ff.

[184]*Ibid.*, II:404-5.

[185]*Ibid.*, II:408.

[186]*Ibid.*, II:409. These concepts of intuition and demonstration are drawn directly from Locke (Locke, *Essay*, bk. IV, chap. 2). The fallacious belief that every step in a demonstration must be self-evident (or even intelligible) continued to obscure the nature of logic until the nineteenth century.

[187]Johnson, *Writings*, II:379, 408. Cf. Locke, *Essay*, bk. IV, chap. 2, sec. 1.

[188]Johnson, *Writings*, II:379.

[189]*Ibid.*, II:379-80.

[190]*Ibid.*, II:380.

[191]Etienne Gilson, *The Christian Philosophy of Saint Augustine* (New York: Random House, 1960), pp. 75-76.

[192]*Ibid.*, p. 77.

[193]*Ibid.*, pp. 83-84.

[194]*Ibid.*, pp. 81-82, 86.

[195]Richard Acworth, S.J., "Two Studies of St. Augustine's Thought: God and Human Knowledge in St. Augustine; The Theory of Illumination," *Downside Review* 75:208-9 (1957).

[196]Gilson, *Augustine*, pp. 80ff.

[197]*Ibid.*, p. 74.

[198]*Ibid.*, p. 79; Acworth, "Augustine," p. 214.

[199]Johnson's book list contains only one reference to Augustine, and it is impossible to tell from that reference just what he read (Johnson, *Writings*, I:505).

[200]Muirhead, *Platonic Tradition*, p. 74.

[201]Johnson, *Writings*, II:380n. Johnson cites Fénelon's *A Demonstration of The Existence and Attributes of God*, and Ralph Cudworth's *The True Intellectual System of the Universe* and *A Treatise Concerning Eternal and Immutable Morality*. The reference to Norris is not specific, but it is almost certainly to his *Ideal World*. The reference to Malebranche is also not specific and it is uncertain whether Johnson had read Malebranche or knew of him only through the copious quotations from his works which are scattered throughout Norris's *Ideal World*.

[202]Cf. Fénelon's *A Demonstration of The Existence and Attributes of God* (London: W. Taylor, 1720), pp. 102-16. The verbal similarities between Fénelon (p. 109) and Johnson, *Writings*, II:379, suggest that Johnson may have had Fénelon's text before him in writing his own.

[203]Johnson, *Writings*, II:374, 379-80, 408.

[204]*Ibid.*, II:374.

[205]*Ibid.*, II:379-80, 408.

[206]*Ibid.*, II:392-94.

[207]Johnson remarked that what Shaftesbury and Hutcheson called the "moral sense" was simply the intellectual light under another name (*ibid.*, II:449). This refers to the strict sense of illumination. Since both illumination and the moral sense permit the judgment that x is good but do not convey the nature of goodness, the analogy is not farfetched.

[208]*Ibid.*, II:407.

209*Ibid.*, II:409, 431ff.

210For a detailed study of Johnson's ethics, see Fiering, "Moral Philosophy," chaps. 7-8.

211William Wollaston, *The Religion of Nature Delineated* (London: J. and P. Knapton, 1750); Johnson, *Writings*, I:505.

212Schneider, *History*, 2d ed., p. 21.

213Johnson, *Writings*, II:448, 471, 472, 480, 482.

214*Ibid.*, II:516-18.

215Wollaston, *Religion of Nature*, 52-69; Johnson, *Writings*, II:476.

216Johnson, *Writings*, II:448.

217*Ibid.*, II:452.

218*Ibid.*, II:442-43.

219*Ibid.*, II:443.

220*Ibid.*, II:380, 391, 443.

221*Ibid.*, II:444.

222*Ibid.*, II:391.

223*Ibid.*, II:448.

224*Ibid.*, II:392.

225*Ibid.*, II:474.

226*Ibid.*, II:476.

227*Ibid.*, II:477.

228*Ibid.*, II:474-76.

229*Ibid.*, II:478.

230*Ibid.*, II:373, 479.

[231] *Ibid.*, II:478.

[232] *Ibid.*, II:466.

[233] *Ibid.*, II:477, 483.

[234] *Ibid.*, II:442-43.

[235] *Ibid.*, II:471-72.

[236] Benjamin Franklin, *Autobiography*, ed. Labaree (New Haven, Conn.: Yale University Press, 1964), pp. 48-72; Miller, *New England Mind II*, pp. 333ff.

[237] Franklin, *Autobiography*, pp. 51-53, 58-59.

[238] Miller, *New England Mind II*, pp. 333ff.

[239] Franklin, *Autobiography*, pp. 58, 64.

[240] *Ibid.*, pp. 113-15.

[241] *Ibid.*, pp. 67-68.

[242] *Ibid.*, p. 71.

[243] Wollaston, *Religion of Nature*.

[244] Benjamin Franklin, *The Papers of Benjamin Franklin*, ed. Labaree (New Haven: Yale Press, 1959), I:55-71; see also Alfred Owen Aldridge, "Benjamin Franklin and Philosophical Necessity," *Modern Language Quarterly* XII:292-309 (1951).

[245] Franklin, *Papers*, I:60.

[246] *Ibid.*, I:61-62. Original in italics.

[247] *Ibid.*, I:62.

[248] *Ibid.*, I:63. Original in italics.

[249] *Ibid.*, I:64.

[250] *Ibid.*, p. I:65.

[251] *Ibid.*, I:66ff.

252Aldridge, "Franklin and Necessity," pp. 292ff.

253Franklin, *Papers*, I:66.

254*Ibid.*, I:69-70.

255*Ibid.*, I:64.

256*Ibid.*, I:62.

257Franklin, *Autobiography*, p. 106.

258Franklin, *Papers*, I:102-4.

259E. M. W. Tillyard, *The Elizabethan World Picture* (London: Chatto and Windus, 1960), p. 38.

260James Parton, *Life and Times of Benjamin Franklin* (Boston: Ticknor and Fields, 1867), I:175.

261Alfred Owen Aldridge, *Benjamin Franklin and Nature's God* (Durham, N.C.: Duke University Press, 1967), pp. 25ff.

262Aldridge has argued that this polytheism remained a part of Franklin's religious beliefs throughout his life (Aldridge, *Franklin and Nature's God*, pp. 31ff), but this seems to us extremely unlikely. In the first place, Franklin's later writings contain a number of explicit statements that there is but one God and no explicit statements that there is more than one. In the second place, the passages cited by Aldridge to support his view leave a good deal to be desired. In the letter of April 14, 1757, to Henry Bouquet (Franklin, *Papers*, VII:182), Franklin does refer to "the Nectar of the Gods" and then a few sentences below remarks in closing "the Gods take care of those they love. A Dieux . . ." It is certainly hard to see anything more than a classical allusion playfully elaborated in this. Again, in the letter of July 28, 1768, to Du Pont De Nemours (Albert Henry Smyth, ed., *The Writings of Benjamin Franklin* [New York: Macmillan, 1906], V:156), Franklin expresses the hope that his philosophy may become the governing philosophy of the human species "as it must be that of superior beings in better worlds." So trite a figure of speech hardly justifies the conclusion that Franklin believed in polytheism. In the letter to Priestley on June 7, 1782, Franklin again refers to superior beings, but elaborates the reference in a humorous story about an angel which is obviously a mere pleasantry. The letter to Abbe Soulavie on September 22, 1782 (Smyth, *Writings*, VIII:599) refers to superior beings smiling at our scientific theories; it seems clearly intended as a reminder of the limited character of our knowledge, not as a theological statement. The letter to Sir Joseph Banks on November 21, 1782 (Smyth, *Writings*, IX:118) contains a long description of some balloon experiments. Franklin is evidently concerned that Banks may think these experiments frivolous and he therefore defends them in spite of their apparent lack of practical value. This defense is followed by the comment that beings superior to us also launch balloons, on one of which we ride around the sun. It is very hard to see anything in this except a slightly humorous ending for a letter. Finally, Aldridge makes much of Franklin's association with David Williams and the Society of Thirteen in the writing of a Deist liturgy for public worship, and concludes that since Williams apparently believed in polytheism, Franklin did also (Aldridge, *Franklin and Nature's God*, pp. 31, 218). The inference however is dubious. The facts appear to be these. In 1773 Williams published an *Essay on Public Worship* in which he urged the creation of a new liturgy for public worship which would contain only those principles upon which all good and religious men agree. Franklin read the *Essay* and was delighted with Williams's proposal. Shortly afterward he arranged to meet Williams, and their meeting became the occasion for the formation of a small philosophical club called the Society of Thirteen, consisting of Franklin, Williams, and eleven others. The society agreed upon the value of Williams's proposal and he was commissioned to carry it out. He did so, and the society, including Franklin, approved the liturgy and had it printed. Subsequently, Williams rented a chapel on Margaret Street, Cavendish Square, where the liturgy was put into practice for four years before financial problems ended the experiment. Although Franklin had left England before the public services began, he was apparently favorably inclined toward the project (Aldridge, *Franklin and Nature's God*, pp. 212ff). Having told this story in considerable detail, Aldridge remarks:

> Williams in his autobiography left a detailed statement of the principles upon which his liturgy and lectures were based. Presumably these were accepted by Franklin as well.
>
> "The God of Newton was probably the regulating Principle or Good of the Solar System. The God of a Nation or of a Sect is always the Spirit of that Nation or Sect, whatever be its nature. These are local Gods.
>
> What Principles may govern or preserve other Systems we know not, and therefore know not their Gods. It is probable that all the Systems of Nature are governed and preserved by a relative Principle or Law, and that governing Principle is the Universal God.
>
> It is to local Gods, those of various Nations, Sects and Parties that Theologists have generally ascribed the domination of the Universe, and the ministers of these Gods have imputed to them their own Properties, to sanctify their own Views, and they have justified the imputation by the Sophism "that causes and effects are similar."
>
> It was my wish to direct the attention of the Society to the universal Good, not to the spirit of a Nation or a Party, to the general feelings of our Nature, and the general results of our Organization, which are ever in harmony with those Circumstances we call Good (Aldridge, *Franklin and Nature's God*, p. 218).

But the conclusion that Franklin accepted Williams's polytheism is not justified. Williams's Autobiography was written long after the *Liturgy*—at least thirty years after—and may or may not reflect what Williams believed when he wrote the *Liturgy*. Nothing in the Autobiography shows or implies that Franklin accepted Williams's polytheism (David Williams, "More Light on Franklin's Religious Ideas," *American Historical Review* 43:803-13 (1938)). What the Autobiography does show, and the other remaining evidence also shows, is that Franklin accepted and endorsed the *Liturgy* as originally published. But the *Liturgy* itself is thoroughly monotheistic. God is addressed in the singular throughout, without any suggestion of other Gods, and the *Liturgy* contains several explicitly monotheistic statements—e.g., "We acknowledge him the only living and true God: God in the heavens above; in the earth beneath, and throughout all worlds; there is none besides him" (David Williams, *Liturgy on the Universal Principles of Religion and Morality* [London, 1776], pp. 2-3). What Franklin's endorsement of the *Liturgy* actually proves is that Franklin was a firm believer in monotheism. Indeed, the question one is left with is how Williams could have written so monotheistic a liturgy if in fact he held polytheistic views in 1776, but that is a question we need not pursue here. In any case, there is no solid evidence to support the claim that Franklin adhered to his early polytheism after 1728 and considerable solid evidence that he did not.

[263]Franklin, *Autobiography*, p. 114.

[264]See p. 84.

[265]Benjamin Franklin to Vaughan, November 9, 1779, in *Benjamin Franklin: Representative Selections*, ed. Mott and Jorgenson (New York: American Book Co., 1936), p. 411.

[266]Franklin, *Papers*, I:264-69.

[267]*Ibid.*, I:265.

[268]*Ibid.*, I:266.

[269]*Ibid.*, I:267.

[270]*Ibid.*

[271]*Ibid.*, I:268.

[272]*Ibid.*

[273]*Ibid.*

[274]*Ibid.*, I:269.

[275]*Ibid.*

[276]*Ibid*.

[277]Wollaston, *Religion of Nature*, pp. 112f, 176f.

[278]Franklin, *Papers*, VII:293-95.

[279]*Ibid*., VII:295.

[280]*Ibid*., VII:294.

[281]*Ibid*., VII:295.

[282]The relation between Mather and Franklin is a subject which would well repay close study. See p. 114.

[283]I. Bernard Cohen, *Franklin and Newton* (Philadelphia: American Philosophical Society, 1956), p. 511; I. Bernard Cohen, "Prejudice against the Introduction of Lightning Rods," *Journal of the Franklin Institute* 253:393-440 (1952).

[284]Franklin, *Papers*, I:213.

[285]Franklin repeated virtually the same creed in a letter to Ezra Stiles on March 9, 1790 (*Franklin: Representative Selections*, pp. 508-9).

[286]*Ibid*.

[287]*Ibid*., II:37-126. See Merton Christensen, "Franklin on the Hemphill Trial: Deism versus Presbyterian Orthodoxy," *William and Mary Quarterly*, Ser. 3, 10:219-24 (1952).

[288]Franklin, *Papers*, II:30.

[289]*Ibid*., II:30.

[290]See above, note 262.

[291]Aldridge, *Franklin and Nature's God*, chap. 13.

[292]Franklin, *Papers*, II:16.

[293]*Ibid*., I:103-4.

[294]*Ibid*., I:262.

[295]Herbert Schneider, *The Puritan Mind* (New York: Henry Holt and Co., 1930), p. 251.

296Franklin, *Papers*, II:378ff.

297Hindle, *Pursuit of Science*, p. 192.

298Eric T. Bell, *Men of Mathematics* (New York: Simon and Schuster, 1937), p. 218.

299Franklin, *Papers*, I:213.

300*Ibid.*, I:103.

301Franklin, *Autobiography*, p. 148.

302*Ibid.*, p. 148.

303*Ibid.*, pp. 148-60.

304Franklin, *Papers*, II:29.

305*Ibid.*, II:17.

306Schneider, *Puritan Mind*, pp. 250ff.

307Franklin, *Autobiography*, pp. 161f.

308Franklin, *Papers*, I:193.

309Franklin, *Autobiography*, pp. 161-63.

310*Ibid.*, pp. 163-65.

311*Ibid.*, p. 164. Original in italics.

312Franklin, *Papers*, I:193.

313*Ibid.*, I:43, 163-67.

314Cf. *ibid.*, 174-75, on the fire company Franklin organized in Philadelphia.

315For an excellent study of Franklin's moral philosophy, see Fiering, "Moral Philosophy," chap. 6.

316Franklin to Samuel Mather, November 10, 1779, quoted in Cotton Mather, *Essays to Do Good* (Dover: Samuel Stevens, 1826), pp. 6-7n.

317Herbert Schneider, *A History of American Philosophy* (New York: Columbia University Press, 1947), pp. 39-40.

Chapter Three

Jonathan Edwards

Chapter Three

Jonathan Edwards

1. Introduction

In 1716, just one year after Samuel Johnson discovered the "new learning," a thirteen-year-old boy named Jonathan Edwards enrolled at Yale College.[1] Like his predecessor, Edwards was soon engrossed in the study of Newton and Locke, and for him, too, these works marked an intellectual awakening. But the effect of these new ideas on Edwards was very different from their effect on Johnson, for Edwards was to become not an apostate from Puritanism, but the greatest champion the Puritan cause ever produced in America. In his defense of Calvinism, Edwards formulated a theology, and a philosophy, which entitle him to the rank of the greatest American theologian and the greatest American philosopher before the Civil War. But because his writing was simply one part of his struggle to revive Puritanism, it must be seen in its context to be understood at all.

We have seen in chapter 1 that one of the most basic tenets of the New England Way was the doctrine that sainthood was visible—that it was possible to distinguish empirically between those who had grace and those who did not. It was this doctrine which permitted the Puritans to limit membership in the church to those who were saved. But that limitation involved certain difficulties with respect to the theory of the sacraments. In the Puritan view, the sacraments have no efficacy in themselves—they do not produce conversion or sanctification; rather, they are "seals" of the covenant, or symbolic acts signifying that the partakers are within the covenant. Accordingly, the sacraments should be limited to those only who are members of the church. This was easy to do with communion, but how to restrict baptism to the saints was not so clear: either baptism had to be limited to those who had already had conversion, which meant a denial of infant baptism and adoption of the Anabaptist heresy, or else it had to be limited to those infants who were certain to experience conversions in later life. The Puritans adopted the latter alternative, because they interpreted the Biblical statement that God had made the covenant of grace with Abraham and his seed[2] to mean that when God gave grace to any man, he also promised grace to all descendants of that man. Hence the children of saints could be safely baptized because, although they were born in sin, they would experience conversion sometime. Thus although the Puritans believed that they were limiting membership in the church to those who were converted, they actually welcomed into the church through baptism a large contingent of children who had not experienced conversion, but who, the Puritans firmly believed, were certain to be converted.[3]

By the 1650s it had become painfully evident that a large proportion of the baptized children were not converting, and the New England churches found themselves facing a contradiction which their system could not solve. For the only explanations which the system itself offered for this situation were all equally unacceptable: either the parents of the unconverted children had never been converted in the first place, or the covenant theology was wrong, or the empirical tests of conversion were inadequate. By the 1660s this situation had become so critical that a synod of the churches had to be called to deal with it. The outcome of the synod was a compromise agreement which was called the Half-Way Covenant: the unconverted but baptized children were granted a limbo status which entitled them to vote and hold office, and, upon formally "owning" the covenant (i.e., professing their acceptance of it), to have their children baptized, but they were excluded from communion. The Half-Way Covenant was not really a solution to the problem—it was an attempt to evade an issue which could not be evaded. Although many churches accepted the Half-Way Covenant, many did not; some continued in the old way, and some—especially in Connecticut—turned toward a presbyterial polity which opened the church to the entire town. Thus by the 1670s the New England Way was in serious trouble over the problem of conversion.[4]

The declining number of conversions clearly indicated to all New England that the faith of the fathers was waning. For whatever reasons, conversions did not occur, and that fact the Puritans were compelled to interpret as somehow due to their own sinfulness. Among all the churches, therefore, ringing condemnations of the sinfulness of the people and equally ringing calls for reformation became common—so common, indeed, that such sermons form a distinct literary form, the jeremiad. Regardless of their other differences, all of the ministers joined in this lament over New England's declension and this call for revival.[5]

It is against this background that the significance of the work of Solomon Stoddard becomes apparent. Stoddard became the minister at Northampton, Massachusetts, in 1669, and for the first eight years of his pastorate adhered to the

Half-Way Covenant. But in 1677 Stoddard introduced a major change in polity: he abandoned the restriction of church membership to the elect, and offered both baptism and communion to all who were not scandalous. This revolution in polity was based upon a revision of the theology—a revision based squarely upon the failure of the older doctrines to yield the predicted results. Stoddard concluded that although the individual who is converted can know that he is converted, it is not possible for others to know for certain whether or not a man has been converted. Accordingly, he held that it was impossible to restrict membership in the church to the elect, since there was no way to tell who was and who was not elect. The function of the sacraments, therefore, could not be to serve as seals of the covenant; rather, Stoddard held, the sacraments, like the sermon, were means to conversion—i.e., God often used the sacraments, as He does the sermon, as a means in bringing about a conversion. So, Stoddard argued, the sacraments should not be restricted to the few—they should be opened to all who earnestly seek them. Thus Stoddard opened the church to the town, thereby abolishing at one stroke the oligarchic rule of the elect. But he was also quick to stifle the democratic implications of this polity by organizing the churches in western Massachusetts into "consociations"—associations of churches on the presbyterian pattern.[6]

Stoddard was not the first to take such steps. John Woodbridge of Killingworth and other Connecticut ministers had already taken this course. But Stoddard became the recognized spokesman for this new presbyterianism and in due course the polity came to be called Stoddardianism.[7] Moreover, these innovations worked. Having created an institutional situation which permitted a popular religious movement and which brought all the resources of the church to bear on the production of conversions, armed with a doctrine which called for revival, and with a sermon style which could induce it, Stoddard began to reap his "harvests." In 1679, 1683, 1696, 1712, and 1718 Stoddard produced what he called "harvests of souls"—full-scale though still minor revivals which brought large numbers of new adherents into the church. Here was an answer, and an effective one, to the problem of church membership, and—possibly—to the problem of the general declension as well.[8]

Jonathan Edwards was born on October 5, 1703, the fifth of the eleven children, and the only son, of Timothy Edwards and Esther Stoddard, daughter of Solomon Stoddard. Timothy Edwards was the minister at East Windsor, Connecticut, and being the local schoolmaster as well, he educated his son at home. Jonathan was extremely precocious and was able to enter Yale in 1716 at the age of thirteen.[9]

The Yale which Edwards attended was in a state of near chaos, torn by warring factions and physically divided between Saybrook and Wethersfield.[10] But the curriculum remained remarkably conservative throughout the turmoil. Edwards cut his philosophic teeth on Burgersdyck, whose blend of Ramus and Aristotle was standard Puritan fare, and Heereboord, who added a Cartesian flavor to the traditional course.[11] But he also read Locke's *Essay*, Newton's *Principia*, and the

Port Royal Logic during these years, and their impact upon him was no less profound than it had been upon Johnson. That impact is recorded in two series of reflections which he wrote during his college days—"The Mind"[12] and "Notes on Natural Science."[13] These two documents were probably written between 1717 and 1720, although exact dating is impossible,[14] and form a record of his philosophic progress during those years. And that progress was indeed remarkable. Edwards's adoption of Newton was complete, and he made Newtonian physics the basis for much of his subsequent philosophy. His attitude toward Locke was more critical, and while he quickly accepted most of the Lockean philosophy, he did not hesitate to disagree with Locke on specific points. The influence of Descartes was primarily methodological, and shows in the deductive form of the manuscripts rather than in the content.[15] Out of this unlikely combination of traditional Ramist Calvinism, Newtonian science, Cartesian logic, and Lockean epistemology, Edwards fashioned a unique philosophic synthesis. Indeed, what is most remarkable about Edwards is the speed with which his philosophical views took shape. By the time he had completed these documents, most of the basic principles of his philosophy were already formulated. Although Edwards continued to do philosophy all his life and kept a running record of his thought in his volumes of Miscellanies,[16] his later work is an elaboration rather than a revision of his early position.

The new learning did not alienate Edwards from Calvinism as it had Johnson; if anything it strengthened his adherence to his ancestral creed. Between 1720 and 1722 he remained at Yale preparing for the ministry, and in the latter year he became the minister of a Presbyterian church in New York City. His tour in New York was brief, and in 1724 he returned to Yale as senior tutor. Meanwhile, his grandfather, Solomon Stoddard, was growing old and was looking for a successor. In 1727 Edwards was ordained at Northampton as colleague pastor to Stoddard. Two years later Stoddard was dead, and Jonathan Edwards, age twenty-six, succeeded to Stoddard's place as the theological leader of Connecticut and western Massachusetts.[17]

More was expected of the heir of Solomon Stoddard than routine pastoral duties—to make good his claim to leadership, Edwards had to prove that he, too, could revive the faith and harvest the faithful. In 1735 he made good the promise by producing the most notable revival which had been seen in New England up to that time. The revival began at Northampton and spread along the Connecticut River until it included most of the towns in the Connecticut valley from Deerfield to the coast. Large numbers of converts were brought into the church, and Edwards's fame spread throughout the colony. The revival was a spectacular success and confirmed Edwards in his grandfather's place, but it was also soon over.[18]

Between 1736 and 1740 Edwards strove to rekindle the faith in Northampton. Then, suddenly, in 1740, came success in abundance. For in that year revivals suddenly appeared not only throughout New England but in other colonies as well, and the "Great Awakening" was on. What caused this remarkable movement, which before it ended had run through all the colonies, remains one of the most perplexing problems of American history, but it is clear that the preaching tour of George Whitefield was one of the precipitating factors. Wherever Whitefield preached, and that was everywhere, he laid them in the aisles. So far as Massachusetts was concerned, Whitefield's brand fell on tinder which Stoddard, Edwards, and generations of jeremiad-preaching Puritans had carefully prepared, and Edwards and his followers fanned the flame into a blaze. For the first time, a revival swept the entire colony from frontier to seaboard and thousands of people were converted. The ministry was delighted, and Edwards rode the whirlwind.[19]

The success was short-lived. The revival quickly ran amuck: emotional religion degenerated into emotionalism. Wild-eyed itinerant enthusiasts like James Davenport began conducting "revivals" which were simply emotional orgies.[20] By 1742, the conservative ministry had turned against the revival, and, under the leadership of Charles Chauncy, were charging that the revival was not the work of God at all, but merely an orgy of emotionalism generated by the hellfire preaching of enthusiasts.[21] Edwards was now caught between the two extremist groups. As against Chauncy and the conservatives he defended the revival as a work of God, but at the same time he had to attack the enthusiasts like Davenport who were destroying it. In his great defense of the revival—*A Treatise Concerning Religious Affections*[22]—Edwards tried to draw the line between those phenomena of the revival which were truly from God and those which were mere emotionalism. But it was too late: the revival was over, the revivalists were under attack, and the New England churches were hopelessly split.[23]

Edwards still held Northampton, but not for long. From the revival he had learned the danger of Stoddard's polity. While this polity had helped to make the revivals possible, it also deprived the ministers of any control over the membership and so opened the way to just those excesses which had ruined the revival. And so Edwards attempted in 1748 to tighten the criteria for membership in the Northampton church by requiring a profession of faith of all applicants. Enraged by this attempt to reassert ministerial control, the town turned against him, stripped him of his church, and forced him to leave.[24]

From 1751 to 1758 Edwards lived at Stockbridge, Massachusetts, as a missionary to the Indians.[25] Now thoroughly in the wilderness, with the revival ruined, his church lost, and the conservatives riding high, Edwards fought his last great battle. During these seven years he wrote four great works—*The Enquiry into the Freedom of the Will*, which was published in 1754;[26] *The Doctrine of Original Sin Defended*, published in 1758;[27] *The Nature of True Virtue* and the *End for Which God Created the World*, both published posthumously in 1765.[28] These treatises were more than just a defense of Calvinism and of the revival: they were an attempt to rebuild Calvinist theology upon a foundation provided by

Locke and Newton, and they represented the culmination of Edwards's lifework. If they failed to stem the decline of Calvinism, they yet represented its finest flower.

In 1756 Edwards's exile ended when he was called to become president of Princeton. The call testified to his position as the leading Calvinist theologian in America, and it returned him to a position where, as head of the colonies' foremost Presbyterian college, his powers would be fully effective. But the opportunity was denied him. Edwards reached Princeton in the midst of a smallpox epidemic. He was inoculated, and died on March 22, 1758.[29]

2. *Philosophy*

In the history of American philosophy, Jonathan Edwards is the greatest figure before the Civil War. Edwards was primarily a theologian and his work in philosophy was done to support his theology; nevertheless, what he did in philosophy was impressive. Like Johnson, Edwards was early converted to the teaching of Locke and Newton, and he saw at once, as Johnson also did, that the new learning destroyed the scholastic basis upon which Puritanism had rested. That realization led Johnson to reject Puritanism, but it produced exactly the opposite effect on Edwards. It became Edwards's lifework to reconstruct the Calvinist position on the basis of Newton and Locke, and so to prove that far from negating the old doctrine, the new science actually supported it.

It is a matter of considerable interest that in this endeavor Edwards should have developed an idealism not unlike Berkeley's—the more so since Johnson, too, became a devotee of such a position. It is natural to ask how Edwards came to such a view and whether or not he, too, was directly influenced by Berkeley. The answer would appear to be that Edwards's development was entirely independent: there is no evidence that Edwards read Berkeley; there is considerable evidence that he did not; and the parallels between the two men, while striking, are not very extensive. The balance of evidence seems to point to the conclusion that Edwards found in Locke some of those same difficulties which Berkeley found, and that in some striking instances he solved them in the same way.[30]

I have suggested already that Edwards's philosophy and theology are not separable. Nevertheless, they are distinguishable, and in the following exposition it will be convenient to deal first and most extensively with Edwards's philosophic writings, and then to show how he used these ideas as a basis for his theology.

The "Notes on the Mind" make it clear that the starting point for Edwards's philosophic reflections was the Lockean theory of ideas. Edwards accepted Locke's definition of an idea as that which is the object of the mind, and his division of ideas into simple, complex, and abstract. By a simple idea, Edwards and Locke mean a phenomenal quality such as red; by a complex idea, a combination of such simple ideas; and by an abstract idea, the idea of that which is common to the members of a class. There is in Edwards's work no trace of Berkeley's attack on Locke's theory of abstraction. Edwards also agreed with Locke in holding that all simple ideas are derived either from sensation or from reflection upon the operations of our own minds.[31]

But Edwards does differ from Locke on the issue of the ontological status of the external world. Edwards's early "Notes on Natural Science" makes it clear that he adopted Newtonian physics completely, together with its implicit atomism.[32] Thus he argues that every body which is not an atom must be composed of atoms.[33] But Edwards then went on to analyze the concept of the atom. With striking insight, he noted that the concept of an atom has nothing to do with absolute size: any body is an atom so long as it cannot be made less than it is. An atom is a *minimum physicae* not by virtue of its absolute size, but by virtue of its indivisibility—i.e., because it cannot be analyzed into parts.[34] But wherein does such indivisibility consist? In an argument which closely parallels Locke's discussion of solidity,[35] Edwards argues that indivisibility and solidity are identical. For according to Locke, that body is solid which, when placed between two other bodies, forever prevents their meeting. But if the body be divisible, and "if it be so that the parts can be broken still finer and finer, they can be broken so fast as not to retard the motion of the [two other bodies] at all."[36] But in this case, the other two bodies will meet, and so the divisible body was not solid. Accordingly, Edwards holds solidity and indivisibility to be the same thing, so that all atoms are perfectly solid.[37]

But from this argument Edwards drew a further conclusion—that solidity is equivalent to body or substance. For suppose a body not solid: such a body is either compound or not. If it is compounded of solid parts, then, although the body itself be not solid still its parts are, so it is resolvable into solid components. But suppose the parts not solid, or the body itself not solid yet indivisible—i.e., suppose a body which when placed between two other bodies does not prevent their meeting. Then the two other bodies must meet, and what has become of the intervening body? Clearly, it is annihilated.[38] Hence without solidity there is no body, so that body and solidity are one. Therefore, ". . . it follows that the certain unknown substance which philosophers used to think subsisted by itself and stood underneath and kept up solidity and all other properties (which they used to say it was impossible for a man to have an idea of) is nothing at all distinct from solidity itself."[39]

Locke defined solidity thus: "That which thus hinders the approach of two bodies, when they are moved one towards another, I call solidity."[40] Solidity therefore consists in resistance: a body is solid if it resists other bodies which seek to invade the space it possesses.[41] But resistance is a dispositional property: its presence is manifest only at the moment when the motion of the invading body is checked. If body is resistance, then the body exists only on those occasions when resistance is manifest. For the body to have continuous existence, the resistance must remain even when not manifest. So body as a continuous existence must consist in a "power of resistance"—i.e., in the fact that should a body invade its space then the motion of the invading body would be resisted. But what is the ontologic status of a "power of resistance"? In the following passage Edwards makes his answer clear:

> Let us suppose two globes only existing; and no mind. There is nothing there, *ex confesso*, but Resistance. That is, there is such a Law, that the space within the limits of a globular figure shall resist. Therefore, there is nothing there but a power, or an establishment. And if there be any Resistance really out of the mind, one power and establishment must resist another establishment and law of Resistance, which is exceedingly ridiculous. But yet it cannot be otherwise, if any way out of the mind. But now it is easy to conceive of Resistance, as a mode of an idea. It is easy to conceive of such a power, or constant manner of stopping or resisting a colour. The idea may be resisted, it may move, and stop and rebound; but how a mere power, which is nothing real, can move and stop, is inconceivable, and it is impossible to say a word about it without contradiction. The world is therefore an ideal one; and the Law of creating, and the succession, of these ideas is constant and regular.[42]

If body is solidity, and solidity is simply the power of resistance, what is it that resists? It cannot be body, since body is nothing but that power to resist. It must therefore be the complex idea itself (the conjunction of the simple ideas such as color) which resists. Resistance, therefore, is a mode of an idea. But since body or substance is merely the power of resistance, it follows that body is ideal, so physical objects exist only as ideas—i.e., as objects of the mind. "The world is therefore an ideal one."

Thus Edwards, like Berkeley, was led to conclude that the *esse* of things is *percipi*. "Those beings which have knowledge and consciousness are the only proper and real and substantial beings, inasmuch as the being of other things is only by these. From hence we may see the gross mistake of those who think material things the most substantial beings and spirits more like a shadow, whereas spirits only are properly substances."[43] Since the being of ideas depends upon perception, only spirits are true substances. The existence of the world therefore depends upon its being known, and while some parts of the universe might be upheld by the action of created spirits, yet it is clear that the whole of it can be maintained by no other agent but God. Strictly speaking, therefore, it is God who is the substance of the world.

> So that this substance of bodies at last becomes either "nothing" or nothing but the Deity acting in that particular manner in those parts of space where He thinks fit. So that speaking most strictly there is no proper substance but God Himself. We speak at present with respect to bodies only. How truly then is He said to be *ens entium*![44]

The fact that God is *ens entium* means that knowledge of the "physical" world is knowledge of God. But to see in just what way knowledge of the one becomes knowledge of the other requires an examination of our knowledge of the "external" world, and so of knowledge in general. Here again Edwards's thought closely parallels Locke's. It will be recalled that Locke defined knowledge as the perception of the agreement or disagreement among ideas. Knowledge, therefore, is propositional and consists not in ideas themselves, but in the perception of the relations among them.[45] This Lockean doctrine is amended by Edwards as follows:

> Knowledge is not the perception of the *agreement*, or *disagreement*, of ideas, but rather the perception of the *union* or *disunion*, of ideas—or the perceiving whether two or more ideas belong to one another.
> *Coroll.* Hence it is not impossible to believe, or know, the Truth of Mysteries, or propositions that we cannot comprehend, or see the manner how the several ideas, that belong to the proposition, are united.[46]

Edwards's position is broader than, and includes, Locke's, and it is necessary to look at its elements in detail.

Both Locke and Edwards rest ultimate certainty upon an indubitable intellectual intuition by which we simply perceive that certain ideas do or do not agree. Thus that "white is not black" is the case, I simply perceive—the proposition is self-evident and indubitable. But in many cases the relation between two ideas is not so obvious, and we are forced to resort to proof. Nevertheless, demonstration itself is ultimately resolvable into a series of self-evident propositions.[47] Thus I prove A to agree with C by using propositions asserting both to agree with B (and the transitivity of agreement), and those propositions must be self-evident. Without such self-evidence, certainty cannot be had and we must rest content with merely probable knowledge.

If such is knowledge, what is truth? Edwards argues as follows:

> Truth, in the general, may be defined, after the most strict and metaphysical manner, *The consistence and agreement of our ideas, with the ideas of God* . . . Truth, as to external things, is the consistency of our ideas with those ideas, or that train and series of ideas, that are raised in our minds, according to God's stated order and law. Truth, as to abstract ideas, is the consistency of our ideas with themselves. As when our idea of a circle, or a triangle, or any of their parts, is agreeable to the idea we have stated and agreed to call by the name of a circle, or a triangle. And it may still be said, that Truth is, *the consistency of our ideas with themselves.* Those ideas are false, that are not consistent with the series of ideas, that are raised in our minds, by [i.e.,] according to the order of nature.[48]

Edwards here distinguishes two sorts of truth, depending upon whether our ideas are abstract or concrete. Truth as to abstract ideas, Edwards holds, means simply self-consistency. So in reasoning about the abstract idea of a triangle, all that can be asked is that our statements be self-consistent, and agree with the abstract definition of the triangle. But with respect to external things, it "is the consistency of our ideas with those ideas, or that train and series of ideas, that are raised in our minds according to God's stated order and law"—i.e., with the given of experience. The Lockean terminology serves to obscure the distinction which Edwards is making here, since both concepts and sense data are called ideas. In the case of external things, it is the agreement of our concept of the thing with the sense data God gives us in experience which constitutes truth. It is consistency with phenomenal experience—not likeness to alleged entities—which is the basis of truth. But if this is so, it must then be asked in what sense there are real external entities.

One must distinguish here between what Edwards takes to be directly known and what he regards as inferred. Strictly speaking, nothing but simple ideas and certain relations among them can be directly known. These constitute the given of experience upon which all else is based. So what can be directly known of the table is simply a conjunction of actually perceived simple ideas. Anything more than this must be inferred.

Inferences are possible only when there are principles of inference, and Edwards admits two such principles:

> We know our existence, and the existence of everything, that we are conscious of in our own minds, intuitively; but all our reasoning, with respect to Real Existence, depends upon the natural, unavoidable and invariable, disposition of the mind, when it sees a thing begin to be, to conclude certainly, that there is a *Cause* of it; or if it sees a thing to be in a very orderly, regular and exact, manner, to conclude that some *Design* regulated and disposed it . . . When we therefore see anything begin to be, we intuitively know there is a cause of it, and not by ratiocination, or any kind of argument. This is an innate principle, in that sense, that the soul is born with it—a necessary, fatal propensity, so to conclude, on every occasion.[49]

The declaration that the principles of efficient and final causality are innate marks a sharp break from the Lockean tradition. Edwards does not explain his reasons for so radical a doctrine but they are not hard to guess. Locke's explanation of causality makes the principle a purely empirical generalization and so fails to explain its apparent necessity and universality.[50] Edwards, like Kant after him, was unwilling to leave so fundamental a principle in so tenuous a status. But in declaring the principles of causality innate, does Edwards really solve this problem? What their innateness proves is that our minds are so constituted that we must interpret sensory experience in terms of causality. Since the truth of a proposition consists in its giving coherence to our experience, the question of the truth of these principles reduces to the question of whether or not they succeed in bringing our experience into a coherent scheme. But must they? As Kant so clearly showed, such a "preformation-system"[51] demonstrates neither the truth nor the necessity of these principles. The fact that we are under a subjective compulsion to so order experience does not prove that a consistent ordering of this kind is possible. Edwards avoids this objection by implicitly assuming a preestablished harmony: both the causal principles and experience are from God and are so designed to yield a consistent picture. But even so, the necessity of the causal principle is not proven. That every event must have a cause must remain for Edwards a contingent fact—contingent upon God's choosing so to order the world.[52]

It is one mark of Edwards's perceptiveness that he learned the meaning of causality from Newton and did not have to wait for Hume. In the "Notes on the Mind," Edwards wrote: "Cause is that, after or upon the existence of which, or the existence of it after such a manner, the existence of another thing follows."[53] Causality, therefore, means invariable sequence: if every occurrence of an A is followed by an occurrence of a B, then A is the cause of B. Between A and B there need be no likeness, nor any other form of connection save only this invariable association. Thus Edwards notes that biological impregnation may be called the cause of the coming into being of a new spirit, since the creation of the new spirit follows upon the physical event, even though the physical event in no sense produces the spirit.

Edwards's idealism commits him to the view that God alone is substance, and that all else is derived from Him. All "external" things, therefore, are really mental and derive their being from God. But this does not tell us what "external" things there are. Edwards's answer is that those things exist which must be supposed to be in order to give a complete causal explanation of experience.

But it may be asked, How do those things exist, which have an actual existence, but of which no created mind is conscious . . . I answer, There has been in times past such a course and succession of existences, that these things must be supposed to make the series complete, according to Divine appointment, of the order of things. And there will be innumerable things consequential, which will be out of joint, out of their constituted series, without the supposition of these. For, upon supposition of these things, are infinite numbers of things otherwise than they would be, if these were not by God thus supposed. Yea, the whole Universe would be otherwise; such an influence have these things, by their attraction and otherwise. Yea, there must be an universal attraction, in the whole system of things, from the beginning of the world to the end; and, to speak more strictly and metaphysically, we must say, in the whole system and series of ideas in all Created minds; so that these things must necessarily be put in, to make complete the system of the ideal world. That is, they must be supposed, if the train of ideas be, in the order and course, settled by the Supreme mind. So that we may answer in short, That the existence of these things is in God's supposing of them, in order to the rendering complete the series of things, (to speak more strictly, *the series of ideas*,) according to his own settled order, and that harmony of things, which he has appointed. — The supposition of God, which we speak of, is nothing else but God's acting, in the course and series of his exciting ideas, as if they, (the things supposed,) were in actual idea.[54]

In order to account for experience, Newtonian science finds it necessary to postulate that the world is fundamentally atomic; therefore, Edwards concludes, the world is fundamentally atomic. The being of the atom does indeed derive from God's mind so that the atom is only mental, but it is also real—there really is such an idea in God's mind—and the world really is atomic. So Edwards agrees with Locke that there are real atoms having real primary qualities, which are described by the simple ideas which compose the complex idea of the atom, and that configurations of these atoms do excite other simple ideas in us—i.e., that God has associated certain ideas in us with certain atomic configurations such that upon contact with those configurations we have those ideas. But Edwards disagrees with Locke in holding that there is no substance but God, and that the existence of the atom and the existence of the idea in me both consist in God's thinking them. To put the matter in other terms, Edwards's conversion of the real world into an ideal one does not in the least invalidate the atomic theory. It simply means that atoms exist, just as the unseen chair in the closed room exists, because God perceives it. Even though no human being will ever perceive the atom, the atom exists because God perceives it. And we know that God perceives it because, in order to give a complete causal explanation of the world, we are compelled to postulate the existence of atoms—i.e., we are compelled to postulate that God perceives them. Edwards's idealism, therefore, in no sense invalidates science: ". . . It is just all one, as to any benefit or advantage, any end that we can suppose was proposed by the Creator, as if the Material Universe were existent in the same manner as is vulgarly thought."[55]

But it is not quite just all one. Newtonian science may remain a true description, but what it is a description of, is not quite what Newton thought. Newton describes nature in terms of atoms moving under inertial and gravitational forces according to the laws of mechanics. In this model, the atoms appear as passive material entities and gravity as an active and wholly unexplained force. But this view Edwards regards as erroneous. The atoms themselves are neither passive nor material. For as we have seen, atoms are resolvable in Edwards's system into localized powers of resistance. But resistance is an active and infinitely powerful force. That it is active may be seen by considering the kinematic phenomena which indicate its presence. What we observe is the approach of one color patch to another. At the moment of contact, the motion of the approaching patch is suddenly altered. Now this alteration, like any other alteration of motion, bespeaks an active force impressed. The usual explanation—that there is a substance there—is hardly adequate. All that the notion of substance contributes is to indicate that these kinematic phenomena require a dynamic explanation, but simply to say that they occur because there is "something" there is no explanation at all. There must indeed be a cause; and that cause, Edwards argues, can only be an active being.[56] And if it is an active being, then it must be God, because the power exerted by that active being is infinitely great. For as Locke had remarked in defining solidity as that which forever hinders the approach of two bodies, "This resistance, whereby it keeps other bodies out of the space which it possesses, is so great, that no force, how great soever, can surmount it."[57] It must therefore be infinite, "For it must be infinite power, or bigger than any finite, that resists all finite how big soever, as we have proved these bodies to do."[58] Here, as Edwards remarks, is "an incontestable argument for the being of God."[59] It follows then that the atom is simply a particular mode of the action of God located at a given time and place.

> . . . the creation of the corporeal universe is nothing but the first causing [of] resistance in such parts of space as God thought fit, with a power of being communicated successively from one part of space to another according to such stated conditions as His infinite wisdom directed (and then, the first beginning of this communication) so that ever after it might be continued without deviating from those stated conditions . . . Hence we see what's that we call the laws of nature in bodies, to wit, the stated methods of God's acting with respect to bodies and the stated conditions of the alteration of the manner of His acting.[60]

Resistance and gravity are thus merely two modes of divine activity, and natural science is nothing but a description of God's manner of action in space and time.[61]

A universe such as Edwards defines may be adequately described by the laws of mechanics, but it is not itself mechanical. For, as Edwards remarks, "there is no such thing as mechanism if that word is taken to be that whereby bodies act each upon other purely and properly by themselves."[62] For if all that exists is the acts and ideas of God, and if the causal relations among these existents are simply invariable associations resulting from arbitrary divine decree, then the universe is truly spiritual, in the sense that its existence and operation from second to second depend entirely and only upon the continuous action of divine power.[63] Thus Edwards's concept of nature combines both the complete determinism and regularity of the Newtonian world and the sense of the immanence of God of the Calvinist world. And for Edwards, as for Johnson and Berkeley, it was idealism which permitted such a combination.

Locke had held that the real essence of things consists in the arrangement of their atomic parts. If we knew the real essences, we could categorize the world into natural classes based on real similarities in things. But since Locke held that we will never know the real essences, all that we can do is to categorize them as they affect us. From particulars we abstract what we find common to them, and this common abstraction constitutes the nominal essence. Our universals are nominal essences and so are arbitrary creations of the mind reflecting an order we impose rather than one founded on real essences.[64] Like Locke, Edwards accepted the view that the real essence of objects is their atomic structure, and so one would expect him to adopt as well Locke's theory of nominal essence. The expectation is born out, but only in part. For Edwards found in the mind universals which he could not account for on Locke's principles. Consider, e.g., the idea of color. Color is clearly a universal. If it is a nominal essence, it must be abstracted from particular colors. But particular colors are simple ideas, and from simple ideas, on Locke's theory, nothing can be abstracted. Therefore color is not a nominal essence. The same argument can be extended to sounds, and to other universals as well.[65] Faced with this problem, Edwards adopted the same solution he used with respect to the status of the causal principle: viz., he grounded the concept in the innate constitution of the mind.

But the union of ideas is not always arbitrary, but

> unavoidably arises[66] from the nature of the Soul; which is such, that the thinking of one thing, of itself, yea, against our wills, excites the thought of other things that are like it . . . So I cannot doubt but, if a person had been born blind, and should have his eyes opened, and should immediately have *blue* placed before his eyes, and then *red*, then *green*, then *yellow*; I doubt not, they would immediately get into one General Idea—they would be united in his mind without his deliberation.
>   . . . So that God has not only distributed things into species, by evidently manifesting, by His making such an agreement in things, that he designed such and such particulars to be together in the mind; but by making the Soul of such a nature, that those particulars, which he thus made to agree, are unavoidably together in the mind, one naturally exciting and including the others.[67]

This is a dangerous doctrine: if there is little reason to believe that nominal essences correspond to real similarities among real essences, then there is even less ground for attributing such a correspondence to innate universals. But it is also a very useful doctrine, for it enables us to assert that certain ideas are joined together, even though we cannot see how they agree. It is on this basis that Edwards extended Locke's definition of knowledge to include the perception of the union or disunion of ideas—not just their agreement or disagreement.[68] And it is this extended definition that permits him to give the status of knowledge to revelations and mysteries which on strict Lockean grounds would not be knowledge at all.[69] That ideas joined together under innate universals do belong together rests upon exactly the same ground as the belief in the Second Coming—viz., the assumption that both are decreed by God.

Nature is at most a derivative world, dependent for its being upon the spiritual world. It is preeminently the spiritual world which it concerns us to know and understand, and so Edwards must explain what we can know of God, and what we can know of created spirits. Edwards has two arguments for the existence of God. The first of these is as follows. Either there is something or there is nothing. If there is something, then something is. If there is nothing, then nothing exists, which is self-contradictory. Therefore something is.[70] The argument, of course, hinges upon the interpretation of "there is nothing" to mean that the existence of something named "nothing" is affirmed, and if this interpretation is accepted, as it often was before Russell, the argument holds. Furthermore, not only does the argument show that something is, but it also shows that this something is a necessary being, since the denial of the existence of this something is self-contradictory. It also shows that the being is omnipresent and eternal: eternal, for if it is logically impossible that nothing exists, then nothing never existed and hence there was always something; and omnipresent, since there can be no place where nothing exists. Hence this being is eternal, omnipresent, infinite, and necessary.[71]

The second argument is drawn from Locke and is the familiar one that the existence of the world is explicable only if there is a self-moving first cause. For if there is no such self-moving first cause, then either the world is uncaused, or caused by a non-self-moving first cause. But on the first alternative, the world is either eternal or due to chance. But in either case, the order and design of the world are inexplicable, which contradicts the principle of final cause. And on the second alternative, if the first cause is not self-moving, then it must have a cause, and that cause, if not self-moving, a further cause, and so we run back in an infinite regress.[72] This argument is really circular, since it assumes the truth of the causal axiom throughout, whereas the only ground for believing this axiom true is the assumption of a preestablished harmony which Edwards rests upon the existence of God. Nevertheless, if it is granted that God is the cause of the world, Edwards can then show by the usual eighteenth-century argument from design that the God who could create so ingeniously contrived a world must be infinitely powerful and wise.[73]

In one of his earliest writings, Edwards asserted that God is space. The reasoning by which he reached this conclusion was that both God and space are necessary, infinite, eternal, and omnipresent; but there can be only one such being, and so God and space are one.[74] Edwards subsequently abandoned this formulation entirely. Although he never came to the point of calling space a form of externality, he did identify it as a simple idea which is necessary in the sense of being presupposed by all other ideas of external things. But as a simple idea, its being, despite its necessity, is the same as that of other "external" things—i.e., it consists in being thought by God. Space, therefore, is simply one of God's ideas which invariably accompanies all ideas of external things.[75]

Thus far, Edwards has dealt with what might be called God's natural attributes as opposed to his moral attributes. Properly to deal with the latter, however, requires first the consideration of the theory of excellency. The doctrine of excellency is one of Edwards's most fundamental beliefs, and it occurs near the beginning of the "Notes on the Mind." The term "excellency," as Edwards there uses it, means beauty; so the problem of excellency is the problem of the nature of the beautiful. Edwards's answer is that excellency consists in symmetry and harmony. "All beauty consists in similarness or identity of relation. In identity of relation consists all likeness, and all identity between two consists in identity of relation."[76] Beauty is therefore an objective property of an aggregate which consists in its harmonious ordering. It follows that a given system may really be beautiful, yet not be perceived as beautiful by any given perceiver. Edwards makes little attempt to justify this definition of excellency, except to cite some cases which seem to exemplify it, so the definition must be taken to be a basic premise of his philosophy.

Edwards's usual way of stating his doctrine of excellency is shown in the following definition: "This is an universal definition of Excellency:—*The Consent of Being to Being, or Being's Consent to Entity*. The more the Consent is, and the more extensive, the greater is the Excellency."[77] "Consent" here means "agreement" or "standing in an harmonious relation to." "Being" refers simply to what there is, as does "entity." The agreement of being with being is therefore excellency, even if the two beings are very minor. But clearly the excellency will be the greater the more beings are involved in the "consent"—i.e., the harmonious arrangement—and the greater the harmony. The greatest excellency will then consist in the fullest consent of being to all being, or to "being in general"—a term which Edwards employs to mean all there is. We have accordingly the following situation—beings A and B, viewed as an isolated system, may be excellent, yet when viewed as part of a larger aggregate they may be completely out of harmony with the whole, and so be ugly. Conversely, A and B, viewed as an isolated system, may be ugly, yet when viewed as part of a larger aggregate, they may nicely contribute to the beauty of the whole and so be excellent. Excellence, therefore, is relative to the system considered, and "true" excellence can only be defined as excellence with respect to the widest possible system, being in general.[78]

The perception of excellence always gives a pleasure to the perceiver which is proportional to the degree of the excellency. Similarly, the perception of ugliness gives a pain to the perceiver which is proportional to its degree. Being's consent to being in general is therefore delightful to perceiving being, and being's dissent from being in general is repulsive.[79] It is important to distinguish here the pleasure which being's consent to being in general gives the perceiver from the pleasure which being's consent to the perceiver gives the perceiver. The latter is merely a harmony between two beings and may well not be excellent, judged relative to the total system of being. On the other hand, should the perceiving mind include all being within itself, as, e.g., God does, then consent to perceiving being would be consent to being in general.[80]

Edwards's concept of excellency clearly applies both to natural and to spiritual beings. In the realm of nature, any symmetrical or harmonious arrangement is excellent. Thus, e.g., the perfect order of the Newtonian universe is a prime example of excellency, and, on Edwards's theory, the perception of this order by any perceiving being must give pleasure. But compared to natural harmony, "Spiritual harmonies are of vastly larger extent: i.e. the proportions are vastly oftener redoubled, and respect more[81] beings, and require a vastly larger view to comprehend them . . ."[82] The meaning of the term "spiritual harmony" here requires some clarification. Edwards distinguishes two types of excellency—what he calls primary and secondary excellency. Any harmoniously or symmetrically ordered aggregate is excellent in this secondary sense, whether the entities involved are natural or spiritual. But primary excellency is that harmony which arises from inclination in a voluntary agent. This is the fundamental meaning of "consent," although Edwards extends the term to include agreements among natural things as well. "There is no other proper consent but that of *Minds*, even of their Will; which, when it is of Minds toward Minds, it is *Love*, and when of Minds toward other things, it is *Choice*."[83] All primary excellence is therefore due to love, and so the formula "being's consent to being must needs be agreeable to perceiving being" becomes "*Mind's love to Mind* must needs be lovely to *Beholding Mind*."[84] Obviously, hatred among spirits must constitute the greatest disharmony and so be ugly and painful to perceiving mind.[85]

The concept of excellency as thus far described is synonymous with beauty, and refers to the symmetry and harmony within the total field of being. In the natural world these harmonies arise from connected orderings such as that induced by Newton's laws: in the spiritual world they result from love. So far Edwards has developed at least a highly plausible aesthetic. But this theory leads to a curious result—viz., that ". . . in a being that is absolutely without any plurality, there cannot be Excellency, for there can be no such thing as consent or agreement."[86] In his early writings Edwards refuses to accept this result and his struggles with it are illuminating.

The early portions of the "Notes on the Mind" show a curious equivocation over the nature of being itself. On the one hand, being is entity, pure and simple. But on the other hand, Edwards states that "Being, if we examine narrowly, is nothing else but Proportion."[87] Yet what could being be the proportion of, if not entity? Edwards's reasoning appears to rest upon his definition of nothing as a state of contradiction. If this definition is accepted then the negation of nothing is the negation of contradiction, so being would be consistency.[88] But again, consistency among what? Edwards vacillates, and part of the reason for his vacillation is that if being is proportion, then being and beauty are synonymous and evil and nothingness equally so. This would tie his theory of excellence neatly to the theory of being, prove the excellence of God, and open the way to a view of sin as mere negation.

But Edwards did not identify being and beauty; rather he redefined excellency to include both being and beauty. Thus he wrote: "Excellency may be distributed into *Greatness* and *Beauty*. The former is the Degree of Being; the latter is Being's Consent to Being."[89] Beauty, therefore, becomes but one form of excellency: mere quantity of being must also be considered excellent. Now since Edwards is already committed to the view that the perception of excellence arouses pleasure in proportion to the degree of excellence, the redefinition of excellence requires a demonstration that pleasure in the beholder is proportional to quantity of being beheld. To support this view, Edwards argued:

> Existence or Entity is that, into which all Excellency is to be resolved. Being or Existence is what is necessarily agreeable to Being; and when Being perceives it, it will be an agreeable perception; and any contradiction to Being or Existence is what Being when it perceives, abhors. If Being, in itself considered, were not pleasing, Being's consent to Being would not be pleasing, nor would Being's disagreeing with Being, be displeasing.[90]

But Edwards did not pursue this attempt to reduce excellency to entity, and in subsequent writings he restricted the term excellency to mean only being's consent to being. Being itself cannot consist in proportion, for proportion is a relative term whose relates must be something other than proportions. Thus a few pages later in "The Mind,"[91] Edwards writes:

> One alone, without any reference to any more, cannot be excellent; for in such case, there can be no manner of relation no way, and therefore no such thing as Consent. Indeed what we call *One*, may be excellent because of a consent of parts, or some consent of those in that being, that are distinguished into a plurality some way or other. But in a being that is absolutely without any plurality, there cannot be Excellency, for there can be no such thing as consent or agreement.[92]

Here it is clear not only that excellency means consent only, but that entity and excellency are not the same. Yet Edwards continued to be attracted to the idea of greatness as an aesthetic category. As he later[93] wrote:

> It is reasonable to suppose that the mere perception of Being is agreeable to perceiving Being, as well as Being's consent to Being. If absolute Being were not agreeable to perceiving Being, the contradiction of Being to Being would not be unpleasant. Hence there is in the mind an inclination to perceive the things that are, or the Desire of Truth. The exercise of this disposition of the

soul, to a high degree, is the passion of admiration. When the mind beholds a very uncommon object, there is the pleasure of a new perception, with the excitation of the appetite of knowing more of it, as the causes and the manner of production and the like, and the uneasiness arising from its being so hidden. These compose that emotion called *Admiration*.[94]

Edwards does not confuse excellence and greatness in this passage, but it seems clear that he is verging on the distinction between the beautiful and the sublime which was to become so important in England during the eighteenth century.[95] And the stress placed in the above quoted passage upon the "uncommon" as the stimulus of "admiration" suggests that these lines may have been written under the immediate stimulus of Addison.[96] Nor is it surprising that Edwards, captivated as he was with the grand discoveries of Newton, should have responded to what he later called "the purity, beauty, sublimity, and glory of the visible heavens."[97] The same enchantment with "inconceivable vastness"[98] which led thinkers like More toward the notion of the sublime is clearly at work in Edwards.[99] What is surprising is that Edwards refused to follow this road to the end. In his later work, the term "excellence" is synonymous with beauty, defined in the strict sense of being's consent to being; and the category of greatness, though it continues to be significant in morality, loses its aesthetic status.[100] Why Edwards chose this course we can only conjecture, but the decision was probably based on the requirements of the theory of virtue.

The theory of excellency forms the basis of Edwards's theory of virtue, and so leads us back to the question of the moral nature of God. Whatever disagreement there may be concerning virtue, Edwards observes, at least this is agreed: that virtue itself is something beautiful.[101] It is accordingly a kind of excellency, and so far as spirits are concerned, it is their chief excellency. It is, therefore, no surprise to find that "true virtue most essentially consists in benevolence to Being in general. Or perhaps to speak more accurately, it is that consent, propensity and union of heart to Being in general, that is immediately exercised in a general good will."[102] The term "benevolence" here requires clarification. Edwards distinguishes two sorts of love: benevolence and complacence.

Love of *benevolence* is that affection or propensity of the heart to any Being, which causes it to incline to its well being, or disposes it to desire and take pleasure in its happiness. And if I mistake not, it is agreeable to the common opinion, that beauty in the object is not always the ground of this propensity: but that there may be such a thing as benevolence, or a disposition to the welfare of those that are not considered as beautiful; unless mere existence be accounted a beauty . . . What is commonly called love of *complacence*, presupposes beauty. For it is no other than delight in beauty; or complacence in the person or Being beloved for his beauty.[103]

True virtue is benevolence to Being in general; it is not complacence. True virtue itself is beautiful, but it is not primarily a love of beauty. It is rather love of being in general, whether being in general is beautiful or not. Absolute benevolence is simply love of being proportional to the quantity of being, and so is greatest when addressed to being in general. But why ought one to love being in general? Had Edwards gone on to develop greatness as a category of excellence one might answer that being in general should be loved because it is excellent, but since Edwards turned away from this road, there is really no answer to this question in Edwards's writings. The fact that such is the ultimate nature of virtue is simply asserted by fiat, and stands as an ultimate premise of Edwards's thought.

Edwards's theory of virtue bears certain analogies to the benevolence morality of Shaftesbury and Hutcheson. It is not certain when Edwards became acquainted with their works, although there was a copy of Shaftesbury's *Characteristics* in the Dummer collection, but it is certain he was well acquainted with their views by the time he wrote the treatise on *The Nature of True Virtue*. It is therefore important to note that Edwards rejected Hutcheson's morality because it was based on benevolence to the creatures rather than toward God. From Edwards's perspective, the benevolence of Hutcheson would produce love to a limited fraction of being rather than love to being in general, and although it might create a harmonious order within that limited system, the result would be a deformity when viewed in respect to the total system of being.[104] Thus, true to the Amesian tradition, Edwards rejected any ethics which was not applied theology.

If it be granted that benevolence to being in general is true virtue, then it follows at once that since God is infinitely the greatest being, and the true substance of all being, then God, being virtuous, loves Himself. That this convicts God of self-love is for Edwards no objection, for self-love is only evil in Edwards's view when the self is something less than being in general. But since God is being in general and contains an infinite quantity of being, God's self-love is infinitely virtuous. It follows then, virtue being itself spiritually beautiful, that God is infinitely beautiful and excellent, for God's self-love is the consent of infinitely great being to being in general. Hence although God does not love Himself for His own beauty but rather for His own being, yet God is infinitely beautiful, and that beauty is His glory.[105]

This analysis leads Edwards to a remarkable view of the trinity. Since God knows all there is, it of course follows that God knows Himself. Moreover, God's knowledge is perfect and amounts to an absolute immediate intuition of all there is. Now a perfect idea in the mind of God is, according to Edwards's idealism, the thing itself: of whatever God has an idea, that idea is the substance of the thing. Therefore, if God perfectly knows Himself, that idea which He has of Himself is the substantial image of God, and is one with the essence of God. Accordingly, "the perfect idea God has of Himself is truly and properly God."[106] It is in this sense that God is self-begetting and self-sustaining. "So that by God's reflecting on Himself the being is begotten, that is, a substantial image of God begotten.''[107] The Godhead is therefore divisible into two aspects: God as knowing subject, and God as known object. The first of these is the first person of the Trinity—God the Father and creator. The second is the second person of the Trinity—God the only begotten Son, who is the image and word of the Father. Both persons are one in substance and are only analytically distinguishable. The situation is analogous to that of the self-conscious man who is both subject thinking and object thought about, except that God's knowledge is both perfect and constitutive. The relation between the Father and the Son is not only one of knowing, but also one of pure love, and this love of God for God constitutes the third person of the Trinity. So the Holy Ghost is literally love—viz., God's love of God Himself.[108]

> & This I suppose to be that Blessed Trinity that we read of in the Holy SS [scriptures]. The F[ather] is the Deity subsisting in the Prime, unoriginated & most absolute manner, or the deity in its direct existence. The Son is the deity generated by Gods understanding, or having an Idea of himself & subsisting in that Idea. The Holy Gh[ost] is the Deity subsisting in act, or the divine essence flowing out and Breathed forth in Gods Infinite love to & delight in himself. & I believe the whole divine Essence does Truly & distinctly subsist both in the divine Idea & divine Love, and that each of them are Properly distinct Persons.[109]

It is this trinitarian analysis of the nature of God which permits Edwards to hold that God is infinitely beautiful. "Again, we have shown that one alone cannot be excellent, inasmuch as, in such case, there can be no consent. Therefore, if God is excellent, there must be a plurality in God; otherwise there can be no consent in Him.''[110] God's self-love is the consent of infinite being to infinite being and it is, therefore, the highest spiritual excellence possible. But it must be remarked that the ground of God's self-love cannot be His own excellence, which is the result of this self-love—it must rather be the greatness of God or the quantity of His existence which serves as the ultimate ground of His self-love. Once this self-love exists, however, God is thereby made infinitely excellent, and that excellence serves as a secondary ground for His love of Himself. It is due to this secondary ground that God can be said to delight in His own excellency.

Edwards's theory of the trinity is certainly a daring extension of his idealism to God Himself, and it raises the question of just how much Edwards thought we can really know of God. On this point Edwards is very clear: our knowledge is at best feeble and fragmentary. We can by the light of reason discover that some attributes must be true of God, but how they can be true we cannot conceive. In an extended passage in the *Miscellanies*, which reminds one of Kant's antinomies, Edwards remarks a long series of propositions about God which must be true but which are beyond our understanding.

> Nothing is more certain than that there must be an universal and unlimited being; and yet the very notion of such a being is all mystery, involving nothing but incomprehensibles, paradoxes, and seeming inconsistencies. It involves the notion of a being, self-existent and without any cause, which is utterly inconceivable and seems repugnant to all our ways of conception. An infinite spiritual being, or infinite understanding and will and spiritual power, must be omnipresent, without extension—which is nothing but mystery and seeming inconsistence.[111]

Similarly God's immutability implies duration without succession, which seems impossible. No more can we comprehend God's knowledge.

> Perfect knowledge of all things, even of all the things of external sense, without any sensation or any reception of ideas from without is inconceivable mystery. Infinite knowledge implies a perfect comprehensive view of a whole future eternity, which seems utterly impossible. For how can there be any reaching of the whole of this, to comprehend it, without reaching to the utmost limits of it? But this can't be where there is no such thing as utmost limits.[112]

Again, how can God see the whole chain of causality from eternity to eternity? For there must be an infinite number of links to the chain, and this fact, Edwards holds, forbids there being a closed totality representable by "all links."[113] These and similar difficulties led Edwards to assert that natural reason, unaided by revelation, could never have penetrated very far into the mysteries of spiritual things. That we have revelation is due to the mercy of God who so enables us to know more than our unaided faculties could attain, and we must not, therefore, be surprised that many things in revelation remain mysterious and obscure. Indeed, this is to be expected and is rather a sign of the genuineness of revelation than the converse. We must, therefore, accept as true many statements given us by revelation even though we cannot understand how they can be true.[114]

Besides God and external nature, whose being is directly from God, Edwards recognizes also the existence of created spirits. By a "mind or spirit" Edwards means "nothing else but consciousness, and what is included in it."[115] The things which are spiritual are, therefore, those things which we would classify as intellectual and emotional. Thus Edwards remarks, "If we would get a right notion of what is Spiritual, we must think of Thought, or Inclination, or Delight."[116] The idea of a spirit is accordingly a complex idea composed of the spiritual powers and attributes attributed to the particular spirit. For as Edwards remarks concerning the idea of God, "This notion of God, or idea I have of Him, is that complex idea of such power, holiness, purity, majesty, excellency, beauty, loveliness, and ten thousand other things."[117] So the same must hold for created spirits.

But the problem of spiritual knowledge is not so easily disposed of, for it remains to explain what sort of simple ideas we have of spiritual things. Like Berkeley, Edwards found it necessary to make a sharp distinction between ideas of sensation and ideas of the operations of our own minds.

> Love is not properly said to be an idea, any more than Understanding is said to be an idea. Understanding and Loving are different acts of the mind entirely; and so Pleasure and Pain are not properly ideas. Though Pleasure and Pain may imply perception in their nature, yet it does not follow, that they are properly ideas. There is an Act of the mind in it. An idea is only a perception, wherein the mind is passive or rather subjective. The Acts of the mind are not merely ideas. All Acts of the mind, about its ideas, are not themselves mere ideas.[118]

Strictly speaking then, we have simple ideas only by sensation when the mind is entirely passive. In what way, then, have we knowledge of the operations of our own minds?

Few doctrines of Locke involve more difficulties than his claim that we derive simple ideas from both sensation and reflection. The simple ideas of sensation are sensory qualities such as red, but there are no sensory qualities of this sort which characterize acts of the mind. So two courses lay open: either the ideas we have of acts of our own minds are not simple ideas, or else the concept of the simple idea must be expanded so as to include other-than-sensory qualities. The first course was taken by Berkeley when he introduced the concept of "notion";[119] the second was taken by Edwards. As the passage quoted above makes clear, Edwards sharply distinguished the acts of the mind from its passive ideas. How then can there be ideas of acts? Edwards found the answer to this problem in the fact that "All sorts of ideas of things are but the repetition of those very things over again—as well the ideas of colours, figures, solidity, tastes, and smells, as the ideas of thought and mental acts."[120] According to this view, to have a true idea of red, the image of red must be present—otherwise, one is merely using the word and no definite sensible idea is present at all. So Edwards argues that to have a true idea of love, the act of love must be actually repeated:

> . . . there is no actual idea of those things [i.e., "those things that we can know only by reflection"] but what consists in the actual existence of the same things, or like things, in our own minds. For instance, to excite the idea of an idea we must have that very idea in our minds; we must have the same idea. To have an actual idea of a thought is to have that thought, that we have an idea of, then in our minds. To have an actual idea of any pleasure or delight, there must be excited a degree of that delight; so to have an actual idea of any trouble or kind of pain, there must be excited a degree of that pain or trouble; and to have an idea of any affection of the mind, there must be then present a degree of that affection.[121]

We have, therefore, an equivocal use of the term "simple idea," depending upon whether the idea concerns internal or external phenomena. Simple ideas proper are ideas of properties of external things, and are ideas in the true Lockean sense. But the term is also used for internal and spiritual acts, and when so used it refers not to any image of the act but to the act itself. The idea of delight is delight; the idea of love is love. It is, therefore, strictly true that no man but a lover can have an idea of love.

It is obvious from this definition of ideas that we often think and talk about ideas without their actually being present. This fact led Edwards to distinguish between what he calls "mere cogitation" and "ideal apprehension." In "mere cogitation" we deal with the signs of ideas, such as words, without the idea itself being present to the mind at all.[122] In "ideal apprehension," on the other hand, "the mind has a direct *ideal view* or *contemplation* of the thing thought of."[123] So in ordinary discourse, we often employ the word "love" as a sign for the idea of love and we talk and think by means of this sign without ever realizing the idea referred to in our minds at all.

On the basis of this distinction, Edwards drew his critical distinction between speculative and sensible knowledge of internal, or spiritual, things.

> . . . or 1. that understanding which consists in mere speculation or under-standing of the head; and 2. that which consists in the sense of the heart. The former includes all that understanding that is without any proper ideal apprehension or view and all that understanding of mental things of either faculty that is only by signs. And also all ideal views of things that are merely intellectual or appertain only to the faculty of understanding, i.e., all that understanding of things that don't consist in or imply some motion of the will or, in other words (to speak figuratively) some feeling of the heart, is mere speculative knowledge, whether it be an ideal apprehension of them or no. But all that understanding of things that does consist in or involve such a sense or feeling is not merely speculative but sensible knowledge. So is all ideal apprehension of beauty and deformity, of loveliness and hatefulness; and all ideas of delight or comfort, or pleasure of body or mind, pain, trouble, or misery; and all ideal apprehensions of desires and longings, esteem, ac-quiescence, hope, fear, contempt, choosing, refusing, assenting, rejecting, loving, hating, anger, and the idea of all the affections of the mind, and all their motions and exercises; and all ideal views of dignity or excellency of any kind; and . . . All knowledge of this sort, as it is of things that concern the heart or the will and affections, so it all relates to the good or evil that the sensible knowledge of things of this nature involves. And nothing is called a sensible knowledge upon any other account but on the account of the sense or kind of inward tasting or feeling of sweetness or pleasure, bitterness or pains, that is implied in it or arises from it.[124]

Ideas derived from reflection simply repeat the internal act of the mind to which they refer. But such ideas may be of two sorts—those which are purely speculative or intellectual, such as the idea of reasoning, which involves no arousal of the emotions, and those which either are ideas of emotion—like love—or involve the emotions. Edwards generalizes the term "sensible" to include the latter but not the former class so that the term "sensible" means for him what derives either from the senses or the sensibility. We can therefore have sensible knowledge of spiritual things such as love and delight, provided that these acts of the mind are truly realized. Accordingly, it is strictly true that a man who has no love to God can have no sensible idea of love to God, since the latter is nothing but love to God. So, although the idea of spirit may be defined as a given sort of complex idea, the elements which compose this complex idea are "ideas" of spiritual things, and only those who have these spiritual realities themselves can be said to have a true idea of spirit.

Since created spirits are not known through the senses, properties such as size and shape clearly have no application to them. Yet created spirits are bound to particular locations such as a particular body, and so the problem arises how that which has neither size nor shape can have place. Edwards answers this as follows:

> . . . Spirits cannot be in place, in such a sense, that all, within the given limits, shall be where the Spirit is, and all without such a circumscription, where he is not; but in this sense only, that all created Spirits have clearer and more strongly impressed ideas of things, in one place than in another, or can produce effects here and not there; and as this place alters, so Spirits move. In Spirits united to bodies, the Spirit more strongly perceives things where the body is, and can there immediately produce effects; and in this sense the soul can be said to be *in the same place* where the body is. And this law is, that we call *the Union between soul and body*.[125]

The spirit is, so to speak, "with" the body but not "in" it.[126] Thus when we say that the world exists only in the mind, it would be absurd to interpret this as meaning that the world is contained within the volume of brain, for the brain itself exists only mentally.[127] Spirits are wherever they act and are acted upon, meaning that ideas received and actions taken are conjoined with particular ideas of place and time. The spirit is in the heart as much as the brain, since it acts in the affections as well as in thought.[128] And the conjunction of the created spirit with those ideas which constitute place or the material body results from a purely arbitrary decree of God, dissolvable at His pleasure, for there is clearly no necessary relation between the soul and these ideas.[129]

Since the soul is immaterial and we have no sensible ideas of it in the ordinary sense, some explanation is called for as to how we acquire our knowledge of it. So far as knowledge of our own souls is concerned, Edwards holds that we have intuitive certainty. "We know our own existence, and the existence of every thing, that we are conscious of in our own minds, intuitively."[130] But with respect to other spirits the case is different. Like all external existences, the existence of other spirits is inferred through the principle of causality. Just as the principle of efficient cause permits us to infer the existence of atoms, so the princple of final cause permits us to infer the existence of other spirits.[131] Since Edwards holds that it is an innate principle of the mind that design implies a designer, so the perception of order tending to a purpose implies a spirit. The behavior of the body gives ample evidence of such design and so the inference is sure that a spirit operates there. Equally, the universe can be metaphorically seen as the body of God, from the behavior of which we infer the existence of the divine spirit.[132]

But when we know a spirit, what is it that we know? What constitutes the being of spirits? Do they exist, like external things, as ideas in God's mind, or is there some peculiar mode of being specific to spirits? In his early writings Edwards denied that spirits existed only in idea. Thus he wrote that the material universe "does not exist as Spirits do, whose existence does not consist in, nor in dependence on, the conception of other minds."[133] This view is similar to Berkeley's view and doubtless derives from Locke's famous chapter on power.[134] But Edwards wrote this before he had formulated his theory of the Trinity, and quite probably before he had clarified his ideas on the nature of our ideas of internal and spiritual things.[135] The discovery that ideas of the mind's actions in fact repeat these acts eliminates one objection to spirits existing in idea—viz., that they would so be rendered passive. And the doctrine of the Trinity involves the explicit statement that the second person (who is certainly a spirit) does exist in idea, and that it is in this sense—viz., as God's idea of Himself—that the Son is the image of the Father. It is, therefore, very hard to see how created spirits could exist otherwise than in divine idea, where idea is properly understood as act. In this sense it is proper to say that man is active (though not that he is self-determining), that he exists in divine idea, that he is wholly dependent upon God, and that he is a communication[136] or emanation[137] of God. And in this sense it is also correct to say, as Edwards does repeatedly, that although created spirits are, yet "He is, as there is none else."[138]

Edwards's definition of virtue as the consent of being to being in general applies equally to created and uncreated spirits. Since God is all being, virtue in Him is self-love. But for created spirits, whose being is derivative, consent to being in general means love to God. As we have already remarked, although mere entity creates obligation, it does not create excellency—the excellency of God rests upon His virtue. Since God is infinitely virtuous, He is therefore infinitely beautiful and excellent, and so one would expect created spirits to be at once attracted to Him. But here one must recall that spiritual things are spiritually discerned: unless the created spirit already has love to God, the beauty of God cannot be perceived.

It is impossible that any one should truly *relish* this beauty, consisting in general benevolence, who has *not* that temper himself. I have observed, that if any Being is possessed of such a temper, he will unavoidably be pleased with the same temper in another. And it may in like manner be demonstrated, that it is such a spirit, and nothing else, which will relish such a spirit. For if a Being, destitute of benevolence, should love benevolence to Being in general, it would prize and seek that which it had no value for. Because to love an inclination to the good of Being in general, would imply a loving and prizing the good of Being in general.[139]

Accordingly, only those who love God can perceive the excellence of God and so delight in His beauty. But the love of God is simply another name for the Holy Ghost. It is, therefore, strictly true to say that only those to whom the Holy Spirit is communicated can see and enjoy the excellence of God. And of course it is only those who do love God who have spiritual virtue and so attain any measure of spiritual excellence themselves. Those who do not love God, either through hatred of Him or preoccupation with their own narrow interests, are without virtue and are therefore lost in sin.

The fact that only the benevolent can love benevolence may well be the reason that Edwards decided against making greatness an aesthetic category. For greatness is, after all, a purely natural attribute, and even sinners should be able to grasp the fact that the totality of being is greater than their own. If greatness alone were aesthetically appealing, the sinner would then be drawn toward God, and so a way would be opened whereby natural men might acquire virtue on the basis of a purely speculative knowledge of God. Such a result would obviously have been unwelcome to Edwards.

In defending his idealism, Edwards is careful to point out that his doctrine is wholly consistent with Newtonian physics and that as far as science is concerned it is "just all one" whether the idealist or the common view is adopted.[140] But clearly in adopting idealism Edwards was after something more than just an alternative ontology to support Newtonian physics. By holding all external things to be ideas in the mind of God, Edwards not only assures an immediate relation to God, but he also raises the question of why these ideas and not others. Since God is a reasoning and designing being, He must have some reasons for creating and ordering the world just so. Science tells us how God operates, not why; it remains for philosophy and theology to determine the end for which God created the world.

There are two sources from which we can derive knowledge concerning the end for which God created the world: Scripture and reason. Scriptural authority is, of course, superior, but the particular Scriptural passages which bear on this point are not unambiguous, so the aid of reason is required. Now if we are to find a solution to this problem by reason, it will obviously be by deriving it from what we know of the attributes of God. But when we examine such attributes as the divine justice, we find that they afford little help. For justice is a disposition to act justly upon all occasions; it does not imply the creation of those occasions. Given that the world exists, it follows from the fact that God is just that He will act justly toward the world; but from the fact that God is just it does not follow that he will create a world so that He may have an occasion for just action.[141] And the case is the same for other divine attributes. Accordingly, Edwards holds, if the end of the creation involves the divine attributes, then it must be in the sense of affording an opportunity or occasion for their exercise, and so we must suppose "that a disposition in God, as an original property of his nature, to an emanation of his own infinite fulness, was what excited him to create the world; and so that the emanation itself was aimed at by him as a last end of the creation."[142]

The Scriptures affirm that the world was created for "the glory of God."[143] On Edwards's view,

> The thing signified by that name, *the glory of God*, when spoken of as the supreme and ultimate end of the work of creation, and of all God's works, is the emanation and true external expression of God's internal glory and fulness . . . Or, in other words, God's internal glory extant, in a true and just exhibition, or external existence of it . . . Now God's internal glory, as it is in God, is either in his understanding or will. The glory or fulness of his understanding, is his knowledge. The internal glory and fulness of God, which we must conceive of as having its special seat in his will, is his holiness and happiness. The whole of God's internal good or glory, is in these three things, viz., his infinite knowledge; his infinite virtue or holiness, and his infinite joy and happiness. Indeed there are a great many attributes in God, . . . but all may be reduced to these, or to the degree, circumstances and relations of these.[144]

There are in fact, according to Edwards, two manifestations of God's internal glory, one *ab intra* and one *ad extra*. The manifestation *ab intra* is the Trinity: the Son being the image of God's knowledge and the Holy Ghost of His love.[145] The manifestation *ad extra* is the image of God created in the elect. "God communicates himself to the understanding of the creature, in giving him the knowledge of his glory; and to the will of the creature, in giving him holiness, consisting primarily in the love of God; and in giving the creature happiness, chiefly consisting in joy in God. These are the sum of that emanation of divine fulness, called in Scripture *the glory of God*."[146] The saints are, of course, the principal part of the creation, for whose sake the rest was made, but the saints themselves exist only that in them the divine glory—i.e., the attributes of God—may be manifest. In this sense, God's end in the creation is Himself, or rather the exercise of Himself,[147] but it can also be said that God aims at the happiness of the saints. For wherein does that happiness consist, but in love to and delight in God? And that love and delight will become ever greater throughout eternity, for Edwards conceives perfect union with God as a limit toward which the elect forever approach. So although the limit is never actually attained, yet "in this view the creature must be looked upon as united to God in an infinite strictness."[148] The happiness of the creature is therefore identical with the happiness of God, so that although God's end in the creation is his own glory only, yet it is also the felicity of his elect.[149]

But if the whole purpose of the creation is the manifestation of God's glory in the saints, why was the physical world also created? Edwards's answer is that nature is a language through which God speaks to His creatures.

> It is very fit and becoming of God, who is infinitely wise, so to order things that there should be a voice of His in His works, instructing those that behold them and painting forth and shewing divine mysteries and things more immediately appertaining to Himself and His spiritual kingdom. The works of God are but a kind of voice or language of God to instruct intelligent beings in things pertaining to Himself.[150]

This answer is traditional to Puritanism, which has always seen sermons in stones, and equally so to idealism. Plato and his followers, including those Cambridge Platonists like Cudworth and Gale whose writings Edwards knew,[151] saw natural things as imitations of the ideas. And Berkeley, working out an idealism so like Edwards's, held nature to be "an universal language."[152] Edwards's solution is therefore not unique, but his particular method of developing this solution is unusual. When Edwards wrote that ". . . as Bodies are but the shadow of being, therefore the consent of bodies one to another, and the harmony that is among them, is but the shadow of Excellency,"[153] he is clearly asserting that natural bodies and their relations are in some sense images of spiritual facts, but in just what sense remains to be explained.

To develop a supernatural reading of nature, Edwards turned to the traditional method of Biblical exegesis known as typology. As we have seen above, typology was an exegetical method which was well established within the Puritan tradition and well accepted in New England. But in applying typology to nature, Edwards found it necessary to deviate from the tradition. In Puritan doctrine, type and antitype were both actual historical events, the type occurring before and prefiguring the antitype, the antitype occurring after and completing the type. But nature, as Newton described it, was ahistorical; the static equilibrium of celestial mechanics knew no development, no change. Hence a typological reading of Newtonian nature could not be historical; the relation of type and antitype had to be atemporal. So when Edwards sought to develop such a reading, he turned the temporal relations of typology into metaphorical relations between natural and spiritual facts. Thus Edwards writes:

> The system of created being may be divided into two parts, the typical world, and the antitypical world. The inferior and carnal, i.e. the more external and transitory part of the universe, that part of it which is inchoative, imperfect, and subservient, is typical of the superiour, more spiritual, perfect, and

durable part of it which is the end, and as it were, the substance and consummation of the other. Thus the material and natural world is typical of the moral, spiritual, and intelligent world, or the city of God.[154]

The distinction between type and trope—a distinction of which earlier Puritans had made much—is here obliterated, and the natural fact becomes a metaphor for a spiritual reality.[155] Viewed from this perspective, the function of science is to offer us an exact delineation of the type, but true understanding of the type can only come when we see its relation to the spiritual antitype, for the sake of which it exists. Nature is therefore subservient to and a revelation of spirit. Newton's laws serve, within the order of nature itself, to explain its behavior, but for typical knowledge we must turn to Scripture.

> The book of Scripture is the interpreter of the book of nature two ways, viz., by declaring to us those spiritual mysteries that are indeed signified and typified in the constitution of the natural world; and secondly, in actually making application of the signs and types in the book of nature as representations of those spiritual mysteries in many instances.[156]

Revelation, by supplying the antitypes, makes possible the true reading of the type which Newton described.

> The whole material universe is preserved by gravity or attraction, or the mutual tendency of all bodies to each other. One part of the universe is hereby made beneficial to another; the beauty, harmony, and order, regular progress, life, and motion, and in short all the well-being of the whole frame depends on it. This is a type of love or charity in the spiritual world.[157]

Nor is it only the general patterns of nature which are typical: every fact may be so interpreted.

> Men as they are born all over filthy, proceeding out of that which is filthy and being begotten in filthiness, so they are born backward into the world, with their backs upon God and heaven and their faces to the earth and hell, representing the natural state of their hearts.[158]

But Edwards goes even further than this. Not only can nature be understood through types, but it cannot be understood without them. For there are classes of natural phenomena which Edwards believed to be inexplicable by science and so to admit of explanation only as types of spiritual facts. Among these he cites the power of the serpent to charm birds and animals,[159] which is an obvious type of the devil's power to delude man, and the miraculous events recorded in the Bible:

And to show that all things in heaven and earth, the whole universe, is wholly subservient, the greater parts of it as well as the smaller, God has once or twice interrupted the course of the greater wheels of the machine, as when the sun stood still in Joshua's time. So, to shew how much He regards things in the spiritual world, there are some things in the ordinary course of things that fall out in a manner quite diverse and aliene from the ordinary laws of nature in other things, to hold forth and represent spiritual things.[160]

Accordingly, the typological reading of nature is not just an adventitious spiritualizing of science. Without typology our understanding of nature would remain incomplete and the relation of natural facts to spiritual facts would remain hidden.

Edwards's typological writings were never embodied in a systematic treatise: at his death they remained in fragmentary form and have only recently come into print. Yet these fragments are of great importance, for they show how clearly Edwards understood the fundamental problem which the new science had raised for religion. Newton had proven once and for all that natural phenomena can be explained in terms of natural laws without recourse to other than natural agents. It was not because Newtonian science denied religion that it was dangerous: it was because it rendered religion unnecessary. Understanding and control of nature were possible without recourse to God. If Edwards was to rebuild Calvinism in America, this enervating implication of the new science had to be attacked and overthrown. Edwards's idealism, by dissolving the too solid mechanism of the Newtonian world into immaterial loci of God's action, was designed to restore the immanence and immediacy of God in nature. His interpretation of causality and law as the mere mode of God's action was designed to maintain the total dependence of the creature upon God. And the doctrine of typology was designed to restore that direct and immediate intercourse between God and man which had existed when God spoke to man through the whirlwind and the lightning bolt. Only by interpreting nature as God's word and by finding in its very order and regularity a divine message could the universe be kept redolent with spiritual life.[161]

3. *Theology*

It was upon the basis of the position outlined above that Edwards strove to rebuild Calvinism in America. In saying this we do not wish to suggest that Edwards's philosophy was developed first and his theology then deliberately erected upon it. Edwards was born and bred a Puritan and he knew Calvin before he ever heard of Newton and Locke. It is perfectly clear that he saw philosophy as a handmaid to theology and that his philosophic doctrines were ever viewed as means to theological ends. Nevertheless, it is legitimate to distinguish his more philosophic work from his more theological, and by doing so one is perhaps the more easily enabled to see how the task of reconstruction was carried out and to appreciate just how skilled a workman Edwards was.

The bedrock of Calvinism was the doctrine of the absolute sovereignty of God. For Puritanism, God was the omnipresent, omniscient, inscrutable, all powerful creator, lord and master of the universe. This is equally so for Edwards. Since all things exist only as ideas in the divine mind there is in a strict sense nothing at all apart from God. It is therefore strictly true that God is the creator and master of the world, that His knowledge of it is absolute (since this is merely knowledge of the content of His own mind), and that He is immanent in every part of it. Nor, despite the boldness of his conception of the Trinity, does Edwards compromise God's inscrutability. The limitations of our minds become evident as soon as we begin to reason about the infinite, and we must resign ourselves to the fact that there are mysteries beyond our understanding. Edwards's God is thoroughly Calvinistic.

The absolute sovereignty of God implies that God foreknows and foreordains all that there is. Predestination was one of the most important and most difficult of Puritan doctrines, and it was one to the defense of which Edwards devoted some of his best work. That total predestination must obtain in Edwards's system is obvious. Since all that is consists of ideas in the mind of God, it is obviously God who ordains all that is. Time and space, being God's creations, cannot apply to God Himself: hence the entire scheme of things, past, present, and future, must be simultaneously present as an ordered set of ideas in the divine mind. And since human history and experience are merely the successive realizations of these ideas in time and space, it is obvious that God knows and determines all that ever is.[162]

That predestination holds true for nature Edwards regarded as decisively proven by Newton. The determinism of the Newtonian system is absolute, and Edwards like most of his contemporaries regarded mechanics as the paradigm of all natural sciences. But that determinism applies equally to the affairs of men was a less obvious, and, to the eighteenth century, a less appealing, doctrine. By the 1740s and 1750s, Arminian optimism was well on the road to victory, both in Europe and America. Even in New England, in the very heart of the predestinarian stronghold, the corrupting influence of the Arminian doctrine had insinuated itself. Not only rationalists but even many seemingly orthodox divines were following English liberals such as Whitby and Taylor in a denial of predestination, and so, whether they knew it or not, were halfway down the road to Arminianism.

For Edwards, the doctrine of predestination was the central pillar of Calvinism: if this doctrine fell, all else was lost; if it stood fast, all else could be saved. It was for this reason that he devoted his greatest treatise to its defense. And the reasons for Edwards's evaluation of its central importance are not difficult to discover. He regarded the Arminian notion of freedom as completely contradictory to the chief doctrines of true religion, and as the last refuge of sin. For if, as the Arminians claimed, the will is self-determining, then not only has God not preordained what is to be, but He cannot foreknow what is to be. God's ordering of the world must then be dependent upon the decisions of His creatures, so that God is no longer sovereign, or omnipotent, or omniscient. Moreover, such a doctrine virtually destroys responsibility for sin. For according to the Arminian doctrine, no man is responsible for any acts except those in which his will is determined by itself. If therefore there were such a thing as original sin—i.e., an inescapable congenital tendency to evil inherent in man—acts committed under the influence of this tendency would not be sinful. Hence original sin, if it exists, is not sin, and all a man need do to escape blame is to plead an irresistible impulse to evil, which, instead of rendering him odious, renders him on Arminian grounds free of guilt. ". . . All wickedness of heart is excused, as what, in itself considered, brings no guilt . . . And how small a matter does this at once bring men's guilt to, when all the main things, wherein their wickedness consists, are passed over."[163] No wonder Edwards believed the Arminian doctrine "almost inconceivably pernicious"[164] and set himself the task of destroying it as a necessary prelude to the reconstruction of the Calvinist position.[165]

Edwards's great treatise on the *Freedom of the Will* opens with a careful and exact statement of the problem. As is usually the case, the statement of the problem is actually the most important part of the whole inquiry, for in defining the question Edwards lays the basis for his own solution. Obviously, the first term which must be defined is the term "will," and Edwards does this as follows: ". . . the will (without any metaphysical refining) is plainly, that by which the mind chooses anything. The faculty of the will is that faculty or power or principle of mind by which it is capable of choosing: an act of the will is the same as an act of choosing or choice."[166] This definition appears clear enough, but something must be said of the term "faculty." Edwards derived his psychology from Locke, and like Locke he wholly rejected the scholastic faculty psychology. Whereas the older theory had conceived of the mind as composed of distinct faculties or agents operating almost like parts of a machine, Locke and Edwards saw the mind as a unity which responds and acts as a whole. The doctrine that the faculties can act upon and determine each other, as when the understanding is said to determine the will, Locke subjected to withering ridicule in a passage which has been quoted and requoted *ad nauseam* but which so accurately makes the point that it will be quoted once more:

For, if it be reasonable to suppose and talk of faculties as distinct beings that can act, (as we do, when we say the will orders, and the will is free,) it is fit that we should make a speaking faculty, and a walking faculty, and a dancing faculty, by which these actions are produced, which are but several modes of motion; as well as we make the will and understanding to be faculties, by which the actions of choosing and perceiving are produced, which are but several modes of thinking. And we may as properly say that it is the singing faculty sings, and the dancing faculty dances, as that the will chooses, or that the understanding conceives; or, as is usual, that the will directs the understanding, or the understanding obeys or obeys not the will: it being altogether as proper and intelligible to say that the power of speaking directs the power of singing, or the power of singing obeys or disobeys the power of speaking.[167]

For Edwards as for Locke to speak of the will is to speak of the choice behavior of a man; to ask if the will is free is to ask if a man's choice is free.[168] Yet Edwards and Locke both continued to employ the faculty terminology (as in the definition of the will above) even though they understood by it simply a mode of behavior of the whole man. To understand Edwards, it is important to bear in mind that he is trying to cram new doctrine into old terms, and that the terms often prove a cumbrous and unwieldy vehicle for his meaning.

If the will is simply the power of choice, then by determination of the will must be meant the causing of one choice rather than another. "To talk of the determination of the will, supposes an effect, which must have a cause. If the will is determined, there is a determiner. This must be supposed to be intended even by them that say, the will determines itself."[169] Having so defined the will and determination, Edwards lays down his first thesis: "it is that motive, which, as it stands in the view of the mind, is the strongest, that determines the will."[170] By a "motive" in this context Edwards means "the whole of that which moves, excites or invites the mind to volition . . . ."[171] The motive may be single but it is usually complex and it comprises the whole set of ideas perceived by the mind which induces to action. The concept is thus very broad: the only restriction is that the motive must be actually apprehended by the mind at the time it serves as a motive, for what is not apprehended cannot affect the mind.[172] And by the "strength" of a motive, Edwards means its tendency to move the mind. "And I think it must also be allowed by all, that everything that is properly called a motive, excitement or inducement to a perceiving willing agent, has some sort and degree of tendency, or advantage to move or excite the will, previous to the effect, or to the act of the will excited. This previous tendency of the motive is what I call the 'strength' of the motive."[173]

Edwards's second thesis is that "the will always is as the greatest apparent good is."[174] The connection between the motive and the good is spelled out by the proposition that "whatever is perceived or apprehended by an intelligent and voluntary agent, which has the nature and influence of a motive to volition or choice, is considered or viewed *as good*,"[175] where the term "good" means "agreeable" or "pleasing" to the mind.[176] By these definitions, the "strongest motive" is correlated to the "greatest apparent good," providing that the latter be restricted to "the direct and immediate object of the act of volition,"[177] not a remote or mediate object. So Edwards's position thus far comes to saying that in every voluntary act men choose that which appears most agreeable to them at the time.

The obvious criticism of this claim is that it appears to reduce to a tautology, for if the strongest motive is equated to the greatest apparent good, and if the will is the mind choosing, it surely seems analytic to say that the mind chooses the greatest apparent good.[178] Edwards saw the difficulty and met it squarely:

> I have rather chosen to express myself thus, that the will always *is* as the greatest apparent good, or as what appears most agreeable, is, than to say that the will is *determined* by the greatest apparent good, or by what seems most agreeable; because an appearing most agreeable or pleasing to the mind, and the mind's preferring and choosing, seem hardly to be properly and perfectly distinct. If strict propriety of speech be insisted on, it may more properly be said, that the voluntary action which is the immediate consequence and fruit of the mind's volition or choice, is determined by that which appears most agreeable, than the preference or choice itself; but that the act of volition itself is always determined by that in or about the mind's view of the object, which causes it to appear most agreeable. I say, in or about the mind's view of the object, because what has influence to render an object in view agreeable, is not only what appears in the object viewed, but also the manner of the view, and the state and circumstances of the mind that views.[179]

It *is* analytic to say that we choose the greatest apparent good. The question is rather why a given motive is the greatest apparent good, or the strongest motive, and Edwards's answer is that at least three factors determine the strength of a motive.[180] The first of these is the "apparent nature and circumstances of the object." By this Edwards means the characteristics of the object which make it "beautiful and pleasant, or deformed or irksome"[181] when considered by itself. He also includes as circumstances of the object the "pleasure or trouble attending the object, or the consequences of it"[182] and the perceived length of time which it will take to obtain the object or its consequences. These are all regarded as objective characteristics of the object itself, although they must be "apparent"— i.e., perceived by us—if they are to be effective. The second factor is the probability of obtaining the pleasure which the object involves; thus Edwards remarks "it is more agreeable to have a certain happiness, than an uncertain one; and a pleasure viewed as more probable, all other things being equal, is more agreeable to the mind, than that which is viewed as less probable."[183] The third factor may be called the salience of the object; i.e., the motive is stronger if "our idea is much more clear, lively and strong."[184] To these three Edwards considers adding a fourth—the state or temper of the mind, due to nature, custom, education, or other causes, which predisposes it to regard one object as agreeable and another as disagreeable. But since this temper will manifest itself in either the first or third of the factors already mentioned, Edwards concludes that its addition would be redundant. Those three factors may be called the determinants of motive strength. Edwards does not discuss their composition—i.e., whether they combine multiplicatively, or, if not, by what other rule—but it is clear that the strength of a given motive will depend upon the magnitude of that composite. Hence when Edwards says that the will is determined by the strongest motive, he must be understood to mean that that motive for which the composite of the determinants of motive strength is the greatest determines the will. That statement is not analytic, for the determinants of motive strength are not identical with the mind's choosing.

Having now defined the relation between will and motive, Edwards turns to the question of necessity. Edwards distinguishes several different meanings of the term "necessity," but that meaning which is relevant to controversies over the will is what he calls "philosophical necessity." By this, as Edwards carefully explains, he means "nothing else than the full and fixed connection between the things signified by the subject and predicate of a proposition, which affirms something to be true."[185] So far as concerns actions in the future, philosophical necessity means nothing more than an invariable connection between antecedent and consequent. ". . . the only way that anything that is to come to pass hereafter, is or can be necessary, is by a connection with something that is necessary in its own nature, or something that already is, or has been; so that the one being supposed, the other certainly follows."[186] So to ask if an act of the will is necessary, or necessitated, is to ask if, upon the occurrence of some antecedent condition, the act certainly follows.

Edwards then draws his famous distinction between moral and natural necessity. "By 'moral necessity' is meant that necessity of connection and consequence, which arises from such *moral causes*, as the strength of inclination, or motives, and the connection which there is in the many cases between these, and such certain volitions and actions."[187] "By 'natural necessity,' as applied to men, I mean such necessity as men are under through the force of natural causes."[188] The distinction then has to do with the nature of the cause, not with the nature of the necessity itself. Since the will is as the greatest apparent good, a man may be said to be under the moral necessity of choosing that thing which appears to him most agreeable: the necessity is moral because the cause is a motive. Since men are material objects possessing weight, they may be said to be under a material necessity of exerting force whenever they voluntarily change position: the necessity is natural because the cause is purely natural. The difference therefore lies in the terms related, not in the nature of the connection.[189]

From moral and natural necessity there follows at once the concept of moral and natural impossibility and so of moral and natural inability. If an action is morally necessary, nonperformance of the action is morally impossible, and similarly if an action is naturally necessary, nonperformance of the action is naturally impossible. An individual who is under a moral impossibility of performing a given act is said to be morally unable to perform it; an individual who is under a natural impossibility of performing an act is said to be naturally unable to perform it. Thus I may be morally unable to stop smoking and naturally unable to fly.[190]

Edwards is now able to state his position regarding the freedom of the will. "Let a person come by his volition or choice how he will, yet, if he is able, and there is nothing in the way to hinder his pursuing and executing his will, the man is fully and perfectly free. . . ."[191] Freedom, therefore, consists in the liberty to do as one wills. Edwards thus maintains that the question of how a man came to will what he does will has no bearing on the question of freedom: however his will came to be as it is, he is free if he can do as he wills. In so defining his position, Edwards draws the line clearly between himself and the Arminians. For the crux of the Arminian position, as Edwards defines it, is that freedom "consists in a self-determining power in the will, or a certain sovereignty the will has over itself, and its own acts, whereby it determines its own volitions; so as not to be dependent in its determinations, on any cause without itself, nor determined by anything prior to its own acts.[192] The issue therefore is this: Edwards says that true freedom is the freedom to do as you will; the Arminians, that it is the freedom to will what you will.[193] But what is really at stake here is not for Edwards simply the definition of freedom, but rather the scope of responsibility. For on Edwards's view, although a man may be excused for failure to perform actions which he is naturally unable to perform, he is not excused for failure to perform actions which he is morally unable to perform.

> It can't be truly said, according to the ordinary use of language, that a malicious man, let him be never so malicious, can't hold his hand from striking, or that he is not able to shew his neighbor kindness; or that a drunkard, let his appetite be never so strong, can't keep the cup from his mouth. In the strictest propriety of speech, a man has a thing in his power, if he has it in his choice, or at his election: and a man can't be truly said to be unable to do a thing, when he can do it if he will . . . Therefore, in these things to ascribe a nonperformance to the want of power or ability, is not just; because the thing wanting is not a being *able*, but a being *willing*. There are faculties of mind, and capacity of nature, and everything else, sufficient, but a disposition: nothing is wanting but a will.[194]

Here is the fundamental issue as Edwards saw it. The Arminians would hold that a man irresistibly drawn to commit a crime is not responsible because his will was not free: Edwards would answer that though he was morally unable to resist, yet he could have resisted had he willed to, and since in committing the crime he did as he willed, therefore he acted freely and is responsible. This was the real issue at stake.

The treatise on the *Freedom of the Will* is less a defense of Edwards's own position than an attack on the Arminian position, and the attack is waged on four points. First, Edwards shows the Arminian doctrine to be absurd because it leads to an infinite regress. The Arminians hold that the will is self-determining. But what can this mean? It means, Edwards argues, either that the acts of the will are uncaused, or that they are determined by prior acts of the will. The first possibility the Arminians themselves reject since the will would then be wholly arbitrary and could be influenced neither by reason nor by the will itself: this would not be freedom, but chaos.[195] But the second alternative is no better. Let W_n be any act of the will. Then W_n must be determined by a prior act of will W_{n-1}. But then W_{n-1} must be similarly determined by a prior act, W_{n-2}, and so on. Now either the series has a first member or it does not. If it does not, then the regress is vicious, for no act of the will is then ever determined. If it does have a first member, then one of three alternatives is true: that the first act is determined by a preceding act of will which is contrary to supposition, or it is wholly arbitrary and uncaused, which leads to the above rejected alternative, or it is determined by something not an act of will. But in the latter case, the will is no longer self-determining, for if the first act is not self-determining, then since the second act is determined by the first, that which determines the first also determines the second. And since the third act is wholly determined by the second act, that which determines the second act also determines the third. And so on, to the W_nth act. Accordingly, that which determines the first act determines every act in the series, and so in no case is the will self-determining.[196] Hence no matter which alternative is taken, the Arminian doctrine collapses in absurdities.

Edwards's argument is relentlessly applied, throughout part two of the treatise, to every conceivable form of the Arminian position. For example, if it is contended that the will is self-determining because it is determined by the understanding, Edwards quickly shows that this destroys its self-determining character.[197] Similarly, against Locke's notion that freedom lies in the power to suspend action, Edwards invokes the same argument by pointing out that the suspension of volition is itself an act of will so that the act of suspension must be determined by a prior act, and that act by yet a prior act, and so on *ad infinitum*.[198] The argument is a telling one, and on Edwards's definition of the Arminian position there is clearly no escape from it.

But Edwards is not content to show that the Arminian doctrine is absurd—he also shows that it is false. For the Arminian argument requires both that the future be really contingent upon individual decisions freely made, and that neither blame nor praise can attach to acts which are necessary—either naturally or morally. But against the first point Edwards argues God's foreknowledge. If any man could really have decided differently than he did, then God could not have known what he would do until the decision was made. But if that is so, then God cannot foreknow anything about the course of human events. Yet even the Arminians admit that God has foreknowledge.[199] Moreover, if blame and praise cannot attach to acts which are necessary, the acts of God are not praiseworthy, for all agree that God is necessarily good. God therefore would be without virtue and would deserve no praise.[200] The same must be true of Jesus, whose moral perfection was necessary.[201] Clearly, for Edwards, or any other Christian, to show that such consequences follow from the Arminian doctrine is equivalent to refuting the doctrine.

But Edwards saves his most deadly shaft for the final section of the treatise. In earlier sections he has shown that the Arminian position is absurd and false; here he attempts to explain why the Arminians have fallen into such egregious errors. "One main foundation [of the Arminian position] is a supposition, that the virtuousness of the dispositions or acts of the will consists not in the nature of these dispositions or acts, but wholly in the origin or cause of them."[202] Thus the Arminians argue that no matter how terrible the act of will, it is not a sin unless its cause is a vicious determination of the will itself, whereas Edwards holds that the act of will is sinful in its own nature, irrespective of its cause. The absurdity of the Arminian position Edwards quickly shows by the now familiar argument. If the viciousness of an act of will lies not in the nature of the act but in its cause, then either it lies in the nature of that cause or in the cause of that cause. If the former, it lies in the nature of an act of the will, which is contrary to supposition: if the latter, we are off again upon an infinite regress. For if the viciousness of an act of the will lies in its cause, and the viciousness of the cause lies in its cause, etc., then we are driven back forever and so the viciousness "lies nowhere at all."[203]

But why do the Arminians believe this strange doctrine?

I suppose, the way that men came to entertain this absurd inconsistent notion, with respect to *internal inclinations and volitions* themselves (or notions that imply it), viz. that the essence of their moral good or evil lies not in their nature, but their cause; was, that it is indeed a very plain dictate of common sense, that it is so with respect to all *outward actions*, and sensible motions of the body; that the moral good or evil of 'em don't lie at all in the motions themselves; which taken by themselves, are nothing of a moral nature; and the essence of all the moral good or evil that concerns them, lies in those internal dispositions and volitions which are the cause of them. Now being always used to determine this, without hesitation or dispute, concerning *external actions*; which are the things that in the common use of language are signified by such phrases, as men's "actions," or their "doings;" hence when they came to speak of volitions, and *internal exercises* of their inclinations, under the same denomination of their "actions," or what they "do," they unwarily determine the case must also be the same with these, as with external actions; not considering the vast difference in the nature of the case.[204]

The Arminian position therefore rests upon a confusion induced by the careless use of language. Physical actions, such as striking a blow, are clearly determined by an act of will as cause, and the virtue or vice of the physical act is as the virtue or vice of the act of will. From this fact, the Arminians have unwarily leaped to the conclusion that the virtue or vice of any act is determined by the virtue or vice of its cause. But in so doing they have failed to see that the term "act" describes something different when applied to the will than when applied to physical behavior. The moral character of an act of will depends upon the nature of the act—not its cause. If the act is one of benevolence to being in general it is virtuous; if not, it is vicious; and the "cause" of the act has nothing to do with its nature.

Here then is the heart of the matter. For Edwards, virtue lies in the nature of the act. Love to God, and all acts of will involving love to God, are inherently virtuous acts; hatred to God, and all acts of will involving hatred to God, are inherently vicious. To say that no act is vicious or virtuous unless its cause is vicious or virtuous and that therefore no man is blamable or praiseworthy except for what he himself caused is to mistake the nature of agency. The notion of agency does not require a man to be the cause of his own first act of will, as the absurdities to which this doctrine leads clearly show: all it requires is that the act be his act, so that he is the agent who performs the given action.[205] To claim otherwise—to vest all praise or blame in the cause and not in the nature of the act, is to destroy virtue and vice. For it will then result that that which is the chief of evils—viz., a fixed and immovable disposition to wrongdoing—is not only not blamable but is as well an excuse against blame because such a disposition coerces the will, while that which is the chief of virtues, even the virtues of God himself—viz., a fixed and immovable disposition to righteousness—is not praiseworthy. Such are the wages of Arminianism.

Edwards's treatise on the freedom of the will is a polemic, and like most polemics it is largely concerned with destroying the opposition. But it is a mistake to view this treatise as a purely negative document: Edwards does something more than lay the Arminians flat on their backs. The treatise contains as well his own detailed analysis of the nature of the will, of freedom, and of virtue and vice respecting the acts of the will, and his argument that true freedom is wholly consistent with absolute predestination. Upon the ground so prepared, Edwards was now ready to defend "the great Christian doctrine of Original Sin."

Edwards opened *The Doctrine of Original Sin Defended* with this definition of original sin:

> By *Origin Sin*, as the phrase has been most commonly used by divines, is meant *the innate, sinful depravity of the heart*. But yet, when the doctrine of Original Sin is spoken of, it is vulgarly understood in that latitude, as to include not only the *depravity of nature*, but the *imputation of Adam's* first Sin; or in other words, the liableness or exposedness of Adam's posterity, in the divine judgment, to partake of the punishment of that Sin.[206]

Clearly then, both the fact of depravity and the question of the origin of that depravity are at issue. Edwards attacks these points in order, and considers first in what depravity consists.

To understand Edwards's position it is essential to understand what Edwards thought the fall of Adam involved. Man's original nature Edwards described as follows:

> . . . when God made man at first, he implanted in him two kinds of principles. There was an *inferior* kind, which may be called *natural*, being the principles of mere human nature; such as self-love, with those natural appetites and passions, which belong to the *nature of man*, in which his love to his own liberty, honor, and pleasure, were exercised: these, when alone, and left to themselves, are what the Scriptures sometimes call *flesh*. Besides these, there were *superior* principles, that were spiritual, holy, and divine, summarily comprehended in divine love; wherein consisted the spiritual image of God, and man's righteousness and true holiness; which are called in Scripture the *divine nature*. These principles . . . are above those principles that are essentially implied in, or necessarily resulting from, and inseparably connected with, *mere human nature*; and being such as immediately depend on man's union and communion with God, or divine communications and influences of God's Spirit: which, though withdrawn, and man's nature forsaken of these principles, human nature would be human nature still; man's nature, as such, being entire, without these divine *principles*, which the Scripture sometimes calls *Spirit*, in contradistinction to *flesh*. These superior principles were given to possess the throne, and maintain an absolute dominion in the heart: the other to be wholly subordinate and subservient.[207]

What happened when Adam fell is described thus:

> When man sinned, and broke God's covenant, and fell under his curse, these superior principles left his heart: for indeed God then left him; that communion with God, on which these principles depended, entirely ceased; the Holy Spirit, that divine inhabitant, forsook the house . . . The inferior principles of self-love, and natural appetite, which were given only to serve, being alone, and left to themselves, *of course* became reigning principles; having no superior principles to regulate or control them, they became absolute masters of the heart . . . Man did immediately set up *himself*, and the objects of his private affections and appetites, as supreme; and so they took the place of God.[208]

As Edwards understood the fall, therefore, it involved the actual and total loss of the divine principles. Fallen or natural man is dominated by self-love. That is, like any biological organism, man seeks primarily the satisfaction of his own needs and desires. These desires may well be various—they may even include an earnest desire for salvation, since heaven is far more desirable a prospect than is hell. But in all cases, the motive involved is the survival and happiness of the man concerned. Edwards regards this conduct as wholly natural: it stems directly from the nature of man and is therefore as necessary a part of human behavior as breathing or eating.

But if we here recall Edwards's definition of virtue as love to being in general, it is at once apparent that this natural behavior of man is not virtuous; indeed, since it is governed by love to only a fraction of being in general—viz., the self—and strives for the advantages of that fraction against the whole universe, such behavior is vicious. It is indeed that very sin of pride, or putting of the self before God, which in the Augustinian tradition forms the root of all evil. Thus men in following the dictates of their nature do necessarily and infallibly commit sin from the time they are born until they die.[209] And if, Edwards adds, there is any serious question as to whether or not men are in fact ruled by self-interest, one need only look to history and daily observation for the proof. That human nature is indeed of this sort "appears in that there have been so very few in the world, from age to age, ever since the world has stood, that have been of any other character."[210]

How completely natural and yet sinful natural men are can perhaps be better understood by recalling the fact that excellency is relative to the system considered. What appears supremely excellent when only a part of being in general is considered may well be a hideous deformity when viewed in relation to all being. Since natural man views all things relative to himself, these things which appear to him as most excellent and agreeable will not be such when viewed relative to God. But natural man's will must be as the greatest apparent good—i.e., as that which appears to him most excellent and agreeable. Hence natural men do gladly will those things which are sinful, and since they are perfectly free to do as they will, their sinful conduct is fully blamable and deserving of punishment. And indeed, as Edwards never tires of stressing, when it is considered how infinitely holy God is, and therefore how great is our obligation to respect and love Him, and therefore how hideous the sinful conduct of natural men really is—that they exalt their deformed and wretched selves above the glorious Lord of all creation—it is but just that their punishment should be terrible, even eternal hellfire.[211]

To such a view, two obvious objections may be raised: it makes God the author of sin, and the imputation of Adam's sin to posterity is unjust. To the first of these Edwards replies that the term "author of sin" is ambiguous. On the one hand, the term may mean that God directly caused Adam to sin, and in this sense Edwards denies that God is the author of sin. On the other hand, it may mean that by withdrawing those spiritual influences without which nature is corrupt God permitted Adam to sin, and Edwards admits that in this sense God is indeed the author of sin.[212] But such an objection, Edwards holds, is no more an objection to his doctrine than to any other, for sin exists, and however it came about it cannot be denied that God has permitted it. And Edwards's theory does not attribute the commission of a sinful act to God; it only holds that God allowed Adam to commit such an act.[213]

The objection concerning imputation is a more complex problem. Why should

Adam's posterity be regarded as having sinned merely because Adam did? Edwards's answer to this problem is as ingenious as it is radical. He asserts that in this respect God may and does regard all men as one. To explain how this can be, Edwards turns to the concept of identity and asks in what the identity of created things consists. And first Edwards notes that the continued existence of any created thing depends upon the continual exercise of God's power—an assertion which, of course, follows at once from his idealism. But if that be so, "it will follow from what has been observed, that God's upholding created substance, or causing its existence in each successive moment, is altogether equivalent to an *immediate production out of nothing*, at each moment. Because its existence at this moment is not merely in part from *God*, but wholly from him, and not in any part or degree, from its *antecedent existence*."[214] What then gives identity to the created thing through a series of such instantaneous renewals? Clearly, "there is no identity or oneness in the case, but what depends on the *arbitrary* constitution of the Creator; who by his wise sovereign establishment so unites these successive new effects, that he *treats them as one*, by communicating to them like properties, relations and circumstances; and so leads *us* to regard and treat them as *one*."[215] And so it follows at once that the objection to God's treating Adam and his posterity as one "is built on a false hypothesis: for it appears, that a *divine constitution* is the thing which *makes truth*, in affairs of this nature."[216] All men are therefore justly chargeable with Adam's sin by virtue of God's decision to treat all as one in this case, for that decision makes them all one in fact.[217]

Traditional Calvinism holds that from among the children of Adam God selects a "saving remnant" whom He predestines to salvation while the rest are bound to hell. Edwards completely accepted this stern doctrine, but his proofs of it were purely Scriptural and need not concern us here.[218] What is of more philosophic and theological interest is the method of salvation. Calvinism held that salvation comes only through the grace of God. Grace is given solely by God's arbitrary decree: it is not in any sense conditional upon the actions or merits of the recipient and cannot be won or earned by any human endeavor. It is, moreover, irresistible and irrevocable. Those to whom it is given become and remain saints; those to whom it is denied are utterly cast away in sin.[219]

This iron doctrine Edwards fully believed, but as usual he modified it and reinterpreted it to fit his own system. Grace is from God alone, but what is grace? Traditionally, grace is the giving of the Holy Spirit. We have seen in discussing the Trinity that for Edwards the Holy Spirit is the love of God. To say then that grace consists in the Holy Spirit coming to dwell in the man means strictly that the love of God comes to dwell in him. That is, Edwards sees grace as a partial restoration of the spiritual principles in man which were lost by the fall.[220] When grace is given, the spirit returns, meaning that love to God comes to dwell in the man, and so becomes an indwelling, permanent, ruling disposition of his heart. As Edwards put it in a stunning metaphor,

But the soul of a saint receives light from the Sun of Righteousness, in such a manner, that its nature is changed, and it becomes properly a luminous thing: not only does the sun shine in the saints, but they also become little suns, partaking of the nature of the fountain of their light. In this respect, the manner of their derivation of light, is like that of the lamps in the tabernacle, rather than that of a reflecting glass; which thought they were lit up by fire from heaven, yet thereby became, themselves burning shining things.[221]

Grace is given by God from without, but being given it lives in the saint. It is in this sense that Edwards speaks of grace as a "new principle" or "new nature," meaning that whereas natural man has as his ruling disposition love to himself, the saint's nature is so transformed by grace that his ruling disposition is love to God.[222] And once this change has truly occurred, it is irrevocable: love to God will remain the ruling disposition forever.

In his description of grace, particularly in the great *Treatise Concerning Religious Affections*, Edwards often describes it as the giving of a "new sense" or as involving the reception of a "new simple idea."[223] In speaking of a "new sense," Edwards seems to intend at least two different things, both of which are important for an understanding of his concept of grace. First, it will be recalled that Edwards uses the term "sensible knowledge" to include that which affects the sensibility as well as that which affects the senses. Sensible knowledge of spiritual things is strictly the ideal apprehension of those spiritual ideas which affect or involve the will and affections. But ideas of spiritual things simply repeat the acts to which they refer. Thus the idea of love is love; the idea of delight is delight. To have a "new sense" of divine things means, therefore, having sensible knowledge of divine things—i.e., having those divine things actually present in the mind as actions of the mind and will. We can have a "simple idea" of love to God only when we actually love God. Natural men, who are bereft of true love to God, cannot have sensible knowledge of love to God and, therefore, have no sense of it; the most they can attain is cogitative understanding which is a mere playing with signs or words. It is only when grace is given and the spiritual realities are in fact present in the mind of the saint that sensible knowledge of divine things is possible at all. Thus it is literally true to say that the saint's experience differs absolutely from the sinner's, for the saint has actual experience of an order of reality of which the sinner knows only by hearsay.

But there is a second, and equally critical, sense in which Edwards holds that grace confers a new sense on the saint. We have seen above that excellency consists in being's consent to being in general. But in order for such consent to appear excellent to perceiving being, it is further necessary that the perceiving being himself consent to being in general. "For if a Being, destitute of benevolence, should love benevolence to Being in general, it would prize and seek that which it had no value for."[224] That is, since Edwards holds that we must approve and desire that which appears most beautiful to us, then to regard the love of one being to another as beautiful we must also love the beloved being. For if this were not the case, we would approve and desire the well-being of that which we do not love, which Edwards regards as contradictory. If this argument is granted, then it follows that natural man cannot perceive the excellence and beauty of God, since he has no love to God but only to himself. But grace is the love of God. So when grace is given, the saint thereby acquires that principle which is the condition of his perceiving the beauty of God.

Edwards's reconstruction of the process of conversion and sanctification appears to be as follows. By fiat God gives grace to a man, meaning that the love of God comes to dwell in the man's heart. This being done, the true spiritual realities are present to the man, and it is now possible for him to perceive the true excellence of God and of all things spiritual.

> Hence we learn that the prime alteration that is made in conversion, that which is first and the foundation of all, is the alteration of the temper and disposition and spirit of the mind. For what is done in conversion is nothing but conferring the Spirit of God, which dwells in the soul and becomes there a principle of life and action. 'Tis this is the new nature, and the divine nature; and the nature of the soul being thus changed, it admits divine light. Divine things now appear excellent, beautiful, glorious, which did not when the soul was of another spirit. Indeed, the first act of the Spirit of God, or the first that this divine temper exerts itself in, is in spiritual understanding or in the sense of the mind, its perception of glory and excellency, etc.—in the ideas it has of divine things. And this is before any proper acts of the will. Indeed, the inclination of the soul, as immediately exercised in that sense of the mind which is called spiritual understanding or the intellect's love, is not only mere presence of ideas in the mind, but it is the mind's sense of their excellency, glory, and delightfulness.[225]

It is this beauty of the divine which constitutes what Edwards calls a "new simple idea":

> . . . it follows, that in those gracious exercises and affections which are wrought in the minds of the saints, through the saving influences of the Spirit of God, there is a new inward perception or sensation of their minds, entirely different in its nature and kind, from anything that ever their minds were the subjects of before they were sanctified . . . if God produces something thus new in a mind, that is a perceiving, thinking, conscious thing; then doubtless something entirely new is felt, or perceived, or thought; or, which is the same thing, there is some new sensation or perception of the mind, which is entirely of a new sort, and which could be produced by no exalting, varying or compounding of that kind of perceptions or sensations which the mind had before; or there is what some metaphysicians call a new simple idea.[226]

It is not grace itself which is the new simple idea, but grace acts like a new sense in that grace is the condition of the new simple idea—i.e., the divine reality and the beauty of divine things—being perceived. So, to use Edwards's famous simile, the idea which a natural man has of spiritual things is like the idea one would have of honey who was born without taste, while the idea the saint has of spiritual things is like the idea one has of honey who can truly experience and relish its sweetness.[227] Given grace, the divine beauty becomes sensible.

The love of God (grace) is the ground of our perception of divine excellence; but the perception of divine excellence is in turn a secondary ground of further love to God.[228] For as God is infinitely beautiful and excellent, so must the saints' love and adoration of God be greatly increased as the true holiness and glory of divine things are made evident. And as God thus appears infinitely desirable, so the affections of the saint are turned away from himself toward God, so that he is no longer ruled by self-love, but rather by love of God. But this means, of course, that God appears as by far the greatest apparent good, so that the will of the saint is morally constrained to seek and serve God wholly and continuously, and to avoid all things which are not to the glory of God. As grace abides and the disposition to seek God is irrevocable, so now the saints become themselves virtuous, for they love God and their actions are ruled by that disposition. So that the saints "though they were lit up by fire from heaven, yet thereby became, themselves burning shining things."[229]

It is obvious that on Edwards's analysis, grace is both irresistible and irrevocable. The giving of grace is wholly arbitrary, and once given the process of conversion and sanctification proceeds under the iron rules of causality which Edwards so elaborately constructed to govern the will. From the giving of grace on, everything is wholly determined. Similarly, without grace the plight of the natural man is utterly hopeless. By his nature he is ruled by self-interest. Lacking the grace of God, he cannot acquire knowledge of divine and spiritual things because those things are not in his experience, nor can he come to any true sense of the excellence of divine things since he has not the conditions upon which such a perception depends. As Edwards argues so thoroughly in the *Treatise Concerning Religious Affections*, no exercise of the natural affections, though inspired by never so great a fear of hell, can simulate the experiences of the saint. It is not a matter of intensity, but of kind: the saint is to the sinner as a man with vision is to a man born blind. Though the former should describe what he sees never so exactly in terms of the other senses, yet he cannot make the blind man have the visual experience itself.[230] Without grace, nothing is seen.

And with grace, what is it that the saint beholds? It will be recalled that Edwards's concept of truth is essentially a coherentist one: that view is true which gives greatest order and harmony to our ideas. And it will also be recalled that excellency consists in symmetry and harmony: beauty is always proportional to the harmony of the perceived aggregate. It follows then that the true and the beautiful are one, or that beauty is one mark of truth. So to see truth as it is, is to see perfect beauty, and the discovery of great beauty is a presumptive mark of truth. The truth of the Newtonian theory lies in the fact that it gives coherence to our experience, and insofar as it does so, it appears excellent to us, since it reveals the perfect harmony of the system of the world. By the same reasoning, the truth of Edwards's typological theory of nature and of history must lie in the coherence it introduces into those realms. But since the antitypes are spiritual things, it is only to the saint that there is given an ideal apprehension of the antitypes. Moreover, it is only the saint who by God's grace is able to contemplate the world not in relation to himself, but in its true relation to God. Hence it is only to the saint that the true relations of type and antitype appear. Accordingly, one who seeks understanding of the world without grace is like a man who seeks to study a garden at night by feeling his way in the dark. "But he who sees by divine light is like a man that views the garden when the sun shines upon it. There is, as it were, a light cast upon the ideas of spiritual things in the mind of the believer which makes them appear clear and real which before were but faint obscure representations."[231] To the saint, therefore, the true harmony and beauty of the world is revealed, so that all nature and all history become, as it were, a transparent medium through which the excellence and glory of God shine forth. That perception of unspeakable beauty is what grace gives—the final experiential proof and seal of salvation.

Notes — Chapter Three

[1]Miller, *Edwards*, 37.

[2]Gen. 17:2-7. See above, p. 12.

[3]Perry Miller, "The Puritan Theory of the Sacraments in Seventeenth Century New England," *Catholic Historical Review* 22:412ff (1937); Morgan, *Visible Saints*, chap. 3.

[4]Miller, "Puritan Theory of the Sacraments," pp. 422ff; Morgan, *Visible Saints*, chap. 4; Perry Miller, "The Half Way Covenant," *New England Quarterly* 6:676-715 (1933); Miller, *New England Mind II*, pp. 93-118; Robert G. Pope, *The Half-Way Covenant* (Princeton: Princeton University Press, 1969), chaps. 3-4.

[5]Miller, *New England Mind II*, bk. I, esp. sec. 2.

[6]Perry Miller, "Solomon Stoddard, 1643-1729," *Harvard Theological Review* 34:277-320 (1941); Solomon Stoddard, *The Safety of Appearing at the Day of Judgement* (Boston: by Samuel Green, for Samuel Phillips, 1687), pp. 109-14; Miller, *New England Mind II*, pp. 227-37, 256ff, 266ff.

[7]Pope, *Half-Way Covenant*, chaps. 3-4, pp. 251ff.

[8]Miller, "Stoddard," pp. 319-20; Miller, *New England Mind II*, pp. 235-36, 266ff; Miller, *Edwards*, p. 136. The Half-Way Covenant itself proved to be a more effective answer than has been recognized. See Pope, *Half-Way Covenant*, chap. 10.

[9]Miller, *Edwards*, p. 37.

[10]Leon Howard, *"The Mind" of Jonathan Edwards: A Reconstructed Text* (Berkeley: University of California Press, 1963), pp. 2-3. Hereafter, this work will be cited as H followed by page numbers.

[11]William Morris, "The Young Jonathan Edwards: A Reconstruction" (Ph.D. diss., University of Chicago, 1955), chaps. 2-3.

[12]"The Mind" poses an acute textual problem. The document was first published by Sereno Dwight in his edition of Edwards's works in 1830. What became of the manuscript after that is unknown; there is no evidence that anyone ever saw it after Dwight. What remains is the text as Dwight printed it, together with a manuscript index to it, and Dwight's description of "The Mind," which reads as follows:

> The Series of remarks, entitled, *"The Mind"*, judging both from the handwriting and the subjects, I suppose was commenced either during, or soon after, his perusal of Locke's Essay on the Human Understanding. It contains nine leaves of foolscap, folded separately, and a few more, obviously written at a later period. The arrangement of subjects, in these papers, is less perfect, than that which he subsequently adopted in other writings. It is as follows. The word, proper to express a given subject, is written at the commencement of a paragraph, which introduces it, in very large letters. Where several subjects are found on one page, they are numbered 1, 2, 3, &c. These numbers, with that of the page, furnished the reference in the index (H 11).

The manuscript consists of a series of notes, some very brief and some amounting to short essays. As Dwight printed the text, neither page numbers nor subject numbers appear; but each note is numbered. Dwight remarks that "the number prefixed to each separate article, will show its place in the manuscript of the author" (*ibid.*, p. 11). It is therefore clear that the numbers represent the order in which the notes stood in the manuscript as Dwight found it, but it is not clear whether these numbers were in the original manuscript or were added by Dwight. If they were in the original, they may or may not have been put there by Edwards; if they were not, they still preserve an ordering of the notes which may well have been that in which Edwards left them at his death. But this numerical order does not match the order given by the index, so that we have at least two different orderings to deal with.

In 1963 Leon Howard published an attempted reconstruction of the manuscript in the form in which it stood when Edwards indexed it. Howard's reconstruction is ingenious and I have followed it here. However, there are several problems which need to be stressed. First, there is the question of how the order as reconstructed by Howard relates to the numerical order. If Howard's model is correct, it must yield both orderings since the manuscript was in one sequence when Edwards indexed it and in another when Dwight printed it. As Howard reconstructs the document, we have a manuscript of fifty-two pages comprised of thirteen folded sheets, some of which had been cut to make half sheets. The sheets, as given by Howard, with the page numbers in brackets and the note numbers unenclosed, are as follows:

Sheet I.	(1)	71, 72
	(2)	blank
	(3)	blank
	(4)	blank
Sheet II.	(5)	61
	(6)	62
	(7)	63
	(8)	64
Sheet III	(9)	1
	(10)	1
	(11)	1
	(12)	1
Sheet IV	(13)	1
	(14)	1
	(15)	1
	(16)	1
Sheet V	(17)	6, 7, 8, 9
	(18)	10, 11, 12, 13
	(19)	65, 65
	(20)	66, 67, 68
Sheet VI	(21)	69, 70
	(22)	blank
	(23)	23, 24, 25, 26, 27
	(24)	28, 29, 30, 31
Sheet VII	(25)	blank
	(26)	41, 42, 43
	(27)	45
	(28)	45
Sheet VIII	(29)	54
	(30)	55, 56, 57, 58, 59
	(31)	59
	(32)	60
Sheet IX	(33)	47, 48, 49
	(34)	51, 53
	(35)	blank
	(36)	blank
Sheet X	(37)	34, 35, 36, 37, 38, 39
	(38)	40
	(39)	14, 15, 16, 17, 18, 19, 20

	(40)	21, 21, 22
Sheet XI	(41)	2
	(42)	3, 4, 5
	(43)	Table of contents to "The Mind"
	(44)	Table of contents
Sheet XII	(45)	Table of contents
	(46)	blank
	(47)	blank
	(48)	blank
Sheet XIII	(49)	blank
	(50)	blank
	(51)	Table of contents
	(52)	Table of contents

Note that there are two notes 21, 25, and 65 and no notes 33, 44, 46, 50, or 52—anomalies which exist in the text as Dwight printed it. Howard concluded that sheets IX, X, and XI had been cut in two, thus creating six half sheets. That leaves ten full sheets, one more than the nine described by Dwight, so one other must have been cut also, but which is not clear. For reasons which will be obvious, I assume that the other sheet cut was sheet VI.

Let us accept Howard's reconstruction and proceed to order these sheets as follows. Put first sheet III followed by sheet IV, so that we have pages 9 through 16 in order. Let this be followed by the half sheet from XI, so that page 41 follows page 16. Then add sheet V. Next, inside sheet V place in order the half sheets bearing pages 39-40, 23-24, and 37-38. Following these, and still within the fold of sheet V, put sheet VII then half sheet 33-34, then sheet VIII, then sheet II, and then half sheet 35-36. This folder is concluded by the second half of sheet V which bears pages 19 and 20. Let all this be followed by half sheet 21-22, then by sheet I, then by half sheet 43-44, and finally by sheets XII and XIII. The completed order of the pages will now be 9, 10, 11, 12, 13, 14, 15, 16, 41, 42, 17, 18, 39, 40, 23, 24, 37, 38, 25, 26, 27, 28, 33, 34, 29, 30, 31, 32, 5, 6, 7, 8, 35, 36, 19, 20, 21, 22, 1, 2, 3, 4, 43, 44, 45, 46, 47, 48, 49, 50, 51, 52. The notes will now be found to be in numerical order from 1 through 72. It thus appears that working from Howard's model and adding the assumption that it was sheet VI which was cut in half, it is possible to reorder the pages in such a way as to yield the numerical order. This result is a further confirmation of the correctness of Howard's reconstruction.

Second, assuming Howard's reconstruction to be correct, we still do not know in what order the notes were composed. We know that the form of the manuscript was unstable, since there are two different orderings in which the sheets stood at different times, and Howard has added evidence that some of the half sheets "floated" from one location to another. Presumably Edwards did not index the manuscript until well after it was written and we cannot be sure that the index represents the original order. The fact that it assumed the numerical order subsequent to the indexing does not prove that it was not composed in that order and later restored to it, particularly if the numbers were in Edwards' hand. And clearly the sheets as reconstructed could have been composed in yet other orders. Chronological inference respecting the notes is therefore peculiarly suspect, especially with respect to the notes on the "floating sheets." This situation is particularly regrettable because the natural explanation for some of the inconsistencies in "The Mind" is that Edwards's views changed and developed in the course of its composition. I have so argued on several points, treating the order of the manuscript as reconstructed from the index as if it were the true chronological order, but the speculative character of this argument needs to be understood. It is true however that in those cases what I take to be the course of development is born out by the fact that what I call his later position matches the position which he did support in writings which are demonstrably later than "The Mind."

[13]Jonathan Edwards, "Notes on Natural Science," in *The Philosophy of Jonathan Edwards*, ed. Harvey G. Townsend (Eugene: University of Oregon Press, 1955). Hereafter this work will be cited as T followed by page numbers.

[14]H 6ff.

[15]H 8f, chap. 3.

[16]T xvi-xviii. Much of the Miscellanies remains unpublished. Selections have appeared in T 74-268, and in various editions of Edwards's works. See T xvii, n. 33.

[17]Miller, *Edwards*, pp. 38-40.

[18]Edwin Gaustad, *The Great Awakening in New England* (New York: Harper, 1957), pp. 18-24.

[19]Miller, *Edwards*, pp. 133-63; Gaustad, *Awakening*, chaps. 3, 4.

[20]Miller, *Edwards*, p. 172; Gaustad, *Awakening*, pp. 36-41.

[21]Miller, *Edwards*, pp. 173f; Gaustad, *Awakening*, pp. 87-96.

[22]Jonathan Edwards, *A Treatise Concerning Religious Affections*, ed. John Smith (New Haven, Conn.: Yale University Press, 1959).

[23]Miller, *Edwards*, pp. 177-95; Gaustad, *Awakening*, chaps. 5, 7, 8.

[24]Miller, *Edwards*, pp. 208-31.

[25]*Ibid.*, pp. 232-33.

26Jonathan Edwards, *A Careful and Strict Enquiry into the Modern Prevailing Notions of that Freedom of the Will, which is Supposed to be essential to Moral Agency, Virtue and Vice, Reward and Punishment, Praise and Blame*, ed. Ramsey (New Haven, Conn.: Yale University Press, 1957).

27Jonathan Edwards, *The Great Christian Doctrine of Original Sin Defended*, in *The Works of President Edwards* (New York: Jonathan Leavitt and John F. Trow, 1843), II:305-510.

28Jonathan Edwards, *Dissertation Concerning the End for which God Created the World*, and *Dissertation on the Nature of True Virtue*, in Edwards, *Works*, II:191-257, 258-304.

29Miller, *Edwards*, p. 233.

30The direct evidence that Edwards was acquainted with Berkeley's writings consists of the fact that the titles of some of Berkeley's works are entered in Edwards's book catalog (Thomas H. Johnson, "Jonathan Edwards' Background Reading," Publications of the Colonial Society of Massachusetts, vol. XXVIII, *Transactions*, 1930-33, p. 211). The titles are not crossed off, but Edwards's marking system in the catalog is still a mystery and no sure inference can be drawn as to whether or not he read, or even saw, the books (Johnson, "Edwards' Reading," p. 206). The indirect evidence that Edwards knew Berkeley's work lies wholly in the parallels between their philosophies. But these parallels are easily exaggerated. It is true that both were Idealists, but Edwards's treatment of primary and secondary qualities does not parallel Berkeley's; he adopts Locke's theory of abstraction and seems wholly unaware of Berkeley's objections to it, and he treats ideas of reflection in a way quite different from Berkeley. The present state of the matter is summarized by the leading student of Edwards as follows: "Actually there is no evidence whatsoever that Edwards read Berkeley, then or later; his journals meticulously acknowledge his debts to every philosopher he managed to read, and nowhere is there any sign of a first-hand acquaintance with Berkeley . . . except for the fact that his mind moved for a few paragraphs along the same path as Berkeley's, a path that was unmistakably laid out by Locke, Edwards and Berkeley have little in common" (Miller, *Edwards*, pp. 61-62).

31H 48-49, 61, 67-70.

32T 9-20.

33*Ibid*., pp. 9-10.

34*Ibid*., p. 13.

35Locke, I:151-57.

[36]T 10.

[37]*Ibid.*, p. 12.

[38]*Ibid.*, p. 11.

[39]*Ibid.*, p. 17.

[40]Locke, I:151.

[41]*Ibid.*, I: 153.

[42]H 63-64.

[43]T 8.

[44]*Ibid.*, p. 17.

[45]Locke, *Essay*, II:167-68.

[46]H 26.

[47]H 80; Locke, *Essay*, II:407ff.

[48]H 51.

[49]H 76-77.

[50]Locke, *Essay*, I:433ff.

[51]Immanuel Kant, *Critique of Pure Reason*, trans. Norman Kemp Smith (London: Macmillan, 1956), B167.

[52]*Ibid.*, B167-68.

[53]H 62.

[54]*Ibid.*, pp. 96-97.

[55]*Ibid.*, p. 93.

[56]*Ibid.*, pp. 30-34.

[57]Locke, *Essay*, I:153.

[58]T 16.

[59]*Ibid.*, p. 16.

60*Ibid.*, pp. 18-19.

61H 30-34.

62T 19.

63*Ibid.*, p. 16.

64Locke, *Essay*, II:25ff.

65H 69.

66I follow Townsend in substituting "arises" for "arising" in the text.

67H 69-70.

68*Ibid.*, p. 26.

69*Ibid.*, p. 26.

70T 1, 9, 74; H53-54.

71T 1.

72*Ibid.*, pp. 76-103.

73*Ibid.*, pp. 76-77, 79.

74*Ibid.*, pp. 1-2.

75H 50.

76*Ibid.*, p. 42.

77*Ibid.*, p. 45.

78*Ibid.*, p. 71, 100-101.

79*Ibid.*, p. 71.

80*Ibid.*, pp. 45-46.

81Reading "more" for "mere".

82H 44.

83*Ibid.*, p. 71.

84*Ibid.*

85*Ibid.*, p. 47.

86*Ibid.*, p. 46.

[87]*Ibid.*, p. 44.

[88]*Ibid.*, pp. 42-44.

[89]*Ibid.*, p. 38.

[90]*Ibid.*, p. 37.

[91]Speculation on the order in which the notes were written is extremely hazardous (see n. 12).

[92]H 46.

[93]I follow Howard's text here. However, n. 49 is on one of the "floating sheets" the original place of which in the manuscript is largely conjectural.

[94]H 87.

[95]Marjorie Hope Nicholson, *Mountain Gloom and Mountain Glory: The Development of the Aesthetics of the Infinite* (Ithaca: Cornell University Press, 1959), chaps. 1, 2; Samuel Monk, *The Sublime: A Study of Critical Theories in XVIII-Century England* (New York: Modern Language Association of America, 1935).

[96]Joseph Addison, *The Works of Joseph Addison*, ed. Henry Bohn (London: George Bell and Sons, 1893), III:397-98, 401-2. The complete *Spectator* was among the books in the Dummer gift (Edwin Oviatt, *The Beginnings of Yale, 1701-1726* [New Haven: Yale Press, 1916], p. 298), and Edwards seems to have particularly liked Addison (Johnson, *Edwards' Reading*, pp. 214-15). Edwards and Addison share the use of the terms beauty, relish, deformity, and greatness, and Edwards's discussion of the uncommon and of admiration are similar to Addison's.

[97]Edwards, *Images or Shadows of Divine Things*, p. 47. The term "sublimity" occurs so rarely in Edwards's writings that its absence is striking. But its occurrence here shows that he was aware of its use in aesthetics.

[98]*Ibid.*, p. 134.

[99]Nicholson, *Mountain Gloom*, pp. 114-43. The influence of More on Edwards may be direct. Edwards was certainly acquainted with the writings of Gale and Cudworth (Clarence Gohdes, "Aspects of Idealism in Early New England," *Philosophical Review* 39:545; T44) and it is entirely possible that he had read some of More's works (W. E. Anderson, "Immaterialism in Jonathan Edwards' Early Philosophical Notes," *Journal of the History of Ideas* 25:181-200 (1964).

[100]Delattre (Roland A. Delattre, *Beauty and Sensibility in the Thought of Jonathan Edwards* [New Haven: Yale Press, 1968]) has presented the strongest argument extant for holding that Edwards continued to treat entity as an aesthetic category, and to regard beauty as the primary category of being. The early discussion in "The Mind" (see n. 12) does support that view. But the reflections which constitute "The Mind" are not definitive; Edwards was developing his ideas when he wrote them, not codifying them. I believe that Edwards abandoned this early view of the relation of entity and beauty even during the time he was writing "The Mind," but certainly by the time he wrote *The Nature of True Virtue*. For in this treatise Edwards is at pains to show that true virtue is not love to being for its beauty, which is complacence, but for its being alone. If being per se were beautiful, this distinction would make no sense. Further, if mere quantity of being were excellent, natural men could not fail to perceive the excellence of being in general—a consequence which certainly contradicts Edwards's theory of virtue. Hence for both logical and ethical reasons, I am convinced that Edwards abandoned this early formulation.

[101]Edwards, *Works*, II:261.

[102]*Ibid.*, II:262.

[103]*Ibid.*, II:263.

[104]*Ibid.*, II:272.

[105]*Ibid.*, II:266-71.

[106]T 259.

[107]*Ibid.*, p. 254.

[108]*Ibid.*, pp. 256-57.

[109]Jonathan Edwards, *Jonathan Edwards: Representative Selections*, ed. Faust and Johnson (New York: American Book Co., 1935), p. 379.

[110]T 258.

[111]*Ibid.*, pp. 230-31.

[112]*Ibid.*, p. 231.

[113]*Ibid.*

[114]*Ibid.*, p. 226.

[115]H 52.

[116]*Ibid.*, p. 107.

[117]T 244.

[118]H 57.

[119]Hicks, *Berkeley*, pp. 145ff.

[120]H 57.

[121]T 115.

[122]*Ibid.*, p. 118.

[123]*Ibid.*, p. 119.

[124]*Ibid.*, pp. 119-20.

[125]H 108.

[126]*Ibid.*, pp. 103-4.

[127]*Ibid.*, pp. 91-92.

[128]*Ibid.*, pp. 65-66.

[129]*Ibid.*, p. 108.

[130]*Ibid.*, p. 76.

[131]T 75.

[132]*Ibid.*, pp. 75-76.

[133]H 89.

[134]Locke, *Essay*, I:308-80.

[135]The quoted passage occurs in note 51 which is on one of the "floating sheets," and it is impossible to determine whether it was written before or after notes 66 and 67 in which Edwards formulated his view of ideas of reflection. See H 21.

[136]H 73.

[137]*Ibid.*, p. 71.

[138]*Ibid.*, p. 73.

[139]Edwards, *Works*, II:266.

[140]H 93.

[141]T 132.

[142]Edwards, *Works*, II:207. Original in italics.

[143]*Ibid.*, II:253.

[144]*Ibid.*

[145]T 152.

[146]Edwards, *Works*, II:254.

[147]*Ibid.*, II:207.

[148]*Ibid.*, II:256.

[149]*Ibid.*, II:257; T 149ff.

[150]Edwards, *Images*, p. 61.

[151]H 99-100; Gohdes, "Idealism," p. 545.

[152]George Berkeley, *The Works of George Berkeley Bishop of Cloyne*, ed. Luce and Jessop (London: Thomas Nelson and Sons, 1948), I:231.

[153]H 46-47.

[154]Edwards, *Images*, p. 27.

[155]Mason I. Lowance, Jr. " 'Images or Shadows of Divine Things' In the Thought of Jonathan Edwards," in Sacvan Bercovitch, ed., *Typology and Early American Literature* (Amherst: University of Massachusetts Press, 1972), pp. 209-48.

[156]Edwards, *Images*, p. 109.

[157]*Ibid.*, p. 79.

[158]*Ibid.*, n. 96.

159*Ibid.*, p. 46.

160*Ibid.*, p. 54.

161*Ibid.*, pp. 24-35.

162T 231; H 51-52, 54, 101.

163Edwards, *Will*, p. 469.

164*Ibid.*, p. 466.

165*Ibid.*, pp. 70-73.

166*Ibid.*, p. 137.

167Locke, *Essay*, I:321-22.

168Miller, *Edwards*, pp. 181-83.

169Edwards, *Will*, p. 141.

170*Ibid.*, p. 141.

171*Ibid.*

172*Ibid.*, p. 142.

173*Ibid.*

174*Ibid.*

175*Ibid.*

176*Ibid.*, p. 143.

177*Ibid.*

178White (Morton White, *Science and Sentiment in America* [New York: Oxford University Press, 1972], chap. 2) in particular has held that Edwards's argument reduces to a "truism." Presumably what White means by a "truism" is an analytic statement, though he seems shy about saying so.

179Edwards, *Will*, p. 144.

[180]The identity of the strongest motive with the greatest apparent good is clear from the fact that the determinants are the same for both—see *ibid.*, pp. 142, 144ff.

[181]*Ibid.*, p. 145.

[182]*Ibid.*

[183]*Ibid.*

[184]*Ibid.*, pp. 145-46.

[185]*Ibid.*, p. 152. White has attacked Edwards's argument on necessity on the ground that it undercuts his own claim that choice is subject to moral judgment. But White seems to think Edwards's argument rests upon what Edwards calls the common notion of necessity, whereas Edwards carefully distinguished that notion from the concept of philosophical necessity upon which his argument is based. See Edwards, *Will*, pp. 149-55; White, *Science and Sentiment*, pp. 45ff.

[186]Edwards, *Will*, pp. 153-54.

[187]*Ibid.*, p. 156.

[188]*Ibid.*

[189]*Ibid.*, p. 158.

[190]*Ibid.*, pp. 156-62.

[191]*Ibid.*, p. 164.

[192]*Ibid.*

[193]Miller, *Edwards*, p. 258.

[194]Edwards, *Will*, p. 162.

[195]*Ibid.*, pp. 180-85.

[196]*Ibid.*, pp. 171-74.

[197]*Ibid.*, p. 191.

[198]*Ibid.*, pp. 209ff.

[199]*Ibid.*, pp. 239-69.

[200]*Ibid.*, pp. 277-80.

[201]*Ibid.*, pp. 281-94.

[202]*Ibid.*, p. 337.

[203]*Ibid.*

[204]*Ibid.*, pp. 341-42.

[205]*Ibid.*, pp. 342-49.

[206]Edwards, *Works*, II:309.

[207]*Ibid.*, II:476-77.

[208]*Ibid.*, II:477.

[209]*Ibid.*, II:477-79.

[210]*Ibid.*, II:341.

[211]*Ibid.*, II:323-26.

[212]*Ibid.*, II:478.

[213]Edwards, *Will*, 397-412; Edwards, *Works*, II:476-81.

[214]Edwards, *Works*, II:489.

[215]*Ibid.*, II:490.

[216]*Ibid.*

[217]*Ibid.*, II:487-95.

[218]*Ibid.*, II:527-46.

[219]Edwards, *Will*, pp. 432-39.

[220]T 249.

[221]Edwards, *Religious Affections*, p. 343.

[222]*Ibid.*, pp. 107ff, 246f, 340-44.

[223]*Ibid.*, p. 205.

[224]Edwards, *Works*, II:266.

[225]T 249.

[226]Edwards, *Religious Affections*, p. 205.

[227]*Ibid.*, p. 209.

[228]Edwards, *Works*, II:265.

[229]Edwards, *Religious Affections*, p. 343.

[230]*Ibid.*, pp. 204, 208, 274-75, 280-81.

[231]Edwards, *Images*, p. 34.

Chapter Four

Philosophy in Academia Revisited— Mainly Princeton

Chapter Four

Philosophy in Academia Revisited— Mainly Princeton[1]

1. Wasteland?

This chapter introduces that long century between the death of Edwards and the emergence of professional philosophies in America—i.e., of idealisms, pragmatisms, and realisms of undoubted competence. This is the period when philosophy, particularly academic philosophy, was dominated by a kind of realism variously called "Common Sense," "naive," or "Natural." Whatever the label, this realism is now uniformly regarded as a wasteland of secondhand ideas servicing orthodox Calvinism; it is pictured as deriving from a Scottish backwater in European thought and as propagated there and in America through unbelievably drab textbooks. This jaundiced appraisal (which, among other things, leaves later idealisms and pragmatisms discontinuous and unrooted in American thought) is echoed with more or less enthusiasm by twentieth-century writers, from Blau and Curti to Riley and Werkmeister. Morris Cohen's history rings with "anemic" and "turgid" used Homeric-like; White's label is "cracker-barrel"; while even the tolerant Schneider talks about the "dusty" and "wormy" texts, though that is perhaps a commentary on Columbia Library's housekeeping.[2]

This chapter together with the next two are intended as character witnesses for the much libeled realists of this country and Scotland. Little brief is held for the sparkle of their texts. But we do want to hold that so far from being a drag on the American Enlightenment, Common Sense Realism was a part of it. It was integral to that astonishing burst of intellectual energy that began in Scotland in the early eighteenth century and extended well into the nineteenth. This Scottish humanism resulted in a flourishing of the sciences and their applications; a resurgence of belles-lettres including history, literary criticism, and anthropology; a revitalization of universities, including medical and legal education; a rethinking of political problems in economic rather than moralistic or natural rights terms; and a liberalizing and naturalizing (and in some cases secularizing) of religion.

More closely allied to French thought than English, it became, directly and indirectly, a part of American tradition. Franklin and Jefferson had personal friends among the Realists. Rush was but one of many who studied medicine in Edinburgh and it was he who suggested ''Common Sense'' as a title to Tom Paine. Madison and Wilson of constitutional fame were involved in the movement. A substantial amount of the Scottish literature was published in America even in the eighteenth century, while the *Encyclopaedia Britannica*, a project designed and overseen by Stewart (whose place in the Scottish school will be examined below), was an important resource issued with some illegality in America. (Its educational use was facilitated by its organization, for at that time it covered whole subjects as a unit.) And for good or ill, Realism left its mark indelibly on courses in philosophy as late as McCosh, president of Princeton (1868-1888), Porter, president of Yale (1871-1886), and Bowen, professor at Harvard (1853-1889).

Moreover the Common Sense Realists were a bridge between the Enlightenment and the pragmatists, not least because they helped determine the way the Kantian philosophy was to be utilized. They introduced psychological and empirical dimensions which thereafter were never long absent from philosophy in America. Even the most conservative of the Realist academics set such store by Newton that they were likely to be empiricists, and often more strongly and consistently than Locke, who was of course counted among their heroes. They sought to give a full account of human behavior based on observation and induction; and if perhaps they relied overmuch on introspection, still they did not sweep under the carpet such patent phenomena as the active role of the knower in perception, judgment, and intention—topics but glancingly treated by the classic empiricism of Locke, Berkeley, and Hume. From the last they learned that all empirical knowledge is only probable, but they could live with less than certain knowledge since it so often sufficed. Convinced that a fully developed science would not conflict with religion, many were surprisingly cordial to the new geology, to ethical naturalism, and to evolution. Such cordiality, when joined to views about design in nature, even led them occasionally to consider the function of knowledge in relation to survival and action, and of institutions to social utilities and happiness. And again, because they believed (in contrast to Kant) that the investigation of the laws of thought was a part of psychology, they devoted themselves to logic, often hoping to illuminate Kant by an appeal to Aristotle, and both by an appeal to the newer developments in inductive and deductive logic and in psychology.

The "Wasteland" criticisms of the twentieth century are themselves in part but a pale echo of a famous and often-quoted article by G. Stanley Hall published in 1880. In part, however, they are a justified reaction to the stereotyped picture of the movement given by some of the tag-end epigoni of Scottish Realism itself, above all—whatever else his virtues—by James McCosh, the immensely influential president of Princeton who made himself the official biographer of the movement. Because the theme of our three chapters runs counter to a negative view so deeply entrenched, and because of its importance as well in the study of later philosophic developments, we have resorted to heroic measures at considerable sacrifice to chronological order. If this seems defensively organized it is because we are laboring under two entrenched but challengeable preconceptions: first, the pedestrian character of Scottish philosophy in its native habitat (which will invite a somewhat lengthy excursion into the Scottish background), and second, the alleged greater sterility of its reflection in America. We are essaying, in effect, an unorthodox appraisal of orthodoxy. We shall first look at Hall and McCosh as protagonists, including an account of McCosh's own position. Then we turn from endings to beginnings and look to the situation in Scotland in which Common Sense Realism had its origin. Thereafter we shall follow the manner in which it was brought to America by John Witherspoon before the Independence and how it was hosted as an official philosophy at Princeton—till we come again to McCosh. We conclude this chapter with a look at the Scottish originals—especially Thomas Reid, Dugald Stewart, and Thomas Brown—both with an eye to determine the correctness of McCosh's account and to suggest the sophistication of the problems which Americans grappled with in that period. This outline serves also as a background to chapter 5 which traces the Scottish Connection that is at the heart of philosophical controversies in the Middle Atlantic and Southern states on problems that range from metaphysics to moral philosophy. Chapter 6 shows the Scottish Connection in the Northeast by considering the development of logic, especially at Harvard.

Hall, Maverick Critic of Realism, and McCosh, August Overseer of the Realist Establishment

Despite differences in the philosophic backgrounds of Hall and McCosh and the fact that they were writing to rather different audiences and to vastly different purposes, there are interesting points of agreement. Both of them construe philosophy so narrowly as virtually to ignore the philosophic issues raised by the social and natural sciences. They were agreed also on the main traits of philosophy in America—its affiliation with religion, its earlier reliance on Scottish realism, and its subsequent flirtation with German idealism. They were joined, too, in acknowledging Edwards as "America's greatest Metaphysician." Like-mindedness stops there. Understandably, the New Englander Hall emphasized New England's activities, while the Scottish-bred McCosh scarcely looked beyond Princeton's philosophic portals, where, it will be remembered, Edwards had briefly been president. But they were dramatically opposed in their diagnoses of the philosophic health of America; where McCosh was an apologist for the realistic orthodox establishment, and therefore for the colleges and universities in which it was established, Hall indicted it with the vengeance of the academically disenfranchised.

G. Stanley Hall, whose adverse opinion of the academic realists did them most harm, was early trained in the Scottish ways; subsequently he was tempted by romantic idealisms, and ultimately was converted to the new in philosophy and psychology. Hall's conversion, like Dewey's, is part of the story. But it was true then, as it is now, that the academic structure militates against philosophical innovation, or at least delays it as long as possible. Thus Hall is one of a group of men (including Dewey and perhaps even James and Peirce) who are not so much transitional figures as men who *were* the transition, who lived it in the various intellectual and emotional crises they underwent, crises no less disturbing because they were the fashion.

On Hall's second stint abroad he was writing (in 1879) for the English journal *Mind* from Germany where he had gone to work with Wundt, Helmholtz, and Fechner. On his first trip he had plunged into the heart of German speculative philosophy, studying especially with Zeller, famous for his work in Greek philosophy, and Trendelenburg, whose Aristotelianized Hegelianism was to become an influence among the St. Louis Hegelians and even on Dewey. On Hall's first return to America, he found himself professionally homeless, with every college uninterested in his German training. Thereupon, he went on to study at Harvard under James and to take America's first Ph.D. in psychology. Since his article in *Mind* ("Philosophy in the United States," 1880)[3] is most influential, is still often cited, and since the names he mentions will figure in the next several chapters, it is worth examining in detail.

Hall's sympathies for a particular part of European tradition, for the problems and the Americans he considered important, are no less revealed and revealing than are the commitments of McCosh. In a roughly descending order of enthusiasms, he notes the vigor and the increase of German influence, but laments its distance from academic centers. The St. Louis Hegelians, especially through their *Journal of Speculative Philosophy* and their full translations, have made available the full range of German thought in pedagogy, aesthetics, and history of ideas as well as philosophy proper. Hall adds somewhat patronizingly that the *Journal* is not self-supporting and might be "if it carried more psychology and less esthetical

matter.'' He notes sadly that neither the American Hegelians nor the Transcendentalists seem to have much influence on education in the colleges.

German influence, where it has penetrated, is dominated by theology—by the
tradition of Edwards and his disciples. President Porter of Yale, ''although a
clergyman of the congregationalist denomination,'' is praised for his exceptional
knowledge of pure philosophy, and said to be ''a vigorous expositor of the
Scotch-Kantian speculation as opposed to Darwinism and materialism.'' We shall
later see how this classification betrays Hall's considerable ignorance of the true
position of the Scots and makes clear his obvious sympathy for the Darwinians.

In the East (a term which, for Hall, is apparently synonymous with ''New
England'') conditions are found to be somewhat better. Emerson, Channing, and
the Unitarians in general have had a wholesome and liberalizing effect on speculative philosophy. Professor Bowen of Harvard, whose antimaterialistic bias was
uncongenial to Hall, is nonetheless praised for his excellent lectures in the history
of philosophy (stressing particularly the works of Kant and Schopenhauer). Hall
does not mention that Bowen had done quite respectable work in logic, nor that he
was a nationally known, albeit controversial, figure in economics (a subject
which, at that time, was often taught as part of moral philosophy).

In the larger Boston area, on the periphery of academic circles, Hall discovers
more congenial currents. British associationistic psychology and evolutionism are
active, as evinced by the work of Fiske, Spencer's American expositor, and
Chauncey Wright, the correspondent of Darwin. Even these two, however, are
found to be unworthy in the end; only C. S. Peirce receives Hall's endorsement.
Hall discusses Peirce's operational criterion of meaning, his notion of chance, and
his doctrine that logic has its roots in a social principle.

Despite his admiration of Peirce, Hall criticizes both the role of logic within
philosophy and its methods of instruction.[4] The theory of the syllogism is taught
from elementary texts, but little time is devoted to it and the methods of induction
are often entirely ignored. Some fifteen years later, Hall still makes roughly these
same points about logic. Deductive logic is the method by which theology and
metaphysics are forced upon unwilling or skeptical minds to the great detriment of
empirical sciences; while inductive logic, which has not yielded a single discovery
through its conscious application, has not shown its academic vitality. He concludes that it would be better if logic were to be dropped entirely from the
curriculum, or at least placed as an elective. The vitality of logic in the academy
will be discussed in chapter 6.

Even though ''the most vigorous and original philosophical instruction is almost
everywhere given in ethics,'' still that course is excoriated for its dogmatism, its
scholasticism, and particularly for its ignorance of the psychological questions on
which ethics seems to depend, viz., those concerning the origin of conscience or
the nature and conditions of pleasure and pain.

The only place in America where the newer research in physiological psychol-

ogy was being taught was at Harvard, by William James—and even that innovation was granted "not without some opposition." Philosophy's most serious
defect, in Hall's opinion, is its lack of psychological orientation. Hall hopes that
courses in "mental philosophy" (relying on such texts as Porter's massive *The
Human Intellect* or even on Locke's *Essay*) will give way to a study of physiological psychology, a chair of which was then being considered by the University of
Baltimore (Johns Hopkins).

Hall directs an even more vitriolic criticism at the denominational colleges,
especially the smaller and Western institutions. In the passage that has become a
locus classicus for historians, he claims that, of three hundred non-Catholic
colleges, two hundred are strictly denominational and sixty more, whose catalogs
claim a nonsectarian base, are Evangelical. Philosophy in such colleges is generally taught by the president, whose convictions are formed by the trustees. "Mental
science" is psychology enchained by theology—a situation which leaves the great
and open questions of metaphysics and experimental psychology to languish.
Many such colleges had been founded in times of religious awakening, and were
later sustained only with difficulty as denominational outposts. In such a climate,
seeming contradictions between science and the Scriptures are, whenever the
chips are down, decided arbitrarily in favor of the Scriptures. Due to this religious
surveillance, and also to the political bias with an eye to which the legislature
disburses college funds, Hall concludes grimly that "there is very small chance
that a well-equipped student of philosophy in any of its departments will secure a
position as a teacher of the subject."

Worst of all in Hall's eyes is the complacency with which academic
philosophers view the situation:

> Andover is well pleased to be thought freer from the rigidity of dogma than
> Princeton, and Oberlin claims more warmth of feeling and less tyranny of
> creed than either. While slight differences among the philosophical *idola* of
> orthodoxy are thus disproportionately magnified, all these institutions unite
> in impressing upon their students the lesson that there is an abyss of skepti-
> cism and materialism into which, as the greatest of all intellectual disasters,
> those who cease to believe in the Scriptures as interpreted according to the
> canons of orthodox criticism, are sure to be plunged.[5]

Except for this reference to Princeton, Hall is curiously silent about it and its
president, McCosh. Princeton was too important an institution, and McCosh too
visible a figure in philosophy, to be omitted except by intent. In that day, for
example, McCosh's texts were very widely used. In truth, McCosh and the
Princeton version of Scottish realism epitomized all that G. S. Hall disliked:
McCosh opposed the teachings of Darwin and Spencer, criticized J. S. Mill,
considered the Germans unsettling, and above all, approached psychology in an

aprioristic and dogmatic fashion. At the time, of course, the proselytizing activities of the Presbyterians in the field of education had brought many of the Middle and Southern colleges under the sway of Princeton and its president.

Hall's article is hardly dispassionate. Yet, since it colors our understanding of the issues down to the present day, the question of the justice of Hall's estimate is crucial. His uncongenial tone may be due simply to the fact that he was not a congenial person. He had a large hand in unseating G. Sylvester Morris from Johns Hopkins; his reviews of the books on psychology by McCosh and Dewey are matched, as regards disdain, only by the bitter dispute with William James (who had the impression that *he*, rather than Hall, had established the first psychological laboratory in America). Even his initially cordial relations with the Hegelians in St. Louis degenerated into a series of bitter arguments over education.

Yet, writing in 1879, Hall had much evidence that seemed to support his view. There *was* a drab parade of texts, a dull abridgment of European classics to yawn over, a demand on the versatility of the president-philosopher who customarily taught the course, a seeming determination, on the part of such philosophers, to defend religious orthodoxy (in the eighteenth century the enemies were infidelity and materialism; in the nineteenth they were agnosticism, Darwinism, and sensationalism). Porter's compendious writings did little to save the situation; McCosh seemed bent on continuing it.

Had Hall waited barely ten years to write his article, fairness might have caused him to take a less petulant tone. By that date, various institutions had established departments of psychology, e.g., the one at Baltimore which Hall organized and directed. There such students as Dewey, Jastrow, and Cattell surrounded Hall; there Peirce was his colleague. In this decade, James published his own *Psychology* and Hall himself founded the *American Journal of Psychology*. Leaving Hopkins, Hall moved to Clark (where he later became president)—an institution which, if not one of the denominational colleges, was nevertheless quite as plagued by dependence on the caprices of its benefactor.

Had Hall written his article at the turn of the century, fairness would not merely have suggested, but required a different appraisal. By that time the philosophic profile was greatly changed, but these later developments, throwing their shadow backward, reveal how much Hall had misread or overlooked. For example, even his appreciative discussion of Peirce was neither accurate nor current, while his report of achievements in inductive logic is simply defective. Similarly, while appropriately insisting on a connection between psychology and ethics, he not only overlooked the sophisticated work being done in moral perception, but his appraisal also ignored the studies of the social and the institutional which had been regarded as the setting for individual duties and which had been a proper part of the course in moral philosophy since the Enlightenment.

Perhaps more importantly, one vainly seeks in the writings of Hall any omen of the philosophic explosion that was even then in the shaping. Companion to this oversight is another, based on a simplistic view of the complexity and maturity of philosophy in the colleges, which led him to miss the continuity that links not only Edwards, but also the Enlightenment and the American Scottish humanism with the emergence of idealisms—the Transcendentalism of Emerson, the Objective Idealism of Royce and Palmer, and the Neo-Hegelianism found in St. Louis. Further, Hall did not see how far academic realism set the problems for future discussion; nor how large a debt was owed to that philosophy for the distinctive reading of Kant which lies so firmly at the base of the pragmatism of Peirce, James, and Lewis. Indeed the new Kantianism that Hall said James got from Renouvier, was in fact also indebted to Reid (including the metaphor "stream of thought"); even Stewart's illustrations survive in Lewis. And strangely enough, Dewey, leaving aside his obligation to James, was independently influenced by this tradition.

McCosh had been imported in 1868 from Scotland, or more strictly from the chair of moral philosophy and logic at Belfast, to guide Princeton's destinies. As a student he had attended Glasgow and Edinburgh and at the latter university had studied with Sir William Hamilton and Thomas Chalmers, but during the great Disruption from the Established (Presbyterian) Church of Scotland, he had followed the conservative leadership of Chalmers into the Free Church. He thus spoke authoritatively (and orthodoxly) for Scottish philosophy. Already mature when he arrived at Princeton, McCosh's enthusiasm for things American was scarcely matched by familiarity with American philosophy, save where it paralleled his own or touched Princeton's. In *The Scottish Philosophy* (1874), he acknowledges the greatness of Edwards and his influence in Scotland.

McCosh occupied no inconsiderable place in the philosophic debates of the day, and the enormous circulation of his writings evidenced that the omission by Hall was no oversight. *The Intuitions of the Mind; Inductively Investigated* (1860) went through four editions. His *Method of the Divine Government, Physical and Moral* (1850) saw seven further editions. These and his other works were "noticed" in the leading English, German, and French philosophical periodicals. He was probably best known however, for his part in the Mill-Hamilton controversy. Hamilton's lectures were published posthumously in 1858: Mill followed them in 1865 with a brutal point-by-point attack in his *Examination of Sir William Hamilton's Philosophy*. McCosh retaliated in 1866 with his *An Examination of Mr. J. S. Mill's Philosophy, Being a Defense of Fundamental Truth*. Unfortunately, McCosh and Mill together have jointly obscured some genuinely interesting points to be found in Hamilton; unfortunately too, McCosh obscures much of his own good argument in polemic—the perception of relations, the original tendencies of thought to follow in patterns, and the discussion of the bearing of physiology on psychology. In particular, his discussion of the interdependence of body and mind is in keeping with a cordiality to evolution as the unfolding of the plan of divine government—i.e., in accordance with "that benevolent law of the survival of the fittest.'' Indeed, he and Guyot the geologist became partners in debating with Woodruff Shields who had come ultimately to believe that the unity of science and religion could not be forced at the present state of knowledge. Armed with optimism and a free reading of the Scriptures unusual for so orthodox a divine, president-philosopher and geologist both could argue for the total harmony of science with religion, e.g., the void in Genesis with the nebular hypothesis. McCosh's appreciation of science and of the importance of philosophically relevant problems of probability, induction, and formal logic was critical in preparing a favorable climate here for Darwin and Spencer, and for the philosophy of science.

McCosh was a realist. That does not convey much to a modern, for the term "realism," although a venerable philosophic position, is a term whose meanings are multifarious. Its intuitive sense is that there is "out there" a mind-independent reality against which the truth of our beliefs is tested and to which successful action must conform. The ordinary man in many ages has taken as real a sizable list of entitites from physical "things," sensations, ideas, events, to intentions, causes, persons, deities. Greek metaphysicians, in an effort to reduce and "explain" such a lengthy inventory, introduced certain ultimate entities into their theories—e.g., atoms—as the reality in terms of which others were to be explained. In the Middle Ages there were ferocious disputes about the reality of universals: the realists are supposed to have believed that universals are quite as real as trees and horses, while the nominalists said that universals were nothing more than names, convenient devices for purposes of communication. When philosophers became more epistemologically oriented and talked about knowing rather than being, the term "realism" developed even finer senses. The new sciences of physiology and psychology, with their rich exploration of the act of perceiving and knowing, necessitated the posing of new questions. Does the limitation of our senses somehow jeopardize our access to what is real? The indirect realist answered that our ideas are caused by external objects, and so interposed ideas, a new set of entities, between the mind and reality. Ideas, rather than being modes of direct access to the real, were representations. Representative theories of perception, such as that of Locke, were usually associated with metaphysical dualisms of mind and body, so that the realm of ideas was generally asserted to be entirely different from that of objects.

Direct realism (pejoratively called "naive realism" by some) is an attempt to restore the direct contact of the mind with reality. Objects are as they seem to us *under standard conditions*. It is a position that is peculiarly relevant to the present account since it seems to have been the position of McCosh. We shall see that it has to face the objections that it cannot account for error, nor furnish a method for adjudicating cases of contradiction between sensations we may happen to have.

The problem of the relation of ideas and "external" reality moves in two directions. Phenomenalism or subjective idealism—its classic adherents are

Berkeley, Hume, and (with reservations) Kant—limits knowledge to the realm of ideas. Materialists (e.g., Priestley or Cooper) turn ideas into a part of the natural material world. Thus the American "new realists" in our own century have argued at length that ideas are as natural as acorns, and that so-called mental phenomena such as conation are no more arcane than embryonic development or any other natural phenomena.

With such a variety of meanings for "realism," the only viable approach is to examine each usage in the context of its own problems and assumptions. A generalized usage becomes promiscuous. But it is precisely this that we find in McCosh.[6] He welcomes into the ranks of realism a quite incredible list of philosophers—Plato, Aristotle, Anselm, Abelard, Descartes, Kant, Hegel, and Berkeley. Only Hume, the Mills, and Spencer escape McCosh's determined classification, and accordingly they form "The Opposition." Scottish realism on both sides of the Atlantic was generally concerned with "Neo-Kantian" problems, e.g., the putative contribution of the knower in the act of knowing, what lies "beyond the limits of knowledge," and the like, but McCosh tends to sidestep such issues, addressing himself primarily to those problems of perceptual realism which arise from his interpretation of Locke's empiricism.

His examination of Locke, whose philosophy he respected, is often careful and insightful. Locke and Aristotle, indeed, seem to be the two philosophers to whom he was most sympathetic. It was a maxim of the latter which he chose to epitomize his own position: "By nature man is competently organized for truth, and truth in general is not beyond his reach." McCosh thought himself an Aristotelian in maintaining that memory is reliable, that reason functions both actively and passively, and that error is not traceable to uninterpreted sense perception. He draws a parallel between Locke's famous distinction of primary and secondary qualities and Aristotle's *sensus communis* (by means of which we grasp unity, motion, and other qualities delivered severally by the senses) and those qualities which depend on one sense only (e.g., smell).

By means of this and other arguments, McCosh assimilates Locke to Aristotle and both to the "realists." Locke, we are told, "intended to be a realist," yet even McCosh had to acknowledge that the main philosophical development of Locke's philosophy was the antirealism or idealism of Berkeley and Hume. For such philosophies McCosh has no use at all: the first fateful step toward phenomenalism (in the Berkeleyan sense) need never have been taken. Locke's philosophy needs to be reexamined and given a realistic interpretation emphasizing his beliefs in the external cause of sensation and in the representational character of certain ideas. The seeds of idealism in Locke, exploited to such horrifying lengths by Berkeley, Hume, Mill, Bain, and Spencer, would then be replaced in a more edifying structure.

McCosh champions the most direct of direct realisms: reality is composed of physical objects, minds, relations, and God. These exist independently of us and are unaffected by our incidental knowledge of them. Sense perception yields true information; hence we know reality directly. Our knowledge of objects is not inferential; it is not the case (contra Hume) that we know only our ideas.

The advantages of such a view are clear. It accords with the natural beliefs Western men have long shared regarding the reality of the external world. It is the native philosophy of the biologist and physiologist—even, in that day, of the physicist (who studied the structure of matter in a straightforward observational fashion that has long since gone out of style). McCosh even claims that it is the comfortable philosopher's view in his nonoracular moments: of a Berkeley when he explored the virtues of coal tar water, or of a Hume when he abandoned skepticism for the writing of history.

Yet one must pay some price for adopting this commonsense view of reality. What, on this account, would be the explanation of error? Perception is not always veridical; what markings (sensory or otherwise) distinguish veridical perceptions from illusions, errors, hallucinations, etc.? How is one to choose among the various senses, as when touch and sight seem to give different information concerning a stick partly immersed in water? Again: what objective property, if any, is revealed by the successive perceptions of smoothness, hardness, and eventual pain which result from increasing the pressure of one's hand on a resistant surface? Considerations like these are serious and generally force the common-sense realist into sophisticated accounts of perception, error, and illusion. But McCosh was very sure of what he perceived. Perception gives us a direct grasp of spatial, temporal, and causal relations which have a real existence, although we may not know them independently of our perceiving objects. Without the direct perception of such relations as these and of identity, could we be aware that objects persist over time and have histories? The abstract relations of mathematics, aesthetics, and morals are equally matters of direct perception; thus, e.g., the rightness of a benevolent act is neither a matter of sentiment, nor an inference, but a perception of the object in its moral relations and these are as "real" as the hand that extends the gift, although perhaps good and bad and obligations may involve a different order of reality. We acknowledge this moral reality whenever we approve the charity. Even our knowledge of religious entities falls into the same pattern of direct perception. As we know things by their qualities, so we perceive, by an inner sense or consciousness, the mind and the self by its qualities or operations of thinking, remembering, resolving, and the like, and this awareness of the self is a constant feature present in all acts of perceiving.

A very broad base has thus been secured in the particular perceptions (intuitions or observations) to which all judgments of common sense commit us and which therefore must form the starting point from which philosophers are to work. Philosophy then proceeds inductively, sharing the method of the empirical sciences, toward the framing of laws. McCosh is closing here with the traditional difficulty of all such empiricisms: whether universal laws can be derived from observations of particulars. He holds that there are some such universal principles that are accessible, though these tend to be the universal principles of thought, being, and belief, rather than the universal laws of science.

His answer to Kant has a kind of commonsensical charm. The a priori categories are after all only available in the first instance by observations of our thinking. If we always find them there, what is the point of deciding in a ponderous way that they are the necessary conditions of our thinking? The criteria for such principles are their self-evidency, necessity, and universality. Self-evidency is not a feeling, nor again is it a constitutive form in the mind imposed on objects, but it is a direct grasping by reason of objects and it affords us personal assurance of an objective external order which can never be weakened. Necessity, at least in Spencer's sense of a proposition whose negative is inconceivable, is a less important and direct criterion, not only because we could never be sure of splitting apart what association has securely tied, but also because it is difficult to determine precisely what is "inconceivable." The criterion of universality, McCosh is quite aware, has its difficulties, since common consent to a particular "truth" has often later been shown to be in error. Clearly McCosh is thinking here in terms of that universality of grammar and the structure of language which allows us to communicate with ourselves and others and to translate one sentence into an equivalent. Error and mistake may arise when observations are careless or hasty, or again in inference, say of a particular case of cause and effect, or in our generalizing; but when we limit ourselves to what is directly given in perception and when that is backed up by self-evidency, necessity, and universality taken corroboratively, mistake is impossible. What is thus secured are the commonsense principles of the external reference of perception, of our own selves, and of a community of like beings to whom we can address ourselves with the assurance of meeting an intelligible response. It is the objective of philosophy to state and defend the reality of these principles assured by intuition, just as it is the objective of physical and mental science to discover their laws.

McCosh also believes that philosophies necessarily take on something of national character and further that they ought to be relevant in the national life. He saw America, no less than Scotland, threatened by the unnaturalized implantations of European thought. Americans were lately "ploughing with the German heifer"—with Kant and Hegel, Jacobi, and Schleiermacher—who were leading us into an incorrigible pessimism and an agnosticism unsettling to theology and students alike. The English associationists are equally threatening insofar as they annihilate self-identity, causation, and arrest "the growth of all higher aims and aspirations, moral and spiritual." It goes without saying that materialism, French sensationalism, and positivism are even more threatening.

According to McCosh, Americans should be open to new philosophic ideas as to immigrants, who, though welcome to our shores, should speak our language and conform to our laws. America should be a republic of philosophy with a Monroe

Doctrine in full effect, i.e., not permitting foreign interference. Its prevailing tone should not be idealistic, neither the idealism of the Germans which is "spun out of the brain" and fits poorly with scientific and philosophic attempts to discover fundamental principles without adding to or subtracting from them, nor that of Berkeley, nor the skepticism of Hume, nor yet the agnosticism of the evolutionary philosophy. We must go back to a purified Locke, to a Locke "who meant to be a realist." McCosh answers with a resounding affirmative to his thesis: *Philosophy of Reality, Should it be Favored by America?* (1894). Yet in all fairness to McCosh he was not promoting the import of Scottish philosophy wholesale into America to meet its practical needs; he wanted loyalty to what is real rather than to what is speculative.

McCosh has appeared to us in two capacities—as the self-constituted arbiter and voice of Scottish Realism in America, and as the expositor of the true Realism in Scotland. As we shuttle back and forth from the one scene to the other, we have to ask whether he fairly represents either Realism in America or Realism in Scotland. In the rest of this chapter we shall try to show that the reality of Realism was much richer, both in America and in Scotland.

2. *Common Sense Realism in America*

McCosh says in his *The Scottish Philosophy* that John Witherspoon introduced Common Sense Realism to America in 1768. This was exactly one hundred years before McCosh received his call, and the circumstances are interestingly parallel, for Witherspoon too was a Presbyterian minister imported to meet a crisis at Princeton. Further, they shared that mixture of liberal, not to say democratic, social outlook which in Scotland was traditionally aligned with conservative religious and philosophic outlook. In both cases it was this conservativism which endeared them to the Princeton trustees and which made it attractive for them to leave Scotland. Especially in the case of Witherspoon the conditions in America which gave rise to the invitation and the conditions in Scotland which led to his departure are of significance not only for the understanding of Witherspoon but also of the course philosophy was to take in America.

Scottish Sources

The role of England in shaping American tradition is well known, but the importance of Scotland has too often been overlooked.[7] For this reason we now turn to Scottish matters—institutional developments, seminal thinkers, and the scientific setting of philosophic problems, including logic and morals. This is not only germane to the rest of this chapter, but also serves as a background for the two succeeding ones.

We start with that Calvinism which was brought to Scotland by Knox and given shape by Melville. The country which received it was impoverished, largely feudal, and virtually untouched by any of the mellowing influences of the Renaissance, except possibly in the universities. Calvinism was intended not merely to modify Romanism, even in the diluted form of Anglicanism, but utterly to refashion a way of life. The Scottish Presbyterians regarded themselves as covenanted, like the Israelites, with God—essentially the stern God of the Old Testament. They appealed directly to the Word of God, looking to the Scriptures for the structure as well as the authority for social institutions. Church government was to be all-encompassing, regulative of almost all behavior from private vices to public morality. And it was to be regulative also of educational and judicial institutions as well as religious ones. In effect, church government was charged with the health, wealth, morals, and wisdom of the nation.

Of course, this government, with its broadly conceived responsibilities, was theocratic in principle, and yielded commitments which many a Scotsman was to carry with him when he emigrated to America. Yet in a peculiar way the church was egalitarian and democratic. In the first place the status of the clergy did not set them apart, for they possessed no special priestly powers, had no privileged access to arcane doctrine, and were not the mediators between God and men. Rather, they were literally pastors who divided the responsibility even of church government with lay elders. In the second place, clergy and elders were importantly representative, since they owed their office to election on the part of the church membership. It thus was a fundamental and cherished right for a congregation to "call" its own minister and not to have him imposed by a patron. Third, upon this democratic base was built that well-known and elaborate administrative and judicial structure—ordered from kirk-session, Presbytery, Synod, to General Assembly. The representative features are preserved throughout the hierarchical structure, and thus the General Assembly, the national body and also the court of final legal appeal, is related by indirect representation to the popular base. Though the Scots had relatively little civil political experience before the mid-eighteenth century, their intimate participation in the functioning of the church provided vivid experience in indirect and complex representation as well as an appreciation for the lines of organization and administration. This was a central part of the heritage of those who came to the New World. Clearly Presbyterianism is good schooling for complex, larger-than-local representative government.

Parallels between church and state forms are obvious. Episcopalianism is monarchical and aristocratic in type. Congregationalism, with its autonomous congregation and internal use of direct techniques in its town meeting policy, embodies direct democracy (though not always realized in America). The Presbyterian structure, whether Scottish, English, or French, exhibits the kind of indirect representation similar to the mixed political form that emerged in the American Constitution. It is certainly not a farfetched hypothesis to suggest that the Presbyterian experience was influential in the forging of the viable political structure of government visible in the Constitution, especially considering the influence of Presbyterianism on James Wilson, Witherspoon, and his student Madison.

The responsibility of the church, especially as ideally formulated in Knox's *First Book of Discipline*, carried with it other commitments defining the relation of church to social institutions other than the state, e.g., to education and to the condition of the poor. Of course there was to be a separation of church and state, intended at that time to preserve the church from invasion by the state.[8] There were to be coordinate legal and ecclesiastical structures, doubtless intended to correspond roughly to the domain of civil responsibility on the one hand, and to moral and religious responsibility on the other. But then as now these domains could not neatly be marked out, and many a man found himself doubly jeopardized for everything from adultery and blasphemy to business dishonesty. Of course the church expected the state to enforce church decisions as well as to finance church operations, including salaries of ministers, church schools, and social relief programs.

There was a measure of reasonableness in this expectation because the church did accept the responsibility for education. A knowledge of the Scriptures, and perforce reading, was necessary for the lowliest of its members. Clearly, too, the education of the ministry must lie in church hands. But because the church was concerned that no talent should be lost either to it or to the nation through poverty, they sought to provide education from the elementary school to the university for those whose capacities qualified them. This concern for the practical relevance of education is early built into the educational system. Further, the church often made itself responsible not only for the righteousness of the poor, but also frequently for their legal and social defense before abuses by the aristocracy and the rising entrepreneurs. And when the evils of rapid urbanization and industrialization became apparent, especially in the slums of Glasgow, the church took on increasing responsibility for industrial apprenticeship and training. This concern with practical training is echoed even in the universities, where from a relatively early time professional schools of medicine and law were established on a par with those of divinity and arts.[9]

About the turn of the eighteenth century, however, coinciding with Scotland's union with England, cultural and economic factors converged with the political ones to put a new face on Scottish intellectual life. If the Renaissance had virtually passed her by,[10] she was to enjoy as high an Enlightenment as was to be found in Europe. Although the new united status of the two countries was primarily a matter of commerce and politics, which left the religious, educational, and legal structures of Scotland intact, still the new emphasis on English language and letters had a softening effect on the cold and harsh expressions of the Scottish piety. Slowly, and not without bitterness, the intellectuals of Scotland polarized into Conservatives and Moderates (New Lights). The former wanted to preserve the uncompromising piety and supernaturalism of the old Calvinism, and they opposed elegance and aesthetic refinement whether it was found in society, at the theater, or even in the phrases of a polished sermon. The Moderates, on the other hand, quite deliberately desired to moderate the old austerity. To the atmosphere of an older Scotland they brought pagan culture—the works of Aristotle, the literature of Rome (especially the works of Cicero and Marcus Aurelius Antoninus), the new politics of Grotius and Pufendorf, the new science of Newton, and the new philosophy of Locke.

The focus of this humanizing was the universities. Themselves part of the Scottish establishment, these seats of learning were staffed by Presbyterians, often ministers. As the Moderates achieved the upper hand in the nation's schools, they also gained power in the General Assembly, and with it a vast influence in the land. From the very beginning the Moderate clergy found allies in the aristocrats, for the latter wanted an educated, cultivated clergy who could be relied upon to soften the eternal din of damnation and to offer a respectable profession for their poorer kinfolk. Thus the intellectually liberal professors were aligned with the patronage system and with social and political conservativism.

The Scottish universities, even the medieval universities of St. Andrews, Aberdeen, and Glasgow, had always looked to European models rather than English ones.[11] Thus early they shared the philosophic fashions of Bologna and Padua and of course of Paris and finally Louvain. These early scholars were members of an international community, sharing one language, one faith, and one outlook on philosophy; and to this community Scotland provided its due share of distinguished intellects. Even during the Reformation (when Edinburgh was founded), and well into the eighteenth century Scottish universities retained their ties to Europe. To kinship with Leiden and Amsterdam in the Low Countries, and to a lesser extent with Halle and Protestant Germany, was added an extensive French association.

These special orientations—the long-continued connection with continental universities and the newer ones with the doctrines of Protestant reformers—resulted in a Scottish tradition that contrasts vividly with that of England. In the first place, the faculties of medicine and law remained intimately connected with the university. This emphasis on professional (as opposed to merely liberal) education paved the way for the new collegiate "chairs" of the eighteenth century, those of chemistry, botany, applied physics, and physiology. In the second place, even when the educational zeal of Knox and Melville faded and the darker side of the Reformation had laid its chill on inquiry, the universities of Scotland continued their agonizing educational self-appraisal and reconstruction. Of importance here is their concern with method, curriculum, and texts, as well as their running dialogue over the relation between church, nation, and university. During the seventeenth century the universities joined in an effort to reform instruction by providing good philosophic texts in place of the classic sources. In 1697 it was agreed that Edinburgh would provide a work on metaphysics, St. Andrews on logic, and Glasgow a compend on ethics. These working texts were published in London in 1701 and represent a real innovation since they were designed to stimulate a general discussion of the problems where heretofore they had been saddled with the authoritative voices of tradition. Second, accompanying the use of these student texts the universities instituted a reform in the manner of teaching which was imitated in American colonial institutions. Formerly it had been the custom to have a single master or tutor undertake the instruction of pupils in all subjects, depending for each subject on the classics; as a general rule the same master or tutor would carry a single class through its entire university career. In the early eighteenth century this system was replaced by a division of academic endeavor which made each professor responsible for a particular subject matter, thus allowing the professor far greater opportunity to develop depth and thorough-ness in his classroom; and the resultant expertise allowed both professor and student to distance themselves from the authoritative classic texts. The professor was freed to be original and ultimately to publish his own text. From this developed the tradition of Scottish lecturing, the fame of which drew students from Europe and America (and even England) to Scotland well into the nineteenth century.

> Teachers not only lectured; they conducted classes. The universities in Scotland managed to maintain the mediaeval curriculum—the trivium, moral philosophy, natural philosophy, and metaphysics, however grave its de-ficiencies as regards sound preparation and classical discipline. To the seemingly accidental circumstance that the Scottish universities provided Philosophers not merely with chairs, but also with classes to teach, Europe probably owes in large part the development of an important and influential School of Philosophy. Between the day of Hutcheson and that of J. S. Mill, a majority of the Philosophers who wrote in English were Professors (or at least alumni) of the Scottish universities.[12]

Philosophy, broadly construed, remained the core of the curriculum. Because of the ties with Europe, and the richer scholastic tradition which those ties implied, the universities of Scotland appear never to have fallen into such intellectual doldrums as Bacon, Hobbes, and Locke describe at Oxford. Aristotle too was neither the hero nor the enemy he was later to become at Oxford, for they knew not only the Aristotle of a late and arid scholasticism, but also the philosopher whose comprehensive science of nature was reworked, e.g., in northern Italy, in order to meet the challenges of the new science.

The reform in teaching methods which created professorships allowed a major choice between logic and moral philosophy as areas of specialization. A certain Gershon Carmichael, educated at Edinburgh but teaching at Glasgow, elected moral philosophy in 1727, but not before he had written an interesting compend of logic, strikingly like the logic text used at Harvard in those days. And like the text at Harvard it is traditional in many respects, reflecting both Aristotelian and Port Royal positions; and yet, in its attempt to treat logic both formally and psychologically, it strikes a modern note, working out carefully the relation between extension and comprehension.

In the field of his later choice, Carmichael interprets moral philosophy in the light of the new politics and law. Grotius, Pufendorf, and the Dutch rationalists Burgersdyk and Heineccius were the standard texts for the Scottish and colonial colleges of the day. Carmichael prepared a much valued edition of Pufendorf which appears to be the text used by the American colleges. What is interesting are the rich and critical notes which have a strong empirical flavor both in their appeals to observation and to social phenomena. In a final book on ethics Carmichael appears to have broken with the rationalist's tradition, turning away from Descartes and the Cambridge Platonists toward empiricism. Carmichael's accomplishment—the early steps toward modernizing logic and moral philosophy—foreshadowed, and it seems likely influenced, the same development toward empiricism as is to be found at Harvard in the study of logic and at Princeton in moral philosophy.

But in Scotland as in America it was the impact of Newton and Locke that capped the intellectual transformations of the time. The former's influence was felt through David Gregory (1627-1720) and Colin Maclaurin (1698-1746). The Gregory family is a famous one in the scientific annals of Scotland. David, senior, had been educated in Scotland and Padua and returned to Scotland to teach mathematics in a well-established tradition of applied mathematics at Edinburgh and succeeded his friend Newton as professor of astronomy at Cambridge on the latter's death. More famous than Gregory in his day, and an equally close friend of Newton, Colin Maclaurin traveled between Glasgow, Aberdeen, and Paris before settling finally as professor of mathematics at Edinburgh, which post he got on Newton's recommendation. Maclaurin's name is perhaps no longer familiar, but in the eighteenth century he was a man to be reckoned with. He shared a prize with Euler and Bernoulli for an essay on the tides. His treatise on fluxions, in addition to applying geometry to mechanics, answers Berkeley's criticism of the mystical elements of the calculus. It was he, too, who received the task of editing Newton's papers after the latter's death. His teaching at Edinburgh early incorporated the work of Newton (before Oxford it is said) and the most advanced science of his day, and his influence was felt not only in Edinburgh, but also among the generations of his students, including Witherspoon, who came to America.

This Scottish tradition in mathematics continued to be vigorous through Playfair, the later Gregorys, and John Leslie who tutored in a Virginia family in 1789. The vitality of mathematics spilled over and reinforced the natural sciences. In large measure this was due to the versatility and the practical interest of the mathematicians themselves. Newton, it may be recalled, worked as much in chemistry as in mathematics, and in Scotland mathematics and chemistry were jointly turned in the direction of inventions, of which Watt's engine is the most famous product. The towering figure in Scotland was Joseph Black (1728-1799) a student of Maclaurin's. His influence was felt not only through his investigations of latent heat, the combustion of nitrogen, but equally through his generosity with regard to his students. It was he who found a place for Watt at Edinburgh, despite that gentleman's deficient academic qualifications. He was one of the finest examples of that eighteenth-century phenomenon, the scientist who is equally concerned for education and for social progress. His work in agriculture was of inestimable service to his nation and reflected the fact that Scottish universities, unlike those of England, developed professional interests that were in close contact with the concrete demands of the country. It was this same concern that early allowed economics as a central part of the moral philosophy course. The notion of a university and its role in national life was precisely that later espoused by Franklin, Witherspoon, Washington, and Jefferson.

Black's work was also important for medicine since it has important ties with physiology and psychology. Many an American, including Rush of Philadelphia, went to Edinburgh to study under him, for that university rapidly became the medical center for the English-speaking world. It was a ready-made model for those Americans who sought to establish medical schools in this country.

Chemistry, of course, figured importantly in the philosophic discussions in American materialism, with Priestley its most intransigent defender. But more important to problems of perception and of voluntary action were the developing studies in physiology. In this context Whytt (1714-1766) was influential in America, for he was in constant correspondence with colonial men of science, especially Cadwallader Colden, scientist, physician, and ultimately lieutenant governor of New York. Whytt was able to distinguish between voluntary motion, which alone requires will and reason, and involuntary or habitual motion. The latter is explained in terms of reflex action which he defines as a sentient principle that translates stimuli into involuntary motion in the spinal cord alone. Whytt demonstrated this reflex action in the laboratory. Not only could involuntary actions be thus stimulated without reasoning or willing, but other actions which are initially reasoned may also drop to the automatic once they have become habitual. His experimental research did much to strengthen the confidence of the associationists in their central principle for explaining behavior.

Whytt's work is only one aspect of the continuing medical contribution to philosophical problems of the mind's relation to body, of the nature of purpose and behavior and voluntary action. Somewhat later, but still in close contact with America, Marshall Hall (1790-1857) clarifies experimentally even more the relation of voluntary to nonvoluntary action. In the early nineteenth century, Charles and John Bell, among others, established the physiological discreteness of motor and sensory fibers. Particular nerve fibers, they demonstrated, carry impulses in only one direction at a given time; thus sensory and motor (sensation and action) are comparable physiological functions. This of course means that action, i.e., response, is systematically related to the stimulus. There is thus no more mystery about sensation than about action, for impressions of outward sense and our ideas are thus connected and the latter have a correspondence with the perceived qualities of the object. Bell's account of the anatomy of expression only reaffirms, in a subtle way, the intimate interplay of mental states with voluntary and involuntary action.

Black and Whytt, the Bells and Hall, are only a few among the Scots who helped form a medical tradition that in turn gave shape to the philosophical problems in America. Of course the Scots were not the only ones contributing to the New World's medical science; Linnaeus in Sweden, and the medicine of the Low Countries, and, somewhat later in the eighteenth century, French physiology were also important elements. And yet the most direct influence in America came from Scotland; even the Revolution, when it came, was no insuperable obstacle to the Americans wanting to study in Scotland. More than one hundred American students mostly from the Middle States satisfied the requirements at Edinburgh before 1800. This is even more relevant to our concerns than might appear, for the university organization of the day allowed, and even encouraged, the reciprocal nourishment of medicine, botany, chemistry, biology, and philosophy.

It is not surprising that such activity in the natural sciences and mathematics was matched by advances in the social sciences; especially the latter were also exploiting the Newtonian model. Studies on population and wealth and efforts to quantify happiness appear early in the century, and culminate in the famous essays of Hume and Adam Smith. Liberal attitudes pioneered the opening of the curriculum to these subjects in the Scottish universities, just as they had early welcomed the experimental sciences. This was a great moment for speculation—for theories about the nature of man, his relation to animals, his origin, the nature of racial differences, and the influence of culture and habit. In all these matters, the Scots were continually being stimulated by (and stimulating) the French.

An integral part of the scene in France and Scotland was the importance given to history. The histories purport to be empirical, but their aim was not so much to describe particular events as to find out the universal laws governing the growth of institutions. These laws were based on a kind of universal psychology which operates more or less uniformly in the development of culture, artistic styles, and individual languages. The science of history was in part normative, for its aim was to discover the laws by which men could reconstruct their institutions. In America, at least, David Hume was more famous for his histories than for his *Treatise*.

Behind all these investigations was a pervasive concern about method that characterized the work of the natural and social sciences, from Hutton in geology to Kames in anthropology, and, of course, Hume and Smith in economics. It is the effort to apply the Newtonian model to human behavior and thereby to develop a science of man and human institutions. The melody was familiar and Newtonian, but the orchestration differed from writer to writer. Some emphasized a simplicity and order of the world which could be formulated in elegant mathematical laws. Such magnificent orderliness most Scots, following Newton himself, interpreted as evidence of God's plan. Others, impressed perhaps by the fact that Newton had refused to speculate on what might lie behind gravitation, preferred to stress the patient gathering of observations and the probabilistic character of scientific generalizations. Hume alone was to challenge the possibility of science.

If Newton provided the model for the sciences generally, it was Locke who sought to apply that model to mind and its phenomena. It goes, almost without saying, that the Scots were all Lockeans. But there are difficulties in taking the Lockean philosophy lock, stock, and barrel; a most important part of his legacy is to be found in the internal tensions of his system—some say magnificent ambiguities—which allow of the various readings which occupy the next centuries. Thus, there are difficulties in making Locke a thoroughly consistent empiricist, since after all he appeals to demonstration in religion, morals, and politics—the famous self-evident truths. His empiricism is also beset with nagging ambiguities in the terms ''experience'' and ''idea'' and in the problem of the reference of ideas which resulted in divisions among Locke's successors, who veered now toward realism, now toward materialism, and now toward idealism. The mainstream of British philosophy was to follow this last, flowing from Locke through Berkeley's immaterialism, to Hume's skepticism and beyond into Mill's phenomenalism. Among the Scots, however, Hume was the exception. Scottish philosophers tended to read their Locke in rather special ways. Those whose background was chiefly mathematical, e.g., Dugald Stewart, were impressed by the universal elements in the human constitution, by the fact that an admittedly private experience is compossible with an intricate system of interpersonal communication. They were persuaded that all languages had a universal syntax, and finally, that mathematics has the kind of certainty that no experience could possibly bestow. Their reading of Locke, and response to Hume, was structured by these claims. Those, on the other hand, who were trained in the natural sciences, especially those familiar with psychology and medicine, e.g., Reid and Brown, tended to view Locke as the physician who was looking for the scientific basis of knowledge, as indeed he was—in his constant probing for the behavior of those particles which would produce the qualitative character of experience. Locke so viewed would surely have been prepared to allow the interaction of mind and body without troubling about the ultimate nature of that interaction or the properties of mind (consciousness). The convergence of these two trends in the Scottish reading of Locke was to make him to most a realist as well as an empiricist.

The Scots brought to the defense of this realism, then, a less impoverished picture of human nature and its resources than Locke or Hume. Locke's account of man leaves that creature essentially passive (a receiving machine), and a social but basically hedonistic animal. It is precisely this deficiency in Locke, this neglect of the dynamic character of man in action, this insensitivity to the finer reaches of aesthetics and morals, that made Shaftesbury's subsequent emendations of the Lockean philosophy so important and influential.

Francis Hutcheson (1694-1746) followed Shaftesbury in a humanizing of philosophy that was influential in Scotland and America. Of equal importance was his leadership (backed by political skill) in humanizing religion and education. A Moderate, his election to the professorship of moral philosophy (succeeding Carmichael) at Glasgow by a narrow margin was a signal victory for the liberals in university and church politics. He in turn labored successfully—though, according to McCosh, somewhat *"unprincipledly"*—to capture the chair of theology for another Moderate, and together they worked to put the "new face" on religion, to naturalize morals, and to introduce into university education those eighteenth-century standards of elegance, style, and learning which were to become a part of Scottish letters from Smith and Hume to Stewart and Hamilton.

But Hutcheson's mark was wider than in matters of style. He influenced philosophically the whole line of Scottish humanists, from Ferguson and Reid to Smith and Hume. And indirectly, through the latter two, his view of utility as the moral standard was to become the thesis of the utilitarianisms of Paley and of Bentham and the Mills. Hutcheson's views of moral sense and goodwill have parallels in the Kantian ethics, and an annotated German edition of his *Inquiry* has been found in Kant's library. His philosophical works were early known and published in America, and American leaders such as Adams and Jefferson acknowledged their debt to him. His influence is also visible in Butler and Price, whose works were popular with the colonists, and even measurably in Witherspoon.

Building on a Lockean empiricism, Hutcheson writes to the broad front of philosophic problems—from metaphysics to morals. An early essay on logic, e.g., introduces psychological concerns and emphasizes induction. Yet, while counting himself a Lockean, he is not above emending that philosophy in places where he regards it as inconclusive or incomplete. Thus Hutcheson sees Locke forthrightly as a realist, but one who failed to do justice to the richness of human experience. Enriching Locke's view of human endowments, he therefore seeks to build upon it a consistently empirical theory of morals, including the economic and social as well as the ethical and the political.

There is no doubt that Locke's view of human nature leaves man singularly impoverished. He is subject to the tyranny of the order in which his ideas initially are experienced. On Locke's account, it is hard to see how a man could make plans or strategies, and even harder to see how he could conform his actions to them. But above all (at least on Hutcheson's view), Locke's man would lack all those richer sensibilities, moral and aesthetic, which enable him to respond to the beauty of nature and art; to appreciate the generosity of a noble character; or even to perceive those evidences of mechanical design in nature to which Locke's own deism commits him—to say nothing of the fantastic harmony of integrated systems that the new microscopic biology was revealing.

Hutcheson's model is basically an aesthetic one, and is explicitly indebted to Shaftesbury—grandson and tutee of Locke's patron. Shaftesbury's works, too, had considerable vogue in America, but Hutcheson's, more detailed and analytic, were more popular. We respond, say, in looking at a painting to a dimension beyond the grossly descriptive lines, colors, and shapes to such qualities as organization, economy, sublimity, and grandeur. Of course, he scarcely questions the objective character of these properties.

The moral situation is analogous: the beauty of a virtuous act (and by extension, a virtuous character) has the power to move us directly to moral approbation quite independently of our willing. Hutcheson calls this capacity to respond to the moral dimension the "moral sense," and while at times he seems to take it as a faculty, generally he is merely naming the moral sensitivity that is aroused in a particular case. The moral sense is universal, common, and shared. It operates more uniformly than might appear from the diversity of responses; such diversity is only apparent and may readily be accounted for by differences in custom, habit, environment, and learning.

As a matter of fact, Hutcheson's moral sense was to create problems of interpretation in America, as well as elsewhere. He intended a theory of natural judgment—similar to and as "rational" as perceptual judgments of distance, color, shape, and size. Yet the moral sense is precariously balanced. It can easily tip over to the side of sentiment, taste, and feelings, as it did in Hume and Smith, and thereby lose much of its rooting in objectivity (beyond, of course, what universal human nature provides). On the other hand, it can easily slip into the "rational" intuition of the Cambridge Platonists, the rational conscience of a Butler, Kant, or Emerson, hardening then into a rational faculty on a par with such other so-called "faculties" as the understanding and the will in the psychology of McCosh.

What Hutcheson intended by sense, at least most of the time, was as suggested, merely to name an obvious characteristic of our psychological activity and to denote an aspect of perceptual functioning. Morals are not so much innate as dependent upon innate activities and capacities—these capacities are just one kind of natural judgment; just as visual perceptions are open afterward to objective and mathematical assessment by the science of optics, so our natural judgments of benevolence, even though very complex, are similarly real and open to appraisals or algebraic calculation. Thus there is an objective standard to which we have direct perceptual—though moral—insight; in fact, it is the general social happiness, or the greatest good for the greatest number, and the worth of actions are to be assessed as they are useful in gaining this objective. The job of moral philosophy lies in pointing out the nature of this highest happiness and what will help and hinder its realization. At the base, then, of Hutcheson's theory is not only the notion that we are as fundamentally other-regarding as self-regarding, but also that such relations provide the fabric of society. Further, these natural affections, both egoistic and altruistic, are attuned to social utilities and to justice, since the world is as benevolent and harmonious as it is orderly and knowable. The teleology is double-edged: a benevolent God has designed the world so that happiness is realizable in it; personal and public happiness are compatible; and we are so equipped that we can discover the relevant laws and contribute to its workings.

Lest we be overimpressed with the naivete of this view, it is worth remembering its strong points: Hutcheson is attempting to answer both Hobbes and the Cambridge Platonists with a theory that takes into account moral sentiments; to point out both in psychology and the order of the world what is necessary to these judgments (thus avoiding a confusion of faculty and standard). Even in the more sophisticated theories of Hume, Smith, Bentham, and the laissez-faire theorists, no less powerful assumptions are made of the neatness and harmony of the universe. He appreciates also the importance that quantifying would have for intersubjective decision, and finally (and of special importance in America) this moral philosophy is no narrow inquiry; it is comprehensive and integrative of all the elements that today we regard as the social sciences.

Hutcheson was tried for heresy before the Presbyterian Synod on the ground that he said happiness was the standard of morality and that knowledge of morals was possible without knowledge of God or revelation, and presumably because (since the moral sense was regulative) a man could be moral without being Christian. Apparently the charges were correct, but they failed by 1738 to add up to heresy. Moderation was on its way.

Witherspoon—Scottish Career

John Witherspoon (1722/3-1794) belonged to the generation of Hutcheson's students and had all the advantages which the Moderates had instituted in the universities—curriculum, teaching, and intellectual tone. But even in his youth Witherspoon was no Moderate and he became in Scotland one of the most outstanding (and outspoken) of conservative Evangelical leaders.[13] The Evangelicals actually had a majority over the Moderates, but in Scotland, as in America, their normal loyalties were split by Whitefieldian revivalism. As a result the conservatives themselves divided into the Popular Party (who remained in the universities and churches) and the Seceders. Ironically, the Seceders fought with the Popular Party over preaching jurisdiction and the signs of authentic conversional experience, and the Popular Party, i.e., Witherspoon's, was left more doctrinal in its faith, more amiable toward Whitefield, and very much the defensive minority within the Establishment.

Witherspoon's days at Edinburgh roughly span those of the slightly older Hume, of Ferguson, Hutton, and James Mill—and at Glasgow, of Reid and Adam Smith. At Edinburgh, Witherspoon added proficiency in Latin and Greek to a childhood ease with French. As may be reconstructed from his writings he read the Roman Stoics and Greek texts in logic and even the aesthetics of Aristotle and the pseudo-Longinus. He also studied the writings of the French Calvinists and Port Royalists as well as the Dutch Cartesians. At this time he won that thorough grounding in Grotius, Pufendorf, and Heineccius that is later evident in his theoretical and practical politics. Mclaurin was his professor of mathematics and natural philosophy and so it may be assumed that he knew Newton's works directly. With Stevenson he read Locke's *Essay*, and of course he knew, as any undergraduate at Edinburgh would, the works of Shaftesbury and Hutcheson, including the ecclesiastical stance of the latter, since the heresy charge was a *cause célèbre* during Witherspoon's first years at Edinburgh.

Versed thus in the old, but more responsive to the new than perhaps he realized, Witherspoon was able to turn the Moderates' learning as well as their tools of style and wit to the defense of his foursquare stand for the traditional faith, for personal piety, and against patronage and public immorality. It was this last that led him to hold that "contributing to the Support of a Public Theater is inconsistent with the Character of a Christian." Although seemingly general, the target was the Reverend John Home's *Douglas*. That a Presbyterian minister should write a play was scandalous enough, but that it should be produced in Edinburgh and witnessed by other Presbyterians, including his former rooming-mate A. Carlyle, was an unmistakable sign of Scottish impiety. Partly through Witherspoon's efforts, Carlyle was censured for attending the performance, but this did little to check the latter's career in the church, while his successes must have certainly contributed to Witherspoon's alienation from the intellectual circles which included Carlyle's friends, Adam Smith and David Hume. The latter two had been instrumental in having the play produced.

Probably a more potent factor in Witherspoon's decision to leave Scotland was the unpleasantness which ultimately followed his eagerness to expose in sermon and in satire the irreligion of the Moderate clergy and the immorality of undergraduates. The most celebrated of the satires is

Ecclesiastical Characteristics,
or the Arcana of Church Policy.
Being an Humble attempt to open the mysteries of Moderation.
Wherein is shewn, A plain and Easy way of attaining to the character of a
Moderate man, as at present in repute in the Church of
Scotland.
1753

Here Witherspoon is shooting at Hutcheson through Shaftesbury for his displacement of Christian virtues by natural ones and of Christian sources by pagan classics.

The way includes such maxims as esteeming professors of divinity, principals of colleges, and ecclesiastical men who are suspected of heresy, as men of "genius, uncommon worth and vast learning." A man who is suspected of loose practices and tendencies to immorality is to be protected,

> especially if faults laid to his charge be as they are incomparably well-termed in a sermon, preached by a hopeful youth that made some noise lately, good-humored vices. The notion of good-humored vices, the reader may please take notice, is an observation of Lord Shaftesbury that the best time for thinking upon religious subjects is when a man is married and in good humor. Whatever, therefore, serves to provide merriment and heighten good humor are so far served for the discovery of religious truth. And since gravity is almost necessarily a consequence of solitude, good-humored vices are certainly social pleasures and such as flow from and show benevolence.[14]

The science of moral virtue is to be taken as analogous to the fine arts and to borrow from them such expressions as beauty, harmony, proportion, and decency. The Moderate must never speak of the confessional of faith except with a sneer, giving sly hints that he doesn't thoroughly believe it, and above all he must make "orthodoxy" a term of contempt and reproach. The Moderate ought also to be filled with contempt for all learning except Leibniz and Shaftesbury which have been whipped into form and shape by the late Mr. Hutcheson. The *Moral Essays* of Hume would also be useful since he is another Scotsman who carries "the scheme of Shaftesbury, Leibnitz and Collins to its most ravishing height." Witherspoon adds as doctrinal the often quoted "Athenian Creed":

> I believe in the beauty and comely proportions of Dame Nature, and in almighty Fate, her only parent and guardian; for it hath been most graciously obliged (blessed be its name) to make us all very good.
>
> I believe that the universe is a huge machine, wound up from everlasting by necessity, and consisting of an infinite number of links and chains, each in a progressive motion towards the zenith of perfection, and meridian of glory; that I myself am a little glorious piece of clockwork, a wheel within a wheel, or rather a pendulum in this grand machine, swinging hither and thither by the different impulses of fate and destiny; that my soul (if I have any) is an imperceptible bundle of exceeding minute corpuscles much smaller than the finest Holland sand; and that certain persons in a very eminent station, are nothing else but a huge collection of necessary agents, who can do nothing at all.
>
> I believe that there is no ill in the universe, nor any such thing as virtue absolutely considered; that those things vulgarly called sins, are only errors in

the judgment, and foils to set off the beauty of nature, or patches to adorn her face; that the whole race of intelligent beings, even the devils themselves (if there are any) shall finally be happy; so that Judas Iscariot is by this time a glorified saint, and it is good for him that he hath been born.

In time, I believe in the divinity of L. S———, the saintship of Marcus Antoninus, the perspicuity and sublimity of A———e, and the perpetual duration of Mr. H———n's works, not withstanding their present tendency to oblivion. Amen.[15]

The *Ecclesiastical Characteristics* became famous overnight and went through many editions. Though written without signature, it was generally known that Witherspoon was its author—although the Philadelphia edition of 1767 appears to be the first in which the authorship is explicit. Witherspoon wrote further satires which became ever more bitter, and with their increased bitterness came a decrease in effectiveness, since overzealous attacks extinguished his subtle irony. Overzealousness led him to further unconsidered attacks on immorality and irreligion. Thus he preached a sermon against a group of young men who, it was reported to him, had mocked the communion during their drinking; he then published the sermon with the names of the parties involved, making himself vulnerable to a suit—which he ultimately lost in the civil courts. Although Witherspoon's congregation paid the action, which amounted to a whole year's living, still the decision of the courts seemed to amount to an antipathy to the Conservative cause. The extensive litigation was a constant source of embarrassment to Witherspoon and continued long after he had moved to America. Not content even with this, he became further involved with one of the litigants, whom he charged with associating with an immoral woman on what turned out to be insufficient evidence. Confronted on all sides by the growing prestige of the Moderates in doctrine, education, and moral style, Witherspoon must have felt the futility of stemming this tide. At this juncture, the invitation from Princeton arrived which, when later seconded by the personal pleading of Benjamin Rush, a medical student in Edinburgh at the time, proved irresistible.

It is not to be thought, then, that Princeton had invited some unknown or uneducated divine to help solve its problems. His sermons and satires had been translated into Dutch; invitations to move to Rotterdam, Dundee, and Dublin had already been proffered. There were even good grounds to believe, as he afterward claimed, that an article of his in the *Scots Magazine*, April 1753, had anticipated Reid's realism. Surely Witherspoon did not have to leave Scotland, but he must clearly have thought that the New World offered greater scope for his orthodoxy and his talents.

Situation in America

Meanwhile, the situation in America which led up to this invitation, though it had its own twists and turns, was in important ways like that of Scotland. New England

Congregationalism had been divided by Whitefield, leaving Edwards as the leader of the evangelical wing, in company with others who felt that Yale no less than Harvard had become inhospitable to those whose deepest concerns lay in personal religion and piety. In the Middle Atlantic and Southern states the Great Awakening had cut through the religious commitments, but there the situation was even more complex since there was already a more extreme left in the deists and materialists, an omnipresent threat in the established Anglicans and Quakers, and a more extreme right in German Pietism.

Even among the Calvinistic churches there was a great range of doctrinal responses, as different churches, reflecting different national backgrounds, interacted with one another—the Dutch Reform and the English Presbyterians in northern New Jersey and New York, and communities of Huguenots from New York to Charleston. The situation was further affected by the immigration after 1720 of ever-increasing numbers of Scotch-Irish Presbyterians who brought with them their own versions of Presbyterianism, a vivid memory of Anglican and English intolerance, and a cleavage between revivalists and orthodox, analogous to the Moderate-Conservative cut in Scotland—slanted, however, toward the orthodox pole. The Old Lights in Massachusetts represented, approximately, the Scot Moderates, and the New Lights, stressing revivalism and the necessity of a private conversional experience for salvation, roughly paralleled the Popular Party.[16]

Of course the Seceders were represented as well, and in the early part of the nineteenth century they were to establish their own colleges. In this environment, more adverse and hostile than in New England, the Congregationalists coming from New England tended to make their allegiances along the lines of revivalism, rather than according to Congregational or Presbyterian structure. (In point of fact, sectarian lines were easily bridged, although doubtless with great soul-searching. Thus Samuel Johnson, first president of Columbia, and William Smith, provost of Pennsylvania, both left Calvinism for Episcopalianism; while the Episcopalian Madison remained in close contact with Presbyterianism most of his life.) As midcentury approached, the Old Lights were in control of higher education at Yale, while Harvard liberals were even more antirevivalist, and the Old Sides appeared to be in control of the ministry in the Middle Atlantic states.

With immigration and expansionism the problem of preparing ministers became a crucial one in the Middle Atlantic and Southern states, for, after all, the only college was the Anglican William and Mary. There grew up about particular ministers schools something like the Dissenting Academies in England, though with more limited educational aims and standards.

The Log College of the Tennents near Philadelphia was typical. Tennent had been educated at Edinburgh and the Log College provided a fairly good classical education; but even there, where a choice had to be made between scholarship and religious conversion, clearly the latter was more important. This was even more true of the other New Side academies, in which the classical education was sometimes negligible. Partly for political reasons, but also out of a genuine concern about the importance of an educated clergy, the Presbyterian Synod at Philadelphia (Old Sides predominating) passed a requirement that all ministers who did not have a degree from a New England college or a foreign university must take a qualifying examination. Clearly, the New Sides could not hope for much under Old Side accrediting, and the Tennents defied the ruling with the support and sympathy of the New England New Lights and those areas of New York and northern New Jersey in which the New Theology had taken roots. To remedy the situation, six graduates from Yale and one from Harvard undertook to establish the college which was later to become Princeton.[17] It was to be a college that would provide an education of high quality for future ministers of New Light persuasion. It took some compromising to finance and to charter the institution as a British college—with the Old Sides in religion to secure the funds, and with Quakers and Anglicans in educational objectives (beyond the preparation of New Side ministers) to secure governmental support. Compromises were indeed made, but the hard core of the trustees did not lose for many a season their initial commitment to Princeton's role as the propagator and defender of the New Side-New Light faith.

This faith was not only threatened from within by the Old Side moderate rationalism to be found in the Middle states and by the liberalism of New Haven and Cambridge, but also from without by the ungodly and so-called "enlightened" materialisms and deisms loosed from Philadelphia and New York, and from the political threat of Quakerism and Anglicanism in the colonial government.

Unfortunately, the troubles at Princeton did not cease with the chartering and the financing of the college. Above all, the next two decades at Princeton were plagued by the early deaths of its presidents, the first four of which, all New England graduates, were as able a group of men as were to be found in the colonies. Jonathan Edwards, e.g., served only a matter of months, and with his death the connections with New England initiative began to dissolve. An effort was made to gain the appointment for Samuel Hopkins, one of Edwards's disciples, but this failed, and the next several presidents were all Middle states men, who reflected subtly the distinctive pressures of that environment, not the least of which was the difficult relation to Anglicanism and the changing complexion of Presbyterianism brought about by the enormous Scotch-Irish immigration. That immigration could not push west parallel to New York, but fanned out south and west, leaving Presbyterianism and Princeton to face southward for its resources, its students, and its problems. New England influence was not wiped out immediately, of course, since a goodly portion of the tutors, including Jonathan Edwards, Jr., Perriam, and Lockwood, kept alive the New England tone and, presumably, something of the Berkeleyan idealism as well.

Anglicanism and Presbyterianism, both Old and New Side, were generally hostile to one another. A brief coalition between Old Sides and Anglicans, however, helped make the University of Pennsylvania possible. Nominally non-denominational (as any enterprise with which Franklin was associated would be), it early was headed by a mismatched team of William Smith—a graduate of Aberdeen, who had turned Anglican and who came from New York to become provost of the new university—and Francis Alison, vice-provost—from Glasgow, and one of the most stalwart and competent of the Old Sides. On the other hand, the Old Side cooperation with the Anglicans was at best an ephemeral affair, for all Presbyterians and Congregationalists were united before the threat of an American Episcopalian Establishment. The provost was an effective operator and Pennsylvania early became the bridge by which many Presbyterians entered Episcopalianism. The Old Side Alison was a philosopher of some distinction too, and as the notes of students show, philosophy was in a generally reputable state. Hutcheson and Shaftesbury, as well as Newton and the moral philosophers, were all well known. The Presbyterians tried in New York to control, or at least to make nondenominational, the college that was to be founded there with public funds. They failed when King's College was established with Samuel Johnson as president, but they did not cease their involvement. And, of course, William and Mary continued as the strongly Anglican college of the South.

The situation was tense, then, in 1766 when Princeton's president Finley died. The Old Sides, seeing the general threat of Episcopalianism, sought to broaden the Calvinist base and were prepared to divide the appointments and the presidency with the New Sides in exchange for their not inconsiderable financial help and moral support. The Old Sides proposed Alison or, alternately, Ewing, who were men of no mean distinction in philosophy. However, the New Side trustees countered this stratagem with the suggestion of Witherspoon as a distinguished outsider. This compromise was accepted.

Witherspoon's Princeton Career

Witherspoon's career at Princeton,[18] and in the larger political and social arena, could scarcely have been a disappointment to the New Side trustees or even to the Old Side ones. He secured a real measure of harmony among the Calvinists, including the German colonists and Dutch Reform, and he fronted the even harder task of unifying Presbyterianism in America. This latter was made somewhat easier by the unity with which the Presbyterians faced the threats first of the Anglican Establishment and then of the developing strains with England. Even before Witherspoon's arrival, the Presbyterians as a church, with Alison the most vocal statesman, had worked toward the repeal of the Stamp Act. Witherspoon soon after his arrival saw the inevitability of the break from Britain and was early a leader in organizing the sentiment, especially of Presbyterians, in support of a move for independence. He sustained that sentiment during the dark hours of the near defeat and the ravaging of Princeton's own buildings and resources. It may not be true, as so often alleged, that Witherspoon was the only minister to sign the Declaration of Independence; but it is true that his deep roots in reformation Calvinism helped him see the War for Independence as a justified and holy war against a tyrant. In any case, it is this recently immigrated Scotsman who was the only college president who was partner to those searing deliberations. The gaining of independence did not see Witherspoon quit politics, for he distinguished himself in the New Jersey assembly and then later in the Constitutional Convention.

Nor could the trustees have had any reason to complain about Witherspoon's service to Princeton, for he materially relieved its financial difficulties and brought Princeton closer to the Scottish university standard, not only by improving the work in the classics and broadening general philosophy, but also by his insistence on natural philosophy as a proper part of the curriculum. Through Witherspoon, Princeton became a national institution with probably the most broadly based student body and certainly the greatest academic influence in the Middle and Southern states.

And yet it is interesting to speculate whether the trustees understood what they were getting in Witherspoon. He brought with him the expected, unimpeachable personal morality and an equally unimpeachable concern for the morals of his students and faculty. Anticipated, too, might have been his liberal social position and even his view of the cordiality between philosophy and science, which Witherspoon made explicit in his inaugural address. But the trustees could scarcely have appreciated how far he was from the position of the New Light founders, nor how profound a change he was to initiate away from the new divinity.

Even in Scotland he seems not to have been very Whitefieldian; certainly in America he never sympathized with strongly conversional experience. And while it may appear that he mellowed at Princeton, it's more probable that the new context into which American religious issues had been thrown made Witherspoon's conservative stand take on a more liberal cast. At least it is clear that he had drunk more deeply of the Scottish Enlightenment than the trustees (and perhaps he himself) had supposed. His difference from Edwards and from the earlier New Light presidents is dramatic. Where Edwards had made the free will issue the basis for his reconstruction of Calvinism, Witherspoon thought the problem ought never to have become a central one, since the problem of choice and of the guiding of our conduct by conscience stands—no matter what the metaphysical base. Thus while Edwards's work dominated and divided the theological discussions in New England for the next hundred years, Witherspoon's cavalier treatment unseated the issue as a focus of discussion in the Middle and Southern states.

In further contrast to Edwards, and it seems his own earlier position at Edinburgh, Witherspoon taught that questions of morality and virtue could be investigated as a branch of science and that our duties could be demonstrated by rational and empirical means. Thus he starts his ethics, not with premises guaranteed by religion or revelation, but from the construction of human nature as learned by observation. Such a program, he tells us, had been opposed (presumably the reference is to Edwards), as reducing infidelity to a system; indeed it looks remarkably similar to the view he had satirized in his "Athenian Creed." Thus whereas Edwards regarded holy affections as supernatural in origin, and limited the natural affections to those which are fundamentally selfish, Witherspoon's *Lectures*[19] builds on a naturalistic view of human nature that goes even further than Hutcheson in broadening the natural affections to include religious ones. We can only conjecture as to the reasons for this seeming "conversion" in Witherspoon's attitude toward moral philosophy—perhaps the moderation he had opposed in Scotland took on a different cast in the New World context. In any case there is a question of consistency between his ethical and theological views.

The sermons are certainly out of phase with the lectures on moral philosophy. But this seems less to represent insulation of a Sunday religion from a workaday empiricism than to point to a distinction between religious and scientific-philosophic undertakings premised on the belief that nothing a completed science will discover would profane revelation. Indeed, the premise is stronger, for Witherspoon is confident that the developments of science will enhance the truth and beauty of Scripture. Thus the study of moral philosophy inquires into the nature and grounds of the principles of duty as they are available to reason through observation and induction. The investigation is thus empirical and nonrevelational precisely because it is philosophic. There are a variety of accesses to the knowledge of this divinely constructed order and philosophy provides one of them.

This working premise about the ultimate reconcilability of science with theology prepares Witherspoon to accept the relevance of physiology and the influence of physical factors upon that compound of body and spirit which is human nature. Going even further, he places man biologically and psychologically within the animal kingdom. No single criterion distinguishes man from other forms; just as man has instincts (which are morally important), there is ample evidence that animals reason, although humans are better able to utilize reason in guiding conduct and in avoiding dangers. It was just this cordiality to science that put Witherspoon within talking distance, though sometimes acrimoniously, of such scientists as Rush and Rittenhouse and other members of the American Philosophical Society.

A similar appreciation of continuities is to be found in Witherspoon's treatment of human faculties. Understanding, will, and affections are not to be read as separate faculties, but as qualities of a single process or as different ways of exerting the same principle: the mind understands, wills, is affected by pleasures and pains. Witherspoon's analysis of the affections is interestingly full, and he acknowledges the importance, and even the value, of anger, malice, love of fame, and gratification; but such self-referring feelings are tempered by a direct delight and interest in the happiness of others. In countering the objection that understanding or reason must be limited to matters of truth and falsity since intelligent beings often do evil, Witherspoon maintains his integrated view of human response. Judgment must be the basis for the full range of choice and decision. Behavior generally may thus be rational in a quite modern and Deweyan sense. Reason further operates as a moral sense or conscience since insight into virtue and duty carries with it the obligation to conform our actions to it. This sense of duty lies behind the primary notion of rights viewed as everything which we are entitled to expect from others and from ourselves and whose neglect is blamable. In other words, there is a moral sentiment that binds us to do what we judge to be right; and that right entails interest beyond our own happiness. The whole argument evidences Witherspoon's belief in the harmony of the moral order, God's will, public interest, and private happiness, as well as in the workings of our affections and sentiments of approbation to reinforce one another in right decision. Thus we are not depraved by original sin, but are competent to see and correct our own departures from original purity, and, by inference, to mold and remake our institutions by choice.

By a natural expansion of the examination of human nature and these materials of ethics, Witherspoon moves on to a discussion of politics. Thus far, of course, he goes with the earlier Lockean tradition, but the reach of "moral" is more extensive. It includes not only our relations to others and duties to God, but also the full setting of social relations from the domestic and economic to international regulation of commerce, the waging of war, and the securing of peace; on Witherspoon's view, nations are moral individuals standing in the relation of natural liberty to one another.

Throughout the *Lectures* the Hutchesonian tone is evident: indeed, he has even adapted Hutcheson's organization of moral philosophy which was his heritage to the whole school of social thinkers from Ferguson to Hume and Smith. But by this broad use of "moral" and by his appeal to observation in his account of human nature and the derived social relations, Witherspoon locates himself well within the mainstream of eighteenth-century efforts to construct a science of man.

Yet he cannot go the whole way with the empiricists, restrained, we suspect, because of the importance to him and to American political thinkers of the Lockean views of natural law in the defense of the Revolution. He cuts through a great deal of "violent and unnecessary controversy" about the nature of the social contract and a precivil society, since the important matter is that we cannot think of society as a voluntary compact without supposing a difference in the rights instituted by the contract and those preexisting it. It is thus unnecessary to raise the question of the historical existence of the contract and prepolitical society. In any case, the contractual basis of established society is evident. Society is the association or compact to abridge some of men's natural rights in order to have the strength of the larger unity, thus protecting the remaining rights. Consent is central to the principles of union as was well enough illustrated in the emergence of a United States. He clearly has in mind the American experience as he writes that consent or contract of union implies the consent of the individual to be a member of that society as well as to the plan of government. It further implies the mutual agreement between subject and ruler and the relation of protection and subjection. There is an important exception: even after consent, recall is permissible if the laws "are found to be pernicious and destructive of the ends of the union, [then] they may certainly break up the society, recall the obligation, and resettle the whole upon a better footing." And again, though departing somewhat from the natural rights conceptions, he cannot go all the way with the utilitarian thesis in the justification of civil liberty, for the advantage of civil liberty need not lie in its furtherance of personal happiness or virtue, or even in its contribution to good government; but it lies chiefly in that it promotes industry and thereby, indirectly, happiness of a kind, and produces every latent quality and improves the human mind. "Liberty is the nurse of riches, literature and heroism."

The *Lectures* appear to have formed the base of Witherspoon's course in moral philosophy from the beginning of his teaching. Although not published until 1800 (after his death and even then against his expressed wish), they were carried as manuscript notes southward to Virginia and the Carolinas, and westward through Pennsylvania and Kentucky. They were used in courses taught by his students and then by students of their students. They were the bearers of Presbyterian influence in the enormous network of Presbyterian-dominated colleges that sprang up in the next four decades. Indeed, their influence went far beyond that in the Middle and Southern states, since they were the most attractive among American texts, which at that time included only Thomas Clap's *Essay on the Nature and Foundations of Moral Virtue and Obligation* (1765), and Johnson's *Ethica* (1746), both of which were narrowly designed.

If the lectures tended to turn philosophy away from New England thought in ways that must have astonished the New Side contingent, his other philosophic teachings must further have reinforced both this direction and their astonishment. Yet in this connection Witherspoon himself must have been surprised when he arrived at Princeton at the range of philosophic commitment to be found on the campus. He surely foresaw the impact of atheism, materialism, and deism which was emanating from the scientists in Philadelphia and New York. He may even have been prepared for the "moderate" Hutchesonianism of Alison and his protégés Ewing, Andrews, and Matthew Wilson, the last of whom Witherspoon blasted in the *Pennsylvania Magazine*.[20] But Witherspoon must have been amazed to find the Berkeleyan-like idealistic interpretation of Locke's philosophy so deeply entrenched among the students and teachers at Princeton. The center of this philosophy seems to have been among the New England tutors—especially Joseph Perriam—but it included such students as Samuel Stanhope Smith and Frederick Beasley. The source of this idealism is rather obscure; it may have been derived from Samuel Johnson's *Elementa Philosophica* which was used as a text at Columbia, Pennsylvania, and William and Mary. Perhaps it came quite directly from the reading of Berkeley, for his halfway step toward idealism in *The New Theory of Vision* was widely circulated at Philadelphia, and William Smith, provost of the University of Pennsylvania, had prepared the London edition of Berkeley's works at midcentury. Jonathan Edwards was too briefly at Princeton to give his idealistic system much currency there, and in any case the idealistic part of his philosophy was not generally known until the 1820s. It is thus unlikely that even Jonathan Edwards, Jr., who was appointed at Princeton in 1767, was a purveyor of his father's idealism to the Princeton group. In any case, Ashbel Green and Frederick Beasley both report that there were adherents of this idealism waiting eagerly to proselytize and to confound the Scotsman on his arrival.

Witherspoon not only excised this idealism almost immediately upon his arrival but substituted for it the realism which was to become the signature of Princeton even beyond the time of McCosh. Witherspoon's realistic loyalties were explicit enough, and although he never wrote a full exposition of his position, it can be reconstructed from his critique of Matthew Wilson and from an early essay in the *Scots Magazine*.[21] The central issue posed in the latter is a perfectly genuine one even today: can the testimony of the unaided senses be reliable when experience by way of scientific instruments gives conflicting sensible evidence?

Witherspoon enters obliquely on this problem by way of challenge and criticism of an essay (of Kames?) which held that the feeling of freedom which we all enjoy is delusive and can be shown philosophically to be so. Kames supports his position by an analogical argument from the deceitfulness of the senses, especially sight, as is shown for example in the disparity between judgments that a surface is smooth when viewed by natural sight while a microscope may show it (truly) to be rough and full of holes. Witherspoon, showing that he had read both the early and late Berkeley, counters with an analysis of secondary qualities, such as sweetness, hardness, color, and heat. Are such qualities to be said to lie in the object or are we to say that the object has the power or aptness to raise these sensations in us? The first choice is manifestly false; no one is deluded into saying that the fire feels the heat or has the sensation. Witherspoon then goes on to defend the second option. To face the problems caused by an apparent smoothness of the table which is revealed as uneven by the microscope, care has to be taken to distinguish just what our senses (truly) provide from what we infer, and to see just what expectations in the way of information are legitimate.

In the first place the senses could scarcely be said to be deceitful if they failed to give us all information truthfully and immediately; deceit only arises when the contrary is put in its place. Sight cannot be said to be deceitful if finer sensibilities would reveal the microscopic roughness, any more than we say of two ordinary listeners that they have been deceived by their hearing when an especially keen observer (or one using an amplifier) detects noises which they have not heard. Both the noise heard or the surface seen naturally and those detected with amplifiers and magnification are true, since these judgments like judgments of littleness and greatness are relative to persons and circumstances, and can be seen to be so when the context of judgment is included in the report.

Witherspoon emphasizes that vision is a special case—most of the illusions and paradoxes generally cited depend on vision in one way or another, as for example the stick which looks bent in water but is straight to touch, or when we judge the moon to be larger than an orange although the images must be equivalent on the retina. We are much quicker to speak of deceit with respect to vision than in cases of taste or sound, when we merely say that the object is not as it appears to be. This brings him to the question of what are the proper primary materials of vision with respect to which it may be taken to be veridical; and he appeals to a Berkeleyan-like view as probable that color and shape are genuine sense materials, while judgments of magnitude, distance, and size are inferred from experiences provided by several senses.

Witherspoon then considers the relation between beliefs and action generally, with particular reference to the kind of effects which would follow for conduct if it were true that the feeling of liberty is delusive. The original essayist had held that philosophers can very well acquiesce in the necessitarian doctrines and yet be responsible persons.

Witherspoon holds that there is no such easy relation between sensation, knowledge, and belief. There are, of course, philosophic discoveries, say about optics and visual angles, which do not contradict what is given in sensation; but in cases where a disparity is discovered, philosophers no less than ordinary men still guide their conduct by their belief. Witherspoon adds the distinctively modern note, that knowledge or belief can even alter the sensible appearance; e.g., on first experience we may be most impressed by the beauty of a rattlesnake, but when we come to know its viciousness, that first impression may be obscured; similarly, a person of great comeliness, when revealed as despicable, may cease to appear beautiful. It is the fact of belief, not the manner in which it was learned, that is determinative. Even this fragment of philosophic argument is sufficient to show Witherspoon's realistic stance; with its concerns about perceptual error, the relation of scientific description to ordinary experience, of scientific accounts of perception to phenomenal experience, and the issue of belief in action, it marks a decisive turning away from New England's problems toward those even then under discussion by the materialists and the physicians of Philadelphia.

Princeton after Witherspoon

Witherspoon's successor as professor of philosophy and eventually as president was his son-in-law, S. Stanhope Smith, the same whom Ashbel Green reports as having recanted his idealism under Witherspoon's pressure. Indeed, since Witherspoon must have been absent from the college a good deal of the time, it is plausible that many of the innovations at Princeton were in large measure inaugurated by Smith, or at least that they were implemented by him. Although a man of prestige in intellectual circles, Smith never got, and doubtless did not want, the kind of authority that Witherspoon had with the Synod and the trustees. In fact, even when he became president, he could not get them to support his liberal experiments with the curriculum, which included among other things the training of nondegree candidates in the natural sciences and the general effort to replace the traditional classics by a stronger program in natural philosophy.

Smith was a man of very special talents. His lectures on moral philosophy[22] are much fuller than Witherspoon's, though roughly in the same pattern; they show a sophisticated contact with the latest discussions—a theme to be considered in the next chapter. But Smith labored under heavy academic cargo; perhaps he was suspect because of his earlier idealism, certainly he was suspect for his emphasis on science by those who feared Princeton's growing secularism. In any case, he was often the target of the charge of Socinianism. Perhaps there were darker reasons at work, for while Smith was still just a professor of philosophy, the notes of a student in his class were subpoenaed by the trustees and surveyed by Ashbel Green for infidelity. There was enough Arianism and liberal philosophy that the taint was never thoroughly erased. Smith defended himself against the only sharp attack—that directed against his claim that polygamy could be moral. He pointed out that polygamy must be justified in some social contexts, since after all such patriarchs as Moses were deeply committed to the habit. What is interesting about this episode is less the change in Witherspoonian climate than the fact that Smith's appeal to the Old Testament was as much a sociological appeal to a cultural context as to the moral authority derivable from the Scriptures.

Smith's experience was in the end disastrous for himself, for Princeton, and perhaps even for the course of philosophy in America. Smith's presidency found the students, accustomed no doubt to a tradition of freedom left over from the Revolution, restive under discipline. There were riots and rebellions and ultimately a fire which Smith suspected the students had set. Under excuse of these difficulties, ultraconservatives, led by Samuel Miller and Ashbel Green, established a seminary for the divinity students, sucking from the college all the advantages and offering nothing in the way of compensation. The resignation of Smith was ultimately forced, and Ashbel Green was neatly engineered by Miller into the presidency.

Ashbel Green was the conversional type even while he was a student. His aim was to return the college to piety and to a classic curriculum stripped almost altogether of the emphasis on science and natural philosophy. This had become even more imperative now because (in his view) Pennsylvania and William and Mary had joined Harvard as dens of infidelity, and Jefferson's atheistic University of Virginia was seducing Princeton's potential Southern students. Green's term was one of increasing catastrophe; not only was philosophy eclipsed by religion but the college was willingly subordinated to the seminary. (One of the reasons why the idealistic episode at Princeton is obscure is that it is filtered through the bias of Green's memoirs, which in any case were written when he was a very old man.)

Between Green and McCosh there were several other administrations all beleaguered by the tragedy of the subordination of college to seminary interests, of increasing financial trouble, of another disastrous fire, and student riots and unrest. Even so the faculty began its slow return to respectability in number and stature. The amazingly versatile Vethake, who was to teach moral philosophy, mathematics, chemistry, natural philosophy, and economics in half a dozen colleges, was appointed in philosophy. Guyot took the chair in geology, and then Joseph Henry replaced Vethake in natural philosophy, bringing great fame to Princeton's science. Of course all were qualified as to faith (the lines were strictly drawn and by this time even a Congregationalist was suspect), but the strengthening of the scientific faculty was to intensify concerns about the relation of science and philosophy to religion. Proposals for chairs to reconcile science and revelation vied with those to apply science to industry, with the former winning out. Charles Woodruff Shields, an apparently "safe" minister, was appointed in 1866 expressly to harmonize religion and science. But even his optimism about defining limits for science immediately came under fire by the trustees as having conceded too much to science.

However the greatest tragedy of all for Princeton was the growing and bitter division in the country that culminated in the Civil War. As differences among Old and New Lights in New England healed, New England students attended colleges in the North and Princeton came to rely more and more on the South to complement its student body. As feelings rose in the country, they were mirrored in microcosm in the college. Northern and Southern Presbyterians broke apart and the faculty, generally Union in feeling, lost the support of the Southerners but never worked up sufficient moral indignation to woo the abolitionists. The tragedy was capped by the war itself.

McCosh Again

In this dark moment, Princeton once again turned to Scotland to find a leader of Scottish persuasion in philosophy, conservative in religion, and democratic in social policy. James McCosh's qualifications were not at all unlike those of Witherspoon, given the passing of a century.

McCosh's tolerance for evolution must have been as much a surprise to the trustees as had been Witherspoon's American Moderatism. But at least they were aware of his place in the inner circle of those leading the exodus from the Scottish Established Church into the Free Church, under Thomas Chalmers (1780-1847). Chalmers was the second of McCosh's famous teachers at Edinburgh. We have already seen how, with Hutcheson, Moderatism had replaced Conservativism in Scottish universities. In turn it was challenged by Chalmers, with McCosh assisting. The reawakening of religious evangelicism was supported with an awareness of the social evils which had resulted from the industrial and commercial revolution. Government and Established Church were responding not at all. In England Bentham's early efforts were directed toward legislative reform; but Chalmers, harking back to the Reformation, saw in the existing parochial structure the potential to carry out the needed reforms; after all not merely an economic but a spiritual reform had to be effected. What was needed was a reawakening of the church, with considerable support from the government, and a moral awakening that would generate a change of habits among the whole population (but of course especially among the poor). Poverty is not the mere lack of funds; it is a complex of inadequate or inequitable laws, of weak moral habits, of social and economic dislocation, and, above all, a failure on the part of the community to accept responsibility and leadership. Chalmers actually put his plan into work in 1822, replacing compulsory taxation by voluntary contribution, districting the parish so that each case could literally be examined individually. He established a kind of job corps, ferreting out opportunities and providing relevant vocational preparation. His work on *Political Economy in Connection with the Moral State and Moral Prospects of Society* (1832), backed up as it was by practical illustration tempered with humanitarianism, had an enormous influence in this country.

But the Scottish government was scarcely prepared to support the needed expansion nor did it wish either to increase the political power of the church, and Chalmers saw in the end that he would not get the required support. In counteraction the government encroached further and further on church jurisdiction in spiritual and ecclesiastical matters, McCosh followed Chalmers, indeed sometimes led, in the legal issues. He saw earlier than Chalmers that secession from the Established Church would be necessary if it were to be truly democratic and popular. These ideas of a democratic and popular church, of a church responsible for and to education, McCosh brought to this country. And it is the larger sphere of education and social concerns that provides the background for his demand that American education and philosophy be socially relevant and take shape in interaction with the particular cultural needs and context of America. McCosh truly belongs to the group—Eliot of Harvard, White of Cornell, Gilman of Johns Hopkins, and Harper of Chicago—who ushered in a new era of higher education in America.

3. *Scottish Originals* [23]

While McCosh's prestige doubtless helped make his version of Realism authoritative—and, as noted earlier, he was in the thick of the controversy between the Realists and John Stuart Mill—and made his book, *The Scottish Philosophy*, largely responsible for the present reputation (or lack of one) of Common Sense, still it did not make his position sound nor his review of the school insightful. We need now to turn to the originals for a more reliable account. Once so important a part even of the European intellectual scene, Scottish Common Sense Realism suffered mortal blows at the hands of empiricists led by Mill as well as by the determined British idealists of the mid- and later nineteenth century. But these opposing schools of British philosophy are by no means without family attachments to the philosophers of Edinburgh, Glasgow, and Aberdeen; and the mass of unfilial attacks has succeeded, abetted by such writers as McCosh, in obscuring the real sophistication of the problems of the Scots. It is as a prelude to the further investigation of realism in America that we need to go back to the detail of their works with an eye to the now-forgotten subtlety which once impressed American readers. There is tough going ahead, but even such bare detail as is offered here was woven into the fabric of American thinking, while familiarity with it was presupposed by every American writer until the time of William James.

The fact of Scottish influence in America is not at issue. Reid and Stewart, Brown and Hamilton, and the lesser lights Beattie and Oswald were read, edited, abridged, and cited from one end of this country to the other. Copies of British or American (sometimes pirated) editions were to be found in the private libraries of Jefferson and Rush, in subscription libraries like the Farmers' Library, in Philadelphia's Logan Library, and of course in the college libraries. Of enormous influence also were the various editions of the Scottish-inspired *Encyclopaedia Britannica*; the extended Supplements of the earlier editions were used as texts in subjects as varied as metaphysics and economics. The problems we are about to discuss were taken seriously by American readers, and the very difficulties with which we are about to struggle are just those that once worried college student and professor.

We plan to locate Scottish realism within British empiricism generally, and then to examine some phases of the arguments of Reid, Stewart, and Brown that were of special influence in America.[23] A hobnailed sketch of Scottish Common Sense Realism begins with Locke's empiricism and his effort to account for all knowledge from sensible experience: "Not an idea is to be found in the mind but what has an origin in sensation." Mind is, of course, the famous "blank tablet," which receives impressions from without. The ideal thesis may be put as follows:

Since the mind, in all its thoughts and reasonings, has no other immediate object but its own ideas, . . . it is evident that our knowledge is only conversant about them.[24]

Now as we have seen above, various kinds of ideas stand in different relations to external stimuli. There are "powers in the objects" which give rise to such ideas as solidity and extension and other primary qualities; in this case our ideas may truly be said to represent these characteristics of the object as they really are. There are also secondary qualities, or powers in the object to produce in us sensations such as those of sound and smell, color and taste, which depend on the perceiver and cannot be said to resemble the qualities in the object. Of the nature of the substance which is said to support these qualities we know nothing at all. Locke does not appear to have doubted that we do have an idea of the self which is known intuitively and of God which can be demonstrated. Locke also appeals weakly, in a later edition of the *Essay*, to laws of simultaneous association.

Berkeley, of course, added his own immensely more sophisticated account of association—showing how, by successive association, sensations or ideas literally become significant, i.e., become signs of future sensations. The relation between signs and their signification is arbitrary, at least in that they are related neither by logical necessity nor causally. Were it not for the benevolence of God who guarantees the order and coherence of ideas, we should not be able to regulate our actions nor attain what is necessary for our preservation and well-being. But Berkeley goes right to the heart of a difficulty in Locke's philosophy, for if all knowledge is to be accounted for in terms of experience, then the distinction between primary and secondary qualities is illegitimate, for the distinction itself has no original in experience. Two reductions are possible: All qualities are primary, i.e., are like those in the object; or all qualities are secondary ones. Berkeley opts for the latter, and in his headlong course toward idealism he gives an account even of space and extension in terms of association of sensations of touch and vision. Berkeley not only restricted ideas to those of secondary qualities, but then went ahead to show that we can do without an external world of material objects existing separately from our perceptions. Yet dispensing with an independently existing world is easier for Bishop Berkeley than dispensing with God or the self which, while not ideas, are notions.

Hume, in his turn, presses the same kind of analysis against Berkeley's spiritual substances, God and the self. In one fell swoop he shows that we have no experience of the self save as a congeries or bundle of impressions; nor any experience of a God who stands as a guarantor of the sign-meaning relation and of the orderliness of our world. Hume caps his skeptical philosophy by arguing that causation, taken as *necessary* connection between events, is no more than a persistent human prejudice based on habit and habitual expectation. There is no guarantee of an order in experience by which past experiences serve as certain clues for what the future will bring. It goes without saying that evidence for an external world is inaccessible through impressions; belief in the externality of objects is merely related to the "vividness" of our impressions.

Common Sense Realism, as too often described, merely refuses the Berkeleyan move and takes the first reduction. The external world is secured by fiat; immaterialism is repudiated by "common sense," for we perceive (at least some properties of) the extramental world directly and veridically. The reality of the self is likewise protected from Hume's agnosticism by making the assertion of its existence a self-evident truth. The reliability of experience and the uniformity of the world's operations are as self-evident as the reality of God. Now perhaps this is a fair statement of the views of some of the Scottish realists, say, for example, Beattie and Oswald; and it even approaches a description of those of McCosh; but the label "Common Sense Realism" also covers more sophisticated views which are appreciative of the power of Locke, Berkeley, and Hume. These latter offer sounder arguments that take apart sensation and perception, that reconsider the doctrine of the association of ideas both in the light of emotional associations and in the light of undoubted facts of planning and purposive behavior.

In contrast to Locke, the Scottish realists developed the notion of the self as active in perception, even though they still considered themselves to be Lockeans. They learned a serious lesson from Berkeley, too—not so much the already familiar Berkeley of the *Principles*, with which Samuel Johnson worked, as the quasi-realistic Berkeley of *The New Theory of Vision*. They took their fellow countryman, Hume, even more to heart: they understood well the limits of empirical knowledge, the uncertainties involved in projecting past regularities into the future, the problems besetting the notion of a self identical through change. They examined Hume's assumption, asking when doubt qualifies as significant doubt. Believing that man is somehow competent to behave in and with nature, and having relieved themselves—at least to their own satisfaction—of Hume's crippling skepticism regarding induction, they even began to develop rudimentary canons of induction in their search for a logic of discovery and an empirical method.

As a matter of fact, they thought their employment of the method of Bacon, Newton, and Locke—the process of scientific induction—was truer to the spirit of empiricism than Hume's debilitating doubts. They were, in the main, more sensitive than Hume had been to the philosophical claims of mathematics on the one hand, and to the relevance of medicine, physiology, and chemistry to philosophy on the other. At a moment when the vision of scientific progress had captured the minds of intellectuals, it seemed that Hume had challenged the very possibility of science. The Scots believed that they could vindicate the claims of science and the Newtonian model and extend it fruitfully to the study of man. Theirs was a sort of extended dialogue with Hume, for they shared much with him.

Hume, as well as they, was a product of the Scottish Enlightenment and its universities. Both were indebted to Hutcheson's encompassing view of man, and both had strong connections with the broad empiricism that developed in France and England during the late eighteenth and early nineteenth centuries.

The particular efforts of the Scots to cope with Humean problems led them down a progressively idealistic path which terminated in the philosophy of Sir William Hamilton (1791-1856), who may be regarded either as the last Scottish realist or as the transitional thinker who begins British Neo-Hegelian Idealism. In America a roughly similar development ended not in Hegelian Idealism, but in specifically native variants: Transcendentalism, Roycean Idealism, and St. Louis Hegelianism. Yet we shall want to show that the Scottish philosophy in America also gave shape to pragmatism.

It was not only in America that the Scots left their mark; Italy, e.g., had its Rosmini who interacted with Realism and who appears in another American connection, namely with the St. Louis Hegelians. In France, through Royer-Collard, Reid's philosophy became the quasi-official weapon in the battle against sensationalism; Jouffroy, Prévost, and Cousin not only rest on foundations laid by Reid and Stewart, but also return that inspiration at secondhand to the American Transcendentalists.

Thomas Reid (1710-1796) rather than Hutcheson is considered to have begun Scottish philosophy in its narrower sense. A modest man, a Moderate in the university disputes, Reid had been educated for the Presbyterian ministry and was well prepared in philosophy under Turnbull and in mathematics with Maclaurin. Thus he had direct access to the post-Newtonian "new philosophy," and with other members of the "wise clan" he would pass the long northern evenings in arguing the modern trends, Edwards's view of will, and Butler's *Analysis*. Reid began by considering himself a thoroughgoing Berkeleyan. He knew that philosopher principally from *The New Theory of Vision*, and seems to have known Locke only via a Berkeleyan interpretation. In 1739 Reid received an early copy of Hume's *Treatise*, the work which disappointed its young author by falling "stillborn from the press." Hume later rewrote it, with considerable revisions, as the *Inquiry* (1762), but Reid appreciated from the beginning those aspects of Humean skepticism which were to prove the bane of empiricism in the subsequent history of philosophy.

Reid tells how he rushed home to read, and he must have been struck by such as the following passages in the *Treatise*:

On the ideal hypothesis:

Now since nothing is ever present to the mind but perceptions, and since all ideas are derived from something antecedently present to the mind; it follows, that 'tis impossible for us so much as to conceive or form an idea of any thing specifically different from ideas and impressions. Let us fix our attention out of ourselves as much as possible: Let us chase our imagination to the heavens, or to the utmost limits of the universe; we never really advance a step beyond ourselves, nor can conceive any kind of existence, but those perceptions, which have appeared in that narrow compass. This is the universe of the imagination, nor have we any idea but what is there produced.[25]

On cause and effect:

When I examine with the utmost accuracy those objects, which are commonly denominated causes and effects, I find, in considering a single instance, that the one object is precedent and contiguous to the other; and in enlarging my view to consider several instances, I find only, that like objects are constantly placed in like relations of succession and continuity. Again, when I consider the influence of this constant conjunction, I perceive, that such a relation can never be an object of reasoning, and can never operate upon the mind, but by means of custom, which determines the imagination to make a transition from the idea of one object to that of its usual attendant, and from the impression of one to a more lively idea of the other.[26]

On induction:

Thus not only reason fails us in the discovery of the *ultimate connexion* of causes and effects, but even after experience has informed us of their *constant conjunction*, 'tis impossible for us to satisfy ourselves by our reason, why we should extend that experience beyond those particular instances, which have fallen under our observation. We suppose, but are never able to prove, that there must be a resemblance betwixt those objects, of which we have had experience, and those which lie beyond the reach of our discovery.[27]

On the self and mind:

The mind is a kind of theatre, where several perceptions successively make their appearance; pass, re-pass, glide away, and mingle in an infinite variety of postures and situations. There is properly no *simplicity* in it at one time, no *identity* in different; whatever natural propension we may have to imagine that simplicity and identity. The comparison of the theatre must not mislead us. They are the successive perceptions only, that constitute the mind; nor have we the most distant notion of the place, where these scenes are represented, or of the materials, of which it is composed.[28]

As Reid took the measure of these paragraphs they threatened the very foundations of empirical science by their challenge to the validity of knowledge: not only was there no external world (this having been reduced to impressions), but the very interpretation of phenomena was reduced to merely psychological relations. As if that were not disturbing enough, the same arguments weaken the surety of self-identity as well as the existence of others. Reid saw that these were not only Hume's conclusions, but also that they were the inevitable results of Locke's philosophy, as shaped by Berkeley and inherited by Hume. Reid took on the task, then, of rethinking the assumptions that underlay their position and led to conclusions so foreign to common sense. Philosophy's job, he urged, is to take the problems set by commonsense beliefs and to make explicit what is already implicit there. Common sense involves beliefs in an external world, in the existence of the self and of others, and in cause and effect. It also includes beliefs that men behave purposively, that knowledge is cumulative, corrigible, and sufficient to govern actions successfully, and finally that the achievements of science are genuine. This disavowal of speculative philosophy, coupled with the appreciation of science and experience, endeared him to the Americans quite apart from his presumed "safeness" for orthodoxy.

But if Reid is to remain the empiricist he wished to be, he has to steer a narrow course between a reduction of everything to impressions and ideas, as Berkeley and Hume had done, and a materialism such as that of Hartley and Priestley. Given such a setting and task, Reid must have found some consolation in another paragraph that he found in Hume's *Treatise*:

> This sceptical doubt, both with respect to reason and the senses, is a malady, which can never be radically cured, but must return upon us every moment, however we may chase it away, and sometimes may seem entirely free from it. 'Tis impossible upon any system to defend either our understanding or senses; and we but expose them farther when we endeavour to justify them in that manner. As the sceptical doubt arises naturally from a profound and intense reflection on those subjects, it always increases, the farther we carry our reflections, whether in opposition or conformity to it. Carelessness and inattention alone can afford us any remedy. For this reason I rely entirely upon them; and take it for granted, whatever may be the reader's opinion at this present moment, that an hour hence he will be persuaded there is both an external and internal world . . .[29]

Yet it must not be supposed either that the common sense Reid generally promoted meant sound, ordinary, good judgment, gumption, or horse sense; nor that his realism amounted to a bald assertion of the mind-independent existence of an external world and veridical perception of its objects. If we look rather at his defense of common sense as a defense of Newton and Locke, and of the physiology and the chemistry which he saw everywhere developing; and if we remember that Reid essentially called attention to the beliefs men patently have and the laws of thought they must acknowledge, then "common sense" is neither a perplexing nor misleading expression. It is not Reid's job to justify beliefs and laws but to discover and examine them, though such discovery and examination may also be normative. After Locke, Reid was somewhat hesitant about labeling "innate" these beliefs or first principles of common sense, and he is agreed with Locke that there is no content save what experience provides. It is not the content but the operations which are innate. Such operations, unlike Locke's comparing and abstracting, have a heavy role in the structuring of our knowledge and in making learning possible. The laws of these operations are available by observation of behavior and language.

Reid nowhere tries to prove the existence of an external world. Proof as such is impossible, though it may be argued for—since the belief that perception has an external reference, and that the self is distinguished from objects, and objects from qualities, is universal and is reflected in the structure of all languages. Reid's position rests on a sophisticated account of perception, which is to be found in his *Inquiry*, although behind that work as well as the later *Essays* is the same pervasive conviction that the self is active—active in sense perception, active also as a voluntary agent, deliberating, determining means in relations to goals and constructing meaningful patterns in art.

His effort to answer the ideal philosophy by a fuller treatment of perception has a negative or defensive side which is an attack on the copy theory of knowledge and on the adequacy of simple association as the full account of the laws of these operations. On its positive side, he offers a constructional theory of perception directed to the problem of how sensations, which exist in and of themselves, become transformed into the (meaningful) perceptions which carry an outward and objective reference. Now a copy theory lay behind the psychology of the day— mental ideas, an external world, and a representative or a copy relation between them. Berkeley and Hume working in this frame showed that within it the existence of an objective reality independently of our perception could not be established. Their skepticism results from this failure. Reid wanted to restructure the model, to lower the sights as it were, and to rethink the notion of reference and objective world. The objects of our experiences are not ideas; we do not have visual sensations, our perceiving is functionally a seeing of objects; we do not know concepts, our concepts are a knowing of objects. In effect, Reid is objecting to the copy theory both as a model and as an objective. Skepticism and failure are in part occasioned by an unnecessarily high level of aspiration.

This effort to restate the question begins with the criticism of the association of ideas as an adequate account of thought and its sequences. Minimally, such association would not be between ideas of objects, but between objects thought of. To confuse the object of thought and the object thought of (the "psychologists' fallacy" that William James discusses) is the result of an impoverished but economical use of language. There are other deficiencies in the theory of association, most of all, that it simply does not account for deliberation and resolute purpose nor for knowledge as it guides action. But Reid does not mean to deny that lawlike explanations of psychological phenomena are possible; it is only requisite to cast these laws in a new and more comprehensive form.

Reid's effort to answer the ideal philosophy carried him into a constructional theory of perception,[30] to which he joined a weak realism (weak, i.e., in that it plays only a minor, almost nonfunctional role in his philosophy). His problem is how sensations are transformed into meaningful perceptions which carry a belief in a reference to real objects. Reid simply denies that we ever know such loose and relationless elements as Locke's "sensations" or Hume's "impressions." Perception is distinguished from sensation (the latter being essentially a construction of the philosophical psychologist). The ultimate unit of experience or perceptions is judgmental from the start and contains in a rudimentary way the structure of knowledge. Reid calls these perceptions or basic judgments *principles*, and they are cognitive; i.e., they include a belief in the outwardness or externality of an object. The conceptual part is not derived from sensation, but is suggested on the occasion of sensing in such a way as to constitute the necessary conditions of perception. The initial reference is thus an initial part of perception; we are led to believe in the externality by as natural a process as experiencing at all; it is as irresistible as it is universal; it is as immediate and unlearned as it is noninferential. We do not first experience isolated shapes, colors, smells, etc., and then put them together to construct an object. Our experience is of objects from the start. Like James, Reid believes that we really never have experiences of pure sensation, of mere unstructured feeling; a pure sensation is a fiction of the psychologists, an abstraction which helps him in his science and is useful for physiological discourse.

The importance of sensation is as a sign of something external: it conducts us to something in the world. This interpretive or judgmental aspect of sensation passes unnoticed, and it is well nigh impossible—even with conscious effort—to capture the sensation alone. Perhaps a trained artist, for short periods, enjoys something like pure sensation; a landscape painter, e.g., might learn to disregard variations of color and shape in their function as cues for the location and size of objects, and regard them instead as pure aesthetic shapes and hues. In the main, however, this sort of nonsignificatory sensation is beyond us. We experience sensations which act as signs in a natural language, itself structured by rules of grammar which "reside naturally in the mind." Because signification is so immediate, so automatic, we have difficulty in distinguishing the sign from that which it signifies. Consequently, our vocabulary contains no distinguishing terms to carry out the separation—and our philosophical neologisms are cumbersome and frequently ambiguous.

Reid further maintains that secondary qualities are related to "their objects" partly because of pragmatic relations. When a man talks about the smell of a fish, he generally refers to a public and objective quality in the fish. But he has the option of using the same expression to refer to a private experience, i.e., the smell-as-subjective-feeling. The private sensation, of course, is very unlike the smell-in-the-object. We locate the quality (in the fish or in consciousness), according to Reid, as urgency requires: strongly distasteful sensations (which amount to pains or revolting conditions) are likely to be located within us rather than within their external cause.

The sign-signified relations admit of no further explication. Why the smell in the fish should affect us in just the way it does is beyond understanding, but *that* it so affects us is ascertainable by ordinary scientific methods. There are other examples of the sign-relation, e.g., in the language of gesture and expression. Similarly there is a language of art; we do not see lines or hear notes and then proceed to infer some emotion, say grief; the grief is felt directly if it is felt at all. Works of art are meaningful compositions and always carry throughout the signature of the artist, and we may even glimpse in the sublimity of nature the Artist behind it. There is even an important sense in which empirical laws—even those of the highest order—are generalizations of systems of natural signs (as when smoke is a sign of fire). There is nothing in the sign taken merely as experience, which betrays the nature of the thing signified. Nor is the relation causal. Yet this relation, generalized, underlies the entire scientific enterprise. Passing from natural languages (in the sense in which we have used that phrase) to social languages such as English, Reid holds that these latter are but extensions of the former. Indeed the social languages with their conventional character and reference could scarcely have been instituted except for the more basic means of communication.

As if all this were not Jamesian enough (William, of course), Reid emphasized "trains" of association, advances the metaphor to "fountains," and finally adds the flourish of "the stream of thought." Indeed similarities to James are inescapable—from the irresistible reference outward and the personal character of experience (James's fringe) to the emphasis on selectivity and voluntary attention.

Perceptions do not arise merely from a complex of sensations, but gain significance by a kind of creative and immediate synthesis. But meaning and knowledge are always general, and that generality needs to be explored, for perceptions are about particular things. The latter are judgments stating only that such and such is a so-and-so; e.g., that this sugar is white. In every judgment of this form properties or attributes are predicated of a subject. The subject acts like a proper name by denoting the object, and the attributes, like common names—i.e., abstract or general terms which can be predicated of many individuals. The application of the predicate to the subject depends upon the sensations resulting from the object which justify our assertions that the object denoted is an object such that the predicate applies. It is true that what is in perception, what is directly known, is the judgment that the object has the predicate, and that the sensations are not immediately known as such; however, in reflective analysis we can distinguish the role played by the sensations in the process of perception from that of the predicate itself. Thus language mediates between the abstract general conceptions referred to by the predicate and our sensory experience.

What then is the status of such predicates? Reid makes no provisions for universals in the mind, and it would seem that he would be forced into a Berkeleyan sort of nominalism. He distinguishes between perceptions, which are always of particular existents, and conceptions, which are represented by general words and do not entail such existence. Conceptions may, in a given case, fail of application. Conceptions are abstractions that come about through recognition of the sameness or difference of two or more individuals. (Reid nowhere considers the objection to this explanation, viz., that "similarity" itself is the name of a universal.) Thus the expression "white" may apply to various individuals, e.g., sugar, linen, or a cloud. It may even correctly apply to objects such as the abominable snowman—that is to say, to nonexistent objects. It must be, he continues, that we come to know in advance of a judgment that one or another conception is applicable in a given situation. Otherwise we would not even know the meaning of the judgment—a prerequisite for determining its truth-value. On the other hand, conceptions or "categories" emerge only from the activity of judging, and are modified by their utility. Conceptions and judgments thus evolve mutually. Conceptions are neither extramental universals, nor universals within the mind. Any conception consists in some particular act of conceiving. "To conceive" means to be able to predicate or apply a term unambiguously—to recognize a sameness among individuals. In effect, we possess some sort of criterion of applicability for such terms as "white." Reid narrowly misses being a nominalist, and his brand of conceptualism seems (given our perspective) to be a first step toward a pragmatic theory of meaning. Since he holds that real essence is unknowable, and that conceptions and categories are produced by experience of their social utility, he clearly opens the way for an instrumental theory of knowledge.

In this connection, Reid distinguishes between extension and comprehension. Extension applies to individuals or classes or existents, while comprehension characterizes the predicates (conceptions). The number of attributes truly predicable of a particular is indefinitely large; inclusion of that individual in some more comprehensive class, however, always results in a diminution of those specific predicates which may be truly applied to the class as a whole. Comprehension and extension thus vary inversely. Reid also distinguishes contingent from necessary laws. Necessary laws (e.g., those to be found in mathematics, though not only there) express relations between propositions, the subject and predicate of which are both conceptions and hence devoid of existential commitment. Now the fundamental principles of belief, of common sense, are of both kinds; yet as axioms, the two classes are equally undemonstrable, since all knowledge must begin with something accepted without proof. It must not be thought, however, that the difference is one of degree of certainty: to say that something is probable may, in ordinary language, be contrasted with certainty; but when a philosopher uses "probable," he does not intend to cast doubt on its certainty, nor even to refer to a degree of evidence, but rather to indicate a manner by which something is evidenced, or a kind of evidence. It is not less certain that Rome is the capital of Italy than that a certain theorem in Euclid is true: they both rest ultimately on undemonstrable principles. What is different is their manner of proof; the latter is merely a relation between conceptions, while the former utilizes conceptions, perceptions, and memory.

Reid seems to be attempting an answer to Hume's skepticism about causation by appealing to induction and probability. He seems to be grappling with a relation between some sort of mathematical probability and a priori assumptions about the warrant which accumulated experience and a series of trials will give. One of his fundamental contingent principles of common sense is: that the future will probably resemble the past. He seems to mean by this that there is a warrant derived from common sense that nature is interpretable and that uniformities can be sought out with profit. "It will rain tomorrow" has some probability, relative to its nonoccurrence, and we can be certain that it has that probability. This is no head-on confrontation with Hume over the subject of causality, but an attempt to bring probability (which is, in some sense, a priori) into contact with experience and the study of actual events. Naturally Reid agrees with Hume that there is no way of demonstrating that the future will be like the past; this is just the reason that Reid refers the belief in the uniformity of nature to a fundamental human intuition or belief. This intuition does not specify any particular instance of uniformity; it only allows us to be certain that some uniformity is observable. What is at stake here is not merely the fact that one's knowledge is cumulative but rather the very possibility for an inductive method in science, which possibility Hume challenged. This assumption of uniformities in nature is constitutive of any inquiry, including Hume's own inquiry. Reid does not settle all the Humean doubts, but in the end he seems to be in much the same position as Russell (at least the Russell of 1945):

what . . . [Hume's] arguments prove—and I do not think the proof can be controverted—is that induction is an independent logical principle, incapable of being inferred either from experience or from other logical principles, and that without this principle science is impossible.[31]

Reid lists quite a number of these fundamental axioms, and this brought down on his head the criticisms of Priestley and others that anything could by this procedure be promoted into an unassailable verity—and in a sense they are miscellaneous and vulnerable. Among the necessary principles are to be found logical axioms such as: "Any contexture of words which does not make a proposition is neither true nor false." Among the contingent principles we find such interesting and controversial theses as: "the thoughts of which I am conscious are mine; I have a personal identity and continued existence over time; we have some degree of power over our actions and the determinations of our will." (*Vide* Wm. James.) These, again, are not demonstrable; but just as the externality of objects was reflected in the grammatical distinction between subject and predicate, so the difference between the perceiver and the object perceived is equally given in experience and reflected in universal syntax.

There is much more that could be said about Reid's analysis of self, but Brown's slightly more sophisticated version seems to have been more influential in America. What is of interest here is the connection of the analysis of the self with Reid's views about activity, causality, and responsibility. Just as Reid had earlier sought to expose the ambiguity in "idea," "probability," "smell," and a host of other terms, he now wishes to show that in "cause" too there lurks a whole set of diverse relations. When "law" is applied without care to the physical order as well as to the moral and political one, confusion results. Primitive animism interpreted the relations of the natural order in terms appropriate to human agency—the tree was moved by its titular spirit; a reverse but equally illegitimate reduction occurs when, in modern times, we take as the paradigm of all causation the relations in the material order. Of course a good bit of our behavior is explicable in causal terms, but such explanation still leaves untouched the patent facts of our translation of sensible and physiological stimuli into meaningful perceptions and awareness. More importantly here, that account of cause leaves unexplained how plans are deliberately chosen and executed; how such meaningful patterns of relations are developed as in a painting or in a melody. In other words, relations of agency-act, designer-system, producer-product must all be distinguished from mechanical cause; they are phenomena of a different order and involve different relations.

The provision for added dimensions to causality is a first step in Reid's voluntarism—and he goes the whole way: we are not only free to do what we will, but the power or freedom to will is ours. The power of agency (and especially moral agency and accountability) is distinctively human, having an experiential base. Reid does not believe this dimension makes human deliberations unapproachable for psychology; on the contrary, what we need are fuller new laws adequate to the phenomena. Associative laws, though they do apply, are insufficient. Man is a natural being in the world of nature; just as we need knowledge of the physical world to bend it to our purposes and make it serve our ends, at the very least we require knowledge of those very interests and purposes in some advanced and sophisticated psychology, which is more than a mere department of physics or astronomy.

Reid's discussion of the active powers and his voluntarism formed part of the lectures which he delivered toward the end of his career, when the amiable protagonist Hume had been replaced by the pugnacious Dr. Priestley. Reid had not answered Priestley's early *Examination* (1774),[32] but he did come to grips with that author's materialism and determinism. When Priestley came to America, he brought this polemic with him, though the debate with the realists here was considerably muted, doubtless partly because Jefferson had sympathies with both sides. As a matter of fact, Reid found an ally in Richard Price, Priestley's friend and coreligionist. Price and Reid both denied the adequacy of the utilitarian reduction of morality to mere happiness, and of mental phenomena to association; both add the activity of the moral agent in a normative or regulative conscience, making duty the peer of happiness. Reid and Price, allied in moral opinions with Butler, were enormously influential in New England as regards these matters, although it was Price, through his intimacy with Channing, who touched the development of Unitarianism, while Reid was left in the common pool as a resource for the orthodox and the unorthodox alike. Reid's views on moral matters did not have the same long-range impact on ethical theory that his distinction between perception and conception had for psychology; but considering the present situation, the following comment on social justice is arresting:

> What was said above, of the natural right every man has to acquire permanent property, and to dispose of it, must be understood with this condition, That no other man be thereby deprived of the necessary means of life. The right of an innocent man to the necessaries of life, is, in its nature, superior to that which the rich man has to his riches, even though they be honestly acquired. The use of riches, or permanent property, is to supply future and casual wants, which ought to yield to present and certain necessity.[33]

Dugald Stewart (1753-1828), the successor to Reid as the doyen of the Scottish School, is its unsung hero. McCosh, and following him, most later writers, find Stewart's work but a feeble though more elegant restatement of Reid. Yet Stewart's treatment of the analytic element in Common Sense principles and mathematical truths adds a new perspective that unites him securely with Peirce and C. I. Lewis (and for that matter even Kant, though he confessed he could not read the German metaphysician). This new perspective puts even his psychological discussions in a very different context from that of Reid. Stewart had personal ties with many of the well-known figures of the day. He had studied with Reid in Glasgow and was competent enough to substitute as lecturer in mathematics for his father and in moral philosophy for Adam Ferguson, when the latter served with the unsuccessful Committee on Negotiations with the Colonies. He was ultimately appointed to the chair of moral philosophy at Edinburgh. He was a friend of Hume and of Adam Smith, whose works he edited. A Moderate, his ecclesiastical liberalism was matched by political sympathies for the American and French Revolutionaries which long made him suspect in Britain. Franklin and Benjamin Rush both knew him, while Jefferson drew directly on his philosophy. His elegant lectures attracted a host of American and French students as well as such British notables-to-be as Walter Scott, James Mill, and Thomas Chalmers. Mill later testified that neither Pitt nor Fox, whose "most admired efforts" he had personally enjoyed was "nearly so eloquent." Stewart's influence in America was enormous, at first exceeding that of Reid whose works had been held up by the war. Important for the broader public was his plan of extended Supplements that converted the *Encyclopaedia Britannica* from a brief work "by two gentlemen of Edinburgh" into a British counterpart of the French *Encyclopédie*. The *Britannica* of course had great currency in America, and American editions were quickly forthcoming. His complete works were published in Boston immediately following his death, and suffered the usual abridgments, which came to be used as texts along with the originals in many colleges. More than twenty years elapsed between the first volume of his *Elements of the Philosophy of the Human Mind* (1792) and the second volume, and the intervening years took him ever further from Reid toward Kantian-like problems. The following discussion depends on his later volume, the American edition of 1829, in company with its (American) commentaries, especially the abridgment by James Walker (of Harvard).

Even from the start, Stewart differed from Reid by refining commonsense principles in ways that reflect his interest in mathematics, formal languages, and linguistics, topics which were at that time also interesting the French. Doubtless piqued by Priestley's and Kant's much-publicized criticism of realism as tantamount to an appeal to vulgar common sense, Stewart makes it altogether clear that common sense refers to processes which are the necessary condition of all reasoning, argument, and inquiry. They might even be called rational "intuitions" after the fashion of the Cambridge Platonists and Price if taken dynamically, i.e., as organizing principles native to the mind as it confronts experience. Stewart's connection with Rationalism is thus intimate and sympathetic; he was attempting to utilize Leibniz's mathematical philosophy in the context of a strong empiricism. With Leibniz he shares not only the expectation that the universal language of arithmetic may one day provide a kind of algebraic instrument or calculus for a formal solution of many problems, but also the view that mathematical reasoning furnishes the paradigm for the kind of universality and necessity which is so often the stepchild of empiricism. Stewart's own work does much to bring together mathematics, logic, and language, although he is careful also to consider the limitations of such a model for all knowledge.

Within mathematics, Stewart distinguishes form from content. The formal component he calls "elements," more or less after Euclid; but what he is trying to identify are the rules by which we move from suppositions to conclusions, i.e., to make explicit those relations by which a conclusion follows necessarily from its premises. Such rules, guiding transformations within a system, are altogether barren; purely formal, they guarantee us nothing in the way of actual experience or existence. They are clearly not demonstrable, since any attempt to establish or disprove them must make at least a covert appeal to them. The only authority to which one can appeal, in establishing the validity of these "principles of validity," is common sense, i.e., reason. Such elements are contributions of the human mind, and their universality and utility convince us, if they do not demonstrate, that they are harmonious with the order of nature.

Content (or the *intended* domain) is provided by definitions (which for Stewart include both Euclidean definitions and postulates). In the case of pure mathematics—algebra, geometry, or arithmetic—these definitions are fixed hypothetical objects, e.g., number, length, etc. Conclusions which are validly drawn will be necessary, precisely because these definitions are fixed so as to stand always and unambiguously for the same hypothetical objects. And since such definitions, e.g., that of a triangle, are wholly matters of intellect and not of sense, there is a certain arbitrary or decisional character about the mathematician's definitions, for he may mold them in shape according to his fancy, subject only to the limitation of consistency. For this reason, alternative definitions may be framed, and with them alternative systems. The distinction between postulates and theorems is ultimately the result of a mathematician's definitions. But once again, the validity of the conclusion as well as its necessity does not lie in any correspondence with reality, since no claim is being made for its applicability to experience; and no empirical observation could overturn it since observations are irrelevant. Any domain may be similarly treated; there can be pure morals, economics, or law, beginning with hypothetical definitions. But in each case the yield is never more than hypothetical and not directly informative about this world. Even, as in the case of mechanics where pure theory and application converge and where the deduced expectations are largely fulfilled, experience still can never fully provide the conditions which would allow universal and necessary empirical conclusions.

The practical value—the values in empirical science and in conduct—arises when the definitions are not hypothetical but categorical—i.e., when they are assigned empirical reference, and when the domain of the theory is some aspect of the actual world. This moment of application involves a dramatic and radical shift in the kind of truth or validity involved. The area of the sensible actual circle drawn on the page before me does not entail any necessary relation to its actual circumference. Empirical truths are always probabilistic and contingent. The utility of formal and hypothetical frameworks is obvious, for there we can see the methods of reasoning unencumbered by particular associations; further, the antiseptic frame may expose structural similarities among different domains that the richness and particularity of experience obscure. Such freedom as the definitions allow has its role in the discovery and invention of new theories. Since we cannot interrogate nature empty-handed, we must present her with some hypothesis if she is to teach us anything. Yet the matter is complex, for while empirical hypotheses must begin in sensible experience, in facts and observations, still it is the theory which provides the context in which such observations become meaningful. Theory or hypothesis thus develops hand in hand with sensible observation and fact.

Stewart is further concerned that hypotheses about this world's business be regarded always as provisional; there must be room for correction and even for replacement in the light of further experience. Indeed, since hypotheses are in some sense arbitrary, there may even be rival and equally consistent hypotheses covering a single set of observations. In that case the choice between them will turn (as James and C. I. Lewis, Duhem and Poincaré were afterward to emphasize) on considerations of utility, elegance, and simplicity. Stewart illustrates the point by reference to the time when the Copernican theory was overcoming the Ptolemaic. No difference of observation was in contest; what was at issue was how the world was to be described, and the decision was to choose the simpler of the two theories.

Up to this point, much of Hume's skepticism has been preserved. In Stewart's analysis of contingent truths there are, then, no necessary connections. Preserving Locke's distinction between primary and secondary qualities, he adds a Humean reservation that there is no guarantee whatsoever that the qualities we experience resemble anything. In fact we do not know essences, neither those of mind nor those of matter, but only qualities grouped as defining criteria. Mind is evidenced by such properties as thinking, remembering, perceiving, and conceiving, while matter has the defining attributes of extension and figure. Finally Stewart agrees with Hume that all knowledge begins in sensible experience, though, of course, this is richer than Hume's impressions, for it includes among other things direct experiences of relations. Yet, in contrast to Hume, this does not mean that all knowledge can be adequately analyzed in terms of sensation. The principles of formal reasoning already constitute a case in point; and when one is dealing with the empirical world and science, further laws of human belief become operative. Like the formal rules of inference, these too are not substantive and can provide no premise for material conclusions. Now such laws are not innate ideas, but the principles or rules involved in the exercise of our reasoning, and are constitutive of experience and inquiry. They are natural tendencies to clarify, to order, and to assimilate experience which the theory of the association of ideas inadequately explains.

Having wrested more out of the sensible originals than Locke or Hume, Stewart is now off to the rescue of the objective world, the self, the uniformity of nature, and God, backing his position with a well-seasoned nominalism and psychology. The self, objects, and the rest of the furniture of experience do not arise with a single sensation or perception; they are induced and depend on a cumulative and relational character of sequences of perceptions. Perception alone will not lead to cognitive awareness nor to retention in memory; when we are attending to one thing, attention may raise the threshold of other stimuli as well as repress them, as love heightens music, and attention closes out noise. Attending, of course, is active; it reduces experientially to a felt effort which must be exerted if we are to remember the experience. Attention is also selective and often is the critical factor in recall. As can be seen, this is already something of a challenge to more

mechanical theories of association. Attention and memory are of course ingre-
dients in belief and action; operations which are performed haltingly at first may
drop into involuntary action or habit; while habitual activity, whether it is a matter
of action or thought, may come to appear wholly involuntary because we forget the
early volitional efforts involved in its formation. The transition from voluntary to
habitual activity serves a biological function; it is perfectly clear that if we could
not learn, nor learn to create a stable world, we should be overwhelmed by the
novelty inherent in each situation. These considerations about habit and involuntary action apply equally to reasoning. Often we can assent to a mathematical proof
without demonstration because the pattern of implicit reasoning is already
habitual.

The keystone of Stewart's psychology is the notion of *conception*, or that power
of the mind which enables it to form a notion of an absent *object* of perception or of
a sensation which it has previously felt. An object, as we can see from prior
discussion, is then formed only through the connecting of many conceptions.
Conception presupposes *the ability to abstract*, i.e., to separate from each other
qualities and circumstances which have been perceived in conjunction. This
ability to isolate properties is the groundwork for any learning whatsoever.
Description does not consist in a minute specification of circumstances, but in a
selection of qualities, and when, afterward, we conceive the object, it is merely an
outline or the model of its most important features. Thus description is already a
function of particular interest, attention, taste, and language, and it always
represents the selective and organizing talents of the conceiver. Conception, since
it does not provide a transcript of anything, is even more than perception a product
of human interest and those prefabrications of language and other subtle aspects of
our social environment. Such attributes as we single out, select, or emphasize are
thus in some sense arbitrary and incomplete; we choose these on grounds of utility
and custom.

Conceptions are always particular; general or universal conceptions (ideas)
exist neither in the mind nor out of it. How then account for universals? Stewart
takes the strong position that universals or general ideas are nothing but dispositions to use signs and language in the ordering of experience. Consider how a child
learns. Perhaps he identifies his father as "Papa," and then proceeds to extend that
term to every male he meets. This tendency to spread the domain or extension of a
term to many individuals depends on observed resemblances, but it never eradi-
cates the reference to particulars. Sometimes we substitute, as above, letting a
functionally proper name stand for a class of individuals so that it represents the
class and becomes a common name in use. At other times we reason with general
names or terms, but in either case we are dealing not with ideas but with signs. The
problem of how we come to interpret signs, assign reference and meaning, is then
not an esoteric matter but the inverse of how we use signs and generalize in the first
place. The use of signs allows us readier access through the particulars of

experience—aiding memory and conserving experiences learned individually and culturally. But our reasoning, thus facilitated by signs, never loses its foothold in particulars. The difference between a proper name and a general term is only shown in the use we make of it; the meaning of a general term (as of a particular one) is not constituted by an image but rather by our ability to use it. On demand one can point out instances of the class or give defining criteria in terms of other signs. Language, taken in its broadest sense, is not only helpful in ordering the world; it is essential in mediating between particular experiences and likenesses or dissimilarities. The systematized use of natural or artificial languages liberates us from particular events and objects, and without the algebraic use of language most of our science would have been impossible.

The problems of induction are like those of abstraction and generalization: the way in which we form classes of individuals is as natural an activity as our generalizing. In either case we have to note similarities of different men in the class of "Papas," or the similarity of events that constitutes the subject of our general inductive laws. It may be noted that Stewart, liberated (whether justly or not) from Hume's skepticism regarding induction, is freer to inquire into the character of likenesses between individuals, the degrees in kind of analogy, and structural similarities like those of maps and models—thus setting the stage for Mill's canons of induction.

For Stewart, the science of the mind, then, is an extension of experimental philosophy. Just as Newton said, we know neither the essence of the objects of the external world, nor that of the mind. The correlations may be investigated empirically but we can never penetrate to ultimate causes—e.g., the relation between sensation and perception, between psychology and physiology. This must remain forever unknowable. This fact, however, no more debilitates our mental science than Newton's admitted ignorance of the cause of gravity hampered him in formulating its laws. As a materialist and an immaterialist may have the same opinions about physics, so they may equally work with the mind. What we know are both ends of a process: we know the fact that external objects produce impressions on sense organs, and that these are followed by a perception of the existence of the qualities of the body by which the impressions are made. It is beyond the reach of philosophy to answer the *why* of the mind-body problem; and attempts either to materialize or to mentalize all the data of perception must remain abortive.

Stewart's work seems to have entered even more than Reid's into the texture of American thinking. Walker and Bowen at Harvard, Porter at Yale, and S. S. Smith at Princeton, not to miss Jefferson and Thomas Cooper, preserved substantive insights from Stewart which do not even figure in McCosh's account. *The Scottish Philosophy* ignores virtually everything which ties Stewart to pragmatism—from his instrumental view of knowledge to the determining force of interest, choice, and purpose in the building of a stable world and reliable expectations.

The third of the realists of importance to the American themes we are recounting was Thomas Brown (1778-1820). He was something of a maverick and his thoroughly naturalistic approach joins the Hartley-Priestley tradition to the later associationism of Bain and the Mills, as John Stuart Mill claimed. Indeed his whole approach has something in common with that of James's *Psychology*; from moments of excellent prose to the emphases on self-activity and on the flow of experience, and even to agonizing over the relation between physiology and psychology. This resemblance to James reveals Brown's affinities with the Scottish realist tradition. He accepts their problems as his own, attempting a reply to Hume which emphasizes the dynamics and the continuity of experience. Like the realists from Hutcheson to Stewart, he enriches the sensitivities and talents of human nature, and agrees with them that the theory of the association of ideas (at least as it had been discussed at that date) is insufficient to account for the palpable features of experience. Like them, too, he attempts to establish a permanently existing world, and to apply a Newtonian method to psychology; but Brown's "Newtonian model" was much more a matter of chemistry than of celestial mechanics.

Brown was educated at Edinburgh in law and medicine under all the notables, including Black, Playfair, and Stewart. James Mill was a collegiate associate. Early in his student days, he undertook an examination of *Zoonomia*, Erasmus Darwin's work on natural philosophy which enjoyed considerable notoriety in the colonies. Darwin, though he had not explicitly denied the realm of spirit, depended heavily on Priestley's materialism in his attempt to biologize epistemology. Brown also investigated Hume's celebrated account of causation, in an effort to defend Sir John Leslie. The latter's appointment to the chair of mathematics at Edinburgh had been endangered after the Evangelicals brought charges of infidelity against him on the grounds of his advocacy of Hume's philosophy. (Earlier, Leslie had been a tutor in Virginia.) Leslie won the appointment, and Brown went on to amplify what had been a small pamphlet into a weighty tome, which had its own vogue in America. The two investigations were not unrelated, for in a sympathetic consideration of Darwin and Hume, Brown developed his own theory of association, which he called "suggestion." Brown is replying, albeit sympathetically, to the materialism of Priestley and Darwin (and the former's determinism), as well as to the skeptical implications of Hume's associative theory. On the whole, however, Brown remains close to all of them, bringing more current advances in physiology to bear on the work of Berkeley and Hume.

Brown starts out with the traditional associational theory,[34] determined to get as much mileage out of it as possible; he even goes Hume one better, reducing the threefold relations of contiguity, resemblance, cause and effect to a single law of contiguity. However, he works out a number of secondary laws which adumbrate our contemporary discussions of memory. Like James, Brown was impressed by the strength of some single, vivid experiences, e.g., of a single hanging, to override a multitude of colorless perceptions which have been established by frequency. Brown also mentions the relative duration of experience, its recency and purity, or coexistence with fewer alternatives as factors in establishing associative trains. Brown, once again anticipating James, goes on to discuss individual differences, i.e., those between different individuals and between the same individual at different times.

For Brown, association takes place on a much wider base than that suggested by Hume. The bases of experience he calls "feelings," which term includes all sorts of internal and external affections, as well as emotions. But even with this broadened base, the classic associationism was found inadequate to account for the things which Brown wants, viz., an objective self, objects, and the feeling of cause and effect. Brown charges that Hume's own theory is inadequate to bear the weight it does; e.g., belief in a self cannot be generated from mere custom. Hume seems to have gone—illegitimately—from a succession of impressions to an impression of succession.

Still other renovations are necessary in the associationist psychology. Even the phrase "association of ideas" was infelicitous, inasmuch as it confines the process to ideas alone. This, according to Brown, is much too narrow a view of the case. When the whiteness of untrodden snow causes us to think of "the innocence of an unpolluted heart," it is not because those two ideas are in proximity to one another, but because they both excite a common emotion. Brown himself prefers the term "suggestion." Hume, in Brown's opinion, had emphasized ideas to the neglect of other elements in mental activity. If, following Hume, one were to make the actual suggestion depend on some association of ideas prior to it,

> we should not merely have assumed the reality of a process, of which we have no consciousness whatever, but should have excluded, by the impossibility of such previous combination, many of the most important classes of sugges- tions,—every suggestion that arises from the relations of objects which we perceive for the first time and . . . every suggestion that does not belong, in the strictest sense to Mr. Hume's single class of contiguity in time.[35]

Of course Brown, like other realists before him, built on Berkeley's *New Theory of Vision*; his debt is far more than the mere word "suggestion." Berkeley, in this early work, like Locke in general, may be read as a realist since the sense of touch, by Berkeley's account, gives access to an external reality. Actually, Berkeley's account of perceptual distance is essential to the empiricists' derivation of knowledge from sensible experience. Visual and tactile perceptions are initially independent experiences, and only through the correlation of original- ly disparate information do we come to use visual clues (e.g., faintness) as anticipatory cues of tactile experiences. The sign-meaning relation is like that of stimulus and response, and is analogous to language in that the relation between sign and thing symbolized is neither logically necessary nor causal, but customary. The proper objects of vision constitute a universal language of the Author of Nature, whereby we are instructed how to regulate our actions so as to attain what is essential to our preservation. (It was this theory, too, which underlay Reid's theory of natural signs.)

Brown further learned from Berkeley that sensible experience is a systematic matter, involving (among other things) anticipation. This is already the antechamber of a pragmatic theory of verification. Brown, however, had stronger physiological resources than his philosophic predecessors which he used to avoid Berkeley's immaterialism to give a convincing theory of the relation of ideas to motor activity and of motor activity to the constructed external world. In effect, we generate constant objects by the feeling of resistance, the muscle sense; mere touch as with the prick of a needle gives a sensation which may have no extensionality at all.

As Whytt and the Bells were showing, sensory as well as motor nerves are important in controlled and voluntary movement, and Brown's notion of externality involves this felt resistance (not in one instance, but differentially), together with memory (i.e., of a temporal order of successions). Both factors operate in the construction of a world of permanent and external objects. A stable and external world, though constructed, is not inferred, for Brown never denied that there is organization at the perceptual level. In effect, we see in terms of patterns and meaningful relations from the start.

Brown, departing once again from Hume, includes in the widened account of the bases of experience direct experience of relations which (at least according to Brown) was a prerequisite for the perceiving of resemblances. The relations which are directly perceived include also analogies, which lie at the heart of science as well as what James was later to call "transitive states," i.e., feelings of "and," "of," "but," and "fringe of continuity." Without this continuity, consciousness would be reduced to a single point. Moreover, even the associationist theory does not require that one mental state be *replaced* by another; we have constant purposes or moods which may endure over a long time, and operate simultaneously with other trains of thought. Ideas too may often fuse or coalesce in a kind of creative synthesis, rather like a chemical reaction, making a composite or complex which has little resemblance to its constituents. Thus, to use a later example, the taste of lemonade is not the sum of separate elements, but already a blend. Mental states themselves are indivisible wholes. The *idea* of an army is not more multiple than the idea of a soldier.

It is clear that the kind of dynamic theory Brown is sponsoring will help him in establishing self-identity. The self is not a faculty, but is found in the flow of experience, in the ways of annexing of one experience to another. Self-identity becomes essentially a set of *my* memories having coherence in change, in just the way objects have a kind of permanence even when they are altering through time.

Selves and objects are constructions out of sets of events that preserve resemblances.

Similar considerations are involved in his moral theory. The complex fusion of emotion and association (suggestion) allows him, like Priestley, to overcome the utilitarian problem, viz., how each self-seeking individual comes to adopt as his goal the general good of society. Our humanity is learned through a social process; we transfer pleasure and moods to their sources: the pleasure we get from drinking milk becomes united with the idea of the mother who gives it to us. In general, we extend to a whole class of actions those approvals and disapprovals that arise in particular instances. However, at the last moment Brown balks at a complete utilitarianism, preferring to cast his lot with Hutcheson, Reid, and Stewart in championing a "moral sense." Of course this is no faculty but the perception of a special kind of "moral" relation between agent and act and situation.

Brown follows Hume as far as possible in the latter's famous analysis of causation:

> holding that *power* is nothing more than immediate invariable *antecedence*; that the immediate invariable *antecedent* in any sequence is the *cause*; and that the immediate invariable *consequent*, in any sequence, is the *effect*. Substances bear a certain relation to one another in time, that is all.[36]

This "power," then, far from being the name of any real, esoteric connection, is only a short expression for invariant sequence. The further question, however, as to whether some proof can be given that the future will resemble the past, shows Brown diverging from Hume. Both hold that no proof can be given of this doctrine. But whereas Hume traced the origin of our belief in the doctrine to custom, Brown asserts that it is "an original feeling, intuitive and immediate on the perception of change" (*Cause and Effect*, p. 199). Brown argues that we cannot abandon this belief: although experience teaches us caution in the assignment of particular causes, it does nothing to destroy our native belief in causation itself, or in invariant causal sequences. He sometimes speaks as though our belief in this invariant succession is a pragmatic assumption necessary to the scientific enterprise, but his more general view is that it is an irresistible belief, which, though arising out of experience, is not derivable from its flow. Brown holds that Hume's position is weak in that it allows neither for an idea, nor for an impression of relation. For example, Hume, while denying that resemblance is an impression, still seems to imply that resemblance, which holds among ideas, is not itself an idea.

Brown, no less than Reid and Stewart, believes that the function of knowledge is practical in the very broadest sense, and he lent his weight and influence in America to the notion of a social philosophy that would seek reform, not only by altering the individual, but also by changing the environment.

It is of importance for us to know, *what* antecedents truly precede *what* consequents; since we can thus provide for the future, which we are hence enabled to foresee, and can, in a great measure modify, and almost create, the future to ourselves.[37]

Sir William Hamilton (1788-1856) brings us to the generation of McCosh's teachers. Educated at Glasgow in medicine and in the humanities at Edinburgh and Balliol College, Oxford, he was admitted to the Scottish bar and became professor of logic and metaphysics at Edinburgh in 1836. He pressed the investigation of medieval logic and established the importance of formal logic and he made Greek philosophy popular among his students. Extended trips to Germany and subsequent familiarity with German philosophy enabled him also to introduce it seriously into English-speaking universities. It is said that he provided Emerson, who heard him lecture at Edinburgh, with a first taste of German philosophy. Certainly Hamilton was the first to wed German critical philosophy with the Scottish tradition, and to expose the latent parallels between Kant and Hutcheson, Reid and Stewart.

But the direct and systematic influence of the Scots seems to have been limited to the writers we have already considered. Hence, for all his prestige, and he certainly didn't lack for editors and commentators, he seems rather to have added fuel than modified the direction of philosophy here. Philosophy in America appears to have been already on track and under its own steam. It was, even as late as Peirce, James, and Dewey, to work out its own parallels. In any case Hamilton's influence seems to be topical, in particular his doctrine of the conditioned (for metaphysics), his reworking of associative laws (for psychology), and his quantification of the predicate (for logic).

As a matter of fact Hamilton turned British philosophy into an avenue which few Americans were to follow. Hamilton certainly incorporated much of the Kantian philosophy—but it was a Kantianism seriously dyed by a later romantic idealism. Hamilton introduced both the mood of Hegel in his treatment of the absolute and the discussion of Hegel by direct reference to the German texts. Perhaps Hamilton is well seen as the first of the British Hegelians rather than the end of Scottish Realism. When the American philosophers finally turned to Kant, they tended to read him straight or against the background of Reid, Stewart, and Brown, or, as in the case of the "literary philosophers," to draw inspiration via Coleridge.

Hamilton starts out by accepting Stewart's qualitative account of what is knowable. We never know the thing in itself, nor mind, except as modified by the knowing process. If to know is to condition, it would follow that we never truly know things as they are. Hamilton's view here is not unlike Kant's up to a point. Yet where Kant cut the noumenal from the phenomenal absolutely, Hamilton appears to differ at two points. First, phenomenal qualities are related and give some, if only a partial, hold on the real. And second, while the phenomena lie within the limited range in which we have knowledge, the questions raised about the knowable seem to lie beyond on, as it were, the same dimension. For whereas Kant holds that the categories and forms are organizing modes for dealing with phenomena and cannot therefore be applied to the noumena or independently real, Hamilton treats the antinomies as legitimate questions about the real, one side of which must be correct because the law of contradiction holds for reality, although which is correct lies beyond the limits of knowledge. It is almost as though there were two baskets, one marked "true" and the other "false"; we may not know to which of the baskets a given proposition belongs, but we may be confident that it belongs in one or the other.

Despite the phenomenalistic or idealistic tendencies, Hamilton believes he can hold to natural realism defensibly. And it is just this step Mill thought he could not take. Defensible or not, Hamilton's argument shows a sophisticated appreciation of the difficulties, and he rests his case on his theory of perception. He distinguishes between presentation and representation, although he is using these terms in a special sense. The presentative is immediate perception of the full concrete particulars, the full sensation, and it carries with it the direct awareness of existence. The representative is derived or mediated knowledge overlaid to a larger extent by learning and past association.

Hamilton's fusion of Scottish common sense and Kantian views led him to regard the mind as contributing essential structural principles to our knowledge. Specifically, all principles which are characterized by universality and necessity arise, Hamilton asserts, from the mind, for more experience could never prove that any principle has these attributes. The truths of formal logic, such as the laws of excluded middle and noncontradiction, are therefore to be regarded as ultimate a priori laws of thought. But the mind contributes more than purely formal principles. In all perception, we are aware of the self as knower and of the object as known—hence it is a necessary truth that all knowledge is knowledge of objects as they stand in relation to us. Similarly, we always perceive the object known as existing—not indeed as existing objectively, independently of us, but existing subjectively as phenomenon. Hence existence is a necessary category of thought through which we must conceptualize the objects of experience. Such principles are necessary truths, but they are truths relating to the conditioned—i.e., to phenomena only—not to things as they are in themselves. Hence our knowledge is a knowledge of the conditioned alone; the unconditioned or noumenal world is forever beyond the grasp of our faculties. Nevertheless, Hamilton holds that we can know at least that there is a noumenal world, although we cannot conceive that world. The argument hinges on the distinction between positive and negative necessity. When I assert that the object of conception exists, I do so by virtue of a positive power of the mind which compels me to conceive it. Yet my thinking may also be constrained by an impossibility of conceiving something, in which case the necessity involved is essentially negative. Thus I cannot conceive space as infinite. Equally, I cannot conceive space as finite, for I cannot conceive space as bounded without thinking of a space beyond the bounds. But by the law of excluded middle, infinite or finite space must be, even though neither possibility is conceivable. The space of experience—space known under the conditions of our knowledge—thus lies between two extremes neither of which is conceivable but one of which must be true. And what is true of space is true of time, and indeed of all conditioned objects of knowledge. As Hamilton put it in his famous "Law of the Conditioned," "The Conditioned is the mean between two extremes—two inconditionates, exclusive of each other, *neither of which can be conceived as possible*, but of which, on the principles of Contradiction and Excluded Middle, *one must be admitted as necessary*." From such antinomies, Hamilton concludes, not that the world of appearance is illusory, but that our powers of conception are weak.

> We are thus taught the salutary lesson, that the capacity of thought is not to be constituted into the measure of existence; and are warned from recognizing the domain of our knowledge as necessarily coextensive with the horizon of our faith. And by a wonderful revelation, we are thus, in a very consciousness of our inability to conceive aught above the relative and finite, inspired with a belief in the existence of something unconditioned beyond the sphere of all comprehensible reality.[38]

Of this incomprehensible reality we can know nothing more than that it is; our beliefs regarding it must rest on faith, not upon rational or empirical demonstration. But this, Hamilton remarks, is what theology has always claimed in holding God to be incomprehensible and known only by faith.

Hamilton's famous Law of the Conditioned had great appeal to those who wished to secure the grounds of their faith while supporting the progress of science. It is hardly surprising that Hamilton's argument was to form the basis for the most ambitious attempt to harmonize evolution with theism—Herbert Spencer's Synthetic Philosophy, and that many of the orthodox rushed to Hamilton's defense when Mill's devastating *Examination* appeared.

Hamilton's reworking of the associative laws, "the law of re-integration," is an effort to restate Brown's suggestion in a more emphatic way, and is also an attack on the notion of ideas as entities. Where Brown had used the term "suggestion" to underscore his conviction that association was not so much a mechanical link as an activity, Hamilton defines reintegration as the power of one idea, not merely to suggest another previously experienced in conjunction with it, but also to suggest or reinstate the whole context and relations in which the initial idea occurred. Hamilton, insofar as he stresses this relational character of mental discourse, appears to provide a base for the subsequent logic of relations developed by the British idealists. In some respects the dynamic character of association and the alternative routes we pursue in trains of thought lead into James's discussion of attention. However Hamilton, under the influence of Kant, developed a really hardened version of faculty psychology in which the functions of the mind are conceived, not dynamically, but departmentally. This faculty psychology, though undoubtedly present in the earlier Scots, was not as evident as their tendency (shared with the Americans) to think of the mind in terms of processes rather than compartmentalized units. James had to combat an entrenched faculty psychology which owed some of its prestige to Hamilton.

Hamilton also wrote extensively on logic, and so lent the great prestige of his name and learning to this discipline. He had a clear appreciation of Aristotelian logic; and if he lacked Stewart's insight into the significance of the formal processes of reasoning in mathematical thought, nevertheless he gave greater attention to the formal elements in logic than had any of his predecessors, and certainly more than Mill. Hamilton somewhat inadvertently furthers the connection between logic and mathematics which Stewart had premiered; the real significance of Hamilton's work in logic will be seen to lie in preparing the way for the development of mathematical logic. It is just this significance of Hamilton's logic which McCosh misses. He attacks Hamilton's extensional interpretation of terms as failing to do justice to the attributive character of ordinary thought. Consequently he attacks the theory of the quantification of the predicate and the various propositional forms to which it gives rise as indefensible deviations from the forms which occur in "spontaneous thought." Moreover, McCosh views Hamilton's reduction of propositions to equations as an illegitimate attempt to identify the subject matter of logic with that of mathematics, for he views equality in the mathematical sense as applicable only to quantity, and so as inapplicable to other domains upon which logic adverts. It is thus not surprising that when McCosh came to write his own logic, he failed to notice the revolution in logic which, building on Hamilton's insight, Boole and De Morgan began in 1847. We shall see the importance of these questions for the American scene in chapter 6.

It is worth suggesting the line that McCosh takes in *The Scottish Philosophy* when criticizing the other major figures as well—few escape his vigilant pen. Hutcheson sensualized and degraded the older philosophy and his account of moral power (the moral sense) is superficial and defective. The identification of virtue and benevolence,

> by bringing down morality from the height at which the great ethical writers, of ancient and modern times, had placed it, . . . prepared the way for the system of Adam Smith, and even for that of Hume.[39]

He chides Reid for his impreciseness in the use of the expression "common sense," and for his view of natural language, signs, and conceptions. Stewart is found wanting in that he dissociates the fundamental laws of belief, i.e., the principles of common sense, from the faculties; that he held the wrong opinion regarding analytic and a priori knowledge; and that he discusses virtue independently of supernatural religion. Brown is given an especially bad press for his preoccupation with physiology, for representing "consciousness" as a general term for states and affections of mind, and for failing to bring out clearly that the moral faculty inescapably declares man to be a sinner. Even his teacher Hamilton is guilty of flirting with German idealism and with Spencer's "Unknown"—and the followers of Hamilton (Mansel, Ferrier, and Maurice) are guilty of "unspeakable Hegelianism." Thomas Chalmers alone is let off scot-free.

The dependence of American intellectual life on Scotland and its educational institutions has not been challenged, but this impact is not always explicitly acknowledged. After the Test Acts had made the nonconformist persona non grata at Oxford and Cambridge, the day of the Scottish universities had struck. England's Dissenting Academies joined forces with the schools of Scotland; Scots and Scotch-Irish flooded the Middle Atlantic states in America, fresh from the lecture halls, especially after 1727. (Curiously, however, few made their way to New England.) These immigrants held important educational posts in the New World (though they had an unaccountable way of turning Anglican when the salary came from Anglican purses). John Blair and William Smith, heads respectively of William and Mary and the College of Philadelphia, James Wilson the lawyer and the physician Cadwalader Colden, Witherspoon of Princeton, and William Smart, Jefferson's friend and teacher at William and Mary—these men are quintessential parts of American intellectual history, and they are all Scottish Enlightenment figures.

There was a return of Americans to Scotland, where the best medical education of the day was to be had. Even a casual survey convinces one that American publishers were abreast of the latest philosophy from Scotland. Kames's *Elements of Criticism* (1762) was on the American shelves by 1770. Adam Smith's *Theory of Moral Sentiments* was first printed in America in 1784, eleven years after its Scottish publication. A Philadelphia edition of Reid's *Essays* was available by 1792, and three years later Hume's *History of England* was marketed (seeing a fourth edition in New York in 1810). Erasmus Darwin's *Zoonomia* (1796) was in its third American edition by 1801. Dugald Stewart enjoyed considerable favor here; excerpts of his unfinished *Elements of the Philosophy of the Human Mind* were published in Vermont in 1808. Three years later, the first American edition of his *Philosophical Essays* was published in Philadelphia. A Boston house released the completed *Elements* in 1828, only one year later than the British edition; by 1829, Harvard undergraduates could obtain a Cambridge edition of his complete works. Yale students in 1824 were studying Brown's *Lectures on the Philosophy of the Human Mind* (and, perhaps significantly, Levi Hedge found it necessary to abridge this work for the students at Harvard in 1827).

The account of the editions of the *Encyclopaedia Britannica* is a most confusing saga, even as it is summarized in the Eleventh Edition. This work was enormously important; its Supplements often served (and appropriately) as college texts. Three industrious but ill-organized Scots began the venture as a counter to "the pestiferous influence" of the *Encyclopédie*. This new work was to be a systematic account, in fairly large chunks, of achievements in all fields of culture. The first three editions are embalmed in a morass of copyright and publishing difficulties, but the fourth represents a radical shift in content, format, and general viewpoint. For this shift, Dugald Stewart seems centrally responsible. Various editions were prefaced or supplemented by treatises on science, metaphysics, and ethics. Some of the most noted social scientists—from Malthus and MacIntosh to McCullough—wrote for the series. The first American edition appears to be the third British edition, though editions were extensively pirated by the Americans.

Even after the *Encyclopaedia* began to be published, not in Scotland, but in Cambridge, England, the work continued to exercise enormous influence here. The British-based publishers rely on their own bias: in the ninth edition Hutcheson, Hume, and Smith are all identified as "Englishmen," while Reid and Stewart remain in the limbo of "Scottish metaphysicians." Once in the hands of the Americans (Sears and Roebuck), the cultural impact noticeably diminished.

Notes — Chapter Four

[1]In this and the following chapters we shall identify the colleges by their present names; thus Princeton instead of the original College of New Jersey.

[2]Although in many respects we are in this chapter running against the trend of these books, they have nevertheless proved invaluable. In particular, we are indebted to Herbert Schneider for many new suggestions, and perhaps we have even persuaded him. The works referred to above are:

Joseph Blau, *Men and Movements in American Philosophy* (Englewood Cliffs, N.J.: 1952).
Morris Raphael Cohen, *American Thought, A Critical Sketch* (Glencoe, Ill.: Free Press, 1954).
Merle Curti, *The Growth of American Thought* (New York: Harper and Brothers, 1943).
I. Woodbridge Riley, *American Philosophy, the Early Schools* (New York: Dodd, Mead, and Co., 1907).
Herbert W. Schneider, *A History of American Philosophy*, 2d ed. (New York: 1963).
W. H. Werkmeister, *A History of Philosophical Ideas in America* (New York: Ronald Press, 1949).
Morton White's comments were made in a lecture.

[3]G. Stanley Hall, "Philosophy in the United States," *Mind*, 1880, pp. 89-105.

[4]Cf. his "On the History of American College Text-books and Teaching in Logic, Ethics, Psychology and Allied Subjects," *Proceedings of the American Antiquarian Society*, April 1894, pp. 137-61.

[5]Hall, "Philosophy in the United States," p. 91.

⁶The works of special interest here in the enormous bibliography of James McCosh are:

The Scottish Philosophy, Biographical, Expository, Critical, from Hutcheson to Hamilton (London: Robert Carter and Brothers, 1874).
Realistic Philosophy (New York: Charles Scribner's Sons, 1882), vol. I, *Expository*; vol. II, *Historical and Critical*.
Philosophy of Reality, Should It be Favored by America? (New York: 1894).
The Intuitions of the Mind, Inductively Investigated (New York: Carter, 1869).
An Examination of Mr. J. S. Mill's Philosophy (New York: Carter, 1869).
The Method of Divine Government, Physical and Moral (New York: Carter, 1850).

A full bibliography will be found in William Milligan Sloane, ed., *The Life of James McCosh* (New York: Charles Scribner's Sons, 1896).

⁷The Scottish Enlightenment is enjoying a renaissance of its own; books and articles are beginning to appear with rapidity. We are especially indebted to the librarians of the Presbyterian Historical Society and to Roger Emerson of the University of Western Ontario whose careful study of the period was the source of helpful suggestions.

⁸The separation of church and state was a point of contention between the Moderates and the High Flyers. Some authorities recognized the right of the state to interfere in the polity of the church but not its dogma. Opponents of patronage generally opposed interference in polity. As for toleration, by about 1715 the state did not enforce uniformity of belief in Scotland. Toleration of Episcopal and other churches was imposed on the Scots during Anne's reign. This, of course, did not mean equality of preferment, especially in the universities.

⁹For medicine this dates from about 1726. Good teachers in law, rather than those simply holding sinecures, begin to appear about 1740, for example John Millar and John Erskine.

¹⁰Many Scots would argue that the Renaissance did come to Scotland and lasted longer, particularly at Aberdeen.

¹¹Cf. John Veitch, "Philosophy in the Scottish Universities," *Mind*, 1877, pp. 74-91, 202-34.

¹²*Ibid.*, 313.

¹³Varnum Lansing Collins's *President Witherspoon, a Biography*, 2 vols. (Princeton, N.J.: Princeton University Press, 1925), is a lively and full study.

[14]*Ecclesiastical Characteristics*, etc. First published 1753. The quotation is from the 1815 edition of his *Works*, vol. 6, p. 23.

[15]*Ibid.*, p. 185.

[16]The revivalist and antirevivalist factions were known by different names in different sections. In New England, the revivalists were called New Lights, the antirevivalists were called Old Lights. In the Middle Atlantic colonies, the revivalists were called New Sides, while the antirevivalists were called Old Sides.

[17]Helpful in tracing out the history of Princeton are Thomas Jefferson Wertenbaker's *Princeton 1746-1896* (Princeton, N.J.: Princeton University Press, 1946), and Leonard J. Trinterud's *The Forming of an American Tradition* (Philadelphia: The Westminster Press, 1949).

[18]For Witherspoon's administration at Princeton, see esp., John McLean, *History of the College of New Jersey* (Philadelphia: J.B. Lippincott, 1877).

[19]*Lectures on Moral Philosophy and Eloquence*, 3d ed. (Philadelphia: Printed by and for William W. Woodward, no. 52 South Second Street, 1810).

[20]"A Few Thoughts on Space, Dimension and the Divisibility of Matter in Infinitum," *Pennsylvania Magazine* II: 225-29 (May 1776).

[21]The articles in question, "Thoughts Concerning Human Liberty," appeared in *The Scots Magazine*, April 1751 and August 1752; they are not signed, or are signed D. W., but tradition attributes them to Lord Kames. Witherspoon's reply, "Remarks on an Essay on Human Liberty," appeared in the same magazine, April 1753, pp. 165-70.

[22]Samuel Stanhope Smith, *The Lectures, Corrected and Improved which have been Delivered for a Series of Years, in the College of New Jersey; on the Subjects of Moral and Political Philosophy* (Trenton, N. J.: Daniel Fenton, 1812).

[23]Of special help here, among secondary sources, is Torgny T. Segerstedt, *The Problem of Knowledge in Scottish Philosophy*, in Lunds Universitets Arsskrift, n.s. 1935, no. 6. See also, Sten Stenson, "History of Scottish Empiricism from 1730-1856" (Ph.D. diss., Columbia University, 1952).

[24]Locke, *Essay*, bk. 4, chap. 1, sec. 1.

[25]David Hume, *A Treatise of Human Nature*, ed. Selby-Bigge (Oxford: Clarendon Press, 1960), pp. 67f.

[26]*Ibid.*, p. 170.

[27]*Ibid.*, pp. 91f.

[28]*Ibid.*, p. 253.

[29]*Ibid.*, p. 218.

[30]Thomas Reid, *Essays on the Intellectual and Active Powers of Man* (Philadelphia: 1792).

[31]Bertrand Russell, *A History of Western Philosophy* (1945), p. 674.

[32]Joseph Priestley, *An Examination of Doctor Reid's Inquiry into the Human Mind on the Principles of Common Sense*, etc., (London: Printed for J. Johnson, rev. ed., 1774).

[33]Reid, *Intellectual and Active Powers*, p. 659.

[34]Thomas Brown, *Lectures on the Philosophy of the Human Mind* (Andover, Mass.: M. Newman, 1822).

[35]*Ibid.*, I:81.

[36]*Ibid.*, I:75.

[37]*Ibid.*, I:78.

[38]Sir William Hamilton, *Discussions on Philosophy and Literature* (New York: Harper, 1853), p. 22.

[39]McCosh, *Scottish Philosophy*, p. 85.

Chapter Five

Philosophy in the Middle Atlantic and Southern States—

Metaphysics and Morals

Chapter Five

Philosophy in the Middle Atlantic and Southern States— Metaphysics and Morals

1. Metaphysics and Epistemology

The preceding chapter discussed Scottish Realism, Princeton Style, and concluded with a sampling of issues from the originals which influenced not only Princeton, but also much of philosophy in America during the eighteenth and a goodly part of the nineteenth century. Taken broadly as the Scottish Enlightenment—as the tradition shaped by Hutcheson—it was neither nationalistic nor parochial. Responsive on the one hand to the continental rationalists and their echo in the Cambridge Platonists and such English successors as Butler and Price, it interacted on the other hand with the science and empiricism that was developing in France and England. Indeed, especially through Hume, Scottish thought influenced the main course of European thought—in science through his analysis of causation and induction, in religion through his riddling of older metaphysical and allegedly scientific deistic proofs based on design and order, in psychology through his

277

account of the self and ideas, and in morals through his emphasis on sentiment rather than reason.

The narrower group of Common Sense Realists, that is, Reid and his successors, presented astonishingly little in the way of a solid front beyond their insistence that thought had a veridical reference, and even there they vary significantly in the details. What they did share were not answers, but commitments to humanism, to empiricism in method, and to the urgency of the problems raised by Hume. Insofar as their efforts to answer Hume led them to a Kantian-like emphasis on the activity of the knower, they made a bridge to German Idealism; and the fact that the Scottish legacy to America lay essentially in the Hutcheson-Reid-Stewart-Brown tradition, with the influence of Hamilton topical rather than systematic, accounts in large measure for the distinctive way the Americans (especially the pragmatists) read Kant—distinctive that is in contrast to the Neo-Hegelian reading of Kant which predominated in England and had deeper roots in the Hamiltonians.

The impact of the Scots was felt at different times in the several colonies but it was important everywhere. Following the imposition of the Test Acts, the English dissenting scholars fled Oxford and Cambridge, going either to the Scottish universities or establishing Dissenting Academies of their own. Despite the legal disabilities under which these academies labored, which prevented their becoming centers of learning equal to the Scottish universities, the relations between the two sets of schools were cordial and Scottish texts were widely used in these schools. The English universities lost their intellectual leadership, even in England, and the Scottish universities of Edinburgh, Glasgow, and Aberdeen, together with the Dissenting Academies, became the British sources to which Americans looked for European learning.

Yet the Scottish philosophy, in either its broader or narrower versions, did not meet the same hearing everywhere in America; it was put to different uses as it was read against backgrounds of varying intellectual sympathies, vocabularies, and tensions. The different colonies and urban centers were truly as many intellectual subcultures; but for the purposes at hand (and with the most cavalier disregard of geography), it will suffice to distinguish New England from the Middle Atlantic and Southern settlements, herein after referred to as the Middle-South. Clearly there are internal differences of importance within each of these divisions, but the wholesale distinction was transparent enough for Samuel Miller to have contrasted the eighteenth-century achievements of New England with the Middle-South, or in his terms, the "East" with the "West."

New England enjoyed a relatively large measure of common educational, religious, and political tradition which was essentially English in origin. There were a high degree of literacy, reasonably well defined social classes, and integrated economic objectives: in short, homogeneity. Harvard and Yale, and toward the end of the century Dartmouth and Brown, operated as steadying forces despite the clashes between New and Old Lights and the fractionings of the post-Edwardseans. Whatever their internal disputes, the New Englanders worked with a common understanding of the domain and the past of philosophy and with the lines of theological discussion finely drawn over a community of issues. It is not surprising, then, that Miller finds the "East" superior in its theological and Oriental studies as well as those in philosophy of mind.

In sharp contrast to the East, the Middle-South was characterized by heterogeneity in every cultural dimension. From New York to Charleston every shade of religious view was entertained—from extravagant evangelicism to atheism. In Philadelphia, Quakers and Anglicans were in daily contact with radical Pietists, and with German Lutherans and Dutch Calvinists who preserved their connections with their European universities. And of course there were always the Scots, and in ever-increasing numbers, the Scotch-Irish. Revivalism when it came cut through this milieu in unpredictable and diverse ways. All the while in the background, and ever more insistently as the century progressed, were felt an urbanely relaxed morality, a scientifically based materialism with deistic overtones coupled with an articulate hostility to institutionalized religion. Again and again the orthodox were stunned into overaggressive reaction.

Such aggressiveness, most frequently organized by the Presbyterians, played havoc with education and gave philosophy a partisan character. Of course each colony played its own variation on the church-state-college relation; but whereas in New England these were generally of one standing order until well after the Independence, in the Middle-South denominations fought and were unequally successful in the control of each of these departments. Even such early colleges as Pennsylvania, Princeton, and Columbia (and to a lesser extent William and Mary and Rutgers), far from being a steadying influence, became centers of factional and debilitating conflict. Even so, according to Miller, "Western" superiority was to be found in the classics and in those important auxiliary branches of philosophy—chemistry, natural history, and medicine—and Miller suggests that the presence of such men as Logan, Franklin, Priestley, Rush, and Colden gave a considerable scientific overtone to the philosophy practiced there.

The differences in the intellectual environment which made for initial differences in philosophy became aggravated as time went on, but the Middle-South states were always left with a broader spread of antagonistic views. This is not to say that there was not a profile of common problems—indeed, they were just those of the Scottish legacy in a commonsense context: to give an account of human nature, activity, and responsibility, to relate that account to natural and moral phenomena, and to work out logic in an empirical context. Yet even the discussions of such problems as these never lost the marks of their different sectional settings, and often they revealed divergent notions of the domain of philosophy and its fitting associates.

Philosophy in the Middle-South

The canonical treatment of the American Enlightenment, after a bow to Jefferson, Franklin, and company, picks up the threads in New England in the successors of Edwards and carries the account through Unitarianism and Transcendentalism to Idealism and Pragmatism. It is not hard to find justification for this emphasis—not only are the materials available and self-consciously publicized, but also they may be easily ordered by using divergence from Edwards as a measure. Further, of course, Samuel Miller was altogether correct regarding the superiority of New England's philosophical activity, viewed in a religious context.

All semblance of this neatness vanishes when one turns to the Middle-South states: the canvas is cloudy and there is scarcely agreement even upon the proper domain of philosophy itself. In orthodox circles there is scarcely a shadow of the excitement which Edwards stimulated in New England and Britain, and such spasmodic attempts as there were to attack or defend Edwards directly lack any special insight. What is interesting, however, are the efforts to reformulate problems such as the freedom of the will to meet the secular demands of natural philosophy. Indeed, it is just the pressure of science, vested in men of affairs such as Franklin and Jefferson, Priestley and Rush, that interacts with and on the academic philosophy to create this untidiness and interest.

But just this role of science in its interaction with philosophy now requires a more comprehensive sense of "philosophy," one suggested by the "American *Philosophical* Society," which appropriates to philosophy much of natural science and morals. Physicians such as Philadelphia's Rush move from medicine to botany and to the causes of moral disease, chemists like Priestley and Cooper argue the nature of choice and the laws of wealth, all without any sense of the disparateness of their problems. Clerical professors such as William Smith and Francis Alison taught natural philosophy (even in medical school) along with moral philosophy, and enthusiastically made observations of the transit of Venus. Witherspoon even engaged Rittenhouse over mathematics, with somewhat disastrous results. And all of these, no less than Franklin and Jefferson, faced the urgent problems of their day from the advancement of learning to the nature of political society as though they were part and parcel of philosophical activity. This broader sense of philosophy is scarcely an American phenomenon, but is rather the eighteenth-century view of the coherence of knowledge and its applications which is to be found from Descartes to Leibniz and Kant, and which was a central feature of the Scottish Enlightenment. It is from this matrix that special disciplines are later to emerge as philosophy *of*—of mathematics, of science, of anthropology, etc.; but knowledge and the methods of its extension were not in that century so compartmentalized. It is important to note, however, that New England philosophy, never strongly entrenched in the Middle-South states, was slowly displaced there by the immigration of the Scots, especially the physicians and ministers. Thus the savor of Edinburgh, Glasgow, St. Andrews, and Aberdeen was transplanted directly into these colonies. Indirectly, too, the Scottish centers of learning were influential through their effects on London medicine and their leadership in the Dissenting Academies. And not less indirectly nor less importantly, the Scottish philosophy served as a target for the more materialistic writers.

Lockean Options

Locke's philosophy rather than Edwards's can be used to bring order into the untidiness, since the Middle-South states sheltered every legitimate, illegitimate, and half-legitimate offspring of that philosopher. We have already noted that Berkeleyan idealism as a development of Locke had a foothold at Princeton when Witherspoon challenged it with his realism, and of course both of these were taken to be in the true Lockean tradition by their advocates.[1] The origins of this Princeton idealism are obscure—it is unlikely that Edwards is the source, since he was guarded in sharing his views, and it seems equally unlikely that the Calvinists would have taken much from Anglican Columbia or its president, Samuel Johnson. Perhaps it was already in the air in Philadelphia since it is safe to say that Berkeley's theory of perception and his challenge to Newton were matters of common discussion in that city. In any case, William Smith, who had been associated with Johnson at Columbia before becoming provost at Pennsylvania, had sympathy enough for Berkeley to publish the London edition of his works as well as to introduce Johnson's texts in the Philadelphia college.[2] William Smith was educated at Aberdeen and, like Johnson, had exchanged an early Calvinism for Anglicanism, but he was invited to Pennsylvania with Franklin's backing to help structure the work at the new college, and it is clear that he imported the plans and the reforms effected in his native universities under the Enlightenment. Indeed, philosophy was to have the central role in his scheme, but that included intellectual and moral as well as natural philosophy.

The Hutcheson-Shaftesbury version of Locke was published in America before the Revolution and was used as a text for nearly three-quarters of a century. It had its greatest advocates at Pennsylvania where Francis Alison raised a generation of students including John Ewing, Samuel Magaw, and John Andrews, who represented well the intellectual and philosophical liberalism of Hutcheson in the Presbyterian circles. Notes from Alison's classes[3] and Ewing's own *A System of Natural Philosophy* (1809) showed that they were no mere commentators but were developing Hutcheson's leads in their own way against a competent background of philosophy and natural science.

Locke and the Scientists

But Locke was turned in a different direction by the men of science—toward materialism. The discussion here in America was of course colored by European materialisms but it was given a character of its own by the originality of such native Americans as Franklin, Jefferson, and Rush and by such imports as Colden, Priestley, Paine, and Cooper. English and French materialisms were following rather independent lines: on the whole, the English depended more directly on Newton's mechanical model and on the longer tradition in the work of such men as Hobbes and Harvey, while the French relied rather on medicine and physiology and were less interested in reducing mind to matter than in accounting for the problems of human behavior left by Descartes. The Americans, native or immigrant, drew from both sources and wrung a richness from the amalgam that was not unlike James's welding of French, English, and German psychologies into a coherent pragmatism. The Scots, unwilling to label themselves materialists, were often complicating factors. Sometimes realist and materialist were at loggerheads —thus Priestley's attack on their philosophy in all probability was the source for Kant's derogatory characterization of common sense. Still, Priestley later tempered his vehemence and Cooper even listed Brown and Stewart among the materialist authorities. There was in fact a love-hate relationship between the realists and the materialists, for they were often in agreement on philosophic detail while remaining poles apart in attitude. Clearly, materialism of any variety has important implications for the problems that we have labeled "common." It gave a special purchase on determinism and the interaction of body and mind, allowing among other things for the effect of the full natural environment, not merely the body and its mechanisms. This materialism, backed as it was by the best scientific minds of the day, constituted a formidable challenge to the clerical establishment.

The new science had provided the eighteenth century with a model which described physical reality as an orderly and intelligible structure which it was within the competence of reason to grasp. The scientific leaders of the American Enlightenment rejected the theological and metaphysical systems which they believed had long imprisoned and deluded reason; and they devoted themselves to empirical research, convinced that the key to nature's secrets lay in the scientific method, a method moreover whereby the understanding of nature could be indefinitely increased. Locke's analysis of that understanding seemed to secure the psychological and epistemological basis for science and empirical knowledge generally. Further, the Newton-Locke model was powerful enough to extend even to social phenomena, and to provide doctrines that served not only as explanations, but also as programs for progress and reform. The Americans were well read in the scientific literature of their time, and indeed they made significant contributions to it.

In fact, Franklin, who was by far the greatest American scientist of the era, materially strengthened the evidence that the Newtonian model was a true description of the structure of the physical universe by his brilliant work in electricity. Before Franklin, electricity was a mystifying anomaly: there was no theory to fit the experimental data then amassed and it was not even known that electrical phenomena occurred spontaneously in nature. Franklin's experimental and theoretical work completely revolutionized the field; he discovered the law of the conservation of electric charge, he demonstrated the electrical character of lightning, and he developed a theory—the one fluid theory—which covered most of the data then known. Yet for all his originality, Franklin worked wholly within the Newtonian scheme. He thought of electricity as a fluid composed of particles, each of which repelled the others while each attracted every particle of matter. These forces are propagated according to the Newtonian model and they vary inversely as some function of the distance. Franklin never proved that that function was the square, though doubtless he suspected it. Priestley, however, deduced the character of the function from the fact that an electrified particle contained within an electrified sphere is neither attracted nor repelled by the sphere. Recalling Newton's proof that, given the inverse square law, the same behavior would characterize a material particle enclosed within a sphere in space (that is to say, the attractions of the various points on the sphere's surface cancel so that the particle remains at rest relative to the sphere), Priestley realized at once that the law governing electrical attraction and repulsion must also be the inverse square. Subsequently, of course, Coulomb gave an experimental proof of this result, thus making the relation between mechanics and electricity complete. In other words, Franklin's theory posited a unique electrical matter, but the behavior of that matter can be described entirely within the framework provided by Newton. Franklin's work thus reinforced belief in the adequacy of that model for the description of all physical reality.

Priestley (1733-1804) was to become the most vigorous of proselytizers[4] for materialism and it was he who provided a base for much of the speculation of the Jeffersonian circle. Priestley was a nonconformist who as a youth attended a Dissenting Academy when he was well enough and when ill remained at home studying metaphysics, logic, natural philosophy, and gaining a phenomenal control of ancient and modern languages. He became a minister, but he also taught a wide range of subjects at the dissenting establishments, all the while conducting experiments and constructing apparatus ingeniously designed to outwit his poverty. In his early years, he became known for a *Chart of History* and for a grammar which attempted to free English from its corseting by classic grammarians. Honors came to him quite early; Edinburgh gave him a doctorate and he was elected fellow of the Royal Society, nominated by Franklin. Franklin also encouraged him to study electricity, and to publish a *History and Present State of Electricity with Original Experiments* (1767). This was no mere account of the state of the science, but an original contribution both to it and to the methodology of science, and as a special bonus it was interesting to boot, reporting, e.g., Franklin's version of the experiments with kite and key. He wrote an equally lively *History and Present State of the Discoveries Relating to Vision, Light and Colors* (1772) which, though more concerned with physics, gave considerable space to perception, raising, e.g., the question of how objects, such as houses in an alley, would have to be placed so as to appear parallel.

Priestley is best remembered for his discovery of oxygen and for his untiring support of the American Revolutionaries; but his scientific contributions were extensive and his political, educational, and economic writings were important and of real service to America. And yet he was also a theological writer of skill. Originally destined for the Presbyterian ministry, the joint impact of science and of Hartley's associationism forced him to leave Calvinism for a very liberal Unitarianism in which Jesus became essentially a great man. It is clear that his liberal religious and political views (he was made a citizen of the French Republic) did not endear him to the ordinary run of Englishmen; and his choice of friends, ranging from Erasmus Darwin to James Watt, was not such as to raise his general prestige or to guarantee his "safeness." In any case, when a violent mob destroyed his chapel in Birmingham and ransacked his house and laboratory, he sought refuge from such persecution in America, arriving in 1794.

Priestley also worked within the Newton-Locke framework, but armed with Newton's strictures on wastefulness in explanation—not to multiply distinctions or hypotheses beyond necessity, to explain similar effects by the same causes, etc.—he chipped away at the dualisms in Locke's philosophy. Locke had appealed to two totally different substances—to matter and to spirit, to body and to mind. While even Hartley had been satisfied with a kind of parallelism between mental and physical processes, Priestley took the full step of reducing everything to an aspect of matter, so that even ideas became a particular kind of matter in motion. But if his theory was a full-styled materialism, it was an extraordinarily qualified one, bent less on a reduction of mind to matter than a search for a middle term. Building on Boscovich's atomic theory and Franklin's notions of the nature of electricity (and with the flavor of Leibniz), he held that matter is not solid and inert but active. The solidity which was taken by Brown and Reid, following Locke, to be derived from experienced resistance is simply not, he claimed, authorized by the facts. Resistance presumes that two objects come into contact, as when we press our hands against a table or when two links of a chain are put by stress into close proximity; but things are never in absolute contact—in the latter case, for example, alteration of the distance with heat and cold can even be grossly observed. Such phenomena can only be accounted for by assuming a power of repulsion as a fundamental property of matter. There are many other arguments, of course, against the assumption that matter is solid or impenetrable, for, of course, light penetrates such "solids" as glass or diamonds. Newton held that the rays of light are not reflected back by impinging against the solid parts of a body but by a power of repulsion acting at some distance from the body; and the part of the beam which overcomes the repulsion goes through the transparent substance in a right line, provided that the object be of a uniform density. On the other hand, the power of attraction must belong to all matter, for if the particles were not attracted an object could not maintain its shape and compactness. Thus for Priestley matter is dynamic, representing ultimately the locus of the forces of attraction and repulsion.

Given such a view of matter there are unorthodox implications for the nature of the self, the external world, and for the notions of free will, educability, and responsibility. Most obviously Priestley's view speaks to the distinction between mind and body. Once matter is taken as active the incompatibility between mind and body simply disappears. Thought always occurs in conjunction with some organized system of matter—in particular, the nervous system and the brain. Further, the destinies of mind and body follow the same course; they mature together and decay together and the illness of one is generally felt as an illness of the other. Sometimes forgotten is the patent fact that vision or perception itself is dependent upon the eye and the optic nerve, and that the integration of touch with sight and the other sensations could not be accounted for without appealing to this organized material system. Only on the assumption that thought and matter are of the same stuff, Priestley held, could one understand interaction with one's own bodily environment or of the larger social and physical environment with the individual man.

As Priestley works out the consequences of this theory for psychology and for the reality of the external world, his ambivalent relations with the Scots come to the surface. Always opposed to Reid and Beattie, he was sometimes sympathetic to Stewart and Hume, and he treated Thomas Brown as a colleague in his own associationist tradition with whom he differed on particular issues. According to Priestley, objects are initially experienced as a whole, and so long as experience remains limited, every aspect of an object will appear equal in importance. Thus to an inexperienced child the garlic taste of spring milk may seem as essential as its whiteness. As experience increases, however, the casual or accidental properties will drop out, leaving the so-called essential properties such as whiteness selectively and inseparably associated with milk. By adding an arbitrary sign like "is" we form propositions which are now regarded as universally and necessarily true. Evidence for this sort of relation depends on experience and induction rather than intuition. If the situations under which the object is experienced are somewhat dissimilar, we then weaken the relation to an analogy and take it to be only probably true, though our confidence increases as the resemblance is the more striking. Of course we can always increase the warrant of knowledge, or move analogy nearer to induction, by collecting more information; this kind of consideration was aimed at drawing the sting from Hume's skepticism.

Mathematical knowledge appears to offer another kind of example of intuitive self-evidency. But here, the self-evidence, say of an equation, derives from the fact that we are merely naming the same thing in different ways. Sometimes when assent is not immediately forthcoming, the identity can be demonstrated through the use of a name or term common to both sides. Still, the pattern of learning exhibited in mathematics resembles that of learning languages. Supposing one is told that the Latin *lac* is the same as the French *lait*, which latter already has the familiar associations of the English *milk*; after some use, *lac* will arouse the associations that *milk* does without any intermediate reasoning; i.e., the notions coalesce.

Such examples, however, are paradigmatic for all kinds of learning. In every case what is at work is merely the associative laws operating on materials received through the senses. Even dogs and children exhibit the same kind of reasoning in rudimentary form as they learn to avoid the fire. Neither logic nor language then is necessary for reasoning and for appropriate responses. Logic and language are critical, however, for mature thought. Children and animals have only limited alternatives of response; as experiences increase the store of associations grows; expectations of pleasure and pain tinge the whole fabric so that sometimes we are overwhelmed with this wealth of association or our responses are checked because the alternatives seem equally attractive. Then we hesitate and deliberate and our final determination is called the will. Now it is exactly this suspense which allows us time to examine our mental processes and our thoughts; that is to say, which allows them to become objects of inquiry in quite the way we study any other object. Philosophers are often tricked into believing that such a study of our thought is all there is to thinking; but this is no closer than the theory of vision and optics is to seeing. Logic and the characteristics of reasoning that we discover are themselves nothing but inductions over judgments actually made. The syllogism, no less than propositions such as "milk is white," is a child of art, not of nature, and this is true of "true" itself.

Priestley's empiricism is complete. All knowledge comes from experience and is not merely awakened by it. The universal and self-evident propositions so relied on by the Scots are nonexistent. It is most unlikely that children, e.g., have any intuition of a difference between a self and an external world until experience helps them to make it. Philosophers may become aware of the sensing media as necessary to the observation of an external world; they may even come to believe that our ideas arise without anything external to them through the immediate agency of the author of our being. Berkeley's position is in no wise absurd; it is merely a more complex and less natural hypothesis than one which assumes both a more general agency of the deity and that the objects are really there. The unity of consciousness is a feeling of unity, of *my* feeling; and the idea of the self which corresponds to *I* is only a complex idea not unlike that, e.g., of our country by which term

we denote a part of the world subject to that form of government by the laws of which we ourselves are bound, as distinguished from other countries, subject to other political systems of government; and the term *self* denotes that substance which is the seat of that particular set of sensations and ideas of which those that are then recollected make a part, as distinguished from other substances which are the seat of similar sets of sensations and ideas.[5]

As with the self, so with the questions of how reasons interact with the passions and how both can affect our physical movements; answers are at least more easily approached on the assumption that these are all functions of a common matter which is able to interact within itself.

Somewhat embarrassingly to the Philadelphia-Princeton Calvinists, Priestley lined up with Edwards as a necessitarian. But his special target, beside the Scottish team of Reid, Beattie, and Oswald, was Richard Price, a personal friend and fellow Unitarian. Against all of them he argued that consciousness of freedom is no evidence for free will at all because awareness of voluntary action entails being able to offer motives as causes or reasons for an action. Further, to take freedom in the sense of randomness or sheer spontaneity is simply to deny a fundamental scientific law that every change must have a cause. Priestley believed that the laws of human behavior, of choice following on preference, followed as fixed and mechanical laws as were to be found elsewhere in nature. Yet Priestley wanted not only to maintain this scientific hardheadedness about the universality of natural laws, but also to accept as facts our self-government in action and in thinking—the ability to make plans and to deliberate which was so central to the Scottish position. The proper opposite of necessity is not the voluntary but the contingent. Voluntaristic views are quite compatible with necessitarian ones when the latter are properly understood. Clearly we have the power to do what we will or please if unhindered by external causes, and importantly we even can suspend judgment; that point is not at issue. The matter does not begin with the willing, for every determination has its roots in the particulars of past experience, in our prior conditioning by pleasure and pain, and in what view one has of the situation and its alternatives (although what are seen as alternatives are also dependent upon past experience).

> What I contend for is that with the same state of mind, the same strength of any particular passion for example, and the same view of things . . . any particular object appearing equally desirable, he [any man] would always voluntarily make the same choice and come to the same determination.[6]

Priestley faced the standard free-will arguments by assuming the posture of his opponents that the will was a faculty. Somewhat fresher are the views he offered when he proceeded to abandon that assumption; indeed they fit easily into a modern approach-avoidance vocabulary. Like Hartley and other associationists, he held the whole man accountable for his behavior; action, judgment, and so-called willing are only particular aspects of the workings under associative laws of the whole man. Initially the child simply acts, striking out in every direction, but soon he identifies some of these motor activities with pleasure and pain. Thus he learns how to act voluntarily, to reach for the choicer apple with virtually no more interruption than that required by the bodily movements. What had been learned slowly now becomes habitual or secondarily automatic. Such phenomena can be accounted for directly in associative terms, though in complex situations we may have to add middle terms or means in the achievement of goals. Thus action following on deliberation follows the same pattern as judgment itself where assent sometimes follows on direct comparison of ideas and sometimes via a common term. We generally limit the term "voluntary" to those actions or patterns of thinking which require time-consuming deliberation, though the mechanisms operative are all the same. Interrupted tasks are the more painful the nearer to achievement the interruption comes, and of course we pursue activities with greater vigor as the anticipated pleasure is the greater and the more certain. Tasks directed toward unrealistic objectives are interrupted with virtually no pain. But in any case we choose that object or that action which appears preferable at the moment, and under similar circumstances of inclination and insight we should always make the same determination.

It follows, then, that remorse, insofar as it is backward-looking and implies that we ought or could have acted differently, is completely inappropriate. What is not inappropriate, however, is a present conviction of the deplorable state of our dispositions at the time that the vicious act was committed. That conviction may now operate so as to make the next act better—i.e., to enable us to do on a similar occasion now what we could not have done before. "And is not this all the benefit that a man can possibly derive from a sense of shame and self-reproach, commonly called remorse or conscience?"

Thus Priestley, in good associationist tradition, looked at man as an eminently educable animal. Further, he presses on to a social theory, looking toward the reform of both man and his institutions as an inevitable product of increasing socialization and of the betterment of the environment. The psychological law of association operating naturally on man and society is sufficient to solve the utilitarian problem of how an individual comes to place his own good in the larger pool of general welfare. Priestley figured importantly in the background of Utilitarianism and Bentham even credited him with the notion of utility, but Priestley differs from them and from Hume in the naturalness by which the associative mechanism reinforces the identification of private and public good, while artificial constraints such as legal reform are but the smallest part in the inevitability of a progress which rests on God's guidance and comprehensive design.

Despite this very qualified materialism, Priestley regarded himself as a Christian, though a Unitarian to be sure. Such materialism, he argued, far from being at odds with Christianity, was essential for its teaching, for had not Christ Himself been *bodily* resurrected? Christian though he might be, his theories understandably left him unpopular with the more orthodox. It is not strange, therefore, that he became a storm center, including among his strong supporters Watt, Erasmus Darwin, and virtually the whole of the wider Jeffersonian family. Jefferson's championing of Priestley and his recommendation of the latter's *An History of the Corruptions of the Christian Religion* (1782) as a text at the University of Virginia were made to order as butts of orthodox attack; and understandable, too, was the rejoicing among Princetonians when Henry disproved the phlogiston theory, in defense of which Priestley had staked his reputation.

The physicians of the day had already been working with Priestley-like assumptions about the interaction and the continuity of mind and body, and often enough, as in the case of Colden, they attempted to make explicit the premises. Medicine, then, was alive to broader philosophic and social issues and one looked to physicians not only for cures, but also for a view of human nature. They were intrigued by the nature of consciousness (or awareness) and its relation to sensation on the one hand and to its physiological base on the other; yet they did not limit themselves to the study of the proximate environment, of the body, but reached out to the context provided by the larger environment of climate, geography, occupation, and economic status. In good eighteenth-century style they studied, too, the effects of habit and racial stock on temperament and often used these as grounds for projected humanitarian reforms.

Medicine in America as well as in Europe was freeing itself from century-old incrustations—survivals of the four humors, of a soul operating on an independent track from the body, of insanity as a seizure of the spirit requiring moral remedies. Perhaps they were no longer hampered by such medieval conceits as led to the search for the geographic origin of disease, as in the case of syphilis, on the assumption that God's economy had placed there the natural remedy; but people still thought of illnesses as directly categorized by symptoms—of colds, yellow fever, jaundice, etc. This was still the age of the great systems of medicine, where metaphysical premises compensated for the sparseness of observation, but for all of that it was a time of turning away from the study of structure to that of function, from anatomy to physiology. The body became even for the most orthodox more than the site of spirit, and its functioning was seen to influence the mind in lawlike ways, while the mind, too, had its observable influences on the health and functioning of the body. Cullen in Edinburgh had provided a lead for the Americans, less by his "system" than by his classification of diseases into both those of bad body habits such as scurvy, and those of the nervous system such as epilepsy. The view of an intimate relation between body and mind was given added strength by those physiological investigations of Whytt and the Bells that we have mentioned earlier. Yet the work in America was never a mere carbon copy of that done in Edinburgh or London; quite independently the Americans were struggling to make clear the general principles of a medical science and to liberate themselves from exclusive reliance on a mechanical model, even that of a Priestley, in favor of a functional and sociological one.

When materialism is placed in a physiological context, when appeal is made to physical, psychosomatic, and sociomedical correlations that are open to general observation, it is not easy to discount it or label it as "infidelity," and Jefferson himself was grateful enough to have Priestley's materialism strengthened by the medical extensions of Benjamin Rush (1745-1813) and Thomas Cooper (1759-1840). It will be remembered that Rush, while studying medicine in Edinburgh, had been instrumental in persuading Witherspoon to come to Princeton. Rush studied under Cullen and the time was to come when he would attempt his own system, though based on fluids rather than irritability. And Rush, too, was of major importance in importing into America the Scottish view of university medical education rather than that of hospital-oriented studies as in England. Being abroad offered him more than medicine; he met Hume—after a stay in Paris where the salon conversation seemed to be of "oeconomics, liberty, and government"—introduced by a letter from Diderot. Rush also had friends among the Realists, especially Stewart.

After his return to America, Rush was caught up not only in medical affairs, but also in the intellectual and political movements which were sweeping the land. It was he who persuaded Thomas Paine to write an appeal for American independence, and though he feared reprisals against his family and practice, that did not deter him when the time came from adding his name to those of the other signers of the Declaration of Independence. His political activities did not cease after the Revolution; he was part of the Pennsylvania Convention that ratified the Federal Constitution, arguing effectively that an undue concern for autonomy had resulted in the downfall of the Greek city-states.

Rush's fine sense for experimental science shows throughout his work, but especially in the experiment he designed to test a proposed treatment for cancer. His apparent medical successes in dealing with yellow fever, together with his undoubted successes in establishing Philadelphia's hospital and medical school, earned him reputation and respect beyond Philadelphia. And he is still remembered for his view of insanity as a disease rather than as evidence of moral deficiency.

His *Enquiry Into the Influence of Physical Causes Upon the Moral Faculty* (1786), dedicated to Benjamin Franklin, was an attempt to deal with the reciprocal effects of mind and body. Rush did not himself construct a philosophical theory about mental substance; his concern was with the patent fact of interaction.

Do we observe the memory, the imagination and the judgement, to be affected by diseases, particularly by fevers, and madness? Where is the physician, who has not seen the moral faculty affected from the same causes? How often do we see the temper wholly changed by a fit of sickness! And how often do we hear persons of the most delicate virtue, utter speeches in the delirium of a fever, that are offensive to decency, or good manners. I have heard a well attested history of a clergyman of the most exemplary moral character, who spent the last moments of a fever which deprived him of both his reason and his life, in profane cursing and swearing.[7]

Rush went on to examine all sorts of interrelations, e.g., the influence of disease on memory and judgment, and of the weather on "the moral sensibility." Extending Cullen, Rush attempted to explain epilepsy in terms of a certain "convulsive operation of the moral faculty upon the bodily system." Yet he did not follow Priestley all the way in the latter's quasi-reduction of mind to force or matter, although he explicitly agreed that the immortality of the soul was not contingent on its immateriality. Moreover, as regards the freedom of the will, Rush attempted to carve out a position halfway between Priestley's determinism and Reid's thoroughgoing voluntarism. While Rush disagreed with Reid on some counts, he was by no means as great an opponent of common sense as was his friend Priestley. In particular, he was in the habit of advising his students to consult Reid on the moral faculty, and he enthusiastically seconded Reid's notion that moral sense is native to the human mind, though education may be required to develop it.

Rush was in the direct line of those eighteenth-century Scots who undertook to develop aspects of a science of man, but unlike most of them he saw the immediate consequences of his medical theories for social reform. For example, he argued that reformation of the criminal is not as well accomplished by exposing him to ignominy as by simple incarceration. The latter was much more to the point, since it left the criminal ample time to experience the salutary effects of shame. It was not criminality alone, but character generally, which responded to the moral, physical, and social environment and it followed, then, that the rational manipulation of such conditions would result in an improved citizenry.

Rush's influence—personal, medical, and especially philosophical—extended well into the nineteenth century. Wherever it is found, whether in the work of his son James (*The Philosophy of Human Nature*, 1812), or the writings of Joseph Buchanan and Thomas Upham, it helped keep alive the view that the physiological and the functional lay at the base of psychological phenomena.

While Rush did not work out the details of materialism in a physiological and medical setting, Thomas Cooper did—extending the theory in a systematic way, even to the social sciences. Cooper arrived in America with Priestley—persecuted by the same English conservatism, since he was a citizen of the French Republic and England had declared war on France in 1793.

Cooper shared Priestley's materialism as a starting point and agreed to its importance for Christianity and for psychology. He was a younger man, acquainted not only with Rush's inquiries, but also with medicine generally, and he faced the body-mind problems in quite a different scientific context than did his mentor.

Cooper had read law at Oxford, but he failed to take the degree, it may be presumed, because his Unitarian sympathies would not allow him to sign the Articles. This legal training served him well, because his first vocations in America were as lawyer and judge—and legal training permeated even the tracts that got him imprisoned under the alien and sedition laws until he was rescued by Jefferson. Even before leaving England, however, his loyalties were divided among law and chemistry and medicine, and he haunted the hospitals in London. In America he taught chemistry, first at Dickinson, and then at the University of Pennsylvania—where he also practiced medicine. He later was invited to the University of South Carolina where he served successively as professor of chemistry, president of the university, professor of geology, and professor of economy. It is not to be supposed that such versatility carried with it any hint of superficiality: for instance, his lectures on geology were regarded as second only to those of Silliman at Yale.

Cooper was not only a younger man armed with different scientific resources, but he also was a different kind of man from Priestley. Where Priestley was a gentle soul who suffered even the ravages of Birmingham without bitterness, Cooper was a vivid and irritating campaigner with a pen equal to his belligerence. He attacked the clergy, whom he saw as a class with a vested interest in protecting their dogma in ways which immunized them from free inquiry and penalized others for undertaking it. As a class he saw them seeking prestige, power, and financial resources, insinuating themselves even into government. Worst of all, the clerical class, including the "aggressive Presbyterians" as well as the "timid Episcopalians," sought control of education. Cooper carries on the polemic:

> The clergy of this country . . . the Calvinistic clergy chiefly, are united in persecuting every man who calls in question any of their metaphysical opinions, or who hints at their views of ambition and aggrandizement . . . they are steadily aiming to obtain the entire control of every seminary of education, throughout the United States; claiming the exclusive superintendance of them as a matter of right. It is high time to warn the people that their liberties are in danger; that they are about to be undermined by a crafty, persevering, insidious foe in the imposing garb of a heavenly friend.[8]

From this, which is but a small sample of an often repeated attack on the clergy, it is easy to understand the hostility which the Presbyterians felt for him. Furthermore, this very vocal antagonism repeatedly lost him opportunities in the academic world. Still, it is an index of the times that his academic career, however stormy and curtailed, lasted virtually until his death.

Though taking his cue from Priestley's attitude toward Christianity, Cooper subjected the Christian evidences to an even more extended and, of course, more vitriolic exegesis than did Priestley. Cooper disavows the fantastic superstructure of Christianity's theology, its metaphysics, and its foolish questions. With spiteful glee he recounts the differences of opinion of trinitarian as opposed to unitarian, of the Romish as opposed to the Greek Church, of the Arian as opposed to the Priestleyan. He strips Christianity down to its barest bones—what he took to be those few plain propositions that are to be found in the New Testament and in the facts of Jesus' ministry. The doctrine of an immortal soul is not even hinted at in these "genuine" sources. More than that, the assumption that the soul is immaterial is a positive denial of the bodily resurrection of Jesus no less than of our own promised resurrection. After all, there is no need of a resurrection of that which has not died; if our soul were already immortal and saved, what substance would the promise have? The evidence shows that it is the material body which is promised immortality. Cooper published these arguments defending the materialism of Christianity in a pamphlet, one of which he sent to Jefferson. Jefferson answered, "That the doctrine of Materialism was that of Jesus himself, was a new idea to me. Yet it is *proved unquestionably*. We all knew it was that of some of the early Fathers."[9]

Given the mutual antipathy between Cooper and the clerics, it is not surprising that he opposed the Scottish metaphysicians on principle, even when the points that separated them were all but indistinguishable. Cooper, as opposed to Reid, maintained that association is sufficient to account for all knowledge, voluntary action, consciousness, and even for attention and effort. The standard Priestley-Hartley associational theory is all there: ideas evolve as we mature and interact with the world; desire arises when ideas are associated with pleasant experiences, and is as real and as genuinely connected with feelings as vision is connected with optic stimulation. The voluntary actions can be distinguished from involuntary ones without appeal to the faculty of a will. Yet Cooper went far beyond the Priestley-Hartley theory, for he drew not only on the British tradition of Hume, Brown, Stewart, and Erasmus Darwin, but also upon the French Ideologues and philosopher-physicians. Priestley developed his theory in notes for an abridged edition of Hartley's works, in which he omitted the outdated physiological part. Actually, the tradition of British associationism, from Priestley well through the Mills and Bain, remained almost indifferent to the developing science of physiology, while the French tradition stayed close to it. Indeed, the Ideologues who were influential upon Jefferson were making positive effort to bring medicine into philosophy and philosophy into medicine. In a way, Cooper's concern to relate sensibility, physiologically understood, to sensation and consciousness was an early attempt to reweld the diverging French and British interests. When viewed in the light of Cooper's efforts, Jefferson's own blending of Stewart with the

Ideologues does not appear to be a naive eclecticism, since the later Scots, especially Stewart and Brown, often make common cause with the French.

In the letter in which he had identified Jesus himself as a materialist, Jefferson concluded that he hoped a "physiological part would follow," meaning that he hoped for further evidence of that kind to fill out his defense of materialism. Cooper did not provide the original physiological materials but instead translated Broussais's *On Irritation and Insanity* (1831),[10] interlarding it with extensive notes and commentary. In publishing it he appended two tracts concerning materialism which were written before he left Europe and which included his account of Christianity together with an outline of associationism. All of this evidences Cooper's very early awareness of the physiological basis of action and knowledge, as he cites, among others, Flourens, Bichat, Pinel, and Broussais. While Broussais is not as well known as the others mentioned, his account and criticism of the history of the problems, together with a truly novel functional view of the organism, is woven into American thought through Cooper and Jefferson to James. It is worth looking at this chapter in French medical philosophy briefly, for it carries us into some of the figures and ideas that had direct influence on the American thinkers.

Broussais's account, as presented by Cooper, of course starts with Descartes, for it was he who colored the thought of the century, and from him French theorists inherited the mechanistic and physiological tinge to their view of the mind-body question. Descartes held that animals are automata, operating on purely mechanical principles. Man's behavior is also largely automatic, but he also possesses a soul, capable of existing separately from the matter of his body, and accounting for those few of his activities which are rational or volitional. The soul is seated in the pineal gland.

In this doctrine, couched in terms of a strong metaphysical dualism, lie the seeds of the difficulty which has occupied so prominent a place in post-Cartesian philosophy: the nature of the interaction of mind and body. The metaphysical grounds for announcing that material substance (*res extensa*) and mental substance (*res cogitans*) are utterly discontinuous were suspect to succeeding generations; they began to think of Descartes's causal interconnections as an egregious case of creaking metaphysics. De La Mettrie (1709-1751), in his *L'Homme Machine*, early challenged the Cartesian discontinuity. He reasoned that if animal behavior can be explained without recourse to the hypothesis of a soul, then why not man's behavior as well? However, at the critical moment, De La Mettrie failed to commit himself definitively to the materiality of the soul.

Condillac (1715-1780), who, together with Voltaire, popularized Locke and Newton among the French, took the next step. He attempted to systematize Locke by dispatching Locke's tentativeness together with the remnants of innate ideas which he thought Locke still preserved in his "internal senses." Condillac, as is well known, made a frank effort to account for all thought on the basis of sensation alone. All psychical functions are merely sensations transformed, and even attention is essentially the passive presence of a sensation or its persistence in memory. Condillac not only chipped away at the dualisms of Locke, but also intensified the method of analyzing complex ideas into their simple, irreducible constituents. The early writings of Condillac left him vulnerable to a charge of Berkeleyan idealism, since he said nothing of the external causes of sensation, nor of the reality of the self. The later *Traitè* (1754), though still leaning on Berkeley, acknowledges that the notions of the external world, though consequences of our practical needs, depend on a material reality, which is nothing but matter in motion. The sense of touch, as in Berkeley, is critical to our access to the external world, for it gives rise to belief in it, in particular, through the sensations of resistance and impenetrability. Condillac thus appears to be as much a materialist as Priestley, though he sides with the Scottish realists' interpretation of Locke.

Condillac was a most prestigious figure, and the succeeding generations of Ideologues paid homage to him, even as they went about seriously modifying his view of sensation so as to stress the individuality of human responses and the richness of the stimuli that lay ready in the physical and social environment.

With the Ideologues we come to men whose influence upon the Americans was felt through personal contacts. Cabanis, e.g., was a friend of Franklin, and Destutt de Tracy, of Jefferson. Jefferson was involved with various successful efforts to translate De Tracy's writings and to have them used in the colleges. Cabanis and Destutt de Tracy were, at least for our purposes, the most important of the Ideologues, a group of intellectual revolutionaries who were, in effect, retired to Helvetius's estate at Auteuil when Napoleon found that he could not convert them into apologists for his regime. The activities of these two physicians extended from politics, theoretical and practical, to education, but what concerns us here is their interest in philosophical psychology. Though these friends were working in closest contact, they each gave rise to interestingly divergent trends within French thought. For whereas De Tracy looked for the manifestations of consciousness in logic, grammar, language, and other social products, Cabanis concerned himself almost exclusively with physiological phenomena. De Tracy's emphasis on activity led later to a voluntarism in America which was ultimately joined to a version of Scottish philosophy. Cabanis's work, rather than becoming an inspiration for a new philosophic tradition, was allied to the history of French medicine and psychology.

Destutt de Tracy (1754-1836) was a zoologist—where "zoologie" is understood broadly as the natural history of living "organisms," which includes social institutions. De Tracy, whose influence on Jefferson was considerable as we shall see, held not only that all ideas are derived from sensation, but also that they *are* sensations. The idea of red is the "sensation" of red. We have both simple sensations (simple ideas) which are individual sense qualities, and compound sensations (complex ideas), which are combinations of simple sensations. Memories of sensations are also sensations. Even judgments are sensations, for a judgment is alleged to consist in the perception of agreement between subject and predicate, where that agreement is "felt," so that to perceive the agreement of S and P is to have the sensation of S agreeing with P.

Sensations are "modifications" of our sensibility, and do not by themselves inform us of external reality. They do, however, prove our own existence. De Tracy wrote that Descartes ought to have altered his celebrated dictum to "I feel, therefore I exist." To feel is to know that that which feels, is. This is not idealism, however: not only do we exist, but there exists a mind-independent reality which we can know. The proof of this is in the impotence of our will. Each bodily movement is accompanied by a peculiar sensation, the "sensation of movement." Let it be supposed that I wish to perpetuate this sensation, but find it stopping at a certain point despite my voluntary exertions. Since it is impossible that I am simultaneously willing *both* the continuation and the cessation of the sensation in question, it must be that the cessation is not of my doing. Hence there is something outside myself which resists my will. The reality of this "something" is not given in my simple sensations; its existence is deduced in the manner indicated. This, of course, is very like the doctrine of Stewart.

De Tracy seeks to derive the properties of matter from the fact that this "something" resists our wills. The derivable properties—inertia, mobility, extension, form, divisibility, impenetrability, etc.—are primary qualities. These properties are not given as elementary sensations, but are inferred in the process of reasoning about sensations. In the same fashion, De Tracy seeks to prove the existence of space and duration. His conclusion, as should be apparent, is that all those features of the world are demonstrably real which are needed for a mechanical description such as Newton's.

If our simple sensations are modifications of our sensibility, as De Tracy claims, what is the relation of these "modifications" to material objects? One notices, he claims, that the feeling of cessation in question is always accompanied by other feelings, e.g., those which are tactile, visual, auditory, etc. One "makes of these sensations the properties of the being which, despite my will, causes the sensation of movement, which I wish to continue, to cease."[11] Are these associated sensations, then, properties of the object itself, or merely effects in us of the object's unknown properties? De Tracy answers that it makes no difference which claim we make. Apart from the existence and primary qualities of the object, which are established by reasoning about our sensations, all we can know about the object is that it causes such and such sensations in us.

So long as we can combine these simple sensations into a consistent concept of an object, we are entitled to call that concept true—for it will be true to our experience, and we can know nothing beyond experience against which it could be tested. Simple sensations, being untestable, are indubitable. The criterion of truth is phenomenal coherence. De Tracy's theory takes an odd turn here, owing to his theory of error. If the sensation of "S agreeing with P" is the judgment that S is P, and if simple sensations are indubitable, it seems to follow that all judgments are indubitable, and that accordingly error is impossible. If there is error, De Tracy explains, then in fact S is not P. The mistake lies, not in our judgment that S is P, but rather in the memory which incorrectly reproduced S or P. What I really sensed was not that S is P, but rather that S' is P (where "S'" is an inaccurate memory of S). The doctrine that all error arises from inaccuracy in the memory is still a coherentist position, since truth depends still on consistent relations among ideas (sensations).

He was quite prepared to accept the continuity of consciousness throughout the animal world and also to see the continuity of thinking with feeling and sensibility. Even the will is merely a kind of impression. Still, there is an active side of perception which is, at least insofar as it involves attention, more than the passive reception of sensory stimuli. Experiences of voluntary effort combined with a felt resistance, for example in the attempt to lift an inordinately heavy object, lead us to infer the existence of an external world, but this is an inference and not a direct sensation. His view of the self as a person is also an inference, derived from feelings of many willed efforts and activities in the face of resistance. It was this emphasis on activity which became woven into the French tradition of voluntarism. Laromiguière (1756-1837) and Maine de Biran (1776-1824) developed the notion of "felt effort" and active attention toward those notions of intention and purposive behavior which are so difficult to account for in a simple stimulus-response model, as the Scottish Common Sense Realists saw. Laromiguière's and Biran's work laid great stress on the notion of personality (which they used to explain the unity and connectedness which Hume had explicated by the formation of habits). Thus De Tracy and his successors interested themselves in very much the same questions as did Dugald Stewart and Thomas Brown. Jefferson could see that the Scots and the French were by no means opposed on such issues as the reality of the external world and its inferred character, and the activity of the self. In the next generation, Frenchmen like Royer-Collard, Jouffroy, and Cousin consciously imported Scottish philosophy. Cousin, especially, formed a bridge for the Kantian stress on the activity of the knower.

Cabanis (1757-1808) was struck by the necessary relation of the sensible with the physical. Sensibility, he argued, is a fundamental property of the nervous system, and it may reach different levels of organization: e.g., in men the highest organization of sensibility will be consciousness or mental activity. Mental activity, however, is necessarily associated with the brain as are other sensations with the appropriate sense organs. Indeed, thinking may be regarded as a functional property of the brain just as digestion is an operation of the stomach—and in neither case is the function separable from its physical housing. The moral and the mental are but the physical viewed from different vantage points, and all are parts of the natural history of man. Cabanis distinguished instinctive reactions from those which are guided by consciousness, though he emphasized the frequency of the former. He also reinstated an "inner sense," although this is to be understood in the physiologically respectable terms of visceral and muscular alterations. He departed from Condillac in another way, holding that the mere unordered addition of sensation to sensation does not amount to experience, for knowledge is more than sequential sensation and consciousness must be understood as but one function of an organism, itself taken to be an active, functioning whole. It was from this sort of physiological premise that later men such as Flourens, Bichat, and Broussais himself took their start.

Flourens was an extraordinarily great experimenter, and the points he struggled so hard to establish are still "debatables" in James's *Psychology*. By extremely neat surgery on pigeons, he was able to show that if the cerebellum is excised, the organism becomes incapable of the control of the voluntary muscles, as in locomotion; while if the cerebrum is excised—without further damage to tissue—the pigeon, though continuing to live, becomes incapable of perceiving, thinking, willing, and—presumably—judging. Flourens thus sees the function of the hemisphere, though different, as dependent on a nervous system, with some localized functions—in contrast to Descartes—and also some generalized functions—in contrast to the phrenologists Gall and Spurzheim, who were, even then, making such a stir in America. Though making no such dramatic experiments, Broussais had a more interesting philosophic picture, for he saw the nervous system as but one among many systems in functional interaction.

The relation of philosophy and medicine that we have just reviewed—as well as Cooper's use of these developments, together with his notes and appendices to Broussais's work—evidences a lack of separation, at this early date, of empirical medicine from "metaphysical" theories. Broussais (and, one presumes, Cooper) was anticipating that the philosophy of the future would ground its theories in a sound physiology. His argument is twofold: first, there is a polemic against the clerical invasion of metaphysics, which Broussais (and Cooper) considers to be wrong in its very method; second, there is an argument aimed at the destruction of the clerical assumptions regarding a separate soul—assumptions which constituted such a disaster to medical treatment, for, naturally, physical medicaments were useless to an immaterial soul. The whole history of remedies for insanity, e.g., shows that they amount to little more than superstition, Rush's theory excepted. In Cooper's words:

> One main intention of Dr. Broussais . . . is to rescue the theory of Insanity from the supposition that it is an affection of the mind or soul . . . Insanity, according to Broussais, is a disease not of the mind, but of the body; and its seat is in the encephalon. Hence it became necessary for him to shew the total want of reasonable evidence attending the hypothesis of a soul, separate and

distinct in its existence from the body, though by some means and in some manner united with it.[12]

Cooper's implied objection is methodological: the hypothesis of a "soul," an entity without any function, violates the criterion of simplicity. Descartes's own lame attempt to locate the soul in the pineal gland carries with it the suggestion that the soul is extended, which, of course, is expressly denied in the *Meditations*. On the other hand, a thorough empiricism requires even the phenomenon of consciousness, and any knowledge about it, to be derived from sense perception. The dodge, so to speak, in which philosophers such as Reid, Cousin, and Kant indulged, took the form of cutting off the two domains: insulating the introspective knowledge of consciousness (a priori knowledge) from empirical psychology and physiology. This thesis represented to Broussais and Cooper an insufferable abuse, before which even the Ideologues had remained silent.

Medicine needs no "soul," yet it does need something called "sensibility," which Broussais understands—more straightforwardly than Cabanis—as a functional property of tissue to respond, and it cannot be studied independently of vital tissue. Similarly, consciousness itself is not an entity, a *res cogitans*, simple and indissoluble, but rather it is a property of functioning material bodies. The point is applicable generally:

> Sensation, perception, feeling, consciousness, are words denoting that property or function of the encephalic nervous apparatus by which we have cognizance of objects extraneous to us. . . . This property or function of the encephalon is termed *Sensibility*. It connects us with the material world extraneous to our bodies, and with the affections or modifications of our internal organs. . . .[13]

In thus placing consciousness among phenomena like sensation and feeling, Cooper-Broussais sounds, to the modern reader, somewhat like William James. The denial that consciousness is an entity and the arguments offered foreshadow the famous Jamesean negative to the question, "Does Consciousness Exist?" There are other similarities also with the pragmatic outlook, from the strong appeal to physiology as necessary to the understanding of the causal factors of behavior to the emphasis on ideomotor activity. Even the general prejudice in favor of functional or operational definition is to be found in Cooper-Broussais.

> We may, without difficulty, and assuredly without hypothesis, reduce all abstract substances, or entities, to functional phenomena, by shewing that they are no more than the representative signs of the modifications or varieties in perception, which every observer remarks in himself.[14]

Perhaps the eighteenth-century writers are even bolder than the pragmatists, for the former were willing to apply their theories even to "life" itself: it too they conceived, not as an entity, but as an aggregate of functions of the systems which compose an organism, while health and disease, which have too often been personified, are characteristics (normal or deranged) of the functioning of tissues.

> Life is the aggregate of those functions which the several organic parts of the body perform on being stimulated into action, by the natural stimuli of caloric, light, air, atmospheric electricity, and food, in the usual and regular proportions and degree.[15]

Broussais's illustration of this point of view was its application to the topic of insanity, which he regarded as an irritation of the brain and nervous system. Medical science, relieved of the worries over the soul, could shed its heavy metaphysical baggage and proceed with experimentation. "Sensibility" is a name for a property of systems operating normally, i.e., without excess of stimulation of an external or internal origin; "irritation" is the pathological, abnormal state. Insanity is not the result of hyperexcitation—it *is* hyperexcitation. This analysis is paralleled in his treatment of volition: the will is not a faculty making decisions, volition is the choosing or the willing.

It is evident from Cooper's footnotes and references to American translations and texts that he was not alone among the philosophically minded physicians to appreciate the merits of the physiological approach. What was going on here was a shift in the discussion of the mind-body relationship from a point of view allied to physics (Priestley), to an intermediate stage in which the influences of the environment were stressed (Rush), to a stage in which the physiological aspects of the organism became crucial, making the mind-body distinction at best methodological (Cooper). The Scots, in whose line Rush followed, had progressed sufficiently to think in terms of systems, e.g., the work of the Bells on the afferent-efferent nerves. What Broussais and Cooper add to this view is the notion of interaction (perhaps even of transaction, to speak modernly) between open systems—a notion which the older Newtonian model of closed systems had some difficulty in handling. The newer model is one of functional interdependence, and though it was tentative and unsung, it contained the seeds of a more mature view, of an evolutionary account of human nature in dynamic interaction with the total environment.

Priestley, Rush, and Cooper were all members of what may be roughly called the Jeffersonian circle. But the central figure of this group was of course Jefferson. Born in 1743 at Shadwell, Virginia, Thomas Jefferson was the eldest son of Peter Jefferson, a wealthy Virginia planter, and Jane Randolph. He entered William and Mary College in 1760, and subsequently studied law under George Wythe, being admitted to the bar in 1767. He was elected to the Virginia House of Burgesses in

1769 and to the Virginia Convention in 1775. In the latter year he was also chosen to represent Virginia in the Continental Congress, and in 1776 was commissioned by that body to write the Declaration of Independence. During the Revolution he served as governor of Virginia, and thereafter was Franklin's successor as minister to France. He served as Secretary of State under Washington, as Vice-President under Adams, and as President of the United States from 1800 to 1808, after which he retired to Virginia where he died in 1826. Despite this remarkable career of public service, Jefferson was also a scientist of importance, an inventor, an educator, a philosopher, and an architect. Indeed, the versatility and range of his mind exceeded even Franklin's, and made him one of the intellectual leaders of America in his day, and the most conspicuous figure of the American Enlightenment.[16]

Jefferson's brilliant success as a political leader who not only won the Presidency, but also built a political coalition to support his program which endured long beyond his term of office has focused primary attention upon his political philosophy, and indeed he is generally regarded as the foremost American political thinker. However justifiable this emphasis is in terms of Jefferson's role in American history, it has had the unfortunate result of obscuring the relations between his political doctrines and the rest of his philosophic views—views which have close ties to those of Priestley, Rush, and Cooper. Jefferson never developed these views in any systematic treatise, so that his doctrines must be culled from his letters and papers, but what emerges from these fragmentary sources is a remarkably consistent and well-thought-out position. In the following pages we shall be more concerned with these general philosophic views rather than with his better known political principles, but in a later section we shall try to indicate the degree to which his political doctrines were based on his views in epistemology and moral philosophy.

In 1820 John Adams wrote Jefferson a letter in which he urged some of Berkeley's skeptical arguments.[17] Jefferson's reply was as follows:

'I feel: therefore I exist'. I feel bodies which are not myself: there are other existences then. I call them *matter*. I feel them changing place. This gives me *motion*. Where there is an absence of matter, I call it *void*, or *nothing*, or *immaterial space*. On the basis of sensation, of matter and motion, we may erect the fabric of all the certainties we can have or need. I can conceive *thought* to be an action of a particular organization of matter, formed for that purpose by its creator, as well as that *attraction* is an action of matter, or *magnetism* of loadstone. When he who denies to the Creator the power of endowing matter with the mode of action called *thinking* shall show how he could endow the Sun with the mode of action called *attraction*, which reins the planets in the tract of their orbits, or how an absence of matter can have a will, and, by that will, put matter into motion, then the materialist may be lawfully required to explain the process by which matter exercises the faculty of thinking. When once we quit the basis of sensation, all is in the wind. To talk of *immaterial* existences is to talk of *nothings*. To say that the human soul, angels, god, are immaterial, is to say they are *nothings*, or that there is no god, no angels, no soul. I cannot reason otherwise: but I believe I am supported in my creed of materialism by Locke, Tracy, and Stewart. . . .

Rejecting all organs of information therefore but my senses, I rid myself of the Pyrrhonisms with which an indulgence in speculations hyperphysical and antiphysical so uselessly occupy and disquiet the mind. A single sense may indeed be sometimes deceived, but rarely: and never all our senses together, with their faculty of reasoning. They evidence realities; and there are enough of these for all the purposes of life, without plunging into the fathomless abyss of dreams and phantasms.[18]

This letter contains Jefferson's most explicit statement of epistemology, and indicates his primary debts. It is likely that Jefferson's early views on this subject were derived from Locke, for whom he had an immense admiration. But during his years in France he became acquainted with the Scottish philosophy of Dugald Stewart,[19] and subsequently with the work of the French Ideologues, Destutt de Tracy and Cabanis.[20] His estimate of these men was extremely high:

I consider him [Stewart] and Tracy as the ablest Metaphysicians living; by which I mean Investigators of the thinking faculty of man. Stuart [*sic*] seems to have given it's natural history, from facts and observations; Tracy it's modes of action and deducation [*sic*], which he calls Logic, and Ideology; and Cabanis, in his Physique et Morale de l'homme, has investigated anatomically, and most ingeniously, the particular organs in the human structure which may most probably exercise that faculty.[21]

The views on epistemology which Jefferson expressed in this 1820 letter quoted above are a curious blend of De Tracy and Stewart.

Jefferson regarded De Tracy's argument for the existence of real objects as affording "the most complete demolition of the Skeptical doctrines which I have ever met with,"[22] so it is not surprising that he relied on De Tracy in answering Adams. The phrase "I feel: therefore I exist" is a direct quote from De Tracy,[23] and the argument for matter, motion, and space clearly follows De Tracy's chapters on the existence and the properties of bodies. But although the references to De Tracy in these sentences are clear, it should also be noted that these doctrines are consistent with Stewart's position, which also derives knowledge of our own existence from sensations,[24] and which is also realistic. The last paragraph, however, presents more difficulties. Strictly speaking, neither De Tracy nor Stewart would admit that the senses can be deceived, but on Stewart's theory such a statement has at least a reasonable meaning—viz., that the sensation is taken to be a sign of an object of which, in this case, it is not a sign[25]—while De Tracy's insistence that the senses are infallible and that error arises only from memory virtually precluded such an expression. The view expressed in this paragraph is in any case a straightforward realism which is strongly reminiscent of Stewart. If Jefferson's formulation is more naive than Cooper's, still he saw more clearly than some subsequent commentators that there was no incompatibility between Stewart and De Tracy.

Jefferson's letter to Adams also throws considerable light on the character of his materialism. Jefferson remarks: "I feel bodies which are not myself: there are other existences then. I call them *matter*."[26] Why did Jefferson call them "matter"? Is this simply an arbitrary definition, in which case his materialism is really vacuous, or is there some reason why these existences are termed "matter"? The answer is probably to be found in Tracy's argument concerning the properties of real objects. Having argued that we know the existence of the real by its resistance to our will, he then seeks to prove that by virtue of that resistance all real bodies must have the properties of inertia, extension, mobility, form, etc. As remarked above, these properties of the real turn out to be essentially those necessary for a mechanistic description. But in that case it is obvious that whatever is, is material in the Newtonian sense of that term. In fact, both De Tracy and Stewart are so dominated by the Newtonian model that they make it constitutive of reality: to be real is to be material, and what is not material, if it could be real, could never be known to be so. Thus Jefferson asserts, "To talk of *immaterial* existences is to talk of *nothings*."[27]

Such a materialistic position leaves Jefferson with certain obvious problems: what is one to do with those things which are traditionally regarded as immaterial, God and the soul? On the grounds Jefferson has taken, either there are no such things, or they are material. Jefferson chose the latter alternative. That God exists he regarded as empirically demonstrable, for in reply to the argument of the atheist, Jefferson wrote:

the Theist pointing 'to the heavens above, and to the earth beneath, and to the waters under the earth', asked if these did not proclaim a first cause, possessing intelligence and power; power in the production, and intelligence in the design and constant preservation of the system; urged the palpable existence of final causes, that the eye was made to see, and the ear to hear, and not that we see because we have eyes, and hear because we have ears; an answer obvious to the senses, as that of walking across the room was to the philosopher demonstrating the nonexistence of motion.[28]

One sees here how strong a hold the axiom that order implies an orderer had on the eighteenth-century mind. That the order he saw was not a "design" was to Jefferson inconceivable. Thus the existence of a God who was the creator and designer of the universe seemed to him undeniable. Jefferson admitted that "of the nature of this being we know nothing";[29] nevertheless, he was quite sure that he did know some things about God. He knew, for instance, that God was a material entity, for "to talk of *immaterial* existences is to talk of *nothings*."[30] Indeed, Jefferson went so far as to claim that those who assert the immateriality of God "are merely atheists, differing from the material Atheist only in their belief that 'nothing made something,' and from the material deist who believes that matter alone can operate on matter."[31] This passage illustrates again Jefferson's equation of matter and existence, but it also suggests a further reason for his denial of immateriality—viz., the difficulty of explaining how immaterial entities can operate on material ones. But Jefferson is here in serious trouble. God is, he asserts, the creator and designer of the universe; it is God who endowed matter with the property of attraction, and, therefore, who established the laws of mechanics.[32] Is God, then, governed by these laws? To be material, in the sense in which Jefferson uses it, would seem to mean having inertia, figure, extension, impenetrability, etc.—i.e., the properties which characterize matter in the Newtonian and Lockean sense. To say that only matter can act on matter is in Jefferson's frame of reference to assert that all action is mechanical. But these assertions make God subject to the laws He is supposed to have created. And conversely, to say He is not subject to them, and does not have the properties of Newtonian matter, is, for Jefferson, to say He does not exist. If the Newtonian model is made constitutive of reality, then it governs God, or there is no God.

Jefferson is certain of other attributes of God besides His materiality. He is certain of His skill as a workman, His power, and His benevolence. As one would expect, it is the perfect economy of nature which is the proof of these attributes. "I hold (without appeal to revelation) that when we take a view of the Universe, in it's parts general or particular, it is impossible for the human mind not to perceive and feel a conviction of design, consummate skill, and indefinite power in every atom of it's composition."[33] And this system of nature is benign: "it has been framed on a principle of benevolence, and more pleasure than pain dealt out to us."[34] God is, therefore, wise, powerful, and benevolent, but he is not immanent. Jefferson was a religious man and a moral man, but he was not a pious man—indeed, I think it would be correct to say that he had no concept of piety. He did not long for personal communion with God or for ecstatic religious experience—in Edwards's phrase, he had no relish for spiritual things. He did not even find it necessary, as Franklin did, to insist upon man's direct dependence upon God as a basis for morality. Jefferson was a devout man, but his devotion was a rational devotion to a rational deity: he was content to know his God through the evidences of the creation and required no more intimate relationship.

In view of these beliefs about God it is not surprising that Jefferson rejected completely all claims for the authority of the Bible and for the supernatural status or inspiration of Jesus.[35] Yet he had great admiration for Jesus, whom he considered to be the greatest moral teacher in history.[36] Jefferson was convinced that the

text of the Gospels had suffered numerous corruptions, and he tried to separate out
the true sayings of Jesus from the rest. The result was "a wee-little book
. . . which I call the Philosophy of Jesus . . .[37] A more beautiful or precious morsel
of ethics I have never seen; it is a document in proof that I am a *real Christian*, that
is to say, a disciple of the doctrines of Jesus . . ."[38] Jefferson has often been called
a deist, and that description is certainly not false, but it would be more accurate to
call him, as he called himself, a Unitarian.[39]

If even God is material it is obvious that the soul must be material, and so
Jefferson asserts.[40] This leaves him with two basic problems respecting the soul:
how to account for thought, and whether or not the soul is immortal. The answer to
the first is contained in the letter to Adams quoted above. He holds "*thought* to be
an action of a particular organization of matter,"[41] and to the objection that
mechanics knows no such action, he replies that mechanics cannot explain how
matter acquired "the mode of action called *attraction*"[42] either, but no one doubts
that it has it. Thus Jefferson adopts the functional view of thought which we have
seen developed in Cooper and Broussais, and his sources for it were clearly the
work of the French thinkers, especially Flourens and Cabanis.

> He [Flourens] takes out the cerebrum completely, leaving the cerebellum and
> other parts of the system uninjured. The animal loses all its senses of hearing,
> seeing, feeling, smelling, tasting, is totally deprived of will, intelligence,
> memory, perception, etc., yet lives for months in perfect health, with all it's
> powers of motion, but without moving but on external excitement, starving
> even on a pile of grain unless crammed down it's throat . . . He takes the
> cerebellum out of others, leaving the cerebrum untouched. The animal retains
> all its senses, faculties and understanding, but loses the power of regulated
> motion, and exhibits all the symptoms of drunkenness . . . Cabanis had
> proved, from the anatomical structure of certain portions of the human frame,
> that they might be capable of receiving from the Creator the faculty of
> thinking. Flourens proves that the cerebrum is the thinking organ, and that
> life and health may continue, and the animal be entirely without thought, if
> deprived of that organ. I wish to see what the spiritualists will say to this.[43]

Here, indeed, was evidence that seemed to prove Jefferson's materialistic view of
thinking.

As one would expect, Jefferson had no doubts about immortality. Having
admitted the existence of a material God who endures forever, why hesitate to
admit a material soul to the same estate? Of the nature of this afterlife Jefferson
evidently thought we could know nothing while in this one except that such a state
exists. Presumably, we shall be held responsible, then, for our conduct now, but
Jefferson has very little to say about this. The benevolence of God was a sufficient
guarantee that the afterlife need not be dreaded.[44]

Locke and Orthodoxy

The views of the Jeffersonians were widely known, in part because of Jefferson's commanding position in the nation's life, but also because men such as Priestley, Rush, and Cooper were distinguished in their own right. Taken together, these men propounded a forceful naturalism which drew support from current work in chemistry, physics, physiology, and medicine in both Europe and America. For orthodox religion, this naturalism posed a serious threat which had to be met. The response of the orthodox was in fact somewhat schizophrenic. On the one hand, it met the situation by political activity directed to control existing colleges, and failing that it often moved to establish "safe" institutions of its own, much to the detriment of higher instruction in America. On the other hand, the orthodox produced their own versions of Locke, which were often subtle and by no means insensitive to the advances in medical knowledge. Thus it happened that orthodox university professors, almost as often as not, fought on the side of the angels—that is, on the side of free inquiry and science.

Frederick Beasley (1777-1845), successively a student at Princeton under S. Stanhope Smith and an Episcopalian minister, became ultimately professor of philosophy and provost of the University of Pennsylvania. He was a source for the early affair of Princetonians with Berkeleyan idealism, and for his own and Smith's conversion to realism by Witherspoon. Writing from Pennsylvania, then in Episcopalian orbit, Beasley attacked the Scottish philosophy vigorously, yet less for its realism than for its pretensions to have corrected the eminent Locke. Reid's realism Beasley found already fully developed in Locke.[45] Reid's mistake was in turning Locke into a representative realist. Assuming the consistency of Locke, Beasley marshaled the passages from the *Essay* which support a realist interpretation. Only at one point did he allow that Locke faltered—i.e., in believing in ideas of primary qualities. Beasley goes on to defend a causal relation holding between physical and mental processes on the basis of a sophisticated Priestleyan physiology. He is at his best in skillful accounts of perception and of classic problems of illusion, e.g., why the moon appears larger on the horizon. Here he used the Berkeleyan associational theory to good advantage, although he gives the account in physical rather than phenomenological terms.

The mere publication of a book like Beasley's, with its detail and skill, indicates the general interest in the prevailing problems of the time, while his effort to defend Locke assumes an intimate knowledge of the text of the *Essay* and of the Scots on the part of his readers. His is a detailed and critical reckoning, though certainly not an original work, showing he knew his way about the common domain of philosophy, psychology, and physiology.

Samuel Miller's *Brief Retrospect of the Eighteenth Century* (1803)[46] is an enterprise of a very different order. Throughout it, there are innumerable signs of the churchman who engineered the resignation of Stanhope Smith and the subordination of Princeton to the theological seminary. Yet Miller's view of philosophy and the scope of his effort (a sketch of the Revolution and of the improvements in science, art, and literature) are encyclopedic. Often relying on secondary sources, and all too often evaluative, still his two volumes stand as an amazing effort at synthesis. He carries a discussion of language from questions of philology, classic and Oriental studies, to universal grammar. He treats the educational innovations in method and practice, gives an account of literary and scientific societies and publications, and includes discussions of "nations lately become literary," comparing the achievements of America with those of Russia and the Germanies. Richest in detail is his account of intellectual life in America: its colleges, booksellers, libraries, presses, and the previously mentioned relative merits of New England and the Middle states.

Miller begins his second volume with an account of the philosophy of mind, lamenting that the methods of Newton have not yet been applied there with the success with which they were employed in the physical sciences. In apparent search for the broader uses of Newton, he reviews the history of philosophy from Descartes and Locke to the idealism of Malebranche and Berkeley, and the skeptical conclusions of Hume. Miller even follows German idealism from Leibniz through Wolff to "the celebrated system of Kant," and although he relies on an article in *The Monthly Review of London*, he gives, all things considered, an accurate account of Kant's phenomenalism, of theoretical and practical reason, and of the distinction between analytic and synthetic propositions. And if his readers studied this carefully they were early equipped with the rudiments of Criticism at the turn of the century.

Miller's ordinary vintage realism was restrained in the body of the text, except to suggest that his endorsement of Edwards's treatment of the freedom of the will was something less than wholehearted. Yet the appendices, notes, and notes to the notes reveal a man of stronger stuff. Here Miller lashes out at the modern materialists, Priestley and Darwin, and offers an extended critique of the *Zoonomia* along the path struck out by Brown's observations, and though scarcely original, once again he shows a complete familiarity with the physiology and the psychology and the relevant arguments.

The *Retrospect* concludes on a wry note. Throughout the text, he contrasts sympathetically the French and Scottish views of perfectibility with the dour view of Calvinism. In his final paragraphs he cites Stewart on the importance of printing for the progress of knowledge and civilization. Stewart sees that science and civilization will be distributed more widely through the acceleration of publishing and the development of a literate public. In turn, this will bring the knowledge of the science of legislation and the advantages of political union, so that political improvement will be joined by general scientific improvement. A philosopher may then combine the cumulative observations and conjectures which exhibit, not only his own intellect, but the cumulative power of mankind.

Yet Miller's final word is as dour as Calvin could have wished, for he admonishes that "this precious art" is not devoted to laudable purposes alone. Among the unlaudable purposes Miller included Priestley's work: "It is to be regretted that so much of what he has written on the philosophy of mind, and almost the whole of his writings on the subject of theology, should be so radically erroneous, and so subversive of all the interests of evangelical truth and practical piety."

But the problems which we labeled "common," those of activity, method, induction, perception, will, and morals, get a sophisticated hearing in the lectures of Samuel Stanhope Smith. Less polemical than Beasley, with less of an ax to grind than Miller, Smith's *Lectures*[47] are much more clearly a text, examining a variety of positions sympathetically. If one may suppose that these well-known lectures were amplified at all, then it is clear that the American reading public and his students and students of students were put into close touch with a sophisticated treatment of the problems of the late eighteenth and the nineteenth centuries.

Smith clearly belongs in the camp of the Scots, not as a mere reporter of their problems, but as one who had an original contribution of his own to make. Above all his work shows that the Scottish tradition, narrowly construed, is not easily separable from the general flow of British empiricism out of Locke or indeed from the wider area of philosophical problems which Leibniz, Grotius, Butler, Paley, and Price all faced. From the start, then, we are not surprised by his empiricism and realism, nor by his humanism; what does surprise us, however, is the naturalistic setting of the whole discussion right in the heart of Princeton. The exchanges such as those which must have taken place among the members of the American Philosophical Society have given his work an interesting biological and sociological perspective.

Philosophic inquiry is to be the investigation of the laws of the physical and moral world, without appeal to revelation. For this inquiry, the only resources which we have, the only opening onto reality, is the total of sensory information. No further justification can be given of the basic role of the sensory in evidence.

We must build inductively from simple sensations. Proceeding initially from effects to causes, this method will never give certainty, not only because of uncertain sensory properties, but also because observations are always finite. We frame hypotheses as to what may be expected, and we have a right to regard these universal laws as legitimate because they are based on a fair sample, and because no experience contradicts them. But these "universal laws" are tentative nonetheless, since it is always possible that further experience will yield a counterinstance. Yet because we have the vivid lesson from the history of science that knowledge is improvable, we must avoid the dangers of a weak and suspicious skepticism no less than those of a bold and positive dogmatism. And he shares something of Stewart's pragmatism, not only in distinguishing the rules of methodology from content, but also in supposing that a choice between two theories may be made on considerations of simplicity.

Smith often seems to be more in line with the direction which Hume and Berkeley gave to Locke's thought than with his commonsense colleagues. Thus he goes directly to human nature for his theory of knowledge, and, as we shall later see, for his moral theory. Yet though his discussions follow the mold of the century, they contain innovations even in the classic mood which seem to have been suggested by the intellectual climate of the Middle states. Of course he accepts the general world view of design, of harmonious interaction between units, but now the model has become biological rather than mechanical. Smith's functionalism is given full sweep as he examines not merely the effects of man upon his environment but the reciprocal effects of the physical and social environment as it weighs upon individuals of whatever species. But humans have a greater flexibility in adapting to their environment than any other creatures.

Man's body is a system for receiving external impressions and translating them into action. The intimate relation of mind and body is ever preserved; here Smith shows that he had learned a serious lesson from the materialists, especially Priestley and Rush. That mind determines body is proved by the delicate fluctuation of emotion, by the language of expression which changes from moment to moment in response to the subtlest stimuli. Smith objects to the idealistic theories, in part, on the grounds that mind has this observably fine influence over body. He suggests, rather in advance of his contemporaries, that certain religious experiences can be explained as deviant operations (distempers) of the nervous mechanisms. While he rejects Priestley's materialism, Smith shows how even on that account error arises in perception. He regards insanity in many cases as consequent upon some distortion of our bodies which has twisted not so much the reason as the organs of perception. So, even though he is not a materialist, Smith is not averse to admitting that physiology is relevant to the study of perception and human behavior. He sees the body, not as something which is, as it were, seduced into motion, but as a dynamic system which continually requires direction.

Perception derives its information from external and internal sources. Since he is a realist Smith believes that perception is generally veridical, but he insists that great care must be taken in interpreting this claim, for it is fraught with ambiguities. "Taste"—taken from the language of sensation—may mean (a) a quality or property of some object, as the taste of fried fish; (b) a series of events within the organism, which might be studied by the physiologist as "the sense of taste"; and (c) the sensation, i.e., what I now taste. The first and the second of these may quite easily be objects of empirical inquiry; the correlation between them and the third meaning may also be explored scientifically, but just how a physical event translates into a form of awareness simply eludes explanation. In effect, he stops where Berkeley did in his *New Theory of Vision*. For Smith as for Stewart, the theoretical disputes between physicists and physiologists about realism and idealism amount to little if anything in practice. And while Smith certainly regards himself as a realist rather than an idealist, he sees the allegiances developed along that dimension as less important than a broader allegiance to empiricism. Perhaps after all Witherspoon was not as entirely successful in wiping out idealism at Princeton as Beasley had reported.

Smith's attempt to grapple with human nature leads him into an amiable confrontation with Hume, for both are analyzing human nature as part of moral philosophy and both are alert to the importance of the study of the powers of the mind and the influence and interrelations of custom and context and environment. Smith's picture of the mind, however, is that of activity in its observed modes, rather than the passive witness of Locke or the bundle of impressions of Hume; the self is, operationally, its functionings. Thus he finds no ground for alarm in Hume's view that reason is the slave of the passions. This is but "an affected singularity of expression" which Smith unpacks to yield an undisturbing and interesting view. Since the passions include, in Hume's account, the active powers of man—desires, instincts, and all the rest—their domain has been so broadened that the task of serving them is no mean office: "to assist them to fulfill their functions in the best manner, to guard them from disorder, and to enable them to attain the most valuable purposes of our being."

In his treatment of reason and will, the notion of activity is similarly preeminent. While referring to these as faculties, he does not commit the central error which James later charged against the faculty psychology, viz., that of using "faculty" as a label in place of an explanation. Almost always Smith means by faculty merely a set of activities open to observation. Thus reason has the following functions—to make observations and experiments of the system of nature; to refer things to general classes or arrange by similarity; most importantly for ethics, to discover general rules and laws of action in the physical and moral world. In the first two we are led by a certain observed uniformity to ascribe to them some common law or power in nature, and in the last, by a uniformity of sentiment among mankind, the same rules or laws of conduct and duty. The final function of reason is to apply general rules to particular cases, or reciprocally, to ascribe to individuals already classified their characters and properties. This is especially evident in the sciences of politics, jurisprudence, morals, and philosophy.

The same sort of strategy is used effectively in the analysis of the will. Since will is an activity, liberty predicated of will makes no sense. It is the mind that is free in its willings or volition, insofar as there is deliberation. Hence there is neither determination by motives nor determination by external causes, nor by the will itself. Incidently, Smith is amiable again with Hume's analysis of cause and effect. He takes both temporal sequence and causal exertion to be primary and distinct, and equally given in experience. The idea of cause has a probable original source in decision expressed in muscular activity.

When Smith faces the question of the moral sense or faculty, so important a concern of Jefferson and of the Scottish tradition, he faces the same problems as Hutcheson, Butler, or Kant—the double facets of morals: the sentiments and the moral law. And he has to avoid the Scylla of a moral sense which is beyond the touch of reason and the Charybdis of a moral sense which is reduced to reason. He is quite prepared for this by his concept of activity and of reason itself. The independence of the moral sense is maintained by its being regarded as parallel to vision, hearing, and taste (in its narrow gustatory and wider aesthetic sense). But of course one would not expect the reduction of any of these senses to others. So too the verdicts of conscience are the verdicts of sentiment addressed to its appropriate objects. But they are also rational because reason and judgment play a part in all senses, even in vision to correct for weaknesses of the eye or deviation from standard conditions in the environment. Perceptions of the moral sense, and the sanctions of conscience which are only the moral sense speaking with authority, bring us to apprehend an object beyond its utility and equity, viz., we feel it to be amenable to a law which, though we do not know it completely, is acknowledged or felt by the plainest understanding as duty. Smith does not find the great diversity of reactions of sentiment and of moral codes as counting against the universality of the moral law. For the judgment of particular actions must always be relative to the state of society and the education of the individual, etc. Reason gives the fuller picture—together with the utility, the systematic relation, and the evidence of overall design—in terms of the consequences of an action and the disposition from which it issues. But without conscience, reason's remonstrances are only advisory.

It is clear enough why Smith was unattractive to the more orthodox—not only was he appreciative of Hume, but his natural theology also has much of the deist's construction and function. There is more than lip service to Christianity, but the function of God in his philosophy is that of the designer who has left sufficient indications of his blueprint so that by observation of the natural world, including human nature, we may understand both the functioning and the inadequacies and the objectives of the system. In effect, Smith is well on his way to a comprehensive extension of the Newtonian model to the pattern of man in nature as a whole. His natural theology provides the evidences, available to human reason (meaning of course by experience), of the nature of God, including his moral character, and of the moral law as sanctioned by God. God and immortality furnish sanctions for morality, but more importantly they provide a standard and an objective in terms of which we can discern and correct our present inadequacies not just on a personal level but on a social and political one as well. God provides some sanctions directly, but these merely buttress the sanctions of conscience and general interest.

The vigorous interest in the classic problems of metaphysics and epistemology which we have explored surely makes suspect Hall's low appraisal of Scottish realism and its influence—which formed the background and organizing challenge set out at the beginning of chapter 4. Nevertheless, it is true that the enlightened treatment of metaphysics and epistemology became submerged in religious dogmatism. Colleges, proliferating senselessly under the Dartmouth decision, became Hall's "three hundred denominational colleges"—the parochial schools of entrenched denominations—while the "safe" philosophy of their presidents often pushed a damaged and obsolescent realist line. Princeton's tragedy, described above, was repeated again and again in the spirit if not the letter of the event. Of the Lockean options, materialism was too heady, physiology too remote, and scientific or independent inquiry too threatening to orthodoxy to flourish in the academy. This loss of vigor was nowhere better illustrated than in McCosh, both in his own position and in his interpretation of the Scottish movement, so long taken as representative.

But whatever the summing up hitherto, the record cannot be closed here, for ethics and moral philosophy, at the core of philosophy, must always be included when we take the measure of philosophic activity. In America this field was thoroughly entwined with practice, from the ideology of the Independence on, including the later impact of theory on the creation of institutions (governmental, legal, economic) as well as the cultivation of public moral and civic virtue. McCosh's contributions to public life are poorly integrated with his ethical theory, while Hall's myopic view, in New England style, considers ethics mainly in its narrowest mode of personal ethical practice. To give the full picture of moral, legal, and political philosophy in the first half of the nineteenth century would here carry us too far afield. We shall limit ourselves majorly to some of the movements in academia, and their relation to the social discussions of the day.

2. Moral Philosophy

While our concerns are still primarily with the Middle and Southern states, it is helpful by way of preliminary to look at New England tradition. From the earliest days of Harvard a course in *Ethicks* divided curricular honors with logic and indeed it was often the climax of a college education. On its founding, Yale followed suit, probably making ethics even more central. Initially the New Englanders took their cues from the same Dutch rationalism that was to fortify their logic, and more importantly, in this context, from the Cartesianism of the Cambridge Platonists and their extended family in Clarke and Wollaston. Indeed More's *Enchiridion Ethicum* early had its place beside Grotius and Pufendorf. When the influence of Locke was felt, it was clear that the New Englanders could not follow him all the way in his ethics—at least to those parts which were extensions of his empirical psychology, since that was but a tempered pleasure-pain theory. What was acceptable, of course, was Locke's political theory with its self-evident truths, divine origins, and natural law overtones. This latter, while it is at tension with Locke's own psychological hedonism, is compatible with the Platonists' moral theory, especially with their emphasis on an ethical order which lies behind political and legal institutions, and to which reason can penetrate deductively. But even to that theory the New Englanders added conservative innovations of their own, giving Cambridge Anglicanism a strong Calvinist twist. Thus Thomas Clap, e.g., who became president of Yale in 1740 and who introduced there the works of the Cambridge Platonists, still held that obligation and virtue could not be determined independently of revealed religion.

The innovations can be roughly summed: ethical theory and practice were to remain for a long time rooted in theology and buttressed by religious sanctions. The strong emphasis on Christian piety and virtue was generally accompanied by a hostility to naturalistic ethics and natural theology, and was formulated as an ethics of duty and obligation, i.e., an ethics of right intentions rather than good consequences. This agent morality most frequently carried with it a view that community morality is directly and immediately dependent upon individual moral character, hence a view of social justice and reform that was cast in terms of individual uprightness and moral regeneration. And an eighteenth-century inclination to see God's design pessimistically, at least for the nonelect, moved later, and smoothly, into sympathy for the iron laws of wages and population, and somewhat later into the Social Darwinism that William Graham Sumner dispensed from Yale.

New England allegiances changed during the eighteenth century from the Cambridge Platonists and company to Scottish Common Sense and a weak utilitarianism; but speaking generally, these earlier commitments seemed to cast their shadows even on the readings of the later sources. Hutcheson, as we have seen, weighted almost equally two strains of his inquiry—first, the nature of the moral sense (i.e., the common sense in moral matters), and secondly the objective features, especially moral ones, which perception provides as the base for a moral calculus. The New England leaders tended to belabor the notion of the moral sense or faculty often at the expense of the second problem. The notion of the moral sense is quite delicately balanced; it can easily slip into a discussion of empirical perceptions and sensibilities, as it did in Hume and Smith, or it can strike out in the direction of a rational intuition or a conscience, as with the Platonists and Butler, Price, and Kant. It was this latter direction that generally caught on among the New England academicians, and surely was a major factor in the popularity of Butler and Price in their ethics courses, leaving Paley (whose Christian utilitarianism was somewhat suspect) as a mere respite between more serious writers. It was this direction, too, which predisposed them later on toward the Kantian categorical imperative; even Emerson arrived at his transcendental intuition by way of the moral sense theory to which he was early exposed at Harvard.

These moralizing tendencies can be found in social attitudes. For example, the abolitionist's stand was essentially a moral or religious sentiment in which slavery was seen not as a functioning economic institution, but as a violation of a higher moral law. In the nineteenth century the Malthusian and Ricardian doctrines were to be taught as a stern moral warning against excessive sexuality on the part of the poor, and against too great expectations of material prosperity (again on the part of the poor). Thus in New England as well as Britain, the fairly optimistic doctrines of Adam Smith and Dugald Stewart took the same pessimistic turn, in this case with a strong infusion of the Calvinistic doctrine of the elect restated in economic terms.

Undoubtedly such tendencies are better illustrated at Yale, and the host of colleges which she mothered, than at Harvard. The generations after Edwards are stamped with this hallmark, from Clap, Dwight, and Day to Porter (Ezra Stiles excepted) at Yale, to Mark Hopkins at Amherst, and Francis Wayland at Brown. Even Harvard's Walker and Bowen in their quite sophisticated economic writings are recognizably in the tradition of a moralistic individualism. Indeed, such individualism seems to be an important part of the New England heritage even in the twentieth century, leaving a genuinely social ethics such as Dewey's or Mead's to Chicago or Columbia.

Now the New England tradition was transferred to the early Middle Atlantic colleges on their founding—by Edwards and his mainly Yale colleagues to Princeton, and by Samuel Johnson to Columbia. And for a brief while, the students read their respective presidents' works—Edwards's *Inquiry* and *Dissertation* and Johnson's *Elementa Ethica*. But this tradition was challenged almost before it could take root, and with the close of their careers the lines of New England philosophy in the Middle South are weakened, and a shift takes place from "Ethics" to "Moral Philosophy," both in the names of the texts and the titles of the courses. This shift is more than terminological. As the eighteenth century wore on, moral philosophy came more and more to reflect those basic interests of the Enlightenment—perfectibility, progress, reasonableness, and naturalism. Moral comes to include reference to customs and habits and to political and social institutions, which according to this new way of thinking could be examined in terms of their functionings, not just in terms of their ethico-religious license. The secularizing of morals makes the burgeoning scientific knowledge relevant, and the materialisms not only provide a context for the discussion of morals, but also as in the case of Rush call for concern with the physical and social environment. Moreover, the new sense of the moral brings education intimately within its purview, querying now not merely the teaching of Christian personal or civic virtue, but also the techniques of cultural diffusion and the encyclopedic principles by which knowledge may be organized.

The social role of education in transmitting the morals of history, the curriculum, and the concrete setting of educational institutions become fundamental topics of philosophic debate. This is the sense in which we are to understand the educational efforts of Franklin and Washington, Priestley and Rush, and above all of Jefferson. Logan constructed a major library in Pennsylvania as a public resource, and even Samuel Miller's *Retrospect* was an attempt to summarize the achievements of the eighteenth century for the education of a nation, or at least of the Presbyterians. In all of this, America was but part of a larger pattern. The French Ideologues and Physiocrats were involved not only with the theory of education but practically with the French educational system of which Cousin later came to be virtually a dictator, while of course the *Encyclopédie* was a towering achievement of the French Enlightenment. The Scots, too, were not only occupied with the revision of school and curriculum in an effort to capture all the talent as a national wealth, but they, too, were embarked on their own encyclopedia which under the comprehensive plan of Stewart become the *Encyclopaedia Britannica*.

This change from ethics to moral philosophy was gradual and uneven. Within the colleges perhaps the most reliable early index was the use of Hutcheson's *Outlines of Moral Philosophy* to replace More's *Enchiridion* and the works of Johnson and Edwards. But it was well on its way when the eighteenth-century French and Scottish authors are imported. Beattie's *Elements of Moral Science* and Ferguson's *Institutes of Moral Philosophy* (1769) share the popularity with Paley's *Principles of Moral and Political Philosophy*. Hume's *Treatise of Human Nature*, though not as popular in America as the others, marks the change completed; it carries the subtitle "An Attempt to introduce the experimental Method of Reasoning into Moral Subjects." Of course Locke continued throughout to be a source, but it was a Locke put to various uses. If we look just to the collegiate curriculum a pattern emerges that involves a change in the very conception of morality. The narrower and personal emphasis on an ethics of duty and obligation, generally with religious overtones, is replaced by a broader view of morality reflecting the sense of *mores*, which includes under moral philosophy virtually all social relations as well as the evolution and the function of institutions. The shift in textbook titles and college course work reflects and reinforces a major trend in the history of American ideas.

Yet even this broader view of morals and moral theory has two distinguishable aspects. A first and earlier view was essentially an extension of individual responsibility onto those classic associates of ethics, i.e., politics and jurisprudence. The language of natural law-natural rights and of contract reigns, and the normative enters in an altogether characteristic way as the projection of individual norms or standards into limited social, i.e., political and legal, relations; while all social relations tend to be reduced to these terms. Colleges and statesmen both turn to the Roman jurists and to Grotius's important work *De Jure Belli ac Pacis*. This scarcely distinguishes among the law of nature, international law, and ethics, and leaves to his successors Pufendorf and Vattel to differentiate between them. It is the last whose gentle influence seems pervasive now in reminder that nations have moral responsibilities and rights in respect to other nations, and now in efforts to humanize war.

A second emphasis with roots in the eighteenth century which flowered in the nineteenth century was a companion to a growing empiricism. It involved a subtle change in the notion of natural law. Here we find a working out of an empirical conception of human nature in terms of wants and needs and the resources which the environment offers to satisfy them. The strongly legal and political view is tempered by a larger view of social relations such as the family and the community. The impact of custom and the empirical relation of institutions to racial and national character are explored in a completely naturalistic way. The contractual view of society is challenged by a genetic one; justification by natural right and government by consent give way to political conformity molded by habit; discussions of private duty moved to examine questions of population and the production and exchange of goods. Morality includes consequences of happiness, and ultimately of the happiness manageably and measurably expressed as wealth. When the normative enters it is intimately related not to abstract rights of equality and estate or some priorly existing moral law, but in terms of the empirical condition of success and of the fulfillment of function and objective. In this view of morality social relations and their institutional aspects have a role in fashioning society's norms rather than merely providing the domains for the application of norms. At this point moral philosophy clearly becomes the matrix out of which the cultural and social sciences were to separate, and the end of the nineteenth century was witness to the separation.

The projection of a moral law into the political and legal is well enough illustrated in Jefferson, while younger Jeffersonians such as Cooper had already moved past this into the naturalistic study of man's social activities. S. S. Smith in his lectures on moral philosophy faces the newer problems with some of the tools fashioned for earlier ones. James Wilson's views of popular sovereignty and the nature of legal institutions mark an early move to a functional analysis. By the first half of the nineteenth century the academic philosophers teaching, e.g., at Princeton, Pennsylvania, and Columbia were treating social and economic problems as central issues in moral philosophy. After all laissez-faire presents no fewer moral issues than natural rights.

Of course America was not alone in this long march toward the development of a fuller science of man; this is a general trend beginning in the Enlightenment, and expanded during the whole of the nineteenth century. But here Americans, speaking to their own condition, intimately involved in constructing social realities at the same time as they evaluated them theoretically, had to tailor European thought to their own needs, and the result was peculiar to themselves. This was most evident in the Middle Atlantic and Southern states.

The emerging pattern can be seen in retrospect as the Newtonizing of the moral sciences. A part of the heritage of Locke was an uneasiness between his empiricism and his political philosophy. His account of morals was a mixed bag. On the one hand there was a strong hedonism, which seemed a natural for the Newtonian model, as the history of the development of utilitarianism showed. But in his explicit moral theorizing the rationalist strain was overt. He regarded the demonstration of moral and political philosophy as paralleling the demonstration in mathematics; and of course his appeal to self-evident principles, at least on the surface, seems freighted with the ghosts of the innate ideas which were the focus of his attack against Descartes. Furthermore, such unobservable entities as natural rights, natural law, and the social contract and the state of nature as historical fact seem scarcely respectable entities for a reputable empiricist. Yet these are central in his political theory; it is his natural rights theory rather than any hedonistic view of man that provides the effective language of revolution. His view did of course justify revolution as a last resort, and this the Americans could appreciate. And it was brimming with individualism, which they could also welcome, not least of all its defense of property. But how could its theoretical framework be seen as other than backsliding from the new empirical philosophy?

Perhaps it is easier to show Locke's consistency than many of his critics have assumed, if we attend to what he was actually doing to the older conceptions even in use of kindred language. His natural rights were quite a distance from the classic natural law theory. The older natural law theory viewed the moral order as expressive of God's will in His government of the universe, bestowing a moral aspect on the physical order itself. Locke's natural right conception, on the other hand, breaks down moral relationships into properties of individuals (the elements), and insofar as (a) rights are properties of individuals, and (b) individuals interact in lawlike ways, we have a clear Newtonian model. These moral properties (as opposed to those mentioned by Hobbes) are not psychological properties; they can rather be taken to be analytic of what it is, according to Locke, to be a man at all. That men are equal, for Locke, is true by definition; "equality" is not the name of an empirical property. Still, this reading of Locke accords with his general treatment of essences and names (his nominalism). Locke, on this interpretation, was certainly an empiricist, but an empiricist whose fault lies not in method but in the use of nonempirical entities. This inconsistency, or disequilibrium, does not affect the political theory; in fact it gives the natural right (considered as a demand, a *sine qua non* of communal existence) a much more secure position, in that the property or characteristic, since it is taken normatively, provides a standard for judging existing states of affairs in any given nation.

The crucial question in the theory is the status of moral properties. Is equality, e.g., reducible to—or does it have a status comparable to that of—psychological and physical properties? Hutcheson's wavering attitude evolves, in the writings of Adam Smith and Hume, into a forthright position: such moral feelings as we discover *must* have just the status of other psychological properties. For Smith and Hume, then, one can perfectly well investigate empirically the laws that govern the occasion and consequences of such feelings. "Natural law" now has come to have a very different sense from that given to it in older theories. Once the contract, the original state of nature, etc., have ceased to be considered empirical entities or facts, a way has been opened for a full empirical science of man. Statistical methods, sociological study of institutions, and a functional consideration of institutions follow almost as inevitable developments of the changed position. Hume, of course, discovered that utility is the underlying principle of approval acts, and Adam Smith finds the same hidden base in sentiments of propriety and duty. Economics, on this Smith theory of the moral sentiments, can be reduced to an empirical study of (among other things) acquisitiveness. Instead of a theory which makes the whole physical order into a moral order, theories like those of Hume and Smith make the realm of morals to be a part of the (generally nonmoral) physical order of things.

There is a third path which starts from a Kantian separation between the natural and moral order, making the latter autonomous, and then in the fashion of German Romanticism, accepting the primacy of the moral order, associates duty and moral obligation with the nation. This development too will have its repercussions in America.

Evidence of the enlarging of the moral and the secularizing of moral philosophy is not hard to come by both within and without the colleges. We shall select to illustrate different phases and diversity of fields. S. S. Smith's strictly moral theory from volume II of his *Lectures* shows the transformation going on in orthodoxy itself with the growth of empirical concern and the pressure of concrete social problems. James Wilson, lecturing on law at the University of Pennsylvania, builds out from Commonsense moral theory an account of sovereignty vested in the people, which was to become an integral part of the American legal tradition. Jefferson, in addition to the historical importance of his political theory, illustrates the development of a normative Lockean option. Finally, we shall look briefly at the emergence of a particular moral science, viz., political economy, with emphasis on Columbia and its New York setting.

Princeton and Samuel Stanhope Smith

Witherspoon's challenge to the New England style had moved the Princetonians away from questions of the freedom of the will and revelation as related to morals and asked in a quite modern way about the grounds of policy as it extends to personal behavior surely, but also in political, legal, and commercial relations. Witherspoon, as we have seen, had moved toward a genetic view of social relations, seeing the family rather than contract as the base even of political relations. As we saw also (chapter 4) this followed in the pattern set down by

Hutcheson, which had no small infusion of the Aristotelian view of social relations; for in Hutcheson the political (narrowly construed) is but one aspect of a plurality of social relations. The heritage of Witherspoon was brought into practical politics by the multitude of Witherspoon's students, the most famous of whom is Madison. It is preserved in the academic world by S. S. Smith, whose *Lectures on Moral Philosophy*[48] was carried throughout the South and West wherever Princeton influence prevailed. S. S. Smith was Witherspoon's successor, but he was more responsive to the growing scientific interest in anthropology, sociology, and economics, and he had also a more direct concern with public law and with civil and international jurisprudence.

Still a young man during the Revolution, Smith worked out these *Lectures* over many decades. They reflect not so much the problems of the Independence as those of the post-Revolution era which, amid many troubles, faced the need and effort to weld factional and jealously guarded interests into an operating social entity. He believed in the necessity of a strong Federal government buttressed by national rather than sectional sentiments, he feared a tyranny of the people more than that of centralized authority, he appreciated the value of a strong and independent judiciary to balance the executive and legislative powers, and he argued for governmental initiative beyond the limits of laissez-faire. And in the background, intensified by the current French experience, are anxieties about the possible consequences of irresponsible suffrage on the one hand and slavery and fears of the decline of republican virtue on the other. And to meet this, he took an institutional approach—the creation of institutions with knowledge of how they develop and how they affect and are affected by character. Less traditionalist than Burke, less voluntarist than Paine, he saw American conditions as providing a unique opportunity for creative design.

Smith is working within the general frame of Witherspoon's lectures, but of course this was not original with Witherspoon. It was the general structure which had emerged in British thought. It was not a question of being original or of making innovations in the pattern; the latter was rather taken to be the topology of the moral. This structuring of the domain is implicit in Grotius (and even Aristotle), but it is explicit in Hutcheson and is an important part of the heritage he bequeathed to the way of teaching moral philosophy in Scottish universities. The classic expression is to be found in Adam Smith's lectures on moral philosophy at Glasgow, which included, in addition to the third part on political economy, published as *The Wealth of Nations*, a second part on morality, *The Theory of Moral Sentiments*, and a beginning part on natural theology which remained unpublished. In fact Adam Smith projected a final section on international law and the regulations of war and commerce which he did not live to carry out. Even Hume is seen to be writing under the same scheme, although less obviously since, not succeeding to a professorship, he did not have to give a course.

Different writers have different emphasis, different orderings of topics, omissions, improvisations, and replacement. Ferguson, e.g., stressed the influence of cultural factors while Hume replaced the parts usually supplied by natural theology with the critical discussions in the *Dialogues Concerning Natural Religion* and others, mostly economists, added a nontheistic discussion of an integrated and harmoniously working world. And of course Scots appealed to French philosophy in diverse ways. Yet the model, which S. S. Smith shares with them, is not hard to make out. An opening discussion of methodology would generally include considerations about the nature of physical and moral science and the appropriate method of investigation (this of course would generally be an empiricism with strong naturalistic overtones). The nature of the human constitution would then touch on the relation of man to other animals, the question of species identity, his original sentiments and springs of action, perception, and the origin and limits of knowledge. Upon this psychological background, the moral habits would be further developed, entailing an account of obligation and virtue, particularly the duties owed to God, self, and others; these latter include not only the stewardship relation, which arises in the limited or domestic situation (husband-wife, father-son, master-servant), but also those which arise from the larger civil and political contexts, and even those arising from relations between nations. Introduced somewhere would be a discussion of natural theology (or its equivalent) presenting the evidences of design, especially as it concerns utility and public happiness, and the sanctions. As suggested above, innovation is not to be expected in the general pattern of inquiry, and S. S. Smith conforms. But what is interesting is the detail and the way in which he has integrated the general topics with American problems.

Smith embarks boldly on just that venture which everyone from Locke to Dugald Stewart and even Samuel Miller have regarded as the desideratum: viz., the extension of the Newtonian model to morals. The same method will yield knowledge of the moral order as was used to explain the physical, and that is largely a matter of subsuming particular phenomena under a more general heading. The domain of moral investigation includes the full range of human activity, from the operation of instincts, propensities, and needs to the affections and voluntary and rational actions. But it includes further all manner of social relations, domestic, civil, political, and cosmopolitan, which go to give man so much of his character. Further, he must be observed in all manner and condition—in poverty and luxury, in adversity and tranquillity, under a variety of institutional and political forms. Beyond that, reference must also be made to the physical environment which leaves so indelible a mark. History itself is a volume of moral experiment, but its laws and lessons are hard to make out, covered as they are by the uniqueness of events and the accidental.

The method then is observational, inductive, and historical, with a just appreciation of the complexity and diversity of the field. Smith has other methodological commitments. He is seeking general laws in the midst of manifold diversity, and universality in the midst of the relative; he believes—in contrast to Hume—that the patient observation of effects will yield laws, and from these uniformities (causes or hypotheses) may be derived further probable effects and legitimate expectations. But this optimism is quickly tempered, for it is converted into a procedural rule—the legitimacy of universal laws grounded on good facts is tenable until countermanded by other observations or shown to have only limited applicability. Such observations, further, are of effects and operations only; we can never penetrate a priori into the essence of human nature or mind (nor of God's nature and design either) nor know anything save what is constructable from the knowledge of those effects and operations. Smith makes a further Stewart-like assumption: given alternative explanations (presumably of equal explanatory power) the simplest is to be taken as true.

Investigation, however, is not merely descriptive but normative as well. Only upon the knowledge of what is—of human nature, of the functions of institutions —is it possible to build what can or ought to be, that is to say what rules of government can augment the dignity and happiness of individuals, the prosperity of states, and the happiness of the world. Only by a knowledge of laws and history are we likely to avoid or postpone the dissolution and degeneration of societies of which history provides so many examples.

An interesting example of Smith's deep commitment to cultural relativity shows his courageous (at least in the bosom of orthodoxy) application of that principle even to moral theory in general and to his own investigation in particular. He is aware of the radical incompatibilities which the history of moral theories reveals: biases of vanity of system, inadequate methods, inadequate observation, and the weaknesses of intellect are seconded by the special biases which the moral philosopher imports from his own setting of culture and habit. Yet—and this is the spirit of the Enlightenment—even philosophies, no less than peoples, institutions, and individuals, are subject to improvement.

Smith first locates man in the animal world, seeking for the unique and identifying factors of human nature. The signs of a nature shared with other species are evident: we too are gregarious and tend to associate spontaneously and multiply. Further, the laws of the physical world operate on us as on other animals; thus our tendency to multiply, no less than theirs, is absolutely limited by the availability of resources, especially food and shelter. Yet man is more widely distributed over the face of the earth than (nearly) any other animal; by his biological and psychological organization man is at once more sensitive to external causes and more flexible and varied in his responses. He lives under the greatest range of conditions, and the pressures of various physical and environmental conditions have wrought enormous changes in stature, complexion, features, hair, color, etc. Indeed, so great is the diversity that the question arises whether there are universal laws about human nature and morality. This search for common elements of human nature sets his problem and accounts for interesting observations about the effects of climate, poverty of soil, diet, geography, etc. This discussion is a part of an argument then raging in Scotland and France and of long-standing interest to Smith. Midway in his Princeton career he wrote "Essay On the Causes of the Variety of Complexion and Figure in the Human Species," the gist of which he presented to the American Philosophical Society.[49] The methodological commitments are put to good use here, for if he can account for physical differences among the races of men through the effects of geography, climate, etc., it will be possible to establish the initially common and universal nature of all men. Perhaps at work in the essay are more ulterior motives. Clearly the Biblical account requires mankind to be a unitary species, although Smith does not use it as evidence. Perhaps more importantly, he wants to defend the New World environment against European charges that it is detrimental and degrading. Rush's thesis follows too, though somewhat obliquely, that favorable environmental conditions—social and physical—can improve the human nature, e.g., of the black.

The major distinction of man from the animals, as might be expected, lies in his use of reason. But reason is weak and operates unpredictably; this unpredictability combines with the random effects of passion, with unforeseeable casualties of history and with a fantastic variety of modifying conditions further to increase the divergence among social groups and the area of indeterminacy for the philosopher.

Still reason lifts us to remedies beyond the capacity of any other animal. For example, while population cannot exceed the necessary resources, still we can learn how far custom has converted indulgence and luxury into necessaries. Further, changes of social organization, say from hunting or pastoral to extensive agriculture, the development of institutions which will increase the production of the land, the cultivation of moral habits of frugality, and the development of commerce and the arts may not only alter considerably the size of the population which can be sustained, but also its comfort and happinesss as well. However, since these institutions arise in particular contexts answering always to specific needs and conditions, they will take different forms.

Differences stemming from physical conditions cooperate with emerging cultural ones to sharpen differences of custom and habit, religion, the state of the arts, and forms of property, justice, and government. Changes, both biological and cultural, survive and make for exponentially increasing differences in the character or genius of peoples. Yet such diversification must not obscure the basic identity of all men. There is a common character which responds in lawlike ways when the complex and modifying factors are taken into account. And there is also a basic universality of sentiment and of reason which makes for the possibility of a moral science. Smith attempts to establish the identity of man empirically and the principles of obligation through analysis based on comparative observation of moral relations.

The development of language serves as a paradigm for Smith (and for the Scots generally) of the growth of institutions. Clearly contract or consent does not institute language; rather, it arises naturally and there is even a sort of language of countenance and expression, so subtle is the link between body and spirit. As artificial signs replace natural ones, the need and the ability to communicate abstractly add further burdens on natural language and result ultimately in all the diverse sophistications and elegances of European languages. There is no necessity (against Kames) to make a weak appeal to the Scriptures and the supernatural to account for natural diversification. In point of fact, the tower of Babel incident was not about language at all, but about a clash of opinions and sentiment arising out of a military effort to extend civil power. Underlying this diversification there is a common structure, a universal grammar, which is evidenced by translation and communication.

Smith distinguishes civil institutions, which determine the relations among men and have their origin in earlier domestic forms, and political institutions which define the apparatus of government and which are but a single aspect of a complex of institutions. Institutions generally reflect the work of reason and of change, the planned and the adventitious; but they are "rational" insofar as they successfully institutionalize justice and utility.

The first form of society is domestic, but with development the internal relationships vary: e.g., the extended family structures become more complex and various; deference to and respect for authority which developed in the familial or tribal situation, and were directed toward the head, may, e.g., be transferred to the wisest or richest in an agrarian society. Where a premium is placed on defense, authority tends to go to the strongest (and hence the young, or to whom the young owe allegiance). The goals of different societies (e.g., for the Jews the preservation of their religious rights, for the Chinese the preservation of tranquillity, for the Romans a continual extension of power and *imperium*) are not only expressions of the wills of individual members, but in turn act as formative influences on other individuals and generations. Marriage generates the fundamental moral relation between man and wife and between child and parent. True to his sociological commitments, Smith first looks at the function of marriage—to secure happiness and to provide for the continuance of a morally responsible citizenry. On these criteria, vagrant sexual associations are ruled out, but history provides many forms of the marriage institution where expectations are legitimized by custom, law, and the particular demands of the environment, e.g., ratio of males to females. What is wrong with polygamy, especially in a modern context, he says, is not that it is vicious or evil, but merely that it arises from an error in judgment. Monogamy is simply a more effective way of ensuring the happiness of individuals and the perpetuation and accumulation of culture. Smith's class notes were subpoenaed on this matter, but he had the undeniable Biblical authority of Moses's domestic arrangements to support him. This is merely another instance where Smith appeals to the Bible, not as supernatural authority, but as a text for the study of social institutions among what was, after all, a highly successful social group. Of course after the New Testament, monogamy clearly is to become the order of the day.

Smith speaks, as do the Scots except Hume, with an eloquent sweetness and delicacy about the companionship which the marital relation affords and the importance for society generally of those finer sensibilities and manners which can arise from intimate family relations and from the recognition of women as persons and equal in the marriage relation (which most emphatically is *not* contractual).

The most general moral relations of justice and benevolence find particular expression, not only between man and wife, but between parent and child. Exercise of authority and its correlative obedience stem initially from affection and gratitude which are given ample time to develop during the long dependence of the children on their parents.

The discussion of the master-slave relation reveals the agonized position of Smith which foreshadowed the difficulties Princetonians generally were to face as they approached the crisis of the Civil War and made them unacceptable both to the Northern Abolitionists as well as the Southern advocates of slavery. It is the appreciation of the factors that weigh on both sides of the issue that accounts for the abandonment of his *Lectures* in the Southern colleges. On the one hand, there is the manifest inhumanity of the institution and the absolute immorality of the relation. Slavery is not merely destructive of the slave but wreaks its moral degradation equally on the master. The historical justifications which are offered, such as debt, crime, and captivity, will not do. Crime and debt are irrelevant; and if in antiquity the victor claimed the right of death over the vanquished and slavery thus at one time appeared to be the more humane option, it does not follow that a civilized society should recognize the right of death in the first place. Utility would advise, and humanity second, the most generous treatment of a captive people. It is even sometimes adduced that it is better and happier for an African to be here than in the vicious conditions of his native land. But even then

> This is making the prejudices of our self-love the judge of their happiness, while at the same time, our own interest is the advocate. — There is no country, however severe the climate, and however barren the soil, from which a native is not unhappy to be exiled. The ideas, the habits, the pleasures of men, are all inseparably blended with the scenes, with the society, with all the objects which have been familiarized to them in the country which gave them birth. A Laplander prefers his snows and rocks to the most cultivated landscapes of France or England. An American savage perceives more delight in his solitary wilds, . . . than he would in the most splendid apartments of a palace. — Men deceive themselves continually by false pretenses, in order to justify the slavery which is convenient for them.[50]

On the other hand, the sentimental liberating of the slaves without recompense would be an injustice, like the usurpation of any property. And further, the emancipation of unskilled and poorly prepared people into the society would create a perilous situation (although this is somewhat balanced by the possibilities of uprisings on the part of the slaves). Smith's remedy for the matter was scarcely popular. Slaves who aspired to freedom were to be alloted a plot of land which they might work if they had the initiative (and Smith assures us from his Virginia experiences that they had the leisure). They could, over a period of years, purchase liberty, and of course fellow slaves were not prohibited from helping one another. Those who succeeded should not be encouraged to stay in the same community, thereby creating a confusing social relation, but would be given a share in the West (a double share for mixed marriages), and a stake. In such a way, that is by the legislator taking thought, both slavery and the differences of race might be expected slowly to disappear, and the nation be strengthened by incentives which it itself had provided.

Beyond the master-slave relation lies the master-servant relation. This is still part of the domestic scene, since "domestic" is being used in a comprehensive sense. What Smith says of the servant appears to apply to free labor generally. Inequalities of wealth will always occur through the misfortunes of history and the differences of talents. Thus a man may sometimes be obliged to offer his labor for sale, but like all commodities its value is subject to supply and demand. But such a sale is for a limited time only, is bound by contract, and such terms are sanctioned by public law. The moral relation can in part be specified: it requires equity on the part of the master and fidelity on the part of the servant. Yet it is more tenuous and extensive, for the master owes a proper sympathy for the unfortunate situation of the servant and should treat him with dignity, while the servant on his part must often merge his interests with those of the master.

The extended family and the broadened domestic situation provide the basis for the more mature forms of social organization. Here are to be found the origins of virtually all the social ties and relations which more complex cultural contexts exhibit—relations of dependence and affection, dominion, sympathy, equity, benevolence, and even that sense of likeness of kind that often becomes a national sentiment. Laid down in connection with the family are also the terms of property and the claims to authority and power. All these derive something of their distinctive character from such sources. With increased complexity of social organization, especially that brought about by the growth of population, conflicts arise over property and power. Authority and power tend always to exceed customary limits; often enough the increase in power is intentionally sought through war, but as frequently the dynamics of the situation conspire unintentionally to alter the lines of power. In times of tranquillity people may not even notice the concentration of power; the situation is always fluid and may easily turn into tragedy, the greatest being when people no longer have the initiative to plan nor the energy to secure their freedom. But social institutions can be developed rationally and self-consciously, at least in part, and it is absolutely essential that they should allow for the security to enjoy the products of one's own labor. Such security would generally entail private property divided in such a way that he who has the least may still have warranted ambitions to enjoy the luxuries open to the richest. Tyranny has neither object nor means until property and wealth have been established. It is precisely to overcome the indeterminacy of power and the evils which result from its tendency to augment itself and to lead to tyranny that it is imperative to have the limits of government defined, preferably in a constitution.

Political institutions are only one kind among many social associations; and while a political institution is of great significance in determining moral relations, it is in turn determined by the larger social context which gives form and operating principles not only to it, but also to the other associations as well.

This fact has two important consequences. If political institutions emerge naturally, and in large measure fortuitously through conflict and accident, there is neither any social contract nor explicit consent save what is effected by custom, habit, and manners. Once freed from the shadows that the social contract theory casts, say about some presocial or prepolitical state, Smith is freer to inquire into the operations and functions of political institutions—especially to raise questions about the relevance of natural resources and setting, the laws of development, and the kind of criteria that are needed to test and reform existing arrangements. This makes way for concrete proposals to improve culture and welfare. As a second consequence, it leads to a new, at least new to the century, way of looking at the relation of the civil to the political domains. Jurisprudence concerns just those matters which are the conditions for civility—the security of life and property and the maximization of those liberties which appear in classic theory as political rights. Once achieved as a permanent framework these are no longer the responsibility of government. Political liberties start, in a functioning government, from public interest and its relation to individual liberties.

The science of legislation concerns that security which is a condition for the development of a state and is directed toward investigating how private interest and national or public interest can be integrated. In contrast to many who assumed a kind of natural identity (at least if natural economic laws were freed from governmental interference), S. S. Smith sees the problem as open to some conscious designing.

Smith uses Montesquieu's distinction between the form and principle of the state. The form is the structure or locus of power determining the operations of the state, best when written and explicit in a constitution, where the limits of power are more readily confined. The principle rests in the spirit of the people which, in the last analysis, is what makes a government run from day to day. That spirit is an amalgam of custom, religion, the state of arts and skills, the readiness to revolution or tranquillity. While despotism rests on fear, as monarchy requires moderation and aristocracy requires honor, still there is no "best form of government." There is no absolutely necessary connection between a particular form of government and the civil liberties actually enjoyed that rest essentially on the sentiment of the community. Where, for example, a despot is enlightened and the limits of power well defined by custom and usage, a greater liberty may operate than in a poorly run democracy. Seldom is it given to a people, as in America, to have the opportunity of choosing their form of government. Then it is a matter of genius to frame the fabric of government in such a way as truly will be adapted to the sentiment of the people, and with such wisdom to frame an explicit definition of power as to allow the healthy working and perpetuation of all segments. All forms of government are in constant change and in unstable equilibrium, but each form of government is pressed by different sources of instability. Democracy rests on the most delicate of balances and is potentially threatened from many sides.

On Smith's view our democracy is least threatened by the judiciary and he sought to strengthen its operations. On the other hand the suspicion of the executive that Americans built into their early government mistook the lessons of a particular moment for universal principles of the science of legislation. During our own Revolution we were concerned to secure individual liberties from usurpation by a central authority; and because the imminent danger of tyranny suppressed other passions than those dedicated to the common good, we trusted overmuch to the wisdom and virtue of the people. The danger in less critical times stems rather from the legislative branch and its responsiveness to the fickleness and passion of mob decision. Suffrage should be limited to those whose identification with the national interest can be counted on. The most responsible are those whose property joins them in sentiment and interest to the soil. Historically, the masses have been most often the cause of ruin. In America, that threat is presently minimal because the population is still small and well informed; but with time it may increase. Clearly (at least to Smith) excessive equality, compounded by all manner of venal electioneering, demagogery, etc., can lead rapidly to the tyranny of the many. In 1793 Smith is anxious whether the French will fail to achieve the democracy to which they aspire, or whether they will be plunged into despotism.

Equal distribution of wealth cannot be guaranteed, only the political rights to the products of one's own effort. On the other hand, when the inevitable differences in rank and wealth are wide and ostentatiously displayed, the republican virtue necessary to democracy has already been corrupted. Government is responsible for increasing the happiness of the people that will result from development of the arts, the greater effectiveness of individual labor, in short for overseeing the conditions that will lead to the identification of public and private interests.

But the kinds of direction and reform that are needed cannot be effected by legal or governmental measures alone. Direct attempts at reform, especially if they offend custom or convulsively attempt to restructure moral attitudes, are doomed to disappointment. Custom and habit are precious, they are intimately related to the pleasures of the people and even to their sentiments of rectitude and morality. Better it is to insinuate changes slowly and by example. Thus slavery cannot be legislated out of existence without danger to national safety. What can be done is to encourage that humanity which would ultimately make emancipation a moral attitude; meanwhile, the nation ought to provide the social conditions which would make the emancipation a successful strategy.

Conservative though he may have been in his general sympathies, Smith lays great store on the need for public education. Education is important not only in preserving the established institutions, but also in directing change:

> . . . if a legislator desires to accommodate the ideas of his people to the institutions he intends to establish, or to give those institutions the greatest stability and duration of which human laws are susceptible, no mean can be found so effectual as a proper direction of the public education.[51]

and again,

> . . . it is a duty of high importance in the legislature of each state to provide for the general information of the citizens in the principles of virtue and good morals, and in the whole system of their civil and social duties. The means of useful instruction should be made accessible to every member of the community. But, besides that universal information which should convey the knowledge of their moral, and civil duties to the lowest order of the citizens, it is perhaps of not less importance that an easy access should be opened to a knowledge of all the liberal arts, and to the higher branches of science to those who have inclination and leisure to pursue them.[52]

Men are at the whim of history and mix reason with their institutions in adventitious ways. Still they can in part rationally determine which form institutions might take to help them to function well. Our efforts at redesign and reform may appear minuscule before the uniqueness of historical events and the imperfection of knowledge; but knowledge and human nature, no less than human institutions, are plastic, are reformable and criticizable. In contrast to many of the laissez-faire theorists, government has large responsibilities for such redesign, although, in contrast to the Benthamites, such reform cannot be executed by legislation only, or mainly, but requires a reform of customs and manners, habits, along the whole front of human institutions.

A fate similar to that of Edwards's work at Princeton overtook Johnson's text at Columbia, although it made its exit more gracefully by being supplemented before it was replaced by the literature reflecting the problems of Grotius, Vattel, and Blackstone, which in turn gave way to those of Adam Smith, Hume, Malthus, and Ricardo. Doubtless the German education of Columbia's John Daniel Gros accounts in part for his view of the state as a moral entity—not so much in the Grotian way which emphasized the moral relations between states, but in the more romantic mode suggested by Kant in *Eternal Peace* and even then being developed by Fichte in Germany.[53] In his *Natural Principles of Rectitude* (1795) Fichte urged that the individual is a free and moral agent, but both his freedom and much of his moral responsibility emerge with and in the state. The state (or better nation) is a rational institution; the evolution of its forms is matched by a moral evolution in its laws and in the moral obligations it generates for its citizens. The highest civic duty as well as the greatest liberty arise through the fulfillment of such obligations. Although Gros distinguishes ethics from the larger political and legal relations, they are inseparably connected as moral relations. This treatment of the nation, almost its personification, is not met again at Columbia until—as we shall see at the close of this chapter—the arrival in 1857 of Lieber, another German university product.

Pennsylvania and James Wilson

The situation in Pennsylvania, especially Philadelphia, had its own character. The Friends, doubtless remembering their own trials, encouraged toleration; but in any case the sectarian rivalries were such as to ensure that no one group's views could prevail when plans for a College of Philadelphia were in the making. Moreover Philadelphia, the largest English-speaking city after London, was rapidly becoming a center for medicine, commerce, the mechanical arts, and the book trade. There was, additionally, a considerable German population whose ties with European intellectual life have still been insufficiently assessed. Thus despite the official importance of religion the college was to be nondenominational.

Franklin and his associates were the decisive influences in the planning and design of the new institution which was chartered in 1755 as a college, and after grave troubles during the Revolution, as a university in 1791.[54] Franklin envisioned a university serving secular and national interests rather than clerical ones. He sought advice from educators and men of letters; he even visited English, Scottish, and German universities with an eye open for practices that might be serviceable. Initially, Franklin's and the trustees' choice for rector fell on Samuel Johnson whose *Noetica* he had published in 1752. But Johnson, who was already occupied in the arrangements for Kings College, forwarded the name of William Smith. What recommended Smith to Franklin was not only his academic qualifications, but also an essay, "A General Idea of the College of Mirania" (1753).[55] What is interesting in the plan is not only its provisions for specialization, but also the effort to design a graded course of study in such a way as to facilitate learning. The proposals of "Mirania" found their way well into the operations of the college after William Smith was inaugurated. As a matter of fact the curriculum was patterned after the New Regulations which Reid had engineered at Aberdeen, Smith's alma mater, as a part of the continuing appraisal of university education in Scotland. The system of professorships following the Scottish pattern was installed from the beginning in preference to tutorial arrangements, although "private hours" were arranged as well.

Moral philosophy was broadly construed to include the law of nature and nations, trade, commerce, law, and government. Locke and Hutcheson, Grotius and Vattel required study but of Johnson's text there was no sign. Francis Alison, a student of Hutcheson's at Glasgow who lost the presidency of Princeton to Witherspoon because of his liberalism, set moral philosophy off on a naturalistic course. Judging from Samuel Miller's student notes (August 26, 1788, under Magaw, a student of Alison's), emphasis fell on the role of utility in morality, on a nonreligious, humanistic interpretation of moral terms such as "good," and on the assembling of a set of rules by which the voluntary agent might order his activities with a view to happiness. Carmichael's edition of Pufendorf appears also to have been a text, in which case the stress must have been less on natural law than on empirical treatment of legal action. Alison himself appears to have developed the natural rights theory in the general direction of a natural continuity between men's needs and those of the other animals; accordingly satisfaction is measured in terms of pleasure in *this* world. These professors began, in a tentative, quasi-sociological fashion, to consider education itself as a social institution having an assignable function and able to be evaluated in terms of successful fulfillment of that function.[56]

Provost Smith regarded the American Philosophical Society as integrated with the university, and there was considerable interchange between the faculty at the college and the society. Clearly the medical facilities of the city were university associated; Rush, who taught at the college, explored insanity and "tristemania" at the celebrated Friends Hospital. Even botanical experiments, together with chemical theorizing, served to tie the medical community with the educational institution. Especially after the Revolution, moreover, the economic concerns of the community were reflected in the college's curriculum. Daniel Raymond reedited his essay on "The Constitution and Political Economy," to use as a text. It was a defense of protectionism, popular in Philadelphia at the time; it had been given its early statement in the pamphlets of Mathew Carey (1760-1839) and later in the works of his son, Henry (1793-1879). The Careys were the major booksellers in the Middle states; Irish Catholic in background (which possibly prevented their appointment to a university chair), they opened their home as a Philadelphia salon ("Carey's vespers"), which provided an important opportunity for the exchange of ideas between gown and town. The university was, like the Careys, largely protectionist in sentiment and Thomas Cooper lost the chair of chemistry to Robert Hare largely on the grounds of the former's laissez-faire sentiments (though this is not to impugn Hare's credentials as a distinguished chemist).

As we have seen, medical lectures intersecting with philosophy were offered even before the Revolution, but formal lectures in law were inaugurated in 1790 before a notable audience that included Washington. They came to hear James Wilson (1742-1798). History, and even the musical *1776*, has treated Wilson niggardly. Victim of debts "which I had no hand in making," he was brought back to Philadelphia in 1906 when a freshly appreciative government reinterred him with honor near his friend Franklin. Yet this very unsung hero had a decisive hand in forming the Constitution and its philosophic grounds.

Born in St. Andrews, Wilson attended the university there, and came into contact with a long tradition of liberal, not to say radical, political thought. George Buchanan (1506-1582) had taught at St. Andrews, developing a theory of the king's subjection to law as well as the grounds of justified revolution. Despite efforts to suppress this doctrine, the tradition was alive in Wilson's day. His collegiate career coincided with one of the richest decades in the history of the Scottish Enlightenment: he attended Glasgow when Adam Smith was rector, and there is internal evidence in his works that he knew Smith's theories at firsthand. Certainly he studied under Ferguson at Edinburgh (at the same time Hume was active there). He seems to have been associated, in one way or another, with Kames, Robertson, Blair, and Stevenson, and to have been a boyhood friend of James Watt.

Scottish legal tradition had deep affinities with Continental thought, stemming ultimately from an idealization of Roman law. Wilson, steeped in this tradition, and equipped with the finest education in the social sciences then available, came to Philadelphia in 1765-66, just as the colonial troubles were coming to a head. He read law with John Dickinson and then served as lawyer, judge, advocate general for France, and was one of the very few who signed both the Declaration of Independence and the Constitution. Under Washington he was appointed to the first Supreme Court. No one was more aware than Wilson of the real novelty of the American experiment.

> The United States exhibited to the world the first instance of a nation unattacked by external force, unconvulsed by domestic insurrections, assembling voluntarily, deliberating fully and deciding calmly concerning that system of government under which they and their posterity should live.[57]

Wilson's starting place was the Common Sense commitment to a moral sense—common because shared by all members of the species. Equality then is grounded in human nature, its common needs and abilities. Upon this universal ability to perceive moral relations Wilson built an explicit theory of representative democracy. More even than Jefferson he believed in the competence of the people to govern themselves reasonably. All justifiable political power stems from the consent of the people. "Consent" does not mean agreement to the terms of a covenant or contract; it is rather the adoption of a rule governing behavior. Thus, to act in accordance with a rule is to consent to that rule where such consent is expressed in complicity and toleration as well as in suffrage and overt action. Any rule which gains consent, i.e., which actually governs behavior, is a custom, and laws are simply special cases of custom. Laws, consequently, are not the power of a superior authority over an inferior. They are rules which develop from the multiplication of voluntary adoptions and choices; they become lasting by proving satisfactory modes of behavior. A proposition is thus not a law merely because it has been decreed by a legislature but because it governs actual behavior. A legislative decree which does *not* govern behavior, or which is incompatible with custom, is not a law. This view of law and consent underlay Wilson's defense of colonial opposition to Parliament and its decrees.

It is not so much that Wilson is combative in his opposition to natural law, but rather that his full attention was turned to man-made law. Doubtless the moral sense can perceive directly the viciousness of harming others, but the ins and outs of positive law surpass in complexity what can be grasped intuitively. Human law is then neither directly a product of divine law as the Lockeans would have it, nor merely a working out of scientific laws as Hume, Smith, and the Benthamites with their laissez-faire overtones would have it. Laws are designed and created in accordance with custom as it expresses funded social wisdom.

Wilson, like many of the colonists in the early stages of the dispute with England, based his arguments on the "rights of Englishmen." Parliament, so he reasoned, is bound by the British constitution, yet even that constitution is not supreme. He is here appealing to the theory of law and consent outlined above, not to any natural right or higher law. His point is that even the British constitution is not law if it is incompatible with the actual customs of the people and fails of their consent. There is a supraconstitutional authority which is not transcendental. Many other colonials, as the debates deepened, were driven toward a natural rights position (with its appeal to self-evident truths); Wilson was able to rest *his* case on his doctrine of consent coupled with an empirical political behaviorism.

With independence came the Articles of Confederation, but it soon became clear that the government of the Articles was too weak. Wilson, like other American leaders, realized that what was needed was not a revision of the Articles, but rather a new design for society. For this new society there was no precedent, neither in the ancient nor in the modern world. Swiss cantons are bound merely by mutual alliance; the Netherlands and the Germanic states offer no model; only in the smallest corner of Britain is there representative government. So a Constitution came to be written, and Wilson was unquestionably one of its major architects. He was chiefly concerned with the empirical questions of the dynamics of power, and of how group interests could be reconciled or at least represented.

> If we take an extended and accurate view of it, we shall find the streams of power running in different directions, in different dimensions, and at different heights . . . but if we trace them, we shall discover, that they all originally flow from one abundant fountain. In this constitution, all authority is derived from THE PEOPLE.[58]

Thus, his history of popular sovereignty once again comes to his rescue. The major difficulty with the Articles of Confederation beyond their weakness was the fact that the states, not individuals, were regarded as constituents. In his view the Constitution was to rectify this error. If the states are taken to be separate entities and as "sovereign," then it is clear they cannot but lose some powers in forming a confederation. But the "state" is only a fiction, a figure of speech. Thus, there exists no shadow entity between the people and their government. Just as a man may have many interests, so the American citizen may have many roles; he may be a citizen of his state *and* a citizen of the United States. Holding all this, Wilson wanted the people rather than the several states to ratify the new Constitution. And this multiplicity of interests gives him a different view from the Federalist Papers of how factions are to be reconciled.

The Constitutional Convention certainly exceeded its authority in drawing up the plan of a new government since it had been called merely to revise the old one. Wilson defended the action of the convention by arguing that a new government was not instituted by the Constitution since the people, in jointly seeking independence, had already been acting (i.e., voluntarily consenting) as a nation. Wilson's most extreme assertion of the sovereignty of the nation came in his decision in the case of *Chisholm* v. *Georgia*. Speaking for the Supreme Court, Wilson held that the Federal courts had jurisdiction over the states, so that a citizen of the nation could sue any state. The underlying issue in the case was, in Wilson's eyes, "do the people of the United States form a nation?"

Wilson saw clearly that there might be difficulties between the states and the Federal government, but he believed that there could be no irreconcilable differences of interest since the states and the nation are different instruments in the service of the same people. Wilson did not wish to diminish the powers of the states, but he believed that the distribution of functions between the states and the Federal government must be governed by a principle of utility.[59]

His theory that sovereignty lies only with the people—and that people may figure in various roles (now as citizens of states, now as citizens of the nation)—offers easy extension to the international level. If the situation is structured in terms, not of power, but rather of the observance of rules for common objectives, then there is no reason why the strength of customary law (already persisting between nations), which is ever extended by commerce, should not be extended—not to a super power, but to "arbitration on an international level."

> Individuals united in civil society institute judges . . . that justice may be done and war may be prevented. Are States too wise or too proud to receive a lesson from individuals? Is the idea of a common judge between nations less admirable than that of a common judge between men? If admissible in idea, would it not be desirable to have an opportunity of trying whether the idea may not be reduced to practice?[60]

It is interesting that Wilson adds his plan for international peace to a score of similar proposals made at the end of the century. His, however, is distinguished (by its commonsense character and its change from a "power model" to a kind of low-keyed appeal to the common interests of mankind) from the efforts of a Gros or a Kant: Wilson, at least, has no romantic tendency to appeal to "the cunning of history" or to glorify the state as an entity in its own right, or to see its development through conflict. Though Wilson stays with international relations (i.e., relations between *nations*), his emphasis on the individual and on the individual's pluralism of interests is a far cry from a view of the state which, as it were, bestows personality on its citizens. In effect, Wilson claims that the American Bill of Rights is contained in the Preamble.

> The boasted Magna Charta of England derives the liberties of the in-habitants . . . from the gift and grant of the King . . . But here the fee simple remains in the people, and by this Constitution they do not part with it. The Preamble of the proposed Constitution . . . contains the essence of all the Bills of Rights that have been or can be devised . . .[61]

The South and Jefferson

The South exhibits well the changes in moral philosophy and the patterns of development which we outlined above. The history of William and Mary ex-presses practically the concern for education, and it rapidly evolved from a predominantly religiously oriented school into an institution for the education of statesmen. Almost from the beginning there were two professors of philosophy, one for physics, metaphysics, and mathematics, and the other for rhetoric, logic, and ethics. Texts were widely chosen from the outset—Grotius, Pufendorf, Locke, and, very early, Hutcheson—indicating that ethical problems were placed in a broad social setting. The location of the college in the then capital of the colony turned attention to political problems which were actively discussed by students and faculty. Even as a student Jefferson engaged in urbane dialogue with William Small of Aberdeen, professor of moral philosophy, and through him with George Wythe, then professor of law, and with Governor Farquier. Reports vary as to how much Jefferson got out of the moral philosophy courses, but Small made a very deep impression on him, and they maintained contact after Small returned to Birmingham, England, where he was identified with the circle of Erasmus Darwin and Priestley.

Difficult days fell on William and Mary after the Revolution, predictably because of its Anglican heritage. Although Jefferson, as governor, worked to disestablish the Anglican Church, he also cooperated with the president, Bishop Madison, to modernize the curriculum, i.e., to teach modern languages and science, and to dissociate moral philosophy from sectarian doctrine. Jefferson not only enlarged the reading requirements, urging the use of Locke's two essays, Rousseau's *Social Contract*, and the works of Paine and Priestley, but also introduced Destutt de Tracy's review of Montesquieu, a work he himself had had a hand in preparing. By doing away with the professorship of divinity, Jefferson was able to engineer another post, a professorship of law and politics (i.e., of administration).

Jefferson's interest in William and Mary waned in later years and he turned instead to the founding of the University of Virginia. The course in moral philosophy at the new university was designed by Jefferson. Philosophy in the large he regarded as ideology with its divisions of universal grammar, ethics, and moral philosophy or the ethics of social relations. Jefferson took an interest in the appointment of the early professors and persuaded Europeans to come there to teach in English literature, modern languages, and other fields, but he was convinced that the American experiment was something so utterly new that new moral paths were being broken and so that moral philosophy needed to be taught by Americans who had shared this experience. He devoted much loving care to the preparation of Destutt de Tracy's formal treatise on economics for use as a text. He recommended also the Declaration of Independence, the Federalist Papers, the Constitution, and the Virginia document of 1799 (a commentary on the Virginia Resolves of 1798) for the work in political philosophy.

Jefferson's own views, moral and political, clearly enter into his recommendations about the curriculum. He was afraid that Federalist political theory would make its way insidiously into the education. Equally clear is his sympathy for moral sense theory in the tradition of Hutcheson and Stewart, and for the economic theory of the physiocrats. As Jefferson states his moral theory:

> I believe . . . that it [the moral sense] is instinct, and innate, that the moral sense is as much a part of our constitution as that of feeling, seeing, or hearing; as a wise creator must have seen to be necessary in an animal destined to live in society: that every human mind feels pleasure in doing good to another; that the non-existence of justice is not to be inferred from the fact that the same act is deemed virtuous and right in one society, which is held vicious and wrong in another; because as the circumstances and opinions of different societies vary, so the acts which may do them right or wrong must vary also: for virtue does not consist in the act we do, but in the end it is to effect. If it is to effect the happiness of him to whom it is directed, it is virtuous, while in a society under different circumstances and opinions the same act might produce pain, and would be vicious. The essence of virtue is in doing good to others, while what is good may be one thing in one society, and it's contrary in another.[62]

This is of course the doctrine of the Scottish school,[63] and in all probability Jefferson derived it from Dugald Stewart. The moral sense, as Jefferson understood it, is not a transcendental intuition, or a theory of illumination: like the other senses to which it is compared, it is an organ of perception which acts only on particular cases. When an act is brought before the mind, the moral sense perceives it to be right or wrong. But the moral sense does not tell us why the action is right or wrong—it enunciates no rules, it tells us nothing about the nature of virtue or vice—it only informs us that this particular act is right or wrong. It is true that by reflecting upon the decisions which the moral sense has made we may be able to induce some general rules of morality, but these rules are not given by the moral sense itself. Thus the moral sense perceives the moral character of acts in the same way that the eye perceives the color of objects. The eye perceives that a given object is red; it does not perceive the "nature" of redness, nor the laws of optics: so the moral sense perceives that a given act is right; it does not perceive the nature of righteousness, nor the laws of virtue.[64]

The essence of true virtue for Jefferson is benevolence. "If it [our act] is to effect the happiness of him to whom it is directed, it is virtuous."[65] The moral sense must, therefore, approve those acts which serve the happiness of others. This doctrine, however, is not one of complete self-sacrifice, for as Jefferson points out above, "every human mind feels pleasure in doing good to another."[66] But if we know what virtue is, why do we need a moral sense at all? Why cannot men simply apply their knowledge of virtue to the particular cases before them? The reason, Jefferson says, is that men are incompetent to do so.

> He who made us would have been a pitiful bungler, if he had made the rules of our moral conduct a matter of science. For one man of science, there are thousands who are not. What would have become of them?[67]

To discover what really conduces to happiness in the long run requires so elaborate a calculation of contingencies that not one man in a thousand could do it correctly; therefore, God has beneficently endowed us with an automatic decision procedure—the moral sense—which directs us to do that which will maximize happiness, even though at the time the decision is made we do not see how that end will be brought about.

The doctrine of the moral sense was an attempt, and a reasonable one, to deal with one of the most difficult problems of philosophy and of moral science—the universality of moral phenomena. Moral distinctions are made in all societies and by all men, or at least by all men not demented or insane, so that morality appears to be a universal characteristic of mankind. But although all men make moral distinctions, the specific content of these distinctions varies from society to society and even from man to man. Thus what is right in one society or for one man can be wrong in another society or for someone else, although for every society and every man there is something which is right or wrong. The postulate that there exists an innate moral sense has the virtue of explaining this universality of morality: what it fails to explain is the variation in specific content. The problem for those who defend this doctrine is thus to account for this relativity, and Jefferson seeks to do this in two ways. In the first place, he argues that

> . . . nature has constituted *utility* to man the standard and best of virtue. Men living in different countries, under different circumstances, different habits and regimens, may have different utilities; the same act, therefore, may be useful, and consequently virtuous in one country which is injurious and vicious in another differently circumstanced.[68]

This argument suffices to explain at least those cases of relativity in which a common end of benevolence is served by different specific acts under different specific cultural conditions. But not all moral variation is of this sort: benevolence is not always the end. To account for these cases, Jefferson resorted to a second theory.

> This is a remarkable instance of improvement in the moral sense. The putting to death captives in war was a general practice among savage nations. When men became more humanized the captive was indulged with life on condition of holding it in perpetual slavery; a condition exacted on this supposition, that the victor had right to take his life, and consequently to commute it for his services . . . At this day it is perceived we have no right to take the life of an enemy unless where our own preservation renders it necessary . . .[69]

Into this developmental wastebasket all cases of relativity which do not fit the first explanation may be swept, and anyone who is not benevolent is simply retarded. Thus the innateness of the moral sense can be maintained in the face of the most patent barbarism, and the theory is so made irrefutable. But not quite irrefutable. For as the passage quoted above makes clear, Jefferson believed that the development of the moral sense can be cumulative through what amounts to the inheritance of acquired characteristics.[70] It is accordingly possible for men living for long periods in debasing conditions to become themselves degraded, as Jefferson held the rabble of Europe to be;[71] and conversely, where men live under conditions which promote the development of the moral sense, they may attain, if not perfection, at least a high degree of moral development.[72] Thus moral philosophy and social philosophy are always closely linked for Jefferson, for although the social order depends upon the moral, the development of morality itself is tied to social conditions. And if those social conditions can be specified, then the moral improvement of the nation can also become an object of science and wise statesmanship.

Jefferson's political theory is fundamentally a moral—i.e., normative—theory. It is not a theory about how people, or nations, actually behave, but about how they should and can behave. Thus when Jefferson argued that all power resides in the people or that no one may infringe the rights of others, he was not describing the actual state of affairs as it was in England or in France under the *ancien régime*— he was making statements about what ought to be the case. Jefferson's classic description of the French monarchy—the government of wolves over sheep[73]—is sufficient proof that he knew very well that not every state conformed to his ideal. But Jefferson also believed that a moral political order could really be created in the world, and that such an order was approximated by the United States. Thus it is a highly practical morality which is being espoused, for men can so design their political structures as to realize the moral order.

The fact that politics is a part of morality is particularly important in understanding Jefferson because it clarifies the status of rights. Natural rights are for Jefferson derived fundamentally from natural—i.e., biological—wants and from the benevolence of God who has so designed the creation that each man may satisfy his natural wants without infringing upon those of his neighbor. But natural rights are moral properties of individuals, as is clear from the fact that to violate a natural right is to commit an immoral act. Since it is the existence of the moral sense which permits us to perceive the rightness or wrongness of actions, it is also the moral sense which enables us to know what the rights of others are. Whether the moral sense perceives these rights as the eye does red, or whether we infer the existence of rights from the fact that certain actions are right and others wrong, Jefferson does not make clear, but in either case the concept of natural right is grounded empirically in the perceptions of the moral sense. This gives to Jefferson's theory of natural rights an empirical basis which contrasts sharply with the apriorism of rationalist proponents of natural rights.

Since Jefferson believed that the political structure of the state can be so designed as to realize the moral order, it is necessary to look in some detail at the machinery he believed could accomplish this task. Jefferson took the idea of the social contract seriously. He believed apparently in the historical reality of the contract, and that governments are instituted to protect the natural rights of men and to promote their happiness.[74] Jefferson also believed, as did every colonist, in the immense importance of written constitutions: two hundred years' experience with colonial charters had so thoroughly demonstrated the utility of such written contracts that no one considered setting up a new government—state or Federal— without one. In accordance with social contract theory, Jefferson believed that power originally, and rightfully, belonged to the people alone, that in establishing the government they had delegated certain powers to the state, and that all powers not so delegated remained with the people. He also held that violation of the contract dissolved its bonds, and that the people were entitled to withdraw power from a government which broke the agreement, even if they had to overthrow it by force.

The fundamental principle of republican government Jefferson believed to be majority rule:

The first principle of republicanism is, that the *lex majoris partis* is the fundamental law of every society of individuals of equal rights; to consider the will of the society enounced by the majority of a single vote, as sacred as if unanimous, is the first of all lessons in importance, yet the last which is thoroughly learnt.[75]

But this is not a doctrine of the general will: the government, even in obedience to the will of the majority, cannot infringe the rights of the minority without violating the social contract. To this principle Jefferson added the principle of representation—that if the people are not able to carry out their will directly, they are entitled to choose representatives to carry it out for them, and to remove these representatives if they fail to fulfill their charge. This device of representation Jefferson regarded as one of the great discoveries of modern times which made possible the extension of republican government to large nations and rendered obsolete most of the classical treatises on politics.[76] Correlative to the principle of representation is the principle that each man should exercise all the powers which he is competent to exercise and delegate to representatives only those which he is not able to exercise himself.[77] Representation therefore does not relieve the individual of responsibilities for the conduct of his own affairs, and Jefferson feared nothing more than the engrossing by rulers, elected or not, of the powers not delegated to them. To guard against such concentration, Jefferson relied upon the principle of the separation of powers. Different powers should be delegated to different agents, each of whom would serve as a check and balance against the concentration of undue power in the hands of anyone. By diffusing power in many hands, Jefferson believed the lust for power of the different agents would produce an equilibrium. If this doctrine owes much to Montesquieu, it is also deeply indebted to the Newtonian model which made such a stable equilibrium appear to be a "natural" solution to the problem of power.[78]

Upon the basis of these principles Jefferson designed the government of the good society. The basic political unit was the individual, conceived typically as a farmer living on his own land and managing his own affairs. Thus even the individual is conceived as an areal political unit. To manage those affairs which the individual cannot manage himself, Jefferson defined areal units five or six miles square which he called wards.[79] These units, which were frankly modeled upon the New England townships, were to be directly governed by their citizens, so that every man would be involved in their management. To deal with those functions which the ward cannot handle, Jefferson proposed to utilize the counties, governed by elected representatives. Similarly, to state governments would be delegated those functions which were beyond the scope of the county, and finally to the Federal government those beyond the scope of the state. Each unit in the hierarchy was to be governed by elected representatives, and the governments of the larger units—the states and nation—were to be organized with the familiar bicameral legislature, executive, and judiciary. That form of organization of course embodies the separation-of-powers principle and the principle of checks and balances, but Jefferson considered the separation of powers between units of the hierarchy even more important than that within the governments of the units. Thus he wrote:

> It is a fatal heresy to suppose that either our State governments are superior to the federal, or the federal to the States. The people, to whom all authority belongs, have divided the powers of government into two distinct departments, the leading characters of which are *foreign* and domestic; and they have appointed for each a distinct set of functionaries. These they have made coordinate, checking and balancing each other, like the three cardinal departments in the individual States: each equally supreme as to the powers delegated to itself, and neither authorized ultimately to decide what belongs to itself, or to its coparcenor in government . . . But, finally, the peculiar happiness of our blessed system is, that in differences of opinion between these different sets of servants, the appeal is to neither, but to their employers peaceably assembled by their representatives in convention.[80]

Nowhere is Jefferson's commitment to the principle of divided sovereignty more evident: each unit is sovereign in its own domain, and it is only by preserving the sovereignty of each unit that genuine separation of powers can be maintained. For this reason, Jefferson was loath to admit that any one unit could assume the power to judge disputes among others, or to which it was itself a party. When, however, as in the case of the alien and sedition laws, he was faced with what he believed to be an unconstitutional act on the part of the Federal government, he took the position that the states may declare an act of Congress to be unconstitutional, and he remained utterly opposed to the doctrine established by Marshall in *Marbury* v. *Madison* that the Federal Supreme Court alone has that power. Thus in case of dispute over delegated powers, Jefferson tended to trust those units lowest on the hierarchy.

The passage quoted above also helps to clarify the principle on which Jefferson believed the delegation of powers should proceed—viz., domestic versus foreign. Whatever concerns only those within a given unit belongs to the jurisdiction of that unit; whatever concerns those outside the unit must be delegated to a more inclusive unit. Thus in saying that men should delegate only what they are not "competent" to do themselves, Jefferson did not mean what they lacked the wealth or resources to do. A state road is a local matter to be dealt with by the state, whether the state has the money to build it or not, while treaties with foreign nations are national matters because they affect all citizens of the nation. Jefferson could therefore oppose Federal involvement in regional affairs while urging state involvement: it was not a question of "government" intervention but of which government.

Jefferson believed that the objective of government was the protection of the individual rights and the promotion of individual happiness, and to the extent that a government succeeded in achieving these objectives, the self-interest of the individual would lead him to support and defend the government. It was very clear to Jefferson that a government, especially a new government, could command the loyalty of its citizens only if it worked—i.e., only if it did effectively further the interests of the citizens, for the happiness which men seek is a happiness in this world. And Jefferson believed that his ideal government, and to a slightly lesser extent, the actual American government, would work. Wedded as he was to an agricultural society, and accustomed to small-scale individual enterprise, Jefferson saw the problem of furthering individual economic interests as largely one of removing constraints upon individual actions and providing security for individual property. Since these were precisely the benefits which he thought his form of government conferred, he was certain of the loyalty of its citizens. Indeed, he regarded the United States government as the strongest on earth because he believed it the only one to whose defense every citizen would rush at the first sign of danger.

The political system Jefferson envisioned is one which seeks to decentralize power as thoroughly as possible. Nevertheless, like any political system its proper functioning depends upon its ability to recruit effective leadership. Jefferson understood this point very well.

> For I agree with you [he wrote John Adams] that there is a natural aristocracy among men. The grounds of this are virtue and talents . . . The natural aristocracy I consider as the most precious gift of nature for the instruction, the trusts, and government of society. And indeed it would have been inconsistent in creation to have formed man for the social state, and not to have provided virtue and wisdom enough to manage the concerns of the society. May we not even say that that form of government is the best which provides the most effectually for a pure selection of these natural aristoi into the offices of government?[81]

Two problems are involved here: the training of the natural aristocracy for their roles, and the placing of the aristocrats in those roles. For the first, Jefferson proposed a scheme of public education which would provide free elementary schools in every ward. The best students from these schools would then be sent on free to grammar schools for further training, and the best of the students completing the grammar schools would then be sent at public charge to William and Mary for advanced training.[82] The objective of the system, which the Virginia legislature declined to enact, was both to provide universal free education and to identify and train talented youths for superior positions within the society. By making the whole process tax supported, Jefferson hoped to provide avenues of mobility which would recruit the most able members of the lower classes (always excepting the slaves) for positions of leadership. The second problem—how to assure the election of the aristocrats—Jefferson believed could be safely left to the good sense of the electorate.

> I think the best remedy is exactly that provided by all our constitutions, to leave to the citizens the free election and separation of the aristoi from the pseudo-aristoi, or the wheat from the chaff. In general they will elect the real good and wise.[83]

If this seems excessively naive, one must recall that Jefferson was an eighteenth-century Virginian, where for more than a century the planter elite had been able to win election to Burgesses regularly without resort to corruption. Jefferson's faith in the wisdom of the electorate was in large part a generalization from his Virginia experience.

Jefferson's efforts to design and implement an ideal government indicate the importance he attached to political structure. But he was far too clear eyed to believe that structure alone could provide a republican government. He even went so far as to claim that, given the proper "spirit" among the people, structure was irrelevant.

> Where then is our republicanism to be found? Not in our constitution certainly, but merely in the spirit of our people. That would oblige even a despot to govern us republicanly. Owing to this spirit, and to nothing in the form of our constitution, all things have gone well.[84]

Certainly Jefferson has here overstated his case, but the point involved is fundamental to his thinking: structure is not enough—republican government is only possible where the people have the right "spirit" and the proper "virtues." By these terms Jefferson meant attitudes and values. Independence, self-control, self-reliance, tolerance—attitudes such as these are necessary conditions for the existence and maintenance of a republican state, and without them any government, regardless of its structure, would become tyrannical. But these attitudes are themselves products of the social order. Clearly education is involved in the shaping of values and attitudes, and this was one of the reasons Jefferson believed universal public education so important. The moral sense is also a source of such dispositions, but as we saw above Jefferson thought that the strength of the moral sense depended upon social conditions. Most of all, Jefferson believed that such values and attitudes could only become dominant in a society where men held property and managed it themselves—where economic security permitted such dispositions to become ruling attributes. "Such men," Jefferson remarked, "may safely and advantageously reserve to themselves a wholsome controul over their public affairs, and a degree of freedom, which, in the hands of the Canaille of the cities of Europe, would be instantly perverted to the demolition and destruction of every thing public and private."[85] Thus one sees again the interplay of the social and moral orders: each depends upon the other in a process relation and changes in one must occasion changes in the other. This is another way of saying that Jefferson saw the political structure of a nation as part of a functioning sociocultural system, depending upon and interacting with other components of the system. A given political structure would produce very different effects when embedded in a different cultural context. For this reason Jefferson did not believe that American political institutions were exportable. Each nation had to develop a structure suited to its own culture. But since the influence between political structure and attitudes and values is reciprocal, by designing the structure in the right way the statesman can further strengthen the attitudes and values of the people which support republican government. Thus Jefferson believed that enlightened statesmanship could lead a nation toward an ever more republican form of society.

The Moral and the Social Sciences

The notion of "moral" with which the writers of the eighteenth and nineteenth centuries were working has become very much larger than that of "the inward and private virtue" of a Johnson or a Franklin, wider even than the classical associations with politics and jurisprudence. By the end of the eighteenth century, it had come to include the study of the entire fabric of custom and tradition. Envisaged then was nothing less than a full science of man based on an empirical psychology, extending to social relations of all kinds and ending with the relations among nations—not in the style of Grotius with his laws of war and peace based on natural law, but in the new mode of commercial interdependence and a new sense of natural laws. As the language of contract, original state of nature, natural rights, and the like gave way to utilitarian formalism, the focus falls increasingly on the complexities of association, production and exchange, poverty and wealth. Theorist and practitioner alike come to conceive of social institutions on a mechanical or biological model and to search for the empirical laws of their functioning and development—the laws of want and need and the actual modes of their satisfaction. Simultaneously the questions, as if by tacit agreement, take on a scientific shape. In the early decades of the nineteenth century they continued to investigate the criteria of institutions and their design, to query whether any given institution was fulfilling its function; and after the 1820s German romanticism adds a further organic and historical dimension to this critique.

Such developments were reflected in courses in moral philosophy which broaden to cover the matters of anthropology, social relations, history, sociology, economics, and rudimentary communication theory. Moral philosophy was the "matrix" out of which each of the particular social sciences was to emerge.[86]

The growing autonomy from moral critique can be suggested by looking at political economy as it begins to take on an identity of its own; methods are developed to handle objective criteria for happiness, and empirical laws began to crystallize for wealth and welfare, population and poverty, division of labor, buying and selling (even of land and labor), and production and distribution generally. Yet, at least until the mid-nineteenth century political economy remained self-consciously rooted in moral theory and involved in concrete moral issues—of slavery, punishment, prison reform, poor laws, and restraints on the insolence of wealth. Of course the domain we now know as economics shook loose from other social issues only slowly and unevenly. The independence from the moral and larger social context is gained decades after the period of our present concern under the protective shield of the neutrality of science. In any case, as "human nature" becomes in principle a fully empirical concept, mathematics and psychology are directly relevant in models of both the economic and moral man.

Once again, New World theory is early inspired by French and British sources. The French Physiocrats, especially Quesnay and Turgot (a friend of Franklin's), and Destutt de Tracy and Du Pont de Nemours (friends of Jefferson), as well as Adam Smith, were facing new problems in trade and agriculture as they moved toward a broadened market economy. Above all mercantilism and the restrictive policies which it spawned needed to be lifted. Mercantilist theory identified national interest with that of the narrow ruling class, saw the visible measure of prestige and power in a favorable balance of trade (in specie wherever possible). Governments glorified the commercial class and justified the most outrageous acts of patronage and special favor to it, and they saw themselves engaged in cutthroat competition with other nations to secure economic power as a national objective. Wide and deep regulation of economic activities was prescribed, including the subordination of colonies by using them for natural resources and by restricting their trade elsewhere, as markets for the manufactures of the dominating power. American colonists, as recipients of these policies, had only too good an opportunity to know them in practice, and to read the theory in Sir James Steuart's *An Inquiry into the Principles of Political Oeconomy*, which Franklin published in 1771.

Inevitably there were differences between the British and French theorists, reflecting the differences in their own economic conditions; e.g., the French located the source of wealth in land and agriculture rather than in labor and commercial enterprise. But both took it as an article of faith that the laws of nature could work in such a way as to make men secure in the cosmos, and that this law of nature embraced a moral harmony and if allowed a chance to operate would destroy those jealousies that lead to war between nations. Laissez-faire (in all probability Franklin's phrase) was thus born in optimistic faith; economics was an extension of moral verities.

Adam Smith's *Wealth of Nations* was enormously influential in America as well as in England, and versions of his work were cited and used everywhere. Of course the ground had been well prepared before Smith's synthesis, including the work of Franklin. And Hume's terse logical arguments demonstrated the futility and inconsistency of mercantilist policies, and lay at the base of Adam Smith's attack on mercantilism. Dugald Stewart was partly responsible for the hearing Smith's theory (and laissez-faire) got, for he edited the *Wealth of Nations*, recommending it personally to Jefferson, and later including in the *Encyclopaedia Britannica* a very popular supplement on economics by McCulloch. This latter became a standard text in America.

It is well to note that Smith's work appeared the same year (1776) as Watt perfected the reciprocating steam engine. There was still to come intensified industrialization, the factory system with its social consequences of poverty, and overcrowding and child labor. Smith had been speaking rather to commerce and trade than to manufacturing and industry, and when these social consequences occurred the problem became how to interpret poverty and disease as part of the natural order. Ricardo applies Smith's principles to Malthus's theory to forge the "dismal science." Gone is the optimism and progress of the Enlightenment, the poor hover on the edge of starvation, and classes are in inevitable conflict—landowner, capitalist, and laborer.

Smith was a spokesman for the middle class, yet there were also radical as well as nationalist elements for which the Americans were to invoke his authority. His support of the free competitive market grew out of his distrust of traders and manufacturers, though the dynamics of their work carried the whole system in that the desire for goods and self-interest was the basic motivation; but he also bore witness to the corruption of wealth attained and the tendency of the wealthy to identify their own interest as the public good. Accordingly the absence of external restraints and freedom to pursue self-interest do not suffice to establish a social harmony. What are required are institutional mechanisms so structured as to compel men to pursue self-interest only in a socially beneficial way, harnessing men's selfish interests to the general welfare. They are also to frustrate men's baser impulses and their antisocial tendencies. Laissez-faire so conceived is a complex and designed institution rather than the absence of an institution; this is what we could expect from a utilitarian as against a Lockean social theory. But with Malthus and Ricardo and the later classical British economists the radical and other parts of his message are forgotten and he is taken to be the voice of unrestricted laissez-faire and free trade.

Once again the Americans reworked theory in the light of their own distinctive circumstances. Some of the doctrines were inappropriate; for example, in contrast to the Malthusian picture there was a need for greater population, and in contrast to Ricardo there was almost limitless land available. In America commerce had distinctive features, not least of which was the urgency for developing common intersectional economic ties. In the minds of some, British and French economic theory was correct, but merely inapplicable to the American situation of the time or premature and inapplicable only in a Utopian sense. But in the minds of others, the theory was simply wrong as proved by its inapplicability in America. Thus some remained strongly laissez-faire—most obviously Jefferson—but for quite different reasons from the original framers of the theory. In addition different aspects appealed to the conservative New England professors of moral philosophy; e.g., Wayland of Brown exalted the commercial class and interests and backed up his position with strongly theological considerations. Others, nominally laissez-faire, like McVickar at Columbia who edited McCulloch's text but supplemented it and materially altered its thrust by reference to American needs. Still others issued a direct challenge—not so much Hamilton himself whose concerns were practical aims of national economic development—but those like Raymond and the Careys who sought out the broader theoretical underpinnings of a national in contrast to a cosmopolitan system. And these latter made common cause with the German view of the nation as organic.

While the focus of the discussion in America tended to be the tariff, dividing along protectionist or free trade lines, this was seldom taken as an isolated issue; in the end, the contest was over the kind of society and the quality of life Americans were to enjoy. Entangled with it were not only questions of a national bank and canals and (later) railroads, but also more ultimate issues of the role and limits of government, the nature of national interest, the role of America among nations, the nature of wealth, the provisions for equality, and the distribution of property.

In the present context, the separation hitherto used between New England on the one hand and the Middle Atlantic and Southern states on the other is less serviceable, for perceived sectional interests made strange philosophical bedfellows. And, of course, western expansion reorients the whole picture. But invariably, academics interacted with nonacademic thinkers and reacted to pressing problems, and as invariably theirs was a conservative message.

Jefferson's polemicizing for the cosmopolitan system was, of course, enormously influential. Personally acquainted with both British and French laissez-faire theorists, he preferred the French version, perhaps because of its emphasis on agriculture and the physiocratic way of viewing of natural law. Importantly too he shared their view of the public interest which was weighted toward the poor. Although Jefferson generally spoke from a political and moral background, still he did much to stimulate the study of economic problems and to make a place for it in the curriculum of the Southern colleges as well as to publicize economic writers. He sponsored Destutt de Tracy's treatise on political economy, translated it in part, wrote a considerable preface, sought its publication, and encouraged its use as a text. Actually Jean Baptiste Say's *Catechism of Political Economy* became the standard text in colleges, even those with strong Hamiltonian protectionist sympathies. Say's work was an elegant and didactic statement of Adam Smith's principles, firmly set in physiocratic soil. He cast the whole in a biological rather than a mechanistic model, which allowed him to emphasize need and utility. Money, he thought, was only a facilitating instrument, for the exchange of product with product is the fundamental fact. Hence, where this is recognized, the prosperity of each is a common concern, whether considered on an individual or an international level. Say's work was more responsive to the developing commerce and industry than Smith's (doubtless because it was written some forty years later). On the whole, then, Jefferson was quite content to let Say be the spokesman for the position.

If Jefferson's outlook expressed and idealized the visible agricultural pattern, Hamilton's in contrast was geared to what the nation could become. It gave a special bent to the Enlightenment's emphasis on progress, calling for the energetic design of political and economic institutions to forge a strong nation, independent of the vagaries of foreign influences. Essential to political independence is economic independence, and this requires a strong central government not only for military purposes, but also for the protection of home industries, the securing of national revenue, and the strengthening of the soft bonds between the states by encouraging economic interdependence. The national government should act directly on individuals without the mediation of states; the Constitution is not essentially a guarantor against the invasion of private life but an instrument for the expansion and diversification of property. Hamilton's program was not merely a means to national independence but expressed his view of the desirable character of national life—progressively expanding economy offering opportunity for development of men's distinctive and diverse powers. As his *Report on Manufactures* (1791) makes clear, this involves the primacy of manufacturing rather than that of agriculture. Hamilton stood for all that Jefferson feared—a nationalism rather than a cosmopolitanism, an urban as against a rural civilization, a national mercantile interest of a necessarily small class as against a broadly based agrarian public. Hamilton foresaw an inevitable widening gap between rich and poor. At stake between the Jeffersonians and the Hamiltonians was not only a view of political and economic institutions and of national destiny, but also a view of the goodness, wisdom, and responsibility of human beings.

Although Hamilton's views had strong overtones of the older mercantilism, he could still enlist the authority of Hume and Adam Smith in support of his position. Thus both (at least on his reading) believed there were occasions where government might intervene legitimately, especially to protect the natural workings of economic laws. Nevertheless, Hamilton looks out in a thoroughly new direction. His interests were always tied to concrete problems and he left to others to work out a larger setting for his policies. But all protectionists were not cut from the same cloth, though of course each in his own way challenged the classical economists. For example, Daniel Raymond and the Careys, Mathew and Henry, approach the matter with very different social philosophies.

It must have taken courage for Raymond, a young lawyer newly set up in his profession and waiting for clients, to challenge Adam Smith directly. While conservatism of his profession is always in the background, still there is a remarkable radical potential in his theory of social justice.[87] If he seems to start with Locke in the view that God gave the resources of the world for the common use of mankind, he parts company in believing that the advent of money and property does not change the situation. And since property and value arise when labor is mixed with these resources, it follows that men have a right to employment and to labor. Private property as presently instituted depends on convention and on law. Those who already have wealth are progressively favored by the operation of the system, resulting in greater and greater inequity in the distribution of property. If the law should take steps to remedy the inequity, it could not be forbidden to do so in the name of a natural right of property, since the property distribution is itself an outcome of man-directed convention.

If effect, Raymond regards classical economics as the apology for the existing inequity. The Malthusian doctrines are excuses for not providing access to the necessities of life. Those who are willing and able to work should be entitled by the system to employment. The government ought to undertake public works in times of unemployment; if they can be used afterward, so much the better; but even if they were merely to be torn down, they would have served a good purpose.

> The property-holders have not an absolute, unconditional right to their property—their right is subordinate to that of the nation; and whatever portion national interests require, should be appropriated to the support of the poor, they have no more right to with-hold, than they have to take possession of their neighbour's field. It is the law alone that gives the richest nobleman in England a better right to his property than the meanest beggar in the kingdom; and the extent of his right is to be ascertained by the strict letter of the law.
>
> If then the law gives them an exclusive right to the whole surface of the earth, upon condition, that they support the poor out of it, let them not complain of the condition, provided they accept of the grant. The law does not require them to support the poor without labour, provided, they are able to labour; but the laws of justice, as well as the laws of the land, require the rich either to furnish the poor with labour, or support them without labour.[88]

The most serious error of all is the way the British economists identify individual wealth with national wealth. If there is, e.g., an enormous inequity of distribution, no amount of wealth in the hands of a few amounts to great national wealth. National wealth is not to be calculated in terms of quantity of capital reserves but in the development of capacities, especially economic ones, and opportunities. Where Adam Smith distinguished productive from nonproductive labor, Raymond rather looks to a larger domain, including the creative work of a Newton or a Boyle. He distinguishes labor applied directly to nature for the production of consumer goods and effective or permanent production, e.g., intermediate instruments for long-term development. Not only is the sum of individual riches not equivalent to national wealth, but clearly individual or class interests may run counter to national ones. Political economy is not the science of how to make an individual wealthy, it is the science of legislation, of government direction, to expand the national wealth in its fullest sense. This includes responsibility for the arts and sciences and for education of the citizenry.

Hamilton's system found one of its most ardent publicists in Mathew Carey, but it was left to his son, Henry, to capture the position in a theoretical framework.[89] His defense of the tariff flowed from a fairly complete social theory and is also an attack on the classic economists, James Mill, as well as Malthus and Ricardo. He attacks their theory of value, the distinction between rent and other commodities, the iron law of wages, and the pressure of population on subsistence, as well as the wider Malthusian thesis. Carey looks for laws of dynamic change rather than static universals. Often he wants a unity of the physical and social sciences and talks in a materialistic if not mechanistic way; on the other hand, he is most sensitive to the variability of human behavior and the necessary reference to particular conditions. The latter leads him to search for concrete data, e.g., the difference between population growth among the Plains Indians and the West Coast Indians as a function of soil and food supply as well as custom. The earlier leads to a normative view of social science and the recognition that many of the conditions are man-made or man controllable. Thus it is that social science is the search for the laws which govern man in his efforts to gain the highest individuality and the greatest power of association with his fellows.

Carey simply denies that there is a distinction in principle between the rent paid for the use of land and the price paid for the use of commodities or personal property. Basically the same laws are at work. All value rests ultimately in labor. Now where Ricardo thought that the richer land was exhausted first and cultivation then proceeded to the poorer land, Carey insists that it is the poor lands that would be developed first, e.g., because they would not have to be cleared, and then move would be made to the richer lands once association and cooperation made it more feasible. Similarly with respect to implements, a better implement, made later, will reduce the value of earlier, more crude implements, even where these made the better ones possible. Hence, reversing Ricardo's picture of the trend, Carey states that as ingenuity, initiative, cooperation, skill, and science are brought increasingly to bear, the value of commodities becomes less—even in the case of land—and they are more readily and broadly acquired. Because of these social factors entering into production (or in Carey's terms, *reproduction*, since it is the function or need satisfaction that is the point, not the mere duplication of the object), the cost of improvement should be borne by society. Thus government has a responsibility for education, for the development of the economic arts, transportation, and science. Government is here serving a shared interest of tenant and landlord, of laborer and manufacturer. Higher wages, an increasing standard of living, greater opportunity for the worker are compatible with the growth of manufacturing, industry, and commerce and their increasing profits.

If value is the resistance needed to be overcome to possess the thing desired, then value measures the power of nature over man while utility measures the power of man over nature. Progress is marked by the increase of the latter and the decrease of man's subservience to nature. Providence would scarcely have given man all the capacities for mastering nature and then left him subject to irreversible laws which would make him nature's slave. The Malthusian thesis may hold for England but it is altogether inappropriate in America where there are virtually inexhaustible lands and a need for increased population. In any case, rates of reproduction depend upon conditions which, when understood, can be controlled. In his vision for America, Carey saw an increasing population, not herded together in huge cities but diffused in small communities, "concentrations," where the "loom is near the plow and the plow is near the anvil." Such centers would serve really to unite different classes and crafts since they would be joined in production and consumption. It is the responsibility of government to foster these and larger sectional economic interdependencies especially between North and South. Government intervention thus may be rational, for government serves society as intelligence serves the organism.

Carey is most often viewed as an economist, and perhaps much of his theory has seemed exotic to later generations, although what seems exotic shifts. But in his own time he was heartily read and translated. He voiced the assurance that underdeveloped nations could take their place among those with diversified and developed economies. Furthermore, his economic theory is but a part of a larger social and moral philosophy.[90] Thus the analysis of the division of labor is also a theory of social development, for upon the particular kind of division of labor rest the kind of technology developed and its possibilities, the kind of interplay between individuals and class conflicts, and in general the kind of social relations that prevail. Once this fundamental role of the division of labor is realized, it becomes the pivotal point for normative assessment. As noted above, social science seeks out the laws which govern man in his efforts to gain the highest individuality; but such individuality depends upon association, and can only achieve richness with complexity and diversity of employment. Freedom is, in the long run, the opportunity to pursue employment of one's own choosing, and Carey attempts to show that it is the counterpart of the solidarity of the community. In this way he seeks to resolve the utilitarian problem of the relation of individual to social good.

Jeffersonian laissez-faire did not lack advocates both in and out of the colleges, but under the political and economic stresses of the twenties and thirties it was thinned out even in the thinking of its early partisans. Thus Thomas Cooper during the last of his many careers at South Carolina College, and as professor successively of chemistry, geology, and political economy, seems to have abandoned many of the values and much of the outlook he once shared with Jefferson. The targets remain the "American system," the protective sentiment issuing from Philadelphia and the diehard Federalists; but his *Lectures on the Elements of Political Economy*[91] (1826) view the subject matter as a basic science which is to be thoroughly nonmoral. He came to reject the theory of natural rights on Utilitarian grounds.[92] The only rights are those granted by a particular society. Property, e.g., is not divine in origin, nor itself guaranteed by anything except the institutions that define it. Yet the institution of property, built on our instinctual accumulative desires, can be seen to function for the greatest general good. Slavery is not an ethical issue or a matter of humane sentiment, but a question of efficient labor supply. He compares the lot of the slave to the dismal conditions of the laborers of Manchester, and arrives at the comforting conclusion that slavery is not necessarily the less humane. Of course men are not equal; the assumption of equality is a conventional device of use in achieving reform but an error upon which sound government cannot be built.[93] On the other hand, some of the liberal mood persists. Gross inequity in the distribution of wealth ought not to be permitted, and those who suffer the inequities ought to have some say in the remedies. Further the rich should bear the burden of taxes, including provisions even for higher public education.[94]

Despite the stormy reception of some of his opinions by the Presbyterian divines, Cooper remained at South Carolina for more than thirty years, most of them as its president. His successor was Francis Lieber.

Parallels in the careers of Cooper and Lieber are striking. Lieber, like Cooper, was foreign born; both came to America after having received a university education abroad. Cooper, in all probability, failed to receive his degree from Oxford due to scruples about signing the Articles, whereas Lieber's own degree from Jena was complicated by several months' imprisonment and flight because of his liberal politics. He was wounded at Waterloo, fought with other romantics for Greek independence, and worked for the creation of a unified Germany. Thus he, like Cooper, came to America with a stock of liberal and philosophical notions which were readily applicable to the new situation. But Lieber came to the Boston of 1820, where he associated himself with a fairly unsuccessful experiment in physical education, and left that to prepare the prestigious *Encyclopedia Americana*. This last was an enormous undertaking, and Lieber enlisted the aid of Henry Carey and many among the American intelligentsia, from Kent and Story in law to Hedge and Furness in literature. This dictionary became a major vehicle by which German thought reached the American public, and Lieber himself was responsible for major articles on German philosophy (including that on Kant) and political economy. He interested himself in the reform of education, and when the University of South Carolina invited him to fill the chair vacated by Cooper, they had every reason to see in Lieber a man of considerable stature. Ironically enough, attacks from the side of orthodox Calvinism were as influential in the departure of

Lieber from the college as they had been for Cooper; this is odd, because while Cooper had been a militant atheist, and anticleric, Lieber himself was an Anglican in good standing. While Lieber's major writings in political economy[95] were done at South Carolina, he welcomed the invitation to Columbia College which they brought him, for he preferred an urban life-style in an Anglican setting.

It was not only their careers that offer parallels: both Lieber and Cooper were deeply committed to the crucial role of economic factors to moral theory; both held that the natural right-contract theory needed modification; both held that laissez-faire was the proper economic doctrine. But there the similarity ends. They disagreed, e.g., on the grounds for their mutual opposition to the natural rights theory, and they took different sides on the important question of the states' right to secede. Whereas Cooper's work (like American academic views in general) depends on British sources, Lieber brings to his writing a Continental perspective in tradition and problem.

Lieber's Columbia appointment was to a professorship in history and political economy, but he engineered a substitution of "political science" for "political economy." In any case, all three subjects were closely wedded in the discipline of moral philosophy. It was through this particular wedding that German influence of a new sort now was imported into the social sciences and used in opposing the Jeffersonian tradition and the policies of Jackson and Calhoun.

In particular, Lieber saw history as practical morality involving institutional growth; we study history not merely to examine precedent, as the German historians emphasized, nor to discover the pattern of history, as the Hegelians had it, but to remind us of the continuities, the depth, and the stability of institutions. He offered the romanticism of Kant and Fichte in opposition to the Jeffersonian radicalism which he associated with the French Revolution. As a Federalist-Whig he detested the policies of Jackson, and he pitted against Calhoun's sectionalism his own analysis of society as a plurality of institutions nourishing the development of a unified American nation rather than fragmenting it into antagonistic groups. In line with the German tradition, the nation is not conceived simply as a political entity (nor of course as a collection of atomic individuals with merely utilitarian objectives) but as an organically developing society embodying the customs and traditions that are the heritage of many generations and into which we are born. These mores are the final determinants of what laws are effective and what institutions will arise.

The state is but one of many institutions; its function is jural. This gives it a moral character, since it furnishes a structure of reciprocal rights and obligations. Unlike Kant and more like Hegel, Lieber sees society itself having its own proper ends. This was his point in preferring "political science" to "political economy," for the former is "politics" in the Aristotelian sense, whereas the latter deals merely with material goods.

An important consequence of Lieber's approach is that the state is not contractual, and there are no absolute and inalienable rights. Authority and property are already present in the family which precedes the state. The problem is then not to account for the origin of authority but to find the institutions that have taken it over. And since power tends to aggregate, the important question is to determine limits to government which will prevent it from becoming arbitrary. This is the groundwork of his theory of liberty. Doubtless remembering his own difficulties with the Prussian government, his brief imprisonment, and longer exile, he is concerned almost exclusively for civil liberties, which are best preserved by representative government against the despotism of political authority or the multitude. Unlike Raymond he has no sense of the need for protection against exploitation by the economically powerful. In dealing with property, Lieber sought the most supportive relationship between government and the commercial and manufacturing and even plantation interests. Although government does not have the task of intervening on behalf of the propertyless, it should take the initiative and intervene to build up the nation, by which he meant largely furthering economic development. The restraints on government must not be such as to emasculate it.

The dynamics of development lie, as in Kant and Hegel, in a dialectic of individualism-socialism, by which he means essentially what Kant meant by the unsocial sociability in which individual competitiveness produces moral progress. Man can only achieve his true individuality or personality in a complex society that offers a rich variety of opportunity. But unlike Kant he foresaw nothing further than nations developing mutual trade and whatever regulation flows from it, neither a world society nor even a Kantian federation that would ensure perpetual peace.

Notes — Chapter Five

[1]In addition to the works listed above (p. 270, no. 2 to chap. 4), Woodbridge Riley's *American Philosophy, the Early Schools* (New York: Dodd, Mead and Co., 1907) pioneered in bringing the materials together. There is, however, a strong difference of perspective in appraising the materials in our present work.

[2]That William Smith published an edition of Berkeley's works is mentioned in many places, but we could not find a copy nor reference to the date. Columbia and Pennsylvania were not, of course, the original names of the colleges. As in the preceding chapter, we use the current and more familiar names of the colleges. Virtually every early college changed its name at least once. For the record of the colleges, the following two books are especially helpful: Donald G. Tewksbury, *The Founding of American Colleges and Universities* (New York: Bureau of Publications, Teachers College, Columbia University, 1932); Herbert B. Adams, *Circulars of Information of the Bureau of Education* (Washington: Government Printing Office, 1887).

[3]Alison's notes and Ewing's books are in the Rare Book Room of the University of Pennsylvania's Van Pelt Library.

[4]*Priestley's Writings on Philosophy, Science and Politics*, ed. Passmore (New York: Collier Books).

[5]*Ibid.*, p. 123. This is from "Matter and Spirit," sec. VIII, 1777.

[6]*Ibid.*, p. 57. This is from "The Doctrine of Philosophical Necessity Illustrated," sec. I, 1777.

[7]Benjamin Rush, *Enquiry Into the Influence of Physical Causes Upon the Moral Faculty* (Philadelphia: 1786), p. 8f.

[8]F. G. V. Broussais, *On Irritation and Insanity*, trans. Thomas Cooper (Columbia, S. C.: Printed by S. J. M' Morris, 1831). It contains also *Two Tracts on Materialism*: "The Scripture Doctrine of Materialism," 1823, and "View of the Metaphysical and Physiological Arguments in favour of Materialism," 1823. There is also an "Outline of the Association of Ideas." These tracts were written by Cooper himself. He publishes here also correspondence from Jefferson. The quotation is on p. 324.

[9]*Ibid.*, p. 328. The letter, reproduced by Cooper, is from Montecello, December 11.

[10]See n. 8, above.

[11]Destutt Comte de Tracy, *Elémens D'Idéologie*, Première Partie (Paris: Courcier, 1817), p. 128.

[12]Cooper, *Irritation and Insanity*, p. 295.

[13]*Ibid.*, pp. iv-v.

[14]*Ibid.*, pp. 117-18.

[15]*Ibid.*, p. iii.

[16]"Thomas Jefferson," in *Dictionary of American Biography*, ed. Malone (New York: Charles Scribner's Sons, 1946), X:17-35.

[17]John Adams to Jefferson, May 12, 1820, in *The Adams-Jefferson Letters*, ed. Cappon (Chapel Hill: University of North Carolina Press, 1959), pp. 563-65.

[18]Jefferson to Adams, August 15, 1820, in *ibid.*, 567-69.

[19]Jefferson to Adams, March 14, 1820, in *ibid.*, 561ff. On this relationship see Adrienne Koch, *The Philosophy of Thomas Jefferson* (New York: Columbia University Press, 1943), pp. 48ff.

[20]See Koch, *Philosophy*, chaps. 7-9.

[21]Jefferson to Adams, March 14, 1820, in *Adams-Jefferson Letters*, p. 562.

[22]Koch, *Philosophy*, p. 63.

[23]See p. 296.

[24]S. A. Grave, *The Scottish Philosophy of Common Sense* (Oxford: Clarendon Press, 1960), p. 182.

[25] *Ibid.*, pp. 183ff.

[26] Jefferson to Adams, August 15, 1820, in *Adams-Jefferson Letters*, p. 567.

[27] *Ibid.*, p. 568.

[28] Jefferson to Adams, April 8, 1816, *ibid.*, p. 468.

[29] Jefferson to Adams, April 11, 1823, *ibid.*, p. 593.

[30] Jefferson to Adams, August 15, 1820, *ibid.*, p. 568.

[31] *Ibid.*, p. 569.

[32] *Ibid.*, p. 568.

[33] Jefferson to Adams, April 11, 1823, *ibid.*, p. 592.

[34] Jefferson to Adams, April 8, 1816, *ibid.*, p. 467.

[35] Koch, *Philosophy*, p. 25; Jefferson to Adams, October 12, 1813, in *Adams-Jefferson Letters*, p. 384; January 24, 1814, *ibid.*, 421; Jefferson to Rush, April 21, 1803, *Basic Writings of Thomas Jefferson*, ed. Foner (New York: John Wiley, 1944), p. 660.

[36] Jefferson to Adams, October 12, 1813, in *Adams-Jefferson Letters*, p. 384; May 5, 1817, *ibid.*, p. 512.

[37] This work, the so-called Jefferson Bible, was published under the title *The Life and Morals of Jesus of Nazareth.*

[38] Thomas Jefferson, *The Living Thoughts of Thomas Jefferson*, ed. Dewey (New York: Longmans, Green and Co., 1943), pp. 93-94.

[39] Koch, *Philosophy*, pp. 26-27.

[40] Jefferson to Adams, August 15, 1820, in *Adams-Jefferson Letters*, p. 568.

[41] *Ibid.*, p. 567.

[42] *Ibid.*, p. 568.

[43] Jefferson to Adams, January 8, 1825, *ibid.*, 605-6.

[44] Jefferson to Adams, November 13, 1818, *ibid.*, p. 529; Koch, *Philosophy*, p. 38.

⁴⁵Frederick Beasley, *A Search of Truth in the Science of the Human Mind*, pt. I (Philadelphia: Potter, 1822).

⁴⁶The larger (but not the full) title of the work reads: *A Brief Retrospect of the Eighteenth Century . . . containing a Sketch of the Revolutions and Improvements in Science, Arts, and Literature, During that Period*.

⁴⁷Samuel Stanhope Smith, *The Lectures, corrected and improved, which have been delivered for a series of years in the College of New Jersey; on the subjects of Moral and Political Philosophy*, 2 vols. (Trenton, N. J.: Daniel Fenton, 1912). Volume I is relevant here.

⁴⁸*Ibid.*, vol. II. Internal evidence makes it clear that the lectures on moral and political philosophy were indeed corrected and improved over several decades, especially in the light of the unfolding American experiences, social and political.

⁴⁹Published in various forms both in America and London. First Philadelphia edition 1787.

⁵⁰Smith, *Lectures*, II:67-68.

⁵¹*Ibid.*, p. 305.

⁵²*Ibid.*, pp. 305-6.

⁵³John Daniel Gros (professor at Columbia (1784-95)) wrote one of the earliest texts in the Middle Atlantic states. See his *Natural Principles of Rectitude, for the Conduct of Man in all States and Situations of Life; demonstrated and explained in a Systematic Treatise on Moral Philosophy: comprehending the Law of Nature— Ethics—Natural Jurisprudence—General Oeconomy—Politics—and the Law of Nations* (New York: T. and J. Swords, 1795).

After Gros, moral philosophy at Columbia was turned toward a kind of utilitarian empiricism and in particular the problems of political economy. Thus John McVickar (professor at Columbia, 1817-57) was enormously influential not only through his lecturing but also through his publishing, especially his *Outlines of Political Economy* (New York: Wilder & Campbell, 1825), which was used at Harvard, Virginia, and William and Mary almost to midcentury. McVickar was personally acquainted with James Mill, Sr., and McCulloch, and other classical British economists. His *Outlines* restate their views, especially McCulloch's *Political Economy* with reference to American problems. Henry Vethake (professor at Columbia, University of Pennsylvania, Rutgers, and the University of the City of New York, among other appointments) moved moral philosophy in the same direction, although he seemed more preoccupied with the social aspects of poverty and population. Vethake was a distinguished man; he was received with honor by the Prussian Academy and was an adviser of the projected New York

University. He seems never to have wanted for academic invitations. Impressive, under the ornate style of the day, is his integrated view of moral philosophy as moral science, Newtonian in model but richly filled out by the materials of the social sciences.

54Cf. Thomas Harrison Montgomery, *A History of the University of Pennsylvania from its Foundation to A.D. 1770* (Philadelphia: Jacobs, 1900).

55William Smith's program was very much influenced by Thomas Reid's concept of education as graded and organized. The actual proposal includes bibliography and outline of courses to be required of the students. It was published in various forms, but the first edition (1753) is in the Rare Book Room of the Van Pelt Library at the University of Pennsylvania.

56Samuel Miller's student notes (under Magaw, a student of Alison's) as well as an annotated copy of Carmichael's edition of Pufendorf, are to be found in the Rare Book Room of the Van Pelt Library at the University of Pennsylvania. We are indebted to Dr. Rudolph Hirsch for steering us to these works.

57James Wilson, *Commentaries on the Constitution* (speech in Convention, November 24, 1787), in Randolph G. Adams, ed., *Selected Political Essays of James Wilson* (New York: Alfred A. Knopf, 1930), p. 168. The works of Wilson are not readily available, and Adams has collected only a few essays, working largely from manuscripts. Adams contrasts the unavailability of Wilson's writings with the ready availability of the Federalist Papers. Wilson was influential in getting the Constitution accepted in the Middle Atlantic states. More a barrister than a pamphleteer, he wrote in a drier and erudite style, and presented arguments that were strong and philosophically well grounded.

There is an edition of the works of Wilson, ed. James DeWitt Andrews (Chicago: Callaghan and Co., 1896).

There is a most interesting and thorough study of James Wilson's life and work by Burton Alva Konkle of the Philadelphia Bar. It is a manuscript in the Friends' Library in Swarthmore College. Konkle was the secretary of the James Wilson Memorial Committee which successfully urged President Theodore Roosevelt to have Wilson's body reinterred near Franklin's in Philadelphia.

58Wilson, *ibid.*, p. 181.

59Wilson moved slowly and reluctantly from a concern to secure the rights of British citizenship for colonials to an appreciation that a more decisive break was needed and inevitable. Even his pre-Revolutionary writings emphasize equality and the happiness (prosperity, welfare) of the people as the only legitimate end of government. That these are not rhetorical flourishes can be seen from his well-thought-out utilitarian and functional theory of government, as well as his view that the people can best judge their happiness.

[60]Wilson, "Man, as a Member of the Great Commonwealth of Nations," in Adams, ed., *Selected Essays*, p. 340.

[61]Wilson, quoted in Andrew Bennett, *James Wilson of St. Andrews* (St. Andrews: J. & G. Innes, Ltd., n.d.), p. 67.

[62]Jefferson to Adams, October 14, 1816, in *Adams-Jefferson Letters*, p. 492.

[63]Grave, *Scottish Philosophy*, pp. 228ff, 244ff.

[64]Jefferson, *Thoughts*, p. 84; Koch, *Philosophy*, p. 3.

[65]Jefferson to Adams, October 14, 1816, in *Adams-Jefferson Letters*, p. 492.

[66]*Ibid*.

[67]Jefferson, *Thoughts*, p. 83.

[68]*Ibid*., p. 87.

[69]Koch, *Philosophy*, p. 18.

[70]Jefferson accepted the doctrine that "the moral and physical qualities of man, whether good or evil, are transmissible in a certain degree from father to son." Jefferson to Adams, October 28, 1813, *Adams-Jefferson Letters*, pp. 387-88.

[71]Jefferson, *Thoughts*, pp. 65, 77.

[72]Jefferson to Du Pont de Nemours, April 24, 1816, in Koch, *Philosophy*, p. 118.

[73]Jefferson, *Thoughts*, p. 46; *The Writings of Thomas Jefferson*, ed. Lipscomb (Washington: Thomas Jefferson Memorial Association, 1904), 6:58.

[74]Jefferson, *Basic Writings*, p. 21; Jefferson, *Thoughts*, p. 50; *Alexander Hamilton and Thomas Jefferson: Representative Selections*, ed. Prescott (New York: American Book Co., 1934), p. 390.

[75]Jefferson, *Writings of Thomas Jefferson*, 15:127.

[76]Jefferson, *Thoughts*, p. 58.

[77]Jefferson, *Representative Selections*, pp. 385, 387; Jefferson, *Thoughts*, pp. 44-45.

[78]Jefferson, *Thoughts*, pp. 51-52.

[79] *Ibid.*, pp. 45-46; Jefferson to Adams, October 28, 1813, in *Adams-Jefferson Letters*, p. 390.

[80] Jefferson, *Writings of Thomas Jefferson*, 15:328-29.

[81] Jefferson to Adams, October 28, 1813, in *Adams-Jefferson Letters*, p. 388.

[82] *Ibid.*, p. 390; Jefferson, *Basic Writings of Thomas Jefferson*, pp. 40-46.

[83] Jefferson to Adams, October 28, 1813, in *Adams-Jefferson Letters*, pp. 388-89.

[84] Jefferson, *Thoughts*, p. 58.

[85] Jefferson to Adams, October 29, 1813, in *Adams-Jefferson Letters*, p. 391.

[86] Valuable accounts of these developments will be found in:

Gladys Bryson, "The Comparable Interests of the Old Moral Philosophy," *International Journal of Ethics* XLII: 304-23 (April 1932).

Gladys Bryson, *Man and Society: The Scottish Inquiry of the Eighteenth Century* (Princeton, N. J.: Princeton University Press, 1945).

Gladys Bryson, "Sociology Considered as Moral Philosophy," *Sociological Review* XXIV: 26-36 (January 1932).

Wilson Smith, *Professors & Public Ethics. Studies of Northern Moral Philosophers before the Civil War* (Ithaca, N.Y.: Cornell University Press, 1956).

Joseph Dorfman, *The Economic Mind in American Civilization, 1606-1865*, 2 vols. (New York: The Viking Press, 1946).

Joseph Dorfman and Rexford G. Tugwell, "Francis Lieber: German Scholar in America," *Columbia University Quarterly* XXX:159-90, 267-93 (September, December 1938).

Joseph Dorfman and Rexford G. Tugwell, *Early American Policy* (New York: Columbia University Press, 1960).

Michael J. L. O'Connor, *Origins of Academic Economics in the United States* (New York: Columbia University Press, 1944).

Anna Haddow, *Political Science in American Colleges and Universities, 1636-1900* (New York: Appleton-Century, 1939).

[87] Daniel Raymond, *Thoughts on Political Economy* (Baltimore: Lucas, 1820); *The Elements of Political Economy*, 2 vols., 2d ed. (Baltimore: Lucas, 1823); *The Elements of Constitutional Law and Political Economy* (Baltimore: James, 1840).

Involved in these three is essentially a single book, where chapters are inserted, altered, withdrawn, and expanded as his thought developed. A useful study is Charles P. Neill, "Daniel Raymond: An Early Chapter in the History of Economic Theory in the United States," *Johns Hopkins Studies in History and Political Science*, 1897.

[88]Raymond, *Political Economy*, pp. 380-81.

[89]Henry Carey, *Principles of Political Economy*, vol. I, 1837; vol. II, 1838; vol. III, 1840. It is interesting that these were published by the publishing house of the Careys.

[90]Henry Carey, *Principles of Social Science*, 1858-60. This was published by Lippincott in Philadelphia.

[91]Thomas Cooper, *Lectures on the Elements of Political Economy* (Columbia, S.C.: S. C. M' Morris and Wilson, 1831). See also "McCulloch's Political Economy," *American Quarterly Review*, 1827, pp. 47-69.

[92]It is generally held that there were few American Utilitarians. Doubtless this is true if it means subscribing to the Benthamite calculus. But the Utilitarian political theory from the critique of Blackstone and that of natural law and natural rights to a functional view of law and government and a hardheaded penetration of fictions in political thought are shared by many Americans beyond William Beach Lawrence and Fanny Wright, the two avowed Utilitarians.

[93]Just as the Careys and Clay made common cause in fighting for protectionism, so Cooper and Calhoun were joined in a defense of states' rights.

[94]In this context it is interesting to note Cooper's statement on the rights of women (although it was written in 1792 in the atmosphere of the French Declaration of the Rights of Man):

> I have repeatedly considered the subject of the Rights of Women, and I am perfectly unable to suggest any argument in support of the political superiority so generally abrogated by the Male Sex, which will not equally apply to any System of Despotism of Man over Man. . . . The fact is that we behave to the Female Sex much in the Manner as we behave to the Poor. We first keep their minds and then their persons in Subjection. . . . (*Propositions Respecting the Foundation of Civil Government* [Manchester: 1792], p. 98a.)

[95]Francis Lieber, *Manual of Political Ethics*, 1838-39; 2d ed., rev. and ed. Theodore D. Woolsey (Philadelphia: J. B. Lippincott, 1877); *On Civil Liberty and Self-Government*, 1851; 3d ed., rev. and ed. Theodore D. Woolsey (Philadelphia: J. B. Lippincott, 1910).

Chapter Six

Philosophy in New England—
Logic

Chapter Six

Philosophy in New England— Logic

The career of philosophy in America after the Enlightenment has generally been told as though its principle practitioners were New England theologians. Thus Edwards and the Awakening, the Unitarian controversy, the emergence of Transcendentalism, and the subsequent connections with later Idealisms have so held the spotlight that other developments have been left in the shadows. These movements in theological philosophy are of real significance, and are dealt with in other places in this work. What needs to be emphasized here is that there were other philosophic issues which were also evoking creative work in the early nineteenth century in New England and that the locus of this work was the college rather than the manse or a cabin by a pond. Questions of logic, induction, and scientific method, of perception and epistemology, and of "moral" philosophy (in the broad sense of the Scots) were pursued with as much vigor at Harvard and Yale as at Princeton and Pennsylvania. To make this point clear, and to show the quality of academic philosophy in New England, we therefore turn to the development of logic at Harvard.

The history of logic since the medieval period is an enormously broad and complex subject, but it is a subject to which the Scottish philosophers made a more significant contribution than is sometimes thought, and it is also a subject which needs to be conceived more broadly than as simply the history of deductive logic. It is traditional to say that during the medieval period Aristotle reigned as the supreme authority in logic, but that he was overthrown during the Renaissance when his deductive logic proved inadequate as a method for the emerging sciences, and that thereafter interest in his logic went into a long period of decline. This picture is certainly not true. In the first place, logic for Aristotle was not synonymous with deductive logic: rather it consisted of a broad profile of subjects ranging from the nature of terms, statements, and relations among statements through syllogistic reasoning and modal logic to the methodology of science or explanation, including the theories of demonstration, definition, argument by analogy, and induction, especially the psychology of concept formation.[1] Thus a revolt against the syllogism narrowly conceived was by no means a revolt against Aristotle or Aristotelian logic in this broader sense. In the second place, the late medieval period was very fruitful both in logical investigations and in the development of science—it was after all that same Jean Buridan, who was one of the celebrated authorities on the theory of supposition, who was also a major contributor to the impetus theory which helped to lead Galileo to his work on the flight of projectiles and the law of falling bodies. What actually occurred during the Renaissance was a very complex interaction of processes, all with significant implications for traditional logic. The Renaissance saw the recovery of the original Greek form of the writings not only of Aristotle and Plato, but also of Archimedes and of many other classic writers, and so brought a realization of the diversity and richness of classical thought of which, until that point, there had been but a very limited appreciation. While this rediscovery led to the intensive study of Plato and other non-Aristotelian writers, it also led to a heightened interest in Aristotle's work and to attempts to extend and amplify it. But at the same time, the new discoveries in mathematics and in physical science raised in a critical form the general problem of what constituted an adequate scientific method. The entire Ramist movement, to which extensive reference has already been made, was in part an attempt to revamp the traditional curriculum in the interests of a more adequate study of science, mathematics, and the classics, and to broaden the scope of the concept of method to include more than deductive logic. It is not mere coincidence that Ramus's *Dialecticae* should have been published in the same year as Copernicus' *De Revolutionibus* and the Latin translation of the last of Archimedes' treatises. Nor is the strength of the Ramist movement at Cambridge —later to be the English center of physics and mathematics—and in Scotland insignificant. But of course the response of Ramus and Talon to this situation was not unique. Descartes was led to his work by exactly the same problems—the realization that traditional views of method were simply inadequate to account either for physical science or for mathematics, and the desire to discover some general method which would accomplish this feat. Bacon's *Novum Organum* was directly inspired by the same dissatisfaction with traditional logic as a method of discovery and the urgent need to invent a new and more comprehensive substitute. Thus the century following 1543 was one which saw repeated efforts to revise the established canons of scientific procedure to fit the rapidly developing fields to which those canons were supposed to apply. The primary concern was not to attack the Aristotelian syllogistic, nor its utility within certain realms, but to create a more general method sufficiently extensive to cover all of the fields in question. Viewed in this perspective, it is clear that for men of that time Ramus, Descartes, Bacon, and Locke were all contributors to a common endeavor and champions of a common cause. Certainly they were so viewed at Harvard College in the seventeenth century.

We have seen above that the Massachusetts Puritans of the seventeenth century were followers of Peter Ramus, and that Ramist doctrines, and particularly Ramist logic, were the core of a seventeenth-century Harvard education. But adherence to Ramus never precluded the study of other texts. Not only were Aristotelian texts used, but the works of Burgersdyck and Heereboord, Dutch Cartesians who were sympathetic to Ramus, were also studied.[2] Nevertheless, Ramus remained the dominant figure in logic until the 1680s. Then, at approximately the same time that Charles Morton introduced the *Compendium Physicae* and so revolutionized the teaching of science at Harvard, William Brattle introduced a new text in logic entitled *Compendium Logicae secundum Principia D. Renati Cartesii*. As the title implies, Brattle's *Compendium* is Cartesian—it is avowedly drawn from the writings of Antoine LeGrand, the French Cartesian who was instrumental in introducing the Cartesian philosophy into England.[3] Moreover, the *Compendium* proved to be remarkably durable: it was used as a text at Harvard until at least 1765, although during this time it underwent considerable, and highly significant, revisions. The introduction of Brattle's text reflects a significant change in the intellectual perspective at Harvard—a change which requires explanation.

The earliest copy of Brattle's text that we have is a manuscript copy dated 1707 while the latest is a published version dated 1758.[4] All the editions of the text have the same structure, although the distribution of emphasis changes over time. They begin with a prolegomenon which describes the nature and use of logic. The main text is divided into four parts corresponding to the four operations of the mind: part one deals with the apprehension of simple terms, part two with the combination of terms into judgments, part three with deductive reasoning or syllogistic, and part four with the ordering of knowledge or methodizing which involves the setting forth of the truth and its communication. This organization is quite traditional, and is equally consistent with Aristotelian or Ramist texts.

A careful examination of the 1707 edition makes clear the degree to which the adoption of Descartes was not a revolt against Ramus but a development of Ramist doctrines. Certainly the epistemological commitments are idealistic in the sense of Descartes: terms represent ideas which "the mind is conscious about or makes unto itself."[5] But the view of simple or absolute terms as ultimate concepts incapable of definition which are known with perfect clarity and distinctness by natural reason, while obviously Cartesian, is also perfectly consistent with Ramist doctrine. Similarly, the theory of axioms which is presented in the section on judgment is as Ramist as it is Cartesian, for both men believed that the natural reason could perceive the truth of certain propositions directly without any intermediary, and that such proof by intuition or self-evidence was ultimate and certain. Again both regarded deduction as serving simply to clear propositions from doubt by deriving them from axioms directly known to be true by natural reason. And both regarded deduction or syllogism as but one division within a general method of science.

As one would expect, the relation of Ramist and Cartesian views is most interestingly in evidence with respect to method. The section on method in the 1707 edition is heavily indebted to Descartes' *Rules*. The term "method" itself is used in a broader and a narrower sense. In the broad sense it refers to the ordering of our ideas in such a way as to avoid obscurity and error and to make knowledge demonstrable to others. It is thus synonymous with the method of teaching, as well as self-teaching, and so retains the pedagogic emphasis of Ramus. But in the narrower sense, method is the organon of inquiry or discovery, and in this sense is said to consist of analysis and synthesis. As in Ramist texts, these two processes are regarded as inverses of each other—Brattle's text compares them to ascending and descending the mountain. But the description of these processes shows an interesting ambiguity which is to be found in both Ramus and Descartes. For Ramus, analysis meant the decomposition of a discourse into its component parts until "ultimate" parts are reached. Thus the discourse is broken down into its component arguments, these into propositions, and these into terms. Synthesis on the other hand meant the composing of a discourse by combining terms into propositions and ordering these to comprise a discourse. On the face of it this description appears to refer to rhetorical composition rather than to inquiry, but we have seen above that Ramus also gave it an empirical meaning, and that this emphasis was greatly expanded in technologia. For if the world is conceived as God's discourse, then "things are God's words in print" and each singular object is a composite which must be analyzed to obtain the simple elements which it is to teach us. Thus for the Puritans analysis is both a method for analyzing other discourses or proofs, and a method of inquiry for the study of nature. And synthesis is then both a method of composing discourses and of building theories out of facts. Descartes' use is no less ambiguous. For applied to mathematical reasonings or deductive proofs, analysis carries us back to the premises from which we start and so to the more general. But applied to empirical knowledge, as, e.g., of the magnet, it carries us to the ultimate or simple natures into which the object can be decomposed and which must serve as the starting point, or premises, for our explanations. Thus analysis can lead us to quite different sorts of things— general principles or simple ideas—which have in common only their relation to the rest of our knowledge since both are ultimate starting points. Synthesis on the other hand is the process of constructing from these elements a derivative knowledge, either by deduction in the one case or by that sort of combination which gives us things from simple properties or complex behavior from simpler elements in the other. The terms analysis and synthesis are therefore applicable both to discourses or arguments and to empirical investigations, but they take quite different senses in these two applications: in the one case analysis proceeds from the less to the more general while in the other it goes from the more complex to the simple.[6] In neither construction, either for Ramus or Descartes, are these terms synonymous with induction or deduction as we now use them, although deduction is one type of synthesis. The Brattle text reproduces the full range of ambiguity associated with these words. Thus in contrasting analysis and synthesis, Brattle remarks:

> Q. In what does Synthesis differ from Analysis? R. In this that Synthesis proceeds from the more general and more simple to the less general and more complex. And analysis on the contrary proceeds by resolving from the less general to the more general or from the complex to the simple.[7]

Nevertheless, particular emphasis is given to the empirical applications of these terms. Thus synthesis is criticized since its practitioners "labor more about certainty than evidence, more about convincing the understanding than enlightening it,"[8] and examples of analysis as seeking the explanations of empirical phenomena received particular stress. One can see here how easily Descartes' views can be superimposed upon those of Ramus, and the same empirical emphasis which the Puritans gave to Ramus reappears in their interpretation of Descartes.

Finally it should be pointed out that there is another and no less important reason why Descartes was acceptable to the Puritans. For if one looks at the psychology which Descartes presents in the *Rules*, one finds that it differs very little from that in Puritan texts. The process by which sense impressions are created and transferred to the brain, and the faculties of the mind—common sense, fancy, and memory—are described in terms which would have been acceptable to any Puritan. Descartes' concept of the understanding is not identical with the traditional one, but the differences involve no weakening of the categorical difference between understanding (or reason) and the other faculties. Moreover, for Descartes the understanding has simple ideas both of material things and of purely intellectual or spiritual things, and the latter, which include all that Locke was to call ideas of reflection, are completely devoid of any taint of sensation or sensible imagery.[9] Thus it was not difficult for the Puritans to view Descartes as a pioneer in logic and method whose work marked an advance beyond Ramus while at the same time it preserved much of technologia intact.

This compatibility shows in the relatively few criticisms which the 1707 text contains of Ramist doctrines. The principal criticism is just the one that would be expected in an era of scientific advance—viz., the criticism of the places or loci.

Brattle argues (at least in 1707) that neither the loci nor the categories of Aristotle are sufficient guides for finding out all the relevant aspects of the phenomenon under study. Brattle proposes instead the categories of matter, measure, rest, motion, position, figure, and mind—categories which show the influence not only of Descartes, but also of the new sciences and very likely of Locke as well. The substitution of matter for substance, the mathematical emphasis evident in measure, and the similarity of the remaining categories to Locke's primary qualities all suggest Lockean influence, although no such citation appears in this early text. Aristotelian categories such as quality are explicitly reduced to the effects of figure and motion, but mind is regarded as irreducible and categorically distinct from all material ideas. Thus it appears that the chief fault in Ramus which the new logic had to correct was the inadequacy of the loci as guiding concepts for empirical science, and this fault is remedied by substituting a new set of categories in place of the old while leaving much of the rest of the structure intact.

Nevertheless, the nominalistic commitments which Brattle may have derived from Locke lead to some interesting consequences which foreshadow subsequent developments. To take one example, there is a discussion of what are called "complex incidents." Complex propositions are those which have at least one complex term; thus complexity of subject or predicate could be illustrated by "men who are featherless bipeds are affected by colds" and "men who wear light clothing are affected by colds." In the first example, the who clause leaves the extension unchanged, while in the second example, it narrows the extension or class. The first is called *explicative*, the second *determinative*. It is interesting to note that the Port Royal logic appears to make this distinction only in terms of the essential-accidental distinction. At least at this point Brattle foreshadows the extensional emphasis that was to become so prominent in the Harvard-Scottish tradition.

A similar problem arises in connection with complexity of the copula. "I said the earth is flat" could be countered with either "No, it is round" or "You never said such a thing." In both cases, the complexity is regarded as incident to the "is." In the first case, it is explicative and the added "I said" does not alter the truth value of the proposition or make it different than merely stating "The earth is flat." In the second case, the complexity modifies what is asserted in the proposition and is determinative of its meaning. The point is an important one in the more complex cases where the determinative complexity offers reasons, evidence, or grounds. The text points out that we need often to refer to the intention of the speaker, to the larger context, or to reformulations in equivalent sentences. We can see thus suggestions of syntactic, semantic, and pragmatic dimensions.

The later editions of the text reveal some quite striking changes. Indeed, the various editions give the appearance of slightly different strata into which the Lockean influence is slowly penetrating, sometimes at real cost to the Cartesian material. There is little direct evidence of Locke's influence in the 1707 edition.

But Lockean doctrine became well known at Harvard in the early eighteenth century, and by 1742 the *Essay* was being used there as a textbook.[10] Accordingly, in the 1735 edition of Brattle's text, *res* is equated with *substantia*,[11] with a reference to Locke so that the conception of substance is definitely Lockean, for although we cannot know substance, we learn more about the nature of things as we experience the dispositions of parts which are proper to one body but not found in all. In the later editions, Locke's influence becomes increasingly explicit, though largely expressed in the footnotes, and particularly directed toward the importance of and the increasing reliance on the senses.[12] At the same time, the distribution of emphasis within the text changes. By 1758, the sections on method have been reduced in size and appear as a mere appendage. On the other hand, the later edition contains a much fuller awareness of the psychology of knowing—of the origin and nature of ideas, the processes of the mind involved in knowledge, etc. Indeed, by 1758 the text has become much less a Cartesian logic than a Lockean essay on human understanding. And this transformation is the most revealing of all. For with Ramus and with Descartes, the problem of logic was the problem of method, and method was conceived in terms of a formal, or formalizable, procedure by which true knowledge could be discovered and articulated. When we analyze the magnet into simple elements, we are applying a formal analytic procedure for the purpose of learning more about the magnet. But with Locke, the problem of method is psychologized; the question is not one of formal procedure but of psychological process. The simple elements into which we resolve the objects of study now become simple ideas out of which the mind builds objects by psychological operations. Thus the declining emphasis upon formal method is the result of the fact that the problems for which Ramus and Descartes required such a method have been psychologized by Locke and so appear in the sections on ideas and judgment. By the late eighteenth century, logic at Harvard College was looking increasingly to Lockean psychology as the foundation of knowledge. And curiously enough, in doing so it was following a course which was remarkably like that which was being pursued in Scotland.

The high status of Bacon, the achievements of Newton, Boyle, and others in empirical science, and the impact of Locke's *Essay* focused attention in England upon the question of the method of discovery in empirical science and upon the epistemological problems involved in such a method. At the same time, the decline of interest in mathematical studies and in the problem of mathematical method which took place in England between Newton and Peacock strengthened this bias toward the inductive and empirical approach as opposed to a deductive and mathematical one. In Scotland, on the other hand, mathematics remained a subject of considerable importance and interest, and the questions of mathematical method and of the relation of classical logic to mathematics continued to be matters of serious interest. As we have seen, Reid and Stewart were both mathematicians of considerable merit and both wrote on Aristotelian logic and its relation to mathematics. Thus while both Reid and Stewart gave primary allegiance to Bacon and Locke, they also regarded themselves as methodologists in a broad sense and so were concerned with the whole gamut of questions raised by Aristotle, Ramus, Descartes, and other continental writers.

This breadth of attitude and understanding is important in grasping the relation of the Scottish writers to Aristotle and his logic, and to method in general. While the Scots were Lockeans, they were Lockeans determined to prove that Locke had "meant to be a realist," and since they viewed Aristotle as a realist too, they found much in Aristotle which was congenial to their point of view. Moreover, committed as they were to the assumption that all knowledge comes from experience, and so to Baconean induction from particular observations, they fully appreciated Aristotle's great achievements as a practicing scientist.[13] Thus their empiricist commitments led them to problems of empirical probability, of beliefs that are less than certain, and to the warrant of action based on incomplete information. On the other hand, their interest in grammar, mathematics, and the direct apprehension of objects made imperative some account of universal and necessary propositions, for they saw very clearly, as Bacon himself had recognized, that such propositions cannot be established by enumerative induction since nature is infinitely more subtle than our experience. Thus the Scottish philosophy found itself face to face with many of the same problems that confronted Kant. But the answer that the Scots gave to these questions was strongly conditioned by their attitude toward both logic and empirical psychology. Despite their respect for Aristotle as an empirical scientist and realist philosopher and their concern with logic and method broadly defined, neither Reid nor Stewart shared Kant's high regard for Aristotle's deductive logic. Reid's "Brief Account of Aristotle's Logic; with Remarks"[14] is a determined attempt to be fair to Aristotle and to say what can be said in favor of the utility of the study of classical deductive logic. Yet Reid openly confesses that he has found the Analytics and Topics so dull that he has never been able to get through them despite repeated trials,[15] that the principles underlying the syllogism are "of undoubted certainty indeed, but of no great depth,"[16] that the conclusions drawn by syllogistic reasoning are generally trivial,[17] and that the syllogism is of no use at all in mathematics,[18] and although Reid is not opposed to some instruction in logic being included in a general education, he obviously considers it inferior both to mathematics and to inductive method.[19] Stewart's essay "Of the Aristotelean Logic"[20] is even more negative. Although as we have seen Stewart possessed a very clear appreciation of the nature and significance of formal reasoning in mathematics, he regarded syllogistic inference as so limited that it was trivial and useless.[21] It was not to deductive logic, therefore, but to psychology that the Scots turned in their search for an answer to their problems, and their appeal is to the intuitive element in empirical experience—much as in Aristotle induction is a psychological process of grasping the particular which yields an apprehension of the universal. The warrant for universal and necessary truths for the Scots is the psychological structure and operation of the mind, not the formal structure of knowledge. Thus the Scottish thinkers were following a course parallel to that illustrated in Brattle's text at Harvard.

Shortly after 1765, Brattle's text was superseded at Harvard by Isaac Watts's *Logic*, a purely Lockean text whose introduction completed the transformation of Cartesianism into Lockean empiricism which we have noted above. Watts's book remained the standard text until Levi Hedge took over the teaching of logic in 1795. Born in 1766, Hedge was the son of a Congregational minister. He graduated from Harvard in 1792 and became tutor there in 1795, a position which he held until 1810 when he become professor of logic and metaphysics. In 1827 he was appointed Alford Professor of Natural Religion, Moral Philosophy, and Civil Polity, which position he held until he retired in 1832. Hedge prepared his own texts for his courses. In 1816 he published the *Elements of Logick*, his most original work and one which he said required fourteen years to prepare, and in 1827 he published an edition of Brown's *Treatise on the Philosophy of the Human Mind* which he also used as a text. It is with Hedge that Scottish views of logic and psychology became dominant at Harvard.[22]

Hedge's *Logick* opens with the following statement:

> *The purpose of Logick is to direct the intellectual powers in the investigation of truth, and in the communication of it to others.* Its foundation is laid in the philosophy of the human mind, in as much as it explains many of its powers and operations, and traces the progress of knowledge from the first and most simple perceptions of outward objects, to those remoter truths and discoveries, which result from the operations of reasoning.[23]

It is thus clear from the beginning that he means to build logic on psychology. The book begins with a description of the affections and operations of the mind. There are for Hedge two kinds of basic intuitions: those derived through perception from sensitive experience, and those of consciousness which provide testimony of internal and intellectual events. Since consciousness is defined to be that notice which the mind takes of its own operations and modes of existence, it is a synonym for reflection. Both perception and consciousness are normally involuntary states of the mind, but they may also be voluntary, in which case Hedge identifies them with attention. In fact, he gives an account of attention that sounds remarkably Jamesean, for he defines the act of attention as nothing more than "an effort of the mind to increase or prolong the consciousness of its own acts."[24]

Perception and consciousness yield several types of intuitive evidence, or sources of intuitive belief.[25] Although we may be mistaken about particular matters known by sense, perception does in general guarantee the reality of objects and events. Similarly, even though the kind of introspection which is required in attending to the successive changes in phenomena of the mind may often lead to error, Hedge holds that there is nevertheless intuitive evidence of one's self, of pleasure and pain, and of thinking and remembering. We have also intuitive evidence from memory without which sustained thinking would be impossible.[26] And finally there are intuitions which give the evidence accompanying mathematical axioms and those abstract truths which are immediately known to be true, as, e.g., every effect must have a cause. Statements of the latter class cannot be proven, since no more self-evident principles can be appealed to in their proof: rather, our assent to them is given as soon as they are contemplated and understood.

Hedge divides reasoning into demonstrative and moral reasoning. Demonstrative reasoning is applicable "wherever the subjects of our reasoning are independent on the existence of things, and are of a nature to afford exact definitions and general propositions of undoubted certainty."[27] Thus demonstrative reasoning is not limited to any one science or field of inquiry. Its most obvious application is in mathematics and in areas where the premises are known by intuition to be certain, but it is also applicable in physics when the premises are entertained hypothetically,[28] and in morals. Hedge quotes with approval Locke's assertion that moral (i.e., ethical and political) subjects are susceptible of demonstration, and that definition is the only way by which the precise meaning of moral words may be known. It is not clear here whether Hedge means simply that demonstration without reference to existence is possible only where there are precise definitions and is relying on Reid's view of intuitions to furnish such definitions, or whether he is following Stewart's view (which he quotes in other contexts) that definitions and self-evident mathematical conclusions are analytic and formal, leaving the empirical and therefore probabilistic issues to lie in problems of interpretation. But in either case, demonstration is applicable so long as the existence of things is not in question and we are concerned only with the consequences of exact definitions and precisely stated general axioms.

But there is another kind of method, which Hedge called "moral," which is a species of proof applicable not only to morals in the narrow sense, but also to all reasoning which is not directly dependent on intuition or on demonstration. Thus moral argument is broadly defined and concerns those situations in which we have to act in the face of incomplete evidence as well as the domain of empirical science where our knowledge and judgment face uncertainty. Moral reasoning differs from demonstration in several respects. First, it concerns matters of fact which are contingent and involve variable connections. Secondly if a demonstrative proof has established a particular conclusion, its denial is absurd and evidence for the denial need not be considered; but if a moral proof has established a conclusion, evidence for the denial must be considered and the denial, even if false, is not absurd. Third, while demonstration depends upon a single chain of arguments, moral reasoning depends upon the combination of many independent arguments. And finally, demonstrative proof does not admit of degree—the conclusion is true if the premises are; but moral reasoning establishes only degrees of belief, depending upon the extent to which evidence for the conclusion exceeds that for its denial. Hence moral reasoning is probable reasoning, not in the popular sense of not commanding full assent, but in a technical sense of involving degrees of belief. Thus while moral reasoning may lead to less than certain conclusions, it may also lead to conclusions having the highest degree of belief—the difference is not in the degree of belief attained, but in the nature of the argument. The neglect of this fact, Hedge remarks, has led philosophers to seek "for a mode of proof altogether unattainable in moral inquiries; and which, if it could be attained, would not be less liable to the cavils of scepticks."[29] It is to discover the circumstances and the modes of ascertaining and increasing such degrees of assurance or warrant of belief that Hedge undertakes his analysis of the kinds of moral reasoning and of the calculation of probabilities or chances.

Hedge distinguishes three types of moral reasoning in descending order of conclusiveness: induction, analogy, and reasoning from facts. It is interesting to note that induction is included in the domain of logic, though doubtless this is because Hedge started by relating logic to the psychology of reasoning and the degrees of warranted belief; on the other hand, he appears to have gone far beyond his starting point in recognizing moral reasoning as a single general method for all empirical knowledge and induction, analogy, and reasoning from facts as related but different methods rather than as all reducible to one. Induction is the inference of general truths from particular cases.[30] While Hedge bases induction on the uniformity of nature,[31] he notes that the degree of belief which we are warranted in reposing in the conclusion of an inductive inference depends both upon the number of observations and the regularity or homogeneity of the reference class. An induction concerning nitric acid is more certain, given a fixed number of observations, than one concerning liquids in general.[32] Thus Hedge raises some of the standard problems about induction in a very clear way. He also presents a rudimentary calculus of probability and distinguishes between mathematical probability and probability relative to experience. Hedge regards analogy as a less satisfactory type of moral reasoning eliciting a lesser degree of assent, although often enough this is the only type of argument applicable. Analogy is difficult to distinguish from induction, but the line can be drawn by noting that the conclusion of an induction is general and is derived from the inspection of individuals of the same species, whereas reasoning by analogy is always across species and is singular in its conclusion—e.g., that the fins of a fish have the same function as the wings of a bird, relative to the water in one instance and the air in the other. By "reasoning from facts" Hedge means to identify that part of our knowledge which is most extensive and useful. "Facts" in this case mean independent, relatively isolated bits of information, especially such as arise from the testimony of others, are parts of our general knowledge, or are matters consistent with our experience but having no alternative probable explanation, such as accounting for a cabin on a desert island by appeal to human construction. Arguments of this type depend upon testimonial and circumstantial evidence, and Hedge presents a careful discussion of such questions as the credibility of witnesses, the use of written and oral testimony and of multiple testimony, and the coherence of evidence and its articulation with the general body of our knowledge.

Hedge's treatment of logic, although brief, becomes clearly intelligible against the background of the Scottish materials, and his writings anticipate a climate that was congenial to the development of pragmatism. By discussing the logic of induction in terms of particular observations, he gives an impetus to extensional logic. His handling of the question of probability as an epistemological one—as the calculation of chances relative to our experience and observation—begins a pragmatic answer to Hume, for there are degrees of probability and warrant rather than total skepticism, and it is his endeavor to formulate the principles which give credibility to our expectations. And finally, he is seeking a critique of knowledge in its relation to decision which practice makes imperative in the presence of uncertainty. These questions were to receive more explicit and sophisticated treatment in Bowen's *Logic*.

Between Hedge's *Elements of Logick* and Bowen's *Treatise on Logic*, there lie not only a period of forty-eight years, but also some major developments within logic as well—developments to which the Scottish realists made substantial contributions. We have repeatedly emphasized the similarities in the problems facing both the Scottish philosophers and the Kantians, and as one might expect a rapprochement between the two schools took place. Specifically, it took place in the work of Sir William Hamilton, the last of the great Scottish philosophic dynasty, and in his day one of the most influential men in Western philosophy. Of the peculiar blend of Kantian and Scottish doctrines which Hamilton effected—a blend which fundamentally influenced many Americans, including not only Bowen but Wright and Peirce, as well as such influential English writers as Herbert Spencer—we shall speak in due course. What needs to be stressed here is the great importance of Hamilton's work in logic. Hamilton was recognized during the 1840s as the outstanding authority on logic as well as metaphysics in Great Britain. But it was one of Hamilton's least fortunate traits that he was very slow to publish his work. Although he stated his ideas freely in his lectures, he allowed years to go by before he wrote them down, and indeed the first expositions of Hamiltonian logic we have are not really Hamilton's own but those which were done by his students, Baynes,[33] Thomson,[34] and Mansel and Veitch.[35] It is thus almost impossible to be sure at what particular time various of Hamilton's ideas reached particular people—a fact which of course led to serious questions of priority—but it is certain that Hamilton brought about major changes in the point of view adopted toward logic in Scotland and England. Unlike Reid and Stewart, Hamilton had a full appreciation of Aristotle's formal logic and did not seek to base it upon psychological grounds. Part of Hamilton's debt to Kant was the clear distinction between logic as formal and as "modified." Pure logic according to Hamilton is the science of the laws of thought and is purely formal[36]—it has no connection with any particular subject matter. "Modified logic" on the other hand, "presupposing a knowledge of the general and contingent phenomena of mind, will thus either comprise Psychology within its sphere, or be itself comprised within the sphere of Psychology."[37] Thus Hamilton divorced logic proper from psychology in a way which prior Scottish writers had not done and insisted upon its formal character. But by formal Hamilton did not mean simply uninterpreted; he is rather using the term in a quasi-Kantian sense to refer to the universal and necessary laws which must govern the structure of thought if it is to be valid.[38] Nevertheless, Hamilton's formulation was of major importance in depsychologizing logic and in focusing attention upon specific laws or axioms of thought which were taken to be basic to logic.

Shortly after Hamilton was chosen professor of logic and metaphysics at Edinburgh in 1836, he began to teach the theory of the quantification of the predicate. It is unfortunately impossible to be sure just when Hamilton formulated this theory; he surely did not have it in 1836, and he surely did have it in 1840: but although Hamilton himself regarded this theory as his great contribution to logic and although he publicly taught it in his lectures, he did not publish it. Hamilton's theory of the quantification of the predicate is today recalled as at best a blundering treatment of the proposition, but this interpretation seems quite incorrect, and since the matter is not without major importance in the history of logic, it deserves at least some brief review here.

Hamilton's theory of the quantification of the predicate is based upon the belief that in the ordinary proposition the predicate of the proposition is always implicitly quantified by the logical quantifiers "all" and "some." In the ordinary use of language, this quantification is left implicit so long as it does not affect the truth of the proposition—thus we say, "all men are mortal" rather than "all men are some mortals." Nevertheless, whenever the implicit quantification does affect the truth of the proposition, it is made explicit, as, e.g., "Peter, John, James, etc., are all the Apostles" or "God alone is good" which is equivalent to saying "God is all good."[39] From reflection upon this fact Hamilton drew a series of conclusions of major importance.

1. That a proposition is simply an equation, an identification, a bringing into congruence, of two notions in respect to their Extensions. I say, in respect to their Extensions, for it is this quantity alone which admits of amplification or restriction, the Comprehension of a notion remaining always the same, being always taken at its full amount.
2. The total quantity of the proposition to be converted, and the total quantity of the proposition the product of the conversion, is always one and the same. In this unexclusive point of view, all conversion is merely *simple conversion*. . . .

3. If the preceding theory be true—if it be true that subject and predicate are, as quantified, always simply convertible, the proposition being in fact only an enouncement of their equation, it follows (and this also is an adequate test) that we may at will identify the two terms by making them both the subject or both the predicate of the same proposition.[40]

Although this quotation is drawn from a later statement of Hamilton's position, it is demonstrable from his publications in 1847 that he had reached all of these conclusions by that time.[41] Accordingly, we may summarize Hamilton's position in 1847 as follows: (1) that terms occurring in propositions are to be interpreted extensionally so far as questions of truth and falsity are concerned, (2) that both subject and predicate are always quantified extensionally by the quantifiers "all" or "some," (3) that the proposition as quantified is always simply convertible, (4) therefore, that the proposition asserts an identity of extension between its two terms, and (5) that the difference between subject and predicate is irrelevant to logic.

On the basis of these views, Hamilton then went on to develop a theory of eight basic forms of propositions, e.g., "all A is all B," "all A is some B," "some A is all B," etc., and an elaborate theory of the syllogism involving these forms. It should be pointed out that Hamilton's development of his theory was imperfect; in fact, two of his eight basic propositions were redundant, he used his quantifiers equivocally, and the theory involved other technical imperfections.[42] But the interest here centers upon the five basic theses concerning the nature of the proposition which he drew from his theory of the quantified predicate.

In 1846 Augustus De Morgan published in the *Transactions* of the Cambridge Philosophical Society an important paper "On the Syllogism."[43] De Morgan was a man of extraordinary and various talent. Born in 1806, he had been educated in mathematics at Cambridge by Peacock, and was elected in 1828 professor of mathematics at University College in London. De Morgan was one of the leading proponents of the theory of symbolical algebra and was an important contributor to that great burst of activity which characterized English algebra at this time. But De Morgan was also interested in logic. As early as 1839 he published a slight volume entitled *First Notions of Logic*,[44] but it was his brilliant series of memoirs on the syllogism which appeared between 1846 and 1862[45] and his *Formal Logic*[46] in 1847 which made him famous as a logician, and it was the first of these memoirs which was the occasion for the extremely unhappy controversy which arose between De Morgan and Hamilton. De Morgan, who was then forty and although well established in mathematics was but little known in philosophy, wrote to Hamilton, then sixty-eight and widely regarded as the foremost authority on logic in England, requesting some information on the history of the syllogism. Hamilton replied, and quite gratuitously offered De Morgan some slight indications that he had been teaching for some time a theory of the syllogism at variance with the classical one. There followed a guarded correspondence in which De Morgan sought to find out more of what Hamilton had done, and received sufficient indications so that he was led to believe that Hamilton might have anticipated him in some of his own doctrines.[47] De Morgan therefore published an addendum to his memoir in which he somewhat amplified his position and also stated that he now believed it possible that Hamilton had anticipated him on some points.[48] In fact, the two theories are quite distinct, although neither man appears to have been perfectly sure of what the other claimed to have discovered. De Morgan's theory might be best described as the attribution of numerical quantity to the subject and predicate: thus De Morgan had noted that if n and m be any two fractions, and if the two premises "A's are n B's" and "mB's are C's" be given, then if n+m is greater than one the conclusion "some A's are C's" is warranted. What De Morgan had not done was to use the ordinary quantifiers "all" and "some" equally with respect to subject and predicate as Hamilton had. Nevertheless, in March of 1847, Hamilton wrote De Morgan charging that De Morgan had plagiarized the notion of quantification of the predicate from him.[49] De Morgan at once demanded a public apology, and despite Hamilton's repeated attempts to avoid either a continuation of the affair or a public dispute, De Morgan would settle for nothing else. Indeed, there seems to be little doubt that De Morgan was delighted with the opportunity of forcing Hamilton into public controversy, for in such an exchange between a relatively young man little known in philosophy and an elder and far more famous one, De Morgan was certain to be the gainer, and in almost every subsequent paper on logic which De Morgan wrote he returned to the attack on Hamilton, even long after Hamilton was dead.[50]

The story of the Hamilton-De Morgan controversy has been told so many times and is so sorry an affair that it would not be worth retelling were it not for the fact that it is invariably told from De Morgan's point of view, and that it is used, together with Mill's subsequent attack on Hamilton,[51] to create the impression that Hamilton was, if not quite a fool, nevertheless a sorry philosopher. Nor in disputing this point is there the slightest need to question the truly great logical contributions of De Morgan—contributions which range from the concepts of the universe of discourse and the complement of a set to the pathbreaking fourth memoir on the syllogism which, as we shall see, opened the way for Peirce's attack on the logic of relations. Nevertheless, one may well believe that the real loser in the controversy was De Morgan. For leaving aside the unquestionable imperfections in the technical development of his doctrines, Hamilton had accomplished an astonishing feat the full significance of which has not been understood. Beginning in the tradition of Reid and Stewart, he had succeeded in disentangling logic from psychology and in formulating it as a formal discipline (in a quasi-Kantian sense) based upon such fundamental laws as excluded middle, non-contradiction, and identity. He had also given a purely extensional interpretation to the terms occurring in propositions, and by applying ordinary quantification to both terms he had reduced all conversion to simple conversion, had abolished the difference between subject and predicate, and had reduced all propositions to equations.[52] In short, Hamilton had taken a field which was entangled in extraneous psychological doctrines, wedded to logically irrelevant grammatical distinctions, encumbered with a mixture of intensional and extensional interpretations and cluttered with multiple rules of conversion, had stripped it down to bare essentials and had rendered it easily mathematizable. Hamilton did not of course mathematize logic; the very thought would have horrified him:[53] yet all that was required to mathematize Hamiltonian logic was an accomplished symbolical algebraist who conceived algebra as a formal, uninterpreted symbolic system, capable of any number of empirical interpretations, and who knew, as William Rowan Hamilton had shown so convincingly in 1844, that new algebraic axioms could be added and old ones dropped to facilitate the application to a particular empirical relational system.[54] If indeed one were to have canvassed England in the spring of 1847 for the man most likely to achieve just this synthesis, there is little doubt as to whom one would have chosen—Augustus De Morgan. But it was not De Morgan who won the prize—it was Boole, and Boole has left no doubt as to how he came to do it. Although at some time in his youth Boole had thought about the possibility of a mathematical logic,[55] he had done nothing with the idea until the Hamilton-De Morgan controversy reached the press in April of 1847.[56] Before the end of 1847, Boole published *The Mathematical Analysis of Logic*,[57] and on page one he remarked, "In the spring of the present year my attention was directed to the question then moved between Sir W. Hamilton and Professor De Morgan; and I was induced by the interest which it inspired, to resume the almost-forgotten thread of former inquiries."[58] As a member of the symbolical algebra school, Boole understood perfectly the purely formal character of algebra and its applicability to many domains;[59] he also understood, as Gauss, Lobachevski, and Bolyai had shown in geometry and William Rowan Hamilton in algebra, that the choice of axioms was arbitrary. Moreover, Boole also saw that if he adopted Hamilton's scheme of the quantification of the predicate, he could then, as Hamilton had claimed, write all propositions as equations and totally free himself from the extraneous grammatical distinctions of subject and predicate. Thus if the letters x, y, z, stand for classes, and are by convention regarded as universally quantified, "all x's are all y's" becomes simply "$x=y$." Boole introduced the quantifier "some" by the use of the operator "v," which he defined to mean "some part of"—thus "vx" means "some part of x." Then "all x's are some y's" becomes "$x = vy$." Borrowing from De Morgan the concept of the complement of a class, Boole also saw that the latter proposition must be equivalent to the statement "nothing is both x and non-y"; he therefore needed a relation among classes which would specify what is common to both. The obvious analogy was multiplication, but since the intersection of a class with itself is itself, this fact gave the rule that $x \bullet x = x$.[60] Boole accordingly adopted this proposition as a new axiom of the algebra. Now there are but two numerical values which obey this new axiom, 0 and 1. Boole gave to 0 the interpretation the null class, and to 1, again borrowing from De Morgan, the universal class. Then De Morgan's notion of the complement is simply represented as $1 - x$, where the operator "$-$" is understood to exclude all members of the class to which it is prefixed from that which it follows. The statement, "nothing is both x and non-y," thus becomes "$x(1-x) = 0$"—a simple linear equation. Thus Boole found himself able to represent the syllogism in Barbara as

$$\text{All Y's are some X's} \quad \text{or} \quad y(1-x) = 0 \quad \text{or} \quad y(1-x) = 0$$
$$\text{All Z's are some Y's} \quad \text{or} \quad z(1-y) = 0 \quad \text{or} \quad zy - z = 0$$

Then by simple elimination we have

$$y(1-x) = 0 \quad : z$$
$$zy - z = 0 \quad : (1-x)$$

$$\overline{}$$

$$(1-x)yz = 0$$
$$(1-x)yz - (1-x)z = 0$$

$$\overline{}$$

$$(1-x)z = 0 \text{ or All z's are some x's.}[61]$$

That is, by selecting the crucial ideas of both De Morgan and Hamilton, Boole was able for the first time to give a really adequate solution to the problem of the relation of mathematical reasoning and the Aristotelian syllogism. By interpreting the premises of the traditional syllogism as linear equations sharing a common unknown, he could by perfectly straightforward algebraic methods eliminate the middle term to produce the conclusion. As Boole went on to show in this book, and much more fully eleven years later in *The Laws of Thought*,[62] traditional syllogistic became now a mere subdivision of a far more comprehensive and powerful mathematical logic which seemed to include all deductive processes of reasoning.[63] As Russell has observed, modern mathematical logic began with the work of Boole.[64]

It is no detraction from the genius of Boole, who surely stands among the greatest logicians in history, to point out how close De Morgan was to the prize, or to suggest that De Morgan's failure to gain it may have been due to his controversy with Hamilton. Just as Eiseley has suggested that Lyell's failure to anticipate Darwin may have resulted from the fact that he had for so long contended against progressionist evolution in geology that he could not conceive of evolution in a nonprogressionist form, so it may be conjectured that had De Morgan not entered the controversy determined to prove that Hamilton's theory was worthless, he might have seen in it what Boole did—precisely the formulation of the logical subject matter which permitted it to be mathematicized within a few short months. And if this is so, the significance of Hamilton's work, so long obscured under the obscenities that De Morgan heaped upon him, needs to be brought much more clearly into the center of the stage. Lewis commented that "without Hamilton, we might not have had Boole";[66] it might be more accurate to say that Boole could not have made the application of mathematics to logic which he did had Hamilton not brought logic into a form in which it could be mathematized. What Hamilton accomplished was important, maugre his errors in technical development; and his students Mansel, Veitch, Thomson, and—at Harvard—Francis Bowen who taught Hamiltonian logic were helping to prepare the way for a newer era.

Francis Bowen was born in 1811 in Charlestown, Massachusetts. He graduated from Harvard in 1833, and, after teaching mathematics for two years at Exeter, became tutor in intellectual philosophy and political economy at Harvard in 1835. In 1853 he was appointed Alford Professor of Natural Religion, Moral Philosophy, and Civil Polity, and remained in this position until he retired shortly before his death in 1890. During the 1840s, Bowen was the editor of the highly influential *North American Review*, and was a prolific writer on a wide variety of subjects ranging from logic to economics. In philosophy he was a follower of the Scottish school, but particularly of Hamilton. In his early writings he was highly critical of German idealism and sharply attacked New England Transcendentalism, but he became increasingly impressed by Kant and in his later years he introduced the *Critique of Pure Reason* as a textbook and he was the first to teach the history of German philosophy at Harvard. Thus in Bowen the rapprochement between Scottish philosophy and Kantianism which we have noted above is even more marked.[67]

Bowen's *Treatise on Logic*[68] was published in 1864. Although it deals with most of the problems raised by Hedge, Bowen's approach is Hamiltonian throughout, and his strongest reliance is upon Hamilton's *Lectures on Logic* and upon the work of Hamilton's disciples, Thomson and Bayne. He refers to De Morgan's work, although his dislike of the man is obvious, but he makes but one reference to Boole and he ignores completely the revolution that Boole had begun seventeen years before. Thus Bowen's work may justly be regarded as an authoritative and highly sophisticated statement of the Hamiltonian view, but uninfluenced by the emergence of mathematical logic.

Bowen's *Logic* opens with a section on psychology in which he attempts to explain the nature of concepts. He distinguishes between intuitions, which in his theory are direct perceptions unmediated by any mental process, and concepts, which are the results of mental operations upon intuitions. The intuitions themselves may be of external things (sensations) or of internal events, but in either case they are immediate and the mind is passive in their reception. Moreover, knowledge by intuition is certain; our intuitions are indubitable. But intuitions as we receive them are chaotic and require to be brought into unity. This unification is achieved through conception, in which the mind compares intuitions, finds similarities among them, and combines them according to these similarities into classes. Thus "Conception is that act of the Understanding or Thinking faculty whereby we unite similar objects into one class by overlooking their points of difference and forming their common attributes into one Concept or Thought, the name of which thus becomes the *common name* of all the individuals included in the class."[69] Conception is therefore a synthesis by which the extension is determined by the intension. Bowen is careful to make a sharp distinction between "marks," or attributes considered only intensionally, and concepts which always include reference to an extension. The formation of a concept is a process involving judgment, for the grouping of objects having common properties into a class is an act of the judgment. There is thus no sharp division between concepts and judgments, and "we may either consider Judgements as the elements of Concepts, or Concepts as the elements of Judgements."[70] Moreover, conception is always to some degree arbitrary, for "all classification is an act of the mind, and is more or less arbitrary, depending on our selection of the attributes or relations in reference to which we classify them."[71] We can guard ourselves against this arbitrariness only by testing and correcting our concepts against our intuitions to determine if the objects classed together in the extension of the concept really have all the characteristics which the intension requires. Thus intuition is the only test of the reality of our concepts, for only intuitions "can determine whether the Concepts properly correspond to the actual objects in nature which they are meant to describe."[72] It is therefore critical for Bowen that the line between intuitions and concepts should be sharply drawn, yet in fact he finds it very difficult to keep this distinction clear. When he discusses cases of apparent sensory deception, he can maintain the certainty of intuition only by so extending the role of conception in cognition that it becomes very difficult to say just what it is that is known by intuition.[73] Indeed, since even the naming of presented objects is for Bowen an act of judgment, the problem of identifying the given element in our knowledge remains one of the main unsolved difficulties in his work.

Despite the emphasis on such "psychological" matters, when Bowen comes to deal with logic itself he takes a position quite different from that of Hedge and the earlier Scottish writers. For Bowen, "Logic is the Science of the Necessary Laws of Pure Thought."[74] Following Hamilton, Bowen asserts that pure logic is entirely formal and depends in no way upon any subject matter or upon psychology. But "formal" in this sense does not mean simply uninterpreted; the term is used in a Kantian sense, not in the sense of formalist mathematics. The axioms of pure logic are "laws of thought" in the sense of necessary and universal conditions of the understanding which are presupposed in all rational thought. These laws are absolute and "cannot be transgressed except by the idiot or the madman."[75] Once stated, they are known to be true by the "immediate testimony of consciousness"[76] and are ultimate premises—indeed, they are constitutive of rational thinking. Pure logic, since it begins with absolute truths and is entirely independent of experience, is a pure demonstrative science, and no questions of "material" or empirical truth are involved. When logic is applied to a particular subject matter, so that the premises are empirical hypotheses, questions of material truth must enter as well as those of validity. But pure logic itself is independent of any empirical interpretation.

Bowen's laws of thought are of course those of Hamilton. The first is that *"all thought must be consistent with itself."*[77] This axiom is embodied in the three traditional principles of identity, excluded middle, and noncontradiction. The second axiom is that *"all thought should be consequent*; that is, that it should never affirm or deny a union of two Concepts without any ground for such affirmation or denial."[78] In analytic judgments, the ground is said to be contained in the meaning of the subject; in ampliative judgments the ground or reason is material and the sufficiency of the ground is an empirical question—all that logic requires is that such a ground exist. The third axiom is that one should "state explicitly in language what is implicitly contained in Thought."[79] It is this axiom which requires the explication of the several senses of the copula "is," and the elaboration of the "implicit quantification" of the predicate in ordinary language which leads to Hamilton's theory of judgment. From these axioms, Bowen then attempts to "derive" all of formal logic.

Bowen's treatment of terms, or concepts, as logical entities, is fairly traditional, but it does involve a very clear discussion of intension and extension and their relations. Bowen states the traditional law of the inverse relation between intension and extension with considerable refinement, pointing out that the inverse relation holds only with respect to essential marks and within a given hierarchy of concepts. With respect to judgment, Bowen's Hamiltonian-Kantian point of view is clearly evident in his definition of it as "that act of mind whereby the relation of one Concept to another, or of an individual thing to a Concept, is determined, and, as a consequence of such determination, that two Concepts, or the individual thing and the Concept, are reduced to unity in Thought."[80] A judgment stated in words is a proposition, and all propositions are regarded as having the subject-predicate form. Bowen is at pains to justify Hamilton's theory of the proposition against the attacks of Mill. While he admits that attributive propositions, such as "snow is white," are intensional, he holds that they can be equally well regarded as extensional and that the difference is one of the psychological set of the user and hence extralogical.[81] Thus he claims that all propositions can be regarded as stating relations among the extensions of their terms, and so, following Hamilton, as equations among the quantified terms.[82]

Bowen's devotion to the Hamiltonian cause does not make him narrowly partisan. He gives a very full account of Aristotle's theory of the proposition and of the Aristotelian syllogistic, although he follows it with an equally extensive treatment of Hamilton's syllogistic theory. Once again, Bowen's quasi-Kantian view of the office of the understanding comes through clearly when he remarks that "as a Judgement is an act whereby the two notions which are its Terms are brought together into one, so a Syllogism—Reasoning proper—Mediate Inference—is that Act of Pure Thought whereby the two Judgements which are its Premisses are collected and summed up into one in the Conclusion."[83] The exposition of immediate and syllogistic inference is detailed and thorough, but no processes of inference beyond syllogism, e.g., none of the mathematical developments of Boole, receive mention.

Bowen then turns to the question of the relation of demonstrative reasoning to science. The central thesis is presented in terms of the following example. If one considers the process by which we come to identify an object as an apple, it is clear that the reasoning involved is demonstrative. For "if I had not already spread out before my mind the Marks which constitute the Intension of the Concept *apple* . . . I could not designate the object now presented to me by that appellation."[84] Thus the reasoning here takes the form

The concept *apple* has the marks such and so
This object is such and so
This object is an apple.[85]

This is reasoning in intension: the major premise serves a purely definitive or legislative function and concerns only our own concepts and their definitions. Since the minor premise is known by intuition, both premises are certain; hence the reasoning is not only deductive but demonstrative. On the other hand, if the reasoning concerns real things whose properties are always to some degree unknown, then the major premise is different and the reasoning becomes

All (real) apples are such and so
This object is such and so
This object is an apple.

The minor premise here is still certain, but the major is not, for instead of being definitive it is now an empirical generalization, and since our experience of real apples is limited, the proposition is probable only. In this case then the reasoning is contingent.[86] Bowen uses this example to develop the difference between demonstrative and contingent reasoning. Logic and mathematics are both demonstrative, for they concern only our own concepts and the laws of thought which are necessarily true. Thus Bowen argues that the certainty of mathematics is derived from the fact that all mathematical reasoning is an explication of the concept of quantity.[87] So long as the reasoning concerns only the concept, and not real quantity, the reasoning is demonstrative. When, however, it is applied to quantity as experienced, it becomes contingent, in the same way that the proposition about apples becomes contingent when taken as a statement about real apples and not a definition.[88] Demonstrative reasoning therefore cannot be an organon of discovery, for it involves only the explication of our own concepts and the consistency of our knowledge:[89] it cannot discover new laws of nature or advance science into new areas.

It is by induction and analogy, Bowen holds, that science actually grows: "hence they are, what Pure Reasoning is not, *organa* for the discovery of truth and the actual advancement of knowledge."[90] By induction we generalize from some to all; thus the major premise about apples is the result of an induction from some apples which we have examined to all apples. Analogy on the other hand is an inference from the fact that two things agree in many respects to the conclusion that they agree in some other respect.[91] Both types of reasoning are probable only, for in each case we infer from cases we have enumerated to cases we have not, but the contingency arises from the limited character of our knowledge, not from any doubt about the cases we have examined. Thus Bowen conceived of induction and analogy as methods for discovering laws and facts respectively, not as methods for proving hypotheses. The problem of induction for Bowen is then the problem of finding warranted generalizations, and since he defines the probability of a proposition as the degree of belief which we may justly repose in that proposition,[92] the problem is that of finding hypotheses of high probability. Bowen's analysis of the factors which contribute to the probability of empirical hypotheses is acute. Thus he comments that the probability of an induction is relative to "the correctness of the preceding Classifications that have been formed of the objects of Science."[93] If we deal with a class such as metals, where past experience has shown that this classification does reflect significant characteristics of the objects, an induction from a limited series of trials is far more probable than if the classification has no such experiential warrant, as, e.g., objects now in this room. Clearly, Bowen is describing what we would today call the entrenchment of the predicates involved, although his formulation of the criterion is neither so general nor so precise as Goodman's. Similarly, Bowen notes that consistency among several inductive conclusions reached independently raises the probability of all the conclusions involved. Thus Bowen's analysis of induction is a highly sophisticated and perceptive discussion of the basis for our empirical beliefs.

But Bowen is not content to rest induction upon past experience alone: a warrant is required for generalizing from past to future experience. He rejects the view that induction is based upon the principle of the uniformity of nature on the ground that this principle is itself derived from induction, so that the argument is circular. Instead, he bases induction upon the principle of causality. That every event must have a cause is, Bowen holds, a synthetic a priori truth[94] which is self-evident to reason and incapable either of further proof or of doubt. But from this principle it follows that no change can occur in nature without a cause and that the same causes always produce the same effects. Hence all the support that the principle of the uniformity of nature appeared to yield induction is in fact obtained from the causal axiom. Thus the ultimate warrant even of empirical knowledge is the self-evident truths of the understanding.

Bowen's *Logic* is a remarkable book. In one sense it looks backward, for it ignores the revolution in logic even then under way. Yet in another sense it looks forward to Peirce (who was Bowen's student), Royce, Lewis, and Quine. There are germs of pragmatism in Bowen's discussion of the relation between intuition and conception, and the dual use of major premises as definitions and as empirical statements inevitably suggests Lewis. But most important, Bowen brought to America an interest in logic as a formal discipline, albeit not in quite the modern sense, and in induction and analogy as the methods of discovery in science. With Francis Bowen, the stage was set for the emergence of modern American philosophy and especially for the Cambridge pragmatists.

Notes — Chapter Six

[1]We appreciate the assistance of Abraham Edel in examining the original texts used in this chapter.

[2]Samuel Eliot Morison, *Harvard College in the Seventeenth Century* (Cambridge, Mass.: Harvard University Press, 1936), pp. 146, 187ff; Benjamin Rand, "Philosophical Instruction in Harvard University from 1636 to 1900," *Harvard Graduates Magazine*, September 1928, pp. 32ff.

[3]Brattle's text is derived from Antoine LeGrand, *Institutio Philosophicae secundum principia D. Renati Descartes, nova methodo adornata & explicata* (Norimbergae: Zieger, 1683).

[4]These four copies are in Houghton Library at Harvard University. They are William Brattle, *Compendium Logicae secundum Principia D. Renati Cartesii*, manuscript copy, 1707; copy published Boston, 1722; copy published Boston, 1735; copy published by Johanne Draper, Boston, 1758.

[5]Brattle, 1707, p. 9.

[6]Rene Descartes, *The Philosophical Works of Descartes*, trans. Haldane and Ross (New York: Dover, 1955), vol. I, rules 1-6.

[7]"Q. In Quo differt Synthesis ab Analysi? R. In hoc quod Synthesis a generalioribus et magis simplicibus, ad minus generalia et magis composita progrediatur. Et Analysis E contra a minus generalibus, ad generalioria; aut a compositis ad simplicia, resolvendo, procedit." Brattle, 1722, 60. A more verbose form of the statement occurs on pp. 39 and 40 of the 1707 edition.

[8]Brattle, 1707, p. 54.

9Descartes, *Works*, I:37ff.

10Rand, "Philosophical Instruction," p. 36.

11Brattle, 1735, p. 10.

12See notes in the 1758 edition.

13Thomas Reid, *The Works of Thomas Reid, D.D.,F.R.S.*, ed. Dugald Stewart (Charlestown, Mass.: Samuel Etheridge, Jr., 1813), I:97.

14*Ibid.*, I:95-164.

15*Ibid.*, I:119.

16*Ibid.*, I:138.

17*Ibid.*, I:135ff.

18*Ibid.*, I:137.

19*Ibid.*, I:153ff.

20Dugald Stewart, *The Collected Works of Dugald Stewart, Esq., F.R.S.*, ed. Hamilton (Edinburgh: Thomas Constable and Co., 1854), III:183-229.

21*Ibid.*, pp. 26, 189, 202-9.

22Rand, "Philosophical Instruction," pp. 36, 42ff; "Levi Hedge," *Dictionary of American Biography*, ed. Johnson and Malone (New York: Charles Scribner's Sons, 1946), VIII:499.

23Levi Hedge, *Elements of Logick; or a summary of the general principles and different modes of Reasoning* (Boston: Cummings and Hilliard, 1818), p. 13.

24The quote occurs in a note added in the third edition—see the edition of Hedge's *Logick* published in 1855 by Phinney and Co., Buffalo, N.Y., p. 172.

25Hedge, *Elements of Logick*, p. 78.

26*Ibid.*, pp. 81-82.

27*Ibid.*, p. 138.

28*Ibid.*, p. 140.

29*Ibid.*, p. 91.

30*Ibid.*

31*Ibid.*

32*Ibid.*

33Thomas Baynes, *Essay on the New Analytic of Logical Forms* (Edinburgh: Sutherland, 1850).

34William Thomson, *An Outline of the Necessary Laws of Thought* (London, 1849).

35Sir William Hamilton, *Lectures on Metaphysics and Logic*, ed. Mansel and Veitch, 2 vols. (Boston: Gould and Lincoln, 1860).

36*Ibid.*, II:43.

37*Ibid.*, II:45.

38*Ibid.*, II:56.

39*Ibid.*, II:517. Original in italics.

40*Ibid.*, II:525-27. It should be noted that Hamilton's theory suffers from some serious difficulties which have been pointed out to us by Peter Geach. First, if the proposition is "simply an equation" then its contradiction must be an inequation, yet Hamilton's propositional schedule contains no such form. Second, Hamilton's universal quantifier is used equivocally, sometimes meaning "all," as in "all S is all P," and sometimes meaning "any," as in "any S is not any P." These two uses are not equivalent. Third, quantifying the predicate, at least in the form done by Hamilton, does not reduce every proposition to a simply convertible form. Consider the proposition "any Q is not some P." If this means "for any Q, say q', there is a P, say p', such that $q' = p'$" then this is not equivalent to "some P is not any Q." For there may be two Ps, p_1 and p_2, both of which are Qs, yet no Q will be both p_1 and p_2.

41Sir William Hamilton, *A Letter to Augustus DeMorgan, Esq. on his claim to an Independent Re-Discovery of a New Principle in the Theory of Syllogism* (London and Edinburgh: Longman, Brown, Green, and Longmans; Maclachlan, Stewart and Co., 1847), pp. 6, 8, 15-16. See also "Extract from Prospectus of 'Essay towards a New Analytic of Logical Forms,' " published as Appendix to *The Works of Thomas Reid, D.D., with Stewart's account of Reid*, ed. Hamilton (Edinburgh, 1846) reprinted in Hamilton, *Lectures*, II:509-12.

42W. Bednarowski, "Hamilton's Quantification of the Predicate," *Proceedings of the Aristotelean Society* 56:217-40 (1956).

43Augustus De Morgan, *On the Syllogism and Other Logical Writings*, ed. Heath (London: Routledge and Kegan Paul, 1966), pp. 1-17.

44Cf. *ibid.*, p. xii.

45Reprinted *ibid.*

46Augustus De Morgan, *Formal Logic* (London: Taylor and Walton, 1847).

47Hamilton, *Letter*, pp. 13ff.

48De Morgan, *On the Syllogism*, pp. 17-21.

49Hamilton, *Letter*, p. 25.

50De Morgan, *On the Syllogism*, Introduction, esp. pp. xviii-xxiv.

51John Stuart Mill, *An Examination of Sir William Hamilton's Philosophy* (London: Longman, Green, Longman, Roberts, and Green, 1865).

52Hamilton, *Lectures*, II.

53*Ibid.*, II:31.

54W. R. Hamilton's quarternions involved noncommutative multiplication.

55William Kneale, "Boole and the Revival of Logic," *Mind*, n.s. 57:150 (1948).

56The published documents of the controversy are Hamilton's *Letter* cited above and Augustus De Morgan, "Statement in Answer to an Assertion made by Sir William Hamilton, Bart.," both of which appeared in April of 1847.

57George Boole, *The Mathematical Analysis of Logic* (Cambridge: Macmillan Barclay and Macmillan, 1847).

58*Ibid.*, p. 1. There is reason to believe that the influence of Hamilton on Boole was much greater than has been suspected. In calling his major work on logic *An Investigation of the Laws of Thought*, Boole chose to use a Hamiltonian title, and one which had already been used by Thomson. Moreover, while Boole used the term "formal" in a mathematician's sense in discussing logic, there are also echoes of Hamilton's quasi-Kantian usage whenever Boole discusses the relation of logic to the processes of thought. Boole clearly did not regard the laws of thought as arbitrary postulates but "as founded in the nature of thought, and as governing its outward manifestation" (George Boole, *Studies in Logic and Probability* [London: Watts and Co., 1952], p. 215), and he compares his own attempts to specify the relation of logic to psychology to that of Hamilton's disciple Mansel in his *Prolegomena Logica* (*ibid.*, p. 212). Boole's own version of this relation, and his conclusion that "we think and reason about the finite, but we do so because our reasoning faculties have a relation to the infinite" (*ibid.*, p. 229) bear suggestive analogies to Hamiltonian doctrines. It should also be noted that Boole, like Hamilton, uses equations to represent propositions but does not use inequations. It would require a more detailed study of Boole's intellectual development than has yet been attempted to define precisely the nature of his relation to Hamilton, but the subject appears to be one worth pursuing.

[59]Boole, *Mathematical Analysis of Logic*, p. 3.

[60]*Ibid.*, pp. 17ff.

[61]*Ibid.*, p. 34. The fact that the proposition "all X are some Y" can be written not only as x = vy but also as x $(1-y) = 0$ shows, as Peter Geach has noted, that the operator "v" can be eliminated by writing x = vy as x = xy. In Boole's retention of the distinct operator "v," one cannot but see the influence of Hamilton.

[62]George Boole, *An Investigation of the Laws of Thought* (New York, Dover, n.d.).

[63]*Ibid.*, pp. 8ff; Boole, *Mathematical Analysis of Logic*, pp. 8ff.

[64]Bertrand Russell, *Our Knowledge of the External World* (London: George Allen and Unwin, 1952), pp. 49-50.

[65]Loren Eiseley, *Darwin's Century* (New York: Doubleday, Anchor, 1958), chap. 4.

[66]C. I. Lewis, *Survey of Symbolic Logic* (New York: Dover, 1960), p. 37.

[67]"Francis Bowen," *Dictionary of American Biography*, II:503-4; Rand, "Philosophical Instruction," pp. 194-200.

[68]Francis Bowen, *A Treatise on Logic* (Cambridge, Mass.: Sever and Francis, 1864).

[69]*Ibid.*, p. 5.

[70]*Ibid.*, p. 20.

[71]*Ibid.*, p. 9.

[72]*Ibid.*, p. 12.

[73] *Ibid.*, pp. 420f.

[74] *Ibid.*, p. 30.

[75] *Ibid.*, p. 34.

[76] *Ibid.*

[77] *Ibid.*, p. 48.

[78] *Ibid.*, p. 53.

[79] *Ibid.*, p. 56.

[80] *Ibid.*, p. 105.

[81] *Ibid.*, pp. 110ff.

[82] *Ibid.*, p. 141.

[83] *Ibid.*, p. 179.

[84] *Ibid.*, p. 351.

[85] *Ibid.*, p. 352.

[86] *Ibid.*

[87] *Ibid.*, p. 359.

[88] *Ibid.*, p. 361.

[89] *Ibid.*, p. 366.

[90] *Ibid.*, p. 380.

[91] *Ibid.*, p. 381.

[92] *Ibid.*, p. 440.

[93] *Ibid.*, p. 385. Original in italics.

[94] *Ibid.*, p. 372.

Chapter Seven

Transcendentalism

Chapter Seven

Transcendentalism

1. Background

As the eighteenth century wore on, the Enlightenment took firm hold among the antirevivalist clergy of eastern Massachusetts—in some cases, too firm a hold. By 1805 a group of these ministers had become so "enlightened" that they found themselves no longer able to accept some of the doctrines of Calvinism. For too firm an adherence to reason, as Samuel Johnson had found a century earlier, is apt to lead to difficulties in the interpretation of revelation. Those "enlightened" ministers demanded a rational Christianity, and rejected those doctrines which seemed to them contrary to reason's teachings. Since the controversy crystallized around the issue of the Trinity, the "enlightened" party was called Unitarians, but the question of the Trinity was only one among a number of questions on which those men differed from the orthodox. They regarded such fundamental Calvinist tenets as innate depravity, infinite atonement, predestination, and election as contrary to reason and as impugning the justice and benevolence of God. From the Unitarian point of view, Calvinism was a form of barbarism unworthy of the name of Christianity—a view summarized in the title of one of the Unitarian pamphlets of the day, *Are You a Christian or a Calvinist?*[1]

But the issue between the Unitarians and the Calvinists lay deeper even than these questions of doctrine: it involved fundamental differences in world view. Like Franklin and Jefferson, the Unitarians were children of the Enlightenment, and they were contending for reason and benevolence in the Enlightenment sense of those terms. In the revolutionary triumphs of science they saw clear proof of the

397

power and scope of human reason, and they were not afraid to follow where it led, even in questions of theology. They conceived of virtue as morality, and their rejection of innate depravity bore witness to their high estimate of the moral capacity of rational men. The Calvinists' assertion that the good works of sinners are doubly damned they denied with a disgust which showed that they no longer understood what the doctrine meant. They opposed religious enthusiasm not only as dangerous but as uncouth, and if they affirmed the orthodox demand for an educated ministry, their concept of what such an education should include was far broader than the curriculum of the Andover Theological Seminary. For the Unitarian clergy were not only theological scholars—they were men of culture, versed in literature and the arts, in modern European thought as well as in the classics. Since Joseph Buckminster, the most brilliant of the early Boston Unitarians and minister of the Brattle Street Church, had returned from Europe in 1806 with the collection of three thousand books which soon after became the basis for the Boston Athenaeum, modern European works had become increasingly common in Boston, and so had the practice of going to Europe to study at firsthand the culture of the Old World. In 1819 George Ticknor returned from four years abroad to become the first professor of modern languages and literature at Harvard, and Edward Everett returned, with a Ph.D. from Göttingen, to assume the chair of Greek. Many who studied under these men, and later became leaders of Unitarianism, and Transcendentalism, followed in their steps—Frederick Hedge, the Emerson brothers, and many others took the grand tour to see for themselves what Europe offered. If the Unitarian leaders were neither so catholic nor so profound as Franklin and Jefferson, and were more bound by traditional Christianity, they were nevertheless responding to the same forces.[2]

Boston Unitarianism was a blend of Enlightenment rationalism and traditional Christianity, and accordingly it combined both the emphasis on reason and nature which characterized the former and the emphasis on supernatural revelation which characterized the latter. Like all rationalists, including the deists, the Boston Unitarians stressed the importance of nature as a source of religious truth and accorded a wider scope and a greater authority to the light of nature than did the Calvinists. Nevertheless, they still regarded the Bible as the primary source of religious knowledge, and as the sole source of our knowledge of the distinctive doctrines of Christianity. The issue between the Boston Unitarians and the Calvinists therefore was not one of the Bible versus nature, but of the proper interpretation of the Bible. The Unitarians held that Scripture must be interpreted in the light of our general knowledge, and Biblical passages which involved assertions that were plainly contrary to known facts of nature and to common sense must be reinterpreted so as to give them a reasonable meaning. But as the Calvinists were quick to point out, this view of interpretation has radical implications. In the first place, it makes reason the judge of what is or is not revelation, and so exalts mere human reason above the Word of God. Secondly, it gives to scientific knowledge an authority equal to Scripture, and so denies the absolute authority of the Bible. But even more important, if conformity to reason and nature is the test of revelation, then everything above reason and nature must be denied, and so all the supernatural elements of Christianity must fall. Once the Unitarian principles are accepted, so the Calvinists charged, there can be no stopping short of Deism or atheism. Unitarianism is not only a new edition of the Arian heresy—it is a halfway house to infidelity: whoever begins as a Unitarian will sooner or later abandon Christianity completely.[3]

There was enough truth to these Calvinist charges to make it imperative for the Unitarians that they be met. Despite their emphasis on reason and nature, the Unitarians were not deists, nor were they Unitarians in the sense of Jefferson or Priestley—they were still Christians and they still believed in supernatural religion. They denied the doctrine of the Trinity, but they nevertheless believed that Jesus spoke with an authority given by God. To prove this fact, the Boston Unitarians turned to the Biblical miracles: the divine authority of Jesus was demonstrated by the fact that He performed miracles. Thus for the Boston Unitarians, the miracles carried the entire weight of supernaturalism. As one Unitarian minister put it,

It has been well said of the miracles, that "they are like the massive subterranean arches and columns of a huge building. It is not on their account that we prize the building, but the building for its own sake. We do not think of the foundation nor care about it, other than to know that it has one. We dwell above in the upper and fairer halls. The crowds go in and out, and rejoice in their comforts and splendours, without ever casting a thought on that upon which the whole so peacefully and securely reposes. Such are the miracles to the gospel. They support the edifice, and upon a divine foundation. They show us, that if the superstructure is fair and beautiful to dwell in, and if its towers and endless flights of steps *appear* to reach even up to heaven, it is all just what it seems to be; for it rests upon the broad foundation of the Rock of Ages."[4]

But if the miracles are the proof of supernaturalism, what is the proof of miracles? Why should we believe in the occurrence of events so utterly at variance with our experience and with natural law? Even if it be granted that miracles would be a reasonable proof of divine authority, what is the proof that they occurred? For these Unitarians that proof was furnished by historical evidences. The Gospels record the testimony of men who were eyewitnesses to these events, and whose credibility as witnesses is unimpeachable. We have therefore as much empirical evidence for the actual occurrence of miracles as we have for any fact of ancient history, and indeed considerably more evidence than we have for most such facts.[5]

It is ironic that the Unitarians should have reached these conclusions just at the time when the German higher criticism was beginning its devastating analysis of the Biblical narratives.[6]

As long as they could believe in the historical evidences of Christianity, the Unitarians felt secure against the Calvinist charge that they were a halfway house to infidelity. But then in 1836 came Transcendentalism. That Transcendentalism was a heresy of a damnable kind was instantly apparent, but what made it acutely embarrassing to the Unitarians was the fact that it was a heresy which sprang from their own ranks. Ralph Waldo Emerson, George Ripley, Frederick Hedge, Converse Francis, O. A. Brownson, William Furness, Theodore Parker, and many other Transcendentalists were Unitarian ministers, and the nonministerial members of the movement, such as Bronson Alcott and Margaret Fuller, had been accounted Unitarians. When Andrews Norton, in the name of his outraged Unitarian brethren, pronounced the Transcendental doctrine "the latest form of infidelity,"[7] he was virtually conceding that the Calvinist prophecy had been right: Unitarianism had spawned heresy, though hardly in the form its critics had anticipated.[8]

Although the genesis of the Transcendentalist movement is complex, it is clear that the issue which precipitated the movement was the problem of miracles. Having rested the whole weight of its supernaturalism on the miracles, and so on historical evidences, the Unitarians were particularly vulnerable to the higher criticism, and as the results of that criticism became known, many of the younger men found their faith severely shaken. But the miracles issue was only a symptom of other problems which were far more basic than those of historical evidences or Biblical interpretation. First, the Unitarians had undertaken to establish the supernatural character of Christianity upon the basis of an empirical epistemology derived from Locke and the Scottish Realists. They had treated problems of religion and morals as empirical problems like those of science, solvable by reason and sense. But having formulated the questions in these terms, they found themselves confronting the problem of how that which is by definition spiritual and immaterial can be known by the senses. Their solution was to appeal to empirical effects produced by spiritual causes, and accordingly to miraculous events—i.e., to events inexplicable by science and so requiring the hypothesis of spiritual action. The collapse of the historical evidences of such events therefore called into question the adequacy of an empirical epistemology as a basis for a spiritual religion.

Second, it is clear that Unitarianism was the outcome of a long process of gradual accommodation between the quasi-scholastic, theologically dominated world view represented by technologia and the scientific world view which emerged with Newton. The early Puritans had believed in a world immediately dependent upon God's will in which natural events were directly related to their own behavior as rewards and punishments. With the scientific revolution, large areas of nature were brought under the rule of natural laws, and so rendered predictable. Since the Puritans believed in predestination, there was in theory no contradiction between an event being predictable and its being a judgment, but once the event could be predicted without reference to any observable human behavior, it soon lost its providential meaning. Such events could still be "spiritualized," and shown to contribute to a divine design in nature, but they no longer represented a direct action of God upon the individual. The gradual narrowing of the circle of special providences and the concomitant expansion of the domain of scientifically explicable phenomena were accordingly accompanied by the conversion of an immanent and all-controlling God into a remote and spectatorial one. By the time Unitarianism emerged, the acceptance of the scientific world view was virtually complete. The miraculous elements were reduced to the inescapable minimum—the Biblical miracles necessary to supply supernatural sanction to Christianity—and so were consigned to ancient history. The resulting faith was rational, but it also notably lacked that sense of the immediate presence of God which was so important a part of the New England piety. For those who became Transcendentalists, rationality was not enough.

Third, the same course of development which had removed the spirit from nature also had the effect of removing it from man. The faculty psychology of the Puritans, whatever its faults may have been, made a perfectly clear distinction between the rational immortal soul peculiar to man and the sensitive soul common to man and animals. The imagination, memory, and common sense belonged to the sensitive soul—reason and conscience to the rational soul alone.[9] But Lockean psychology combined the functions of the reason and the common sense into a single faculty, the understanding, and although animals might possess less understanding than men, the differences were a matter of degree, not of kind. In a similar way, Lockean psychology undermined the traditional Protestant theory of conscience. As Miller has pointed out,

> Protestantism inherited the dominant Aristotelian tradition, the empirical doctrine of the faculties . . . Yet Protestant theology made imperative a new emphasis upon a theory of conscience which had more in common with the dissenting, the mystical or Platonic tradition, than with the one transcribed in Protestant textbooks. It was supremely necessary for Protestantism to maintain that there still linger in the mind of fallen man certain inborn moral certainties, not derived from experience . . . It was easy enough to account for such innate principles in purely theological terms: they are remains from the image of God; man in the fall lost his "moral powers", but not his "moral image". . . .[10]

We have already seen that this doctrine played an important part in New England Puritanism.[11] Yet it is a potentially dangerous doctrine, for in postulating innate ideas having divine authority, it carried mystical implications which even the

Aristotelian doctrine of the faculties was not always sufficient to suppress. But what Aristotle could not achieve, Locke could. Such Platonic innatism was categorically denied by Locke, and the whole theory of conscience had to be recast to fit the new epistemology. This reformulation was accomplished by the Scottish Common Sense Realists in the theory of the moral sense. Indeed, one of the chief reasons why all Protestant groups in America welcomed Scottish Realism was that the moral sense has the virtues of the Protestant conscience without its faults: it was an innate moral guide, yet it was merely a perceptive faculty and not a source of principles or doctrine. Princeton Presbyterians and Harvard Unitarians could celebrate the divine spark within, secure in the knowledge that a Scottish epistemology would never lead to antinomianism.

The miracles controversy was the occasion for the emergence of Transcendentalism, but the real causes of the movement lay in the profound failure of Unitarianism to provide a basis for a spiritual religion. Its epistemology made direct religious experience impossible, its rationalism secularized the natural order, and its psychology submerged man in that secular nature. When James Marsh, the president of the University of Vermont, published the first American edition of Coleridge's *Aids to Reflection* in 1828,[12] he spelled out the issue in the bluntest terms in his preliminary essay.

> . . . so long as we hold the doctrines of Locke and the Scotch metaphysicians . . . we not only can make and defend no essential distinction between that which is *natural*, and that which is *spiritual*, but we cannot even find rational grounds for the feeling of *moral obligation*. . . .[13]

Transcendentalism was an attempt to rescue man from nature and reestablish his spiritual character. That is why Emerson's great manifesto was entitled *Nature*.[14]

Although the Transcendentalists were a remarkably able group of men, they were also a very small group of men: the movement probably never had more than fifty adherents and only a few of these were leaders in its development. Most of its members were Unitarian ministers, and, as that fact suggests, the movement was fundamentally a religious movement with religious objectives. Given the character of religion in this period, these religious objectives often involved social objectives, and many of the Transcendentalists were involved in a variety of social reform movements. They were also involved in philosophic problems, because they were concerned about the ground of religious knowledge, and so about epistemology in general. But few of them have left detailed and explicit formulations of their position. Of these few, the most important for us are Emerson and Alcott. Insofar as Transcendentalism had a leader, that leader was Emerson. His book, *Nature*, comes closer to being a credo of the movement than any other publication, and he was recognized by his peers as the ablest spokesman of the group. Although in later phases of the movement Theodore Parker became the most effective champion of Transcendental doctrines in the battle over church reform, Emerson's formulation of the position remains the classic one. Alcott, on the other hand, was not a minister, and lacked the professional and social qualifications to be a leader in such a company. He was also a tedious writer, but exactly because his writing was pedestrian it often contained clearer statements of the Transcendental position than are to be found in the glistering prose of some of the others. Furthermore, it was Alcott who was the major link between the Transcendentalists of New England and the Hegelian movements in the West, particularly in St. Louis, and it was Alcott who was to preside in his old age over the Concord School of Philosophy when Western idealism came to New England.

Transcendentalism has sometimes been interpreted as an importation of German idealism. There were some among the Transcendentalists who were directly influenced by German thought, but there were not many. Only one, Frederick Hedge, son of the Harvard logician, Levi Hedge, was a thorough student of German language and literature, and his articles on Coleridge and on German literature which appeared in the *Christian Examiner* from 1833 to 1835 helped to bring a more accurate knowledge of German thought to New England. Others, such as George Ripley, certainly knew a good deal of German literature at firsthand. Yet the direct influence of German thought seems to have been slight; certainly neither Emerson nor Alcott had any direct acquaintance with German idealism until after they had formulated their own Transcendentalist positions. On the other hand, the influence of British Romanticism—particularly of Coleridge— was enormous. Yet the British Romantics were influential for a particular reason: it was because their doctrines provided answers to a set of problems which had arisen in the native New England context, and because the New Englanders were already moving toward this position before they read the British, that they were prepared to acclaim Coleridge a prophet of light. Since both Emerson and Alcott were assiduous journalizers, and since the journals of both men are extant for the period during which they formulated their Transcendentalist positions, it is possible to follow the way in which these two radically different men from very different backgrounds, grappling with the same basic problems of religious knowledge, worked out independently Transcendentalist positions which were virtually identical.[15]

2. Emerson's Early Views

Ralph Waldo Emerson was born in Boston in 1803. He was the son of William Emerson, one of the ministers who had helped to establish the Unitarian Church. Emerson's father died in 1811, leaving his family in straitened circumstances. Nevertheless, the Emerson boys went to Harvard: Waldo entered in 1817 and graduated in 1821. After trying his hand at schoolteaching, he entered Harvard

Divinity School in 1825 and after graduating was ordained minister at the Second Unitarian Church in Boston in 1829—a position which he resigned in 1832 when his changed religious views made his continuance impossible and his wife's inheritance made it unnecessary.[16]

From 1820 on, Emerson kept a journal, and in this, and his letters[17] and other writings, one can follow the evolution of his views. As one might expect, he studied philosophy at Harvard, where he was indoctrined with Scottish Realism by Levi Hedge and Levi Frisbie,[18] but the indoctrination was only partly successful. Emerson's early writings show that he accepted the theory of the moral sense in quite an orthodox form,[19] but he found the Scottish replies to Berkeley and Hume something less than convincing. Although he described Hume's skepticism as an "outrage upon the feeling of human nature"[20] and praised Reid's attempt to refute it, he also observed that Reid's arguments "have not been made with such complete success as to remove the terror which attached to the name of Hume."[21] Thus Emerson's position in the early twenties is rather unusual: he accepted the moral sense as a secure basis for morality, yet he was unconvinced by the realists' answers to Humean skepticism.

What roused Emerson from his dogmatic slumbers, however, was not Hume— it was the higher criticism. Emerson's elder brother, William, went to Germany in 1823 to prepare for the ministry and while there met the full force of this criticism. The impact was shattering. When William returned home in 1825 his faith was so badly shaken that he abandoned the ministry as a career.[22] The effects of this event, and of the critical doctrines which induced it, upon Waldo are clearly evident in a letter which he wrote to his aunt in 1826:

> The objections the German scholars have proposed attack the foundations of external evidence, and so give up the internal to historical speculators and pleasant doubters . . . There will be to good men henceforward a horrid anticipation when the majestic vision that has, for ages, kept a commanding check upon the dangerous passions of men—has rivetted the social bonds and brought forward so many noble spirits and prodigious benefits to the help of struggling humanity—shall roll away, and let in the ghastly reality of things. Regard it as a possible event, and it is the prospect of a dark and disastrous tragedy. These great Eleusinian Mysteries which have hoarded comfort from age to age for human sufferings,—the august Founder, the twelve self-denying heroes of pious renown, . . . the martyrs, . . . the boundless aggregate of hearts and deeds which the genius of Christianity touched and inspired . . . all these must now pass away and become ridiculous. They have been the sum of what was most precious on earth. They must now pass into the rhetoric of scoffer and atheist as the significant testimonies of human folly, and every drunkard in his cups, and every voluptuary in his brothel will roll out his tongue at the Resurrection from the dead; at the acts, the martyrdoms, the unassailable virtues and the legendary greatness of Chris-

tianity. God forbid. It were base treason in his servants tamely to surrender his cause. The gates of hell will not prevail against it. But it were vile and supine to sit and be astonished without exploring the strength of the enemy. If heaven gives me sight, I will dedicate it to this cause.[23]

It is obvious from this letter that Emerson was deeply shaken by the work of the German critics and fully recognized its significance: either Christianity was now reduced to a pleasant fable, or some new ground of belief had to be found.

Faced with difficulties of this magnitude, Emerson turned to the one principle he had never doubted, the moral sense.[24] In his college courses under Hedge and Frisbie, Emerson had studied such works as Stewart's *Elements of the Philosophy of the Human Mind*, and so had acquired a perfectly orthodox interpretation of the moral sense: he regarded it as a faculty which perceived the rightness or wrongness of particular acts. In 1821 he read Price's *Review of the Principle Questions and Difficulties of Morals* in which he found presented a somewhat different view of the basis of moral knowledge. Since Price was a rationalist with certain Platonic overtones, it has sometimes been thought that Emerson derived some of his later idealism from Price.[25] This conclusion, however, appears doubtful. Price does go beyond the orthodox moral sense position in two important ways: he argues that moral distinctions are made by the understanding rather than by a "moral sense" as Hutcheson had claimed, and he holds that the understanding can perceive not only the rightness or wrongness of particular acts, but also certain general moral truths. But in claiming this, Price is really only extending to morality the power of "intuition" which the Scots gave generally to common sense, whereby we know the truth of such principles as the axiom of causality. Moreover, Price's view of the understanding is perceptive, not legislative; the understanding perceives moral distinctions, it does not decree them. And despite Price's comments about abstraction, there is certainly little evidence of Platonic innatism in his work. Furthermore, there is no evidence that Emerson interpreted Price as an idealist, or that Emerson's own view of the character of the moral sense was changed by reading Price. Emerson continued to speak of the moral sense as the foundation of morality and to describe it as a faculty which perceives the moral character of particulars.[26] But both before and after reading Price, Emerson gave to the moral sense a religious interpretation which stressed its spiritual character in a way that clearly identified it with the traditional concept of the image of God within. Thus in 1822 he wrote of it:

> . . . that sovereign sense whereof we speak leaves the material world and its subordinate knowledge to subordinate faculties, and marshalls before its divine tribunal the motives of action, the secrets of character and the interests of the universe. It has no taint of mortality in the purity and unity of its intelligence; it is perfectly spiritual.[27]

Emerson's view is still orthodox, although it goes about as far in spiritualizing the moral sense as a Unitarian could go. Yet in doing so, Emerson was following a path which Unitarianism itself clearly suggested.

Orthodox Calvinism had hedged the doctrine of the Image of God with the doctrine of innate depravity. Whatever divine spark man might carry within, he was still a corrupt and evil being with a ruined mind and a feeble conscience. But the doctrine of innate depravity was one of the tenets of Calvinism which the Unitarians rejected. The Unitarians of course admitted man's capacity for sin, and even that all men do sin, but in denying the inherent depravity of man they laid a stress on the capacities of man's moral nature which gave new emphasis to the theory of conscience. This trend reached its culmination in the works of William Ellery Channing.

Channing is one of the greatest figures in American religious history, and one of the most complex. After Buckminster's early death, he became the acknowledged leader and the most brilliant spokesman for Boston Unitarianism, yet his theological position was far more original and extreme than that of most of his Unitarian brethren. Channing was not a Transcendentalist, yet his statements of his own doctrine could often be given a Transcendentalist interpretation; and Emerson, Alcott, and the other young dissidents in the late twenties and early thirties did so interpret them. Accordingly, these young men idolized Channing and thought of him as their leader, when in fact he was nothing of the kind. So Channing played a curious role in the emergence of Transcendentalism: without intending to do so he helped set these young men on the road to idealism.[28]

Channing's fundamental doctrine was what Robert Patterson has called the doctrine of "essential sameness."[29] Instead of holding, as did the Calvinists, that God differs in kind from man, Channing held that man and God are essentially similar, however they may differ in degree. Attributes may therefore be used univocally to describe both God and man, and although these attributes—e.g., goodness—may be possessed by God in higher degree than by men, nevertheless human goodness is of the same kind as God's. Man is therefore essentially like God: his nature too is divine, and the more virtuous he becomes the closer he comes "to that perfection of the soul, which constitutes it a bright image of God."[30]

From this doctrine of essential sameness, Channing drew the conclusion that we derive our knowledge of God from our own souls.

Whence do we derive our knowledge of the attributes and perfections which constitute the Supreme Being? I answer, we derive them from our own souls. The divine attributes are first developed in ourselves, and thence transferred to our Creator. The idea of God, sublime and awful as it is, is the idea of our own spiritual nature, purified and enlarged to infinity. In ourselves are the elements of the Divinity.[31]

Channing's meaning here is clear enough in terms of the doctrine of essential sameness: since God's attributes differ from ours only in degree, we can learn the nature of those attributes from the study of ourselves. Channing did not mean to assert that the idea of God is innate in the soul, or that the soul somehow communicates knowledge to us, yet when he speaks of the conscience he so emphasizes its divine character that he is open to such interpretation. Thus he writes:

> . . . the moral perfections of the Deity . . . are comprehended by us, only through our own moral nature. It is conscience within us, which, by its approving and condemning voice, interprets to us God's love of virtue and hatred of sin; and without conscience, these glorious conceptions would never have opened on the mind. It is the lawgiver in our own breasts, which gives us the idea of divine authority, and binds us to obey it. The soul, by its sense of right, or its perception of moral distinctions, is clothed with sovereignty over itself, and through this alone, it understands and recognizes the Sovereign of the Universe. Men, as by a natural inspiration, have agreed to speak of conscience as the voice of God, as the Divinity within us.[32]

This statement does not really go beyond asserting an orthodox doctrine of the moral sense, yet it suggests a good deal more than it says. Channing is so enraptured by the divinity of man's nature that it is hard to tell where men ends and God begins. Moreover, in emphasizing the soul as the source of our ideas of God, Channing shifts the focus away from external evidences, from historical record and from nature. For him, this is only a shift of emphasis: it did not imply a distrust of the Biblical narratives or of arguments from design.[33] Yet Channing even went so far as to assert that it is from ourselves that we derive the knowledge that enables us to interpret physical nature:

> It is plain, too, that likeness to God is the true and only preparation for the enjoyment of the universe. In proportion as we approach and resemble the mind of God, we are brought into harmony with the creation; for, in that proportion, we possess the principles from which the universe sprung; we carry within ourselves the perfections, of which its beauty, magnificence, order, benevolent adaptations, and boundless purposes, are the results and manifestations. God unfolds himself in his works to a kindred mind.[34]

Channing half recognized the danger of these words, for he immediately hedged them with qualifications, yet even here he was still within the bounds of an empirical epistemology. Francis Wayland and other Scottish realist writers of the time held essentially similar views.[35] Nevertheless, Channing's words can also yield a far more radical meaning than he intended, and this meaning Emerson and Alcott were soon to draw.

The Unitarian views of man's moral nature, and particularly Channing's extreme formulation of these views, encouraged Emerson's emphasis on the moral sense and led him to attribute to it an authority and scope which strained empirical epistemology to the breaking point. Thus by 1824 Emerson wrote:

> . . . the highest species of reasoning upon divine subjects is rather the fruit of a sort of moral imagination, than of the "Reasoning Machines", such as Locke and Clarke and David Hume. Dr. Channing's Dudleian Lecture is the model of what I mean, and the faculty which produced this is akin to the higher flights of fancy.[36]

Thus Emerson was well prepared for idealism when he read the first American edition of Coleridge's *Aids to Reflection* in 1829. This book was the turning point for Emerson, as it was for most of the other Transcendentalists. Marsh's preliminary essay to the volume was a powerful attack, not only upon Locke, but upon the Scottish philosophy as well, and categorically denied that a spiritual religion could be based upon an empirical epistemology. "And where," Marsh demanded, "I would beg to know, shall we look, according to the popular system of philosophy, for that 'image of God' in which we are created?"[37] But Coleridge's idealism, Marsh claimed, provided a secure basis for a spiritual religion.[38] The crucial doctrine was the distinction between the reason and the understanding. By the understanding, Coleridge meant the faculty which performs all those operations of comparing and contrasting, abstracting and combining, by which empirical knowledge is derived from sensory experience. But by the reason he meant something quite different: "Reason is the Power of universal and necessary Convictions, the Source and Substance of Truths above Sense, and having their evidence in themselves."[39] Reason thus comprehends the moral insight, but in a much more powerful form, for, as Coleridge argues, conscience is merely one use of Reason.

> . . . in reference to *actual* (or moral) truth, as the fountain of ideas and the *Light* of the Conscience, we name it the *practical* Reason. Whenever by self-subjection to this universal Light, the Will of the Individual, the *particular* Will, has become a Will of Reason, the man is regenerate: and Reason is then the *Spirit* of the regenerate man, whereby the Person is capable of a quickening intercommunication with the Divine Spirit.[40]

Reason and conscience therefore are modes of action of the spirit within: they are spiritual faculties, and so are categorically distinguished from the understanding. Thus Coleridge provided a psychological basis for differentiating what is spiritual in man from what is natural. But he did more than this—he made the Reason both a source and a test of truth. It is a source of truth since certain universal and necessary propositions are propounded directly by the Reason.[41] Moreover, since the Reason is the spirit, it is capable of immediate "intercommunication" with

God, and so of receiving principles directly from Him. Hence Coleridge's epis-temology offers a basis for immediate personal experience of spiritual things of a sort impossible on empirical grounds.

It was Coleridge who convinced Emerson that a spiritual religion could not be based upon an empirical epistemology. Emerson adopted Coleridge's psychology, and identified Reason with God. "Our compound nature differences us from God, but our Reason is not to be distinguished from the divine Essence."[42] And it was the idealistic epistemology, with its claim that religious truth is self-evident to Reason, which furnished Emerson a solution to the problem of historical evidence.

> Internal evidence outweighs all other to the inner man. If the whole history of the New Testament had perished, and its teachings remained, the spirituality of Paul, the grave, considerate, unerring advice of James would take the same rank with me that now they do. I should say, as now I say, this certainly is the greatest height to which the religious principle of human nature has ever been carried, and it has the total suffrage of my soul to its truth, whether the miracle was wrought, as is pretended, or not. If it had not, I should yield to Hume or any one that this, like all other miracle accounts, was probably false. As it is true, the miracle falls in with and confirms it.[43]

Miracles do not prove the truth of the New Testament: the truth of the New Testament proves the miracles. Christianity is true because the Reason declares it to be true. Yet the task of formulating the idealistic position so as to support these conclusions remained, and engrossed Emerson during the early thirties. The result of these efforts was the thin book called *Nature* which he published in 1836. This book is Emerson's definitive statement of his position—a position which changed very little during the remainder of his life, and it is also the classic statement of New England Transcendentalism. But before analyzing *Nature*, it is necessary to trace Alcott's development to this same position.

3. Alcott's Early Views

Amos Bronson Alcott was born in Wolcott, Connecticut, in 1799, the son of farming parents of slender means. Since the Congregational Church was the established church in Connecticut until 1818, Wolcott had of course a Congrega-tional church, and it seems quite clear that during Alcott's youth the Wolcott church was Edwardsean, though not strongly revivalistic. But despite the fact that Alcott's father was a member of this church, his mother was not, for she had been raised an Episcopalian, and her brother, Tillotson Bronson, was one of the leading Episcopal clergymen in the area, the principal of the Cheshire Academy, and the editor of the *Churchman's Magazine*—an Episcopal journal. At this time Con-necticut had no Unitarian churches, but the Episcopal Church played a role in

Connecticut which was in many ways comparable to that of the Unitarian Church in Massachusetts, and was besides allied with the Jeffersonian party against the Congregationalist-Federalist coalition in a campaign to disestablish the Congregational Church—a campaign which succeeded in 1818. It was therefore significant that the Alcott family as a whole shifted to the Episcopal Church in 1808, for although Alcott never became a devout Episcopalian, the Episcopal Church formed one of the few avenues by which rationalistic and anti-Calvinist ideas could reach him. Thus although Alcott had received his meager formal education from the local Congregational minister, he early turned against Calvinism in all its forms.[44]

Although Alcott's formal education was limited to the Wolcott common school and one year of study with his uncle at Cheshire, he and his older cousin William read all the books they could obtain and early resolved to dedicate themselves to teaching as a career. Alcott was particularly influenced by *Pilgrim's Progress*, from which he learned to see himself as Christian and life as a mission and a trial, and by James Burgh's *Dignity of Human Nature*,[45] a book designed to teach young men the way to salvation. But the important thing about Burgh's book for the Alcott cousins was that it was a purely Lockean treatise which attempted to show how on Lockean grounds young men might be led to prudence, knowledge, and virtue. Although Burgh is orthodox enough to pay lip service to the doctrines of original sin, the whole message of the treatise is not only Arminian but openly asserts that all men by proper education can be made virtuous, and so implicitly suggests that all can be saved. It was from Burgh and Bunyan, then, that the Alcotts found their calling. Barred by poverty from the ministry, strongly anti-Calvinist, and yearning for a field of creative moral action, education presented an ideal career through which they could follow "safe in Christian's way." For in the Connecticut of that day, the common schools were essentially Congregational parochial schools, taught by Congregational ministers or men they approved, and designed to instill religious orthodoxy along with the three Rs. To attack Calvinism in the schools was as revolutionary an action in Connecticut then as to attack it in the pulpit in Boston.[46]

In 1818 Bronson Alcott set out to teach. Armed with a certificate of qualification signed by his uncle Tillotson, but unable to find a job near home, he went south to Virginia hoping to find a school there. But Alcott quickly discovered that his plan was hopeless, and, making the best of a bad situation, took to peddling instead. In spite of his failure to get a school, he found Virginia delightful. The planters let him use their libraries, and it was there in 1818 that he first read Locke's *Essay*. Lured by the charms of the South, and the need to make a living, Alcott made a number of such trips south, but by 1823 his inability to make a profit peddling and his conviction that only a life with moral purpose was worthwhile led him to follow the example of his cousin William and return to teaching in Connecticut.[47]

From 1824 to 1828 Bronson Alcott taught school in Connecticut. Beginning at

Bristol in 1824, he then moved to a school in Cheshire which failed in 1827, and in the winter of 1827-28 taught again at Bristol.[48] During this time Alcott worked furiously to develop a theory and practice of education, and read every book on education and psychology he could lay hands on, including Reid, Stewart, Cogan, and many more.[49] Alcott remained faithful to the Lockean psychology and epistemology, and despite his reading of the Scots he did not then adopt the theory of the moral sense—rather he conceived moral knowledge as learned from experience in exactly the same way as any other sort of empirical knowledge. That is, Alcott conceived the world of experience as evidencing a moral order so ordained by God that virtue leads to happiness and vice to misery—hence by induction from particular cases, one can learn what is virtuous and what is vicious.[50] But Alcott found Locke inadequate in his treatment of the emotions, and to amplify his psychology he turned to Thomas Cogan's *A Philosophical Treatise on the Passions and Affections*.[51] Cogan's work involves an elaborate classification of the emotions, but more important it involves a very clear thesis concerning the relation of the affections to the will. According to Cogan, whatever we perceive to serve our own well-being we regard as good, and whatever we perceive as threatening our well-being we regard as evil, and since Cogan holds that as the affections are so is the will, it follows that our actions are determined by the affections. Accordingly, a virtuous character is the result of the attachment of the affections to real goods, and a vicious character is the result of the attachment of the affections to mistaken goods.[52] Hence Alcott concluded that regeneration consists simply in the transfer of the affections from the self to God, and that once this is fully accomplished sanctified behavior must invariably follow.[53] And so Alcott concluded that "By attending to the education of children then, we prevent the necessity of regeneration. We prevent them from being depraved."[54] That is, for Alcott there is no original sin; all character is due to education, and the right education of children can prevent the occurrence of all sin. By education, Alcott believed he could save the world. It is perhaps not surprising that in Congregational Connecticut Alcott found little sympathy for so radical a view, or for the brilliant pedagogic innovations he introduced to implement it. By 1828, it was time for Alcott to leave Connecticut.

In June of 1828, on the advice of Samuel May—the first and only Unitarian minister then in Connecticut, and the man whose sister Alcott was to marry in 1830, Alcott went to Boston to take charge of the Salem Street infant school.[55] And Boston was indeed the place for Alcott. For Boston of the 1820s and 1830s not only teemed with reform movement, it was also the scene of the Unitarian-Calvinist battle. Alcott was enthralled, and went to hear the great Unitarian clergy week after week, absorbing their liberalism, their culture and urbanity, their doctrines, and their concern about miracles. And very quickly Alcott recognized that the miracle question was the crucial question upon which Unitarianism stood or fell.

The features of this age are indeed protentions of contention. The theology of America is yet to be determined—and we see no other alternative but that the question must come to this—Is the Bible an inspired book, or not?[56]

Alcott did not believe that Jesus was divinely inspired, nor did he believe that any supernatural intervention was required to explain the character and opinions of Jesus.[57] He believed in the perfectibility of man in this world by natural means, and Jesus simply confirmed his views. But he did require evidence that the doctrines Jesus taught had divine sanction, and at this point miracles provided his only proof.

It was natural that in these circumstances Alcott should have turned to Channing.[58] He heard Channing preach at every opportunity, and for two and a half years his journals are crammed with accolades to Channing which show clearly that Alcott regarded him as the intellectual and spiritual leader of the city.[59] He took careful notes on Channing's sermons and was particularly struck by Channing's theory of conscience, yet throughout he remained steadfast in his adherence to Locke, and in his usual slow but thorough way tried to work out a combination of these doctrines which would reconcile them with each other. And here too Channing was his guide, for Channing recommended that he read De Gérando's *Self-Education*.[60] Alcott bought the book and read it in August of 1830,[61] and when in December of that year he left Boston to take charge of a school in Germantown, Pennsylvania, he carried with him De Gérando's book and a journal filled with notes on Channing's sermons.

De Gérando's book was ideally suited to Alcott's needs, for it contained in explicit form a version of the Scottish theory of the moral sense. According to De Gérando, man contains five "natures" or faculties together with the motives to which they give rise: the sensual, social, intellectual, moral, and religious.[62] While the intellectual nature is simply the Lockean understanding, the moral nature, with which Alcott included the religious, is distinctly non-Lockean. The moral nature is a perceptive faculty: it does not simply apply ideas of right or wrong, it perceives the rightness or wrongness of the actions brought before it. But the perception is particular: the conscience does not hand down general laws, but acts only on particular cases. It is thus the ability to perceive the moral quality of particulars which this faculty gives us, and since it is a faculty of our nature it is innate in all men.[63]

Alcott had met the doctrine of the moral sense before, but not in the context of the miracles controversy, and his adoption of it in 1831 was quite clearly owing to the fact that it provided him with an answer to the problem of historical evidence. This is spelled out in his Journal for August 28, 1831.

I . . . believe in the truth recorded in the New Testament. I know them to be true: they are founded on the very nature of man: they are proved by the very

moral attribute of our nature; they respond to the dictate of conscience
. . . As to the historical proofs of any fact, they are but the external sign of its
existence: they are the mere expression . . . He whose mind is not thus
prepared to test all truth, is far from knowledge: he receives the opinions
. . . of others, where . . . it is his duty to exert his own powers: he opens the
door for error to enter, and pollute the pure throne of the Soul: he usurps his
own conscience, that divine principle within which . . . obeyed, is designed
to be applied to the appreciation of all moral truths: and like the powers of the
fire under the crucible, to melt down and separate the pure metal of truth from
the dross of error.[64]

It is at once apparent that Alcott has generalized the conscience into a faculty of
moral and spiritual insight capable of judging not only the rightness of particular
acts, but also the truth of general principles. In so doing he followed Channing's
suggestions, but he has here gone far beyond anything Channing had contemplated. For Alcott, the entire controversy over historical evidence is now passé: the
truth of Scripture and of Christianity rests solely upon the declaration of his own
conscience and needs no further warrant.

By late 1831, Alcott was repeating the argument of Channing's "Likeness to
God" in a way which shows that he had identified the voice of conscience with the
voice of the spirit within and was painfully close to regarding it as an avenue of
direct communication with God.

Thus man's duty is within him. It is his appreciation of his own nature, which
gives him the idea of a divinity . . . The deity within him is more excellent
than any which is revealed to him from without . . . Without, is but the
semblance of God, within, he dwells and reveals himself . . . Among all the
works of God, there are none so worthy of study as ourselves. That wonderful
fabrick which contains within it the purest resemblance to himself on earth;
that temple within which he himself dwells, whose image is himself, whose
oracle is conscience, and whose priest is reason;—that temple, within the
human heart . . . the haven of truth: this is worthy of man's study.[65]

Here it is obvious that conscience is the voice of the indwelling spirit, and although
Alcott was not yet ready to admit direct communication, he was not far away.

Meanwhile, Alcott was pondering the problem of nature. According to his
theory, nature is designed by God to teach moral and spiritual truths to man, but
nature does this only by presenting particular facts from which we must derive
explaining generalizations by induction. Once a moral generalization is made,
conscience may declare it true or false, but conscience does not give us the
generalization itself—that must come from the action of the understanding. Yet
how are such generalizations found? Channing had suggested that since nature
symbolizes the divine attributes, the more we approach God the more easily we

can understand nature. This suggestion Alcott now found strikingly confirmed and amplified in Francis Wayland's "Discourse on the Philosophy of Analogy."[66]

Francis Wayland was one of the intellectual leaders of America in this period. He was the president of Brown University, a Baptist minister, a Scottish Realist, and a prolific writer on moral, intellectual, and social philosophy. In the "Discourse on the Philosophy of Analogy" Wayland addresses himself to the question of the origin of our true hypotheses, and argues that neither induction nor deduction can account for them.

> To speak with exactness, demonstration and induction never discover a law of nature; they only show whether a law has or has not been discovered. And as truth is one, and error infinite, it is manifest, that were we in possession of no other means of advancement, we might weary ourselves forever in interpreting the answers of nature, and find, in the end, that we had only taken a few from an infinity of possibilities of error.[67]

How then do we find true hypotheses? Wayland's answer is that the origin of true hypotheses can only be explained by reasoning from analogy, which in turn depends upon two basic principles.

> First, a part of any system which is the work of an intelligent agent, is similar, so far as the principles which it involves are concerned, to the whole of that system. And, secondly, the work of an intelligent and moral being must bear, in all its lineaments, the traces of the character of its Author. And, hence, he will use analogy the more skillfully who is most thoroughly imbued with the spirit of the system, and at the same time most deeply penetrated with a conviction of the attributes of the first Cause of all things.[68]

Accordingly, we are told that Christians excel at the discovery of true hypotheses, while infidels are limited to making applications of known principles![69]

Wayland's "Discourse" had an important influence on Alcott, for it broke the hold which Baconian induction had exercised over his mind by showing him that true generalizations cannot simply be recognized by the comparison of particulars. Rather, as both Channing and Wayland suggested, man can find such generalizations only because he recognizes in nature something which corresponds to characteristics which lie within himself, and the nearer he approaches the perfection of God the stronger that correspondence will be. Thus Alcott was clearly on the road to a theory of correspondence between man and nature which could make the moral nature within a source of knowledge of the world without when in September of 1832 he first read Coleridge's *Aids to Reflection*.[70]

Coleridge's *Aids* played the same role in Alcott's development that it did for Emerson and for other Transcendentalists. By introducing a new psychology which endowed man not only with a Lockean understanding to deal with sense, but also with a Reason and Conscience which are purely spiritual and which are in fact modes of action of the divine spirit within, Coleridge restored to man that purely spiritual component of the mind which Lockean psychology so effectively obscured. Moreover, Coleridge's Reason, being identical with the divine spirit, is a source of universal and necessary truths a priori—an avenue of direct communication between God and man. Reason therefore must contain the archetypal divine ideas of which the world is the realization, and all that is required to understand nature is access to the truth within.

From this point on, Alcott's progress toward Transcendentalism was rapid. By February 1833 he was writing in his journal that

> The human soul has had a primordial experience in the infinite Spirit. The infinite is embodied in the finite, to be developed and returned again to the source of infinite energy from whence it sprang. This is spiritual and earthly experience, and all the phenomena of humanity arise from the union and evolution of these elements. The finite is but the return of the soul on the path of the infinite—the wheeling orb attracted toward, and yet preserved in the cycle of, the central sphere.[71]

This is of course the Platonic theory of lapse, according to which the soul comes from God in full possession of the archetypal ideas, and the function of nature is merely to recall these ideas to us by presenting us with symbolic expressions of them in experience. Alcott was not yet a full-blown Transcendentalist but he reached the flood tide of idealism when he wrote in his journal on June 18, 1834:

> May we not believe that *thought* gives life and meaning to external nature— that what we see, hear, feel, taste, and experience around us, acquires these properties, by the self-investing powers of our own spirits. Is not the living spirit of all things in our spirits, and do they not, through the vivid action, the picturing, life-starting agency, of this same spirit, rise up, tinted, and shaped, before us, even as in starting from the bed of rest, the external world becomes visible to us, with the opening of our eyes, not so much to *let in* the light, as to *let out* our spirits upon the scene which they color and animate, with beauty and life! The *reality* is in the *mind*, *sense* but gives us an *outward type* of it—an outward *shaping* to reduce it to the cognizance of the *understanding*: and, in *space* and *time*, to *substantiate*, the indwelling forms, of our *spirits*. We throw ourselves outward upon nature, that we may the better look upon ourselves; and this process is rendered more conscious to us, in the *act of waking*, than in any other.[72]

And by August of 1835 Alcott had concluded that what is within the mind is God.

> Every man hath a Spirit entrusted to him. It is his Endowment, or rather in the *sense*, and *apprehension* of this endowment, doth his *individual life* consist.

He is a *man* by just so far as he apprehends, or feels, this endowment: "in it he lives, and moves, and hath his individual being:" the endowment seemeth to be his; but he hath the use of it alone, for in its absolute nature, this same endowment is the Godhead itself—the Divine Spirit incarnate, and living *in* him—feeling, thinking, willing, acting, in accordance with his derivative life! The *Father* sustaining the *Son*![73]

Each man is a particular embodiment of God, created to effect some special divine purpose, and that duty or calling represents the man's "genius." If he is true to his genius he serves the Lord, and the power which works in him is God working through him. Every man is therefore divine, and as nature is but the creation of the same spirit which dwells within, when God acts through us we command nature.

We must *be* and *do* what the ideal *images* from the Infinite and Eternal: and which Plato taught and Jesus *lived*, and then revelations, like those made to them—yea, more inspiring than those—will assuredly be given to us . . . Would we meditate and act as they did, we should attain to the same clearness and energy; and our *thoughts* and *lives*, would operate as a revelation, and a miracle, on the minds of those *below* and *around* us. For we should then live a spiritual life, while in flesh; and *in*, and *from* us, "would the Godhead spire forth bodily" . . . Miracles! What are they!—Operations of the Ideal—and those who are faithful, shall work them. . . .[74]

What then was to be the peculiar calling of Bronson Alcott?

I shall *redeem* infancy and childhood; and if a *Savior of Adults* was given, in the person of Jesus; let me, without impiety or arrogance, regard myself as the Children's *Savior*.[75]

In July of 1834 Alcott returned to Boston, and on September 22 he opened his famous Temple School, where he believed he was to fulfill the mission to which God had called him.[76] In 1835 he met Emerson, and quickly discovered a comrade in arms. Emerson was already at work on *Nature* and had his own position fully formulated, so the meeting of minds was mutual. Alcott lent Emerson some of his recent journals, and in *Nature* Emerson paid tribute to Alcott by paraphrasing part of his journal under the guise of the Orphic poet. Meanwhile, Alcott had begun the discussions of the Gospels with the children in his school which he was to publish in 1836—the same year *Nature* appeared. If *Nature* is the classic statement of New England Transcendentalism, Alcott's *Conversations with Children on the Gospels*[77] is the epitome of its sublime innocence and arrogance. We shall therefore look first in detail at *Nature* and then briefly at Alcott's volume, and at the subsequent history of the movement.

4. Nature *and* Conversations

Nature opens with a direct challenge to the Unitarian conservatives.

Our age is retrospective. It builds the sepulchres of the fathers. It writes biographies, histories, and criticism. The foregoing generations beheld God and nature face to face; we, through their eyes. Why should not we also enjoy an original relation to the universe? Why should not we have a poetry and philosophy of insight and not of tradition, and a religion by revelation to us, and not the history of theirs?[78]

This statement amounts to a flat assertion that religion must be based upon our own experience, not upon historical evidence. But how, if men are as Locke described them, and nature is as Newton described it, is "a religion by revelation to us" to be found? This is Emerson's problem—to show that the natural does not preclude the spiritual.

"All science has one aim," Emerson asserts, "namely, to find a theory of nature."[79] But how are we to understand the term "nature"?

Philosophically considered, the universe is composed of Nature and the Soul. Strictly speaking, therefore, all that is separate from us, all which Philosophy distinguishes as the NOT ME, that is, both nature and art, all other men and my own body, must be ranked under this name, NATURE.[80]

This is certainly not the usual use of these terms. "Soul" here refers to the mind (but not the brain) of the individual knower; "nature" refers to everything which is phenomenally given. So "nature" is here used in a much broader sense than in the ordinary statements about physical "nature." Other men may have "souls," but since I know these men only as phenomena, they belong to nature. Whatever is known through the senses, whatever is phenomenally given, is nature.

Is it possible for nature, so defined, to be a source of revelation?

If the stars should appear one night in a thousand years, how would men believe and adore; and preserve for many generations the remembrance of the city of God which had been shown! But every night come out these envoys of beauty, and light the universe with their admonishing smile.[81]

What is asserted here is that nature is now a revelation if it is properly seen. But it is obvious that not everyone sees nature in these terms.

To speak truly, few adult persons can see nature. Most persons do not see the sun. At least they have a very superficial seeing. The sun illuminates only the eye of the man, but shines into the eye and the heart of the child. The lover of nature is he whose inward and outward senses are still truly adjusted to each other; who has retained the spirit of infancy even into the era of manhood.[82]

Whether nature is a revelation or not thus depends upon the perceiver—upon the soul. If the soul is in the right state, he will experience not only revelation but communion with God.

> Standing on the bare ground,—my head bathed by the blithe air, and uplifted into infinite space,—all mean egotism vanishes. I become a transparent eyeball; I am nothing; I see all; the currents of the Universal Being circulate through me; I am part or parcel of God.[83]

Now what Emerson is describing here is quite clearly a religious experience of the most intense kind—a sense of spiritual union with God and of insight into the divine mind. This is Emerson's pledge of the possibility of immediate communion with God, and it is the only possible pledge—the assertion that he has had this experience. Having given this pledge, his task is now to explain the nature of this experience and the conditions of its occurrence.

A theory of nature, Emerson asserts, must explain "to what end is nature."[84] That this formulation of the problem involves final cause was not an objection, since none of the groups against whom he was writing denied that nature was the purposeful creation of an intelligent first cause. The problem then is to discover what that purpose is. "Whoever considers the final cause of the world," Emerson says, "will discern a multitude of uses that enter as parts into that result."[85] These uses Emerson classifies into four types—commodity, beauty, language, and discipline, and he discusses each in turn.

By commodity, Emerson means "all those advantages which our senses owe to nature."[86] Under this heading he includes all the material benefits which we derive from nature. These material benefits provided one of the favorite arguments of the natural theology for the being and attributes of God: thus we have seen both Franklin and Jefferson arguing that nature's usefulness in satisfying our biological wants proves the benevolence of God.[87] Nature's use as commodity is important, Emerson admits, but he refuses to consider it an ultimate use. "A man is fed, not that he may be fed, but that he may work."[88] So in asserting that nature is a commodity we have not answered the question of its purpose—there must be further uses to which these are merely instrumental.

The second use is beauty, which Emerson divides into three types—sensual, moral, and intellectual. That nature is beautiful as well as useful was a standard argument for the benevolence of God: nature would have served its purpose as commodity even if it were ugly, so in making it beautiful God has given us a consumer's surplus.[89] But such sensual delights are the least of nature's beauties: there are higher forms of beauty which are moral and intellectual. "Beauty is the mark God sets upon virtue."[90] Emerson does not explain here why this should be the case, since his opponents would hardly contest the fact, but his concept of intellectual beauty suggests the answer. Thus he writes:

> What is common to them all,—that perfectness and harmony, is beauty. The standard of beauty is the entire circuit of natural forms,—the totality of nature; . . . Nothing is quite beautiful alone; nothing but is beautiful in the whole. A single object is only so far beautiful as it suggests this universal grace.[91]

What Emerson is propounding here is a coherentist theory of aesthetics. Beauty consists in the harmony and order of the involved aggregate. So in his journal, Emerson remarks, "We take them out of composition, and so lose their greatest beauty. The moon is an unsatisfactory sight if the eye be exclusively directed to it, and a shell retains but a small part of its beauty when examined separately."[92] It is the ordered whole which is beautiful; the parts are beautiful only as components of that whole. But order can be moral as well as intellectual. If virtue is defined, as it usually is in religious systems, as obedience to moral law, then moral beauty obeys the same standard as intellectual beauty. Virtuous actions are beautiful because they conform to the moral order.

Beauty is an ultimate end of nature: "no reason can be asked or given why the soul seeks beauty."[93] Nevertheless, Emerson holds, beauty is not the chief ultimate end of the universe. Although beauty does not exist for the sake of something else, yet it is a sign of something beyond itself, and it is that something else which the theory of nature must specify.

The third use of nature Emerson calls language. What he means by this is spelled out in the three famous propositions:

1. Words are signs of natural facts.
2. Particular natural facts are symbols of particular spiritual facts.
3. Nature is the symbol of spirit.[94]

That words which describe nature are signs of natural facts is of course obvious: what the first statement asserts beyond that is that even words used to describe moral or intellectual facts, which are not a part of nature on Emerson's definition, began as signs of natural facts. So if we examine the etymology of our terms for moral and mental phenomena, we find that these terms originally referred to some fact in nature. "*Right* means *straight*; *wrong* means *twisted*,"[95] etc. All words therefore are at root signs of natural facts, whether they have retained their original meaning or not.

But how is it that words which are signs of natural facts can be used to describe spiritual facts? The reason Emerson asserts is that "every natural fact is a symbol of some spiritual fact. Every appearance in nature corresponds to some state of the mind, and that state of the mind can only be described by presenting that natural appearance as its picture.''[96] There is thus a fundamental correspondence between man and nature such that each spiritual fact has at least one natural fact which is its objective correlate.[97] In support of this proposition Emerson presents three arguments. First, it is a fact that figurative language can convey thought.[98] But if there were no real relation between natural and spiritual facts, Emerson holds that a figurative language would be impossible, for how would the natural fact come to stand for the spiritual one? It would seem at first glance that this argument is easily answered by pointing out that such relations can be established by convention. But Emerson would reply that this argument is question-begging, since the point at issue is precisely the origin of the convention. For a natural fact to suggest a spiritual one, the two must be in some way related. Emerson gives the following examples of this natural symbolism. ''An enraged man is a lion, a cunning man is a fox, a firm man is a rock, a learned man is a torch. A lamb is innocence; a snake is subtle spite; flowers express to us the delicate affections.''[99] In these cases it would appear that the relation is based upon similarity—upon possession of common properties—and one naturally wonders why Emerson refused to draw that conclusion. The answer would appear to be that for Emerson a natural fact cannot be like a spiritual fact. In Lockean terms, an idea of sense cannot resemble an idea of reflection, for the one is a sense impression and the other is not. The common properties which seem to underlie his illustrations are more complex than is at first apparent. A cunning man is like a fox because they act alike, but this already assumes a relation between a psychological characteristic—cunning—and overt behavior, which is a natural fact, and that relation is not a relation of similarity. Again, to find a property common to innocence and a lamb is no easy task: the lamb may be young, white, stupid, etc., but none of these qualities are themselves like innocence. But if similarity will not do, it would seem that a strong case can be made for causality. The cunning man is like a fox because his cunning causes him to act like a fox. But Emerson had read Hume. What this statement means is only that certain behaviors—natural facts—are associated with certain spiritual facts, and Emerson refused to rest content with such an association as an ultimate fact—he demanded to know why that association is there, and the assertion that the relation is one of natural symbolism is designed to answer that demand.

Emerson's second argument is that this natural symbolism is universal and can be shown to underlie all languages.

Because of this radical correspondence between visible things and human thoughts, savages, who have only what is necessary, converse in figures. As we go back in history, language becomes more picturesque, until its infancy, when it is all poetry; or all spiritual facts are represented by natural symbols. The same symbols are found to make the original elements of all languages.[100]

This view of the origin and development of language was not unique to Emerson; it was advanced by Swedenborgian writers such as Sampson Reed, and was based in considerable part upon their interpretation of the then newly rediscovered Egyptian hieroglyphs. The discovery of the Rosetta stone and the subsequent success of Jean François Champollion in translating the hieroglyphs were subjects of wide interest in the intellectual world of the early nineteenth century. Champollion's analysis of the hieroglyphs into three classes of signs—those literally representing the object meant, those symbolically expressing an idea by an image of a physical object, and those representing sounds by an image of a physical object—was converted by some of his interpreters into an analysis of the development of language by assuming that the three classes represented three historical stages. In this view, the literal representations were the earliest and most primitive, the symbolic next, and the phonetic last in order of appearance. Combined with the religious doctrine of the fall, and the traditional Christian view that nature embodies God's wisdom, this historical interpretation can easily become the claim that the language of Eden was composed of literal representations, and that the development of symbolic and phonetic signs represents man's fall from the intuitive understanding of nature which he had in his innocence. This is clearly Emerson's doctrine here.[101]

Third, this natural symbolism offers Emerson a way of accounting for the effectiveness of art. The great poet and great orator express themselves in natural symbols and hence their meanings are driven home with peculiar force. "Hence, good writing and brilliant discourse are perpetual allegories. This imagery is spontaneous. It is the blending of experience with the present action of the mind. It is proper creation."[102] It is not surprising in view of this statement that Emerson should have been particularly fond of seventeenth-century poetry, particularly that of Herbert.[103]

The correspondence of natural and spiritual facts permits us to express our thoughts by appropriate orderings of natural images. "But how great a language to convey such pepper-corn informations!"[104] What of the orderings of natural facts as they exist in nature? Do these also have a meaning?

The world is emblematic. Parts of speech are metaphors, because the whole of nature is a metaphor of the human mind. The laws of moral nature answer to those of matter as face to face in a glass . . . The axioms of physics translate the laws of ethics.[105]

Natural facts form a language, and nature itself is a discourse through which God speaks to His creatures. As the artist creates natural images which convey his thought, God creates natural facts which convey His, and the whole order of nature is a revelation to us. Thus, Emerson, like Edwards, Berkeley, and so many idealists before him, seeks to solve the problem of keeping God immanent in nature by converting nature into a symbolic expression of God. The solid mechanism of the world machine is thus dissolved into an allegory of the moral law.

Yet the poetic meaning of nature somehow escapes most men.

> This relation between the mind and matter is not fancied by some poet, but stands in the will of God, and so is free to be known by all men. It appears to men, or it does not appear.[106]

And there is the problem: why doesn't it appear to all? Emerson's answer is ingenious. If nature is a discourse, it must be analyzed by the rules of literary criticism.

> "Every scripture is to be interpreted by the same spirit which gave it forth,"—is the fundamental law of criticism. A life in harmony with Nature, the love of truth and of virtue, will purge the eyes to understand her text. By degrees we may come to know the primitive sense of the permanent objects of nature, so that the world shall be to us an open book, and every form significant of its hidden life and final cause.[107]

What Emerson is asserting here is the empathetic theory of criticism. To understand the meaning of a literary work, Emerson holds, the reader must share the state of mind of the author. A symbol or metaphor is unintelligible unless it arouses the same feelings and ideas in the reader as in the author, and for this to occur the reader must already share the author's associations and emotions—in short, he must empathize, or "sympathize," with the author. We need not here enter into a discussion of the merits of this theory of criticism: it still has defenders today, although the prevailing literary views are against it. What does concern us is Emerson's application of it to the interpretation of nature. The author of nature is of course God. If we must empathize with God to understand nature, then we must think and feel as God does before the meaning will appear. And to think and feel as God does is to realize in ourselves his virtues and holiness: it is likeness to God which is the key to understanding, as Channing had said. Nature may be free to be known to all men, but it is only to the virtuous that the inner meaning will appear. Those who are corrupt are by that fact out of sympathy with God and therefore find nature unintelligible.[108]

"In view of the significance of nature, we arrive at once at a new fact, that nature is a discipline."[109] Nature is symbolic that it may teach us, and Emerson goes on to specify the character of this discipline. On the lowest level, objects of sense are a discipline to the understanding whereby we are taught "the necessary lessons of difference, of likeness, of order, of being and seeming, of progressive arrangement; of ascent from particular to general; of combination to one end of manifold forces."[110] But Emerson is more concerned with nature as a discipline of Reason.

> Man is conscious of a universal soul within or behind his individual life, wherein, as in a firmament, the natures of Justice, Truth, Love, Freedom, arise and shine. This universal soul he calls Reason: it is not mine, or thine, or his, but we are its; we are its property and men.[111]

These "Ideas of the Reason" as Emerson calls them[112] are clearly Platonic Ideas, here conceived as ideas in the mind of God. Since the Reason is identical with the spirit, the ideas are innate in us, and are accessible to us through Reason. But how are they accessible? Emerson's answer is a variant of the Platonic theory of recollection. We become aware of the ideas by finding them illustrated in nature. "That which was unconscious truth, becomes, when interpreted and defined in an object, a part of the domain of knowledge—a new weapon in the magazine of power."[113] Thus the idea is brought into consciousness by our experience of its particular instances.

Now it is clear that what Emerson is discussing here is the problem of induction. Emerson recognized very early that explaining hypotheses cannot be mechanically induced from particulars, and for this reason he was always hostile to that type of scientific procedure which consists in the mere collection and classification of data. What he honored in science and in thought generally was the flash of insight, the sudden and inexplicable leap to the right generalization.[114] But how is that flash of insight to be explained? Where do we get the generalization, and why is it elicited by these particulars? Emerson's answer is that the idea is innate but unconscious, and that the particulars are its natural symbols. Hence these phenomena suggest the hypothesis as particular words do their meanings. Every instance thus "expresses" the law of which it is an instance, so that to know the law instanced by a fact is to know its meaning. Emerson has a peculiar way of stating this: he says that the facts become "transparent," and that the laws "shine" through them. This is merely a poetic way of saying that the meaning of the facts is understood.[115]

Considered as a discipline, it is the function of nature to call out our innate ideas by presenting us with natural symbols for them, and so to realize these ideas in the conscious mind. The result of this process is of course the description of the true order of nature, for these ideas are the laws which govern nature, and "that law, when in the mind, is an idea. Its beauty is infinite. The true philosopher and the true poet are one, and a beauty, which is truth, and a truth, which is beauty, is the aim of both.''[116] The identity of truth and beauty results from the fact that both involve coherence. A hypothesis is true if it permits the deduction of the observed phenomena: accordingly, it gives order to these phenomena.[117] But as Emerson has defined beauty, it consists in the order and harmony among the component parts of an aggregate. Beauty is therefore a mark of truth. Hence, beauty, although it is an ultimate end of nature, is properly the sign of something else, namely, truth.

Is discipline then the final end of nature?

A noble doubt perpetually suggests itself,—whether this end be not the Final Cause of the Universe; and whether nature outwardly exists.[118]

Is nature ideal? ''Be it what it may, it is ideal to me so long as I cannot try the accuracy of my senses.''[119] Emerson thus ranges himself on the side of subjective idealism and defends the adequacy of this view at some length. But Emerson does not stop with subjective idealism.

Three problems are put by nature to the mind; What is matter? Whence is it? and Whereto? The first of these questions only, the ideal theory answers. Idealism saith: matter is a phenomenon, not a substance . . . Yet, if it only deny the existence of matter, it does not satisfy the demands of the spirit. It leaves God out of me. It leaves me in the splendid labyrinth of my perceptions, to wander without end.[120]

If then we turn to the questions, whence is nature and whereto, ''we learn that the highest is present to the soul of man . . . that spirit, that is, the Supreme Being, does not build up nature around us but puts it forth through us, as the life of the tree puts forth new branches and leaves through the pores of the old.''[121] Not only does the spirit within contain the ideas which are elicited by natural symbols, it also creates the natural symbols and paints them before our eyes.

The world proceeds from the same spirit as the body of man. It is a remoter and inferior incarnation of God, a projection of God in the unconscious. But it differs from the body in one important respect. It is not, like that, now subjected to the human will. Its serene order is inviolable by us. It is, therefore, to us, the present expositor of the divine mind. It is a fixed point whereby we may measure our departure. As we degenerate, the contrast between us and our house is more evident. We are as much strangers in nature as we are aliens from God.[122]

It is at this point that the real radicalism of Emerson's position becomes evident. Emerson defined nature as including both the body and all ''external'' objects: these differ only in that the body is under the control of the will while ''external'' nature is not. The function of external nature is therefore to be the ''present expositor of the divine mind.'' By drawing out the ideas within, it teaches us the content of God's mind. But Emerson is saying something much more extreme than this. Our understanding of nature depends upon our empathy with God: hence our fall may be measured by our inability to understand nature. Yet we have already seen that children understand nature, that some adults do also, and that men who are virtuous identify themselves with God and so achieve this insight. And they achieve more than insight. For since nature is an ideal creation of spirit, in the degree to which man identifies himself with the spirit, he becomes the spirit, and he so acquires the same power over nature which God has.

> Meantime, in the thick darkness, there are not wanting gleams of a better light,—occasional examples of the action of man upon nature with his entire force,—with reason as well as understanding. Such examples are, the tradition of miracles in the earliest antiquity of all nations; the history of Jesus Christ . . . These are examples of Reason's momentary grasp of the sceptre; the exertions of a power which exists not in time or space, but an instantaneous in-streaming causing power. [123]

Those who are fully redeemed acquire the power to subject ''external'' nature to their will as the body is subject to the will, and even the power to create and change nature. Jesus achieved this identification with the spirit more fully than other men, and so achieved the power to command nature, as the miracles show. But what was true of Jesus can be true of every man. So, as Emerson wheels into his peroration, his message is that you too can work miracles.

> Build therefore your own world. As fast as you conform your life to the pure idea in your mind, that will unfold its great proportions. A correspondent revolution in things will attend the influx of the spirit. So fast will disagreeable appearances, swine, spiders, snakes, pests, mad-houses, prisons, enemies, vanish; they are temporary and shall be no more seen. The sordor and filths of nature, the sun shall dry up and the wind exhale. As when the summer comes from the south the snow-banks melt and the face of the earth becomes green before it, so shall the advancing spirit create its ornaments along its path and carry with it the beauty it visits and the song which enchants it; . . . The kingdom of man over nature, which cometh not with observation,—a dominion such as now is beyond his dream of God,—he shall enter without more wonder than the blind man feels who is gradually restored to perfect sight. [124]

By identifying himself with the God within, man becomes a channel through which the spirit works, and so, since nature is merely the spirit's imagery, he can rewrite it for himself. All those perversions which the fall brought into the world can then be swept away, and the world restored to its ''original and eternal beauty.'' [125]

In the same year that *Nature* appeared, Alcott published his *Conversations with Children on the Gospels*. If Emerson gave Boston conservatives their clearest view of what the new doctrine was, Alcott gave them the most appalling indication of its implications. Believing as he did that Jesus was the most perfect example of the divinity of human nature,[126] that others can only be understood through empathy, and that infant children are as free from sin and as near to God as any beings on earth, Alcott concluded that the children should be able to understand the Gospels much more easily and fully than adults, who had grown corrupt and had lost their spiritual vision. But this was not enough: not only did he use the views of the children to explain the Gospels, he used them to prove the truth of Christianity. For since all men contain the same spirit, and every man is a Christ, the only way to prove that what Jesus spoke was the message of the spirit is by the testimony of the spirit itself. And since the spirit is in its purest form in infant children, the fact that these children found the Christian doctrines to be self-evident was, to Alcott, the strongest possible proof of their truth.[127] And so in all seriousness Alcott proposed to the Boston orthodoxy that they should rest their hopes of salvation upon the testimony of six-year-old children! Andrews Norton was not amused!

5. *Toward Midcentury*

It is not hard to see why Unitarians considered Transcendentalism as infidelity. No more radical religious doctrine has ever been preached in America. Even the wildest enthusiasts of the Great Awakening had never dared to claim what Emerson and Alcott claimed—that they were one with God and that they too could work miracles. Moreover, the Transcendentalist revolt came at a time when the appearance of heresy within their ranks was acutely embarrassing for the Unitarians. Emerson had at least the decency to resign his pulpit, and Alcott, lacking the financial and social resources of some of his fellows, could be and was easily ruined, his school closed, and all possibility of further teaching positions ended. Yet not all the Transcendentalists were so easily dealt with: Theodore Parker refused to resign his pulpit, and when the Unitarian orthodoxy tried to force him from it, he fought them on the very grounds of Congregational autonomy with which they had maintained their pulpits against similar attacks by the Calvinists, and won. Indeed, what is remarkable about Transcendentalism is how quickly it ceased to be heresy. Men who had been infidels in 1836 were accounted sages fifteen years later; Emerson was a highly popular Lyceum lecturer and even Alcott came to be regarded as a mystic whose "conversations" and writings might be obscure but were hardly dangerous, and who was finally to preside as dean of the Concord School of Philosophy.

Yet this mellowing of the atmosphere betokened no change of position by Emerson or Alcott—rather, it marked a shift in the American intellectual climate which made their writings less and less revolutionary. We have remarked before the gradual confluence of Scottish Realism and Kantianism—a confluence evident in Hamilton and in such students of his as Bowen, who was one of the bitter critics of Transcendentalism in the 1830s. Moreover, the role of Scottish moral sense intuitionism in the development of Transcendentalism is clear and obvious in both Emerson and Alcott. What Emerson, Alcott, and their fellows had seen more clearly than anyone since Edwards was that the Lockean epistemology, even as revised by the Scots, was not an adequate support for a spiritual religion or even for moral knowledge. But while Edwards and Johnson could rest with a Berkeleyan type of idealism, the Transcendentalists had read Hume, and they knew that some other epistemological basis had to be found. In the 1830s their brand of Romantic idealism was revolutionary, but by the 1850s English romantic literature was well known in America, Frederick Henry Hedge had published his *Prose Writers of Germany*, which contained excellent translations of some of the leading German writers, Americans by the dozens were studying in Germany, and the appreciation of the importance of Kant, Fichte, Schelling, and Hegel was rapidly increasing in America. And as German thought became better known, it also became apparent that it could serve many of the same functions which Scottish Realism had served—that it could also guarantee universal and necessary truths and could provide a basis for morality and religion. Viewed in this context, Transcendentalism was less revolutionary, and as Emerson and Alcott toured the nation, and particularly the West, they found not only sympathy for their doctrines, but in some places—notably in St. Louis—thoroughly knowledgeable Hegelians who considered the Transcendentalism of New England tame and out of date. Thus for all its radicalism and provinciality, Transcendentalism was an important movement: if it pointed toward a basic failure in the received doctrines of empiricism, it also pointed the way toward a more general movement in philosophy and theology which was to carry Scottish Realism toward a midcentury marriage with Idealism.

Notes — Chapter Seven

[1]John Lowell, *Are You a Christian or a Calvinist? Or, Do You Prefer the Authority of Christ to that of the Genevan Reformer?* (Boston, 1815); William R. Hutchinson, *The Transcendentalist Ministers* (New Haven, Conn.: Yale University Press, 1959), chap. 1; George Willis Cooke, *Unitarianism in America* (Boston: American Unitarian Association, 1902), chap. 5; Sidney Earl Mead, *Nathaniel William Taylor, 1786-1858* (Chicago: University of Chicago Press, 1942), chap. 11; Joseph Haroutunian, *Piety Versus Moralism* (New York: Henry Holt, 1932); Clarence Faust, "The Background of the Unitarian Opposition to Transcendentalism," *Modern Philology* 35:297-324 (1938); Octavius B. Frothingham, *Boston Unitarianism, 1820-1850* (New York: G. P. Putnam's Sons, 1890).

[2]Perry Miller, ed., *The Transcendentalists* (Cambridge, Mass.: Harvard University Press, 1950), chap. 8; Van Wyck Brooks, *The Flowering of New England, 1815-1865* (New York: E. P. Dutton and Co., 1936).

[3]Faust, "Background," pp. 297-323; Hutchinson, *Ministers*, chap. 1.

[4]Orville Dewey, "On Miracles," The Dudleian Lecture, 1836, in *Discourses and Reviews upon Questions in Controversial Theology and Practical Religion* (New York: C. S. Francis and Co., 1846), pp. 235-36. In basing supernaturalism upon miracles, the Unitarians were of course following Locke. Cf. Robert Leet Patterson, *The Philosophy of William Ellery Channing* (New York: Bookman Associates, 1942), pp. 46ff.

[5]Faust, "Background," pp. 302ff; Hutchinson, *Ministers*, chap. 3; Patterson, *Channing*, p. 52.

[6]Marvin R. Vincent, *A History of the Textual Criticism of the New Testament* (New York: Macmillan Co., 1899), chaps. 10-17; Albert Schweitzer, *The Quest of the Historical Jesus* (New York: Macmillan Co., 1948), chaps. 1-10.

[7]Andrews Norton, *A Discourse on the Latest Form of Infidelity . . .* (Cambridge, Mass., 1839).

[8]Faust, "Background," pp. 313ff; Miller, *Transcendentalists*, Introduction.

[9]See above, pp. 42-43.

[10]Perry Miller, *New England Mind I*, p. 270.

[11]See above, pp. 44-45.

[12]Samuel Taylor Coleridge, *Aids to Reflection, in the Formation of a Manly Character, on the Several Grounds of Prudence, Morality, and Religion*, edited with a Preliminary Essay by James Marsh (Burlington, Vt.: Chauncey Goodrich, 1829).

[13]Marsh, "Preliminary Essay," p. xxx. Marsh was an interesting and important figure in his own right. Cf. the excellent brief study of him in Ronald Vale Wells, *Three Christian Transcendentalists* (New York: Columbia University Press, 1943), chap. 2.

[14]Ralph Waldo Emerson, *Nature* in *Nature, Addresses, and Lectures* (Boston: Houghton Mifflin and Co., 1885), pp. 7-80.

[15]On the Transcendentalist movement, see Hutchinson, *Ministers*; Alexander Kern, "The Rise of Transcendentalism, 1815-1860," in Harry Hayden Clark, ed., *Transitions in American Literary History* (Durham, N.C.: Duke University Press, 1953), pp. 245-314; Frothingham, *Transcendentalism*. For a recent study of Ripley, see Charles Crowe, *George Ripley, Transcendentalist and Utopian Socialist* (Athens, Ga.: University of Georgia Press, 1967).

[16]Ralph Rusk, *The Life of Ralph Waldo Emerson* (New York: Charles Scribner's Sons, 1949), chaps. 1-11.

[17]Ralph Waldo Emerson, *The Letters of Ralph Waldo Emerson*, ed. Rusk, 6 vols. (New York: Columbia University Press, 1939).

[18]Merrell R. Davis, "Emerson's 'Reason' and the Scottish Philosophers," *New England Quarterly* 17:209-28 (1944); John E. Schamberger, "Emerson's Concept of the 'Moral Sense': A Study of its Sources and its Importance to his Intellectual Development" (Ph.D. diss., University of Pennsylvania, 1969), chaps. 3-4.

[19]Ralph Waldo Emerson, *Journals of Ralph Waldo Emerson* (Boston: Houghton Mifflin and Co., 1909-10), I:97, 162f, 186, 209; II:89.

[20]Ralph Waldo Emerson, "The Present State of Ethical Philosophy," in *Two Unpublished Essays. The Character of Socrates. The Present State of Ethical Philosophy*, Introduction by E. E. Hale (Boston: Lamson Wolffe and Co., 1896), p. 68.

[21]*Ibid.*, p. 69.

[22]Rusk, *Emerson*, pp. 107-13.

[23]Emerson, *Journals*, II:83-85.

[24]Emerson, *Journals*, I:209. For studies of the relation between Emerson and the Scottish Realists, cf. Davis, "Emerson's 'Reason' and the Scottish Philosophers," pp. 209-28; John Q. Anderson, "Emerson and 'The Moral Sentiment,' " *Emerson Society Quarterly* 19:13-15 (1960); Schamberger, "Emerson's Concept of the 'Moral Sense' "; Joel Porte, *Emerson and Thoreau: Transcendentalists in Conflict* (Middletown, Conn.: Wesleyan University Press, 1966).

[25]Schamberger, "Emerson's Concept of the 'Moral Sense,' " chap. 4; Porte, *Emerson and Thoreau*, chap. 4.

[26]Emerson, *Journals*, I:97, 162f, 186, 209; II:89.

[27]*Ibid.*, I:164.

[28]Miller, *Transcendentalists*, pp. 21-22.

[29]Patterson, *Channing*, p. 78.

[30]William Ellery Channing, "Likeness to God," in *The Works of William E. Channing, D.D.* (Boston: James Munroe and Co., 1846), III:228; Patterson, *Channing*, p. 78.

[31]Channing, "Likeness," p. 233.

[32]*Ibid.*, p. 234.

[33]Patterson, *Channing*, pp. 204ff.

[34]Channing, "Likeness," p. 230.

35Francis Wayland, *"A Discourse on the Philosophy of Analogy" delivered before the Phi Beta Kappa Society of Rhode Island, Sept. 7, 1831* (Boston: Hilliard, Gray, Little, and Wilkins, 1831).

36Emerson, *Journals*, I:361.

37Marsh, "Preliminary Essay," p. xli.

38*Ibid.*, pp. xxxviiiff.

39Coleridge, *Aids*, p. 137.

40*Ibid.*, p. 137.

41*Ibid.*, p. 142.

42Emerson, *Journals*, III:235.

43*Ibid.*, II:325.

44Odell Shepard, *Pedlar's Progress: The Life of Bronson Alcott* (Boston: Little, Brown and Co., 1937), pp. 1-30; Kenneth Walter Cameron, *Emerson, Thoreau and Concord in Early Newspapers* (Hartford: Transcendental Books, 1958), p. 325. See the memoir of Tillotson Bronson in *Churchman's Magazine* n.s. 5:259-69 (1826); Richard Purcell, *Connecticut in Transition, 1775-1818* (Washington: American Historical Association, 1918).

45James Burgh, *The Dignity of Human Nature*, 3d American ed. (New York: Evert Duyckinck, 1812).

46Shepard, *Pedlar's Progress*, chap. 1; F. B. Sanborn and W. T. Harris, eds., *A. Bronson Alcott: His Life and Philosophy* (Boston: Roberts Brothers, 1893), chap. 1.

47Shepard, *Pedlar's Progress*, chap. 2; Sanborn and Harris, *Alcott*, chap. 2.

48Shepard, *Pedlar's Progress*, pp. 75-79; Sanborn and Harris, *Alcott*, pp. 68-74; Dorothy McCuskey, *Bronson Alcott, Teacher* (New York: Macmillan Co., 1940), chap. 2.

49Amos Bronson Alcott, "Journal," 1826, August 24, November 18; 1827, July 9; "Autobiographical Collections," II:1827. The Alcott manuscripts, including the journals and autobiographical collections, are in Houghton Library at Harvard University.

50Alcott, "Journal," 1827, pp. 111-12—undated pages at the end of the 1826-27 Journal.

51Thomas Cogan, *A Philosophical Treatise on the Passions* (Boston: Wells and Lilly, 1821).

52*Ibid.,* pp. 22-25, 35-46, 55-59, 71, 81, 292f.

53Alcott, "Journal," 1827, March 4.

54*Ibid.,* 1827, April 1.

55Shepard, *Pedlar's Progress*, pp. 120-22; Sanborn and Harris, *Alcott*, p. 110.

56Alcott, "Journal," 1828, June 12.

57*Ibid.,* 1829, September 19.

58For Alcott's reaction to Channing, see "Journal," 1829, January 6, November 8; Amos Bronson Alcott, *The Journals of Bronson Alcott*, ed. Odell Shepard (Boston: Little, Brown and Co., 1938), 1828, October 26; 1829, February 15; 1834, April 22.

59Cf. Alcott, "Journal," 1828, October 26; 1829, February 15.

60Alcott, "Journal," 1830, September 7; Baron De Gérando, *Self-Education: of the Means and Art of Moral Progress* (Boston: Carter and Hendee, 1830).

61Alcott, "Journal," 1830, August 2, September 7; 1831, February 21, May 23; 1832, January, n.d.; esp. 1834, May 25.

62De Gérando, *Self-Education*, pp. 10-11.

63*Ibid.,* pp. 62ff.

64Alcott, "Journal," 1831, August 28.

65*Ibid.,* 1831, September 24.

66*Ibid.,* 1831, December 13; Wayland, *Discourse*.

67Wayland, *Discourse*, p. 12.

68*Ibid.,* pp. 14-15.

69*Ibid.,* pp. 16-17.

70Alcott, "Journal," 1832, September, n.d.

[71]Alcott, "Journal," 1833, February, n.d.

[72]Alcott, "Journal," 1834, June 18.

[73]*Ibid.*, 1835, August 2.

[74]*Ibid.*, 1834, October 22.

[75]*Ibid.*, 1834, October 27; 1835, January 15, March 8, December 15.

[76]Sanborn and Harris, *Alcott*, p. 176.

[77]A. B. Alcott, *Conversations with Children on the Gospels*, 2 vols. (Boston: James Munroe, 1836-37).

[78]Emerson, *Nature*, p. 9.

[79]*Ibid.*, p. 10.

[80]*Ibid.*, pp. 10-11.

[81]*Ibid.*, p. 13.

[82]*Ibid.*, pp. 14-15.

[83]*Ibid.*, pp. 15-16.

[84]*Ibid.*, p. 10.

[85]*Ibid.*, p. 18.

[86]*Ibid.*, p. 18.

[87]See pp. 106, 304.

[88]Emerson, *Nature*, p. 20.

[89]Paley, *Natural Theology*, p. 177.

[90]Emerson, *Nature*, p. 25.

[91]*Ibid.*, p. 29.

[92]Emerson, *Journals*, III:293.

[93]Emerson, *Nature*, pp. 29-30.

94*Ibid.*, p. 31.

95*Ibid.*

96*Ibid.*, p. 32.

97Emerson's theory of correspondence is largely derived from the doctrines of the Swedish mystic, Emanuel Swedenborg. Emerson first became acquainted with Swedenborg's theory through Sampson Reed's *Observations on the Growth of the Mind* (Boston, 1826). Cf. the selection in Miller, *Transcendentalists*, pp. 53-59. Emerson read Reed's book in 1826 (Emerson, *Journals*, II:124). Cf. the discussion of correspondence theory in Sherman Paul, *Emerson's Angle of Vision* (Cambridge, Mass.: Harvard University Press, 1952).

98Emerson, *Nature*, pp. 34-35.

99*Ibid.*, p. 32.

100*Ibid.*, pp. 34-35.

101John T. Irwin, "The Symbol of the Hieroglyphics in the American Renaissance," *American Quarterly* 26:103-26 (1974).

102Emerson, *Nature*, p. 36.

103F. O. Matthiessen, *American Renaissance* (New York: Oxford University Press, 1941), pp. 100ff; Norman Brittin, "Emerson and the Metaphysical Poets," *American Literature* 8:1-21 (1936).

104Emerson, *Nature*, p. 37.

105*Ibid.*, p. 38.

106*Ibid.*, p. 39.

107*Ibid.*, p. 40.

108*Ibid.*, p. 35.

109*Ibid.*, p. 42.

110*Ibid.*, pp. 42-43.

111*Ibid.*, p. 33.

112Emerson, *Journals*, III:235.

[113]Emerson, *Nature*, p. 41.

[114]Stephen Whicher, *Freedom and Fate: An Inner Life of Ralph Waldo Emerson* (Philadelphia: University of Pennsylvania Press, 1953), pp. 89-90.

[115]Emerson, *Nature*, p. 39; Emerson, *Journals*, III:261.

[116]Emerson, *Nature*, p. 59.

[117]*Ibid.*, pp. 10, 59.

[118]*Ibid.*, p. 52.

[119]*Ibid.*, p. 53.

[120]*Ibid.*, pp. 66-67.

[121]*Ibid.*, pp. 67-68.

[122]*Ibid.*, pp. 68-69.

[123]*Ibid.*, p. 76.

[124]*Ibid.*, pp. 79-80.

[125]*Ibid.*, p. 77.

[126]Alcott, "Journal," 1835, March 18, August 11.

[127]*Ibid.*, 1835, July, n.d., August 11, September 18, 19, 20, 21, October 14.

INDEX OF NAMES

INDEX

INDEX OF SUBJECTS